Western Australia

Jeff Williams

Western Australia

2nd edition

Published by
Lonely Planet Publications
Head Office: PO Box 617, Hawthorn, Vic 3122, Australia
Branches: 150 Linden St, Oakland, CA 94607, USA
               10a Spring Place, London NW5 3BH, UK
               1 rue du Dahomey, 75011 Paris, France

Printed by
The Bookmaker International Ltd
Printed in China

Photographs by

Glenn Beanland	Chris Lee Ack	Paul Steel
David Curl	Ron & Viv Moon	Western Australian Tourist
Roger du Buisson	Bernard Napthine	Commission
Keren Flavell	Richard Nebesky	Tony Wheeler
Richard I'Anson	Denis O'Byrne	Jeff Williams

Front cover: Riding camels along the beach, Broome (Andrea Pistolesi, The Image Bank)

First Published
April 1995

This Edition
February 1998

Although the authors and publisher have tried to make the information as accurate as possible, they accept no responsibility for any loss, injury or inconvenience sustained by any person using this book.

National Library of Australia Cataloguing in Publication Data

Williams, Jeff, 1954 Dec. 15- .
Western Australia.

2nd ed.
Includes index.
ISBN 0 86442 544 9.

1. Western Australia - Guidebooks. I. Title.

919.410465

text & maps © Lonely Planet 1998
photos © photographers as indicated 1998

Jeff Williams

Jeff Williams is a Kiwi from Greymouth on NZ's wild west coast. He currently lives in Brisbane, Queensland, out near the coast on Moreton Bay, with his wife Alison and their five-year-old son Callum. When not working for Lonely Planet he works on a series of unpublished and unfinished novels, goes for bike rides with Callum and writes freelance articles for magazines. He has authored, co-authored or contributed to *New Zealand; Tramping in New Zealand; Australia; South Africa, Lesotho & Swaziland; Africa on a shoestring*; and *Washington DC & the Capital Region*. His next job is in West Africa.

From the Author

Jeff would like to thank his mate Russell Wilson for babysitting Callum in Western Australia; Callum, who travelled the length and breadth of this vast state for the second time (and shared his unique sense of humour); Stef and Angela Frodsham in East Fremantle; in Perth, Paul from Paul & Scotty's Ozi Inn, Rory from Rory's Backpackers, Angela from the Easyrider bus; in Exmouth, Mal Poole from Exmouth Diving Centre; the kind folks at the Wander Inn in Bunbury; and the staff of the Albany, Broome, Carnarvon, Esperance, Geraldton, Karratha, Kalbarri, Kalgoorlie-Boulder and Margaret River tourist offices. Also, Katie Cody, Ann Jeffree and Mary Neighbour at Lonely Planet for guiding this book smoothly through production (and Paul Harding for a great brief). Lastly, but not leastly, a big thanks to Alison, who kept the home fires burning.

From the Publisher

This 2nd edition was edited and proofed by Katie Cody (as coordinating editor), Miriam Cannell, Anne Mulvaney, Tom Smallman and Mary Neighbour. Ann Jeffree drew the maps and illustrations and coordinated the layout. Thanks to Mark Griffiths who assisted with drawing maps and Paul

Harding for the final editorial check. The cover was designed by Simon Bracken.

Thanks

Many thanks to the travellers who used the last edition and wrote to us with helpful hints, useful advice and interesting anecdotes:

Les Barnett, Paula Bayford, Paul & Jill Bromhead, Angela Brooks, Clare Butler, Sandra Butler, Connie Chai, Kathy Croak, Chaitanya Dasa, Tony Ferrell, N Grob, Monica Grusell, C Hall, Ian Harrison, Bronwyn Hayes, Marianne Jannemann, Gregory Jones, Justine Knights, Rex HuTon Kwong, Nathan Laurie, N Lessmann, Kathryn Levi, Deborah Ling, Stephen Litvin, Jane Luscombe, Jill Maguire, Daniel Morrissyd, D Nahouri, Caroline Norton, R & J Pilcher, Norman Poulter, Mallory Rome, Jane Simpson, Philippa Smith, A Sompopsakul, Christina Tassell, Jacob-Peter Westerhof, Timo Wolf

Warning & Request

Things change – prices go up, schedules change, good places go bad and bad places go bankrupt – nothing stays the same. So, if you find things better or worse, recently opened or long since closed, please tell us and help make the next edition even more accurate and useful.

We value all of the feedback we receive from travellers. Julie Young coordinates a small team who read and acknowledge every letter, postcard and email, and ensure that every precious morsel of information finds its way to the appropriate authors, editors and publishers.

Everyone who writes to us will find their name in the next edition of the appropriate guide and will also receive a free subscription to our quarterly newsletter, *Planet Talk*.

The very best contributions will be rewarded with a free Lonely Planet guide.

Excerpts from your correspondence may appear in new editions of this guide; in our newsletter, *Planet Talk*; or in updates on our Web site – so please let us know if you don't want your letter published or your name acknowledged.

Contents

Boxed Asides

Map Legend

BOUNDARIES

.... International Boundary
.... State Boundary
.... Disputed Boundary

ROUTES

A25 ..... Freeway, with Route Number
.... Major Road
.... Minor Road
.... Minor Road - Unsealed
.... City Road
.... City Street
.... City Lane
.... Train Route, with Station
.... Metro Route, with Station
.... Cable Car or Chairlift
.... Ferry Route
.... Walking Track

AREA FEATURES

.... Building
.... Cemetery
.... Beach
.... Market
.... Park, Gardens
.... Pedestrian Mall
.... Reef
.... Urban Area

HYDROGRAPHIC FEATURES

.... Canal
.... Coastline
.... Creek, River
.... Lake, Intermittent Lake
.... Rapids, Waterfalls
.... Salt Lake
.... Swamp

SYMBOLS

○ **CAPITAL** .... National Capital	.... Airport	.... One Way Street
◉ **CAPITAL** .... State Capital	... Ancient or City Wall	℗ .... Parking
● **CITY** .... City	.... Bank	)(........................ Pass
● **Town** .... Large Town	.... Beach	.... Petrol Station
● Town .... Small Town	.... Cave	★ .... Police Station
	.... Church	.... Post Office
■ .... Place to Stay	.... Cliff or Escarpment	⁂ .... Ruins
⚑ .... Camping Ground	.... Dive Site	❖ .... Shopping Centre
⌂ .... Caravan Park	○ .... Embassy	◎ .... Spring
⌂ .... Hut or Chalet	↑ .... Golf Course	.... Surf Beach
	✚ .... Hospital	.... Swimming Pool
▼ .... Place to Eat	✳ .... Lookout	☎ .... Telephone
▣ .... Pub or Bar	▲ .... Monument	.... Temple
♨ .... Cafe	◪ .... Mosque	▣ .... Tomb
	▲ .... Mountain or Hill	❶ ..... Tourist Information
○ .... Point of Interest	🏛 .... Museum	⊖ .... Transport
	♣ .... National Park	.... Zoo

Note: not all symbols displayed above appear in this book

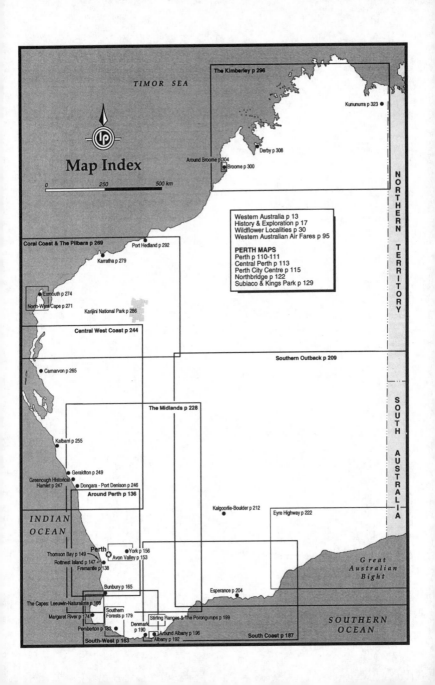

Map Index

0   250   500 km

TIMOR SEA

The Kimberley p 296

Kununurra p 323

Derby p 308

Around Broome p 304
Broome p 300

NORTHERN TERRITORY

Western Australia p 13
History & Exploration p 17
Wildflower Localities p 30
Western Australian Air Fares p 95

PERTH MAPS
Perth 110-111
Central Perth p 113
Perth City Centre p 115
Northbridge p 122
Subiaco & Kings Park p 129

Coral Coast & The Pilbara p 269

Port Hedland p 292

Karratha p 279

Exmouth p 274
North-West Cape p 271

Karijini National Park p 286

Central West Coast p 244

Southern Outback p 209

Camarvon p 265

SOUTH AUSTRALIA

The Midlands p 228

Kalbarri p 255

Geraldton p 249

Greenough Historical
Hamlet p 247   Dongara - Port Denison p 246

Around Perth p 136

Kalgoorlie-Boulder p 212   Eyre Highway p 222

INDIAN OCEAN

Perth
Thomson Bay p 149   York p 156
Rottnest Island p 147   Avon Valley p 153
Fremantle p 138

Great Australian Bight

SOUTH AUSTRALIA

Bunbury p 165

The Capes: Leeuwin-Naturaliste p 168

Esperance p 204

Margaret River p 174   Southern Forests p 179   Stirling Ranges & The Porongurups p 199

Pemberton p 183   Denmark p 190   SOUTHERN OCEAN

South-West p 163   Around Albany p 196   South Coast p 187
Albany p 192

Introduction

Western Australia (more commonly known as WA, 'Double-U ay') is isolated by desert from Australia's population and power centres to the east. But, paradoxically, this potential weakness has heralded a number of strengths, enhancing the feeling that WA is somehow different, almost a separate country. And let's face it, WA is also big! But we all know that size isn't everything – Australia's largest state is packed with wonders and much of its allure is the realisation that many of these are just being 'discovered'.

Chances are you will be the only person swimming in the idyllic lagoons of Ningaloo Reef on a particular day; yours will be the sole four-wheel drive (4WD) driven into remote Rudall River National Park for some weeks; you were one of a handful of people who camped inside a gorge in the spectacular Purnululu (Bungle Bungles) National Park in the past month; when fishing, you had a couple of hundred km of beach to yourself; and you and your partner were the only people who saw a particular huge expanse of wildflowers in bloom this year. Not only are all of the above examples possible, they'll also be the norm for some time to come.

This is a state of incredible contrasts: sophisticated cities to ghost towns, the rugged Kimberley to the billiard-table flat Nullarbor, the lush forests of the south-west to the sunbaked red and brown hues of the arid centre, and the brilliant blue waters of the oceans to the dazzling white saltpans on the fringe of civilisation. And the land, sea and sky are intensified by the light in a most vivid and unforgettable manner.

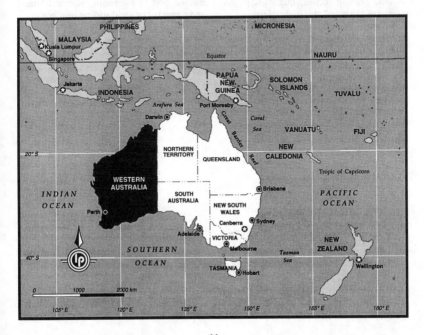

The only remaining frontier in non-desert Australia is in the north of the state. The Kimberley, remote, rugged and three times the size of England, has repulsed attempts at settlement and is still the least-populated area of northern Australia. To the south is the equally wild Pilbara. The spectacular Hamersley Range includes memorable views over gorges of the Karijini National Park. Sandwiched between the Kimberley and the Pilbara is the exotic town of Broome, now a major tourist mecca.

Western Australia is the perfect ecotourism destination. Shark Bay, renowned for its friendly dolphins at Monkey Mia, has an additional wealth of flora & fauna which led to its being designated as a world heritage area. North-West Cape, with unforgettable Ningaloo Reef and the absorbing Cape Range, is Australia's best ecotourism destination. The fauna seen here includes the world's largest fish, the whale shark (which you can swim with), manta rays, humpback whales, nesting turtles, dugongs, plus a myriad of birds and rare marsupials.

An irresistible lure for any traveller is the wildflowers (approximately 8000 species are found in the state). The forests of the south contain mighty jarrah, karri, marri and tingle trees and more wildflowers. Birdlife and animals are prolific and the wide variety of habitats supports many species.

The regions of the Great Southern and the south-west are missed by many visitors to Australia. A pity, as they also possess a wealth of natural attractions – limestone caves, archipelagos teeming with wildlife, forests of ancient trees including the giant karri and the rare tingles, the Fitzgerald River Biosphere Reserve and the rugged Stirling and Porongurup ranges. To the north lies the goldfields region, with historic ghost towns and the frontier city of Kalgoorlie-Boulder.

The hub of WA is undoubtedly its vibrant cosmopolitan capital, Perth (often called the most isolated city in the world). Perth may be isolated, but it is also very classy with a complete range of accommodation, places to eat and entertainment. Not far away are the historic port of Fremantle, Rottnest Island and a number of great surfing beaches.

Western Australia includes something for all types of traveller. So go west!

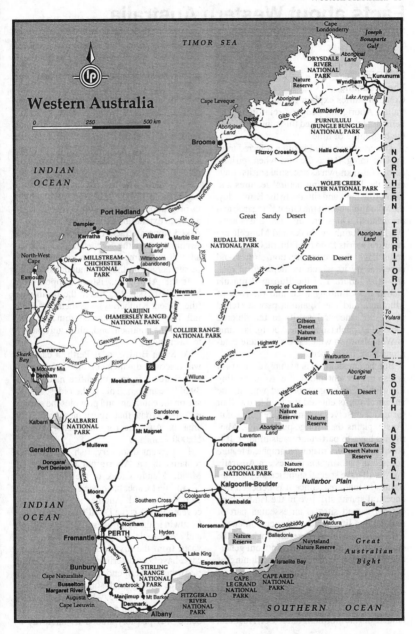

Facts about Western Australia

HISTORY

The Dreaming

Creation stories explain the origins of Australian Aboriginal peoples, reinforcing the belief that they inhabited this continent since the beginning of time.

The creation period is often referred to as the Dreaming. It was the time when spiritual beings (also known as ancestral spirits) travelled the land forming natural features and instituting laws and rituals. In the Kimberley, the Wandjina, Marlu the Great Kangaroo and the Maletji Dogs are all ancestral spirits. Warlu the Rainbow Snake and Mangela are ancestral spirits from the Pilbara. Other local areas have their own creation stories and ancestral spirits which are depicted in rock art – the Jaburara of the Burrup Peninsula etched the Climbing Men into the rock of Murajuga and the Ngaluma people etched images of ancestral spirits in the dolerite rocks of Depuch Island (the Aboriginal name is Womalantha), which is a site where ceremonies are performed.

But the Dreaming is not simply the past – it is also the present and future. After creating life and everything associated with it, the ancestral spirits entered the land to dwell or formed themselves into natural features of it. This explains the strong spiritual link Aborigines have to particular tracts of land. It is possible that every major geographical feature you see in your travels in Western Australia (WA) will have special significance for Aborigines in that area. Since it is believed that ancestral spirits still live in the land, taking care of sacred sites is an essential part of maintaining life, health and social order.

However, with the arrival of whites, the continuity of life handed down from generation to generation, since the beginning of time, was disrupted.

The Archaeological Record

It is thought that Aborigines may have landed on the northern shores of Australia some 60,000 years ago, at a time when large parts of the continental shelf were exposed.

Evidence from this period, such as campsites and artefacts, would now be under the sea. The expansion of polar ice caps and reduction in rainfall experienced during Pleistocene 'ice ages' would result in lower sea levels. At the end of each period of glaciation, the sea rose, inundating the continental shelf. The last rise in the sea level began about 12,000 years ago, stabilising at its present position some 6000 years ago. To a certain extent this explains the presence of flaked stone artefacts on the islands of the Archipelago of the Recherche near Esperance. It is assumed many more sites would be submerged on the now inundated shelf.

If the Aborigines island-hopped from South-East Asia it is likely the north-west (the present Kimberley) was their first landfall. They would have spread from here to all parts of the continent and, ultimately, across to Tasmania.

At Swan Bridge, near Perth, a campsite was discovered which contained stone tools and charcoal from a campfire made about 39,500 years ago. This is the oldest known site on the continent and provides the strongest proof to date that Aborigines lived in the area, or Australia for that matter, at least 50,000 years ago.

In a recent discovery, fish and shellfish remains in an Aboriginal rockshelter at Mandu Mandu Creek in the Cape Range, North-West Cape, have been dated as being 34,000 years old. Another ice-age site discovered in WA is the Devil's Lair, near Cape Leeuwin in the south-west of the state. Bone and stone tools, choppers and flakes excavated from the dry floor of this limestone cave, have been determined to be 33,000 old.

At the northern end of the Weld Ranges, near Cue in the Murchison district, the Aborigines mined ochre which was used in ceremonies as long ago as 30,000 years. The ochre was possibly traded as far away as

Aboriginial rock painting

Queensland. This ochre mine, Wilga Mia, features in tales from the Dreaming.

There is a great deal of evidence of a sophisticated culture further south, with examples of Aborigines' daily food-gathering. They trapped fish in the estuaries, capturing and killing now-extinct megafauna such as the large kangaroo-like *Sthenurus* and the hippopotamus-sized wombat *(Diprotodon)*. Many shell middens (remains of shellfish meals), quarries and fishtraps remain.

The Aborigines also learnt to use the local flora in everyday life, both for food and materials for a broad range of objects. Wood was used to fashion clubs, bowls, spears and boomerangs. Slender banksia was soaked in water to make a sweet drink and the *Macrozamia* (a cycad with cones) was cooked and eaten after it too was soaked, while the small leaf clematis was roasted and pounded into a mash.

About a dozen local groups of the Nyoongar people occupied the area of the Swan River Valley and it is estimated there were over another dozen tribal groups between Geraldton and Esperance. The Aborigines travelled along *bidi* (tracks) to trade or meet for feasts and ceremonies.

Aboriginal prehistory is still being pieced together – only further archaeological dis-coveries and painstaking research will clarify the origins and identity of the Aborigines of the west and, indeed, Australia.

The First Foreigners
There is no doubt that the first 'outsiders' to make contact with the Aborigines were traders from the islands that are now Indonesia (who are remembered in song cycles and in paintings). Their impact, however, was likely slight and confined to coastal area.

Uncertainty surrounds the great Asian fleet under the Chinese lord, Cheng Ho (Zheng He), who allegedly visited the north-ern Australian shores in the 15th century. A small carved figure of the Chinese god of good life, Shao Lao, was found lodged in the roots of a banyan tree near Darwin – it dated from the Ming Dynasty (1368-1644). However, no account of its origin survives.

The Europeans
The Portuguese, traversing the Indian Ocean in the 15th century, may have been the first to discover the west coast. A 16th-century book talks about a voyage to the Kimberley coast and a Portuguese map, dated 1602, indicates a landing in the region of Collier and Brunswick bays.

As early as 1606, the Dutchman, Willem Jansz, sailing in the *Duyfken*, explored the western coast of Cape York. He was unaware of the significance of his discoveries and did not know that he had touched a new conti-nent.

Another Dutchman, Henrik Brouwer, dis-covered a shorter route from the Cape of Good Hope to Batavia (Jakarta) in 1611. The ships would sail into the Roaring Forties in the Southern Ocean, use the tremendous winds to head east then strike north to their intended destination. These powerful winds often carried the ships too far west where they would hit the western coast of Australia.

The first known Europeans to land on or near the WA coast were Dutch. Dirk Hartog sighted land near Shark Bay on 25 October 1616. He and a party of fellow Dutch rowed ashore from the *Eendracht* and landed on the island that now bears his name. He left, at what is now called Cape Inscription – the famous pewter Hartog Plate recording the landing.

The next recorded contact was by Lenaert Jacobszoon and Willem Jansz of the *Mauritius* in 1618. They landed at Cloates Island near Exmouth and named the Willems River. The following year Houtman discovered and named the Abrolhos Islands, scene of the notorious wreck of the *Batavia*, some 10 years later.

In 1622, the crew of the *Leeuwin* explored the south-west coast. That same year the first English came ashore – the crew of the *Trial* (also spelled *Tryal*), wrecked on a reef near the Montebellos Islands.

What followed was exploration interspersed with tragedy (see the boxed aside 'Dutch Shipwrecks' in the Central West Coast chapter). Francis Thijssen and Pieter Nuijts in the *Gulden Zeepaard* sighted the southern part of the continent near Cape Leeuwin and sailed a further 1600km east across the Great Australian Bight. And the following year, Gerit Frederikszoon de Witt, in the *Vyanen*, sighted land at 21° south by accident.

The first navigator to really chart the western coast was Abel Tasman. In 1644, with the *Limmen*, *Zeemeeuw* and *Bracq*, he sailed up the north-west coast from near Exmouth Gulf, continuing further north towards the Gulf of Carpentaria.

William Dampier

The first of the English to chart the coast was William Dampier. A buccaneer and passenger of the *Cygnet*, he landed at the subsequently named Cygnet Bay (near the modern-day Dampier Peninsula) in 1688. The ship, under the command of Captain Read, was forced to spend over two months in Australian waters as it needed careening. The Aborigines encountered at Cygnet Bay were described by Read as 'the miserablest people in the world', observing that they had no houses and slept in the open.

Dampier left the *Cygnet* and returned to England in 1691 after spending more than 12 years on his first voyage. In 1697 he published an account of his voyage entitled *New Voyage Around the World*. His stature enhanced, he obtained command of the HMS *Roebuck* and embarked, in January 1699, on another voyage of discovery. In early August 1699, he found himself off the Houtman Abrolhos Islands.

Dampier, using the chart Tasman had prepared in 1644, sailed northwards. He encountered many sharks and turtles at the place he named Shark's (now Shark) Bay. Further north, the ship passed a group of small islands, which are now the Dampier Archipelago. The ship then landed at Roebuck Bay, near present-day Broome. Unfortunately, a skirmish between the sailors and local Aborigines resulted in Dampier shooting one of them. He later apologised 'for what happened'.

The lack of water and the health of his scurvy-ridden crew drove Dampier to abandon further exploration and head for Timor. By July 1700 the *Roebuck* was in Batavia and in bad need of an overhaul. The *Roebuck* sank at Ascension Island on its return voyage to England; the crew were eventually rescued in July 1701.

Willem de Vlamingh

In 1696, another group of Dutch navigators, Willem de Vlamingh in the *Geelvinck*, Gerrit Collaert in the *Nijptangh* and Cornelius de Vlamingh in the *Het Weseltje*, searched New Holland for a group of survivors from a Dutch East India Company (Verenigde Oost-Indische Compagnie) ship lost in 1694.

They sighted the coast on Christmas Day and landed on the mainland at Cottesloe Beach. Exploring parties ventured inland, saw the black swans and gave the river, on which Perth is now sited, its name. He also mistook the quokkas (small wallabies) on the island west of Perth to be rats and named the place Rottnest (or Rat's Nest).

De Vlamingh sailed north and landed on Hartog Island where he found, you guessed it, the Hartog Plate, placed there in 1616. Leaving plates must have been the go in the 17th century – de Vlamingh swiped Hartog's and substituted his own. (The former is now

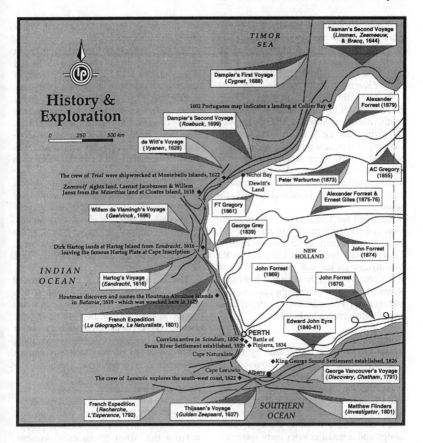

History & Exploration

TIMOR SEA

Tasman's Second Voyage (*Limmen, Zeemeeuw, & Bracq*, 1644)

Dampier's First Voyage (*Cygnet*, 1688)

1602 Portuguese map indicates a landing at Collier Bay ◆

Alexander Forrest (1879)

Dampier's Second Voyage (*Roebuck*, 1699)

de Witt's Voyage (*Vyanen*, 1628)

The crew of *Trial* were shipwrecked at Montebello Islands, 1622 ◆

Zeewolf sights land. Laenart Jacobszoon & Willem Jansz from the *Mauritius* land at Cloates Island, 1618 ◆

Nichol Bay ◆

Dewitt's Land

Peter Warburton (1873)

AC Gregory (1855)

Willem de Vlamingh's Voyage (*Geelvinck*, 1696)

FT Gregory (1861)

Alexander Forrest & Ernest Giles (1875-76)

George Grey (1839)

NEW HOLLAND

John Forrest (1874)

Dirk Hartog lands at Hartog Island from *Eendracht*, 1616 - leaving the famous Hartog Plate at Cape Inscription

INDIAN OCEAN

Hartog's Voyage (*Eendracht*, 1616)

John Forrest (1869)

John Forrest (1870)

Houtman discovers and names the Houtman Abrolhos Islands ◆ in *Batavia*, 1619 - which was wrecked here in 1629

French Expedition (*Le Géographe, Le Naturaliste*, 1801)

Edward John Eyre (1840-41)

Convicts arrive in *Scindian*, 1850 ◆
Swan River Settlement established, 1829 ◆

PERTH
Battle of Pinjarra, 1834

Cape Naturaliste

King George Sound Settlement established, 1826 ◆

Cape Leeuwin
Albany

George Vancouver's Voyage (*Discovery, Chatham*, 1791)

The crew of *Leeuwin* explores the south-west coast, 1622 ◆

French Expedition (*Recherche, L'Espérance*, 1792)

Thijssen's Voyage (*Gulden Zeepaard*, 1627)

SOUTHERN OCEAN

Matthew Flinders (*Investigator*, 1801)

0   250   500 km

in the Rijksmuseum in Amsterdam and the latter is in the Maritime Museum in Fremantle.) From Hartog Island, de Vlamingh continued to survey the coast and look for survivors; sailing as far north as Exmouth Gulf before heading for Batavia.

Later Exploration

Captain James Cook, aboard the *Endeavour* (1768-1771), came nowhere near the western coast of Australia, and the First Fleet, bound for Botany Bay in 1788, sailed well below the south-western coast of the continent.

In 1791, almost 100 years after de Vlamingh and Dampier, George Vancouver, in command of the *Discovery* and *Chatham*, sailed within sight of land at Cape Nuyts (Vancouver Island and the Canadian city are named after him.). He discovered and named Cape Chatham, and two days later found the harbour of King George III Sound where he formally took possession of the country for Britain. He left the coast near Esperance for Tasmania.

The following year a French expedition transported by two ships – the *Recherche* and *L'Espérance* – visited the west coast looking for traces of the French explorer La Pérouse who had disappeared in 1788. The place names Esperance and Archipelago of the Recherche, relate to this visit, as does Point d'Entrecasteaux, named after the captain of the *Recherche*.

In 1800, the French navigator Nicolas Baudin set out to complete a survey of the southern coast of Australia. His two ships *Le Géographe* and *Le Naturaliste* anchored in Géographe Bay, near present-day Busselton, on 27 May 1801. They explored the coast as far as Shark Bay where, today, the naturalist of the expedition, François Péron, is remembered in the name of the cape at the tip of the peninsula.

They left for Timor in order to re-provision the expedition, returning in 1802. Baudin met Matthew Flinders – who, in 1801, passed near Cape Leeuwin in the *Investigator* on his way to Bass Strait – at Encounter Bay, near the mouth of the Murray River. Many of the place names given by the cartographer Freycinet were later replaced with English names by Flinders.

Colonisation

It was probably the exploration by French mariners such as Baudin that prompted colonists on the eastern coast of Australia to take interest in the vast west. Reports of a dry, barren land had previously discouraged attempts at settlement and it was not until 1826 that Major Edmund Lockyer, some troops and a small convict party were sent from Sydney in the brig *Amity* to establish a military outpost at King George Sound. The small outpost was never intended to be permanent and in 1831 the garrison and convicts were withdrawn.

Also in 1826, Captain James Stirling had sailed to the area of the Swan River to see if it was suitable for settlement. He was enthusiastic about its potential and pushed for the establishment of a colony when he returned to Britain in 1828. In November 1828, Captain CH Fremantle, in command of HMS *Challenger*, sailed to take possession of the territory; on 2 May 1829, at the mouth of the Swan River, he formally annexed all terri-tory outside the colony of New South Wales (NSW) for the Crown.

Stirling's proposals had received much publicity in Britain and many people flocked to take advantage of the favourable terms of settlement – one acre of land for every one shilling and sixpence (worth 15 cents today but considerably more then) of equipment, money or stock which potential settlers took with them. Stirling was appointed as Lieu-tenant Governor of the settlement and was provided with the 63rd Regiment along with administrators.

The *Parmelia* and *Sulphur* transports arrived in Cockburn Sound on 1 June 1829 and the new colony was officially pro-claimed on 18 June. For almost two months, the settlers camped on Garden Island until a suitable site for the new colony had been determined. By the end of 1830 there were about 1500 settlers.

The first 10 years of colonisation proved arduous. The land given the settlers was often of poor quality, food was scarce and money in short supply. In 1848 there were over 40,000 people in the colony but just over a thousand labourers. Shortages eventually led the colony to ask the British government for help in the form of convict labour.

Aboriginal Resistance

During the long history of Aboriginal occupation of WA, hunting and gathering was done successfully in small nomadic groups, despite the often harsh environment. However, colonisation proved to have dire consequences for the local Aborigines, espe-cially the Nyoongar people of the south-west.

In 1829, the Swan River settlement was established on land known already to the Nyoongar as Mooro; the site of Perth at the foot of Mt Eliza was known as Boorloo. The Aborigines, after seeing the settlers shoot their food sources such as kangaroo, took cattle and sheep in response. But, under European law they were seen as thieves.

Aboriginal-European relations reached their nadir during Governor Stirling's control. In 1832-33, the Aborigines began forming groups in order to resist the settlers. In October 1834, an official expedition led by Stirling, designed to eliminate resistance by the Nyoongar – led by the warrior Calyute – set out for the Murray River. The Nyoongar were ambushed and many were killed. Two of Stirling's men were wounded and one, Captain Ellis, died later of his wounds. The Battle of Pinjarra (as it came to be known) lasted for about an hour and a half; the wounded Aborigines were hunted down and killed. About 50 were slain but Calyute survived. Nyoongar resistance effectively ended at that point and the following year the Murray River leaders pledged their support to Governor Stirling and the Crown.

The Convicts

The first group of convicts transported to WA at the request of the colony, arrived off Fremantle in the *Scindian* on 1 June 1850. It was at this time that transportation was ending in the eastern colonies (1840 in NSW and 1852 in Tasmania).

Many convicts were set to work constructing public buildings and roads in Perth and Fremantle. Works from this period include the jail at Fremantle, a road linking Perth to Albany, Government House, the Perth Town Hall, the Pensioners' Barracks and a summer residence for the governor on Rottnest Island.

The colony was seen as a natural prison, where escape was made difficult by distance. The lash was employed sparingly, usually for cases of brutal assault, but chains were used around Perth and Fremantle. Convicts worked for the government until eligible for a conditional pardon or 'ticket of leave' (four years for a seven-year sentence and five years three months for a 10-year sentence) when they could do wage labour, virtually as free men, for other settlers. They were also subject to certain reporting conditions and could not return to Britain.

The first Comptroller General, Captain Edmund Henderson, oversaw the operation until 1863 (he was also largely responsible for the setting up of Scotland Yard). When an ex-Comptroller General of convicts in

Tasmania and a veteran of Norfolk Island, Dr JS Hampton, arrived to take over as governor, the convicts were treated more strictly. The settlers spread out from Swan River to Champion Bay, Bunbury, Busselton and Albany, with convicts providing labour.

Transportation of convicts to WA ceased by January 1868 with the 37th transport, the *Hougoumont*. Aboard were 63 Irish Fenians including the writer and editor John Boyle O'Reilly. In 1869, O'Reilly escaped from Bunbury on a US whaler. From New York he helped organise the rescue of six other Fenians – the *Catalpa* picked them up near Rockingham in 1876.

Over 9600 convicts were sent to WA, their labour important to the development of the colony. Anthony Trollope, the English novelist, visited the colony after transportation had ended and observed:

Such roads have been made as the other colonies do not possess. Public buildings have been erected, and an air of prosperity has been given to the two towns – Perth and Fremantle, the only towns in the colony – which could hardly have come to them yet but for this convict aid...

'Cinderella' Colony

In comparison to the colonies in the east, WA was much poorer, prompting the reference 'Cinderella' colony. But its apparent poverty did little to deter further exploration.

Explorers had been hard at work since 1839 when George Grey walked from Shark Bay to Perth. Edward John Eyre's party set out from South Australia in 1840, with Eyre and an unwilling Aborigine, Wylie, finally reaching Albany in 1841 after food shortages had forced them to depend on Wylie's hunting and food gathering ability. In 1861 Frank T Gregory set out from Nickol Bay (near modern-day Karratha) along the Fortescue River to the Hamersley Range.

The Forrests, John and Alexander, were active explorers for 10 years from 1869 to 1879. In 1869, John led an expedition in search of Ludwig Leichhardt and got as far inland as Lake Ballard; in 1870, he and four others travelled from Perth to Adelaide. In

The Baron of Bunbury

John Forrest, later Lord Forrest, Baron of Bunbury, was born near Bunbury in 1847. He is the giant of WA's modern history, having achieved fame in the fields of exploration and politics. In physical appearance he was also a giant, with a huge frame, bushy whiskers and an equally dominating presence.

In 1869 he led an expedition to search for Ludwig Leichhardt's party and reached the Lake Ballard area north of modern-day Kalgoorlie. Next, in 1870, he became the first to follow the Great Australian Bight west to east when he travelled from Perth to Adelaide.

On his third expedition in 1874, he explored the hinterland from which flow the Gascoyne, Murchison, Ashburton, De Grey and Fitzroy rivers. From there he pushed on across the Gibson Desert to the Peake telegraph station on the Adelaide to Darwin telegraph line, thus completing a more northerly west-east crossing. He published an account of his journeys, *Explorations in Australia*, in 1875.

As Commissioner of Crown Lands and Surveyor-General from 1883 to 1890, he made, in 1884, a fourth expedition to a large part of the Kimberley plateau. In 1890 Forrest entered politics as Premier of WA, heading a coalition of independent members of parliament (there were no political parties in WA at that time).

Forrest resigned from state politics in 1901 and entered the first federal parliament as Postmaster General in the first federal ministry. Later he held portfolios for Defence, Home Affairs, Treasury and was, for a brief period, acting Prime Minister. His two chief political successes were the goldfields water supply scheme and the transcontinental railway. In 1918, the year of his death, he became the first Australian-born citizen to be raised to the British peerage. ■

1873, a party led by Peter Warburton left Alice Springs in an attempt to cross to Perth, nearly starving to death before they reached the north-west coast near the Oakover River. In 1875-76, Alexander and Ernest Giles crossed the continent from South Australia to Perth and in 1879, Alexander, in a much feted expedition, went from De Grey River to Daly Waters in the Northern Territory.

As new regions were discovered, systems of roads, railways and telegraph lines were established to link communities. Perth was connected to the Overland Telegraph Line in 1877, providing communication to London and Adelaide.

Gold Rushes

Gold was discovered at Halls Creek in the remote Kimberley in 1885, and in 1886 diggers on the Queensland fields made the anti-clockwise trek towards new riches. The terrain in the Kimberley was inhospitable and the track from the wharves at Wyndham and Derby the most ferocious that miners in Australia had yet negotiated.

The Pilbara was next to reveal its riches. In 1888, diggers swarmed over Pilbara Creek, fanning out through the dry gorges to Marble Bar, Nullagine and the Ashburton River. Despite the intense heat, the lure of gold proved irresistible and some diggers were rewarded with finds of huge nuggets.

Gold was found near Nannine, inland from Geraldton, in 1890. The Murchison field now bloomed and Cue, Day Dawn, Paynes Find, Lake Austin and Mt Magnet joined the list of gold towns in the outback.

More discoveries followed, especially

around Southern Cross in the Yilgarn. Major strikes were made in 1892 at Coolgardie and nearby Kalgoorlie, but of all the goldfield areas, Kalgoorlie remains the only large town.

Coolgardie's period of prosperity lasted only until 1905 and many other gold towns went from nothing to populations of 10,000 then back to nothing in just 10 years. However, WA profited from the gold boom for the rest of the century. Gold put WA on the map and finally gave it the population to make it viable in its own right, rather than just an offshoot of the eastern colonies.

Economic depression and unemployment often attracted fossickers back to the gullies and rivers, especially during the Great Depression. In other places mining never actually stopped – witness the Golden Mile in Kalgoorlie-Boulder.

Federation & After

The colony of WA adopted a new constitution in 1890 and the gold discoveries brought wealth and independence. Initially there was scepticism about whether or not the eastern colonies would care about the remote west in a federation. But when it came to vote to federate, the eastern diggers on the west's goldfields ensured a 'yes' vote. The new Australian constitution was accepted and WA retained its boundary at the 129th meridian. The first premier was the explorer Sir John Forrest (see the boxed aside 'The Baron of Bunbury' in this chapter).

Rapid expansion in primary production and a wheatbelt was established between Perth and the eastern goldfields soon after WWI. The Depression hit WA hard (wheat and wool prices fell dramatically). This carried on to local manufacturing, geared to supply farmers, and many workers lost their jobs and were forced to go on the 'dole' (unemployment benefit).

The Depression heightened feelings of neglect in the west and added to the perception that the isolated state had lost much because of Federation. During the 1930s, discussion about secession from the federation occurred, with proponents blaming the

Edith Dirksey Cowan (1861-1932)

Edith Cowan was born 2 August 1861 at Glengarry, near Geraldton. A leading social reformer who was passionately interested in women's issues, she was awarded the Order of the British Empire (OBE) in 1920 and the following year was elected by constituents of West Perth to the Legislative Assembly. In her three-year term she highlighted the need for improved migrant welfare, sex education and infant health centres. She also encouraged women to enter the legal profession through her sponsorship of the Women's Legal Status Act in 1923.

After losing her seat she continued advocating women's rights until she died on 9 June 1932. (Interestingly, the first woman Cabinet Minister was also West Australian – Mrs AFG Cardell-Oliver, Member of the Legislative Assembly (MLA) for Subiaco, in the Ministry of 1947.) ∎

eastern states for the prevailing economic woes. Electors in the compulsory 1933 referendum voted by almost two-to-one to leave the Australian Commonwealth – only six electoral districts of 50 recorded a no majority, five in the goldfields and the Kimberley. Secession never occurred as it was deemed WA had no legal right to request legislation on the constitution. The referendum, however, was an important signal to the federal government. (You can see a copy of the Secession Petition in the Museum of WA.)

Paradoxically, the state Australian Labor Party which had not supported secession, was swept into power in 1933 and remained there until the narrow Liberal-Country Party victory in 1947.

WWII

During WWII the west felt the brunt of war first-hand. The great naval engagement between HMAS *Sydney* and the German auxiliary cruiser *Kormoran* was fought on 19 November 1941. The result was the sinking of both ships and the loss of the entire crew (645 personnel) of the *Sydney*.

Broome, Wyndham, Derby and Onslow were bombed by the Japanese in February

1942 and it is believed that the Japanese came ashore and reconnoitred part of the Kimberley. In Broome, 70 people were killed and 16 Royal Dutch Air Force flying boats destroyed while moored near the old jetty. In Wyndham, the SS *Koolama* was bombed and sunk.

Many military bases were established in the west. Fremantle became an important naval base for Allied operations in the Indian Ocean and Exmouth Gulf was the centre of *Operation Potshot*, an advance US submarine refuelling base.

A great number of Italian prisoners of war, captured in North Africa, were allocated to work on farms; many stayed on after the war and their descendants live in WA today.

Post-War to the Present

After the war the west began to prosper, mainly as a result of the exploitation of the state's vast mineral wealth. In 1948 iron ore was shipped from Yampi Sound and since then the state has not looked back – it is now one of the main iron-ore exporters in the world. Mines such as Tom Price, Mt Newman and Goldsworthy flourished in the Pilbara and an elaborate infrastructure of transport and shipping was set up to support this massive growth. Migrants came into the state to bolster the workforce and women took a greater role in all areas of industry. In the Kimberley, the mighty Ord River Scheme was established in 1961, bringing fertility to the desert.

The state politics of the post-war years has seen three distinct periods of ascendancy by either the ALP or the conservative coalition. The ALP ran the state for six years from 1953 until 1959 when the Liberal & Country League (LCL)-Country Party (CP) coalition came to power.

Except for the three-year interruption of the Tonkin Labor government (1971-1974), the LCL-CP coalition held power from 1959 to 1983. In this time two strong Liberal leaders, David Brand and Sir Charles Court, ruled almost unopposed. Labor, led by the young and popular Brian Burke, was returned to office in 1983.

The Labor Government of the late 1980s was embroiled in a series of scandals called 'WA Inc'. The term – used loosely to describe a series of titanic collapses involving businessmen and the Labor government – led to a Royal Commission into governmental corruption. The government suffered heavily at the hands of voters in the 1993 election. The conservative Liberal-Country Party coalition government, headed by Richard Fairfax Court, son of former premier Sir Charles Court, took reign and introduced austere economic policies. While the scandals surrounding WA Inc proved painful, they appear not to have had any effect on the state's international reputation.

Today, a larger and far more technologically advanced mineral boom forms the basis of the state's prosperity. During the rapacious 1980s with a number of high-flying entrepreneurs added their marks to the Perth city skyline. At this time Fremantle played host to the 1986 America's Cup (Australia was the holder after defeating the USA in 1983). Their defence, however, was unsuccessful.

The display of 'paper' wealth was conspicuous and the entrepreneurs fell heavily when the economic bubble burst, partly a result of the October 1997 stockmarket crash. A number of key players such as the late Laurie Connell and Alan Bond served prison terms for their indiscretions during the period of WA Inc, indeed Bond is expected to remain in prison until 2000. In July 1994, former premier, Brian Burke, was sentenced to jail for two years for rorting travel expenses. Legal actions on other prominent figures are still outstanding.

Aboriginal Protest & Land Rights

In May 1946, the first real act of Aboriginal self-determination was enacted in the Pilbara. Then, 800 Aboriginal workers walked off their stations in the Port Hedland region in protest at their degrading conditions, 'slave wages' and the enforcement of the archaic Native Administration Act.

Led by white prospector Don McLeod and two Aborigines, Clancy McKenna and

Dooley Binbin, the strikers congregated in camps. In the atmosphere of post-war security, little news of the protest was leaked to the press and Binbin and McKenna were arrested for communist subversion. When food coupons were withheld from the protesters they returned to traditional methods of food gathering.

The protest culminated with a station-to-station march in 1949 and, after protesters were arrested, the Seaman's Union banned the handling of wool from the 'slave stations'. The government conceded to the protesters demands so that the shipping ban would be lifted (but soon after backed out of the deal). Meanwhile, the strikers had taken up other occupations and never returned to the stations.

Land rights became a prominent issue in June 1966 when a group at Wave Hill station (owned by the British Vestey corporation) walked off their jobs, requesting that some of their land be returned to them. It wasn't until 1973 that the federal Whitlam Labor government announced that it would buy back two cattle stations in the north-west and return them to the Aborigines. Ironically, it was part of the Wave Hill station which was returned to the traditional Gurindji owners.

In 1992 the High Court handed down the Mabo decision. The result of a claim by Torres Strait islander, Eddy Mabo, it challenged and overturned the established concept of *terra nullius* – that Australia was empty or uninhabited on white arrival. The court's ruling – that Aborigines were the first occupants and had the right to claim land back where continuous association was demonstrated – set off a heated and deeply divided debate on land rights and mining interests within WA. The state government even went as far as passing legislation which conflicted with Commonwealth legislation though little impact on new resource projects has yet been felt.

In 1993, the Labor federal government introduced the Native Title Act, which formalised the High Court's Mabo ruling. The content of the bill had, somewhat surprisingly, been agreed upon by all the major players involved – the miners, the farmers, the government and Aborigines. In reality, the act gives Aboriginal people few new rights. The application of native title is limited to land which no-one owns or leases, and also to land which Aboriginal people have continued to have a physical association. The acts states that existing ownership or leases extinguish native title, although native title may be revived after mining leases have expired. If land is successfully claimed by Aboriginal people under the act, they will have no veto over developments, including mining.

When the Howard Liberal-National coalition government was elected in March 1996 they promised to retain the Native Title Act, but matters were further complicated when the High Court handed down the Wik decision, which established that pastoral leases don't necessarily extinguish native title. This has resulted in some fairly hysterical responses and, especially in WA and Queensland, threatens to undermine the reconciliation process between Aboriginal and non-Aboriginal Australians.

In the face of the Wik decision, which alienated the grass roots supporters of the National Party; new 'compromise' proposals (in Bill form for Parliament) were introduced. The Labor opposition saw the Native Title Act to be 'gutted' if the government's Wik legislation became law, Aborigines saw it as derailing the reconciliation process, and the National Farmers Federation even found fault with it. There is continuing uncertainty regarding native title, and the 'development-rampant' west anxiously awaits an outcome.

GEOGRAPHY

Western Australia is Australia's largest state with a size of 2,525,500 sq km, a third of the country's land mass. It extends 1621km from the Indian Ocean to the 129th meridian where the Northern Territory and South Australia begin. It extends 2391km north from the Southern Ocean to the Timor Sea. The most northerly point is Cape Londonderry and the most southerly, Torbay Head.

Western Australia has a small coastal strip

in its south-west corner. Hills rise behind the coast here, but not as dramatically as the Great Dividing Range in the eastern states. Further north it's dry and relatively barren. Fringing the central-west coast is the Great Sandy Desert, an inhospitable region running almost to the sea.

There are a couple of interesting variations, such as the Kimberley, in the extreme north of the state – a wild and rugged area with a convoluted coast and spectacular inland gorges. It gets good annual rainfall, but all in the Wet or 'Green' season. There are small, remote patches of tropical rainforest here.

Further south is the Pilbara, an area with more magnificent ancient rock and gorge country and the treasure-house from which the state derives its vast mineral wealth. The Pilbara has two of the state's most interesting national parks – Karijini, based in the gorges of the Hamersley Ranges; and Millstream-Chichester, an oasis in the desert. Near Karijini is Mt MeHarry, WA's highest point at 1245m. Incidentally, the highest waterfall is King George Falls (80m), the highest town is Tom Price (740m) and the longest river the Gascoyne (865km).

From the coast there are a number of large islands and archipelagos. Large islands include Augustus, Barrow, Bigge, Bernier and Hartog. Some of the archipelagos are Bonaparte, Buccaneer, Dampier, Houtman Abrolhos and Recherche. There are also numerous prominent peninsulas and capes that jut into the Indian Ocean – Dampier, North-West Cape, Péron and Naturaliste.

The world's largest west-coast reef, Ningaloo, stretches south from North-West Cape to Coral Bay, some 260km. It is Australia's closest point to the continental shelf.

Christmas & Cocos (Keeling) Islands

Often forgotten are Australia's Indian Ocean protectorates – Christmas Island and the Cocos (Keeling) Islands, about 2300km and 2750km north-west of Perth respectively. Both places are wildlife havens and island paradises.

The average temperature on Christmas is 27°C, but being near the equator it is humid and rain falls between December and April. In the Cocos (Keeling) group temperatures are similar with two distinct periods referred to: the hot and sultry 'doldrums' from October to March and the cooler 'trades' from April to September.

Christmas Island is some 137 sq km and over 60% of this is national park. Although the island was named on Christmas Day 1643, the first recorded landing, by William Dampier, did not occur until 1688. From 1897 until 1987 phosphate was mined and there is still limited mining now. Today, tourism plays a large part in the island's prosperity and there are a backpackers' hostel, lodge and a casino/resort on Waterfall Bay (it was recently closed but is due to reopen). The Christmas Island Visitor Information Centre (☎ (08) 9164 8382; fax 9164 8080) will happily provide further details.

Each year in December/January, at the end of the Dry, there is a spectacular migration when millions of red crabs move from the rainforest to the ocean to spawn.

The Cocos Islands, with their Cocos Malay culture are strongly characterised by the Muslim faith and adherence to prayer. The first recorded sighting of the Cocos was in 1609, but the islands were not settled until the 1820s when the Clunies-Ross family established an estate on Home Island. Today there is limited tourist accommodation on West Island and the chance to enjoy local seafood cooked in the Malay style. Travellers are just beginning to learn of the existence of this idyllic island group.

On all these islands there is much opportunity to see tropical rainforest and orchids, masses of land crabs (18 species are found on Christmas alone), reptiles, bats and rare seabirds. Diving, snorkelling, surfing, fishing and beachcombing are all popular activities.

For information, contact the Christmas Island Visitor Information Centre (☎ 9164 8382), Coates Wildlife Tours (☎ 9324 2552) or Island Bound Holidays (☎ toll-free (1800) 804 420, 9381 3644). A package tour from Perth to Cocos Island with lodge accommodation is $1090/1330 for six/14 nights; to Christmas Island it is $1140/1410 in the lodge, $1300/1780 at the resort. Australians do not need a passport and there is no departure tax; duty free shopping is possible. ■

Away from the coast, however, most of WA seems a vast empty stretch of outback: the Nullarbor Plain in the south, the Great Sandy Desert in the north and the Gibson and Great Victoria deserts in between. There are many interesting features dotted throughout the arid regions to break the monotony, including Mt Augustus, the world's largest rock (monadnock).

The south-west is much more different than the bulk of the state. The Mediterranean climate and higher rainfall has made this a much greener place with large tracts of forest (see the Flora section later in this chapter) intersected by rivers and streams. The forests only occur where the rainfall exceeds 500mm, and by far the bulk of forest is jarrah with nearly 15,000 sq km followed by the karri with about 1500 sq km.

There are two interesting mountain ranges which punctuate the rolling, grassy plains – the Porongurups and the Stirlings. The Stirlings rise abruptly more than 1000m above sea level, and stretch east-west for 65km. Prominent peaks include Bluff Knoll, Toolbrunup, Mt Trio, Mondurup and Ellen Peak, all above 800m. The Porongurups are 40km south, distinguishable by their huge 1100-million-year-old granite domes. Both ranges support unique species of animals and plants.

The coastline in the south is exciting with numerous rugged headlands, granite boulders, rock shelves and sheltered bays.

GEOLOGY

From Perth you can look to the Darling Ranges which are, in fact, the edge of the Yilgarnia escarpment. Yilgarnia is one of the oldest lands in the world and was formed in the early stages of the Archae (a subdivision of the Pre-Cambrian) period, about 2600 million years ago. It was altered for about 1500 million years, covered up in many places and sank below sea level in others. The Archipelago of the Recherche is a part of Yilgarnia.

North of the Yilgarnia are the world's oldest rocks – those that are almost original crust – dated at 4.1 billion years old. These are the zircon crystals of Mt Narryer, inland from Shark Bay, formed a mere 500 million years after the earth began to coalesce.

When did life start on earth? So far WA holds the first tangible proof. In the Pilbara, fossilised stromatolites (see the boxed aside 'Stromatolites' in the Central West Coast chapter), found in a layer of siltstone, have been dated at 3.5 billion years old. At sea level, in Shark Bay, stromatolites thrive in the hypersaline waters of Hamelin Pool.

Nearby, the Hamersley Ranges constitute the backbone of the Pilbara. The rocks, which form the gorges of Karijini National Park, are over 2.5 billion years old. They originated as iron and silica-rich sediment deposits that accumulated on the sea bed. Horizontal compression forced these sediments to buckle and develop cracks, until the whole was elevated to the surface to form dry land.

The Kimberley had its origins in the Proterozoic period more than two billion years ago. Sediments referred to as the Halls Creek Group were laid down and underwent intense folding and faulting. About 150 million years later, the sediments forming the Kimberley basin were also laid down, remaining remarkably stable in spite of two mobile zones nearby. Approximately 750 and 670 million years ago the region was gripped by two severe glacial epochs.

It is in the Devonian era, 370 million years ago, that the most visible geological features were formed; this was before mammals or reptiles had evolved. In the Devonian era, a barrier reef grew south-east of Derby where the Canning Basin area was covered by a tropical sea. It is surmised that this reef, 300km of which is exposed, could have extended some 1000km to join with another exposed reef in the Bonaparte Basin near Kununurra.

The limestone reefs – of which Geikie Gorge, Windjana Gorge and Tunnel Creek national parks are part – rise from 50 to 100m above the river valleys. Obviously the limestone was more resilient to the weathering and other geological changes which occurred.

The geological oddity of the Kimberley is the Purnululu (Bungle Bungle) Range. The ancient beehives, gravels and sandstones encased in silica, which make up this massif, are 350 million years old. It is believed that rivers flowing south and east from nearby formations washed sand and pebbles into the area. This gradually compacted to form sandstone which was uplifted over time and gouged out by the Wet (monsoonal rains occurring between December and April). The covering of silica (orange in colour) and lichen (green) protected the domes from complete erosion, leaving the curious beehives you see today.

East of Purnululu is the Wolfe Creek meteorite crater, one of the best preserved craters in the world, formed thousands of years ago when a meteor weighing thousands of tonnes hit the earth. The crater floor is 50m below the rim and the outer slopes are 35m high.

CLIMATE

Western Australia has a variety of climates from the tropical savannah in the north (the Kimberley), through the desert and semidesert of the centre to the Mediterranean climate of the south-west. The main influence of topography is a decrease in rainfall the further you get from the coast. The trade winds separate the northern south-east trade winds from the westerlies in the south.

The tropical north has hot, 'sticky' wet summers and warm dry winters. The climate is characterised by the Wet. Before the Wet there is an incredible period called the 'build-up'. The horizon is black as ominous clouds roll through the sky and there are occasional flashes of lightning. No rain falls until one day, a deluge ... the Wet has started. Once the Wet begins, the roads are subject to flash flooding at any time.

Occasionally, there are tropical cyclones. These usually develop well offshore and produce heavy rain, high winds and the lashing of coastal areas. Port Hedland gets a cyclone about once every two years. Cyclones produced WA's biggest wind gust (267 km/h, Tropical Cyclone Olivia, April

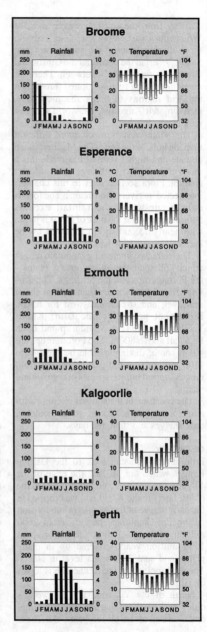

1996) and heaviest rainfall (747mm in one day in 1975).

May to November the nights are mostly cool and crisp and the days are sunny with blue skies.

The area of WA which could be classified as desert or semidesert is east of a line drawn roughly from Geraldton through Southern Cross to midway between Albany and Esperance, and south of a line drawn from Broome to Halls Creek. These areas have hot dry summers, mild dry winters. (Desert areas get less than 250mm of rainfall annually.)

About 200km south of Port Hedland, on the Great Northern Highway, is Marble Bar, reputedly the hottest place in Australia. Australian seasons are the opposite of the northern hemisphere's and temperatures are expressed in degrees Celsius (see the conversion chart at the back of the book). October to March, expect daytime temperatures of 38°C and above. There was a period in the 1920s when the temperature topped 37°C for 160 consecutive days. On one occasion, in 1905, the mercury soared to 49.1°C. The highest temperature ever recorded was 50.7°C at Eucla (near the South Australian border).

The Mediterranean climate of the south has hot, dry summers and mild, wet winters. Perth, in the centre of this region, has maximums of around 30°C from December to March, but minimums are rarely below 10°C. February is the hottest month, July the coldest. Rainfall is lightest from November to March when it seldom rains (20mm and below) and heaviest May to August (120 to 200mm). Perth's annual rainfall averages 975mm.

Summer sees the crowds flock to Rottnest Island and the southern and northern beaches; in winter, only the hardy are seen out windsurfing and surfing as the beaches are inhospitable places with strong westerlies whipping up large waves.

One peculiarity of the local weather is the 'Fremantle Doctor', a wind that blows in from the sea in the late afternoon. It is often welcomed by Western Australians as it clears away the oppressive heat.

The Great Southern area is much influenced by the prevailing winds and many storms blow in from the southern ocean. To the north, the Stirling Ranges create a weather pattern all their own. In late spring and early summer (October to December), when it begins to warm, the ranges are an ideal place to visit. Winter (June to August) in this range is cold and wet and the temperatures can drop suddenly. Hail and rain are common and snow occasionally falls.

ECOLOGY & ENVIRONMENT

In spite of the lack of resources, a fair degree of political opposition and a small population base, the 'green movement' is alive and well in the west. The peak body which coordinates the 60 or so environmental groups is the Conservation Council of Western Australia (CCWA; ☎ 9220 0652), 79 Stirling St, Perth 6000. The government department charged with the care of WA's natural resources is Conservation & Land Management (CALM). Its methods of forest conservation and management are often at odds with ecological organisations. Consequently, the environmental watchdogs are very much opposed to a number of CALM's policies, especially logging in the south-west forests and mining

Other useful environmental organisations include:

Environment Centre of WA Inc
  Resource and information base for both the public and various organisations, publishes *What's On...Environmentally* monthly (☎ 9335 2137).
South-West Forests Defence Foundation
  Organisation to prevent destruction of the beautiful native forests, especially karri, in the south-west (☎ 9325 2813).
Western Australian Forest Alliance
  Another organisation to prevent destruction of the beautiful native forests in the south-west, in particular the Giblett block, based at the CCWA (☎ 9220 0651).
Wilderness Society
  Dedicated to the protection of wilderness areas and publishes the monthly *Wilderness WA Newsletter* (☎ 9335 9512) 12 William St, Fremantle 6160.

FLORA

For information on wildflowers found in WA see the illustrated Wildflower section on page 29.

Trees

Forests are in the south-west corner of the state. The following species grow only in WA.

In WA's south-west, there are eucalypts, and other species of tree, that you will see nowhere else. In the Kimberley, the curiously shaped boab tree *(Adansonia gregorii)* is a characteristic feature of the landscape – for more information see the boxed aside 'Boabs' in the Kimberley chapter.

A good book is *Key Guide to Australian Trees* by Leonard Cronin. A useful general book on flora & fauna is the *Environmental Guide to Flora & Fauna: Australia's Outback* by Frank Haddon.

Jarrah These majestic hardwood trees *(E. marginata)* grow up to 40m and live up to 400 years. In coastal areas, poor soils reduce their growth to about 15m, and the average height in forests is closer to 30m. The stringy bark has deep vertical grooves and is dark-grey or reddish-brown. The botanical name refers to a thick margin around the leaves.

Karri Another giant hardwood tree, karri *(E. diversicolor)* has a pale, smooth bark which changes to the colour of pink in autumn. Reaching upwards of 90m in height, this is the world's third tallest hardwood tree after Australia's mountain ash *(E. regnans)*. Karri grows in red clay loams where there is more than 750mm of rain per year. *Diversicolor* refers to the difference between the top and underside of its leaf.

Marri This hardwood tree *(E. calophylla)* is often called redgum as it oozes drops of red gum from its grey bark. They are different from jarrah as they have a larger fruit (honkey nuts) and their branches are more widespread. In dry areas they only grow to about 10m but in forests they reach up to 60m. It grows widely throughout the south-west and along the Darling Scarp.

Tingle There are three species of this rare and restricted eucalypt (found in a small area near Walpole-Nornalup National Park).

The red tingle *(E. jacksonii)* has a similar look to jarrah except that it is much larger. Its thick trunk has spreading buttresses up to 20m high and the tree is one of the top 10 largest living things on the planet. The 'red' relates to the colour of timber.

Much smaller is the yellow tingle *(E. guilfoylei)*, but it still has a buttressed base. Identification is difficult as the flowers and gum-nuts are often over 30m above the ground.

The last of the tingles is Rates tingle *(E. brevistylis)*, only recently discovered northeast of Walpole. It is not easily distinguished from the red and yellow tingles.

There are a number of places where you can get close to the tingles in the Walpole-Nornalup forests, most notably the Tingle Tree Walk east of Walpole and in the aptly named Valley of the Giants.

Wandoo This tree *(E. wandoo)* is one of Australia's dense and durable hardwoods. Commonly referred to as the white gum, wandoo forms a major part of the south-west eucalypt forests. The powder-bark wandoo *(E. accedens)* is found on the hills of the wheatbelt and is distinguished from common wandoo by the powder on its bark which rubs off easily.

Tuart Also rare and restricted is the tuart *(E. gomphocephala)*, which is found between the Hill River and Busselton and is at its best in the Ludlow Forest. Its height is determined by the salt-laden winds, but it can reach upwards of 40m. Its presence is an indication of limestone soils.

Red Flowering Gum Another rare and restricted eucalypt is this gum *(E. ficifolia)* which is found on the headland of Point Irwin, between Walpole and Peaceful Bay. It has brilliantly coloured flowers, varying from vermilion, crimson, orange and pink. It is a small tree, reaching only 5m, with a short trunk.

WILDFLOWERS

Western Australia is famed for its wildflowers, which bloom mainly from August to November. Even some of the driest regions put on a technicolour display after just a little rainfall. It is estimated that there are more than 8000 species of flowering plants in the state.

The south-west has over 3000 species, many of which, because of the state's isolation, are unique. They're commonly known as everlastings because the petals stay attached even after the flowers have died. The flowers seem to spring up almost overnight, and transform vast areas within days.

You can find wildflowers almost everywhere in the state, but the jarrah forests in the south-west are particularly rich. The coastal parks, such as Fitzgerald River and Kalbarri, also put on brilliant displays. Near Perth, the Badgingarra, Tathra, Alexander Morrison, Yanchep and John Forrest national parks are excellent places to see wildflowers. There's also a wildflower display in Kings Park, Perth.

Books

A good book or a knowledgeable guide will enhance your appreciation of the many wildflowers you will encounter. The excellent *Wildflower Discovery – a Guide for the Motorist*, which details wildflower trails north and south of Perth, is available free from the Western Australia Tourism Commission (WATC) in Perth. *Discovering the Wildflowers of Western Australia* by Margaret Pieroni ($7.95) is the best of the semi-technical books with a description and illustration of over 200 plants. Probably harder to get but a valuable resource is *Flowers & Plants of Western Australia* (Rica Erickson et al, reprinted 1983).

Wildflower Names

Many people will recognise the common names of flowering plants: wattle, gum, featherflower, cone flower, mulla mulla, honey myrtle and

---

Wildflower Festivals

During the flowering season there are a number of wildflower shows and festivals, including the following:

August	Mullewa Wildflower Show
September	Albany Wildflower Festival
	Augusta Annual Spring Orchid Show
	Bindoon Wildflower Weekend
	Busselton Wildflower Exhibition
	Cranbrook Wildflower Display
	Kalgoorlie-Boulder Spring Flower Show
	Mingenew Wildflower Show
	Nannup Wildflower Display
	Ongerup Wildflower Display
	Ravensthorpe Wildflower Show
October	Kings Park Wildflower Festival
	Kojonup Country Wildflower Festival
	Walpole Orchid Show

Wildflower Regions

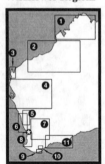

1 – The Kimberley
2 – The Pilbara
3 – North West Cape
4 – The North West
5 – Wildflower Way
6 – North of Perth
7 – South-East Wheatbelt
8 – South of Perth
9 – Albany Region
10 – Stirling &
    Porongurup Ranges
11 – Bremer Bay to
    Esperance

Note: These extents are representational only. The actual spring wildflower display engulfs the state – even 'the desert blooms'.

mountain bells. With a bit of practice you will soon recognise the names of the genera (those above are *Acacia*, *Eucalyptus*, *Verticordia*, *Isopogon*, *Ptilotus*, *Melaleuca* and *Darwinia*. The next step is to identify *Acacia gregorii* as Gregory's wattle, *Verticordia forrestii* as Forrest's featherflower, and so on.

In this section, genera abbreviations are used if it is obvious from the text what the genus is. For example, Stirling Range banksia *(Banksia solandri)* – becomes *B. solandri*.

South of Perth
Early September to November

The North Dandalup, south of Perth, is a great place to see Darling Range wildflowers such as colourful peas, Swan River myrtle *(Hypocalymma robustum)*, green kangaroo paw *(Anigozanthos viridis)* and golden dryandras *(D. nobilis)*.

Further inland, near Collie, expect to see the beautiful silky yellow banjine *(Pimelea sauveolens)* and the *P. spectabilis*, with its large white flowers. Also found here are blue lechenaultia *(L. biloba)* and mauve pepper-and-salt *(Eriostemon spicatus)*, which is related to boronia.

In the Leeuwin-Naturaliste region there is an amazing variety of flowering plants from the swamp bottlebrush *(Beaufortia sparsa)* in Scott National Park to the common hovea *(H. trisperma)* and yellow flags *(Patersonia xanthina)* along Caves Rd. There is also the flying duck orchid *(Paracaleana nigrita)* in the jarrah forests.

A number of interesting species also exist on the Swan Coastal Plain. The Yanchep rose *(Diplolaena angustifolia)* is found on sand and limestone; the rough daisybush *(Olearia rudis)* is widespread; the chenille honeymyrtle *(Melaleuca huegelii)* is common along the coast from Geraldton to Augusta; Mangle's kangaroo paw *(Anigozanthos manglesii)*, the floral emblem of WA, ranges from Shark Bay to Manjimup; Stirling's mulla mulla *(Ptilotus stirlingii)* and the snottygobble *(Persoonia saccata)* grow in sandy woodlands along the coastal plain; and the vibrant redcoat *(Utricularia menziesii)* ranges from Perth to the south coast and as far east as Esperance.

The Stirling & Porongurup Ranges
September to November

There is a great variety of flowering plants in and around the Stirling Range and Porongurup national parks. In the Stirlings, 1500 species of flowering plants occur and around 60 are endemic.

Some 10 species of Darwinias, or mountain bells, have been identified. Near Cranbrook you can see the magnificent Cranbrook bell *(D. meeboldii)*. The lemon-yellow bell *(D. collina)* is found on Bluff Knoll, the pink mountain bell *(D. squarrosa)* occurs higher up in the range on the Bluff Knoll Trail and the large red and white Mondurup bell *(D. macrostegia)* is found on Mondurup Peak.

The Stirling Range banksia *(B. solandri)*, the stunning Stirling Range coneflower *(Isopogon baxteri)* and the mountain pea *Oxylobium atropurpureum)* are also restricted to this range. There are also many black gins *(Kingia australis)*, named after the explorer Philip King, near Bluff Knoll; part of the *Xanthorrhoeaceae* family, these are truly beautiful when in flower (any month).

In the vicinity of the Stirling Range caravan park are orchids and near the damp flats of the range is a good place to look for the dwarf kangaroo paw *(Anigozanthos gabrielae)*. The natural display in the Porongurups includes the tree hovea *(H. elliptica)*.

Albany Region
June to November

The national parks of the Albany region provide much reward for the keen observer. In West Cape Howe, the coastal heath supports many species of banksias, dryandras and hakeas. The scarlet banksia (B. coccinea) is common in areas of deep sand, as is Baxter's banksia (B. baxteri), while the red swamp banksia (B. occidentalis) prefers wetter areas. The insect-eating Albany pitcher plant (Cephalotus follicularis), the only member of its plant family, is also found in this park.

In William Bay National Park, west of Denmark, the five-petalled sticky tail-flower (Anthocercis viscosa) is found, and along Ficifolia Rd, near Walpole, you may be lucky enough to see the red-flowering gum (E. ficifolia; see the main Flora & Fauna section) in bloom.

North of Albany, on the sandy heaths, the hidden featherflower (Verticordia habrantha) flowers from September to November. The Albany cat's paw (Anigozanthos preissii) grows only within 50km of Albany in sandy jarrah woodlands. A perennial favourite is the Southern Cross (Xanthosia rotundifolia) which is common in sandy soil from Albany to the Stirling Range.

The region is rich in orchids including the slender zebra orchid (Caladenia cairnsiana), the crab-lipped spider orchid (C. plicata), the clubbed spider orchid (C. longiclavata), the curious hammer orchid (Drakaea elastica), one of four species endemic to WA, the king leek orchid (Prasophyllum regium) and the pouched leek orchid (P. gibbosum).

Bremer Bay to Esperance
September to November

There is a wealth of flowering plants in this region. North-west of Bremer Bay, near the towns of Ongerup and Gnowangerup, in the open heath under woodland, there are pockets of the tough perennial herb pincushions (Borya nitida), the barrel coneflower (Isopogon trilobus), the sprawling red combs (Grevillea concina), the ouch bush (Daviesia pachyphylla) and several varieties of poison peas, part of the Gastrolobium species.

Along the Jerramungup-Ravensthorpe road is a wide road reserve which is dense with wildflowers. The ubiquitous bush cauliflower (Cassinia aculeata), the robust ashy hakea (H. cinerea), the Ravensthorpe bottlebrush (B. orbifolia) and a host of banksias can be seen along here.

To the south of the Jerramungup-Ravensthorpe road is the Fitzgerald River Biosphere Reserve, one of two such reserves in WA (see the South Coast chapter for more information).

The most coveted flowers in this reserve are the strange-looking royal hakea (H. victoria), the only native plant in WA with variegated leaves; the pinky red pin-cushion hakea (H. laurina); the creamy or orange chittick (Lambertia inermis); the striking scarlet banksia; the four-winged mallee (E. tetraptera) and the warted yate (E. megacornuta); the red or white (or combinations of both) heath lechenaultia (L. tubiflora); the silky triggerplant (Stylidium pilosum); the Qualup bell (P. physodes), the only pimelea with a bell-like inflorescence; the thorny hovea (H. acanthoclada); the weeping gum (E. sepulcharis), which only grows on a few ranges at the eastern end of the Barrens Range; the Barrens clawflower (Calothamnus validus); the oak-leafed dryandra (D. quercifolia); Barrens lechenaultia (L. superba); and the beautiful Barrens regelia (R. velutina) – any one of these species is reason enough to turn off the main highway.

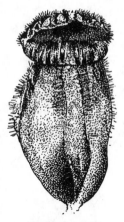

A low-growing plant found in swampy areas around Albany, the Albany Pitcher Plant (or Flycatcher) uses a sweet-smelling fluid to lure crawling and flying insects to their death. The striking red-purple pitchers are not flowers but modified leaves. The plant also has more conventional green oval-shaped leaves, and produces tiny, inconspicuous pale green flowers.

The Ravensthorpe Range is also noted for its rare flora. Get information from the Ravensthorpe information centre then go in search of ouch bush, the rattle pea *(Daviesia oppositifolia)*, the common blue dampiera *(D. linearis)* and the cushion fan-flower *(Scaevola pulvinaris)*.

In the national parks around Esperance there are a wealth of wildflowers. In the Cape Le Grand region, look for thickets of the showy banksia *(B. speciosa)* and the spreading shrub of the Teasel banksia *(B. pulchella)* in the deep sand of the sand plains. The rocky hills and heaths of Stokes National Park are great places to seek the bell-fruited mallee *(Eucalyptus pressiana)*. Other flowering plants to look out for include the nodding banksia *(B. nutans)*, the Southern Plains banksia *(B. media)*, the shining honeypot *(Dryandra obtusa)*, the coastal hakea *(H. clavata)* and the remarkable crab claws *(Stylidium macranthum)*. The stunning pink enamel orchid *(Elythranthera emarginata)* is found in a number of habitats in the Esperance region.

South-East Wheatbelt
September to November

A lot more than wheat grows in this region. In the Dryandra State Forest, often described as an 'ecological oasis', you will spot many golden dryandras, the purple tangled grevillea *(G. flexuosa)* and pink rainbows *(Drosera menziesii)*. Orchids also abound in this forest.

Just a few examples are listed but the tourist offices have information on flowering plants in their areas. In particular, go in search of the unusual cricket ball hakea *(H. platysperma)* between Coorow and Hyden; the common cauliflower *(Verticordia brownii)* towards Lake King; the spectacular King dryandra *(D. proteoides)* on the ridges between Northam and Narrogin; red bonnets *(Burtonia hendersoni)* near Hyden; star-leaf grevillea *(G. asteriscosa)* between Kulin and Bruce Rock; cluster boronia *(B. capitata)* known only from the Pingelly region; Pritzel's featherflower *(Verticordia pritzelii)*; the widespread scarlet honeymyrtle *(Melaleuca fulgens)*; curved mulla mulla *(Ptilotus declinatus)* around Katanning; the perennial herb, downy stackhousia *(S. pubescens)*; the dark pea-bush *(Brachysema lanceolatum)* between Wagin and Bremer Bay; and the fringed mantis orchid *(Caladenia dilatata)*.

North of Perth
Late July to end of November

Brand Highway, north of Perth, is the place to see green kangaroo paws and red kangaroo paws *(Anigozanthos rufus)* near the Gingin cemetery, the open-branched dryandra *(D. kippistiana)* and many other species of dryandra in the Red Gully Reserve, and cowslip orchids *(Caladenia flava)* beside Regan's Ford. Badgingarra National Park has a great profusion of wildflowers including the black kangaroo paw *(Macropidia fuliginosa)*. Not far past Badgingarra is Coomallo Creek, with 200 or more wildflowers in the vicinity – black kangaroo paws, yellow kangaroo paws *(A. pulcherrimus)*, scarlet *(Verticordia grandis)* and painted featherflowers *(V. picta)*, the endemic Coomallo banksia *(B. lanata)* and the Western Australian Christmas tree *(Nuytsia floribunda)*, one of the few flowering mistletoes in the world (best seen between November and January).

There is an abundance of banksias including the unusual propeller banksia *(B. candolleana)* around Eneabba. The summer months see the superb starflower *(Calytrix superba)* bloom on the open sandy heaths; it has the largest flowers of any calytrix.

Ashby's Banksia
(Banskia ashbyi)

Baxter's Kunzea
(Kunzea baxteri)

Black Kangaroo Paw
(Macropidia fuliginosa)

Broad Leaf Lambstail
(Lachnostachys verbascifolia)

Cat's Paw
(Anigozanthos humilis)

Christmas Tree
(Nuytsia floribunda)

Cootamundra Wattle
(Acacia baileyana)

Common Blackboy Grass Tree
(Xanthorrhoea preissii)

Cowslip Orchid
(Caladenia flava)

All photographs courtesy of Western Australian Tourist Commission

Crab-lipped Spider Orchid
(*Caladenia plicata*)

Dampiera
(*Dampiera linearis*)

Everlastings
(*Helichrysum bracteatum*)

Firewood Banksia
(*Banksia menziesii*)

Geraldton Wax Flower
(*Chamelaucium uncinatum*)

Karri Boronia
(*Boronia gracilipes*)

Lemon-flowered Gum
(*Eucalyptus woodwardii*)

Lesser Bottlebrush
(*Callistemon phoeniceus*)

Mangles' Kangaroo Paw
(*Anigozanthos manglesii*)

All photographs courtesy of Western Australian Tourist Commission

Oak-Leaved Dryandra
(Dryandra quercifolia)

Pear-fruited Mallee
(Eucalyptus ipyriformis)

Pincushion Hakea
(Hakea laurina)

Pink Enamel Orchid
(Elythranthera emarginata)

Pink Featherflower
(Verticordia monadelpha)

Prickly Bitter-pea
(Daviesia decurrens)

Royal Hakea
(Hakea victoria)

Scarlet Banksia
(Banksia coccinea)

Southern Cross
(Xanthosia rotundifolia)

All photographs courtesy of Western Australian Tourist Commission

Sturt's Desert Pea
(Clianthus formosus)

Swamp Bottlebrush
(Beaufortia sparsa)

Tall or Pink Boronia
(Boronia elatior)

Tree Hovea
(Hovea elliptica)

Yellow Feather Flower
(Verticordia acerosa)

White Spider Orchid
(Caladenia patersonii)

Wilson's Grevillea
(Grevillea wilsonii)

Wreath Lechenaultia
(Lechenaultia macrantha)

All photographs courtesy of Western Australian Tourist Commission

Mingenew, on the Midland road, is a centre of the fledgling wildflower-growing industry. This area has a large variety of wattles which shade the bright pink schoenia (S. cassiniana) and a number of everlastings. There are many wildflower drives nearby – keep an eye out for red pokers (Hakea bucculenta) growing in sand among tall scrub and prickly plume grevillea (G. annulifera), a many-branched shrub which grows on sandy heaths.

Wildflower Way
Late July to end of November
This region boasts fields of everlastings (Helichrysums and Helipterums) stretching off into the distance (just like in the brochures), plus many other varieties of flowering plants.

Head north from Perth on the Great Northern Highway to get to the famous Wildflower Way. A small deviation off the highway is Piawanning, where you can see the biggest eucalypt flower – the spectacular mottlecah (Eucalyptus macrocarpa).

The Wildflower Way starts at Wubin and passes through Perenjori and Morawa before it ends at Mullewa. If the rains come, this road is sandwiched between fields of everlastings which are at their best for a six to eight week period.

Other beautiful flowers to seek out are the truly magnificent wreath lechenaultia (L. macrantha), found between Wubin and Mullewa; rose Darwinia (D. purpurea), found near granite outcrops around Mullewa; the widespread native foxglove (Pityrodia terminalis), a grey-felted perennial herb; pink spike hakea (H. coriacea) in gravelly soils between Mullewa and Southern Cross; bottlebrush grevillea (G. paradoxa) growing on heaths; and the scarlet honeymyrtle, found in gravelly soil among scrub.

If you head towards Geraldton, returning down the coast to Perth, look out for the famous Geraldton wax (Chamelaucium uncinatum), a long-time favourite in gardens.

The North-West
July to September
The Kalbarri National Park has tremendous displays of wildflowers over a long season, July to September – banksias, grevilleas and eucalypts are abundant.

The road into Shark Bay and the North-West Coastal Highway from Shark Bay to Carnarvon, passes through a region which has a surprising number of flowering plants. Look out for bright podolepsis (P. canescans), hairy mulla mulla (Ptilotus helipteroides), tall mulla mulla (P. exaltatus), pincushion mistletoe (Amyema fitzgeraldii), the omnipresent Sturt's desert pea (Clianthus formosus), native fuschia (Eremophila maculata), the Shark Bay poverty bush (Eremophila maitlandii), and the strange, rare, samphire bulli bulli (Tecticornia arborea).

North-West Cape
April to September
The wildflower display in the Cape Range National Park is dependent on rainfall and, if rain falls, the best time to see it is winter and early spring.

The Cape Range grevillea (G. varifolia) is particularly beautiful as are the rock morning glory (Ipomoea costata) and the Yardie morning glory (I. yardiensis). The pretty yulbah (Erythrina vespertilio) is common in the canyons of the range; the leafless toucan flower (Brachysema macrocarpum) grows in sand or limestone; white cassia (C. pruinosa)

Because sun orchids like Queen of Sheba (Thelymitra variegata) do not need a constantly moist atmosphere they are found in semi-arid conditions north of Perth. Single plants grow in low heath or open woodland where the soil is sandy. The flower varies in colour over its distribution range, but the most common form is purple with darker tones with a crimson and yellow edge. The species is named because their flowers only open on sunny days.

occurs on open rocky hillsides; native plumbago *(P. zeylanica)* which grows in shaded parts of gorges, is the only species of plumbago native to Australia; the green birdflower *(Crotalaria cunninghamii)* which resembles a hummingbird in flight, is found in the coastal dunes; and mat mulla mulla *(Ptilotus axillaris)* grows in open spaces in rocky soil.

One of the most unusual (but aptly named) plants you will see is the cockroach bush *(Cassia notabilis)*. The distinctive yellow pom poms of Gregory's wattle *(Acacia gregorii)* can be found in sand or limestone country between North-West Cape and Lake Macleod.

The Pilbara
April to October

The best time to see wildflowers in the Pilbara is after the winter rain when a thin, green blanket of growth spreads across the countryside.

In disturbed soils, the popular Sturt desert pea, purple mulla mulla and the northern bluebell *(Trichodesma zeylanicum)* can be seen. Perennials include sennas, native fuschias, an abundance of wattles and the holly-leafed grevillea *(G. wickhamii)*.

In sandy coastal areas, the Dampier pea *(Swainsonia pterostylis)* and the coastal caper *(Capparis spinosa)* are common. The beautiful flowers of the white dragon tree *(Sesbania formosa)* are the largest of any native legume in WA; they are seen along rivers on the plains of the upper north-west.

The gorges of the Hamersley Ranges are home to many flowering plants. The striking mistletoe *(Lysiana casuarinae)* is found on many host plants; the weeping mulla mulla *(Ptilotus calostachyus)* occurs on open plains among spinifex; and the paperbark cadjeput *(Melaleuca leucadendron)*, found in many of the gorges, has terminal white 'bottlebrush-like' flowers.

The Kimberley
April to November

As well as spectacular scenery, the Kimberley has plenty of wildflowers at a time when the pickings are pretty slim in the rest of WA.

Two species of *Stenocarpus*, with flowers similar to a grevillea, occur in the Kimberley; the little wheel bush *(S. cunninghamii)* grows among sandstone rocks in gorges. Common on rocky sandstone hills are the magnificent scarlet gum *(E. phoenicia)* and the bushy shrub Xanthostemon *(X. paradoxus)*.

Unlike the featherflowers in the south, this species occurs as a tree in the Kimberley. The tree featherflower *(Verticordia cunninghamii)* grows in sand among sandstone rocks and blooms from June to August.

There are nine orchids in the Kimberley and the most common species is *Cymbidium canaliculatum*, seen throughout the region in a number of trees. The waxy flowers of the native hoya *(H. australis)* are found where this scrambler clings to sandstone cliffs. And *Melastomas*, attractive shrubs which are found throughout the tropics, hide in shady places.

The Cranbrook Bell (Darwinia meeboldii) *can be seen flowering near Cranbrook in the Stirling Range from September to November. The delicate cream and scarlet-edged flowers hang like bells. Pollination is carried out by native birds.*

FAUNA
Animals

Australia's most distinctive fauna are the marsupials (kangaroos and koalas) and monotremes (platypuses and echidnas). Marsupials give birth to partially developed young which they suckle in a pouch. Monotremes lay eggs but also suckle their young. In all, WA has 141 native mammal species, two of which are marine mammals – the Australian sea lion and the New Zealand fur seal. Also the leopard seal, dugong, 16 species of dolphin and 19 species of whale have been recorded off the coast. Two mammals, the numbat and honey possum, have only been recorded in WA.

Good books on the subject are *Whales & Dolphins of New Zealand and Australia: An Identification Guide* (1990) by Alan N Baker; *Whales and Whalewatching in Australia* (1989) by Mark Tucker and *Key Guide to Australian Mammals* (1991) by Leonard Cronin.

The native animals you're most likely to see in the wild are wallabies, wallaroos, kangaroos and possums. However, that doesn't mean that there isn't a huge range of small, mainly nocturnal animals going about their business unobserved.

Western Australia has the country's most restricted mammal, the Shark Bay mouse *(Pseudomys praeconis)*, found only on Bernier Island near Shark Bay. Similarly, the western-barred bandicoot *(Perameles bougainville)* and banded hare-wallaby *(Lagostrophus fasciatus)* are now found only on Bernier and nearby Dorre Island.

There are many other marsupial species found in WA, many of them rare and fascinating. The curious pebble-mound mouse (see the boxed aside 'Pebble-Mound Mouse' in the Coral Coast & the Pilbara chapter) and the rabbit-eared bandicoot or bilby (see the boxed aside 'The Bilby' in the Kimberley chapter) are just two more examples.

And there are further rare and interesting native species. The Gilbert potoroo *(Potorous tridactylus gilberti)*, a sub-species of the long-nosed potoroo or kangaroo rat, was recently re-discovered in WA, after being thought extinct for 80 years.

Kangaroos The extraordinary breeding cycle of the kangaroo is well adapted to Australia's harsh, often unpredictable environment. The young kangaroo, or joey, just millimetres long at birth, claws its way from the uterus unaided to the mother's pouch where it attaches itself to a nipple. A day or two later, the mother mates again, but the new embryo does not begin to develop until the first joey has left the pouch permanently.

At this point the mother produces two types of milk – one formula to feed the joey at heel, the other for the baby in her pouch. If environmental conditions are right, the mother will then mate again. However, if food or water is scarce, the breeding cycle will be interrupted until conditions improve and the chances of survival are better.

As well as many species of wallaroos and wallabies (some endangered, such as the black-footed rock and tammar), there are two main species of kangaroos in WA – the western grey *(Macropus fuliginosus)* and the red kangaroo *(Macropus rufus)*.

Quokkas By far the west's most famous example of a wallaby-type marsupial is the quokka *(Setonis brachyurus)*. The quokka is mostly found on Rottnest Island (named when the quokkas were mistaken for rats by de Vlamingh), but it also occurs in the southeast forests. It is a small robust wallaby, about a half-metre tall with a tail about 300mm long. Its fur is grey and brown with a reddish tinge on the upperside and a pale grey below. It can survive for a long time without water and reputedly drinks seawater.

Possums There is a wide range of possums throughout Australia – with the ability to adapt to all sorts of conditions. Apart from the common ringtail and common brushtail, a number of other species are found in WA, including the scaly-tailed possum *(Wyulda squamicaudata)* and the 'ultra-cute' honey possum *(Tarsipes rostratus)*.

The little arboreal honey possum weighs up to 20gm, is 40 to 90mm high and has a prehensile tail from 50 to 100mm long. The honey possum uses its long snout and long brush-tipped tongue to dip into tubular wild-flowers such as grevillea or to penetrate the stiff brushes of banksias and bottlebrushes. They are nomadic, according to the seasonal availability of favoured wildflowers.

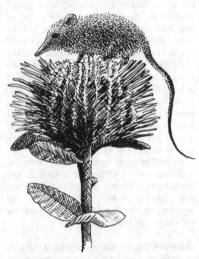

The tiny arboreal honey possum uses its long snout and tongue to feed from the banksia.

Dunnarts These little mouse-sized creatures have pointed muzzles, and large ears and eyes. Of the 18 species known, about half are found only in the western half of the continent. These include the very rare long-tailed dunnart *(Sminthopsis longicaudata)* and sandhill dunnart *(S. psammophila)*.

They are common in the south-west of the state and species found there include the fat-tailed *(S. crassicaudata)*, little long-tailed *(S. dolichura)*, Gilbert's *(S. gilberti)*, white-tailed *(S. granulipes)*, grey-bellied *(S. griseoventer)* and the common *(S. murina)* dunnart. It is these small innocuous species that suffer most when their habitat is slashed or burnt.

Numbats The beautifully patterned numbat *(Myrmecobius fasciatus)* – a marsupial ant-eater – is the state's fauna symbol. It is a member of the native cat family, but is vastly different from other members. It has a pointed face and its tongue can extend 10cm beyond the nose tip. It is thus ideally suited to search for termites in the fallen wandoo trees of south-west Australia; the species is extinct in the eastern states.

About the size of a rabbit (head and body 30cm and the tail another 20cm), it is easily recognisable by the white transverse stripes across its reddish-brown fur. There is also a dark stripe across the eye from its ear to its mouth. It is endangered because of habitat destruction and predation from foxes.

Wombats Wombats are slow, solid, power-fully built marsupials with broad heads and short, stumpy legs. The common wombat *(Vombatus ursinus)* is *not* found in WA but the southern hairy-nosed wombat *(Lasiorhinus latifrons)* can be found in the far east of the state around Eucla.

Koalas The koala *(Phascolarctos cinereus)* is distantly related to the wombat and found along the eastern seaboard. They are *not* found in the wild in WA (only in special reserves – eg Yanchep National Park).

Platypuses & Echidnas The platypus and the echidna are the only living representatives of the most primitive group of mammals, the monotremes. The amphibious platypus *(Ornitho-rhynchus anatinus)* has a duck-like bill, webbed feet and a beaver-like body. It is *not* found in the wild in WA.

The short-beaked echidna *(Tachyglossus aculeatus)* is a spiny anteater that hides from predators by digging into the ground and covering itself with dirt, or by rolling itself into a ball and raising its sharp quills.

Dingoes Australia's native dog is the dingo *(Canis familiaris dingo)*, domesticated by the Aborigines and a stable breed for at least 3000 years, possibly much longer. Its ancestor is the Indian wolf. After the Europeans arrived and Aborigines could no longer hunt freely, dingoes again became 'wild', and by preying on sheep they earned the wrath of graziers. These sensitive, intelligent dogs are legally considered vermin. The discovery of dingo bones has been used to verify the radiation of Aboriginal groups from the north-western corner of Australia.

Common Dolphins The *(Delphinus delphis)* is found all along the WA coast as it favours warm, temperate waters. It is dark-grey to purple-black on its upper body and white on its underside. It is easily recognised by the gold hourglass pattern on its side. The dorsal fin is sickle-shaped and it has a long, slender beak. The single calf is suckled by the mother for one to three years. Adults are from 1.7 to 2.4m long.

Bottlenose Dolphins The *(Tursiops truncatus)* is found all along the WA coast as it also favours warmer waters. Dark-grey in colour, it is easily recognised as being the 'Flipper' dolphin most of us are familiar with. The dorsal fin is sickle-shaped and it has a relatively short beak in which the lower jaw extends beyond the upper jaw. The calf is suckled by the mother for 12 to 18 months. Adults are 2.3 to 4m long. This is the dolphin people come to see at Monkey Mia and Bunbury.

Australian Sea Lions This sea lion seal *(Neophoca cinerea)* is endemic to Australia. It is found in cool, temperate waters and rocky coastlines such as those on the south-west coast of WA. It has a bulky but streamlined body, blunt snout and dog-shaped head. The males are chocolate brown and the females range from silver-grey to fawn. They have front flippers and webbed hind legs. Males are 1.8 to 2.3m long, females 1.3 to 1.8m.

Dugongs This is a herbivorous aquatic mammal *(Dugong dugon)*, often known as the 'sea cow', found along the northern Australian coast from Shark Bay to the Great Barrier Reef – the Shark Bay population is estimated to be over 10,000, about 10% of the world's dugong population. It is found in shallow tropical waters and estuaries where it feeds on seagrasses, supplemented by algae. Its bulky body is grey to bronze on the upperside and lighter beneath, and it has a broad snout; males have a pair of protruding tusks. Dugongs can live for over 70 years.

Fur Seals Two types of fur seal are found in Australian waters but only one type lives in WA, the New Zealand fur seal *(Arctocephalus forsteri)*. You're likely see it sunning on off-shore islands such as those in the Archipelago of the Recherche. The fur seal is smaller than the sea lion and its head has a more pointed snout with long whiskers. The seal pups congregate in pods and are suckled for about a year. Males grow to between 1.5 and 2.5m, females to between 1.3 and 1.5m.

Southern Right Whales The southern right whale *(Eubalaena australis)* – so-called because it was the 'right' whale to kill – was almost hunted to the point of extinction. But since the cessation of whaling it has started to return to Australian coastal waters in increasing numbers and can be seen in the waters of the Great Australian Bight and near Albany.

A baleen whale, it is easily recognised by its strongly down-curved mouth with long baleen plates that filter water for planktonic krill (a tiny, shrimp-like crustacean). These plates were once used to make corsets. Its head and snout have callosities (barnacle-like protuberances); these are unique to each whale and aid in the identification of individual whales. The southern right whale grows to 18m and travels alone or in small family groups.

Humpback Whales Now a regular visitor to the west and east coasts of Australia, this massive marine mammal *(Megaptera novaeangliae)* is a joy to behold. It breeds in winter in subtropical and tropical waters and in the west you are likely to see them any-where from Cape Leeuwin to North-West Cape, even off the city of Perth, as they migrate northwards from their feeding grounds in the polar seas.

The back and sides are grey-black, the belly and throat are black and white and the baleen plates black. The body has a humpback and there are two long flippers which have a row of knobs at the front edges. The young, over 4m when born, are weaned at seven months but stay with the mother for two to three years. Adult humpbacks are from 14 to 19m and live for over 30 years, mating every two to three years. They are also spectacular jumpers and leapers.

Endangered Species

Sadly, many species of mammal are on the endangered list in WA. Destruction of habitat and predation, and the damage caused by introduced species are the greatest factors contributing to the decline in numbers (even near extinction) of species – included are dunnarts, numbats, potoroos, bilby, pebble-mound mouse and stick-nest rat. Similarly, the survival of 30 species of bird is threatened.

Introduced Species

The Acclimatisation Society devoted itself to 'improving' the countries of the British Empire by introducing plants and animals. Unfortunately, its work proved a disastrous blunder.

Exotic animals thriving in WA include foxes, rabbits, cats, donkeys, pigs (now bristly-black razorbacks with long tusks) and goats. These species have been disastrous for the native animals, both as predators and as competitors for food and water.

Probably the biggest change to the ecosystem has been caused by another exotic animal: the sheep. To make room for sheep, wholesale clearing of the bush took place, and plains were planted with exotic grasses. Many small marsupials became extinct when their habitats changed.

Disruption of Aboriginal land-management meant that there was no longer regular burning of the bush and plains. This caused less-frequent but disastrous bushfires which fed on the accumulated growth (previously this was dependent on regular low-intensity fires for germination).

Birds

About 510 species are found in WA of which 380 are breeding species and 130 are non-breeding migratory species. Fourteen species are endemic, ie found only in this state. Over 30 species are threatened and seven of these declared in need of special protection. (See also Birdwatching in the Facts for the Visitor chapter.)

Emus The only bird larger than the emu *(Dromaius novaehollandiae)* is the African ostrich, also flightless. The emu is a shaggy-feathered bird with an often curious nature. After the female emu lays the eggs, the male hatches them and raises the young. Emus are common throughout the state.

Black Swans This is the most famous of WA's birds and very much a state symbol. The long slender-necked swan *(Cygnus atratus)* is black except for white flight quills, red eye and red beak. It is found in all water habitats where it builds its bulky nest of sticks, either as a floating island or on a small island. In Northam, on the Avon River, there is a colony of the introduced mute swan *(Cygnus olor)* – white with a yellow bill.

Parrots & Cockatoos There is an amazing variety of these birds. The noisy pink-and-grey galahs *(Cacatua roseicapilla)* are among the most common, although the sulphur-crested *(C. galerita)* and pink Major Mitchell *(C. leadbeateri)* cockatoos have to be the noisiest. Other species of cockatoo seen in the state are little corellas *(C. pastinator)*, long-billed black *(Calyptorhyncus baudinii)*, red-tailed black *(C. banksii)* and Carnaby's *(C. latirostris)* cockatoos.

Lorikeets, rosellas and parrots are also numerous throughout the state. It is refreshing to see large flocks of budgerigars *(Melopsittacus undulatus)* darting about in formation and just as quickly settling on the ground, rather than the usual lone forlorn creature in a cage.

Parrots are seen just about everywhere but it is the careful observer that tells them apart – cockatiels *(Nymphicus hollandicus)* and

Bourke's *(Neophema bourkii)* in the arid areas, elegant parrots *(N. elegans)* along the coast, rock parrots *(N. petrophila)* also along the coast from Esperance to Shark Bay, red-capped parrots *(Purpureicephalus spurius)* in the south-west, regents *(Polytelis anthropeplus)* throughout the goldfields, Alexandra's parrot *(P. alexandrae)* in the extremely arid centre, red-winged parrots *(Aprosmictus erythropterus)* in the Kimberley, blue bonnets *(Northiella haematogaster)* on the Nullarbor and 28s or Port Lincoln ringnecks *(Barnardius zonarius)* just about everywhere from the Pilbara south.

Visitors to the eastern states will be familiar with the ubiquitous eastern rosella *(Platycercus eximius)*. This species is not seen in the west, but in the north-east of the state, the northern rosella *(P. venustus)* is found in the hills near water. In the south-west, the western rosella *(P. icterotis)* inhabits open woodland and farmland.

Raptors Birds that prey on other species have long been a subject of fascination for birdwatchers and species of all three families found in Australia can be observed in WA.

The osprey *(Pandion haliaetus)* is found along the coast from the Kimberley to Esperance and several actually nest in Broome. The white-bellied sea eagle *(Haliaeetus leucogaster)* is also found along the coast and you will definitely see it in the Archipelago of the Recherche; the majestic wedge-tailed eagle *(Aquila audax)* is seen throughout the state feeding on road kills; and the brahminy kite *(Milvus indus)* is seen in north-west mudflats and mangroves.

Kookaburras A member of the kingfisher family, the kookaburra is heard as much as it is seen – you can't miss its loud, cackling laugh, usually at dawn and sunset. Kookaburras can become quite tame and pay regular visits to friendly households.

In WA, the laughing kookaburra *(Dacelo novaeguineae)* is found in the south-west; in the Kimberley and the coastal centre of the state, the blue-winged kookaburra *(D. leachii)*, unfamiliar to most people in the east, can be found.

Fish
There is a bewildering variety of fish found in WA waters. They range from minute tropical fish to the world's largest, the whale shark *(Rhiniodon typus)*. Around 1040 of the 1500 or so species are tropical and the remainder either southern temperate (400 species) or freshwater (60 species).

Reptiles
There are at least 750 known species of Australian reptiles and 439 of these are found in WA. The two main deserts, the Great Sandy and Great Victoria, each support about 75 species of reptile. One of the world's rarest species, the western swamp tortoise, is found in one nature reserve near Perth.

Snakes There are a number of species of snake in WA, all protected. Many are poisonous, some deadly, but very few are at all aggressive and they'll usually get out of your way before you even realise that they are there. (See Dangers & Annoyances in the Facts for the Visitor chapter for ways of avoiding being bitten and what to do in the unlikely event that you are.)

The best known of the local venomous species is the dugite *(Pseudonaja affinis)*, which is confined to the southernmost part of WA, including the Perth metropolitan area and Rottnest Island. The greenish-brown to greenish-grey dugites prefer sandy areas and places where house mice are plentiful.

One species of blind snake *(Rhamphotyphlops leptosoma)* is known only from the area around Kalbarri. Other venomous snakes found in the west are the desert death adder *(Acanthopus pyrrhus)*, mulga snake *(Pseudechis australis)* and black-striped snake *(Vermicella calonota)*; the latter occurs within a 35km radius of Perth.

Crocodiles There are two types of crocodile in Australia: the extremely dangerous saltwater crocodile *(Crocodylus porosus)*, or 'saltie' as it is known, and the less aggressive freshwater crocodile *(Crocodylus johnstoni)* or 'freshie'. These living relics existed 200 million years before humans.

Salties are not only confined to salt water. They inhabit estuaries, and, following floods, may be found many kilometres from the coast. They may even be found in fresh water more than 100km inland.

Freshies are smaller than salties – anything over 4m should be regarded as a saltie. Freshies are also more finely constructed and have much narrower snouts and smaller teeth. Salties, which can grow to 7m, will attack and kill humans. Freshies, though unlikely to seek human prey, have been known to bite, and children in particular should be kept away from them.

You'll probably see many freshies in the Kimberley (along the banks of Geikie Gorge), and there are many known haunts of the saltie along the northern coast, including the big crocs at the Wyndham abattoir outfall.

Lizards There is a wide variety of lizards, from tiny skinks to prehistoric-looking goannas which can grow up to 2.5m, although most species you'll meet in WA are much smaller. Goannas can run very fast and when threatened will use those big claws to climb the nearest tree – or perhaps the nearest leg! The 'racing' goanna (known as the 'bungarra') is most often seen.

Blue-tongue lizards, slow moving and stumpy, are children's favourites and are sometimes kept as pets. Their even slower and stumpier relations, shingle-backs, are common in the Darling Ranges near Perth.

More fleet footed are the frilled lizards *(Chlamydosaurus kingii)* and bizarre and ugly (or beautiful if you are of the same species) thorny or mountain devil *(Moloch horridus)*. The latter can change colour by a variation of skin pigments to match the desert sand or clay surface.

Marine Turtles These are often seen in the waters off the north-west coast of Australia. Four species can be observed coming ashore

on islands and beaches to nest – green *(Chelonia mydas)*, loggerhead *(Caretta caretta)*, flatback *(Chelonia depressa)* and hawksbill *(Eretmochelys imbricata)*. All four species are protected; Aborigines, however, whose diet traditionally includes turtle, can hunt them. The flatback is believed to nest only on Australian coasts.

Turtles nest between September and April, although they can be seen in north-west waters throughout the year. Nesting occurs nightly during warmer summer months and the best time to observe them is two hours before or after high tide.

Turtles live a long life and are thought to be about 40 to 50 years old before they breed. The incubation temperature determines the sex of the hatchlings; outside the temperature range of 24 to 32°C, no egg development occurs. For guidelines to watching nesting check with a CALM office.

Amphibians The only amphibians that occur in Australia are frogs. Western Australia has 25 species of tree frog and 51 species of ground frog, one-third of Australia's known species.

Male green turtles may spend their whole lives at sea, while females only come ashore to lay their eggs.

NATIONAL PARKS & RESERVES

Western Australia has about 60 national parks and nearly 20 forest recreation areas which are administered by Conservation & Land Management (CALM); overseeing almost 200,000 sq km. They cover a diverse range of landforms, marine environments and flora & fauna. Unlike other states, such as Victoria and NSW, they do not cover a large area of this huge state. They tend to focus on special features. Exploration of these parks will be rewarded with breathtaking scenery, fascinating glimpses into ancient cultures and objects of interest at almost every turn. About 10 of Australia's 30 most interesting natural features are found in this state; reasonable odds considering it takes up one-third of continental Australia. Of course, this begs the question: what are WA's most interesting natural features?

Try the Purnululu (Bungle Bungle) Range, the Devonian Reef national parks, Ningaloo Marine Reserve, Cape Range, Shark Bay World Heritage area, Karijini (Hamersley Range), Millstream-Chichester, the Montebellos, Nambung (the Pinnacles), Fitzgerald River Biosphere Reserve, Walpole-Nornalup, Leeuwin-Naturaliste and the Stirling Ranges. More than 10, there are still others worthy of top 30 status.

CALM publishes pamphlets on all of the main parks, forests and marine reserves and has a number of interesting publications for

sale. See National Parks in the Books section of the Facts for the Visitor chapter.

In addition to the national parks, there are 1100 nature reserves and seven marine conservation reserves.

The main CALM office is in Perth. The address is 50 Hayman Rd (PO Box 104), Como, WA 6152 (☎ 9334 0333). There are a number of CALM regional offices:

Central Forest
    North Boyanup Rd, PO Box 733, Bunbury 6230 (☎ 9725 4300)
Goldfields
    Hannan St, PO Box 366, Kalgoorlie 6430 (☎ 9021 2677)
Greenough
    7th Floor, Town Towers, PO Box 72, Geraldton (☎ 9921 5955)
Kimberley
    Konkerberry Drive, PO Box 942, Kununurra 6743 (☎ 9168 0200)
Metropolitan
    5 The Esplanade, Mount Pleasant 6153 (☎ 9364 0777)
Northern Forest
    3044 Albany Highway, Kelmscott 6111 (☎ 9390 5977)
Pilbara
    Welcome Rd, SGIO Building, PO Box 835, Karratha 6714 (☎ 9186 8288)
Shark Bay District Office
    67 Knight Terrace, Denham 6537 (☎ 9948 1208)
South Coast
    44 Serpentine Rd, Albany 6330 (☎ 9841 7133)
Southern Forest
    Brain St, Manjimup 6258 (☎ 9771 1988)
Wheatbelt
    Hough St, PO Box 100, Narrogin 6312 (☎ 9881 1113)

GOVERNMENT & POLITICS

Western Australia is one of the six states which make up the Australian federation together with the ACT and the Northern Territory.

The state is represented vice-regally by a Governor who performs official and ceremonial functions pertaining to the Crown. Western Australia contributes 12 senators to the Senate at federal level (four Labor, six Liberal and two Green following the last election) and a proportional number of Members of Parliament (MPs) based on population figures. In the last federal election –

Rainforest

Not until 1965 was it realised that WA had its own patches of rainforest – along the north-west coast between Broome and the Northern Territory and in parks and reserves such as Prince Regent River, Drysdale River, Point Spring, Coulomb Point and Purnululu.

The rainforests are distinguished by closed evergreen canopies and a profusion of vines and plants. Of the 20 types of rainforest found in Australia, three types occur in the Kimberley. If you can, get a copy of the Conservation & Land Management's (CALM) pamphlet The Kimberley Rainforests. ■

March 1996 – there were 148 MPs with 14 from WA. Interestingly, two of the elected members of the Senate were Green candidates, representing environmental issues. Currently, the Greens, Democrats and Independents hold the balance of power in the Senate and therefore greatly influence the passage of legislation.

The state Parliament consists of two parts (a Legislative Council and a Legislative Assembly). The principal minister is called the Premier. After the last state election for the Legislative Assembly the Liberal and National parties in coalition formed the government (with 35 of the 57 seats); the Premier, Richard Court, is the leader of the coalition, and Hendy Cowan is his deputy. These two parties also held the majority (18 of 34 seats) in the upper house (Legislative Council). The main opposition is the Australian Labor Party.

ECONOMY

Western Australia is fundamentally based on the production and export of mineral and agricultural products, and continues to play a crucial role in Australia's economic recovery. During the 1980s the WA economy experienced strong growth and the Gross State Production (GSP) increased over that period by 57% in contrast to the overall national growth in Gross Domestic Product (GDP) of 34%.

In the period 1995-96, WA led the nation in exports with 24.9% of the Australian total. In 1995-96, mining was the state's most valuable export, gold contributing 17.7% ($3.35 billion) of the value of exports and iron ore 15% ($2.85 billion). Agriculture, forestry and fisheries were also valuable exports, the most significant being wheat at 9.6% ($1.83 billion). North Asian economies received over 65% of these exports.

The state still has a relatively small manufacturing sector and continues to receive more interstate imports than it exports. The main sources of foreign imports are the USA, Japan and Singapore. Exports to foreign countries, however, are currently three times the value of imports.

Tourism is one of the real growth industries. In 1994-95 tourism was worth $2.2 billion, about 4.5% of GSP, and some 9% of the state's workforce were engaged in the industry. Still, by far the greatest number of visitors (80%) are from intrastate. Singapore and the UK topped the bill as main sources of overseas tourists in 1995-96.

POPULATION & PEOPLE

Western Australia with nearly 1.8 million people, about a tenth of the nation's population, is very sparsely populated. Compare this to NSW, only a third the size of WA, which has a population approaching six million. The annual growth rate in WA is less than 2%.

Immigration contributes to the state's population's growth and diversification. There is a large population of British migrants (at 170,000 almost as big as Melbourne's quota) as well as migrants from Ireland, South Africa, New Zealand, Germany, India, Greece, Italy, Poland, the Netherlands and the former Yugoslavia. Its proximity to Asia also means that it has a sizeable Asian population – particularly from Malaysia, Singapore and Vietnam. Perth has more Singaporeans than either Sydney or Melbourne, both three times its size.

There are estimated to be 47,250 Aborigines in the state, about 16% of the nation's total (and roughly the same number before European colonisation).

ARTS

While Perth and WA lack the supposed cultural status of, say, Melbourne and Victoria, they certainly lack nothing in regard to solid artistic and cultural bases. There is a resident symphony orchestra, a ballet company, a number of theatre companies, an impressive art gallery, the innovative Perth Institute of Contemporary Art (PICA), literary publishing houses and a string of contributors in all facets of artistic and cultural endeavour over the years. The Perth Cultural Centre, Northbridge, and the Perth Concert Hall are solid foci for the arts.

You just have to look at the varied list of festivals and events to realise that the state has much to offer culturally. (See Public Holidays & Special Events in the Facts for the Visitor chapter.)

The geographical epicentre of fine arts in the west is the Perth Cultural Centre in Northbridge (see the Perth chapter) which includes the Alexander Library, WA Museum, Art Gallery of WA and the Perth Institute of Contemporary Art (PICA). There are many other galleries in Perth, Fremantle and the south-west region.

Obtain a copy of the *Gallery Guide* from the Art Gallery of WA as it lists all the current exhibitions at nearly 20 galleries in and around Perth.

The west has a rich tradition of fine arts with painting, indigenous art, sculpture and ceramics well represented.

Aboriginal Art & Culture

Probably the richest cultural heritage of this state is to be found amid the spinifex and rocks. Visitors can witness Aboriginal culture first-hand, either in modern communities or at traditional sites.

In Perth, the Museum of WA and Art

Experiencing Aboriginal Western Australia

Culture Many tourists come wishing to experience Aboriginal culture first-hand and many leave disappointed. Readers are encouraged to make contact with the Aboriginal communities they pass through, observing the usual courtesies and obtaining permits where necessary as outlined below. Don't, as many white Australians do, ignore these people as if they were passing 'ghosts'.

As yet there are no major Aboriginal events or festivals in the west. Stompem Ground, based in Broome, was a start but seems to have died a quick death as entrepreneurs, who had lost sight of its original purpose, moved in. National Aboriginal Islander Day Observance Committee (NAIDOC) Week, in early July, brings together many groups in Perth with displays of indigenous art and cultural performances.

There is also plenty of opportunity to participate in the daily lives of Aboriginal groups in the north-west (see the Coral Coast & the Pilbara and The Kimberley chapters).

In several places there are engrossing self-guided walking trails. Some heritage trails include the Yaberoo Budjara near Yanchep, the petroglyphs (rock engravings) of the Burrup Peninsula and the excellent Jaburara Trail in the range above Karratha.

Permits You need a permit to enter Aboriginal land, but getting one is only really a problem in the remote communities in the east of the state.

In the Kimberley and Pilbara a permit is usually easily obtained after a courtesy visit to community administration offices. Some insensitive travellers have gone through the gates of communities on the Dampier Peninsula and set up their caravans outside people's houses – imagine if someone set up their tent in your backyard without asking!

Permits can be issued only by the Aboriginal Affairs Department (☎ 9483 1222) in Perth; individual Aborigines apparently can't give permission. Often, access is informally allowed, but there can be problems controlling inconsiderate campers.

Tours on Aboriginal Land There are a number of tours which incorporate aspects of Aboriginal life and culture. These represent the best opportunity for travellers to have some form of meaningful contact with Aboriginal people.

In the Kimberley, there are a number of options, mostly initiatives of local Aborigines. Operators include Over the Top Tours, Lombadina Tours, Darngku Heritage Cruise (Geikie Gorge), Kooljaman Resort and Wundargoodie Tours (see The Kimberley chapter for more details).

The Purnululu Aboriginal Corporation and CALM jointly manage the Purnululu (Bungle Bungle) National Park, one of the first national attempts to balance the needs of local people with the demands of tourism. The traditional owners are planning to take tours into the Bungles.

Similarly, the traditional occupiers of Karijini (Hamersley Range) National Park in the Pilbara – the Panyjima, Innawonga and Kurrama people – have returned to help in the administration of their former lands. ■

Gallery of WA have comprehensive collections of Aboriginal art and culture. Other branches of the museum in Geraldton and Albany also have displays covering pre-colonisation and the modern life of Aborigines. One of Australia's best collections of Aboriginal art is on display in the Art Gallery of WA.

A fine collection of traditional and contemporary Aboriginal art and artefacts can be found in the Berndt Museum of Anthropology, in the Social Sciences Building, University of WA, Crawley. There is an active, successful indigenous publishing house in Broome – Magabala Books (☎ 9192 1991), 28 Saville St.

Music
One of the first things you should do is buy a tape of Aboriginal music to play in the car as you drive through WA. The hauntingly beautiful tones seem to vivify the landscape and allow the 'whitefellas' a bit of a chance to experience the magic of the Dreaming.

All choices of music are available in WA. It could be listening to a pub band in Freo or enjoying a night under the stars at a winery wooed by the strings of the Western Australian Symphony Orchestra (WASO).

Classical Wine is the natural accompaniment to classical music in this state – performances at the Leeuwin Estate are extremely popular. The WASO performs regularly at the Perth Concert Hall and under the direction of David Measham has made many acclaimed recordings. There is also a state youth orchestra, the WAYO.

The Perth Concert Hall has an annual calendar of events as varied as the WASO playing pop one night to the Academy of St Martins in the Field Octet performing serious classical the next.

The west has also provided a cavalcade of composers and performers. The former group includes Janet Dobie of Armadale, George Tibbits of Boulder and Jennifer Fowler of Bunbury.

Renowned performers include the saxophonist Peter Clinch, baritones Bruce Martin (a Wagner specialist) and Greg Yurisich, soprano Glenys Fowles and mezzo-soprano Lorna Sydney. The indomitable arts administrator Herbert C ('Nugget') Coombs was born in Kalamunda.

Rock & Pop There's a healthy pop scene in Perth. It wasn't always so. While a lot of good musicians grew up in WA, they inevitably gravitated to Sydney and Melbourne, leaving Perth, with a reputation as a 'cover city'.

In the early 1960s, a grinning, dentally-challenged Ronald ('Bon') Scott served time in a juvenile detention centre in Perth, dreaming of a song he was later to sing with the successful band AC/DC, *Jailbreak*. He later drifted to Melbourne where, in 1969, his group the Valentines became the first Australian band to be arrested for possession of marijuana. Bon later unleashed his raunchy vocals on an unsuspecting world as the lead singer of AC/DC and sadly ascended into 'rock 'n' roll heaven' after a bout of heavy drinking in 1979.

In the 1980s, Dave Faulkner wandered across the Nullarbor to Sydney to form the immensely successful Hoodoo Gurus; the guitarist in the Innocent Bystanders became Johnny Diesel; and a legend in the west, Dave Warner, crooned the poignant lines of *I'm Just a Suburban Boy*, summarising the ethos of Perth for those not covered wiv' glitter.

Perth also gave us the Dugites, the Scientists, Chad's Tree and The Triffids. The latter band drew rave critical reviews in the UK and France for their countrified rock, showcased in their album *Treeless Plain*.

These days there are plenty of venues around Perth where you can go and see any type of modern music from grunge to covers (yes, these kinds of bands still exist) of Elvis, U2 and Midnight Oil (see Entertainment in the Perth chapter). You can find out where the action is in *Xpress* magazine, available free from record shops and pubs. There seems to be an inner city (read 'cool' scene) and a suburban pub music scene (read 'not so cool').

Jazz Jazz lovers have a number of regular venues in Perth including pubs in North Fremantle and Applecross. The WA Jazz Society meets every Monday night at the Hyde Park Hotel in Bulwer St, Perth.

Country & Western An inexplicably large following is reserved for country & western music in Perth. Perhaps it is easier to understand if you are in the bush in a wheatbelt or goldfields town. In such an environment, you're likely to hear Willy Nelson, Waylon Jennings and Tammy Wynette with unfailing regularity. Maybe it has something to do with 'Western' in the title of country & western. Northam, in the Avon Valley, is the Nashville of the west and host of a festival which is well attended. The annual calendar of events throughout the state will keep country & western fans yodelling, yelping and boot scooting until the wee small hours.

Contemporary Aboriginal In the north-west you may have the opportunity to see a contemporary Aboriginal band. The Broome Musicians Aboriginal Corporation (BMAC) was established to promote and develop music amongst the Aboriginal community and protect musicians from the usual rip-offs associated with the industry. There is a distinctive 'Broome sound' which combines corroboree influences, folk music from a number of sources such as Polynesia and Asia, and even Gregorian chant. There have been a succession of bands: the Broome Beats, Tombstone Shadows (aka Crossfire, aka Scrap Metal), Maja, Chocolate Solja, Black Label, Sunburn and Bingurr. In the eastern states it is hard to find any of this music so the record shops in the west are your best bet.

Literature

Western Australia's literary tradition is remarkably fecund, encompassing the unpolished, rough humour of the early writers from the north-west and goldfields to sophisticated works from a string of modern writers.

By far the most prolific of WA's writers was Katharine Susannah Prichard. She wasn't born in WA but settled there in 1916. She wrote extensively on WA themes, often infusing her own communist beliefs into many of her works. *Black Opal* (1921) deals with the independent ownership of mines in the mythical town of Fallen Star Ridge; *Working Bullocks* (1926) was an account of the timber-getters in the karri forests of the south-west; *Coonardoo* (1929) examines the taboo subject of black-white sexual relationships; and *The Roaring Nineties* (1946), *Golden Miles* (1948) and *Winged Seeds* (1950) were parts of an enormous socialist realist trilogy about the goldfields.

Henrietta Drake-Brockman, a contemporary of Prichard's, was known mainly for her work *Men without Wives and Other Plays* (1955). Her novels include *Blue North* (1934) which is set in the pearling town of Broome and *Sheba Lane* (1936), also set in Broome, but when it is no longer a rollicking frontier town.

Two respected novelists to come out of the University of WA were Peter Cowan and Randolph Stow. Cowan has written a number of collections of short stories (*Drift*, *The Unploughed Land*, *The Empty Street*, *The Tins* and *Mobiles*) since the end of WWII. Most of his stories have a theme of isolation very much influenced by the WA bush. Stow was an accomplished novelist, poet and librettist. His work has deservedly won many awards and his *The Merry-Go-Round in the Sea* (1965), a semi-autobiographical look at life through the eyes of a child in Geraldton, is one of Australia's most popular novels.

Not strictly a novel, but dramatic in its presentation, is Dame Mary Durack's saga of her own family in *Kings in Grass Castles* (1959). The sequel to this monumental work on life in the Kimberley was *Sons in the Saddle* (1983). In addition to these she wrote children's books and the novel *Keep Him My Country* (1955).

One of the great modern WA writers is English-born Elizabeth Jolley. She has won numerous writing awards for her unusual short stories and novels. Her short fiction includes *Five Acre Virgin and Other Stories*

Albert Facey

One of the great stories of a 'battler' is Albert Barnett Facey's autobiography *A Fortunate Life* (1981), which won the NSW Premier's Award for non-fiction in 1981.

Facey was born in Maidstone, Victoria, in 1894 and grew up in the Coolgardie goldfields and outback WA. His father died before he was two and his mother deserted him (and his sister and two brothers). The family was subsequently raised by his grandmother. He started work at eight and was variously employed doing station work, working on the railway, droving and boxing in an itinerant troupe.

He returned to Perth in 1915 after fighting and sustaining injury at Gallipoli (his brother Joseph was killed there). Facey married, joined the WA Tramways, then became a farmer as part of the Soldier Settlement Scheme near Wickepin (see under The Fortunate House in the Midlands chapter). After the war he learned to read and write and eventually compiled the notes which formed the basis of his best-selling autobiography.

The Depression and his injuries forced him to return to Perth in 1934. He rejoined the Tramways and became active in the union. Three of his sons went off to fight in WWII and one was killed when Singapore fell. Facey died in Perth in 1982.

A Fortunate Life is a marvellous heart-wrenching story, giving an historic glimpse of the lives of ordinary Australians from the turn of the century to the 1970s. The story has subsequently been dramatised and made into a TV series. ■

(1976), *The Travelling Entertainer* (1979), *Woman in a Lampshade* (1983) and novels *The Newspaper of Claremont Street* (1981), *Mr Scobie's Riddle* (1982) and *Miss Peabody's Inheritance* (1983). *Lovesong* (1997) covered the controversial subject of paedophilia.

Jack Davis' *The First-Born and other Poems* (1970) was a watershed in Aboriginal literature. The work was 'discovered' almost by accident after Davis had pinned it on a board outside his office in the Perth Aboriginal Centre. He was later named Aboriginal Writer of the Year (1981) and, in 1985, won the inaugural Sydney Myer Performing Arts Award.

Another outstanding talent is the Aboriginal writer, Archie Weller. His *The Day of the Dog*, tracing the fall of the traditional male role in Aboriginal society, garnered great reviews and was highly commended in the Vogel Literary Awards (1980).

Sally Morgan's autobiography, *My Place*,

charted her Aboriginality and outlined her grandmother's family history. Winner of the inaugural Human Rights and Equal Opportunity Commission Humanitarian Award (1987), she also won, in 1988, the WA Week Literary Award for non-fiction.

Many of the works of Dorothy Hewett (born in Perth in 1923) can be linked to the Great Southern region of the state and include the collections of poetry found in *Windmill Country* (1965), *Rapunzel in Suburbia* (1979) and the plays *The Man from Mukinupin* (1980) and *The Fields of Heaven* (1982).

The young and highly successful Tim Winton, born in 1960, has written a number of novels including the immensely popular *Cloudstreet* (1991) and the recent *The Riders*. His first novel, *An Open Swimmer*, was joint winner of the Vogel Award in 1981 and his second, *Shallows* (1984), won the prestigious Miles Franklin Award. His other novels include *Scission* (1985), *In the Winter*

Dark (1988), *Jesse* (1988) and *Lockie Leonard, Human Torpedo* (1990).

Magabala Books in Broome is the first Aboriginal publishing house in Australia. It aims to preserve Aboriginal culture and history through the written word, and bridge the gap between, and promote their culture to, non-Aborigines. Forthcoming titles include *Lori* by John Wilson and *Don't Go Around the Edges* by Daisy Utemmorah.

Architecture

The most dominating aspect of Perth's architecture is the line of uninspiring skyscrapers that tower above the Swan River. Fortunately, a few fine stone and brick buildings survive (see the Perth chapter) and, not far out of the city, there are gracious Victorian homes. Fremantle's architectural heritage survives thanks to the efforts of residents who fought to preserve it.

The goldfields architecture, often referred to as 'Boom architecture', is the most noticeable aspect of a number of towns in the west. Nowhere is this more apparent than along Kalgoorlie's Hannan St (see the boxed aside 'Architectural Styles' in the Southern Outback chapter). The wealth from gold also contributed to the fine architecture seen in Gwalia, Coolgardie and Cue.

Western Australia has many examples of vernacular homes, those which show ingenious adaptation to the climate and clever use of local, available building materials. Examples are Bedamanup Homestead in Gingin, the houses of Yalgoo, the timber slab and stone cottage in West Arthur, Old Blythewood near Pinjarra, the shell-block church in Denham and the fieldstone buildings of Milligan Homestead near Kellerberrin.

One of the most famous architects in the WA was the enigmatic and controversial Monsignor John Hawes (see the Central West Coast chapter).

Film

The west does not have a large film industry although its location and climate would make it an ideal replacement for California, should the need ever arise.

The WA Film Commission, founded in 1978, has produced some good films but they have yet to achieve widespread exposure. Examples of their films are *Harlequin* (1980), *Roadgames* (1980) and the TV series *Falcon Island*. The feminist film *Shame*, starring Deborah Lee-Furness and directed by Steve Jodrell, is set in an isolated WA community, and examines attitudes towards rape.

The Film Corporation of WA is a private company which has produced *Runnin' on Empty* (1982), *We of the Never Never* (1982) and *Winds of Jarrah* (1983).

The west has given us actors such as Kate Fitzpatrick, Rolf Harris, Alan Cassell, Phillip Ross and that 'cop of cops', Alwyn Kurts (immortalised in TV shows such as *Cop Shop*).

A number of films concentrating on Aboriginal themes have started to filter out of the west such as *Milli Milli* by Wayne Barker and Paul Roberts.

Theatre

Theatre is alive and well in the west. For real-life soap opera you can watch the local TV news. The Perth Theatre Company (PTC), Theatre West, Black Swan, Barking Gecko and Hole in the Wall theatre companies reside in Perth. The city also has a number of venues for live theatre, the most striking being the beautiful Edwardian-style His Majesty's Theatre at 285 Hay St (for more information see the Perth chapter).

A number of playwrights were either born or began their careers in the west. The expatriate Alan Seymour gave us *One Day of the Year* (1962), an examination of the generational differences one Anzac Day. The son of Katharine Sussanah Prichard, Ric Throssell, has continued his family's literary tradition, producing a string of satires and plays with serious themes. Dorothy Hewett, known for her poetry, has also written many plays.

The prolific WA writer, Jack Davis, has had plays produced throughout Australia and, in 1986 with *The Dreamers*, became the first Aborigine to have a play performed in the UK.

The first Aboriginal stage musical came from Broome. Jimmy Chi's *Bran Nue Dae* has since been produced throughout Australia. *Sistergirl*, a tragicomedy about racial reconciliation, is the first play by WA writer Sally Morgan, and another production that has fared well in Australia.

Painting

In the 1890s there was an influx of people who had formal training as painters such as FM Williams, AW Bassett, George Pitt Morrison and James WR Linton. The well known artist Daisy Rossi, whose wildflower and garden paintings were widely exhibited, was prominent during and after WWI.

The 1930s heralded a discernible change in subject matter – Aboriginal portraiture and cityscapes became serious themes. In the late 1930s, Herbert McLintock, as Max Ebert, made an impact with his figurative surrealist compositions; he later joined a group of realists in Sydney and was an official war artist during WWII.

Following WWII, artists branched out from Perth in search of subject matter. Two good interpreters of the outback were the German Elise Blumann and Australian Elizabeth Durack. Blumann painted Aborigines living on the fringe of European society and Durack looked to the familiar Kimberley for many of her ideas.

Elizabeth Durack later (aged 81) became embroiled in the 1997 'Eddie Burrup' art scandal when she entered her paintings signed 'Burrup', in an Aboriginal art award. In Australia's highly sensitive and culturally cringing art world her actions caused an earthquake; in the ancient Kimberley they caused no more than a ripple on the surface of Lake Argyle.

Well known modern WA painters have looked to the local landscape and the special light in the west for their inspiration. Robert Juniper, Guy Grey Smith and George Haynes are three artists to have achieved recent success. While their art would not be considered avant-garde in the eastern states, it nonetheless reflects an inspired interpretation of the aridity and untamed nature of their surroundings. A good place to see the work of Juniper is in the Holy Trinity Church in York where his paintings and glass designs are featured. Sally Morgan, the respected WA writer, is also a nationally recognised artist widely exhibited throughout Australia and was awarded an AM (Member of the Order of Australia) in 1990.

The Art Gallery of WA in Perth has a fine collection of local and overseas art. The major attraction is a world famous indigenous collection. A local publication, *Arts Unlimited*, details happenings and exhibitions and has interviews with local artists and critiques of their work. There are numerous galleries dotted throughout Perth and the south-west.

RELIGION

A shrinking majority of people in Australia are at least nominally Christian. Most Protestant churches have merged to become the Uniting Church, although the Church of England has remained separate. The Catholic Church is popular (about a third of Christians are Catholics), with original Irish adherents boosted by the large numbers of Mediterranean immigrants.

Non-Christian minorities abound: Buddhist, Jewish and Muslim (the town of Katanning in the wheatbelt has a significant Muslim population made up of Christmas Islanders).

LANGUAGE

Any visitor from abroad who thinks Australian (that's 'strine') is simply a weird variant of English/American will soon have a few surprises. For a start many Australians speak other languages such as Italian, Lebanese, Vietnamese, Turkish or Greek.

Those who do speak the native tongue are liable to lose you in a strange collection of Australian words. Some have completely different meanings in Australia to those in English-speaking countries north of the equator; some commonly used words have been shortened almost beyond recognition. Others derive from Aboriginal languages, or from convict slang.

There is a slight regional variation in the Australian accent, while the difference between city and country speech is mainly a

Sandgropers

You will often hear Western Australians colloquially referred to as sandgropers. The actual sandgroper is a subterranean insect known as a cylindrachetid, believed to be a descendant of the grasshopper group. Five species of sandgroper have been found in Australia, one in Papua New Guinea and one separate species in Argentina.

Their bodies are perfectly adapted for 'groping' or burrowing in the sandy soils of the Swan Coastal Plain where they are found. They have a swimming motion through sand – propelled with powerful forelegs, their streamlined bodies with mid and hind legs tucked away offer very little resistance.

Like grasshoppers they develop from egg to adult with no larval stage. They appear to be vegetarian although some studies show that at least one species is omnivorous.

Human sandgropers have a diet of Swan Lager, like sunbathing and footy, eat in Freo's cafe strip and holiday at the beach. They have yet to perfect the sand swimming technique. ■

matter of speed. If you want to pass for a native, try speaking in a slightly nasal tone, shortening any word of more than two syllables and then adding a vowel to the end of it. You can also make anything you can into a diminutive (even the Hell's Angels can become mere 'bikies'). And don't forget to pepper your speech with as many expletives as possible. For more information, see Lonely Planet's *Australian phrasebook*. The Australian language glossary at the back of the book may be a good start.

Aboriginal Language

At the time of contact with Europeans there were around 250 separate Australian Aboriginal languages, comprising about 700 dialects, and these languages were as distinct from each other as English and French. Often three or four adjacent groups would speak what amounted to dialects of the same language, but another adjacent group might speak a completely different language.

There are a number of words, however, that occur right across the continent, such as *jina* (foot) and *mala* (hand), and similarities also exist in the often complex grammatical structures.

Aboriginal Kriol is a new language which has developed since European arrival in Australia. It is spoken across northern Australia and has become the first language of many young Aborigines. It contains many English words, but the pronunciation and grammatical usage are along Aboriginal lines, the meaning is often different, and the spelling is phonetic. For example, the English sentence 'He was amazed' becomes 'I bin luk kwesjinmak' in Kriol.

There are a number of generic terms which Aborigines use to describe themselves, and these vary according to the region. The most common of these is Koori, used for the people of south-east Australia. Nunga is used to refer to the people of coastal South Australia, Murri for those from the north-east, and Nyoongar (or Nyungar) is used in the country's south-west.

Facts for the Visitor

PLANNING

When to Go

Any time is a good time to be in WA, but as you'd expect in a state this large, different parts are at their best at different times.

The southern part of the state is most popular during the summer months, as it's warm enough for swimming and it's great to be outdoors. In the centre of the state it's too hot to do anything much, while in the far north, the summer is the Wet (or Green) season and the heat and humidity can make life pretty uncomfortable. On the other hand, if you want to see the Kimberley green and free of dust, be treated to some spectacular electrical storms and have the best of the fishing while all the other tourists are down south, this is the time to do it.

Spring and autumn give the greatest flexibility for a short visit as you can combine highlights of the whole state while avoiding the extremes of the weather. This is also the best time for wildflowers and these can be absolutely stunning after rain.

The other major consideration when travelling in WA is school holidays. Families take to the road (and air) en masse at these times and many places are booked out, prices rise and things generally get a bit crazy. Holidays vary somewhat from state to state, but in WA the main holiday period is from late December to late January; the other two-week periods are roughly mid to late April, mid to late July, and early to late October.

Maps

You can buy a range of maps from the headquarters of the RACWA (☎ 9421 4444), 228 Adelaide Terrace, Perth. Included are *Perth: City & Suburbs, Perth Region, Lower South-West, Geraldton Region, Kalgoorlie/Boulder Region, Esperance Region, Perth-Port Hedland* and *Port Hedland-Darwin*. UBD publishes two excellent street directories, *Perth* ($24.95) and *Western Australia: Cities and Towns* ($24.95), with 145 maps of all major and minor towns.

The Perth Map Centre (☎ 9322 5733), 891 Hay St, has a full range of maps including the excellent StreetSmart touring series.

If you need topographical maps you can get them from CALM and the Central Map Agency (☎ 9323 1344), Lands Administration, Cathedral Ave, Perth.

What to Bring

Anything you might need can be bought locally – a hat for the sun, sunscreen, mosquito repellent, comfortable clothing, boogie or surfboard, bicycle, tent, sleeping bag, camping supplies, water bottles, and the essentials for a medical kit. And attitude – that's up to you.

SUGGESTED ITINERARIES

It is a big state – two weeks lets you look at Perth, Fremantle, Rottnest, the Pinnacles and the south-west. A month is needed to explore further afield – either south and west to Kalgoorlie, Albany and Esperance, or north to Kalbarri, Monkey Mia, Exmouth and Broome. Six weeks if you want to see all of the above. Add a couple more weeks if you wish to add the Pilbara and Kimberley. Three months is the minimum if you want to more than scratch the surface of this vast state.

HIGHLIGHTS

Western Australia certainly has highlights aplenty to match its size. All the flora & fauna superlatives are justified and it is fast becoming one of the great ecotourism destinations of the world.

Try this for a list of natural wonders: marvel at stromatolites, the oldest form of living mass, which first appeared 3.5 billion years ago; swim with the largest fish, the whale shark; 'fly' through the water with manta rays; feed bottlenose dolphins; witness the annual migration from the northern hemisphere of thousands of birds; swim with sea lions; climb the karri, one of the world's largest trees, or walk above the huge tingles at the Valley of the Giants; waltz through a profusion of wildflowers at any time of the year; explore the Fitzgerald River International Biosphere Reserve amongst numerous unique plant species; wade to the largest western coast coral reef in the world; watch turtles lay their eggs; follow a humpback whale as it breaches spectacularly; spot a pebble-mound mouse; and watch a rare black-footed wallaby leap up a remote gorge.

But wait, there's more: touch the earth's oldest rocks in the Pilbara and Yilgarnia (Darling Escarpment); fly over the mysterious Purnululu Range; wander across an uplifted barrier reef from the Devonian era in the Kimberley; witness the awesome power of the tidal waterfalls of Talbot Bay; lose yourself in the labyrinthine Karijini (Hamersley) gorges; explore the magnificent Leeuwin-Naturaliste and Nullarbor caves; climb to the top of the ancient Stirling Range; admire the brilliant blues of the Indian and Southern oceans; descend into the world's second-largest meteorite crater, at Wolfe Creek near Purnululu in the Kimberley; or climb the world's biggest rock, Mt Augustus.

Other and no less spectacular highlights are Wave Rock near Hyden; the vibrant capital of Perth; historic and cosmopolitan Fremantle; get-away-from-it-all Rottnest Island; the amazing Pinnacles Desert; Kalbarri and its surrounding national park; exotic Broome; 'old' Albany; the huge mining constructions of the Pilbara; and the historic towns of the goldfields.

If it was mandatory to select three favourites – North-West Cape & Ningaloo Reef, Karijini (Hamersley Range) National Park and Fremantle would get the nod.

TOURIST OFFICES
Local Tourist Offices
The Western Australia Tourism Commission (WATC) has an office in Perth – the Western Australian Tourist Centre (☎ 9483 1111), Albert Facey House in Forrest Place, on the corner of Wellington St opposite the train station. The office is open 8.30 am to 6 pm Monday to Thursday, 8.30 am to 7 pm Friday, 8.30 am to 5 pm Saturday, 10 am to 5 pm Sunday. It has plenty of brochures but the staff seem more intent on selling you accommodation than offering advice.

Often the best sources of information will be staff at the backpackers' hostels. They know the best tours to take, what's on, where to go, what to see and how to get there.

Interstate Tourist Offices
There are WATC agents in the various states and territories:

Australian Capital Territory
    Goddard & Partners, 40 Allara St, Canberra 2600 (☎ (02) 6248 9399)
New South Wales
    NRMA Travel, 151 Clarence St, Sydney 2000 (☎ (02) 9260 9222)
Queensland
    Harvey World Travel, 204 Adelaide St, Brisbane 4000 (☎ (07) 3221 5022)
South Australia
    RAA Travel, 41 Hindmarsh Square, 5000 (☎ (08) 8202 4589)
Victoria
    WATC, Level 11, 50 Franklin St, Melbourne 3000 (☎ (03) 9663 2766)

Tourist Offices Abroad
Overseas representatives for WATC include:

Germany
    WATC, Kaiserstrasse 8, 60311 Frankfurt (☎ 4969 288868; fax 4969 288875)
Japan
    WATC, Australian Business Centre, New Otani Garden Court Building, Level 28F, 4-1 Kioi-cho, Chiyoda-ku, Tokyo 102 (☎ 81 3 5214 0797; fax 5214 0799)
Malaysia
    WATC, 4th Floor, UBN Tower, Letterbox 51, 10 Jalan P Ramlee, Kuala Lumpur 50250 (☎ 60 3 232 5996, 232 8300; fax 232 0254)
Singapore
    WATC, No 05-13 The Adelphi, 1 Coleman St, Singapore 179803 (☎ 65 338 7772; fax 338 4373)
UK
    Western Australia House, 115 The Strand, London WC2R OAJ (☎ 44 171 240 2881; fax 379 9826)

VISAS & DOCUMENTS
Passport
Your most important travel document is a passport, which should remain valid for at least six months after your intended stay. If it's about to expire, renew it before you go. This may not be easy to do away from your home country.

Applying for or renewing a passport can take from a few days to several months, so don't leave it till the last minute. Things will probably happen faster if you do everything in person, but check first on what you need to take with you. Once you start travelling, carry your passport at all times and guard it carefully.

Visas
All visitors to Australia need a visa. Only New Zealand nationals are exempt, and even they receive a 'special category' visa on arrival.

Visa application forms are available from either Australian diplomatic missions overseas or travel agents. There are several different types of visas, depending on the reason for your visit.

There are two main types of visitor visas.

Tourist Visas Tourist visas are issued by Australian consular offices abroad; they're the most common and generally valid for a stay of up to six months in a 12-month period. If you intend staying less than three months, the visa is free; for six months the fee is $35.

When you apply for a visa, you need to present your passport and a passport photo and sign an undertaking that you have an onward or return ticket and 'sufficient funds'.

Working Visas Young visitors from the UK, the Republic of Ireland, Canada, Holland, Japan and Korea may be eligible for a 'working holiday' visa. 'Young' is loosely interpreted as around 18 to 26, and working holiday means up to 12 months, but the emphasis is supposed to be on casual employment rather than a full-time job, so you are only supposed to work for three months. Officially this visa can only be applied for in your home country, but some travellers report that the rule can be bent. A fee of about $140 is payable.

See the Work section later in this chapter for information on work available in WA.

Visa Extensions
The maximum stay given to visitors in Australia is one year, including extensions. Visa extensions are made through Department of Immigration & Ethnic Affairs offices in Australia and, as the process takes some time, it's best to apply about a month before your visa expires. There is an application fee of $135 – and even if they turn down your application they can still keep your money! To qualify for an extension you are required to take out private medical insurance to cover the period of the extension, and have a ticket out of the country. Some offices are more strict in enforcing these conditions than others.

If you intend staying longer in Australia, the books *Tourist to Permanent Resident in Australia* and *Practical Guide to Obtaining Permanent Residence in Australia*, both published by Longman, might be useful.

Photocopies
You should make two photocopies of your most valuable documents before leaving home. Make sure you include your passport and visa, driver's licence, airline ticket, travel insurance and a list of your travellers cheque numbers. Keep one copy at home. Carry the second copy with you, but separate from the originals. If your documents are lost or stolen, replacing them will be much easier.

Travel Insurance
This not only covers you for medical expenses and luggage theft or loss, but also for cancellations or delays in your travel arrangements under certain circumstances (you might fall seriously ill two days before departure, for example) - and everyone should be covered for the worst possible case, such as an accident requiring hospital treatment and a flight home. Cover depends on your insurance and type of ticket, so ask

both your insurer and your ticket-issuing agency to explain where you stand. Ticket loss is also (usually) covered by travel insurance. Buy travel insurance as early as possible. If you buy it the week before you fly, you may find, for example, that you're not covered for delays to your flight caused by strikes or industrial action.

Check the fine print: some policies exclude 'dangerous activities' like scuba diving or motorcycling. If such activities are on your agenda, you don't want that policy. Finally, make sure the policy includes health care and medication in the countries you may visit to/from Australia.

Driving Licence & Permit

Foreign driving licences are valid for the first three months of your visit. If you're staying longer, it's worth obtaining an International Driving Permit (IDP) from your local automobile association before you leave – you'll need a passport photo and a valid licence. IDPs are valid for one year.

While you're there, ask your automobile association for a Letter of Introduction or other proof of membership, which will give you reciprocal rights to the services of the RACWA (see Automobile Association in the Getting Around chapter).

Student & Hostel Cards

Carrying a student card entitles you to a wide variety of discounts throughout NSW. The most common card is the International Student Identity Card (ISIC), issued by student unions, hostelling organisations or 'alternative style' travel agencies.

It's also worth bringing a youth hostel membership card (Hostelling International, Youth Hostel Association etc). As well as entitling you to discounts, it's valid for membership of the YHA in WA.

EMBASSIES & CONSULATES
Australian Embassies & Consulates Abroad

Australian diplomatic missions overseas include:

Canada
    Suite 710, 50 O'Connor St, Ottawa K1P 6L2
    (☎ (613) 236 0841); also in Toronto and Vancouver
China
    15 Dongzhimenwai Dajie, Sanlitun, Beijing, 100600 (☎ (10) 532 2331)
Denmark
    Kristianagade 21, 2100 Copenhagen
    (☎ (3126 2244)
France
    4 Rue Jean Rey, Paris, 15eme (☎ (01) 40 59 33 00)
Germany
    Godesberger Allee 107, 53175 Bonn (☎ (0228) 81 030), also in Frankfurt and Berlin
Greece
    37 Dimitriou Soutsou St, Ambelokpi, Athens 11521 (☎ (01) 644 7303)
Hong Kong
    23/F Harbour Centre, 25 Harbour Rd, Wanchai, Hong Kong Island (☎ 2827 8881)
India
    Australian Compound, No 1/50-G Shantipath, Chanakyapuri, New Delhi 110021
    (☎ (11) 688 8223); also in Bombay
Indonesia
    Jalan HR Rasuna Said Kav C15-16, Jakarta, Selatan 12940 (☎ (021) 522 7111); also in Denpasar
Ireland
    Fitzwilton House, Wilton Terrace, Dublin 2
    (☎ (01) 676 1517)
Italy
    Via Alessandria 215, Rome 00198 (☎ (06) 852 721); also in Milan
Japan
    2-1-14 Mita, Minato-ku, Tokyo 108 (☎ (03) 5232 4111); also in Osaka, Fukuoka and Nagoya
Malaysia
    6 Jalan Yap Kwan Seng, Kuala Lumpur 50450
    (☎ (03) 242 3122)
Netherlands
    Carnegielaan 4, 2517 KH The Hague
    (☎ (070) 310 8200)
New Zealand
    72-78 Hobson St, Thorndon, Wellington
    (☎ (04) 473 6411); also in Auckland
Papua New Guinea
    Independence Drive, Waigani, Port Moresby
    (☎ 325 9333)
Philippines
    Dona Salustiana Ty Tower, 104 Paseo de Roxas, Makati, Metro Manila (☎ (02) 817 7911)
Singapore
    25 Napier Rd, Singapore 1025 (☎ 737 9311)
South Africa
    292 Orient St, Arcadia, Pretoria 0083
    (☎ (012) 342 3740)
Sweden
    Sergels Torg 12, Stockholm (☎ (08) 613 2900)

Switzerland
> 29 Alpenstrasse, CH-3006 Berne (☎ (031) 351 0143); also in Geneva

Thailand
> 37 South Sathorn Rd, Bangkok 10120 (☎ (02) 287 2680)

UK
> Australia House, The Strand, London WC2B 4LA (☎ (0171) 379 4334); also in Edinburgh and Manchester

USA
> 1601 Massachusetts Ave NW, Washington DC 20036 (☎ (202) 797 3000); also in Los Angeles, Chicago, Denver, Atlanta, Honolulu, Houston, New York and San Francisco

Foreign Consulates

The principal diplomatic representations to Australia are in Canberra. There are also representatives in Perth. About 30 countries are represented in WA by consular staff or trade representatives. The important ones for travellers are:

Canada
> Honorary Consul, 44 St George's Terrace, Perth 6000 (☎ 9221 1770)

France
> Honorary Consul, 21/146 Mounts Bay Rd, Perth 6000 (☎ 9321 1940)

Germany
> Honorary Consul, 8th Floor, 16 St George's Terrace, Perth 6000 (☎ 9325 8851)

Ireland
> Consulate General, 10 Lilika Rd, City Beach 6015 (☎ 9385 8247)

Japan
> Consul, 21st Floor, 221 St George's Terrace, Perth 6000 (☎ 9321 7816)

Netherlands
> Honorary Consul, 83 Mill Point Rd, South Perth 6151 (☎ 9474 1282)

New Zealand
> Consul, 16 St George's Terrace, Perth 6000 (☎ 9325 7877)

Sweden
> Honorary Consul-General, 23 Walters Drive, Osborne Park 6017 (☎ 9244 3699)

Switzerland
> Honorary Consul, 5 Marie Way, Kalamunda 6076 (☎ 9293 2704)

UK
> Consul-General, 95 St George's Terrace, Perth 6000 (☎ 9322 3200)

USA
> Consul-General, 16 St George's Terrace, Perth 6000 (☎ 9221 1177)

CUSTOMS

You can bring most articles in duty free when entering Australia, provided Australian Customs are satisfied they are for personal use and that you'll be taking them with you when you leave. There's also the usual duty-free per-person quota of one litre of alcohol, 250 cigarettes and dutiable goods up to the value of A$400.

Two issues need particular attention. Number one is illegal drugs – don't bring any in with you. If you are arriving from South-East Asia or the Indian subcontinent you will be under even closer scrutiny from Customs.

Number two is animal and plant quarantine – declare all goods of animal or vegetable origin and show them to an official. Authorities are naturally keen to prevent weeds, pests or diseases getting into the country. Fresh food and flowers are also unpopular. There are also restrictions on taking fruit and vegetables between states; in WA there are quarantine stations at the South Australian and Northern Territory borders.

Weapons and firearms are either prohibited or require a permit and safety testing. Other restricted goods include products (such as ivory) made from protected wildlife species, non-approved telecommunications devices and live animals.

When you leave, don't take any protected flora or fauna with you. Customs come down hard on smugglers.

MONEY
Costs

Compared to the USA, Canada and European countries, Australia is cheaper in some ways and more expensive in others. You pay more for clothes, cars and other manufactured items. On the other hand, food is both high in quality and low in cost.

Accommodation is also reasonably priced. In virtually every town where backpackers are likely to stay, there'll be a backpackers' hostel with dorm beds from $12 or less, or a caravan park with on-site vans for around $25 for two.

The biggest cost in any trip to WA is going to be transport, simply because it's such a vast state. If there's a group of you, buying a second-hand car is probably the most economical way to go.

Carrying Money

The usual rules apply – don't flash your cash, carry as much as you need, and stash it safely (in a hidden money belt). Australia has its share of opportunistic thieves, often locals. There are plenty of reports of theft by fellow travellers, especially in backpackers' hostels, so put your valuables in the hostel safe. Keep cameras, videos and laptops in sight at all times.

Travellers Cheques

For a short stay, travellers cheques are the most straightforward and generally have a better exchange rate than foreign cash in Australia.

American Express, Thomas Cook and other well known international brands of travellers cheques are all widely used in Australia. A passport will usually be adequate for identification; but it would be sensible to carry a driver's licence, credit cards or a plane ticket in case of problems.

Commissions and fees for changing foreign-currency travellers cheques seem to vary from bank to bank and year to year. It's worth making a few phone calls to see which bank currently has the lowest charges. Some charge a flat fee for each transaction, which currently varies from nothing at some banks to $6 at the Commonwealth Bank.

Buying Australian dollar travellers cheques is worth looking at. These can be exchanged immediately at the cashier's window without being converted from a foreign currency or incurring commissions, fees and fluctuating exchange rates.

ATMs

Automatic teller machines (ATMs) can be used day or night, and it is possible to use the machines of some other banks: Westpac ATMs accept Commonwealth Bank cards and vice versa; National Bank ATMs accept ANZ cards and vice versa. Banks are currently developing an agreement whereby any bank cash card can be used in any ATM. There's a daily limit on how much you can withdraw from your account which varies from bank to bank.

In WA, ATMs are only available in reasonably large towns. Plan ahead on the roads between large towns and bring cash or hope that the local fuel station/store has EFTPOS (see later in this section).

Credit Cards

Credit cards are widely accepted in Australia and are an alternative to carrying large numbers of travellers cheques. The most common credit card is the Australian Bankcard. Visa, MasterCard, Diners Club and American Express are also widely accepted.

Cash advances from credit cards are available over the counter and from many ATMs, depending on the card.

If you're planning to rent cars while travelling around Australia, a credit card makes life much simpler; they're looked upon with greater favour by rent-a-car agencies than nasty old cash, and many agencies simply won't rent you a vehicle if you don't have a card.

Local Bank Accounts

If you're planning to stay longer than just a month or so, it's worth considering other ways of handling money that give you more flexibility and are more economical. This applies equally to Australians setting off to travel around the country.

Most travellers these days opt for an account which includes a cash card, which you can use to access your cash from ATMs found all over Australia. You put your card in the machine, key in your personal identification number (PIN), then withdraw funds from your account. Westpac, ANZ, National and Commonwealth bank branches are found nationwide, and in all but the most remote town there'll be at least one agency where you can withdraw money. In many of the really small towns in WA, the post office acts as the local bank.

Opening an account at an Australian bank is not all that easy these days, especially for overseas visitors. A points system operates and you need to score a minimum of 100 points before you can have the privilege of letting the bank take your money. Passports, driver's licences, birth certificates and other 'major' IDs earn you 40 points; minor ones such as credit cards get you 20 points. Just like a game show really! However, if visitors apply to open an account during the first six weeks of their visit, just showing their passport will suffice.

EFTPOS Many businesses, such as service stations, supermarkets and convenience stores, are linked to the Electronic Funds Transfer at Point Of Sale (EFTPOS) system which allows you to use your bank cash card to pay for services or purchases direct, and sometimes withdraw cash as well. Bank cash cards and credit cards can also be used to make local, STD and international phone calls in special public telephones, found in most towns throughout the country.

Currency
Australia's currency is the Australian dollar, which comprises 100 cents. There are 5c, 10c, 20c, 50c, $1 and $2 coins, and notes for $5, $10, $20, $50 and $100.

There are no notable restrictions on importing or exporting currency or travellers cheques except that you can't take out more than A$5000 in cash without prior approval.

Currency Exchange
In recent years the Australian dollar has fluctuated quite markedly against the US dollar, but it now seems to hover midway between the 70c to 80c mark – a disaster for Australians travelling overseas but a real bonus for inbound visitors.

Canada	C$1	=	A$0.98
Germany	DM 1	=	A$0.77
Hong Kong	HK$10	=	A$1.75
Japan	¥100	=	A$1.12
Korea (South)	W100	=	A$0.14
New Zealand	NZ$1	=	A$0.87
UK	UK£1	=	A$2.19
USA	US$1	=	A$1.35

Changing Money
Changing foreign currency or travellers cheques is done quickly and efficiently at almost any bank.

Tipping
In Australia, tipping isn't entrenched the way it is in the USA or Europe. It's only customary to tip in more expensive restaurants, and only if the service has been especially good; 10% of the bill is the usual amount. Taxi drivers don't expect tips (of course, they don't hurl it back at you if you decide to leave the change). In contrast, just try getting out of a New York cab without leaving your 10 to 15%.

Taxes & Refunds
If you don't have an Australian Tax File Number, interest earned from your funds will be taxed at 48%. You may be able to reclaim this by filing a tax return when leaving the country if the total you have earned officially falls below the tax-free threshold (currently around $6000).

POST & COMMUNICATIONS
Post
Australia's postal services are relatively efficient but not too cheap. Most post offices open from 9 am to 5 pm Monday to Friday, but you can often get stamps from local post offices operated from newsagencies or from Australia Post shops, found in large cities, on Saturday mornings.

Sending Mail It costs 45c to send a standard letter or postcard within Australia, while aerograms cost 70c.

Air-mail letters/postcards cost 75/70c to New Zealand, 85/80c to Singapore and Malaysia, 95/90c to Hong Kong and India, $1.05/95c to the USA and Canada, and $1.20/1 to Europe and the UK.

Parcels are reasonable. By sea mail a 1/2/5kg parcel costs $14.50/18/28.50 to New Zealand and India, and $15/19/31 to the USA, Europe or the UK. Air-mail rates are considerably more expensive.

Receiving Mail All post offices hold mail for visitors and the Perth GPO has a busy poste restante. You can also have mail sent to you c/- American Express in Perth if you have an Amex card or travellers cheques.

Telephone

Local Calls Local calls from public phones cost 40c for an unlimited amount of time. Make calls from gold or blue phones in hotels, shops, bars etc or phone booths. Local calls from private telephones cost 30c.

STD Calls It's possible to make long-distance Subscriber Trunk Dialling (STD) calls from virtually any public phone. Many public phones accept Telstra phonecards, which are very convenient. The cards come in $5, $10, $20 and $50 denominations, and are available from retail outlets such as newsagents and pharmacies which display the phonecard logo. You keep using the card until the value has been used in calls. Otherwise, have plenty of 20c, 50c and $1 coins ready.

Some public phones are set up to take only bank cash cards or credit cards, and these too are convenient, although you need to keep an eye on how much the call is costing as it can quickly mount up. The minimum charge for a call on one of these phones is $1.20.

STD calls are cheaper at night. In ascending order of cost:

Economy – 6 pm Saturday to 8 am Monday;
 10 pm to 8 am every night
Night – 6 to 10 pm Monday to Friday
Day – 8 am to 6 pm Monday to Saturday

International Calls From most STD phones you can also make International Subscriber Dialling (ISD) calls.

Dial 0011 for overseas, the country code (44 for the Britain, 1 for North America, 64 for New Zealand), the city code (0171 or 0181 for London, 212 for New York etc), and then the telephone number. It's possible to make ISD calls with either of Australia's two main telephone companies, Telstra or Optus, from private phones in certain areas. Phone

Optus (☎ toll-free (1800) 500 005) for details on how to access their services.

A standard Telstra call to the USA or the UK costs $1.35 a minute ($1.05 off peak); New Zealand is $1.10 a minute (70c off peak). Off-peak times, if available, vary depending on the destination – see the back of any White Pages telephone book for more details.

Country Direct gives travellers in Australia direct access to operators in nearly 50 other countries, to make reverse-charge (collect) or credit-card calls. For a full list of the countries hooked into this system, check any White Pages telephone book. They include:

Canada	☎ (1800) 881 150
France	☎ (1800) 881 330
Germany	☎ (1800) 881 490
Japan	☎ (1800) 881 810
New Zealand	☎ (1800) 881 640
UK	☎ (1800) 881 440
USA	☎ (1800) 881 011 (AT&T)
	☎ (1800) 881 100 (MCI)
	☎ (1800) 881 877 (Sprint)

Other Calls Many businesses and some government departments operate a toll-free service from around the country with a prefix of 1800. Many companies have six-digit numbers beginning with 13 which are charged at the rate of a local call.

Phone numbers with the prefixes 014, 015, 016, 018 or 041 are mobile or car phones. The three mobile operators are Telstra, Optus and Vodaphone. Calls to mobile numbers can be expensive.

Numbers starting with 0055, usually recorded information services, are provided by private companies, and your call is charged in multiples of 25c (40c from public phones) at a rate selected by the provider varying from 35c to 70c per minute. Numbers beginning with 190 are also information services, but are charged on a fixed fee basis which can be expensive.

Western Australian Area Code This is a large state, but it only has a single area code (08) and all telephone numbers have eight digits.

Fax, Telegraph & Email Services

Just about all small towns in WA have some sort of fax, telegraph or email service. This is due to a government initiative to 'bring the world' to these isolated centres. Telecentres, where you can fax, send emails or surf the Net, have been established in places where before there was not even a proper post office. (I received and sent a couple of weeks worth of emails from Nannup, a timber town in the south-west.)

See Online Services later in this chapter for information on service providers and costs.

BOOKS
Lonely Planet

Lonely Planet publishes *Australia, Outback Australia, Australia phrasebook* and *Bushwalking in Australia* (for a review, see Bushwalking later in this chapter). Lonely Planet also publishes state guides *Victoria, Northern Territory, New South Wales, South Australia, Tasmania* and *Queensland* and city guides *Melbourne* and *Sydney*.

Travel with Children by Maureen Wheeler provides practical information and health advice for younger children and includes the travel experiences of the Wheelers and other families.

Guidebooks

This is the only comprehensive guide to WA. The Australian Geographic Society has produced some good guides to more isolated parts of the state such as the Kimberley and the Canning Stock Route.

A number of commercial guides (with advertising throughout) are available free at tourist offices, hostels and hotels. These include *Tourist Guide to Western Australia, Your Guide to the Amazing North, Your Guide to the Golden West & Beautiful South, Hill's Tourist Guide to Western Australia & Eyre Highway* and *Your Guide to Perth & Fremantle.*

History

A Short History of Australia by Manning Clark is a succinct, fascinating and readable history of Australia. Robert Hughes' bestseller *The Fatal Shore*, a colourful and detailed historical account of convict transportation, has a brief section on this era in WA. Geoffrey Blainey's *The Tyranny of Distance* is a captivating narrative of white settlement and his *The Rush that Never Ended* covers some of the WA goldfields history.

The most comprehensive history of WA is the 836-page *A New History of Western Australia* (1981), edited by CT Stannage. It has nearly 20 contributors and includes excellent coverage of the clash of white and Aboriginal cultures, colonisation, education, religion, sport, unionism and party politics. Shorter, but now dated, is Frank Crowley's *A Short History of Western Australia* (revised edition 1969).

Important historical biographies include *Alexander Forrest: His Life and Times* (1958) by GC Bolton; R Duffield's *Rogue Bull: The Story of Lang Hancock, King of the Pilbara* (1979); Mary Durack's three family sagas *Kings in Grass Castles* (1959), *Sons in the Saddle* (1983) and *To Be Heirs Forever* (1976) (see also Literature in the Facts about WA chapter); *Thomas Peel of Swan River* (1965) by A Hasluck; *Bishop Salvado: Founder of New Norcia* (1943) by JT McMahon; and *The Chief: CY O'Connor* (1978) by M Tauman. Short biographies can be found in the *Dictionary of West Australians 1829-1914* (1979, three volumes) compiled by R Erickson.

The best of the autobiographies is *A Fortunate Life* (1981) by AB Facey. This microcosm of life in post-federation Australia, it is Albert Facey's account of his misfortunes in what was the extraordinary life of a seemingly ordinary person (see also the Albert Facey boxed aside in the Facts about Western Australia chapter).

Good historical accounts of Perth are *The Beginning: European Discovery and Early Settlement of Swan River, Western Australia* (1979) by RT Appleyard & T Manford; and the Perth chapters in *The Origins of Australia's Capital Cities* (1989), edited by Pamela Statham. For Fremantle's history, see *The Western Gateway* (1971) by JK Ewers.

Australian Aboriginal Culture

There are a number of good books which examine Aboriginal culture and sacred places in Aboriginal history. The best coverage is given in Josephine Flood's *Archaeology of the Dreamtime* (1983) and *Riches of Ancient Australia* (1993).

The excellent *Sacred Places in Australia* (1991), a photo-essay by James Cowan & Colin Beard, looks at the sacred areas of the Pilbara, Depuch Island, the Kimberley and Purnululu. More specific to WA are *Thalu Sites of the West Pilbara* (1990) by David Daniel; *Devil's Lair: A Study in Prehistory* (1984) by Charles Dortch.

The local Aboriginal language is covered in *A Nyoongar Wordlist from the South-West of Western Australia* (1992), edited by Peter Bindon & Ross Chadwick.

For an understanding of Aboriginal art, RM & CH Berndt's *Aboriginal Australian Art* (1988) describes the art in its own traditional settings and tells how to 'read' what is painted, carved or etched. IM Crawford's *The Art of the Wandjina* (1968) describes the fascinating paintings of the Kimberley. Also focusing on the region is *Painting the Country: Contemporary Aboriginal Art from the Kimberley Region* (1989).

Many modern writings focus on the theme of Aboriginal alienation in white society. One account is *Outback Ghettos* by Patty O'Grady, which deals with the separation of Aboriginal children from their natural parents. Another is *Encounters in Place: Outsiders and Aboriginal Australians 1606-1985* by DJ Mulvaney.

The two-volume *Encyclopedia of Aboriginal Australia,* edited by David Horton, is an excellent comprehensive and inclusive history of Australia.

Fiction & Drama

For a full description of fiction and drama see Literature and Theatre in the Facts about WA chapter.

National Parks

The national parks custodian, CALM, provides pamphlets on all of the main parks,

forests and marine reserves. In addition it has a number of interesting publications for sale. Recommended are: *Discover Wild Places, Quiet Places* (south-west); *Shark Bay: Discover Monkey Mia and Other Natural Wonders; Wildflower Country* (Jurien Bay to Shark Bay and Inland to Meekatharra); *From the Range to the Reef* (Cape Range and Ningaloo) and *North-West Bound* (Shark Bay to Wyndham).

CALM also produces the excellent and informative quarterly *Landscope: WA's Conservation, Forests & Wildlife Magazine* ($5.95). The magazine has comprehensive articles and often focuses on one area, eg Shark Bay.

ONLINE SERVICES

There are service providers in all the capital cities and in many regional centres, especially at Telecentres (see earlier). Online costs vary, but a typical price is about $5 per hour, with no minimum charge. To receive your emails is much cheaper, say $3 for about 10 pages.

The excellent CALM Internet site NatureBase has information on national parks, walking tracks and developments in the forests. Your Guide to Perth & Fremantle is at www.countrywide.com.au. Also, Gateway to Perth at www.gtp.com.au is a fertile source. The WA Maritime Museum, one of the country's best museums, reveals its treasures at www.mm.wa.gov.au.

Skywest Airlines is at www.skywest.com.au and Greyhound buses are at www.greyhound.com.au.

A number of backpackers' hostels are on the Web and their home pages, although still experimental, have lots of good information. The best organised Web sites are undoubtedly those for the Perth sex industry!

The Rottnest Island Authority sells an excellent CD ROM which outlines the island's attractions, accommodation, transport services and tours.

NEWSPAPERS & MAGAZINES

The *West Australian* and the *Australian* are available each morning from Monday to

Saturday. The Saturday issue of *West Australian* has a supplement *West Magazine*. The *Sunday Times* is available on Sunday.

Some smaller towns have their own newspapers which focus on local news and events, including *Kalgoorlie Miner*, *North-West Telegraph* and *Kimberley Echo*.

International newspapers are available in Perth at the Plaza Newsagency, Plaza Arcade (off Hay St Mall) as well as at the Public Library in James St. Interstate newspaper such as the *Age*, are usually available in the afternoon of the day of publication.

Weekly newspapers and magazines are widely available. These include Australian editions of *Time* and *Rolling Stone*, and the national news magazine *Bulletin* which incorporates an edition of the US *Newsweek*. The British newspapers *Daily Express*, *Guardian* and *Independent* have Australian editions – popular in Perth because of its large number of expats.

RADIO & TV

Unfortunately, WA has probably the worst radio coverage of all the states of Australia, due, most likely, to its small listener base in the country. Perth, however, is well served with both commercial and non-commercial radio and the Australian Broadcasting Corporation (ABC) does its best in the country.

In Perth, the ABC's stations are the AM Regional 6WF (720 kHz), AM Radio National 6RN (810 kHz) and ABC Classical 97.7 FM. The popular youth station JJJ (Triple J) FM can be found on 99.3 MHz in Perth. Other radio stations are MMM (Triple M) FM (96.1 MHz, rock 'n' roll), PMFM (92.9 MHz, rock 'n' roll), 6MM (1116 kHz, Hits and Memories), 94.5 FM (music), 101 FM (community interest and music programmes) and Special Broadcasting Service (SBS) National (96.9 MHz, ethnic programmes).

Some Aboriginal communities have their own stations and make the best of minimal resources. Examples include Wangki Yupurnanupurru Radio (WYRS) in Fitzroy Crossing and Radio Goolari in Broome.

Perth has five TV stations. The three commercial networks are channels 7, 9 and 10.

The ABC (Channel 2) is government funded and supposedly free of bias, as is the Special Broadcasting Service (SBS) 0-28. The best world news service is on SBS at 6.30 pm.

Country stations generally receive two TV stations: the ABC and a local commercial network, Golden West Network (GWN). A lot of places are too remote to get good reception unless they have good antennae or satellite dishes. In the country, head to the pub to watch cable TV.

VIDEO SYSTEMS

Overseas visitors thinking of purchasing videos should remember that Australia uses the Phase Alternative Line (PAL) system which isn't compatible with other standards unless converted.

PHOTOGRAPHY & VIDEO

If you come to WA via Hong Kong or Singapore, it's worth buying film there but otherwise Australian film prices are not too far out of line with those of the rest of the Western world. Including developing, 36-exposure Kodachrome 64 or Fujichrome 100 slide film costs around $25, but with a little shopping around you can find it for $20.

There are plenty of camera shops in the main centres and standards of camera service are high. Developing standards are also high, with many places offering one-hour developing of print film. You can buy 400 ASA film from photographic suppliers and shops.

Photography is no problem, but in the arid areas you have to allow for the exceptional intensity of the light. Best results in the outback regions are obtained early in the morning and late in the afternoon. As the sun gets higher, colours appear washed out. You must also allow for the intensity of reflected light when taking shots of Ningaloo Reef or at other coastal locations. In the outback, especially in the summer, allow for temperature extremes and do your best to keep film as cool as possible, particularly after exposure. Other film and camera hazards are dust in the outback and humidity in the tropical region of the Kimberley.

As in any country, politeness goes a long way when taking photographs; ask before taking pictures of people. Note that many Aboriginal people do not like to have their photographs taken, even from a distance.

TIME

Australia is divided into three time zones: Western Standard Time is plus eight hours from GMT/UTC, Central Standard Time is plus 9½ hours (Northern Territory, South Australia and parts of WA near the border) and Eastern Standard Time is plus 10 (Tasmania, Victoria, New South Wales, Queensland). When it's noon in WA, it's 1.30 pm in the Northern Territory and South Australia and 2 pm in the rest of the country. During the summer things get slightly screwed up as daylight saving time (when clocks are put forward an hour) does not operate in WA or Queensland, and in Tasmania it lasts for two months longer than in other states.

This time difference isn't really a problem in the south where the Nullarbor provides a good distance buffer but it is in the north, in East Kimberley, where a mere border crossing changes the time significantly.

In winter, when it's noon in Perth, it is 6 am in Paris, 5 am in London, midnight in New York and 9 pm in Los Angeles. In Auckland it is 4 pm, in Tokyo 1 pm .

ELECTRICITY

Voltage is 220-240 V and the plugs are three-pin, but not the same as British three-pin plugs. Users of electric shavers or hairdryers should note that, apart from up-market hotels, it's difficult to find converters to take either US flat two-pin plugs or the European round two-pin plugs. Adapters for British plugs can be found in good hardware shops, chemists and travel agents.

WEIGHTS & MEASURES

Australia went metric in the early 1970s. Petrol and milk are sold by the litre, apples and potatoes by the kg, distance is measured by the metre or km, and speed limits are in km per hour (km/h).

For those who need help, there's a conversion table at the back of this book.

LAUNDRY

Fortunately, most accommodation places in WA (even backpackers' hostels) have a small laundry where you can attempt to remove the red Pilbara dust from your favourite white T-shirt – usually without much luck.

In the main towns there are laundrettes, but again the places to stay are geared up with heavy duty washers and dryers, and even sell washing powder. To wash and dry one load, is about $4 to $6.

HEALTH

Australia is a remarkably healthy country to travel in, considering that such a large part of it lies in the tropics. So long as you have not visited an infected country in the past 14 days, no vaccinations are required for entry.

Medical care in Australia is first-class and only moderately expensive. A typical visit to the doctor costs around $35. If you have an immediate health problem, phone or visit the casualty section at the nearest public hospital, or in the outback make contact with the Royal Flying Doctor Service.

The heat in the north and desert areas of WA is probably the main hazard and with it come problems such as heat stroke, dehydration and sunburn.

Travel Insurance

Make sure that you have adequate health insurance. Ambulance services in Australia are self-funding (ie they're not free) and can be very expensive, so you'd be wise to take out travel insurance for that reason alone. Make sure the policy does not exclude engaging in adventure activities (scuba diving, climbing, motorcycling), if that is what you intend to do.

The national health organisation is Medicare. If you are from Britain, New Zealand, Sweden, Italy or the Netherlands, you are entitled, thanks to international agreements, to 'immediate and necessary treatment' (but not emergency dental work). If your visa is valid, you can obtain a Medicare card.

Medical Kit Check List

As doctors are few and far between outside of the South-West of WA, consider taking a basic medical kit including:

☐ **Aspirin** or **paracetamol** (acetaminophen in the US) – for pain or fever.

☐ **Antihistamine** (such as Benadryl) – useful as a decongestant for colds and allergies, to ease the itch from insect bites or stings, and to help prevent motion sickness. Antihistamines may cause sedation and interact with alcohol so care should be taken when using them; take one you know and have used before, if possible.

☐ **Antiseptic** such as povidone-iodine (eg Betadine) – for cuts and grazes.

☐ **Calamine lotion** or **aluminium sulphate** spray (eg Stingose) – to ease irritation from bites or stings.

☐ **Bandages** and **Band-aids**

☐ **Scissors**, **tweezers** and a **thermometer**

☐ **Insect repellent**, **sunscreen** and **chap stick**

Environmental Hazards

Fungal Infections These occur more commonly in hot weather and are usually found on the scalp, between the toes or fingers, in the groin and on the body. Moisture encourages these infections. To prevent such fungal infections wear loose, comfortable clothes, avoid artificial fibres, wash frequently and dry carefully. If you do get an infection, wash the infected area at least daily with a disinfectant or medicated soap and water, and rinse and dry well. Apply an antifungal cream or powder like tolnifate (Tinaderm). Try to expose the infected area to air or sunlight as much as possible and wash all towels and underwear in hot water, change them often and dry them in the sun.

Heat Exhaustion Dehydration and salt deficiency can cause heat exhaustion. Take time to acclimatise to high temperatures, drink sufficient liquids and do not do anything too physically demanding.

Salt deficiency is characterised by fatigue, lethargy, headaches, giddiness and muscle cramps; salt tablets may help, but adding extra salt to your food is better.

Heat Stroke This serious, occasionally fatal, condition can occur if the body's heat-regulating mechanism breaks down and the body temperature rises to dangerous levels. Long, continuous periods of exposure to high temperatures and insufficient fluids can leave you vulnerable to heat stroke.

The symptoms are feeling unwell, not sweating very much (or at all) and a high body temperature ($39°C$ to $41°C$ or $102°F$ to $106°F$). Where sweating has ceased the skin becomes flushed and red. Severe, throbbing headaches and lack of coordination will also occur, and the sufferer may be confused or aggressive. Eventually the victim will become delirious or convulse. Hospitalisation is essential, but in the interim get victims out of the sun, remove their clothing, cover them with a wet sheet or towel and then fan continually. Give fluids if conscious.

Dehydration In hot climates make sure you drink enough – don't rely on feeling thirsty to indicate when you should drink. Not needing to urinate or small amounts of very dark yellow urine is a danger sign.

Always carry plenty of water with you on long trips – up to 20 litres if you intend going off road. Excessive sweating can lead to loss of salt and therefore muscle cramping. Salt tablets are not a good idea as a preventative.

Prickly Heat Prickly heat is an itchy rash caused by excessive perspiration trapped under the skin. It usually strikes people who have just arrived in a hot climate. Keeping cool, bathing often, drying the skin and using a mild talcum or prickly heat powder or resorting to air-conditioning may help.

Sunburn You can get sunburnt surprisingly quickly, even through cloud. Use a sunscreen, hat, and barrier cream for your nose and lips. Calamine lotion or stingose are good for mild sunburn. Protect your eyes with good quality sunglasses. Be careful of the sun between 10 am and 3 pm.

Infectious Diseases

Hepatitis There are almost 300 million

chronic carriers of Hepatitis B in the world. It is spread through contact with infected blood, blood products or body fluids, for example through sexual contact, unsterilised needles and blood transfusions, or contact with blood via small breaks in the skin. Other risk situations include having a shave, tattoo, or having your body pierced with contaminated equipment. The symptoms of type B may be more severe and may lead to long term problems.

HIV/AIDS HIV, Human Immunodeficiency Virus, may develop into AIDS, Acquired Immune Deficiency Syndrome, which is a fatal disease. HIV is a major problem in many countries. Any exposure to blood, blood products or body fluids may put the individual at risk. The disease is often transmitted through sexual contact or dirty needles – vaccinations, acupuncture, tattooing and body piercing can be potentially as dangerous as intravenous drug use.

HIV/AIDS can also be spread through infected blood transfusions; some developing countries cannot afford to screen blood used for transfusions.

If you do need an injection, ask to see the syringe unwrapped in front of you, or take a needle and syringe pack with you. (Fear of HIV infection should never preclude treatment for serious conditions.)

The AIDS Council of WA (☎ 9429 9900) is at 664 Murray St, PO Box 1510, West Perth; the Affected Persons HIV/AIDS Support Group (☎ 9429 9900), PO Box 993, Canning Bridge, 6153; and the AIDS/STD Infoline is ☎ 9227 3777 (weekdays from 9 am to 10 pm, Saturday 10 am to 4 pm).

Sexually Transmitted Diseases Gonorrhoea, herpes and syphilis are among these diseases; sores, blisters or rashes around the genitals, discharges or pain when urinating are common symptoms. While abstinence from sexual contact is the only 100% effective prevention, using condoms is also effective. The treatment of gonorrhoea and syphilis is with antibiotics. The different sexually transmitted diseases each require specific antibiotics. There is no cure for herpes or AIDS.

Cuts, Bites & Stings
Insect Bites & Stings Bee and wasp stings are usually painful rather than dangerous. However in people who are allergic to them severe breathing difficulties may occur and require urgent medical care. Calamine lotion or Stingose spray will give relief and ice packs will reduce the pain and swelling. There are some spiders with dangerous bites but antivenenes are usually available. Scorpion stings are notoriously painful. Scorpions often shelter in shoes or clothing.

For snake bite treatment, see Dangers & Annoyances.

Cuts & Scratches Wash well and treat any cut with an antiseptic such as povidone-iodine. Where possible avoid bandages and Band-aids, which can keep wounds wet. Coral cuts are notoriously slow to heal and if they are not adequately cleaned small pieces of coral can become embedded in the wound. Severe pain, throbbing, redness, fever or generally feeling unwell suggest infection and the need for antibiotics promptly as coral cuts may result in serious infections.

Women's Health
Sexually transmitted diseases are a major cause of vaginal problems. Symptoms include a smelly discharge, painful intercourse and sometimes a burning sensation when urinating. Male sexual partners must also be treated. Medical attention should be sought and remember in addition to these diseases HIV or hepatitis B may also be acquired during exposure. Besides abstinence, the best thing is to practise safe sex using condoms.

Antibiotic use, synthetic underwear, sweating and contraceptive pills can lead to fungal vaginal infections when travelling in hot climates. Maintaining good personal hygiene, and loose-fitting clothes and cotton underwear helps to prevent these infections.

Fungal infections, characterised by a rash,

itch and discharge, can be treated with a vinegar or lemon-juice douche, or with yoghurt. Nystatin, miconazole or clotrimazole pessaries or vaginal cream are the usual treatment.

TOILETS

You will find grungy public toilets in most towns, but travel in WA usually means it's a long distance between 'long drops'. Otherwise it is the redback trap at Widgiemooltha, or that lovely edifice between Broome and Port Hedland – the Great Sandy Desert. A roll of toilet paper is a must if you're travelling by car.

There is heaps of territory to piss or shit in WA, and no one will chastise you if you are slightly off mark. In the desert leave your shit on the surface – it will dry, desiccate and eventually blow away. Burn your toilet paper, if at all possible, but keep in mind fire danger.

WOMEN TRAVELLERS

Western Australia is generally a safe place for women travellers, although you should avoid walking alone late at night in any of the major towns, especially central Perth, Albany and Kalgoorlie. There are still a number of unsolved abductions and murders in metropolitan Perth. Women should not consider hitching in WA.

Useful organisations are:

Centre for Women's Health
    Bagot Rd, Subiaco (☎ 9340 2222)
Sexual Assault Referral Centre
    24-hour Crisis Line Perth (☎ 9340 1828);
    Country areas freecall (☎ (008) 199 888)
Single Women's Refuges: 24 hours
    Nunyara (☎ 9328 7284); Wyn Carr House
    (☎ 9430 5756); Multicultural Service
    (☎ 9325 7716)

GAY & LESBIAN TRAVELLERS

The West, in spite of its current conservative politics, has active and proud gay and lesbian communities. Northbridge and North Fremantle are the places to hang out. In October, there is a Gay Pride march (Perth Pride) and in the same month, a Reclaim-the-Night march. In November a Gay Olympics

is held. For gay and lesbian-friendly places to eat, stay and party, see the Perth chapter or read the free *West Side Observer* and the lesbian newsletter *Grapevine*.

Useful organisations include:

Perth Outdoors Group
    PO Box 47, Northbridge, 6865 (☎ 9354 2737)
Gay Activities Group Services
    PO Box 8234, Perth 6849
Lesbian & Gay Pride WA
    PO Box 30, North Perth, 6006 (☎ 9470 6911)
AIDS Council of WA
    664 Murray St, PO Box 1510, West Perth
    (☎ 9429 9900).

DISABLED TRAVELLERS

The office of the Australian Council for the Rehabilitation of the Disabled (ACROD; ☎ 9222 2961), 189 Royal St, East Perth, produces information sheets for disabled travellers, including lists of state-level organisations, specialist travel agents, wheelchair and equipment hire and access guides. It can also help with specific queries by post and staff are grateful if you send a stamped addressed envelopes.

People with Disabilities (WA) Inc (☎ 9386 6477) in Perth will also be able to help. Its freecall number outside the Perth metropolitan area is ☎ (1800) 193 331 and the TTY (talking telephone) number is ☎ 9386 6451.

Other useful organisations are:

Blind Association
    16 Sunbury Rd, Victoria Park (☎ 9311 8202)
Deaf Society of WA (Inc)
    16 Brentham St, Leederville (☎ 9443 2677;
    TTY 9433 1960)
Paraplegic-Quadriplegic Association of WA (Inc)
    10 Selby St, Shenton Park (☎ 9381 0173)

SENIOR TRAVELLERS

This state is sympathetic to the 'older' traveller – indeed a caravan park in Carnarvon has a minimum age entry of 50.

Everything becomes relative when you realise that Cliff Young in 1997, at a mere 76 years of age, *ran* from Perth to Kununurra, averaging 75km a day.

You can get more information from the

state government's Seniors' Information Service (☎ 9328 9155). There are further listings in Telstra's Yellow Pages.

TRAVEL WITH CHILDREN

Travel with your kids if you have them. The kilometres will be made more interesting, but no easier, by their presence. This book was written/updated with a one-year-old/four-year-old in tow. Get a copy of Lonely Planet's *Travel with Children*, by Maureen Wheeler, for more tips. (See Books earlier for a review.) Remember there are huge distances between points of interest and it is hard to convince a kid that the Great Sandy Desert is more than sand.

There are many opportunities for children to see wildlife up close, such as encounters with pelicans and dolphins at Monkey Mia.

EMERGENCY

In case of a life-threatening emergency call ☎ 000. This call is free from any phone, and the operator will connect you to either the police, ambulance or fire brigade. Local emergency numbers can be found in the Perth White Pages telephone directory. Oth-

erwise you can call the police on ☎ 9222 1111 in Perth and ☎ 9430 5244 in Fremantle.

In remote areas a number of travellers will be equipped with Flying Doctor emergency radios. For those crossing the Nullarbor and equipped with HF radios, the Royal Flying Doctor Base (VNZ) at Port Augusta monitors the following frequencies from 6 am to 9 pm daily: 2020, 4010, 6890 and 8165 kHz. Kalgoorlie (VJQ) RFDS monitors 5360 kHz from 8 am to 5 pm Monday to Friday, from 9 to 10 am on weekends. In the north-west, the Royal Flying Doctor Base (VKL) at Port Hedland monitors 4030 and 6960 kHz from 7 am to 5 pm Monday to Friday, 8.30 to 10 am Saturday (but not on Sunday). The frequency for Derby (VJB) is 5300 kHz, and for Meekatharra (VKJ) 4010 and 6880 kHz.

There is an interpreter service available on ☎ 9325 9144.

DANGERS & ANNOYANCES
Animal Hazards

There are a few unique and sometimes dangerous creatures, although it's unlikely that you'll come across any of them, particularly if you stick to the cities.

The best known danger in the outback, and the one that captures visitors' imaginations, is snakes. Although there are many venomous snakes, there are few that are aggressive, and unless you have the bad fortune to stand on one it's unlikely you'll be bitten. Some snakes, however, will attack if alarmed and sea snakes can also be dangerous.

To minimise your chances of being bitten, always wear boots, socks and long trousers when walking through undergrowth. Don't put your hands into holes and crevices, and be careful when collecting firewood.

Snake bites do not cause instantaneous death and antivenenes are usually available. Keep the victim calm and still, wrap the bitten limb tightly, as you would for a sprained ankle, and then attach a splint to immobilise it. Then seek medical help. Don't attempt to catch the snake if there is even a remote possibility of being bitten again. Tourniquets and sucking out the poison are now discredited procedures.

Avoid spiders as there are a couple of really nasty ones. If you're bitten, seek medical attention straight away.

Leeches are common, and while they will suck your blood, they're not dangerous and are easily removed by the application of salt or heat.

The box jellyfish, also known as the sea wasp or 'stinger', is found in the north-west during summer and can be fatal. The stinging tentacles spread several metres out from the sea wasp's body; by the time you see it you're likely to have been stung. If someone is stung, they will probably run out of the sea screaming and collapse on the beach, with weals on their body as though they've been whipped – and they sometimes stop breathing.

Douse the stings with vinegar (available on many beaches or from nearby houses), do not try to remove the tentacles from the skin, and treat as for snake bite. If there's a first-aider present, they may have to apply artificial respiration until the ambulance gets there. Above all, stay out of the sea when the sea wasps are around – the locals are ignoring that lovely water for an excellent reason.

When reef walking you must always wear shoes to protect your feet against coral cuts which quickly become infected. There are stonefish – venomous fish that look like a flat piece of rock on the sea bed – throughout the tropical water of WA. Also watch out for the scorpion fish, which has venomous spines.

Crocodiles Up in the north-west, saltwater crocodiles can be a real danger (they have killed a number of people including travellers and locals). Be careful before diving into that inviting, cool water to find out if it's croc-free. There are some local rules to remember:

- Don't launch your boat from the same spot all the time.
- Don't throw fish guts or old bait into the water.
- Camp well away from the banks.

Flies & Mosquitoes

For four to six months of the year you'll have to cope with those two banes of the Australian outdoors – the fly and the mosquito.

The flies are not too bad in the towns and cities; it's in the country that it starts getting out of hand, and the further 'out' you get the worse the flies seem to be. Flies are a real problem in north-west Australia and are responsible for much of the conjunctivitis and trachoma found in the Kimberley. Try hard to prevent flies from getting near the eyes of infants and young children. Repellents such as Aerogard, Rid and Bushmens go some way to deterring them, but don't let any of this stuff get near the eyes of kids.

Mosquitoes can also be a problem, especially in the warmer tropical and subtropical areas. Mosquitoes in the Kimberley are responsible for the transmission of a number of diseases such as Ross River virus and Australian encephalitis. Cover up bare skin and wear a mosquito repellent if you go outside at dusk.

On the Road

Cattle and kangaroos are often a hazard to the driver. A collision with one will badly damage your car and probably kill the animal. Unfortunately, other drivers are even more dangerous, particularly those who drink. Australia has a high road toll, particularly in the countryside, so don't drink and drive and please take care.

See Car in the Getting Around chapter for more on driving hazards. *Never* leave a child in the car, especially with the windows closed, where they can dehydrate and die quickly.

Cyclones

These are a feature of the weather pattern of the north-west and the northern coastal areas. A cyclone is a circular rotating storm of tropical origin in which the mean wind speed exceeds 63 km/h (gale force). Speeds of 100 km/h, however, are common and a speed of 248 km/h was recorded at Onslow in 1975. Some winds can extend up to 200km from the centre or 'eye' of the cyclone. Heavy rain falls as the system decays which it does 24 to 48 hours after hitting land, and flooding often occurs. The cyclone season in the west is officially 1 November to 30 April.

Cyclones are erratic, so it is important to listen to ABC radio for information – a battery-powered radio is the best option as power supplies may be cut. There are also two recorded Severe Weather Service lines: Port Hedland (☎ (08) 11554) and Perth (☎ (08) 11542), which report the latest developments.

There are three cyclone warning stages:

- blue – cyclone may affect the area in 48 hours
- yellow – cyclone moving closer and inevitable in 12 hours
- red – cyclone is imminent

The all clear is sounded when the cyclone has passed, but there may still be wind and heavy rain. If you have any doubts, seek local advice. The Bureau of Meteorology provides a free pamphlet *Surviving Cyclones*.

Bushfires & Blizzards

Bushfires happen every year in Australia. Don't be the mug who starts one. In hot, dry, windy weather, be extremely careful with any naked flame – this means no cigarette butts out of car windows. On a Total Fire Ban Day (listen to the radio or watch the billboards on country roads), it is forbidden to use a camping stove in the open. The locals will happily dob you in if you break the law, and the penalties are severe.

If you're unfortunate enough to find yourself driving through a bushfire, stay inside your car and try to park off the road in an open space, away from trees, until the danger's past. Lie on the floor under the dashboard, covering yourself with a wool blanket if possible. The front of the fire should pass quickly, and you will be much safer than if you were out in the open.

Bushwalkers should take local advice before setting out. Don't go on a Total Fire Ban Day – delay your trip until the weather has changed. Chances are that it will be so unpleasantly hot and windy, you'll be better off in an air-con pub sipping a cool beer anyway.

If you're out in the bush and you see smoke, even at a great distance, take it seriously. Go to the nearest open space, downhill if possible. A forested ridge is the most dangerous place to be. Bushfires move very quickly and change direction with the wind.

Having said all that, more bushwalkers die of cold than in bushfires! Even in summer, temperatures can drop below freezing at night in the mountains of the south-west.

LEGAL MATTERS

There is not much to worry about in WA, just a few simple rules. Don't buy illegal drugs such as marijuana; don't drink and drive; don't smoke cigarettes where they are forbidden; don't litter (sensitive Aussies rightly hate it); don't whip your clothes off on a beach where most people are fully clothed for swimming (there are plenty of beaches where you can bare it all); don't light any fire on a Total Fire Ban Day; and don't try and bring fruit or vegetables across the SA and NT borders.

If the shit hits the fan and you have breached this simple set of rules, you are allowed to contact a legal representative. You can also contact the Rights and Equal Opportunities commissions for further advice. Local consulates will do what they can when their nationals call for help, which may not be much if you've broken the law.

BUSINESS HOURS

Most shops close at 5 or 5.30 pm weekdays, and either noon or 5 pm on Saturday. In some places Sunday trading is starting to catch on, but it's currently limited to suburban areas such as Subiaco, Northbridge and Fremantle. In most towns there is one late-shopping night each week when the doors stay open until 9 pm. Central Perth and Fremantle have extended hours: Monday to Thursday until 7 pm, Friday 9 pm, Saturday 5 pm and Sunday from 12 noon to 6 pm.

Banks open from 9.30 am to 4 pm Monday to Thursday, and until 5 pm on Friday. Some bank agencies also open on Saturday, but generally all banks are closed on Saturday, Sunday and public holidays.

There are exceptions to WA's opening hours and all sorts of places stay open late and at weekends – milk bars, convenience stores, supermarkets, delis and bookshops.

PUBLIC HOLIDAYS & SPECIAL EVENTS
Public Holidays
The Christmas holiday season is part of the long summer school holidays and accommodation is usually fully booked. The following is a list of the main national and WA public holidays:

1 January
   New Year's Day
26 January
   Australia Day
Second Monday in March
   Labour Day (WA)
Good Friday and Easter Saturday,
   Sunday and Monday
25 April
   ANZAC Day
First Monday in June
   Foundation Day (WA)
First Monday in October
   Queen's Birthday (WA)
25 December
   Christmas Day
26 December
   Boxing Day

Special Events
Perth has a number of special events including the big Festival of Perth from mid-February to early March, a cultural festival of local national and international arts from theatre, dance, film, music and visual arts – the oldest such festival in Australia – at venues throughout the city. Migrants have added a number of festivals to the calendar also, including the Perth Italian Festival in September, an Oktoberfest in, of course, October, and the Japanese-style Shinju Matsuri (Pearl) Festival in Broome. There are exhibitions of indigenous art and cultural performances in Perth during National Aboriginal Islander Day Observance Committee (NAIDOC) Week in July.

Both Broome in the Kimberley and York

in the Avon Valley have achieved reputations as festival centres (for more details see those sections). Outside Perth, WA's major annual festivals and events include the following (for more information see the relevant chapters):

January
   Lancelin to Ledge Point Sailboard Race, Mount Barker Summer Wine Festival, Esperance Oz Rock Festival & Sailboard Classic, Fremantle Sardine Festival
February
   Geraldton Kite Festival & Wind on Water, Margaret River Wine & Food Festival, Great Southern Wine Festival, Leeuwin Estate Concert (Margaret River)
March
   Kalbarri Sports Fishing Classic, Bunbury Show & Aqua Festival, Pemberton King Karri Karnival, Rottnest Festival
April
   Kalgoorlie Great Gold Festival, Broome Waterbirds Odyssey, Margaret River Surf Masters (be wary of invitations on the 1st, April Fool's Day)
May
   Broome Fringe Arts Festival, Toodyay Moondyne Festival & Colonial Fair
June
   Carnarvon Rodeo, Cossack Fair and Regatta, New Norcia Festival of Flowers
July
   Exmouth Exmo Week, Broome Aboriginal Culture & Arts Festival, Derby Boab Festival, Katanning Islamic Celebration
August
   Avon Descent, Mullewa Wildflower Show, Karratha FeNaCLNG Festival, Broome Shinju-Matsuri (Pearl) Festival, Kununurra Ord River Festival, Denmark Winter Festival
September
   York Jazz Festival, Kojonup Wildflower Festival, Ravensthorpe Wildflower Show
October
   Chittering Sheep Dog Trials, Toodyay Folk Festival, Geraldton Sunshine Festival, Nannup Wildflower Display
November
   Geraldton Blessing of the Fleet, Discover Bunbury, York Flying 50 Vintage/Veteran Car Race, Margaret River Surf Classic & Show, Manjimup Timber Festival, Wilyabrup Wine and Craft Show
December
   Broome Mango Festival, Derby Boxing Day Sports

ACTIVITIES

Western Australia bills itself as the 'state of excitement' and there is little doubt that a huge range of activities exist. Bushwalking and birdwatching are both inexpensive activities that require a minimal cash outlay and there is no shortage of wilderness in which to do them. Surfers (windsurfers, bodysurfers and boardsurfers) and divers are well catered for in this state, especially around Perth and in the south-west. Over the vast state there are plenty of places to go horseriding, 4WD driving and cycling. Canoeing, sea kayaking and rafting are also popular in both the north and south of WA.

Rockclimbing is popular, as are the associated activities of canyoning and abseiling. 'Spelunking', or caving, is also widely practised and WA has some of the best caves in the country including those in the south-west and Nullarbor.

Other activities include gold prospecting, fossicking for rocks and fishing. For the vast range of possibilities delve into CALM's *Perth Outdoors* (1992).

Western Australians are a sporting lot. Australian Rules Football is the most popular sport with over 50,000 players, and netball is next in line with more than 40,000. Bowls, tennis, indoor cricket, golf and cricket follow, and are popular with both sexes.

Bushwalking

There are some great bushwalks in this state, ranging from short trips in the forests of the south-west to the long Bibbulmun Track or untracked coastal walks. Many involve substantial climbs and the traversing of picturesque ranges.

The beauty of WA is that the walks are in vastly different environments. There is the tropical Kimberley, the dry Pilbara with its magnificent gorges, Kalbarri and the Murchison River, the Darling Range near Perth and the great variety of the coastline and forests of the south-west.

For bushwalkers who like to have something high to climb, there is Mt Augustus, twice the size of Uluru (Ayer's Rock); Pyramid Hill in the Pilbara with its stunning views; the precipitous peaks of the Stirling Range and the Porongurups; and Peak Charles, Mt Ragged and Frenchman's Peak near Esperance.

There is a surfeit of spectacular coastline punctuated by a number of interesting walks. Of particular interest are the walks in Fitzgerald River, William Bay, Leeuwin-Naturaliste, Walpole-Nornalup and d'Entrecasteaux national parks. It is not unusual to see humpback whales at sea and wildflowers cascading down coastal tracks.

Interesting walks in the hills around Perth include the 640km Bibbulmun Track that

Bibbulmun Track

This track was first thought of about 25 years ago, and even though it was initially routed from Kalamunda near Perth to Northcliffe in the south-west (and later as far as Walpole), it was usually referred to as the 'Perth-Albany Track'.

The track was officially opened in 1979 as part of the celebrations to mark 150 years of white settlement and the first group of walkers made it from one end to the other. In the early 1990s it was proposed that the track be upgraded, realigned in several places and extended a further 180km from Walpole to Albany.

When completed the Bibbulmun will cover some 950km and pass through a variety of forest types. There will be campsites spaced every 10 to 20km, most with a three-sided shelter which sleeps eight to 12 people.

Currently, it is estimated that about 5000 walkers use the track each year, but most are only on the track for two or three days. For more information ring ☎(08) 9334 0265 or email: bibtrack@calm.wa.gov.au. A new guide book and maps to the track, indicating campsites and realigned sections of track, is being produced. ■

runs along old forest tracks between Perth and Walpole on WA's south-eastern coast. Information on this and many other tracks is available from CALM (☎ (1800) 199 287), 50 Hayman Rd, Como, WA 6152.

Clubs There are a number of bushwalking clubs in WA. The umbrella organisation is the Federation of WA Bushwalking Clubs (☎ 9341 5353) in Perth.

Equipment There are a number of equipment suppliers in Perth who can provide bushwalking information:

Big Country Camping & Tramping
    884 Hay St, Perth 6000 (☎ 9321 2666)
Mainpeak Pty Ltd
    31 Jarrad St, Cottesloe 6011 (☎ 9385 1689)
Mountain Designs
    862 Hay St, Perth 6000 (☎ 9322 4774)
    3 Queensgate Centre, William St, Fremantle 6160 (☎ 9335 1431)
Snowgum
    581 Murray St, Perth 6005 (☎ 9321 5259)
Wilderness Equipment
    Bayview Centre, corner Stirling Highway & Leura Ave, Claremont 6010 (☎ 9385 3711)

Books Suitable bushwalking books, all published by CALM, are *Beating About the Bush: Discover the National Parks and Forests near Perth* (1986) by Andrew Cribb; *Family Walks in Perth Outdoors*; *Perth Outdoors: A Guide to Natural Recreation Areas In and Around Perth* (1992); and the recently revised *Guide to the Bibbulmun Bushwalking Track* which covers the over 600km walk from Perth to the south-west corner of the state (see the boxed aside 'Bibbulmun Track').

Lonely Planet's *Bushwalking in Australia* (1992) by John & Monica Chapman has details of the Stirling Range Circuit and a Nuyts Wilderness walk, both two day walks.

Australia's *Wild* magazine has a number of articles on WA's bushwalks, including an account of an arduous trip in country near the Drysdale River in the Kimberley.

Heritage Trails Network The Heritage Trails Network, launched during Australia's Bicentenary in 1988, is an excellent series of trails covering historical, cultural or natural points of interest throughout the state. Somewhat neglected now, the trails are usually marked with interpretive displays and directional markers. Information on the Heritage Trails Network can be obtained from tourist offices or the WA Heritage Committee (☎ 9221 4177), 108 Adelaide Terrace, East Perth 6004. There is a dated *Heritage Trails in WA* book published by the committee.

Bird-Watching

This state is one of the best places in Australia for birdwatching because of the variety of species and the ease with which you can observe them. The state is a birdwatcher's delight, so much so, that two of the four official Royal Australian Ornithologist Union's (RAOU's) observatories are in the WA (at Eyre and Broome).

The search for the noisy scrub bird, rainbow pitta, Gouldian finch, shy hylacola, peregrine falcon, wedge-tailed eagle, chestnut breasted quail thrush, gibber chat, western bristlebird, sandstone shrike-thrush, yellow-rumped pardalote, pink cockatoo and purple-gaped honeyeater will take you to all parts of the state.

For details about sightings of rare and endangered birds, contact the RAOU (☎ 9364 6202), 218/15 Ogilvie Rd, Canning Bridge, or see issues of *WA Birdnotes*.

To help you make the distinction between species you will need *Field Guide to the Birds of Australia* (1989) by K Simpson & N Day; *Field Guide to the Birds of Western Australia* (1985) by GM Storr & RE Johnstone; and *The Slater Field Guide to Australian Birds* (1990) by Peter Slater et al.

Cycling

This is a very popular activity in WA. Rottnest Island is virtually free of motorised traffic and many visitors pedal their way around the island. Perth has a great path system for cyclists including the Around the Rivers ride, which is made up of 12 connected paths. The Cycle Touring Association has heaps of information on cycling in the state; contact them through Bike West (☎ 9430 7550;

jkrynen@dot.wa.gov.au), Suite 16, Fremantle Mall, 27-35 William St, Fremantle, or the Department of Transport (☎ 9389 0611), 136 Stirling Highway, Nedlands 6009. The South West Development Commission produces an excellent map *Cycling Down South*.

Bicycle Touring in Australia (1991) by Leigh Hemmings covers the south-west of the state. For more info about practicalities, see Bicycle in the Getting Around chapter.

Horse & Camel Trekking

The horse and camel were the animal pioneers of this country, enabling both the explorers and settlers to make inroads into the inhospitable interior. Today, there are many places in the state where you can go either horse or camel trekking.

For further information, contact the local tourist offices for details of those companies taking treks. The type of trek ranges from a leisurely camel ride along Cable Beach near Broome to an overnight or moonlight horse ride in Kalbarri National Park.

The more adventurous could contemplate an overnight trip south of Wyndham in the rugged East Kimberley. There are also a number of horseriding and trekking operations in the south-west of the state. Specific information relating to trekking is given in the relevant chapters. The Canning Stock Route, by camel, even looms as a possibility!

Rockclimbing

It was widely thought, over a decade ago, that WA had the greatest remaining areas of unclimbed rock – this is still true. Most activity has been concentrated in the south-west of the state, close to Perth, but the Pilbara, North-West Cape and the Kimberley have endless climbing possibilities. The Kimberley, for instance, is twice the size of Victoria and much of it is covered with rock.

In the south-west corner of the state are Churchmans Brook and Mountain Quarry near Perth, the sea cliffs of Wilyabrup, humongous West Cape Howe, the Gap, Peak Head, the Stirlings, the Porongurups and Peak Charles. Back in 1972, the 280m Coercion (Grade 16), a route on Bluff Knoll, was climbed by a party of three. A 'doddle' (easy climb) by today's standards, it was fairly spectacular then.

A new wave of climbers have moved in and claimed previously unclimbed lines on many of the features. Slowly, the massive cliffs of the Pilbara, the Dampier Archipelago, North-West Cape and the Kimberley are succumbing to ascents by spider-like humans (check with local CALM officials as to where climbing is permitted).

Canyoning and abseiling, necessary skills of the exploratory climber, are popular activities in their own right. The Miracle Mile canyoning trip in the Karijini (Hamersley Range) gorges with guide Dave Doust has become popular with foreign backpackers. Abseiling into the Murchison gorges near Kalbarri with another guide, Gordon, has also won renown. There are many other locations for these activities.

Outdoor outfitting shops can advise you on where and when the Climbing Association meets. The *Redpoint* climbing magazine comes out on a regular basis.

For beginners, Adventure Out (☎ 9472 3919) conducts instructional courses at Churchman Brook, near Armadale; the cost for a two day programme is $195. A two day lead rockclimbing course conducted at Wilyabrup, near Margaret River, costs $260.

Caving

There are plenty of opportunities for adventure caving in WA. This type of caving, which is vastly different to tours through electrically-lit 'commercial' caves, involves specialist knowledge and skill. Many caves are in the Leeuwin-Naturaliste karst system and a number, such as Brides and Dingo's, have to be accessed using ropes. Cape Range National Park of North-West Cape has a number of unexplored caves (although human moles are rapidly drifting north and underground).

Adventure Out (☎ 9472 3919) has a two day adventure discovery trip to the Margaret River region which includes abseiling, climbing and caving for $260; caving is conducted in Brides Cave at Calgardup.

Surfing

The WA coast is a mecca for surfers from all over the world. It is the south-west, and the Margaret River area in particular, that are so well known. Yallingup and Prevelly Park both host top-level surf competitions attracting the best board riders in the world. Around Bunbury, Geraldton, Kalbarri, Carnarvon and Albany there is also good surfing. Chances are, if you are here with your board, then we don't have to tell you where to go.

Nat Young's *Surfing & Sailboard Guide to Australia* and coffee-table publication *Atlas of Australian Surfing* cover the west coast beaches.

For further information, contact Surf Point Lodge, Gnarabup (☎ 9757 1777) near Margaret River.

Riding the perfect wave at Margie's

Scuba Diving & Snorkelling

With over 6000km of coastline in WA, there is plenty of 'divers-ity' for those heading underwater. Good diving areas include the large stretch of coast from Esperance to Geraldton, and between Carnarvon and Exmouth. You can also get out to the islands and reefs in small boats.

The more popular diving spots include Esperance, Bremer Bay, Albany, Denmark, Windy Harbour, Margaret River, Busselton Jetty, Bunbury, Rottnest Island, Shoalwater Islands Marine Park (near Rockingham), Lancelin, Houtman Abrolhos Islands (near Geraldton), Carnarvon and North-West Cape (Exmouth, Coral Bay, Ningaloo Reef).

Perhaps the most spectacular underwater experience would be diving with the world's largest fish, the whale shark, or swimming with the graceful manta rays. This is possible off Ningaloo Reef and Exmouth (see Exmouth in the Coral Coast & the Pilbara chapter). There is a strong possibility you will also see green and loggerhead turtles, dolphins, dugongs and humpback whales, depending on when you visit.

Watching Marine Mammals

Although commercial operators will happily take you to spot marine mammals, most notably humpback whales and bottlenose dolphins, many are seen purely by chance. There are few other accessible places in the world where the spotting of such a variety of marine mammals is so easy. Notes on common marine mammals are included in the Flora & Fauna section earlier in this chapter.

Whales, particularly the humpback, are commonly seen (anywhere from Cape Leeuwin north to Dampier, even between Perth and Rottnest Island). Another 'watched' whale is the southern right, seen in numbers off the Great Australian Bight, near Albany and by Cape Leeuwin.

Dolphins observed in the west are the common dolphin and bottlenose dolphin. The bottlenose attracts thousands of tourists to Monkey Mia on Shark Bay and to Bunbury south of Perth. You can also swim with the bottlenose off Rockingham, south of Perth. Common dolphins are likely to be seen on boat trips in places like the Archipelago of the Recherche.

Other marine mammals include the Australian sea lion at Carnac Island (opposite Perth); any one of the 10,000 dugongs that frequent Shark Bay; and NZ fur seals basking along the southern coastline.

The world's biggest fish is the benign whale shark, easily seen off Ningaloo Reef near Exmouth and Coral Bay (see the Coral Coast & Pilbara chapter).

Sailing

Western Australia brought home the America's Cup for a brief period from 1983 to 1987 when *Australia II* triumphed over the US yacht *Liberty*. There are a number of opportunities to learn basic or advanced sailing, or just go for a sail, in and around Perth and Fremantle. The Swan River is a great place to begin and there is another school at Sorrento at Hillary's Boat Harbour. Fun catamarans are available for hire at a number of southern and northern beaches.

Fremantle is one of the six world legs in the Whitbread Around the World Yacht Race, concluding the arduous 'bash' across the Southern Ocean from Cape Town.

Fishing

The coastal regions of WA offer some of the best fishing in the world. Some of the more popular areas include Rottnest Island, Albany, Geraldton and the Houtman Abrolhos, Mackerel Islands, Shark Bay, Carnarvon and the coastline to the north, the North-West Cape and Broome.

Fishing licences (available for $55 from the Fisheries Department (☎ 9482 7333), SGIO Building, 3rd Floor, 168 St George's Terrace, Perth, or country offices) are only required if you intend catching marron and rock lobsters or intend using a fishing net. The department publishes fishing guides including one for environmentally sensitive Ningaloo Reef.

The *Caravan, Camping & Fishing Guide to the Northwest* (1990) by Don & Lyn Yelland is useful and its philosophy is not to clean out the fish stocks but 'to aim to catch a feed for oneself and family and, for a variety of personal reasons, to enjoy the experience along the way'.

Canoeing

There is ample scope to paddle a canoe or kayak in WA. By canoe we mean the Canadian which is open, seating two or three people; whereas a kayak has an enclosed cockpit and seats one or two.

For information contact the Amateur Canoe Association of WA (☎ 9387 5756). Other groups of paddlers include Ascot Kayak, Canning River, Darling Range, Peel Districts, South-West and Swan canoe clubs.

The most famous river is the Avon which is 'descended' by a rabble of powered and unpowered craft in the annual Avon Descent, held in August. There are many other calmer stretches of water that can be enjoyed in a canoe or kayak. Canadians are used for the trip down the Murchison River which gives access to the picturesque gorges of Kalbarri National Park. The forest-to-sea tour on the Blackwood River in the south-west is rated one of Australia's best trips in *Canoe Touring in Australia: Seven of the Country's Best River Journeys* (1993) by L Hemmings.

Kayaks and Canadians can be hired in Perth. A kayak or two-person Canadian costs about $40 for the week or $35 for a weekend and a three-person Canadian about $5 more.

The state's Department of Sport & Recreation (☎ 9387 9700) publishes a series of free *Canoeing Guides*; No 12 in the series, *Avon River: Northam to Toodyay*, is particularly useful.

White-Water Rafting

From Perth white-water rafting trips are available with Adventure Out (☎ 9472 3919). In summer, the Collie River is suitable for two-person rafts; and in winter the Murray River, about a 90-minute drive south of Perth, can be tackled in seven-person rafts. Other rafting places in the state are the Murchison River (after a cyclone) and the Ord River spillway near Kununurra.

Sea Kayaking

This adventure sport has a good following in the west. Sea kayaking requires a good deal of skill and should only be undertaken with good equipment and the necessary training.

In the north-west, the tidal changes are huge and there are dangers from crocodiles and sharks. Adventure Out (see White-Water Rafting above) should be able to put you in contact with like-minded enthusiasts. Perhaps the best trip is along Ningaloo Reef with Sea Kayak Wilderness Adventures (☎ 9949 1990).

Windsurfing

This is immensely popular, especially at Perth's city beaches. Scarborough on a windy day is ablaze with multi-coloured sails and wave riders leaping over intimidating, incoming breakers.

Beaches in the south-west, such as Mandurah, Rockingham, Busselton, Dunsborough and Bunbury are also popular. So are northern beaches – Seabird, Lancelin (probably the sailboard mecca), Ledge Point and Geraldton. This type of craft features heavily in Geraldton's Festival of the Winds. Each year, in January, there is an ocean race from Ledge Point to Lancelin.

For more information contact the tourist offices in the towns mentioned here.

LANGUAGE COURSES

If English isn't your first language and you want to study it, places specialising in teaching English include:

Edith Cowan University International English Centre
  Goldsworthy Rd, Claremont (☎ 9442 1403)
Phoenix English Language Academy
  223 Vincent St, North Perth 6006 (☎ 9227 5538; fax 9227 5540)

WORK
Working Holiday

If you come to Australia on a 12-month 'working holiday' visa, you can officially work for three out of those 12 months, but working on a regular tourist visa is strictly not on. Many travellers on tourist visas do find casual work, but with a national unemployment rate of 11% and youth unemployment as high as 40% in some areas, it is becoming more difficult to find a job – legal or otherwise.

Many travellers who have budgeted on finding work return home early, simply because the work they hoped to find just isn't available. If you are coming to Australia with the intention of working, ensure you have enough funds to cover your stay, or have a contingency plan if the work is not forthcoming.

Having said all that, it *is* still possible to find short-term work, it's just that the opportunities are far fewer than in the past.

To receive wages in Australia you must be in possession of a Tax File Number, issued by the Taxation Department. Forms are available from post offices and you'll need to show your passport and visa.

The best prospects for casual work include factories, bar work, waiting on tables or washing dishes, domestic chores at outback roadhouses, nanny work, fruit picking and collecting for charities.

The Commonwealth Employment Service (CES) has over 300 offices around the country, and the staff usually have a good idea of what's available. The CES also produces an annual agricultural joblist in *Harvest Table*. If federal plans to privatise this service go ahead check with the equivalent.

There are also a number of private employment agencies that can assist you to get work. Computer temps, word processors and programming contractors are seemingly always in demand. For both CES and private agencies check Employment Agencies in the Yellow Pages. Best of luck.

Try the classified section of the daily newspapers under Situations Vacant, especially on Saturdays and Wednesdays. The various backpackers' magazines and hostels are good information sources – some local employers even advertise on their notice boards.

Think very carefully about the heavily advertised 'collecting' jobs and make sure you are satisfied that a reasonable percentage of the funds you collect gets to an actual charity. Most backpackers last less than a day in these jobs, which gives you some idea of what they're like. Didn't you come here for a holiday? See the table below for a list of crops and their seasons.

Fish Processing

Crayfish process workers are required from mid-November until the end of June. Try the CES offices in Fremantle, Mandurah, Dongara, Kalbarri and Geraldton. Scallop and prawn processors are required in Carnarvon, March to October.

Oats, Barley & Wheat Harvesting/ Seeding

Some work is available in the wheatbelt during harvesting and seeding. Seeding occurs from April to June in the north, March to June in the central belt and April to June in the south. Harvesting is from October to January in the north, October to December in the central belt and November to December in the south. The main towns are Merredin, Northam, Wagin, Gnowangerup, Katanning, Williams, Narrogin, Geraldton, Bindoon, Chittering, Moora, Salmon Gums, Albany and Moora. Check at the CES offices listed earlier.

ACCOMMODATION

Western Australia is well equipped with youth hostels, backpackers' hostels and caravan parks with campsites – the cheapest shelter you can find.

A typical town of more than a thousand people (say Mullewa in the Midlands) will have a basic motel at around \$50/70 for singles/doubles. An old hotel in the centre of town with rooms (shared bathrooms) would be around \$25/40. A caravan park – probably with unpowered tent/powered caravan sites would be around \$7/12 for two, and a nearby bed & breakfast (B&B) or guesthouse (in this case a station stay) may have budget singles for \$20 and full board for \$60.

You'll rarely have much trouble finding *somewhere* to lay your head in WA, even when there are no hostels, although some surprisingly small and seemingly insignificant towns have backpackers' hostels these days. If there's a group of you, the rates for three or four people in a room are worth checking. Often there are larger 'family' rooms or units with two bedrooms.

The best free guide to accommodation is the *Western Australia Accommodation Listing* available from all tourist offices. It comprehensively lists the accommodation in each town, including Perth. There is also the giveaway backpackers' booklet *Backpackers Guide to WA* available at hostels around the state. This has an up-to-date list of hostels, giving prices and details of each.

Another source of comprehensive accommodation listings is the RACWA's annual directory. It's updated annually so prices are current, and it is available from the club for \$6 if you're a full or reciprocal member.

Summer Harvest Times & Regions

Crop	Season	Region
Wildflowers	February-March, July-December	Coorow
Fruit	June-July	Kununurra
Fruit	June-December	Carnarvon
Fruit	December-June	South-West
Grapes	February-April	Mt Barker, Margaret River, Swan Valley
Apples/Pears	November-May	Manjimup, Pemberton, Bridgetown, Donnybrook
Watermelons & Rockmelons/Vegies	May-October	Kununurra
Strawberries	November-January	Near Perth
Zucchini/Squash	May-September	Kununurra
Bananas	All Year	Kununurra

The state Youth Hostel Association (YHA; ☎ 9227 5350) has its main office at 236 William St, Northbridge. The helpful staff give out all sorts of information and make bookings for tours and accommodation.

Paraquad (☎ 9381 0173) will advise about accommodation with disabled access.

Camping & Caravanning

Camping in WA is a great (sometimes the only) accommodation option. There are many caravan parks, especially in the southwest, and you'll almost always find space available, even in peak periods. If you want to get around WA cheaply, then camping's the way to go – from $10 to $14 for two per night.

One massive drawback is that campsites are often intended more for caravanners (house trailers for any North Americans out there) than for campers and the tent campers get little thought in these places. Fitzroy Crossing and Kalgoorlie are two notable exceptions with the best facilities for campers in the state.

Also remember that in most large towns, campsites are well away from the centre. This is not inconvenient in small towns but, in general, if you're planning to camp around WA, you really need your own transport. This is as true for Perth as it is for any other large Australian city.

Western Australian caravan parks are generally well kept, conveniently located and excellent value. Many sites also have on-site vans which you can rent for the night (from $25 to $35). These give you the comfort of a caravan without the inconvenience of actually towing one.

On-site cabins are also widely available, and these are more like a small self-contained unit. They usually have one bedroom, or at least an area which can be screened off from the rest of the unit – just the thing if you have small kids. Cabins also have the advantage of having their own bathroom and toilet, although this is sometimes an optional extra. Many have air-con, a must in the Pilbara and Kimberley at certain times of the year. They are also much less cramped than a caravan, and the price difference is not always that great – $25 to $35 for an on-site van, $40 to $50 for a cabin for two. Some cabins can accommodate six to eight and cost about $70.

Camping in the bush, either in national parks and reserves or in the open, is for many people one of the highlights of a visit to WA (and costs a mere $5 for two). In many places it is a necessity as there is no formal accommodation. In the outback you won't even need a tent, just a swag. Nights spent around a campfire under the stars are unforgettable.

Hostels

You'll find hostels all over the state, with more official hostels and backpackers' hostels popping up all the time.

YHA Hostels YHA hostels provide basic accommodation, usually in small dormitories or bunk rooms, although more and more of them are providing twin rooms for couples. The nightly charges are cheap – usually between $10 and $18 a night. Many of WA's hostels are housed in grand old buildings (some quite run down) but there are now purpose-built places (eg Kimberley Klub, Broome) which rival more expensive accommodation.

With the increased competition from backpackers' hostels, many YHA hostels have done away with the old fetishes for curfews and doing chores, but still retain segregated dorms. Many even take non-YHA members, although there may be a small 'temporary membership' charge. To become a full YHA member in Australia costs $26 a year (there's also a $16 joining fee, although if you're an overseas resident joining in Australia you don't have to pay this). You can join at any youth hostel.

Youth hostels are part of an international organisation, Hostelling International (HI, formerly known as the International Youth Hostel Federation or IYHF), so if you're already a member of the YHA in your own country, your membership entitles you to use the Australian hostels. Hostels are great places for meeting people and great travellers' centres, and in many busier hostels foreign visitors outnumber Australians. The annual *YHA Accommodation Guide* booklet, available from any YHA office in Australia and from some YHA offices overseas, lists all YHA hostels around Australia with useful little maps showing how to find them.

You must have a regulation sheet-cum-sleeping bag or bed linen – for hygiene reasons a regular sleeping bag will not do. If you haven't got sheets they can be rented at many hostels (usually $3), but it's cheaper, after awhile, to have your own. YHA offices and larger hostels sell the official sheet bag.

Most hostels have cooking facilities and 24-hour access, and there's usually some communal area where you can sit and talk. There are usually laundry facilities and often excellent notice boards. Many hostels are permanently full and as a result have a maximum-stay period.

Not all of the 20-plus hostels in WA are actually owned by the YHA. Some are 'associate hostels', which generally abide by hostel regulations, but are owned by other organisations or individuals.

Backpackers' Hostels In recent years the number of backpackers' hostels in WA has increased dramatically – Perth has more per capita than any other capital city in Australia! The standard of these hostels varies enormously. Some in Perth are rundown inner-city hotels where the owners have tried to fill empty rooms; unless recently renovated, these places are generally gloomy and depressing.

Others are former motels, so each unit, typically with four to six bunks, will have fridge, TV and bathroom. When the climate allows, there's usually a pool too. The drawback with these places is that the communal areas and cooking facilities are often lacking, as motels were never originally designed for communal use.

Some hostels are purpose-built as backpackers' hostels; these are usually the best places in terms of facilities, although

sometimes they are simply too big and therefore lack personalised service. The managers often have backpackers running the places, and usually it's not too long before standards start to slip. Some of these places, particularly in Broome and Perth, actively promote themselves as 'party' hostels, so if you want quiet, avoid.

Prices at backpackers' hostels are generally in line with YHA hostels, typically $12 to $18, although the $10 bed is still alive and well (but perhaps not clean) in some places.

As with YHA hostels, the success of a hostel largely depends on the friendliness and willingness of the managers. One practice that many people find objectionable in independent hostels (it never happens in YHAs) is the 'vetting' of Australians, who may be asked to provide a passport or two forms of ID. This is a method of keeping unwanted customers out. Never hand over your driver's licence or passport as surety.

Guesthouses & B&Bs

These are the fastest growing segment of the accommodation market. New places are opening all the time, and the network of accommodation alternatives throughout the state includes everything from rambling old guesthouses, up-market country homes and romantic escapes, to a simple bedroom in a family home. Many of these places are listed throughout the book. Tariffs cover a wide range, but are typically in the $50 to $120 (per double) bracket. Get a copy of the free pamphlet *Winter Breaks* from the WATC or tourist offices.

Hotels & Pubs

For the budget traveller, hotels in WA are generally older places, while motels are newer. Not all hotels have rooms to rent, although many still do. A 'private hotel', as opposed to a 'licensed hotel', provides accommodation and does not serve alcohol. A 'guesthouse' is much the same as a 'private hotel'.

New hotels are mainly of the five-star Hilton variety. So, if you're staying in a hotel, it will usually mean an older place, often with rooms without private facilities. Unfortunately, many older places are on the drab, grey and dreary side. Others, fortunately, are colourful places with lively interiors. Many hotels have backpackers' accommodation for about $15 per person.

In some older towns, or in historic centres like Kalgoorlie, the old hotels can be magnificent. The rooms may be old-fashioned and unexciting, but the hotel façade and entrance area will often be quite extravagant. In the outback, the old hotels are often places of real character. And, of course, a place to meet characters. Try the Widgiemooltha, Whim Creek, the 'Spinny' in Derby or the Crossing Inn near Fitzroy Crossing.

Another good thing about hotels (guesthouses and private hotels, too) is that the big breakfasts are usually excellent. Generally, hotels have rooms for around $25 to $40. When comparing prices, ask if breakfast is included.

Motels

If you've got transport and want a modern place with your own bathroom and other facilities, then you're moving into the motel bracket. Motels are everywhere, but they're usually away from city centres. Prices vary and, unlike hotels, singles are often not much cheaper than doubles. The reason is quite simple – in old hotels many rooms really are singles, relics of the days when single men travelled the country looking for work. In motels, the rooms are almost always doubles. You'll find motel rooms for less than $40, and in most places have little trouble finding something for $50 or less. Most motels provide at least tea/coffee-making facilities and a small fridge.

Holiday Flats & Serviced Apartments

Holiday flats and serviced apartments are often much the same as motels. Basically, holiday flats are found in holiday areas, serviced apartments in cities. A holiday flat is much like a motel room but usually with a kitchen or cooking facilities, cooking utensils, cutlery, crockery and so on, so you can fix your own food. They are not serviced like

motels – you don't get your bed made up every morning and the cups washed out. In some holiday flats you have to provide your own sheets and bedding.

Holiday flats are often rented on a weekly basis but even in these cases, it's worth asking if daily rates are available. Paying for a week, even if you stay only for a few days, can still be cheaper than having those days at a higher daily rate. If there's more than two of you, another advantage of holiday flats is that you can often find them with two or more bedrooms. A two-bedroom holiday flat is about 1½ times the cost of a comparable single-bedroom unit.

In holiday areas like the South Coast or Kalbarri, motels and holiday flats are one and the same thing. In big cities, on the other hand, the serviced apartments are often a little more obscure, although they may be advertised in the newspaper's classified ads.

The Country Women's Association (CWA) offers accommodation in country areas throughout the state. It has holiday units in Albany, Busselton, Port Denison-Dongara, Esperance, Guilderton, Hopetoun, Jurien, Broome, Lancelin and Rockingham. As a general rule, a double costs $30 for members, $5 extra for each non-member.

Farm & Station Stays

Western Australia is a land of farms (known as 'stations' in the outback where they are greater in size and characterised by their red dust) and one of the best ways to come to grips with Australian life is to spend a few days on one. Many farms offer accommodation where you can sit back and watch how it's done, or get actively involved in daily activities.

The WATC or the WA Farm & Country Holidays Association can advise you on what's available; prices are pretty reasonable. The association puts out the accommodation guide *Farm Holidays & Country Retreats* which lists over 40 places in the south-west, a land of farms rather than of stations. The region around Margaret River is popular for farm stays.

Apart from Queensland, WA is probably

the best place to stay on a real station; you'll find numerous pamphlets in the accommodation racks in tourist offices. The Gascoyne, Pilbara and Murchison areas are popular areas for station stays (see Station Stays in the Coral Coast & The Pilbara chapter).

Most stations have comfortable accommodation in the main homestead or cottages, and budget accommodation in out buildings or former shearers' quarters. They also allow caravans and campers for a reasonable site fee, but do not have the facilities of caravan parks.

The B&B, Farm & Station Stay Guide to WA ($9.95) is a good reference.

Other Possibilities

There are plenty of parks where you can camp for free, or roadside rest areas where short-term camping is permitted. The state has thousands of square kilometres of bush where nobody is going to complain about you putting up a tent – or even notice.

In Perth, if you want to stay for a while, the first place to look for a shared flat or a room is the classifieds in the daily newspaper; Wednesday and Saturday are best days.

FOOD

Perth/Fremantle has more restaurants per head of population than anywhere in Australia, but outside the metropolitan area there is nowhere near the variety except in some resorts such as Margaret River and Broome.

There was once a time when Australia's food (mighty steaks apart) had a reputation for being mediocre. Miracles happen and Australia's miracle was immigration. Greeks, Yugoslavs, Italians, Lebanese and many others flooded into Australia in the 1950s and 1960s introducing their cuisine to the local population. You can have excellent Greek *moussaka* (and retsina to wash it down), delicious Italian *saltimbocca* and pasta, or good, heavy German dumplings; you can perfume the air with garlic after stumbling out of a French bistro, or try all sorts of Middle Eastern treats.

The Chinese have been sweet & souring since the gold-rush days, while more recently, Indian, Thai and Malaysian restaurants have been all the rage. Recent arrivals, such as the Vietnamese, are now ladling out their delicious, cheap *pho* in Perth.

Australian Food

Although there is no real definition of Australian cuisine, there is certainly some excellent Australian food to try, much of it defined by an innovative use of Asian spices and ingredients. For a start, there's the great iconic Australian meat pie – every bit as sacred an institution as the hot dog is to a New Yorker. While there are a few places that do a really good job on this classic dish, the standard pie is an awful concoction of anonymous meat and dark gravy in a soggy pastry case. Mrs MacGregor's is one of the better varieties.

Even more central to Australian eating habits is Vegemite. This strange, dark-coloured yeast-extract substance looks like tar and smells like, well, Vegemite – this strange spread is something only an Australian could love. Australians spread Vegemite on bread and become so addicted to it that anywhere in the world you find an Aussie, a jar of Vegemite is bound to be close at hand.

The good news about Australian food is the range of ingredients, their freshness and quality. There is a fine market garden industry in the state, so nearly all the produce is grown in WA.

Everybody knows about good Australian steaks ('This is cattle country, so eat beef you bastards', announce the farmers' bumper stickers), but there are lots of other things to try.

Western Australia has a superb range of seafood: fish like spangled emperor, coral trout, many species of cod, groper, pink schnapper, King George whiting, sand whiting and the esteemed barramundi, or superb lobsters and other crustaceans like Exmouth Gulf prawns.

Unique to the south-west of the state are delicious marron or freshwater crayfish. The French settlers named the crustacean after the large edible chestnut which had a dark exterior, sweet taste and white flesh.

Don't miss the chance to try marron pan-fried in lemon, dill and garlic.

Even vegetarians get a fair go in WA; there are some excellent vegetarian restaurants and, once again, the vegetables are as fresh as you could ask for.

Fast Food

If you want something familiar and utterly predictable, there are McDonald's, KFC, Pizza Hut and all the other well known names (if you're coming from Darwin, the first of these multinational takeaways you see will be in Geraldton). There are also Chinese restaurants with bronzed ducks in the window, Middle Eastern places with spiced doner kebab or shashlik, and many other places from Italian to Mexican.

For real value for money, Australian delis are terrific and they'll put together a superb sandwich.

Australians love fish & chips just as much as the British and quality can vary enormously.

The places to avoid eating at all costs are the dreary roadhouses that punctuate the nothingness between towns. They were designed to serve fuel and the food tastes as if it has been cooked in it.

Pubs

In the evening the best bargains can be found in the pubs. Look for 'counter meals', so called because they used to be eaten at the bar counter. Some places are still like that, while others are up-market, almost restaurant-like. Although the food is usually of the simple 'surf and turf' (fish or steak) and chips, the quality is often excellent and

prices are commendably low. The best places usually have serve-yourself salad tables where you can add as much salad, French bread and dressings as you wish.

One catch is the strict hours. The evening meal time may be just 6 to 7.30 or 8 pm. Pubs doing counter meals often have a blackboard menu outside, but some of the best places are quite anonymous. Counter meals vary enormously in price but in general the better class places with good serve-yourself salad tables will be in the $7.50 to $15 range.

Self-Catering

Stock up with fresh produce from supermarkets in towns either side of large drives.

DRINKS
Nonalcoholic Drinks

Australians knock back cola and flavoured milk like there's no tomorrow and there are also excellent mineral waters.

Coffee lovers will be relieved to find good Italian cafes serving cappuccino and other coffees, and often into the wee small hours and beyond. Freo's South Terrace is where you will find those who know the difference between Vittorio, Braziliano and Lavazza.

Alcoholic Drinks

Beer Each Australian state has its own beer brands and there's always someone singing the praises of each one. The Swan Brewery, the west's biggest producer of beer, has two major brands, Swan and Emu. Swan comes as Draught, Gold and Lager; Emu comes as Export and Bitter. The Swan Brewery in Canning Vale has a free tour (see the Perth chapter) and it throws in a couple of free beers.

Another smaller brewery, Matilda Bay, in North Fremantle, produces boutique beer which is popular in all states. The beers are Redback (with a light version), Fremantle Bitter and Matilda Bay Pils and Bitter. There are many small boutique breweries in various pubs and two drops worth a mention are the Perth Brass Monkey's Stout and Fremantle's Sail & Anchor Seven Sea Real Ale. To the yuppie crowd, a Redback with a slice of lemon in the neck is still a popular call. Guinness is occasionally found on draught – in Irish pubs such as Rosie O'Gradys and The Bog in Perth.

A word of warning to visitors: Australian beer has a higher alcohol content than British or American beers. Standard beer is generally around 4.9% alcohol, although most breweries now produce 'lite' beers, with an alcohol content of between 2% and 3.5%.

People who drive under the influence of alcohol and get caught lose their licences. The maximum legal blood-alcohol concentration level for drivers in most parts of Australia, including WA, is 0.05%.

All around Australia, beer, the containers it comes in, and the receptacles you drink it from, are called by different names. In WA, beer comes in stubbies and tinnies. Here, a 275ml beer is a middy and a 450ml beer is a schooner. And, no one drinks warm beer here unless their fridge has broken down or the Esky is out of ice.

In *Mark Shield's Beer Guide*, the following WA beers received a very favourable four or five stars: Brass Monkey Stout; Dogbolter; Emu Bitter; Emu Export; Emu; Redback Pils; Matilda Bay Bitter; and Swan Western Bitter.

Wine Western Australia has the perfect climate for wine producing. There are some superb wine-growing areas and best known are the Swan Valley, the Margaret River region and the area around Mt Barker. Houghton's, in the Swan Valley, produces Australia's best selling bottled white wine, white burgundy – the one with the blue stripe. Some of the Margaret River wineries, such as Cape Mentelle and Leeuwin Estate, have a strong following in the eastern states.

An even more economical way of drinking WA wines is to do it on the cheap (or free) at the wineries. In the wine-growing areas, most wineries have tastings: you just zip straight in and say what you'd like to try. An increasing number are charging a tasting fee for their limited edition wines.

All over WA you'll find restaurants advertising that they're BYO. The initials stand for 'Bring Your Own' and it means that they're not licensed to serve alcohol, but you are permitted to bring your own with you for a small corkage fee. Transform the wine which you purchased from the cellar into BYO that night!

ENTERTAINMENT

It's often hot and dusty, you've been driving for days without the whiff of a beer or the clink of a cool glass of semillon, and you have seen 2½ of the seven geological wonders of the world and sniffed more wildflowers than you care to remember. You deserve a night out in the most isolated capital city in the known universe.

Perth has plenty of diversions for those who seek them and is the epicentre for the state's cultural attractions (in fact very little goes on outside here). Friday nights in Northbridge, Subiaco and Leederville are a wonder to behold, an almost nonstop frenetic party until dawn. The crowds spill out of the restaurants, rage in the nightclubs and swamp the many cafes along the streets. Business people in expensive suits, dags in ill-fitting, mismatched clothing, gays and lesbians, dinky-di's and the glamorous – they are all on show.

The regional centres have one or two pubs where those in the know hang out. Just ask someone at the tourist centre where you should go. In most of the towns in WA there is only one pub (Widgiemooltha or Whim Creek for instance) while Hannan St, the main street of Kalgoorlie, is choked with grog shops as befits a frontier mining town.

Cinemas

Although cinema took an initial hammering from the meteoric rise of the home-video market, it has bounced back as people rediscover the joys of the big screen.

The big operators such as Greater Union and Hoyts have movie theatres scattered across Perth and Fremantle has its own Coastal Cinemas. In the west drive-ins are still a feature, thanks to the weather. For the uninitiated this means you watch a film on a giant screen from the comfort of your car while parked in a car park! The most authentic outdoor cinemas in the state are Sun Pictures, Broome, and Derby Picture Gardens, both in the Kimberley.

Seeing a new-release mainstream film costs around $11 ($7.50 for children under 15) in the big cities, less in country areas.

You will also find arthouse and independent cinemas in Perth. These generally screen films that aren't made for mass consumption or specialise purely in re-runs of classics and cult movies. The Lumiere, Astor and Paradiso all fall into this category.

Discos & Nightclubs

Yep, no shortage of these either, but they are confined to Perth and larger towns. Clubs range from the exclusive 'members only' variety to barn-sized discos where anyone who wants to spend the money is welcome. Admission ranges from $6 to $12.

Some places have dress standards, but it is generally left to the discretion of the people at the door – if they don't like the look of you, bad luck. The up-market nightclubs attract an older, more sophisticated and affluent crowd, and generally have stricter dress codes, smarter decor – and higher prices.

Dance & Theatre

Most performances take place in Perth and Fremantle but occasionally the cultural viper reaches Bunbury and Albany, even as far afield as Broome. In Perth, you could watch a performance of *Giselle* at His Majesty's Theatre, David Williamson's *Siren* at the Playhouse Theatre, *Tap Dogs* at the Regal Theatre or *Diary of a Madman* at the Subiaco Theatre. There always seems to be a cavalcade of talent in this town.

Opera & Classical Music

In the south-west of the state there is a dedicated band of classical music listeners. Performances include the West Australian Symphony Orchestra or West Australian Opera at the Perth Concert Hall or Kiri Te Kanawa at the Leeuwin Estate Winery near Margaret River. A good monthly guide to

culture and the arts is *The Western Review* or on the Internet at www.twr.com.au.

Pubs

Many suburban pubs have discos and/or live music, and these are often great places for catching live bands. There are comprehensive listings in newspapers, particularly on Friday and Saturday, and in the entertainment magazine *Xpress*.

In out-of-the-way parts of WA you may come across pubs with bars where Aborigines and whites drink separately. Typically the Aborigines will drink in a section with no furniture and bars, while whites drink in a more 'gentile' area. This might seem like segregation but Aborigines are more than welcome in the 'gentile' area provided they meet the required standards of dress and behaviour.

SPECTATOR SPORT

One of the best things about travel in this state is watching the parochial WA crowd support local teams in national competitions. Some of the places to catch all the action are listed with the following sports.

Australian Rules Football

This game has been heartily embraced by the west. Although its headquarters are in Victoria, the game has achieved national status with major teams in Adelaide, Sydney, Brisbane, Perth, Geelong and Fremantle.

The Perth-based West Coast Eagles (drawn from the Western Australian Football League teams of Claremont, East Fremantle, East Perth, Perth, South Fremantle, Swan Districts, Subiaco and West Perth) were the first non-Victorian Australian Rules team to win a premiership in the 96-year history of the Australian Football League (AFL). On 26 September 1992, in their sixth season in the national competition, they had a 28 point win over Geelong before a crowd of 95,000 at the Melbourne Cricket Ground. The score was 16.17 (113) to 12.13 (85). This was as audacious an act as Australia wresting the America's Cup from the New York Yacht Club. In the 1994 Grand Final, the Eagles did it again, beating Geelong by 20.23 (143) to 8.15 (63).

The Fremantle Dockers has now joined the West Coast Eagles in the national league.

Many illustrious players have come from the west, including Geelong ruckman Graham 'Polly' Farmer, who could handball over 30 to 40m, give his rovers an 'armchair ride' (a good team player makes it easy for his team mates) and grab some real 'screamers' (a great mark). Other capable WA players with the 'attributes' are/or were St Kilda's Nicky Winmar, ex-Fitzroy captain Ron Alexander and Essendon Best & Fairest (three times), and 1976 Brownlow winner, Graeme Moss.

Cricket

In the 1991-92 cricket season, WA won the Sheffield Shield for the thirteenth time since being admitted to the competition in 1947-48. They beat NSW by 44 runs at the WACA. This was their eleventh success since 1970-71, equalling the combined efforts of all other states in the same period. In the limited-overs competition the tables were turned and NSW beat WA by 69 runs.

Some of the world's greatest cricketers have come out of WA. The commentators cry 'Caught Marsh, bowled Lillee' is synonymous with Australian cricketing success in the late seventies. The Fremantle Doctor (a late afternoon wind) honed the skills of the pace bowlers Graham McKenzie and Dennis Lillee and the swing bowlers Bob Massie and Terry Alderman with often devastating results. And a little known fact: the first test ever played at the WACA was in December 1970 when Greg Chappell made his maiden century (108) in his first test.

Basketball

There is a WA women's and a WA men's team in the national competition. Games are played at the Perth Entertainment Centre during the winter months. The Quit Western Australian Institute of Sport (WAIS) Breakers won the national women's title in 1992 and the male team Perth Wildcats (☎ 9324 1844) just failed in their bid to win three consecutive national titles in 1992. For women's match details, contact the WA Basketball Federation (☎ 9386 5525).

Other Sports

The Perth Thundersticks play in the National Hockey League (NHL) after being admitted to the NHL in 1992 when they won the national final (in 1992 against the Brisbane Blades 4-3, after a sudden-death shoot out). The male team Perth Heat participate in the National Baseball League (NBL), and have held the national crown.

Motor racing is held on Sundays from March to October at Wanneroo Park Raceway, Pinjar Rd, Wanneroo. Throughout spring and summer, speedcar and motorcycle races are held on Friday night at the Royal Agricultural Showground at Claremont.

Perth fields the Western Reds in the Super League rugby-league competition.

Gambling

The saying goes that Australians would bet on two flies crawling up a wall, and Western Australians are no different. In fact, in Derby, they have an annual cockroach race at the Spinifex ('Spinny') Hotel.

Apart from flies and cockroaches, local gamblers bet on the horses (trotters and gallopers), the dogs (greyhounds) and on the football. You can bet at any Totalisator Agency Board (TAB) betting shops, found in most shopping areas and in pubs (there are over 250 in the state). Prize money is listed per $1, but the minimum bet is 50c per unit. The PubTABs usually have a Sky TV facility so punters can have a beer while they check out the races.

In the metropolitan area, the trots are held at Gloucester Park every Friday, the races (WA Turf Club) are held at Ascot (check the newspapers for dates) and the dogs chase the bunny at Cannington every Thursday and Saturday.

Those that know the difference between Fan Tan and blackjack can visit the Burswood Casino, on the Great Eastern Highway, across the river from the city (see the Perth chapter). There are various numbers for prize games, ranging from the usual Lotto to Scratch & Win tickets.

All eyes are directed at the floor at the legalised Two-Up 'school' in the tin shed,

6km north of Kalgoorlie. Two-up is a game where two pennies are tossed into the air with a wooden stick (the kip) and the result of the bet hinges on the call, either heads or tails. If you haven't played it at one of the casinos, check it out in this rustic setting; business gets under way at 4 pm and goes on until about 10 pm.

THINGS TO BUY
Aboriginal Art
Aboriginal art is much cheaper in the west than the eastern states. The works of some of the Kimberley artists, such as Mingi May Barnes, are exhibited throughout the world.

Aboriginal art is an integral part of ancient and modern Aboriginal culture. Artistic expression is very much linked to the Dreamtime and the same totemic images recur regardless of the medium on which they are etched or painted. The medium could be the body, a carved creature, cave walls or the sides of a significant rock.

In the last couple of decades, artists began to transfer their paintings to canvas, employing long-lasting acrylic paints. The mosaics (painted canvases) incorporate complex interweaving of the geography of the country with traditional stories. Mosaic painters may have learnt the details of at least a thousand paintings each.

Apart from canvas paintings, you will see motifs painted on carved animals (widely available in the far south-east of the state), women's utensils such as coolamons, clapping sticks, water carriers, dancing boards and didjeridu. There are also colourful batik scarves, dilly bags and even T-shirts.

Places to buy Aboriginal paintings and crafts are Waringarri Aboriginal Arts in Kununurra; Mangkaja Aboriginal Arts Centre in Fitzroy Crossing; in Broome and Derby at various places; and from outlets in and around Perth such as Creative Native, 32 King St, Perth; Indigenart, 115 Hay St, Subiaco; or Ganada, Atwell Arcade, Fremantle.

Carved Emu Eggs & Boab Nuts A number
of places, especially in the north of the state, sell exquisitely carved emu eggs and boab nuts. Derby is a good place to buy carved boab nuts; enquire at the tourist centre. Bottle-green emu eggs are particularly beautiful and seen in many of the galleries selling traditional Aboriginal crafts.

Australiana
Australiana is rather a vague cultural term which refers in this section to collections of 'souvenirs'. It's those things you buy as gifts, supposedly representative of Aussie culture.

A lot of these items are neither Australian in character nor made in Australia. Some delightfully tacky souvenirs include: ashtrays embedded with New Zealand paua shell (masquerading as pearl shell) with 'Greetings from Broome' emblazoned on them; and tea towels depicting a cross between a sperm and a humpback whale with a bubble above the air spout proclaiming: 'Welcome to Rottnest Island'.

One genuine article is the neoprene or polystyrene beer-can cooler. Prized among collectors of such amber-fluid containers is the one from Widgiemooltha pub, between Kalgoorlie and Norseman.

You can buy wildflowers seeds, but check whether you can take them home. Many of them have successfully been transplanted within Australia, in widely different conditions.

Last but not least, don't forget WA wines. The wine-growing areas – Margaret River, the Swan Valley, Pemberton and Mount Barker – produce a diversity of styles.

Aussie Clothing
The humble elastic-sided Blundstone work boot, which originated in Tasmania, has 'made it' in Europe and rivals the ubiquitous Doc Martens. Moleskin trousers, once a practical form of wear in the Kimberley, are popular with both men and women. Woollen bush shirts are another handy item for cool northern hemisphere climates. These can be topped off with an Akubra hat, made of rabbit skin. The last item in the perfect 'get up' for the outback traveller is the 'swag', a canvas bedding roll made in WA (see Camping & Caravanning in the Accommodation section earlier in this chapter).

Gold, Diamonds, Pearls & Opals

The main street of Kalgoorlie has plenty of jewellery shops where you can buy earrings, bracelets and pendants which incorporate gold nuggets. These have sometimes been tumbled to give a slightly polished appearance or are attached in a raw state. They are relatively inexpensive – but ensure the fittings are of good quality.

World famous Argyle diamonds are mined south of Kununurra. The pink diamonds can be purchased from outlets in Kununurra such as Nina's Jewellery and Kimberley Fine Diamonds, or in a number of shops in Perth.

Broome pearls, reputed to be the best, are cultured from the beautiful silver-lipped oyster; they are probably the most expensive in the world. There are many pearl galleries in Broome.

Handicrafts

Many of the handicrafts for sale feature local motifs such as wildflower designs or dried-and-dyed wildflower arrangements.

One favourite handicraft is carved and turned timbers from the giant forests. Popular are tables made of timber burls (unusual circular growths which occur on the tree trunk), turned wooden bowls and exquisitely carved fauna depicting whales and dolphins. The timber used includes local jarrah, the rare curly jarrah, sheoak, WA blackbutt, wandoo, karri, marri, coastal banksia and the grass tree .

Getting There & Away

AIR

A few overseas airlines use Perth as their gateway to Australia but, in reality, many visitors come to the west after passing through the eastern states. Most flights land in the east, and then there is a giant leap across the continent to WA, with more time and expense.

There are lots of competing airlines and a variety of air fares from Asia or Europe, but even so, flights are often heavily after booked. If you want to fly to Australia at a popular time of year (December to February) or on a popular route, plan ahead.

Australia has a large number of international gateways. Sydney and Melbourne are busiest with flights from everywhere. Perth also gets many flights from Asia and Europe and has direct flights to Asia and Africa.

Buying Tickets

Buying airline tickets these days is like shopping for a car, a stereo or a camera. Rule number one if you're looking for a cheap ticket is to go to an agent, not directly to the airline. The airline can usually only quote the regular fare. An agent, on the other hand, can offer all sorts of special deals, particularly on competitive routes.

Ideally, airlines would like every seat occupied on all their flights, with every passenger paying the highest fare possible. Fortunately, life usually isn't like that and airlines would rather have a half-price passenger than an empty seat. When faced with the problem of too many empty seats, they will either let agents sell them at cut prices, or make one-off special offers on particular routes – watch the travel ads in the newspapers.

Round-the-World Tickets Round-the-World (RTW) tickets are very popular and many will take you through Perth. The airline RTW tickets are often bargains and since Australia is pretty much the other side of the world from Europe or North America,

> **Warning**
> The information in this chapter is particularly vulnerable to change – prices for international travel are volatile, routes are introduced and cancelled, schedules change, rules are amended, special deals come and go, borders open and close. Airlines and governments seem to take a perverse pleasure in making price structures and regulations as complicated as possible and you should check directly with the airline or travel agent to make sure you understand how a fare (and ticket you may buy) works.
>
> In addition, the travel industry is highly competitive and there are many lurks and perks. The upshot of this is that you should get opinions, quotes and advice from as many airlines and travel agents as possible before you part with your hard-earned cash. The details given in this chapter should be regarded only as pointers and cannot be any substitute for your own careful, up-to-date research. ■

it can work out no more expensive, or even cheaper, to keep going in the same direction right round the world rather than U-turn when you go home. This is a good option for getting to Perth, either after entering Australia from the eastern states or using the city as the first port of call.

The official airline RTW tickets are usually put together by a combination of two airlines, and allow you to fly anywhere on their route systems as long as you do not backtrack. Other restrictions are that you (usually) must book the first sector in advance and cancellation penalties then apply. There may be restrictions on how many stops you are permitted and usually the tickets are valid from 90 days up to a year.

An alternative type of RTW ticket is one put together by a travel agent using a combination of discounted tickets from a number of airlines. A UK agent like Trailfinders can put together interesting London-to-London

RTW combinations including Perth for £850. The two main operators through Perth are Qantas and British Airways, so check the possibilities with them.

Circle Pacific Tickets Circle Pacific fares are similar to RTW tickets and use a combination of airlines to circle the Pacific – combining Australia, New Zealand, North America and Asia. These would be of little value to people trying to get to WA, as a costly sidetrip would be necessary.

Typical prices for these tickets, which allow say four Pacific stopovers, are from US$2500 from the US west coast and $2750 from the east coast.

Travellers with Special Needs

If you've broken a leg, are vegetarian or require a special diet, are travelling in a wheelchair, taking a baby, terrified of flying, or whatever, let the airline staff know as soon as possible so that they can make the necessary arrangements. Remind them when you reconfirm your booking (at least 72 hours before departure) and again when you check in at the airport. It may also be worth ringing round the airlines before you make your booking to find out how they can handle your particular needs.

Airports and airlines can be helpful, but they need advance warning. Most international airports provide escorts from the check-in desk to the aeroplane where needed, and there should be ramps, lifts, accessible toilets and phones. Aircraft toilets, on the other hand, are likely to present a problem; travellers should discuss this with the airline at an early stage and, if necessary, with their doctor.

Guide dogs for the blind often travel in a specially pressurised baggage compartment with other animals, away from their owner; smaller guide dogs, however, may be admitted to the cabin. Guide dogs are subject to the same quarantine laws as other animals when entering or returning to countries free of rabies.

Deaf travellers can ask for airport and in-flight announcements to be written down for them.

Children under two travel for 10% of the standard fare (or free on some airlines) as long as they don't occupy a seat. They don't get a baggage allowance either. 'Skycots' should be provided by the airline if requested in advance; these will take a child weighing up to about 10kg. Children aged between two and 12 years can usually occupy a seat for half to two-thirds of the full fare, and get a baggage allowance. Pushchairs can often be taken as hand luggage.

North America

There are various connections across the Pacific from Los Angeles, San Francisco and Vancouver to Australia including direct flights, flights via New Zealand, island-hopping routes or more circuitous Pacific-rim routes via nations in Asia. Qantas, Air New Zealand and United all fly USA-Australia; Qantas, Air New Zealand and Canadian Airlines International fly Canada-Australia. Nearly all of these entail an additional fare to WA as the usual gateway is the east coast.

To find good fares to Australia check the travel ads in the Sunday travel sections of papers like the *Los Angeles Times*, *San Francisco Chronicle-Examiner*, *New York Times* or Canada's *Globe & Mail*. The straightforward return excursion fare from the USA west coast to Melbourne/Sydney is around US$1050 and US$1250 to Perth from the USA west coast, depending on the season – most travellers to WA would look into open jaws options.

In North America, good agents for discounted tickets are the student travel operators, Council Travel (☎ (1800) 743 1823) and STA Travel (☎ (1800) 777 0112), both of which have lots of offices around the country; and in Canada, Travel CUTS (☎ (416) 979 2406), which also has many offices.

New Zealand

Air New Zealand and Qantas operate a network of trans-Tasman flights linking

Air Travel Glossary

Apex Apex, or 'advance purchase excursion' is a discounted ticket which must be paid for in advance. There are penalties if you wish to change it.

Baggage Allowance This will be written on your ticket: usually one 20kg item to go in the hold, plus one item of hand luggage.

Bucket Shop An unbonded travel agency specialising in discounted airline tickets.

Bumped Just because you have a confirmed seat doesn't mean you're going to get on the plane – see Overbooking.

Cancellation Penalties If you have to cancel or change an Apex ticket there are often heavy penalties involved; insurance can sometimes be taken out against these penalties. Some airlines impose penalties on regular tickets as well, particularly against 'no show' passengers.

Check In Airlines ask you to check in a certain time ahead of the flight departure (usually 1½ hours on international flights). If you fail to check in on time and the flight is overbooked the airline can cancel your booking and give your seat to somebody else.

Confirmation Having a ticket written out with the flight and date you want doesn't mean you have a seat until the agent has checked with the airline that your status is 'OK' or confirmed. Meanwhile you could just be 'on request'.

Discounted Tickets There are two types of discounted fares – officially discounted (see Promotional Fares) and unofficially discounted. The lowest prices often impose drawbacks like flying with unpopular airlines, inconvenient schedules, or unpleasant routes and connections. A discounted ticket can save you other things than money – you may be able to pay Apex prices without the associated Apex advance booking and other requirements. Discounted tickets only exist where there is fierce competition.

Full Fares Airlines traditionally offer first class (coded F), business class (coded J) and economy class (coded Y) tickets. These days there are so many promotional and discounted fares available from the regular economy class that few passengers pay full economy fare.

Lost Tickets If you lose your airline ticket an airline will usually treat it like a travellers' cheque and, after enquiries, issue you with another one. Legally, however, an airline is entitled to treat it like cash and if you lose it then it's gone forever. Take good care of your tickets.

No Shows No shows are passengers who fail to show up for their flight. Full-fare passengers who fail to turn up are sometimes entitled to travel on a later flight. The rest of us are penalised (see Cancellation Penalties).

On Request An unconfirmed booking for a flight; see Confirmation.

Open Jaws A return ticket where you fly to one place but return from another. If available, this can save you backtracking to your arrival point.

Auckland, Wellington and Christchurch in New Zealand with most major Australian gateway cities. Another flight, about the same distance, will be required to reach Perth entailing more time and expense.

From Auckland, New Zealand, to Sydney or Melbourne you're looking at around NZ$530 one way and NZ$630 return. To Perth it's a whopping NZ$930 one way, NZ$1030 return.

The UK

The cheapest tickets in London are from the numerous 'bucket shops' (discount ticket agencies) which advertise in magazines and papers like *Time Out* and *TNT*. Pick up one or two of these publications and ring round a few bucket shops to find the best deal. The magazine *Business Traveller* also has a great deal of good advice on airfare bargains. Most bucket shops are trustworthy and reliable, but the occasional sharp operator appears – *Time Out* and *Business Traveller* give some useful advice on precautions to take.

Trailfinders (☎ (0171) 938 3366), 42-50 Earls Court Rd, London W8 and STA Travel (☎ (0171) 581 4132), 74 Old Brompton Rd, London SW7 and 117 Euston Rd, London NW1 (☎ (0171) 465 0484) are good, reliable agents for cheap tickets.

Overbooking Airlines hate to fly empty seats and since every flight has some passengers who fail to show up (see No Shows), airlines often book more passengers than they have seats. Usually the excess passengers balance those who fail to show up, but occasionally somebody gets bumped. If this happens guess who it is most likely to be? The passengers who check in late.

Promotional Fares Officially discounted fares like Apex fares which are available from travel agents or direct from the airline.

Reconfirmation At least 72 hours prior to departure time of an onward or return flight, you must contact the airline and 'reconfirm' that you intend to be on the flight. If you don't do this the airline can delete your name from the passenger list and you could lose your seat. You don't have to reconfirm the first flight on your itinerary or if your stopover is less than 72 hours. It doesn't hurt to reconfirm more than once.

Restrictions Discounted tickets often have various restrictions on them – advance purchase is the most usual one (see Apex). Others are restrictions on the minimum and maximum period you must be away, such as a minimum of 14 days or a maximum of one year. See Cancellation Penalties.

Standby A discounted ticket where you only fly if there is a seat free at the last moment. Standby fares are usually only available on domestic routes.

Tickets Out An entry requirement for many countries is that you have an onward or return ticket, in other words, a ticket out of the country. If you're not sure what you intend to do next, the easiest solution is to buy the cheapest onward ticket to a neighbouring country or a ticket from a reliable airline which can later be refunded if you do not use it.

Transferred Tickets Airline tickets cannot be transferred from one person to another. Travellers sometimes try to sell the return half of their ticket, but officials can ask you to prove that you are the person named on the ticket. This is unlikely to happen on domestic flights; on an international flight, tickets may be compared with passports.

Travel Agencies Travel agencies vary widely and you should ensure you use one that suits your needs. Some simply handle tours while full-service agencies handle everything from tours and tickets to car rental and hotel bookings. A good one will do all these things and can save you a lot of money but if all you want is a ticket at the lowest possible price, then you really need an agency specialising in discounted tickets. A discounted ticket agency, however, may not be useful for other things, like hotel bookings.

Travel Periods Some officially discounted fares, Apex fares in particular, vary with the time of year. There is often a low (off-peak) season and a high (peak) season. Sometimes there's an intermediate or shoulder season as well. At peak times, when everyone wants to fly, not only will the officially discounted fares be higher, so will the unofficially discounted fares or there may simply be no discounted tickets available. Usually the fare depends on your outward flight – if you depart in the high season and return in the low season, you pay the high-season fare. ■

The cheapest London to Perth bucket shop tickets are about £440 one way or £780 return. Such prices are usually only available if you leave London in the low season – March to June. In September and mid-December, fares go up about 30% while the rest of the year they're somewhere in between (Perth is only slightly cheaper than Sydney or Melbourne). The main operators through Perth (to Europe) are Qantas via Singapore and Bangkok, and British Airways via Singapore.

Many cheap tickets allow stopovers on the way to or from Australia. Rules regarding how many stopovers you can take, how long you can stay away, how far in advance you have to decide your return date and so on, vary. Most return tickets now allow you to stay away for any period between 14 days and a year, with stopovers permitted anywhere along the route. As usual with heavily discounted tickets, the less you pay the less you get.

From Perth you can expect to pay around A$1440 one way, and A$2000 return (low season) with Qantas to London and other European capitals, with stops in Asia on the way. A combination tickets, say Thai International and Malev Hungarian, can be a little cheaper ($1350/1690).

Continental Europe

You can't fly directly from Continental Europe to Perth. Continental operators such as Lauda Air, Alitalia, Olympic and KLM fly to the eastern states, necessitating further cost to cross to WA. Alternatively, you could change to an Asian or Australian airline in Asia, although as single flights usually work out cheaper than flights involving stopovers there is little advantage in doing this, unless Perth is your main destination.

Africa

The flight possibilities from here are not so varied and you're much more likely to have to pay the full fare. There is only a handful of direct flights each week between Africa and Australia and then only between Perth and Harare (Zimbabwe), Johannesburg (South Africa) and Nairobi (Kenya). A much cheaper alternative from East Africa is to fly from Nairobi to India or Pakistan and on to South-East Asia, then connect from there to Australia.

Operators on the Africa route are Air Mauritius from Nairobi via Mauritius, South African Airways from Johannesburg and Qantas from Harare. Costs for these flights are around US$700/1200 for one way/return (February to March).

Asia

Ticket discounting is widespread in Asia, particularly in Singapore, Hong Kong, Bangkok and Penang. There are a lot of fly-by-nights in the Asian ticketing scene so a little care is required. Also the Asian routes have been caught up in the capacity shortages on flights to Australia. Flights between Hong Kong and Australia are notoriously heavily booked while flights to or from Bangkok and Singapore are often part of the longer Europe-Australia route so they are frequently full. Plan ahead. For more information on South-East Asian travel and on to Australia, see Lonely Planet's *South-East Asia on a shoestring*.

Typical one-way fares to WA from Asia include Hong Kong-Perth for around HK$5000 or Singapore-Perth for around S$700.

From Australia, in low season, some typical return fares from the west coast include Singapore $600, Kuala Lumpur $1010, Bangkok $1110, Hong Kong $1310 and Tokyo $1690.

A cheap way out of Australia is take one of the flights operating between Darwin and Bali ($469/789). Perth-Bali you could expect to pay $469/739 for one way/return with Garuda.

Asian operators through Perth are the Indonesian airlines Sempati Air and Garuda Indonesia, Qantas, Ansett International (to Denpasar), Thai International, Cathay Pacific, Malaysian Airlines and Singapore Airlines.

Arriving & Departing

Australia's dramatic increase in visitor arrivals has caused severe bottlenecks at the entry points, particularly at Sydney where delays on arrival or departure are frequent. You can save yourself a lot of time and trouble by making Perth, Brisbane, Cairns, Melbourne or another gateway city your arrival point.

For information about how to get to the city from Perth airport, see Getting Around in the Perth chapter.

When you finally leave, remember to keep $27 aside for the departure tax.

Domestic Flights

The major domestic carriers are Ansett (☎ 13 1300), which also flies a few international routes, and Qantas Domestic (☎ 13 1313), which is also the international flag-carrier flying as Qantas. Both fly between Perth and the other capital cities, and both have subsidiaries which fly smaller planes on shorter inter and intra-state routes.

You don't have to reconfirm domestic flights on Ansett and Qantas, but you should phone on the day of your flight to check the details. For Ansett, call ☎ 13 1515; for Qantas Domestic, call ☎ 13 1223.

Qantas operates from other interstate cities and tourist destinations to Perth but *does not* offer a service within the state.

Regular one-way and return seats cost the same as Ansett Australia although both have special deals from time to time. You have to check and book with the airlines at least 28 days in advance so you can be eligible for special fares. It would not be unusual to get a Melbourne-Perth return for $400 with 28 day's notice, $470 with three week's notice or $510 with 14 day's notice; compared with the regular return fare of $1075, this is a substantial saving.

All airports and domestic flights are non-smoking.

Fares Few people pay full fare on domestic travel, as the airlines offer a wide range of discounts. These come and go and there are regular 'spot specials', so keep your eyes open. Because discounting is so unpredictable, we quote full economy fares in this book.

Full-time university or higher-education students get 25% off the regular economy fare when producing a student ID or an International Student Identity Card (ISIC), but you can usually find fares discounted by more than that.

There are no longer stand-by fares, but there are discount fares which allow same-day travel on certain flights, usually those which are uncomfortably early or late.

The cheapest fares are advance-purchase deals. Some advance-purchase fares offer up to 33% off one-way fares and up to 50% or more off return fares. You have to book one to four weeks ahead, and you often have to stay away for at least one Saturday night (for some unexplained reason). There are restrictions on changing flights and you can lose up to 100% of the ticket price if you cancel, although you can buy health-related cancellation insurance.

International travellers (Australians and foreigners) can get a 25% to 40% discount on Qantas or Ansett domestic flights simply by presenting their international ticket (any airline, one way or return) when booking. It seems there is no limit to the number of domestic flights you can take, but there might be time limits, say 60 days after you arrive in Australia. Note that the discount applies only to the full economy fare, and in many cases it will be cheaper to take advantage of other discounts offered.

Economy one-way fares (not including discounts) from other parts of Australia include: Darwin $589, Melbourne $539, Adelaide $499, Sydney $601, Uluru $437, Cairns $621 and Brisbane $661.

Air Passes With so much discounting these days, air passes do not represent the value they once did, so much so that Qantas does not offer any passes.

Ansett Australia still has its Kangaroo Airpass, which gives you two options – 6000km with two or three stopovers for $949 ($729 for children) and 10,000km with three to seven stopovers for $1499 ($1149 for children). There are a number of restrictions on these tickets, but they can be a good deal if you want to see a lot of country in a short time. You do not need to start and finish at the same place.

Restrictions include a minimum (10 nights) and a maximum (45 nights) travel time. One of the stops must be at a non-capital-city destination and be for at least four nights. All sectors must be booked when you purchase the ticket, although these can be changed without penalty unless the ticket needs rewriting, in which case there's a $50 charge. Refunds are available before travel commences, but not after you start using the ticket.

There are also special deals available only to foreign visitors. Currently, Ansett Australia's International Connection Fare can be bought and booked overseas, but you can alter your bookings and buy extra legs after arrival. For example, one-way fares from Perth to Sydney are $486, to Adelaide $390, Melbourne $436 and Darwin $474.

LAND

The south-west of WA is isolated from the rest of Australia; interstate travel therefore entails a major journey. The nearest state capital to Perth is Adelaide, 2700km away by the shortest road route. To Melbourne it's at least 3440km, Darwin is around 4160km and Sydney 4200km away. But in spite of the vast distances, you can still drive across the Nullarbor Plain from the eastern states to Perth and then all the way up the Indian Ocean coast and through the Kimberley to Darwin on sealed roads.

Bus

It pays to shop around for fares. Students and YHA members get discounts of at least 10% with many long-distance companies. On straight point-to-point tickets there are varying stopover deals. Some companies give one free stopover on express routes, others charge a fee, maybe $5 for each stopover. This fee might be waived if you book through certain agents, notably some of the hostels.

With Greyhound Pioneer Australia (☎ 13 2030) major interstate routes/fares (with km-points deals) from Perth are:

Destination	Fares	Km points
Sydney via the Nullarbor	$313	4400
Melbourne via the Nullarbor	$270	3500
Adelaide via the Nullarbor	$214	2750
Darwin via the North-West Coastal Highway	$415	approx 5000
Darwin via the Inland Route (SH 95)	$415	approx 4250

Bus Passes If you're planning to travel around Australia, check out Greyhound's excellent bus pass and km-points deals –but make sure you get enough time and stopovers. Greyhound's Adelaide to Perth, Perth to Darwin via the Coastal Highway and return to Adelaide through the Centre route would be an attractive option for many people; the cost is $925 but the fare does not allow backtracking. Added to this would be the cost of a fare to Adelaide from either Sydney/Melbourne, say about $100/60.

With the Greyhound Km-Pass, 5000km is $379, 8000km $574, 10,000km $704, 15,000km $1024 and 20,000km $1344. You can get off at any point on the scheduled and have unlimited stopovers within the life of the pass.

There are also set-duration passes which allow travel on a set number of days during a specified period. There are no restrictions on where you can travel, and passes range from $499 for seven days of travel in a month up to $980 for 21 days travel in two months.

Train

There is only one interstate rail link, the famous Indian-Pacific Railway. Along with the Ghan to Alice Springs, the long Indian-Pacific run is one of Australia's great train journeys – a 65 hour trip between the Pacific Ocean on one side of the continent and the Indian Ocean on the other. Travelling this way, you see Australia at ground level and by the end of the journey you really appreciate the immensity of the country (or, alternatively, you are bored stiff).

From Sydney, you cross NSW to Broken Hill, then continue to Adelaide and across the Nullarbor. From Port Augusta to Kalgoorlie, the seemingly endless crossing of the virtually uninhabited centre takes well over 24 hours, including the 'long straight' on the Nullarbor – at 478km this is the longest straight stretch of railway line in the world. Unlike the trans-Nullarbor road, which runs south of the Nullarbor along the coast of the Great Australian Bight, the railway line crosses the actual plain. From Kalgoorlie, it's a straightforward run into Perth.

Classes, Reservations & Costs To Perth, one-way fares from Adelaide are $492 for an economy Holiday Class sleeper, $758 for a 1st-class sleeper or $230 in an economy seat ('coach') with no meals; and from Sydney $763 economy, $1172 1st class or $378 in coach. Caper (advance-purchase) fares offer good reductions (around 30%).

The rail distance from Sydney to Perth is 3961km. You can break your journey at any stop along the way and continue on later as long as you complete the one-way trip within two months; return tickets are valid for up to six months.

Westbound, the Indian-Pacific departs Sydney at 2.55 pm on Thursday and Monday, arriving in Perth at 7 am Sunday and Thursday. Heading east, the train departs Perth at 1.35 pm on Monday and Friday, arriving in Sydney at 9.30 am on Thursday

Building the Trans-Continental Railway

The promise of a trans-continental railway link helped lure gold-rich WA into the Australian Commonwealth in 1901. Port Augusta (South Australia) and Kalgoorlie were the existing state railheads in 1907 and, that year, surveyors were sent out to map a line between those towns. In 1911 the Commonwealth government legislated to fund north-south (The Ghan) and east-west (Indian-Pacific) routes across the continent; nearly 90 years later the former has not been completed.

The first soil was turned in Augusta in 1912 and, for five years, two self-contained gangs – a total of 3000 workers – inched towards each other. They endured sandstorms, swarms of blowflies and intense heat as they laid 2.5 million sleepers and 140,000 tonnes of rail. The soil and rock was removed with pick and shovel and the workers were supplied by packhorse and camel. The whole job was completed with a minimum of mechanical aids, one of the few machines being the Roberts track-layer.

There was no opening celebration as planned (to mark the spot where the track gangs met in the sandhills near Ooldea) as Australia was embroiled in WWI. The first Transcontinental Express pulled out of Port Augusta at 9.32 pm on 22 October 1917, heralding the start of the 'desert railway from Hell to Hallelujah'. It arrived in Kalgoorlie on 24 October at 2.50 pm (42 hours 48 minutes with time difference taken into account) after covering over 1682km.

The participants in the building of the railway are reflected in the names of the stations along the stretch – Forrest, Deakin, Hughes, Cook, Fisher, O'Malley and Barton. Bates commemorates Daisy Bates, who devoted herself to the welfare of Aborigines and for a time lived alongside the line near Ooldea. Denman was the Governor-General who turned the first sod in 1917.

A good read is Patsy Adam Smith's *The Desert Railway* (1974) which has many photographs depicting the building of the line. The history of the line is covered exhaustively in *Road Through the Wilderness* (1991) by David Burke. ∎

and Monday. Book at least a month in advance (or nine months in advance if you wish to go in wildflower season).

The main difference between Holiday Class economy and 1st-class sleepers is that 1st-class compartments are available as singles or twins, economy as twins only. First-class twins have showers and toilets; 1st-class singles have toilets only, with showers at the end of the carriage. In the economy-seating compartments, the showers and toilets are at the end of the carriage. Meals are included in the fare for 1st class only; 'coach' and economy-seat passengers have the option of purchasing meals from the buffet car. First-class passengers also have a lounge compartment complete with piano.

Cars can be transported between Sydney/Adelaide and Perth ($650/460). This makes a good option for those not wishing to drive the Nullarbor in both directions.

Between Adelaide and Perth you can also travel on the weekly Trans-Australian. Fares are the same as the Indian-Pacific fares, and the trip takes 38 hours. Reservations for all services are made with Australian National Railways in Adelaide and Port Augusta; both on ☎ 13 2232.

An Ausrail Pass gives eight days travel for $380, two weeks for $460, three weeks for $591 and a month for $720; this is far more useful on the east coast where there is a wider network of rail services.

Car, Motorcycle & Bicycle

See the Getting Around chapter for details of road rules, driving conditions and information on buying and renting vehicles.

The main road routes into WA are combinations of Highway 1 (the Great Northern Highway from Port Hedland) and the North-West Coastal Highway (still part of Highway 1); Great Northern Highway (Highway 1) and State Highway 95 (Inland Route, also referred to as Great Northern Highway) from Darwin to Perth; and a combination of State Highway 94 (Great Eastern Highway) and the Eyre Highway (Highway 1) from the eastern states.

Distances to eastern state capitals are: Adelaide (2700km), Brisbane (4357km), Darwin (4165km), Melbourne (3438km) and Sydney (4200km).

Hitching

Hitching across the Nullarbor is definately not advisable; waits of several days are not uncommon. Driving yourself is probably the cheapest way of getting to WA from the eastern states – if there is a group of you. You'll probably spend around $500 to $550 on fuel, travelling coast to coast. Coming from Darwin, we never saw anyone, in a period of two months, hitching on main roads in the Kimberley or Pilbara.

ORGANISED TOURS

Another interesting route into WA is from Yulara near Uluru to Perth via the Warburton Rd. There are a number of escorted tours including Austracks 4WD Outback Adventures (☎ (1800) 655 200); the cost for its six day trip is $399. Marlu Camping Safaris (☎ 9302 1320) has an 11 day Red Centre tour for $720.

STUDENT TRAVEL

STA Travel is the main agent for student travellers in Australia. The main office in WA (☎ 9382 3977) is in Rokeby Rd, Subiaco, 6008.

Getting Around

AIR

Western Australia is so vast (and at times so empty) that unless your time is unlimited you will probably have to fly at some point. In WA, large companies use aircraft to shuttle workers from Perth to the outback.

There are only two main domestic carriers within Australia – Qantas Domestic and Ansett Australia – despite the fact that the airline industry is deregulated. So far, deregulation has made little difference to flying within WA. Ansett Australia controls most traffic, with its local operator Skywest operating most small WA routes. Ansett has a comprehensive network of flights connecting Perth with regional centres. The frequency of some flights seems ridiculous given the state's small population – until you realise how many mining projects are based there.

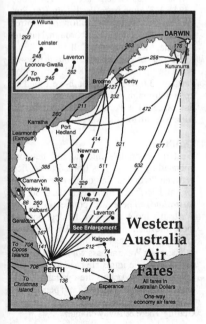

Western Australia Air Fares

All fares in Australian Dollars

One-way economy air fares

Ansett Australia (☎ 13 1300) operates regular services from Perth to the following destinations: Kalgoorlie, Geraldton, Carnarvon, Derby, Learmonth (Exmouth), Paraburdoo, Newman, Karratha, Port Hedland, Broome and Kununurra. These are linked with interstate flights to Darwin, Sydney, Adelaide, Melbourne, Uluru (Ayers Rock), Cairns and Townsville. Additionally, there are flights to the Australian protectorates, Cocos/Keeling Islands and Christmas Island, in the Indian Ocean ($708/1416 one-way/return).

Skywest Airlines (☎ 9478 9999, 13 1300) operates services from Perth to the following destinations: Albany, Carnarvon, Derby, Esperance, Exmouth, Kalgoorlie, Laverton, Leinster, Leonora, Geraldton, Monkey Mia, Mt Magnet, Cue, Meekatharra and Wiluna.

There are other smaller operators within the state. Western Airlines (☎ 9277 4022) operates a service from Perth to Kalbarri, Useless Loop and Monkey Mia. There is also a regular service to Rottnest Island (☎ 9478 1322): usually three flights in the morning and three in the afternoon.

Travelling from airport to town is reasonably cheap and convenient by airline bus. A taxi shared between three or more people can often be cheaper than the bus. For transport to/from Perth airport, see the Perth chapter.

BUS

Bus travel is generally the cheapest way from A to B, but the main problem is finding the best deal. A great many travellers see WA by bus because it's one of the best ways to come to grips with the state's size and variety of terrain, and because the bus companies have route networks far more comprehensive than the limited railway system. All buses look pretty similar and are equipped with air-con, toilets and videos.

Greyhound Pioneer Australia (☎ 13 2030) is the only national bus network operating in WA. As well as interstate destinations, it has departures from Perth to Dongara-Port

Denison ($38), Geraldton ($42), Kalbarri ($77), Monkey Mia ($126), Port Hedland ($155), Exmouth ($203), Broome ($240), Derby ($263), Kununurra ($377), Meekatharra ($112), Newman ($139), Port Hedland via Newman ($155), Northam ($42) and Kalgoorlie ($86).

Its buses run from Perth along the coast to Darwin ($415) and to Adelaide/Melbourne via Kalgoorlie and the Eyre Highway ($214/270). Greyhound is the most extensive service in the state with an interconnecting service that would allow an almost-loop trip such as Perth to Kalbarri, Monkey Mia, Exmouth and Broome, and return via the inland route. (A return fare on Greyhound is double, less 10%.)

Perth Goldfields Express (☎ 9328 9199, 9021 2954) does the Perth-to-Leinster run via the Great Eastern Highway and Kalgoorlie; one way from Perth is Leinster ($100), Leonora ($90), Kalgoorlie ($65) and Merredin ($50).

The largest operator in the mid-west and south-west is Westrail, and its buses run in conjunction with limited rail services.

Westrail Bus Services (from Perth)

Destination	Fare
Williams-Albany	$36
Bunbury-Pemberton	$31
Northam-Geraldton-Meekatharra	$67
Geraldton	$38
Geraldton terminal-Kalbarri	$23
Northam-Narrogin-Albany	$35
Esperance	$53
Bunbury-Augusta	$29
Bunbury terminal-Denmark*	$29
Mukinbudin	$29
York-Kulin-Hyden-Esperance	$53
Kalgoorlie terminal-Esperance	$33
Northam-York*	$10
Bunbury terminal-Manjimup-Albany (King Karri)*	$33.50
Albany terminal-Margaret River*	$10
Albany terminal-Pemberton*	$10
Albany terminal-Esperance*	$46

* Not Originating at the East Perth terminal (EPT)

Westrail services York, Geraldton, Kalbarri, Esperance, Bunbury, Kalgoorlie, Margaret River, Augusta, Pemberton, Mukinbudin, Hyden, Albany and Meekatharra. Reservations (☎ 13 1053) are necessary on all Westrail bus/train services.

It has a number of main routes, most of which originate at the East Perth terminal (EPT). See the Westrail Bus Services table.

Concession-card holders (pensioners, seniors, unemployed/low-income earners and students) can get a fare reduction on Westrail. Children under 16 travel for half fare and children under 10 may not travel unaccompanied. There is a free luggage allowance of 50kg (two items) and bicycles (suitably packed) or surfboards can only be accepted if room permits. There is a 28 day Southern Discovery pass for $140; you can travel in one direction in a loop – Perth, Kalgoorlie, Norseman, Esperance, Augusta, Bunbury, Perth, or vice versa. Backtracking is allowed on the Bunbury-Augusta sector.

South-West Coachlines (☎ 9754 1666; 9324 2333) runs from Perth City Bus Port, Wellington St, to the following centres: Bunbury, Busselton, Dunsborough, Nannup, Augusta, Manjimup and Collie.

The only true backpackers' bus in the west is the Easyrider (☎ 9383 7848). It runs from Perth to 13 towns in the south-west, picking up and dropping off at budget accommodation places. The Perth-Augusta-Pemberton-Albany-Perth loop is a very reasonable $129.

TRAIN

Western Australia's internal rail network, operated by Westrail, is limited to services between Perth and Kalgoorlie (the *Prospector*), and Perth and Bunbury in the south (the *Australind*). There are connections with Westrail's more extensive bus service (for more information see Getting There & Away in the Perth chapter).

There is a Westrailpass which can be used for all travel on intrastate road and rail passenger services; tickets are available for 14 day, one month and three month periods. For information on the Indian-Pacific see the Getting There & Away chapter.

CAR

More and more travellers are finding the car the best way to see the state – with three or four travelling together, the costs are reasonable and the benefits many, provided you don't have a major mechanical problem. However, because so many travellers are buying cars these days, you may find it difficult to find people to share the journey.

Road Rules

Driving in WA holds few surprises. Australians drive on the left-hand side of the road. There are a few local rules.

The main one is the 'give way to the right' rule. This means that if you're driving on a main road and somebody appears on a minor road on your right, you must give way to them – unless they are facing a give-way or stop sign. Most intersections are now signposted to indicate the priority road.

The general speed limit in built-up areas is 60 km/h, the freeways are 90 km/h and in some country areas it's 110 km/h; lower limits are designated by roadside speed-limit signs. The police have radar speed traps and speed cameras and are very fond of using them in carefully hidden locations – don't exceed the speed limit as the boys and girls in blue may be waiting for you.

Australia was one of the first countries in the world to make the wearing of seat belts compulsory. All new cars in Australia are required to have seat belts back and front and if your seat has a belt then you must wear it – you're liable to be fined if you don't. Western Australia is the only state which does not require small children to be belted into an approved safety seat – a foolish omission which should be rectified.

Although overseas licences are acceptable in Australia for genuine visitors, an International Driving Permit is preferred.

On the Road

Western Australia is not crisscrossed by multi-lane highways. There simply is not enough traffic and the distances are too great to justify them.

In general, roads in WA are well-surfaced two-lanes on all of the main routes. You don't have to get very far off the beaten track, however, to find yourself on dirt roads, and anybody who sets out to see the state in reasonable detail will have to expect to do some dirt-road travelling. If you seriously want to explore, then you'd better plan on having a 4WD and a winch.

A few useful spare parts are worth carrying if you're travelling on highways in the Kimberley, Pilbara or remote south-eastern parts of the state. A broken fan belt can be a real nuisance if the next service station is 200km away.

Driving standards in Australia aren't the highest in the world and drink-driving is a

Road Distances (from Perth)	
Route	Km
North-West Coastal Highway	
Cataby	163
Dongara	365
Geraldton	427
Billabong Roadhouse	657
Overlander Roadhouse	705
Carnarvon	905
Minilya Roadhouse	1035
Nanutarra Roadhouse	1263
Karratha	1537
Great Northern Highway	
Wubin	272
Meekatharra	765
Kumarina	1021
Auski Roadhouse	1384
Port Hedland	1761
Sandfire Roadhouse	1907
Roebuck Roadhouse	2193
Willare Roadhouse	2323
Fitzroy Crossing	2554
Halls Creek	2842
Warmun (Turkey Creek)	3005
Kununurra	3201
Eyre Highway (Nullarbor)	
Norseman	726
Balladonia	917
Caiguna	1099
WA/SA Border Village	1448
Nullarbor Roadhouse, SA	1284
(over Christmas only)	

real problem, especially in country areas. In recent years random breath tests in built-up areas have been used in an effort to reduce the road toll. If you're caught with a blood-alcohol level of more than 0.05% (0.08% in the Northern Territory) be prepared for a hefty fine, a court appearance and the loss of your licence. If possible, get copies of the booklets *Drive Safe* and *How to Enjoy Touring in Western Australia*.

Fuel Petrol is available from stations sporting the well known international brand names. In WA, prices vary enormously from place to place. In a trip from Kununurra to Perth, expect a price variation of 35c per litre for diesel or petrol, decreasing as you get closer to major centres and increasing on lonely stretches of road.

In the outback, the price can soar and some outback service stations are not above exploiting their monopoly position, especially those between Kununurra and Geraldton where fuel transport costs feature heavily in the equation. In general, the price ranges throughout the state from about 70c a litre to $1.05. If you have a 4WD then long-range fuel tanks assist in making large savings on fuel costs.

Along the coastal route, the Great Northern Highway or the Eyre Highway (Nullarbor), fuel supplies are widely spaced. There is 24 day availability at the following places (these roadhouses are under no obligation to stay open for 24 hours, so always be prepared to have to drive further).

Hazards Cattle, emus and kangaroos are common hazards on country roads, and a collision is likely to kill the animal and seriously damage your vehicle. Kangaroos are most active around dawn and dusk, and they travel in groups. If you see one hopping across the road in front of you, slow right down – its friends are probably just behind it. Many Australians avoid travelling altogether between 5 pm and 8 am, because of the hazards posed by animals.

Finally, if one hops out in front of you (as a family of emus did to us), hit the brakes and only swerve to avoid the animal if it is safe to do so. The number of people who have been killed in accidents caused by swerving to miss an animal is high – better to damage your car and probably kill the animal than kill yourself and others with you.

At some stage you are bound to find yourself on a dirt road, eg the Stirling Ranges, Gibb River Rd and the access roads to Karijini and Millstream-Chichester national parks. Driving on the dirt requires special care as a car performs differently under braking and turning when on dirt. You should under no circumstances exceed 80 km/h on dirt. If you go faster you will not have enough time to respond to a sharp turn, stock on the road or an unmarked gate or cattle grid. So take it easy. See the sights and don't break the land speed record.

Travelling in WA, especially in the north-west, means having to pass a road train. On some days you will see more road trains than cars. These articulated trucks and their loads can be up to 53.5m long, 2.5m wide and travel around 100 km/h. Overtaking is a tricky process and requires a clear view ahead. At times you will have to drive off the bitumen to get past. Exercise caution and remember that it is much harder for the larger road train to be kept in control than your car; basically, show some courtesy.

Flooding is a real problem up north during the Wet because of cyclonic storms. If you travel at this time, delays should be expected. You can check whether roads are open, following heavy rain, by telephoning one of the following numbers:

Perth
    ☎ (08) 9323 4354 or ☎ (1800) 013 314
Carnarvon
    ☎ (1800) 013 315
Port Hedland
    ☎ (1800) 013 316
Derby
    ☎ (1800) 013 317
Darwin
    ☎ (089) 8922 3394

Note: Elsewhere in WA ring the Perth number for a prompt which requests the region you're ringing from.

Distances One thing you have to adjust to in the west is the vast distances. The truth is that many places of interest are a bloody long way away from Perth. There are rest areas, where tired drivers can revive. Ask for the maps from the RACWA which indicate free coffee stops and rest areas.

See the Road Distances table below for some examples of the distances from Perth to regional centres.

Outback Travel

You can drive around Australia on Highway 1 or through the centre all the way from Adelaide in the south to Darwin in the north almost without ever leaving sealed road. Occasionally, there are sections of dirt when the road is being repaired after the Wet floods.

If you really want to see outback WA, there are lots of unsealed roads where the official recommendation is that you report to the police before you leave one end, and again when you arrive at the other. That way, if you fail to turn up at the other end they can organise search parties (there are at least a couple of stories each year of motorists being stranded for weeks).

Nevertheless, many of these tracks are now better kept and you don't need a 4WD or fancy expedition equipment to tackle them. You do need, however, to be carefully prepared and to carry important spare parts. Backtracking 500km to pick up some minor malfunctioning component or, much worse, to arrange a tow, is unlikely to be easy.

You will need to carry a fair amount of water in case of disaster – around 20 litres a person is sensible – stored in more than one container. Food is less important – space may be better allocated to an extra spare tyre.

The state automobile associations can advise on preparation and supply maps and track notes. Most tracks have an ideal time of year – in the centre it's not wise to attempt the tough tracks during the heat of summer (November to March) when the dust can be severe, chances of mechanical trouble are much greater and water will be scarce and hence a breakdown more dangerous. Similarly in the north, travelling in the Wet may be impossible due to flooding and mud.

If you do run into trouble in the back of beyond, stay with your car. It's easier to spot a car than a human being from the air, and you wouldn't be able to carry your 20 litres of water very far anyway.

Make sure you practise gate etiquette. The rules are quite simple: if you find a gate open leave it open and if you find it closed make sure you close it after you have passed through. Farm owners can be understandably irate if you neglect to do this.

Road Distances (from Perth)

Town	Km
Albany	409
Augusta	320
Broome	2230
Bunbury	180
Carnarvon	904
Cervantes	245
Coral Bay	1131
Cue	650
Dampier	1555
Denham	834
(Monkey Mia)	859
Derby	2381
Esperance	730
Eucla	1436
Exmouth	1260
Fitzroy Crossing	2554
Geraldton	430
Hyden	340
Kalbarri	589
Kalgoorlie	597
Karratha	1535
Lake Argyle	3284
Manjimup	307
Marble Bar	1476
Margaret River	277
Mount Barker	360
Newman	1184
Onslow	1386
Pemberton	335
Port Hedland (via coast)	1640
Roebourne	1560
Southern Cross	368
Tom Price	1548
Walpole	426
Wyndham	3205

Some of the favourite outback tracks in the west follow.

Warburton Rd/Gunbarrel Highway This route runs west from Yulara past the Aboriginal settlements of Docker River and Warburton to Laverton in WA. From there you can drive down to Kalgoorlie and on to Perth. The route passes through Aboriginal reserves and you should get permission to enter the reserves in advance.

A well-prepared conventional vehicle can complete this route although ground clearance can be a problem and it is very remote. From the Yulara resort at Yulara to Warburton is 567km, and it's another 568km from there to Laverton. It's then 361km on sealed road to Kalgoorlie. For 300km, near the Giles Meteorological Station, the Warburton Rd and the Gunbarrel Highway run on the same route. Taking the old Gunbarrel (to the north of the Warburton) all the way to Wiluna is a much rougher trip requiring 4WD. The Warburton Rd is now commonly referred to as the Gunbarrel.

Tanami Track Turning off the Stuart Highway just north of Alice Springs, the Tanami Track goes north-west across the Tanami Desert to Halls Creek in WA. It's a popular short cut for people travelling between the centre and the Kimberley. The road has been extensively improved in recent years and conventional vehicles are quite OK although there are occasional sandy stretches on the WA section.

Be warned that Rabbit Flat Roadhouse, in the middle of the desert, is only open Friday to Monday.

Canning Stock Route This old stock trail runs south-west from Halls Creek to Wiluna in WA. It crosses the Great Sandy and Gibson deserts, and since the track has not been maintained for over 30 years, it's a route to be taken seriously. Like the Simpson Desert crossing you should only travel in a well-equipped party and careful navigation is required.

Two good books on the route are Ronele & Eric Gard's *Canning Stock Route: A Traveller's Guide for a Journey through History* (1990) and the *Australian Geographic Book of the Canning Stock Route* (1992).

Gibb River Rd This is the short cut between Derby and Kununurra, and runs through the heart of the spectacular Kimberley in northern WA. Although fairly badly corrugated in places, it can be negotiated with care by conventional vehicles in the dry season and is 720km, compared with about 920km via the bitumen Northern Highway. For more information see Gibb River Rd in the Kimberley chapter.

Rental

If you've got the cash there are plenty of car-rental companies ready and willing to put you behind the wheel. Competition in the WA car-rental business is pretty fierce so rates tend to vary and lots of special deals pop up and disappear again. Whatever your mode of transport, it can be very useful to have a car for local travel. Between a group it can even be economical. There are places in the state – if you haven't a car – where you'll have to choose between a tour and a rented vehicle since there is no public transport and the distances are too great for walking or even bicycles.

The three major companies are Budget, Hertz and Avis, with offices in the main towns – all three have offices in Kalgoorlie, Albany, Broome, Geraldton, Carnarvon, Exmouth and Kununurra, for example.

The big firms have a number of advantages. First of all, they're the ones at the airports – Avis, Budget, Hertz and, quite often, Thrifty. If you want to pick up a car or leave a car at the airport, then they're the best ones to deal with. In some, but not all airports, other companies also arrange to pick up or leave their cars there.

One-way rentals are generally not available into or out of the Northern Territory or WA. Special rules may also apply to one-ways into or out of other 'remote areas'.

Daily unlimited rates are about $60 a day for a small Class A car (Ford Festiva, Holden

Barina, Mazda 121, Nissan Micro), about $70 a day for a Class C medium car (Holden Mondeo, Toyota Camry, Nissan Pulsar), $75 a day for a big Class D car (Holden Commodore, Ford Falcon) and about $100 for a Class E car (Holden Statesman or Ford Fairlane), all including insurance and collision damage waiver (CDW).

There is a whole collection of other factors to bear in mind. For a start, you must be at least 21 to hire from most firms. If you're going to want it for a week or longer then they all have lower rates.

There's a plethora of smaller hire companies and lots of competition, which are still pretty big in terms of numbers of shiny new cars. In many cases local companies are markedly cheaper than the big boys, but in others, what looks like a cheaper rate can end up quite the opposite if you're not careful (many readers' letters confirm this). In Perth there is a lot to choose from and this list is by no means exhaustive:

Ace Rent-a-Car
    311 Hay St, Perth (☎ 9221 333)
Action Hire Cars
    652 Albany Highway, Victoria Park
    (☎ (1800) 627 688)
ATC Rent-a-Car
    126 Adelaide Terrace, Perth (☎ 9325 1833)
Bayswater Car Rental
    160 Adelaide Terrace, Perth
    (☎ 9325 1000, 9430 5300)
Carousel Rent-a-Car
    1276 Albany Highway, Cannington
    (☎ 9451 9999)
City Centre Car Rentals
    41 Milligan St, Perth (☎ (1800) 806 141)
Delta
    3-5 Gordon St, West Perth
    (☎ 13 1390, (1800) 637 388)
Ezidrive Car Rentals
    640 Newcastle St, Leederville
    (☎ (1800) 355 575)
Network
    259 William St, Northbridge (next to Britannia
    YHA Hostel) (☎ 9227 8810)
Thrifty Car Rental
    33 Milligan St, Perth
    (☎ 9481 1999, (1800) 652 008)

Companies are eager to get you to rent if you are restricting yourself to Perth and sur-

rounding environs. Tell them you plan to go further afield and the daily rate zooms upwards. Mere mention of the outback attracts price hikes like uncovered meat does flies.

And don't forget the 'rent-a-wreck' companies. They specialise in renting older cars – at first they really were old, and a flat rate like '$15 a day and forget the insurance' was the usual story. Now many of them have a variety of rates, typically around $35 a day. If you just want to travel around the city, or not too far out, they can be worth considering. A couple of contacts are:

Letz Rent a Car
    126 Grandstand St, Belmont (☎ 9478 1999)
Rent a Heap
    368 Guildford Rd, Bayswater (☎ 9272 2206)
Road Runner Rentals
    33 Great Eastern Highway, Rivervale
    (☎ 9470 2150)

4WDs A 4WD enables you to get off the beaten track and see some great wilderness and outback regions (such as Purnululu or the Kimberley).

Renting a 4WD vehicle is within the budget range if a few people get together; but include a return to Perth. Something small like a small Suzuki Vitara or similar costs around $85 per day; for a Toyota Landcruiser or Nissan Patrol you're looking at around $100, which should include insurance and

some free kilometres (typically 150km – extra kilometres are about 25c each). Check the insurance conditions, especially excess, as they can be onerous.

A few places to check are:

Osborne Rentals
130 Hector St, Osborne Park (☎ 9451 1070); 528 Hannan St, Kalgoorlie (☎ 9021 4722)
South Perth 4WD Rentals
80 Canning Highway, Victoria Park (☎ 9362 5444)
Woody's 4WD Hire
corner of Frederick & Herbert Sts, Broome (☎ 9192 1791)

Campervans Brits Australia (☎ (1800) 331 454) hires fully equipped 4WD vehicles fitted out as campervans. These have proved extremely popular in WA in recent years, although they are not cheap at $197 per day in high season for unlimited kilometres, plus CDW ($20 per day). In low season the vehicle may be hired for as low as $140, and there are discounts for hires of more than 21 days. It has offices in all the mainland capitals, so one-way rentals are also possible.

Other companies which hire out camper vans are Dolphin Campervan Hire (☎ (1800) 658 776), 3 Chalkly Place, Bayswater (Mazda pop-up vans which sleep a couple comfortably and which are equipped with an erect rooftop camper conversion); Camperworld (☎ 9478 2755), rear of 44 Great Eastern Highway, Guildford; and Camperent WA (☎ 9364 5529), 708 Canning Highway, Applecross.

Purchase

Australian cars are relatively cheap to purchase – now apparently second only after US car prices. If you're buying a second-hand vehicle, reliability is all important. Mechanical breakdowns in the outback can be very inconvenient (and dangerous) – the nearest mechanic can be a long way down the road. Shopping around for a used car involves much the same rules as anywhere in the Western world but with a few local variations.

Used-car dealers in Australia are just like used-car dealers from Los Angeles to London – they'd sell their mother into slavery if it turned a dollar. For any given car you'll probably get it cheaper by buying privately through newspaper ads (Saturday's *West Australian)* rather than through a car dealer. Buying through a dealer does give the advantage of some sort of guarantee, but a guarantee is not much use if you're buying a car in Perth and intend setting off for Sydney next week. Used-car guarantee requirements vary from state to state – check with the RACWA in Perth.

There's much discussion amongst travellers about where is the best place to buy used cars. Popular theories exist that you can buy a car in Sydney or Melbourne, drive it to Darwin or Perth and sell it there for a profit. Or is it vice versa? It's quite possible that prices do vary, but don't count on turning it to your advantage.

What is rather more certain is that the further you get from civilisation, the better it is to be in a Holden or a Ford. New cars can be a whole different ball game of course, but if you're in an older vehicle, something that's likely to have the odd hiccup from time to time, then life is much simpler if it's a car for which you can get spare parts anywhere from Kununurra to Kellerberrin. When your fancy Japanese car goes kaput near the remote Mt Augustus or Collier Range national parks, it's likely to be a month wait while the new part arrives fresh from Fukuoka. On the other hand, when your rusty old Holden goes bang there's probably another old Holden sitting in a ditch or scrap yard with spare parts aplenty.

Remember that in Australia, third-party personal injury insurance is always included in the vehicle registration cost. This ensures that every registered vehicle carries at least minimum insurance. You're wise to extend that minimum to third-party property insurance as well.

When you come to buy or sell a car, there are usually some local regulations to be complied with. In WA a car has to have a compulsory safety check (Road Worthiness Certificate – RWC) before it can be registered in the new owner's name – usually the seller will indicate if the car already has a RWC. Stamp duty has to be paid when you buy a car and, as this is based on the purchase price, it's not unknown for buyer and seller to agree privately to understate the price! It's much easier to sell a car in the same state that it's registered in, otherwise it will have to be re-registered in the new state. It may be possible to sell a car without re-registering it, but you're likely to get a lower price.

One way of getting around the hassles of buying and selling a vehicle privately is to enter into a buy-back arrangement with a car or motorcycle dealer. However, dealers frequently find ways of knocking down the price when you return the vehicle, even if a price has been agreed on in writing – usually by pointing out expensive repairs that allegedly will be required to gain the dreaded RWC needed to transfer the registration.

The cars on offer have often been driven around Australia a number of times, usually with haphazard or minimal servicing, and are generally pretty tired. The main advantage of these schemes is that you don't have to worry about being able to sell the vehicle quickly at the end of your trip, and can usually arrange insurance, which short-term visitors may find hard to get.

One local possibility is Deals on Wheels (☎ 9493 3155), 1844 Albany Highway, Maddington. Just because they appear here does not mean they are recommended. But as an example, in 1997, they were selling a 1979 Kingswood for $2000, an 81 Ford Falcon panel van for $3000, and an 83 Mitsubishi Star Van for $8000.

Finally, make use of the RACWA – see the section below for more details on services.

Self Drive Tours Within WA lists 15 or so of the state's most popular drives; it is available free from the WATC. Gregory's *Touring Guides* cover the Great Southern, south-east and goldfields, Mandurah and Murray and Northern Agricultural regions.

Automobile Association

The Royal Automobile Club of Western Australia (RACWA; ☎ 9421 4444), 228 Adelaide Terrace, provides pilot services to first-time visitors to the city. Its bookshop has an excellent travel section, and detailed regional maps can be obtained at its Road Travel counter. It can advise you on any local regulations you should be aware of, give general guidelines about buying a car and, most importantly, for a fee (around $70) will check over a used car and report on its condition before you agree to purchase it. It also offers car insurance to its members. The addresses of road travel specialists in bordering states are:

South Australia
   Royal Automobile Association of South Australia (RAA), 41 Hindmarsh Square, Adelaide 5000 (☎ (08) 8223 4555)
Northern Territory
   Automobile Association of the Northern Territory, 79-81 Smith St, Darwin 0800 (☎ (08) 8981 3837)

MOTORCYCLE

Motorcycles are a very popular way of getting around. The climate is just about ideal for biking much of the year, and the many small trails from the road into the bush often lead to perfect spots to spend the night in the world's largest camping ground.

The long, open roads are really made for large-capacity machines above 750cc, which Australians prefer once they outgrow their 250cc learner restrictions. But that doesn't stop enterprising individuals – many of them Japanese – from tackling the length and breadth of the continent on 250cc trail bikes. Doing it on a small bike is not impossible, just tedious at times.

If you want to bring your own motorcycle into Australia you'll need a *carnet de passage*, and when you try to sell it you'll get less than the market price because of restrictive registration requirements (not so severe in WA). Shipping from just about anywhere is expensive.

However, with a little bit of time up your sleeve, getting mobile on two wheels is quite feasible, thanks largely to the chronically depressed motorcycle market. Australian newspapers and the local bike press have extensive classified advertisement sections where $2500 gets you something that will easily take you around the country if you know a bit about bikes. The main drawback is that you'll have to try and sell it again afterwards.

An easier option is a buy-back arrangement with a large motorcycle dealer in a major city. They're keen to do business, and basic negotiating skills allied with a wad of cash (say, $8000) should secure an excellent second-hand bike with a written guarantee that they'll buy it back in good condition minus say $1500 after your four month, round-Australia trip. Popular brands for this sort of thing are BMWs, large-capacity, shaft-driven Japanese bikes and possibly Harley-Davidson's (very popular in Australia). The percentage drop on a 600cc trail bike (for, say, $3000) will be much greater, though the amount should be similar – if you can find a dealer willing to come to the party.

You'll need a rider's licence and a helmet. A fuel range of 350km will cover fuel stops up the Inland Route and on Highway 1 around the coast. Beware of dehydration in the dry, hot air – force yourself to drink plenty of water, even if you don't feel thirsty.

The 'roo bars' (outsize bumpers) you'll see on interstate trucks and many outback cars should be a warning never to ride at night, or in the early morning and evening because of the number of native animals, cattle and sheep which stray onto the roads at these times. It's wise to stop riding by around 5 pm. Many roadhouses offer showers free of charge or for a nominal fee. They're meant for truck drivers, but other people often use them too.

It's worth carrying some spares and tools even if you don't know how to use them, because someone else often does. If you do know, you'll probably have a fair idea of what to take.

The basics include: a spare tyre tube (front wheel size, which will fit on the rear but usually not vice versa); puncture repair kit with levers and a pump (or tubeless tyre repair kit with two or three carbon-dioxide cartridges); a spare tyre valve, and a valve cap that can unscrew same; the bike's stan-

dard tool kit for what it's worth (aftermarket items are better); spare throttle, clutch and brake cables; tie wire, cloth tape ('gaffer' tape) and nylon 'zip-ties'; a handful of bolts and nuts in the usual emergency sizes (M6 and M8), along with a few self-tapping screws; one or two fuses in your bike's ratings; a bar of soap for fixing tank leaks (knead to a putty with water and squeeze into the leak); and, most important of all, a workshop manual for your bike (even if you can't make sense of it, the local motorcycle mechanic can). You'll never have enough elastic straps (octopus or 'ocky' straps) to tie down your gear.

Make sure you carry water everywhere stored in good quality carriers – at least two litres on major roads in WA, and much more off the beaten track. In 1993, a foreign motorcyclist headed off to do the Warburton Rd with a couple of cheap plastic containers of water which subsequently leaked. A major search ensued and the rider was lucky to be found alive.

So finally, if something does go hopelessly wrong in the outback, park your bike where it's clearly visible and observe the cardinal rule: don't leave your vehicle!

BICYCLE

Whether you're hiring a bike to ride around Rottnest Island or wearing out your Bio-Ace chain-wheels on a trans-Nullarbor marathon, you'll find that WA is a great place for cycling. There are lots of bike tracks in Perth, and in the country you'll find thousands of kilometres of good roads which carry so little traffic that the biggest hassle is waving back to the drivers. Especially appealing is that in many areas you'll ride a very long way without encountering a hill.

It's possible to plan rides of any duration and through almost any terrain. A day or two cycling around the Margaret River wineries south of Perth is popular, and longer rides, particularly around the coast, can be tackled by well-prepared cyclists.

Cycling has always been popular here, and not only as a sport: some shearers would ride for huge distances between jobs, rather than use less reliable horses. It's rare to find a town that doesn't have a shop stocking at least basic bike parts. A list of approved bike shops should be available from the Cycle Touring Association of WA, PO Box 174, Wembley WA 6014.

If you're coming specifically to cycle, it makes sense to bring your own bike. Check your airline for costs and the degree of dismantling/packing required. Within WA you can load your bike onto a bus to skip the boring bits. Bus companies require you to dismantle your bike (and some don't guarantee that it will travel on the same bus as you).

You can get by with standard road maps, but as you'll probably want to avoid both the highways and the low-grade unsealed roads, the government series is best. The 1:250,000 scale is the most suitable but you'll need a lot of maps if you're covering much territory. The next scale up, 1:1,000,000, is adequate. These, and the excellent series of RACWA maps, are available in Perth and elsewhere.

Until you get fit you should be careful to eat enough to keep you going – remember that exercise is an appetite suppressant. It's surprisingly easy to exhaust yourself and end up camping under a gum tree just 10km short of a shower and a steak.

No matter how fit you are, water is still vital. Dehydration is no joke and can be life-threatening. It can get very hot in summer, and you

should take things slowly until you're used to the heat. Cycling in 35°C-plus temperatures isn't too bad if you wear a hat and plenty of sunscreen, and drink *lots* of water.

Of course, you don't have to follow the larger roads and visit towns. It's possible to fill your mountain bike's panniers with muesli, head out into the bush, and not see anyone for weeks. Or ever again – outback travel is very risky if not properly planned. Water is the main problem in the 'dead heart', and you can't rely on it where there aren't settlements. That tank marked on your map may be dry or the water from it unfit for humans, and those station buildings probably blew away years ago. That little creek marked with a dotted blue line? Forget it – the only time it has water is when the country's flooded for hundreds of kilometres.

Always check with locals if you're heading into remote areas, and notify the police if you're about to do something particularly adventurous. That said, you can't rely too much on local knowledge of road conditions – most people have no idea of what a heavily loaded touring bike needs. What they think of as a great road may be pedal-deep in sand or bull dust, while cyclists have happily ridden along roads that were officially flooded out.

Bicycle helmets are compulsory wear in all states and territories.

Cycling the Nullarbor

The Nullarbor (Eyre Highway) is a real challenge to cyclists, attracted by the barrenness and distance, certainly not by the interesting scenery. As you drive across you see many of them, at all times of the year, lifting their waterbottles to their parched mouths or sheltering under a lone tree.

Excellent equipment is needed and adequate water supplies have to be carried. The cyclist should also know where all the water tanks are. And beware the sun – adequate protection should be applied even in cloudy weather. Realise that the prevailing wind for most of the journey will be west to east, the most preferable direction to be pedalling.

Spare a thought for the first cyclist to cross the Nullarbor. Arthur Richardson set off from Coolgardie on 24 November 1896 with a small kit and water bag. Thirty-one days later he arrived in Adelaide having followed the telegraph line, on the way encountering hot winds, '1000 in the shade' and 40km of sandhills west of Madura station.

In 1900, Richardson became the first person to pedal around Australia. leaving Perth on 5 June 1899 and arriving back on 4 February 1900. He left amid much publicity just as another group had left in a counter-clockwise direction from Melbourne. The epic journey is described in his *Story of a Remarkable Ride* (1900). ∎

HITCHING

Hitching is never entirely safe in any country in the world, and we *don't* recommend it. Travellers who decide to hitch should understand that they are taking a potentially serious risk. However, many people do choose to hitch, and the advice that follows should help to make their journeys as fast and safe as possible.

Travel by thumb can be a good way of getting around and it is certainly interesting. Sometimes it can even be fast, but it's usually foolish to try and set yourself deadlines when travelling this way – you need luck. Successful hitching depends on several factors, all of them involves common sense.

The most important is your numbers – two people are really the ideal, any more may make things difficult. Ideally, those two should comprise one male and one female – two guys hitching together can expect long waits. It is not advisable for women to hitch alone, or even in pairs.

Another major consideration is knowing when to say no. Saying no to a car-load of drunks is pretty obvious, but it can be time-saving to say no to a short ride that might take you from a good hitching point to a lousy one. Wait for the right, long ride to come along.

If you're visiting from abroad, a nice prominent flag on your pack will help, and a sign announcing your destination can also be useful. Uni and hostel notice boards are good places to look for hitching partners. Remember not to stand in the road.

FERRY

Transperth has a ferry service from the city to South Perth and a number of operators who travel from Fremantle, Hillary's Boat Harbour and Perth to Rottnest Island. For information on these services, see Getting Around in the Perth chapter and Getting There & Away under Rottnest Island in the Around Perth chapter.

LOCAL TRANSPORT

Outside Perth local transport is limited. See the Getting Around section in the Perth chapter for local transport options.

Taxi

Taxis are available in most of the cities and towns where locals are heavily reliant on them as a means of beating the booze buses and police patrols. Shared among a number of people they are reasonable and a good means of getting around.

ORGANISED TOURS

There are all sorts of tours available in WA including some interesting camping tours, many of which originate in Perth. Adventure tours include 4WD safaris – some of these go to places you simply couldn't get to on your own without large amounts of expensive equipment. The tours listed here are only a sample of what is available; check with the local tourist information office.

AAT Kings Australian Tours
  Bus, 13 day Broome and Kimberley trip which including a Tanami Desert crossing ($1998) – and a $99 fare to the point of departure from anywhere in Australia; this trip suits a less adventurous crowd (☎ (1800) 33 4009).
All Terrain Safaris
  4WD adventure tours including four day Pinnacles/Monkey Mia ($339), south-west ($329), Perth to Broome and Gorges ($765) and Perth return via Gorges (also $765) (☎ (1800) 633 456).
Around Australia Adventures
  Bus, budget and value trips to Wave Rock ($75 including lunch), Monkey Mia four day safari ($299) (☎ (1800) 649 364, 9493 6660).
Australian Pacific Tours
  Bus, the 20 day Westcoaster is a Perth to Darwin trip which includes Monkey Mia, Hamersley Gorges, Broome, and a flight over Purnululu and Kakadu; $2265 (☎ 9221 1163).
Milesaway Tours
  4WD, five and eight day trips in the south-west including Hyden, Stirling Ranges, Margaret River, Albany and Esperance; from $340 (☎ 9755 3574).
Overland 4WD Safaris
  4WD, five day trip which includes Wooleen Station, Monkey Mia, Kalbarri Gorges, the Pinnacles; $399 (☎ 9354 4396).
Pathfinder (Ansett)
  Bus, 12 day Kimberley Top End Explorer includes Broome, Geikie Gorge, Wyndham, Lake Argyle and a flight over Purnululu; $2300 (☎ 9354 4396).

S-Cape Adventure Tours
4WD tours to the south-west, up the coast to Broome ($595) and as far afield as 12 days to the Kimberley ($995) (☎ (1800) 633 352).

Travelabout
4WD, options include a 10 day Hamersley Range tour, a 16 day Purnululu-Kakadu tour and four day Monkey Mia-Kalbarri-Pinnacles tour; $750, $1300, $280 respectively (☎ 9244 1200).

West Coast Explorer
4WD adventure tours from Perth via Broome to Darwin, $1390 for 15 days, $1190 for 12 days and $735 for seven days (☎ toll-free (1800) 651 210).

Western Travel Bug
Bus, five day trips to the south-west and as far out as Esperance and Wave Rock/ Hyden (☎ toll-free (1800) 627 488, 9561 5236).

Perth

• *pop 1,300,000*

Perth is a vibrant and modern city, pleasantly sited on the Swan and Canning rivers, with the cerulean Indian Ocean to the west and the ancient Darling Ranges to the east. It's claimed to be the sunniest state capital in Australia and the most isolated capital city in the world and it is closer to Singapore than Sydney. Of WA's 1.7 million people, almost 80% live in and around Perth – and a fair percentage of the 80% are intent on enjoying the type of easy-going lifestyle which an equable climate fosters.

The city centre, with its sterile concrete and glass skyscrapers, unfortunately dominates a site which has the potential, with its picturesque riverside location, to be stunning. The domineering edifices hide a handful of 19th century buildings and facades, and beleaguered patches of greenery.

Away from this cluttered rectangle of commerce and public service, there is indeed a beautiful city, enhanced by the Indian Ocean beaches, the hillside hideaways, romantic Fremantle, cosmopolitan Subiaco and the select, comfortable suburbs which fringe the Swan River.

History

The site that is now Perth had been occupied by groups of the Nyoongar tribe for thousands of years. They, and their ancestors, can be traced back some 40,000 years (verified by discoveries of stone implements near the Swan Bridge).

In December 1696, three ships in the fleet commanded by de Vlamingh – *Nijptangh, Geelvinck* and *Het Weseltje* – anchored off Rottnest Island. On 5 January 1697, a well-armed party landed near present-day Cottesloe Beach then marched eastwards to the Swan River near Freshwater Bay. They tried to contact some of the Nyoongar to enquire about the fate of survivors of the *Ridderschap van Hollant*, lost in 1694, but were unsuccessful. They sailed north, but not

before de Vlamingh had bestowed the name 'Swan' on the river.

Perth was founded in 1829 as the Swan River Settlement, but it grew very slowly until 1850, when convicts were brought in to alleviate the labour shortage. Many of Perth's fine buildings such as Government House and Perth Town Hall were built using convict labour. Even then, Perth's development lagged behind that of the eastern cities, until the discovery of gold in the 1890s increased the population four-fold in a decade and initiated a building boom. Many of these 19th century buildings have since disappeared amid a deluge of concrete and questionable architectural taste.

Western Australia's mineral wealth has undeniably contributed to Perth's growth, sparking farther construction in the outer suburbs. A somewhat squeaky-clean, nouveau-riche image has been tainted by scandals such as WA Inc but it all seems to add to the town's frontier image.

Orientation
The city centre is fairly compact, situated on a sweep of the Swan River. The river, which borders the city centre to the south and east, links Perth to its port, Fremantle. The main shopping precinct in the city is along the Hay St and Murray St malls and the arcades that run between them. St George's Terrace is the hub of the financial district.

The railway line bounds the city centre on the northern side. Immediately north of the railway line is Northbridge, a popular restaurant and entertainment enclave with a number of hostels and other cheap accommodation. The western end of Perth rises to the pleasant Kings Park, which overlooks the city and Swan River, and then farther on to cosmopolitan Subiaco. Farther to the west, suburbs extend as far as Scarborough and Cottesloe beaches on the Indian Ocean.

Maps The Royal Automobile Club of Western Australia (RACWA), 228 Adelaide Terrace, has an excellent travel section, and detailed regional maps can be obtained at its Road Travel counter. The Perth Map Centre (☎ 9322 5733), 891 Hay St, has a full range of maps including the excellent StreetSmart touring series.

Information
Tourist Offices The Western Australian Tourist Centre (WATC) (☎ 9483 1111) is in Albert Facey House in Forrest Place, on the corner of Wellington St and opposite the train station. The centre is open from 8.30 am to 5.30 pm Monday to Friday and 9 am to 1 pm Saturday. You can call them free from outside Perth (☎ (1800) 812 808).

It has a wide range of maps and brochures on Perth and WA, and an accommodation and tours reservation service. The Pinnacles Travel Centre, corner of Hay and Pier Sts, acts as the information centre on Saturday afternoon and on Sunday morning.

Guides to Perth including *Hello Perth & Fremantle*, *What's On in Perth & Fremantle*, *Your Guide to Perth & Fremantle*, *West Coast Visitor's Guide* and the *Tourist Maps: Perth to Fremantle* are free from the tourist centre, hostels and hotels. Perth's tourist radio is broadcast at 87.6 FM.

Money Currency exchange facilities at Perth airport and city banks are open from 9.30 am to 4 pm weekdays (and until 5 pm Friday). Foreign banks include BNP (☎ 9221 3011) and Chase Manhattan (☎ 9320 8440). Most large stores, fuel outlets and supermarkets accept credit cards (such as Bankcard, Visa, Amex, MasterCard and Diner's Club) and have EFTPOS.

Post & Communications Perth's GPO (☎ 9326 5211) is in Forrest Place which runs between Wellington St and the Murray St Mall. There are phones for international calls in GPO foyer. The GPO provides a post office service between 8 am and 6 pm Monday to Friday, 9 am to noon Saturday. You only have to telephone ☎ 13 1318 to be automatically connected to the post office nearest to where you are calling from. The STD telephone area code for the state is ☎08.

Bookshops Some good city bookshops include Angus & Robertson, 199 Murray St and 625 Hay St; Dymocks, Hay St Mall which have the biggest travel sections in the CBD, including a full range of LP. All Foreign Languages, 101 William St, specialises in travel, foreign language guides, phrasebooks and dictionaries and

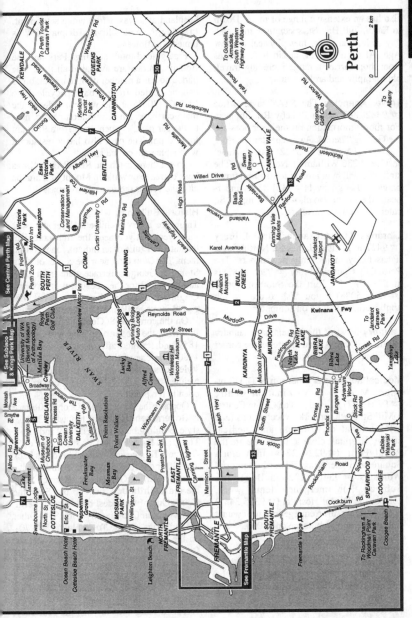

Perth

also has an extensive range of maps. Down to Earth, 790 Hay St, specialises in travel, gay & lesbian titles, metaphysical & New Age. Also on Hay St, at No 806, Boffins Bookshop carries a range including travel, photography and architecture.

Travel Agencies The STA Travel office (☎ 9382 3977) is in Rokeby Rd, Subiaco. For more information on their services see the Getting There & Away chapter.

The YHA (☎ 9227 5122) has its travel service at 236 William St, Northbridge. The staff here will hunt around for the best travel bargains. Let's Travel (☎ 9321 8330) underneath the Globe Hotel, 479 Wellington St, caters for budget travellers.

Libraries The Alexander State Library (☎ 9427 3111) is in James St, Northbridge; it has many major daily newspapers. The Perth City Council library (☎ 9265 3381) is at 573 Hay St. Join the Subiaco library (☎ 9381 5088) if you wish to prepare job applications and CVs on computer.

Laundry Most of the hostels have laundry facilities. There is a laundrette on the corner of William and Wellington Sts.

Medical Services & Emergency The Travellers Medical & Vaccination Centre (☎ 9321 1977), Level 5, The Capita Centre, 1 Mill St, Perth, provides vaccinations (and international certificates) and medical advice. Hospitals close to the centre are the Royal Perth (☎ 9224 2244) in Victoria Square and the King Edward Memorial Women's (☎ 9340 2222) in Bagot Rd, Subiaco. For emergency dental work, contact the Dental Hospital (☎ 9325 3452) in Goderich St. In an emergency only contact police, fire and ambulance on ☎ 000.

Kings Park
There are superb views across Perth and the river from this 4 sq km park, the lungs of the city centre. It includes a 17-hectare **Botanic Garden** with over 2000 different plant species from WA and a section of natural bushland as it was before white settlement. In spring, there's a cultivated display of WA's famed wildflowers.

Free guided tours of Kings Park and the Botanic Garden are available all year. The park also has a number of bike tracks; bikes can be rented from Koala Bicycle Hire (☎ 9321 3061) at the western side of the main car park. An information centre, next to the car park, is open daily from 9.30 am to 3.30 pm. The park also has a restaurant with a pleasant coffee shop.

To get there, catch the Red CAT to Kings Park entrance or walk up Mount St from the city, then cross the freeway overpass.

Historic Buildings
There are a few architectural remnants of yesteryear, but you need the archaeological tenacity and guile of an Indiana Jones to find them. The **Cloisters**, near the corner of King St and St George's Terrace, date from 1858 and are noted for their beautiful brickwork. Originally a school, they have been integrated into a modern office development.

On the corner of St George's Terrace and Pier St is the **Deanery,** which was built in 1859 and restored after a public appeal in 1980. It is one of the few existing cottage-style houses that survive from the period. Neither the Cloisters nor the Deanery are open to the public.

Opposite the Deanery on St George's Terrace is **Government House**, a fantastic Gothic-style, building built between 1859 and 1864. The grand **Palace Hotel**, on the corner of St George's Terrace and William St, dates back to 1895 and is now a banking chamber.

In the Stirling Gardens, off Barrack St, is the old **courthouse**, next to the Supreme Court. One of the oldest buildings in Perth, it was built in Georgian style in 1836. Other old buildings include **Town Hall** (1867-70), on the corner of Hay and Barrack Sts; the **Central Government Buildings** on the corner of Barrack St and St George's Terrace, which can be recognised by their patterned brick; the restored Edwardian **His Majesty's Theatre** (originally opened in 1904) on the corner of King and Hay Sts; the **Treasury,**

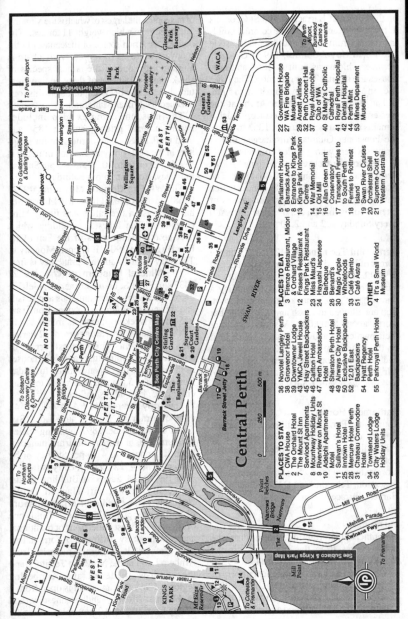

Central Perth

0   250   500 m

PLACES TO STAY
1   CWA House
2   The Orchard Hotel
7   The Mount St Inn
8   Serviced Apartments
9   Mountway Holiday Units
9   Riverview on Mount St
    Adelphi Apartments
    Motel
11 Sullivan's Hotel
25 Inntown Hotel
28 Mercure Hotel Perth
31 Chateau Commodore
    Hotel
34 Townsend Lodge
35 City Waters Lodge
    Holiday Units
36 Novotel Langley Perth
38 Grosvenor Hotel
39 Downtowner Lodge
43 YMCA Jewell House
45 Hay Street Backpackers
46 Carlton Hotel
47 Perth Ambassador
    Hotel
48 Sheraton Perth Hotel
49 Airways City Hotel
50 Exclusive Backpackers
52 12.01 East
    Backpackers
54 Hyatt Regency
    Perth Hotel
55 Parkroyal Perth Hotel

PLACES TO EAT
3   Firenze Restaurant, Midori
    & Orchard Village
12 Frasers Restaurant &
    Kings Park Restaurant
23 Miss Maud's
24 Hayashi Japanese
    Restaurant
26 Benardi's
30 Magic Apple
    Wholefoods
33 Café Cilento
51 Café Astra

OTHER
4   It's a Small World
    Museum
5   Parliament House
6   Barracks Arch
8   Entrance to Kings Park
13 Kings Park Information
    Centre
14 War Memorial
15 J Wood
16 Allan Green Plant
    Conservatory
17 Transperth Ferries to
    South Perth
18 Ferries to Rottnest
    Island
19 Swan River Cruises
20 Orchestral Shell
21 Supreme Court of
    Western Australia
22 Government House
27 WA Fire Brigade
    Museum
29 Ansett Airlines
32 Perth Concert Hall
37 Royal Automobile
    Club of WA
40 St Mary's Catholic
    Cathedral
41 Royal Perth Hospital
42 Dental Hospital
44 Perth Mint
53 Mines Department
    Museum

on the corner of Barrack St and St George's Terrace, an example of a fine colonial building dating from 1874; and the Gothic-style **Old Perth Boys' School**, 139 St George's Terrace, which was built in 1854 and now houses a National Trust gift shop. The latter is open Monday to Friday from 9 am to 5 pm.

The distinctive **Barracks Arch**, at the western end of St George's Terrace, is all that remains of a barracks built in 1863 to house the Pensioner Guards – discharged British Army soldiers who guarded convicts.

The **Pioneer Cemetery** in Bronte St, East Perth, was used from 1830 to 1899. The National Trust (☎ 9321 6088) conducts free one hour tours of the chapel and graves of interest (or is that places of grave interest?) every Sunday at 2 and 2.30 pm.

Perth Mint The mint (☎ 9421 7425), on the corner of Hill and Hay Sts, originally opened in 1899. It is now open for public tours. A variety of coins are on display including a numismatist's delight, a 1kg nugget coin. You are allowed to touch an 11.3kg gold bar worth about $200,000. Visitors can mint their own coins and watch gold pours, held on the hour from 10 am to 3 pm weekdays and 10 am to noon on weekends. Entry is $5 (children $3). It is open weekdays from 9 am to 4 pm, weekends from 9 am to 1 pm.

Parliament House
Tours of the Parliament buildings on Harvest Terrace can be arranged from Monday to Friday through the Parliamentary Information Officer (☎ 9222 7222) – you will get a more extensive tour when Parliament is not in session. Take the Red CAT and get off at Harvest Terrace.

Museums
On Francis St, Northbridge, north across the railway lines from the city centre, is the **Museum of Western Australia** (☎9328 4411), which includes an excellent gallery of Aboriginal culture, a marine gallery with a 25m blue whale skeleton, vintage cars, a gallery of dinosaur casts and a good collection of meteorites, the largest of which is the Mundrabilla specimen which weighs 11 tonnes. (The outback is a rich source of meteorites.) In the courtyard, set in its own preservative bath is **Megamouth**, one of the largest species of shark. Only about five of these benign creature have ever been captured – this one beached itself near Mandurah.

The museum complex also includes Perth's original **prison**, built in 1856 and used until 1888 – a favourite spot for hangings in the past. Entry to this fine museum is free; it is open from 10.30 am to 5 pm Sunday to Friday, from 1 to 5 pm Saturday.

The **WA Fire Brigade Museum** (☎9323 9468), on the corner of Irwin and Murray Sts, has displays on fire safety and fire-fighting equipment. The limestone building which became the headquarters of the Perth City Fire Brigade in 1901. It is open Monday to Thursday from 10 am to 3 pm; entry is free.

The **Mineral Museum of WA** (☎9222 3333), in Plain St on the corner of Adelaide Terrace, features rocks, minerals and fossils and spevcial exhibitions. It's open from 9 am to 5 pm on weekdays; entry is free.

It's a Small World Museum, at 12 Parliament Place, has the largest array of collectable toys, miniatures and dolls houses in the country. It is open Sunday to Friday from 10 am to 5 pm and Saturday 2 to 5 pm; entry is $5/4 for adults/children.

The **Army Museum of WA** (☎9380 2854), on the corner of Bulwer and Lord Sts, Northbridge, in the 1897 building called 'Dilhorn', has a display of army memorabilia. It is open 1 to 4.30 pm Sunday or by appointment (☎9227 9269); entry is free.

In the Social Sciences Building of the University of WA, off Hackett Drive, Nedlands, is the excellent **Berndt Museum of Anthropology** (☎9328 7233). This is one of Australia's finest collections of traditional and contemporary Australian Aboriginal art and artefacts. It combines material from Arnhem Land in the Northern Territory and the south-west, desert and Kimberley regions of WA. The museum is open from 2 to 4.30 pm Monday and Wednesday, and Friday from 10 am to 2 pm; entry is free.

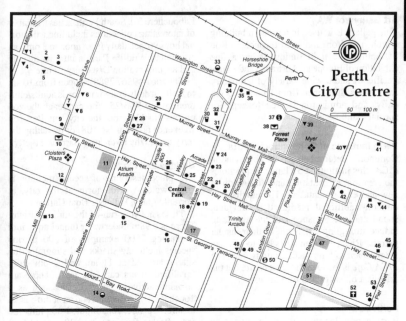

Perth City Centre

PLACES TO STAY
13   Parmelia Hilton
26   Perth Travelodge
     Hotel
29   Princes Hotel Perth
32   Wentworth Plaza
     Hotel
34   Royal Hotel
36   Globe Backpackers
41   Grand Central Hotel
43   Murray St Hostel
45   Sebel of Perth Hotel
46   Criterion Hotel

PLACES TO EAT
1   Fast Eddy's
2   Katong Singapore
     Restaurant & Taj
     Tandoor
4   Medici Café
5   Lenox Cafe & Bar
6   Frost Bites
7   Creations Café
8   Buzz Bar

24   Fast Food Strip
     (Pizza Hut,
     McDonald's,
     Hungry Jack's)
28   No 44 King St
30   Moon & Sixpence Bar
31   Bobby Dazzler's
39   McDonalds
40   Ann's Malaysian
     Restaurant
44   Japanese Sushi Bar
48   Venice Café

OTHER
3   Club 418
9   Perth Map Centre
10   Post Office
11   His Majesty's Theatre
12   The Cloisters
14   Perth City Bus Port
15   Old Perth Boys'
     School
16   Garuda
17   Palace Hotel

18   Qantas Airlines
19   Malaysia Airlines
20   Piccadilly Cinema
21   Ansett Australia
22   American Express
23   British Airways
25   Thomas Cook
27   Creative Native
     Gallery
33   Wellington St Bus
     Station
35   Let's Travel
37   WATC
38   General Post Office
42   Cinecentre
47   Town Hall
48   South African Airlines
50   National Australia Bank
51   Central Government
     Buildings
52   St George's Anglican
     Cathedral
53   Playhouse Theatre
54   The Deanery

Art Gallery of WA

This gallery is housed in a modern building which runs from James St through to Roe St, behind the train station. It has a fine exhibition of European, Australian and Asian/Pacific art and a wide variety of temporary exhibitions. It is open from 10 am to 5 pm daily, and admission is free (except for special exhibitions).

Perth Institute of Contemporary Arts

Commonly referred to by its abbreviation PICA, this institute at 51 James St promotes the creation, presentation and discussion of new and experimental art. The emphasis is on non-traditional media such as video, sound and performance and the aim is to induce struggling artists out of their insular garrets. PICA is open Tuesday to Sunday from 10 am to 5 pm; admission is free. The *PICA Cafe* is the local Internet centre but the price is a bit stiff at $6 for one hour.

Perth Zoo

Perth's popular zoo is set in attractive gardens across the river from the city at 20

Now endangered, the numbat is the state symbol.

Labouchere Rd, South Perth. It has a number of interesting collections including a nocturnal house (open daily from noon to 3 pm), an Australian Wildlife Park, a numbat display and a Conservation Discovery Centre.

The zoo (☎9367 7988) is open from 10 am to 5.30 pm daily and admission is adults/children/family $8/3/25. You can reach the zoo on bus No 110 from the city Bus Port (on weekends take bus No 108) or by taking the ferry across the river from Barrack St jetty.

Underwater World

One place deserving of special mention is Underwater World, north of the city, at Sorrento Quay, Hillary's Boat Harbour.

This is not your run-of-the-mill aquarium. There is a 98m underwater tunnel aquarium displaying 2500 examples of 200 marine species including sharks and stingrays; the sharks are fed at 11 am and 2 pm daily (qualified divers can take part). There are also interactive displays inside such as a Touch Pool, Microworld and an audio-visual theatre. Outside, rehabilitated dolphins are fed (after performing) at 10.30 am and 1.30 and 4 pm. In season they conduct three hour whalewatching trips to see humpbacks.

Underwater World (☎9447 7500) is open daily from 9 am to 5 pm and entry costs $15.50 ($7.50 for children, $39 for families). To get there take the Joondalup train to Warwick Interchange; transfer to bus No 423 and get off at Sorrento.

Parks & Gardens

On the Esplanade, between the city and the river, is the **Allan Green Plant Conservatory**. It has a tropical and semitropical environment display; entry is free.

Also close to the city, on the corner of St George's Terrace and Barrack St, are the **Supreme Court Gardens**, a popular place for city workers to have lunch. The **Queen's Gardens**, at the eastern end of Hay St, is a pleasant little park with lakes and bridges; get there on a Red CAT bus (weekdays only).

Lake Monger, Wembley, is a hang-out for local feathered friends, particularly the famous black swans.

Beaches

Perth residents claim that the city has the best beaches and surf of any Australian city.

There are calm beaches on the Swan River at Crawley, Peppermint Grove and Como.

The string of surf beaches on the Indian Ocean coast is the best place to head to, where there are patrols by the Surf Life Saving Club (SLSC). Perth's very popular nude beach is **Swanbourne** (bus No 205 or 207 from stand No 44, St George's Terrace).

Other surf beaches include **Port** near Fremantle; **Cottesloe**, a very safe swimming beach (bus Nos 70 to 73 from the city Bus Port and No 205 and 207 from stand 32, St George's Terrace); **Leighton** (bus No 103 from stand 34, St George's Terrace); the usually safe **City Beach** (bus Nos 81, 84 and 93 from Raine Square, Wellington St); the normally safe **Floreat**; popular **Scarborough**, known for its beachside cafe society, but which is great for experienced surfers and sailboarders (the Joondalup train to Glendalough station then bus Nos 400 and 929 to the beach); and **Trigg Island**, another surf beach that is dangerous when rough and which is prone to rips (bus No 250 from Wellington St).

To the north lies a string of good beaches. **Watermans Bay, North Beach, Hamersley** and **Mettams Pool** are small, safe bays suitable for families and inexperienced swimmers. **Burns** and **Mullaloo** are both safe family beaches and **Sorrento**, south of Hillary's Boat Harbour, is patrolled because the on-shore winds make the surf rough. To get to the northern beaches take bus No 929 (the Sunset Coaster) from either Whitfords or Glendalough stations on the Joondalup train line.

Markets

There are many lively markets around Perth – ideal if you're into browsing and buying. The **Subiaco Pavilion**, on the corner of Roberts and Rokeby Rds near Subiaco station, is open Thursday to Sunday. On weekends and public holiday Mondays there are also all-day street markets, comprising 130 or so stalls, near Subiaco station.

The **Wanneroo Markets**, north of Perth at Prindiville Drive, Wangara, have a large licensed food hall and a variety of stalls; it's open on weekends from 9 am to 6 pm. Take a train to Whitfords station, then bus No 469.

Other markets include the historic **Fremantle Markets** (see the Around Perth chapter); the weekend **Stock Rd Markets**, on the corner of Stock Rd and Spearwood Ave in Bibra Lake; **Gosnells Railway Markets**, on the corner of Albany Highway and Fremantle Rd, open Thursday to Sunday; the **Canning Vale Markets**, on the corner of Ranford and Bannister Rds, open from 7.30 am every Sunday with room for more than 1000 stalls; the **Midland Sunday Markets**, Crescent Car Park, Midland, open from 8 am to 4 pm; the **Mardi Gras Markets**, Bonnar Drive in Malaga, open Friday from noon to 8 pm, weekends from 9 am to 5.30 pm; and the **Depot Markets**, on the corner of Lord and Royal Sts, in the East Perth food halls, open Friday to Sunday from 10 am to 5.30 pm (the food hall is open until 8 pm).

Other Attractions

Across Narrows Bridge is one of Perth's landmarks: the **Old Mill**, built in 1835. It's open in the afternoon, except Tuesday and Friday; admission is free. To get here, take Transperth bus Nos 108 or 109 from St George's Terrace.

Between Hay St and St George's Terrace is the narrow, touristy **London Court**, a photographer's delight. Although it looks very Tudor English, it dates from just 1937. At one end of this shopping court, St George and the dragon do battle above the clock each quarter of an hour, while at the other end knights joust on horseback. Mega-kitsch, without any Shakespearian tragedy, but cute.

The **Scitech Discovery Centre** in the City West centre, on the corner of Sutherland St and Railway Parade, West Perth, has over 160 hands-on and large-scale exhibits and is well worth a visit. It is open daily but entry is not cheap – $10/7/25 for adults/children/family.

The finely restored Old Mill.

Perth Suburbs

Armadale The **Pioneer World** at Armadale, 29km south-east of the city, is a working model of a 19th century village; it's open daily from 10 am to 5 pm and admission is $4/2 for adults/children. You can get there on bus No 219 or a train from Perth station.

Tumbulgum Farm (☎ 9525 5888), 6km south of Armadale on the South Western Highway. It is open Wednesday to Sunday from 9.30 am to 5 pm; entry is $8/4.

On Mills Rd East, near Gosnells, try riding a miniature railway through the **Cohunu Koala Park**, while watching native animals in natural surroundings. There are also plenty of waterbirds and a large walk-in aviary. It is open daily from 10 am to 5.30 pm, the park's about a 35 minute drive from Perth; there's an admission fee.

Other Suburbs There's a potpourri of other options; ask at the tourist centre for opening times. In Subiaco, the **Museum of Childhood**, at 160 Hamersley Rd, houses an interesting collection of memorabilia; it is open daily, except Saturday. Across the Canning River towards Jandakot Airport, on Bull Creek Drive, is the excellent **Aviation Museum** with its large collection of aviation relics; it is open daily (entry $5/2).

Adventure World, 15km south of Perth at 179 Progress Drive, Bibra Lake, is a large amusement park; it's open daily, October to April, from 10 am to 5 pm.

If you wish to throw yourself headlong off a 40m tower then jump to **Bungee West** on Progress Drive, Bibra Lakes.

Swan River

There are many attractions up the Swan River, easily combined with a winery tour (see the Perth map). **Tranby House**, on Maylands Peninsula, is beautifully restored. Built in 1839, it's one of the oldest and finest colonial houses in WA. It's open from 2 to 5 pm daily and 11 am to 1 pm also on Sundays; entry is $2.50/1.50 for adults/kids.

The **Rail Transport Museum** on Railway Parade, Bassendean, has locomotives and all sorts of railway memorabilia; it is open from 1 to 5 pm on Sunday; entry is $4/1.

Guildford has a number of historic buildings, including **Mechanics Hall**, in Meadow St, and the **Folk Museum & Gaol** which is open Sunday from 2 to 5 pm (March to December). **Woodbridge** in Third Ave, was built in 1855 and is a fully restored and beautifully furnished colonial mansion overlooking the river. It's open daily (closed Wednesday); there's a $2/1.20 entry fee.

In Arthur St, West Swan, is **Caversham Wildlife Park & Zoo**, which has a large collection of Australian animals and birds. It's open 10 am to 5 pm daily; entry is $5/2.

Also in West Swan, on Lord St, is the 26 sq km **Whiteman Park** (☎ 9249 2446), Perth's biggest reserve. There are picnic and barbecue facilities at Mussell Pool, the Trade Village with craft shops and displays, over 30km of walkways and bike paths and vintage steam train ($4/2 for adults/children) and tram ($2/1) rides; entry is $5 per car.

Swan Valley Vineyards

Vineyards are dotted along the river from Guildford to the Upper Swan and are open for tastings and sales.

Olive Farm Wines, 77 Great Eastern Highway, South Guildford, is the oldest in the region, established at the same time Perth was settled in 1829. Houghton Wines, on Dale Rd, Middle Swan, was established later but produced the first commercial vintage in 1859. Its white burgundy is the biggest selling bottled white in Australia.

Lamont Winery, on Bisdee Rd in Millendon, produces traditional, full flavoured wines which you can enjoy with an alfresco lunch (the author's favourite).

Other wineries in the Swan are Jane Brook Estate, Toodyay Rd, Middle Swan; Sandalford, West Swan Rd, Upper Caversham; Henley Park, on the corner of West Swan Rd and Swan St, Henley; Evans & Tate, Swan Rd, Henley Brook; and the Westfield, Mann, Twin Hill Wines, at the junction of Gnangara Rd and Great Northern Highway.

Golf

There are several world-class public golf courses in and around Perth, taking advantage of the availability of space to good effect. Good courses include the 36-hole City of Perth Golf Complex (☎ 9484 2500) in Floreat; Lake Claremont Public Golf Course (☎ 9384 2887); the 18-hole Hamersley Public Golf Course (☎ 9447 7137), in Karrinyup; the Fremantle Municipal Golf Course (☎ 9430 2316); and the Burswood Park Golf Course (☎ 9362 7576).

Some up-market courses are the Vines Resort (☎ 9297 0222) in the Swan Valley, a 30 minute drive from Perth; and the Joondalup Country Club (☎ 9400 8811), about 30 minutes north of Perth.

Watersports

Perth thrives on aquatic sports. At **Cables Waterski Park**, at Troode St in Spearwood (just off Rockingham Rd, south of Perth), cables haul waterskiers along at 20 to 50 km/h. It is open daily; an hour's waterskiing costs $12.

Windsurfing is very popular both on the Swan and on the Sunset Coast beaches; you can hire boards from Pelican Point Windsurfing (☎ (018) 915 136) on Hackett Drive at Crawley. **Yachting**, for those who prefer bigger craft, is also popular. This can range from funcats on the Swan in South Perth or yachting on the Indian Ocean. Funcat Hire (☎ (018) 926 003) in Coode St, South Perth can provide the former; and Viking Sailing School (☎ (019) 402 782), 64 Dampier Ave, Mullaloo, the latter.

Surfing and **diving** are other water pursuits – the Sunset Coast and Rottnest Island are good spots. For diving info contact the Perth Diving Academy (☎ 9430 6300), Malibu Diving Centre (☎ 9527 9211), Dolphin Scuba Diving (☎ 9353 2488) or Diving Ventures (☎ 9421 1052).

Rivergods (☎ 9324 2662), 862 Hay St, organises **whitewater rafting** in both summer (Collie River) and winter (Avon River), **sea kayaking** to Seal and Penguin islands, and **Canadian canoeing** on the Blackwood River; prices for trips depends on duration and the type of equipment used.

Whale Watching

Numerous activities bring you into contact with whales and other marine mammals near Perth.

Whalewatching is possible out of Perth as there are a number of tour operators. The trip with Mills Charters (☎ 9401 0833), which runs its tours in conjunction with Underwater World (in their boats *Blue Water* and *Blue Horizon*) is very informative. The search is for the humpback whale, returning to Antarctic waters after wintering in the waters of north-west Australia. The trip leaves from Hillary's Boat Harbour and costs $25 and $20 for weekends and weekdays respectively (children $20 and $15). Other operators are Oceanic Cruises (☎ 9430 5127) in Freo, and Boat Torque (☎ 9246 1039) at Hillary's.

Organised Tours

The WATC has detailed information about the tours around Perth; it can also book them.

Land-Based Tours Half-day city tours of Perth and Fremantle are about $30, and for around $55 you can get tours to the Swan Valley wineries, Cohunu Koala Park, or Underwater World and the beaches north of Perth.

A favourite is the free tour of the **Swan Brewery** (☎ 9350 0650), 25 Baile Rd, Canning Vale. The tour takes 1½ hours (followed by a couple of beers) and departs at 10 am from Monday to Thursday and 2.30 pm on Monday to Wednesday. Remember to make reservations.

Other day tours, to places like Avon Valley, Mandurah, New Norcia or the south coast, range from $55 to $75. Some of the larger tour operators include Feature Tours (☎ 9221 5411), Pinnacle Tours & Travel Centre (☎ 9417 5555) and Great Western Tours (☎ 9490 2455).

There are daily trips to the Pinnacles with Safari Treks (☎ 9271 1271) for $80; it also has trips to Wave Rock on Monday, Wednesday and Saturday ($70). Travelabout Outback Tours (☎ 9244 1200) also has one day tours to the Pinnacles. The Redback Safaris (☎ 9371 1183) trips to the Pinnacles and Margaret River are recommended by many hostel owners and backpackers (both trips are $70).

Coach Bush Eco Tours (☎ 9336 3050) have been recommended by readers. Their one day Metro Tours are an excellent introduction to outdoor Perth and take in national parks and lakes ($96). On Saturday it has a superb trip to the Dryandra Woodlands ($105), on Monday the three day Southern Heartlands including Dwellingup Forest ($299, accommodation and meals included) and periodic four day trips to the Houtman Abrolhos Islands and Kalbarri ($475).

A good alternative for backpackers is Western Travel Bug's (☎ 9561 5236) five day south-west tour from Perth to Margaret River, Pemberton, Walpole, Albany and back to Perth for $365. S-Cape (☎ (1800) 633 352) has a tour which incorporates the Stirlings and Wave Rock ($329); it includes canoeing on the Blackwood River, caving near Margaret River and horse-riding. The tour lasts five days in summer, four in winter (from May to September).

Australian Harley Holidays (☎ 9361 3718) has hog-wild bikie tours from $350 per day ($80 per hour).

Cruises There are also a number of cruise companies that operate tours from the Barrack St jetty, including Captain Cook Cruises (☎ 9325 3341) and Boat Torque (☎ 9221 5844). Tours include scenic cruises of the Swan River, winery visits, trips to Fremantle and lunch and dinner cruises. Boat Torque also has a full-day Swan River cruise for $65 (children $45); and Captain Cook Cruises has a three hour Scenic River Cruise around Perth and Fremantle for $24/12 (luncheon cruises are $37/25).

From September to May, the Transperth MV *Countess II* departs daily except Saturday at 2 pm from the Barrack St jetty. It's a three hour cruise towards the Upper Swan River; the cost is about $15.

Special Events

Every year for several weeks around February/March the Festival of Perth offers entertainment in the form of music, drama, dance and films. In early June, West Week is held to celebrate WA's foundation – there are historical recreations, arts & crafts events, concerts and sporting events.

The Royal Perth Show takes place every September. The Artrage Festival is in October and the Northbridge Festival is hosted at the same time as the Festival of Perth.

Places to Stay

Perth has accommodation for all tastes and pockets. There are numerous caravan parks scattered around the metropolitan area. The main area for budget beds is Northbridge, while hotels, motels and holiday flats of all standards are spread throughout Perth.

Camping, Caravans & Cabins Perth, like many other large cities, is not well endowed with campsites convenient to the city centre. There are, however, many caravan parks in the suburbs (distances are from the city):

Armadale Tourist Village (27km south-east)
South-West Highway, Armadale; powered sites $12, holiday units for two $38 (☎ 9399 6376).

Forrestfield Caravan Park (18km east)
351 Hawtin Rd, Forrestfield; tent sites $12, cabins for two $40 (☎ 9453 6378).

Gosnells Caravan Village (21km south-east)
2462 Albany Highway, Gosnells; tent/powered sites $12/16, on-site vans $30, park cabins for two $40 (☎ 9398 2746).

Karrinyup Waters Resort (14km north)
467 North Beach Rd, Gwelup; tent/powered sites $15/17, on-site vans from $29, park cabins for two from $55 (☎ 9447 6665).

Kenlorn Tourist Park (9km south-east)
229 Welshpool Rd, Queens Park; tent sites $12 (weekly rates available), on-site vans $20, park cabins for two $30 (☎ 9356 2380).

Midland Caravan Park (19km east)
2 Toodyay Rd, Midland; powered sites $13, cabins from $30, chalets for two from $45 (☎ 9274 3002).

Perth Central Caravan Park (8km east)
34 Central Ave, Redcliffe; tent/powered sites $14/18, on-site vans for two $35 (☎ 9277 1704).

Perth Tourist Caravan Park (18km east)
Hale Rd, Forrestfield; tent sites $13, cabins $55 (☎ 9453 6677).

Starhaven Caravan Park (14km north-west)
18 Pearl Parade, Scarborough; tent sites $15, on-site vans $28, holiday units for two $50 (☎ 9341 1770).

Swan Valley Tourist Village (19km north-east)
6581 West Swan Rd, Guildford; tent/powered sites $13/14, on-site vans from $28, holiday units for two $45 (☎ 9274 2828).

Wanneroo Caravan Park (25km north)
Jacaranda Drive, Wanneroo; powered sites for two $13, on-site vans from $70 per week (☎ 9405 1176).

Hostels There are many hostels and backpackers' in Perth – probably more than the city can support. As a result, competition is fierce. Some are good, others need lots of improvement. Most provide pick-ups from the airport or bus terminals.

Northbridge *Rory's Backpackers* (☎ 9328 9958), also listed as *Backpackers Perth Inn*, at 194 Brisbane St, is in two clean (and joined) renovated colonial houses with pleasant gardens and a barbecue area. Rory, who has been in the industry a long time, has a range of rooms and revamped facilities.

Dorm beds are $14, twins, doubles and triples about $34.

Also good, with two capable owners, is *Paul & Scotty's Ozi Inn* (☎ 9328 1222) at 282 Newcastle St. The large renovated house has all necessary facilities and friendly staff. Dorms are $14, twins and doubles with TV and air-con are $34. Paul & Scotty's run a good budget travel centre at 499 Wellington St, the Traveller's Club (☎9226 0660). Nearby, there is an overflow place, the *Workhouse* for longer-term (perhaps noisier) patrons ($11 per night) working in the city.

At 253 William St is the large, central and much-improved *Britannia YHA* (☎ 9328 6121). The better single-only rooms are at the back on the verandah, rooms near the hallways can be noisy; dorm beds are from $14. Around the corner at 42-46 Francis St is the *Northbridge YHA* (☎ 9328 7794), popular with travellers who warm to the friendly staff. This ageing, but renovated former guesthouse has all the facilities; again dorm beds are from $14.

The *Shiralee* (☎ 9227 7448), 107 Brisbane St, has pleasant recreation areas and all facilities are clean and shipshape; dorms are $14, air-con twins and doubles are $34. A little farther east, at 133 Summers St, East Perth, is the pleasant *Rainbow Lodge* (☎ 9227 1818), a large rambling place with a number of recreation areas (and free breakfast); dorms are $12 ($75 per week), twins and doubles are $28.

Redbackpackers (☎ 9227 9969), at 496 Newcastle St, has been much improved (and it needed it). Dorms are $14, twins are $32 and doubles $34. The small *Backpack City & Surf* (☎ 9227 1234), tucked away next to the Buddhist Centre at 41 Money St, is an unusual place with a large central corridor where travellers get together with their rooms in sight; it is well run and worth the $13 for dorm beds, and $32 for twins and doubles. It arranges trips to the beach where they have a 'sister/brother' hostel.

Another good alternative is the *North Lodge* (☎ 9227 7588) at 225 Beaufort St; it's clean, friendly and has all the usual facilities and comfortable dorm/twin bedrooms. Also

PERTH

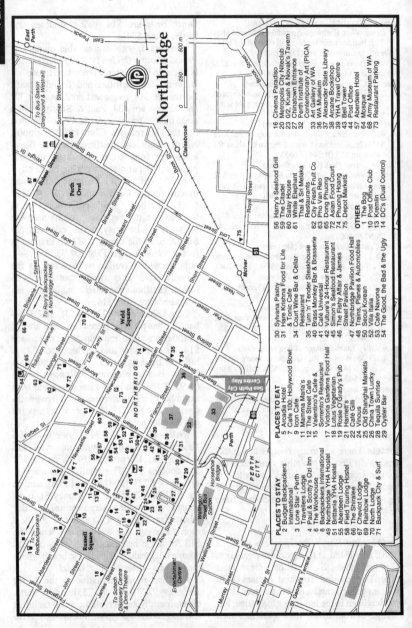

Northbridge

0   250   500 m

PLACES TO STAY
2 Budget Backpackers
   International
3 Lone Star - Perth
   Travellers Club
4 Paul & Scotty's Ozi Inn
6 The Workhouse
8 Backpackers International
49 Northbridge YHA Hostel
51 Britannia YHA Hostel
55 Aberdeen Lodge
58 Field Touring Hostel
66 The Shiralee
67 Cheviot Lodge
69 Rainbow Lodge
70 North Lodge
71 Backpack City & Surf

PLACES TO EAT
5 Arcadia Hotel
7 Cafe 100: Hollywood Bowl
9 Icon Cafe
11 Mamma Maria's
12 The Street Cafe
15 Valentino's Cafe &
   Sorrento's Restaurant
17 Victoria Gardens Food Hall
18 Lotus Vegetarian
19 Rosie O'Grady's Pub
21 Harriett's
22 Café Gilli
24 Vinous
25 Old Shanghai Markets
26 China Town Lucky
28 Tequila Sunrise
29 Oyster Bar
30 Sylvana Pastry
31 Hare Krishna Food for Life
34 Court Wine Bar & Cellar
   & Tonic Cafe
35 Turn 'n' Tender Steakhouse
40 Brass Monkey Bar & Brasserie
41 Café Universal
42 Vulture's 24-Hour Restaurant
45 Simon's Seafood Restaurant
46 The Fishy Affair & James
   Street Pavilion
47 Northbridge Pavilion Food Hall
48 Trains, Planes & Automobiles
50 Seoul Korean
52 Villa Italia
53 Cafe Navona
54 The Good, the Bad & the Ugly
56 Harry's Seafood Grill
59 The Citadel
60 Satay House
61 White Elephant
   Thai & Sri Melaka
   Restaurants
62 City Fresh Fruit Co
63 Pho Rico
72 Asian Food Court
74 Phuong Hoang
75 Depot Markets

OTHER
1 The Bog
10 Post Office Club
13 Kremlin
14 DC's (Dual Control)
16 Cinema Paradiso
20 Metropolis City Niteclub
23 0/2, Krush & Novak's Tavern
27 Chinatown Entrance
32 Perth Institute of
   Contemporary Art (PICA)
33 Art Gallery of WA
36 WA Museum
37 Alexander State Library
38 Arcane Bookshop
39 YHA Travel Centre
43 Bell Tower
44 Post Office
57 Aberdeen Hotel
64 Mosque
68 Army Museum of WA
73 Restaurant Parking

in Northbridge is *Cheviot Lodge* (☎ 9227 6817) at 30 Bulwer St; it's open 24 hours, is close to the interstate rail terminal and there are no bunk beds.

If these places don't satisfy your every whim, try: the *Budget Backpackers' International* (☎ 9328 9468), at 342 Newcastle St, with comfortable lounge and good kitchen facilities (dorms from $14 per night); the *Lone Star – Perth Travellers Lodge* (☎ 9328 6667), confusingly with several other names, at 156-158 Aberdeen St, made up of two recently renovated houses (dorms are $13, twins $30); *Field Touring Hostel* (☎ 9328 4692), 74 Aberdeen St (dorms $13, twins $26), organises overseas expeditions; and *Backpackers International* (☎ 9227 9977), on the corner of Lake and Aberdeen Sts (dorms from $12, twins $28, doubles $35).

Away from the budget strip is *Beatty Lodge* (☎ 9227 1521), at 235 Vincent St where dorms are $12, singles $24, twins $38 and doubles $40. Currently, it is student 'digs' near a large foreign language school. Hot of the press, *Witch's Hat* (☎ 9228 4228) at 148 Palmerston St, Northbridge, is named for its Edwardian turret (a dorm bed is $16, twins and doubles are $40).

Inner City The *Hay Street Backpackers*, 266-268 Hay St, East Perth, is good value with good facilities, a pool, dorms for $15, and doubles $36 (with en-suite $42), but like all hostels in the city area, is separated from the action of Northbridge and Leederville. After 6 pm the centre closes down to become as quiet as a morgue!

Not far away, *12.01 East* (☎ 9221 1666), in a converted office building at 195 Hay St, has dorms from $13, twins from $30 and doubles from $36; the rooms are clean and air-con and some have fridges in the rooms. Underneath is a 'chill out' area where you can play pool etc – much needed in this dead part of the city. Just around the corner at 158 Adelaide Terrace is *Exclusive Backpackers* (☎ 9325 2852) in a beautifully restored building adjoining a trendy restaurant. It lacked 'backpackers' when we visited but any who visit will get a little bit of luxury for

their money – it costs about $15 for a dorm, $40 for a twin or double.

Closer to the city centre is the *Townsend Lodge* (☎ 9325 4143) at 240 Adelaide Terrace; with dinner (Monday to Friday) included for $18 per person in lockable single rooms. If you stay one week you get a free night. The *Murray Street Hostel* (☎ 9325 7627), 119 Murray St (dorms from $13), and *Globe Backpackers* (☎ 9321 4080), 479 Wellington St (dorms from $12), are both in an area that is busy during the day and, fortunately, within walking distance of Northbridge.

Scarborough This area is a good alternative to Northbridge, being close to the surf. *Mandarin Gardens* (☎ 9341 5431), at 20-28 Wheatcroft St, has dorm rooms for $14. This hostel is 500m walk to popular Scarborough Beach, has a pool and sizeable recreational areas. It also has flats from $40 to $85 per night.

Backpack City & Surf (☎ 9245 1161), at 119 Scarborough Beach Rd, needs a bit of work to make it comfortable; the plus is that the first night in a dorm is only $7 ($11 each night after); they transfer you from their city location in Money St, Northbridge.

The compact *Western Beach Lodge* (☎ 9245 1624), 6 Westborough St, is clean and airy; rates are $12 in dorms, $30 in doubles (with en-suite $34). Also in Scarborough, *Indigo Lodge* (☎ 9341 6655), on the West Coast Highway, has dorms for $13, singles for $22, and twin and double rooms for $36. To get there, take bus No 400 from the Perth city Bus Port. The *Swanbourne Lodge* (☎ 9341 6655), behind the hotel at 141 Claremont Crescent, was still being renovated when we visited. It needed considerable work (and ejection of its permanent dwellers) if it is to be a successful travellers' place.

Y's & Guesthouses The *YMCA Jewell House* (☎ 9325 8488), at 180 Goderich St (the continuation of Murray St after Victoria Square), has over 200 comfortable, clean and modern rooms; singles/doubles are $30/38 and weekly rates are six times the daily rate. It is open 24 hours and has off-street parking.

The *Grand Central Hotel* (☎ 9221 2682), once a 'Y' at 379 Wellington St, was closed for renovations when we visited. No one is sure what style the accommodation will take in future – rumours are that it will be pricey.

Central, good value and recommended by readers is the *Downtowner Lodge* (☎ 9325 6973), at 63 Hill St, opposite the Perth Mint. The rooms are clean and pleasant, and it's a very tranquil, friendly, nonsmoking place; twin rooms are $36 and there are weekly rates.

The *Country Women's Association (CWA) House* (☎ 9321 6081) is at 1174 Hay St, West Perth (the entrance is at the rear). The rooms are very comfortable and some have good city views at $35/60 for singles/doubles (some have en-suites). Family suites have connecting rooms for the kids; a light breakfast is included.

Out at Swanbourne, the 'gay friendly' *Swanbourne Guesthouse* (☎ 9383 1981), 5 Myera St, has excellent self-contained rooms from $55/65; breakfast is included.

Motels & Holiday Flats Perth and the surrounding suburbs have an abundance of motels and holiday flats (see the *Western Australia Accommodation & Tours Listing* available from the tourist office for more information). A selection follows.

City Waters Lodge Holiday Units (☎ 9325 1566), at 118 Terrace Rd, by the river, is central and good value with cooking facilities, bathroom, TV and laundry; it is $72/77 for singles/doubles.

North of the city centre at 166 Palmerston St are the self-contained *Brownelea Holiday Units* (☎ 9227 1710) from $55 a double. The *Adelphi Apartments Motel* (☎ 9322 4666), at 130a Mounts Bay Rd, has well-equipped units for $58/68.

The *Mount St Inn Serviced Apartments* (☎ 9481 0866), 24 Mount St, West Perth, is between the city and Kings Park and has magnificent views over the city and river; rooms are from $116 for two. Nearby, across the overpass, are the *Mountway Holiday Units* (☎ 9321 8307), at No 36; singles/ doubles are from $39/45. In the same vicinity

is the *Riverview on Mount Street* (☎ 9321 8963), at No 42; rooms are from $55/60.

The *Murray Lodge Motel* (☎ 9321 7441), 718 Murray St, West Perth, next to Shenton Park, is an economic place with singles/ doubles for $54/62. *Kings Park Motel* (☎ 9381 3488), 225 Thomas St, Subiaco, has rooms (some self-contained) from $85/90.

Across the bridge, on the South Perth side in Applecross, the *Canning Bridge Auto Lodge* (☎ 9364 2511), at 891 Canning Rd, has rooms from $50 for two. Along the Swan River are the *Swanview Motor Inn* (☎ 9367 5755), 1 Preston St, in Como, with rooms for $74/79; the *Metro Inn* (☎ 9367 6122), 61 Canning Highway, from $98 for two; and the *Regency Motel* (☎ 9362 3000), 61-69 Great Eastern Highway, Rivervale, from $38/45.

Hotels There are a number of old-fashioned hotels around the city centre. The *Criterion Hotel* (☎ 9325 5155), a refurbished Art Deco building at 560 Hay St, has friendly staff and clean renovated singles/doubles for $95/115, breakfast included. The *Royal Hotel* (☎ 9324 1510), corner of Wellington and William Sts, has rooms from $30/45, and 'executive' rooms from $75. The *Court Hotel* (☎ 9328 5292), 50 Beaufort St, is a 'gay friendly' place with B&B from $30/60.

Sullivan's Hotel (☎ 9321 8022), at 166 Mounts Bay Rd (about 2km from the centre and next to Kings Park), is a very popular family-run place with comfortable rooms for $90. It has a pool, restaurant and off-street parking and is on the CAT route.

If you are chasing something up-market, you won't be disappointed with what's available in the city centre:

Airways City Hotel
195 Adelaide Terrace, doubles from $80 (☎ 9323 7799)
Burswood Resort Hotel
Great Eastern Highway, doubles from $290 (☎ 9362 7777).
Chateau Commodore Hotel
417 Hay St, doubles from $110 (☎ 325 0461).
Hyatt Regency Perth Hotel
99 Adelaide Terrace, doubles from $245 (☎ 9225 1234).

Inntown Hotel
corner of Pier and Murray Sts, singles/doubles $59/69 (☎ 9325 2133).

Mercure Hotel Perth
10 Irwin St, doubles from $173 (☎ 9325 0481).

Novotel Langley Perth
corner of Adelaide Terrace and Hill St, doubles from $183 (☎ 9221 1200).

Orchard Hotel
corner of Wellington and Milligan Sts, doubles from $140 to $220 (☎ 9327 7000).

Parkroyal Perth Hotel
54 Terrace Rd, doubles from $145 (☎ 9325 3811).

Parmelia Hilton
Mill St, doubles from $255 (☎ 9322 3622).

Perth Ambassador Hotel
196 Adelaide Terrace, doubles from $100 (☎ 9325 1455).

Perth Travelodge Hotel
778 Hay St, doubles from $115 to $200 (☎ 9321 9141).

Princes Hotel Perth
334 Murray St, doubles from $144 (☎ 9322 2844).

Sebel of Perth Hotel
37 Pier St, doubles from $200 (☎ 9325 7655).

Sheraton Perth Hotel
207 Adelaide Terrace, doubles from $240 (☎ 9325 0501).

Wentworth Plaza Hotel
300 Murray St, doubles from $55 to $95 (☎ 9481 1000).

The *Cottesloe Beach Hotel* (☎ 9383 1100) is a renovated Art Deco place right on Cottesloe Beach on the corner of John St and Marine Parade. It has spacious rooms with fridge, TV and tea & coffee-making facilities, from $55/75.

The *Radisson Observation City Resort Hotel* (☎ 9245 1000), The Esplanade, Scarborough, with more than 300 rooms is an incongruity on the not-so-heavily-developed Sunset Coast beach strip. Its size is matched by its prices; doubles are from $170 to $249 and suites from $320 to $1600!

Places to Eat

Perth is a great place to dine out, with bounteous local produce, wines and beers. All tastes and budgets are easily satisfied.

City Centre The city centre is a particularly good place for lunches and light meals. If, for you, this includes fast food then you will be well satisfied on the east side of William St between Murray and Hay Sts.

The *Down Under Food Hall* downstairs in the Hay St Mall, near the corner of William St, has Chinese, Mexican, Thai, Indian and many other types of food. It is open Monday to Wednesday from 8 am to 7 pm, Thursday to Saturday from 8 am to 9 pm.

The *Carillon Arcade Food Hall*, in the Carillon Arcade on Hay St Mall, is slightly more up-market than the Down Under Food Hall and has the same international flavour with Italian, Middle Eastern and Chinese food from $6 to $8. It also has sandwich shops, a seafood stall and fast-food outlets. It is open until 9 pm every evening, although some of the food stalls close around 7 pm.

On James St, at the back of Chinatown are the *Old Shanghai Markets*; the *Victoria Gardens* is on the corner of Aberdeen St, overlooking Russell Square; and there is a much smaller *Asian Food Court* on the corner of William and Little Parry Sts.

Magic Apple Wholefoods, at the other end of the spectrum at 445 Hay St, does delicious pitta bread sandwiches, cakes and fresh juices. The busy *Benardi's*, at 528 Hay St, has good sandwiches, quiches, home-made soups and salads.

Ann's Malaysian, at the northern end of Barrack St is a good place for a quick economical lunch or takeaway. At 117 Murray St, between Pier and Barrack Sts, is a small, pleasant and reasonably priced Japanese *sushi bar*, well worth a visit if you like raw fish. The *Hayashi Japanese Barbecue*, at 107 Pier St, has excellent-value set lunches for around $11 and dinner for two is about $30. *Bobby Dazzler's*, at the Wentworth Plaza, prides itself on its Australian menu and is a good place for a bite and a drink.

The *Venice Cafe*, at the St George's Terrace end of the Trinity Arcade (shop No 201), is a pleasant European-style cafe with tables out the front and light meals such as lasagne, quiche, home-made pies and salad from $5 to $6.50. Local tour gurus recommend *No 44 King Street*, in King St, for small serves of fashionable but expensive food. Just around the corner at 300 Murray St is the *Moon & Sixpence Bar*, popular with the lunchtime office crowd (and backpackers), who feast on pasta from $5.

Farther east of the malls, there are good lunchtime places, probably wall to wall with shoulder pads and suits at weekday lunchtimes: the *Stamina Indonesian* in the Chateau Commodore, Hay St, has starters from $3 and mains from $7.50); and on Adelaide Terrace, both the *Cafe Astra*, at No 156, and *Cafe Cilento*, at No 254, have good food, and considering the usual clientele, are reasonably priced.

Towards the western (Kings Park) end of the city centre, there's a string of places, including a cluster of restaurants near the corner of Wellington and Milligan Sts. These include *Firenze* which has $11 lunchtime pasta specials; the licensed *Midori* serving Japanese and Korean; the deservedly popular *Fast Eddy's*, on the corner of Murray and Milligan Sts (with great breakfasts and burgers); and the cheap, highly recommended *Katong Singapore* at 446 Murray St, for those tantalising nyonya delights (and let's not forget the reasonable Indian *Taj Tandoor* just beside it).

Across the road are the brassy, distinctly up-market *Lenox Bar & Cafe*, at 437 Murray St, and next door the equally glittering *Medici Café*.

Shafto Lane, between Murray and Hay Sts, has a number of eateries including the oh so chic *Buzz Bar* for up-market lunches; the trendy *Frost Bites* (formerly the Iguana) on the Murray St corner, which is open from 11 am until late, Monday to Saturday; and *Creations*, a stylish outdoor cafe with a good lunch menu.

For a splurge, *Kings Park* and *Frasers* restaurants, atop Mt Eliza in Kings Park, both have great city and river views.

Northbridge North of the city centre, the area bounded by William, Lake and Newcastle Sts, is full of ethnic restaurants to suit all tastes and budgets. William St (and the streets which run perpendicular to and west of it) is the hub – this area rivals Melbourne's Lygon and Brunswick Sts for variety and certainly for value.

The best bet is to walk around and take in the sights and smells – you will soon find something to your liking at an appropriate price. Although the following restaurants represent only about half your choice in this area, it is still prudent to book tables on weekends. Self-caterers will find *Cheapaway*, on the corner of Roe and Fitzgerald Sts, good value.

Starting west of the train station is Roe St with its entrance to Chinatown. On the way you will pass the award-winning *Oyster Bar*, which serves those beloved crustacea and other seafood (a three-course lunch is $17.50); and *Tequila Sunrise*, a Mexican place that is open seven nights. Two ferocious guardians indicate the entrance to Chinatown, and tucked away on its own here is *China Town Lucky*, an intimate little place next to the entrance to a rambling food hall (with its main entrance on James St) – these exude aromatic, pungent smells reminiscent of Singapore, Bangkok and Guangzhou.

There is a real cornucopia of ethnic tastes on William St. Heading north, near the Roe St corner you'll find a couple of Asian res-

---

Seafood

Perth is famous for its seafood restaurants, many of which let you select your meal direct from glass tanks. Reputable places in Northbridge are *Simon's*, 73 Francis St (with $19.50 lunch specials), *Harry's Seafood Grill*, 94 Aberdeen St (around $20 for lunch, $27 for dinner), *Fishy Affair*, 132 James St, and the deservedly famous *Oyster Bar* at 20 Roe St.

In the Hyatt Centre on Adelaide Terrace is *Jessica's*, a renowned seafood place with set price menus for lunch and dinner – expensive but a dining experience. The *Surf Club Fish Cafe*, on Port Beach, North Fremantle, is recommended for the food, the view and its facilities for kids. ∎

taurants; the moderately priced and popular *Romany*, one of the city's long-running Italian eateries; *Sylvana Pastry*, a comfortable Lebanese coffee bar with an amazing selection of those sticky Middle Eastern pastries; the hip *Tonic Cafe*; and the vegetarian *Hare Krishna Food for Life*, at No 200. The latter has cheap ($4, $3 with a concession) meals, and $2 meals on Tuesday and Friday between 5 and 6 pm.

On the left-hand side – for the next five blocks of William St heading north – are the *Brass Monkey Bar & Brasserie* with a great selection of beers and good-sized counter meals (lunches are about $7.50); the trendy *Café Universal* which is more of a cappuccino haunt; *Vulture's* 24 hour restaurant; the *Seoul Korean* with excellent lunches for about $7, dinners for about $15; the busy *Villa Italia*, which serves fine coffee and light meals including good pasta; the trendy *Citadel* for coffee and lunches (including barbecue on Sunday); a string of Asian restaurants, including *Sri Melaka* (with nyonya choices and a full banquet for $17), at No 313; the *White Elephant Thai* at No 323; and the *Satay House* on the corner of Newcastle St.

Beyond Forbes St, is the *City Fresh Food Co*, the place for self-caterers to buy healthy fruit and vegetables; and the Vietnamese *Pho Van Reo* which serves tasty pho for $5.50 a bowl. The reliable *Dong Phuong*, at 434a William St, is open every night (except Tuesday).

On the corner of James and Lake Sts is a large collection of places, most Italian, giving this sector of Northbridge a 'little Italy' feel. Not far from the junction you will find *Fishy Affair* (see Seafood earlier); the Italian contingent *(Valentino's Café, Sorrento's Restaurant* and *Café Gilli)*; *Harriett's*, a stylish brasserie; *Novak's Tavern*, open daily; and *Vinous* open daily from 10 am until late. At the latter they have a superb Aussie burger ($18), unlike any you've probably tasted – all Australia's food icons are represented, from vegemite damper to kangaroo meat.

The large *Northbridge Pavilion Food Hall*, on the corner of Lake and James Sts, is

also good-value with Japanese, Italian, Indian, Thai, vegetarian and Chinese food. It's open from Wednesday to Sunday and has some outdoor seating and a couple of bars; the juices at *Naturals* are truly refreshing.

Between James and Francis Sts, on Lake St, there are a number of sidewalk cafes including the *Street Cafe* – as well as landmarks like the *Northbridge Pavilion Food Hall*, *Trains, Planes & Automobiles* (with occasional all-you-can-eat specials) and the *Kremlin*. A little farther north on Lake St are the *Cafe 100: Hollywood Bowl*, at No 100; and the *Arcadia Hotel*.

The pickings are also rich along Aberdeen St. The feast starts on the corner of William St with the *Citadel* (see earlier); then continues with *Cafe Navona*, another good Italian place; the *Good, the Bad & the Ugly*, which combines steakhouse fare with Tex/Mex; the *Aberdeen Hotel*; and *Harry's* (see Seafood earlier).

Don't forget *Mamma Maria's*, at 105 Aberdeen St. This place has a pleasant ambience and a deserved reputation as one of Perth's best Italian eateries. Its two-course weekday lunches are $12, and two should be able to dine here for $40.

Just across from unpretentious Mamma's is a trendy place, the Mediterranean *Icon Cafe*, a nice breakfast spot (8 to 11 am, Friday and Sunday).

Appropriately plonked on the corner of Milligan St, is *Rosie O'Grady's Pub*, a popular venue after work with good-value meals. Across the road, at 220 James St, is the new *Lotus Vegetarian* with an Australian, Malaysian, Indian and Chinese buffet for about $8.

On Beaufort St, near the eastern end of Francis St, are the Macedonian *Court Wine Bar & Cellar Restaurant*; the *Turn 'n Tender Steakhouse*, at No 96; and a little way north on Beaufort, the excellent Vietnamese restaurant *Phuong Hoang*.

Leederville The area of Oxford St between Vincent and Melrose Sts, and Newcastle St, in the suburb of Leederville, have earned popularity with the 'cappuccino set'. Many cafes and eateries, as well as the art-house *Luna Cinema*, are found here.

Cafes include *Villa, Oxford 130, Mazzini's, Giardini's* and *Fat Bellies* (which fulfils the promise in its name). The cuisines of the world are represented in an eclectic collection of eateries: *Cosmos Kebabs, Banzai Sushi & Noodle Bar, Woodstock Rock Pizzeria, Anna Vietnamese, Shalimar Indian* and *Hawkers Hut Asian*.

This restaurant enclave is fast becoming a chic alternative to the hustle and bustle of Northbridge. *Cafe Fourteen-7* and nearby *Green & Co*, Oxford St, have been recommended by many readers for their food, as have the entertainment venues, the *Leederville Hotel* and *hip-e-club*.

Subiaco This enclave, known as 'Subi' has a number of eateries, mostly on (or just off) Rokeby Rd. Heading north from Nicholson Rd, you'll come to *Cassini's Cafe*, the *Little Lebanon* with its friendly staff and superb Middle Eastern fare and, not far beyond, *Chez Jean Claude*, a French patisserie.

Just before Bagot Rd are the expensive French restaurant *Chanterelle*, where a meal is about $60 for two; the reliable *Amarin Thai* and the busy *Rokeby's Bar & Café*. At the Barker St corner is the popular *Bridie O'Reilly's* and close by on Rokeby Rd is the *Witch's Cauldron*, at No 89, with its renowned garlic prawns. Across from Forrest Way Mall in Churchill St, is the small *Maggie's Kitchen*, a pleasant spot for a hearty cheap breakfast ($5.50).

There are more places on Hay St where it intersects with Rokeby Rd. The *Subiaco Hotel*, on the east corner, faces the Art Deco Regal Theatre and a little farther east, at No 420, is the BYO *Redd's Cafe*.

Next door to the theatre is the chic *Oriel Cafe & Brasserie*, at No 483, which is rather expensive but always buzzing (it is open 24 hours). The *Mezza Villa*, on the corner of Railway Rd and Rokeby St, has a good atmosphere, staff and food.

The Subiaco Mews hides a few decent eateries such as the *Subiaco Steakhouse* with

its reef and beef lobster & fillet for $25; the Subiaco Village has *Henry's Cafe & Grill*; and the Subiaco Pavilion has a food hall with 15 or so stalls.

Entertainment

Perth has plenty of pubs, discos and nightclubs (see the Around Perth chapter for details of the Fremantle scene). The *Xpress*, a weekly music mag available free at record shops and other outlets, has a gig guide. See the *West Australian* for listings of theatre, cinema and nightclubs.

Northbridge, Leederville and Subiaco are the places to go after dark, especially at weekends when the city centre remains dead, despite efforts to revitalise it.

Cinemas The *Cinema Paradiso*, 164 James St in the Galleria, Northbridge; the *Luna* in Oxford St, Leederville; and the *Astor*, on the corner of Beaufort and Walcott Sts in Mt Lawley, usually have quality art-house films. All of the Oscar-nominated favourites are on in the Hoyts, Greater Union and Village suburban cinemas; budget night is Tuesday.

Theatres Popular theatres include *His Majesty's Theatre* (☎ 93221 2721) on the corner of King and Hay Sts, the *Regal Theatre* at 474 Hay St, Subiaco, and the *Hole in the Wall*, Subiaco Theatre Centre, 180 Hamersley Rd, Subiaco.

Other theatre venues are the *Playhouse*, Pier St, Perth; the *Stirling Theatre*, Cedric St, Stirling; and the *Effie Crump Theatre*, upstairs in the old Brisbane Hotel, Beaufort St, Perth. You can enjoy the work of a local playwright or an internationally renowned production.

Sessions times and programmes for these and other cinemas and theatres in Perth are available daily in the *West Australian*. newspaper

Classical Music The *Perth Concert Hall* (☎ 9325 9944) in St George's Terrace and the large *Entertainment Centre* (☎ 9321 1575) in Wellington St are venues for concerts and recitals by local and international acts.

JEFF WILLIAMS

PAUL STEEL

TONY WHEELER

PAUL STEEL

ROGER DU BUISSON

PAUL STEEL

A	B
C	D
E	F

Perth

A: Miners' Monument, Perth Mint
B: Perth skyline at night
C: Hay St Mall

D: Trains, Planes & Automobiles
Restaurant, Northbridge
E: View of South Perth
F: Havana Restaurant, Northbridge

GLENN BEANLAND

GLENN BEANLAND

JEFF WILLIAMS

JEFF WILLIAMS

A	B
	C
D	

Around Perth

A: Lighthouse, Wadjemup Hill, Rottnest Island

B: The Quokka (*Setonix brachyurus*), a wallaby-like marsupial

C: Bricks made by convicts, Round House, Fremantle

D: Up close with a large male sea lion, Carnac Island

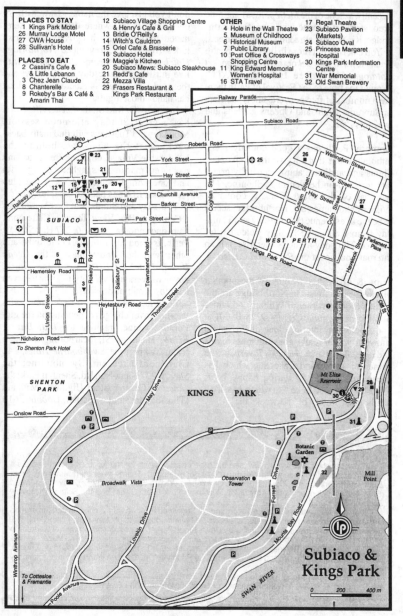

PLACES TO STAY
1 Kings Park Motel
26 Murray Lodge Motel
27 CWA House
28 Sullivan's Hotel

PLACES TO EAT
2 Cassini's Cafe &
    Little Lebanon
3 Chez Jean Claude
8 Chanterelle
9 Rokeby's Bar & Café &
    Amarin Thai

12 Subiaco Village Shopping Centre
    & Henry's Cafe & Grill
13 Bridie O'Reilly's
14 Witch's Cauldron
15 Oriel Cafe & Brasserie
18 Subiaco Hotel
19 Maggie's Kitchen
20 Subiaco Mews: Subiaco Steakhouse
21 Redd's Cafe
22 Mezza Villa
29 Frasers Restaurant &
    Kings Park Restaurant

OTHER
4 Hole in the Wall Theatre
5 Museum of Childhood
6 Historical Museum
7 Public Library
10 Post Office & Crossways
    Shopping Centre
11 King Edward Memorial
    Women's Hospital
16 STA Travel

17 Regal Theatre
23 Subiaco Pavilion
    (Markets)
24 Subiaco Oval
25 Princess Margaret
    Hospital
30 Kings Park Information
    Centre
31 War Memorial
32 Old Swan Brewery

**Subiaco &
Kings Park**

0   200   400 m

Recently, a clone of the *Metropolis*, a long-time Freo stalwart, opened in Roe St, Northbridge; it is already attracting mainstream acts.

You can find out more in the Perth Theatre Trust News *Applause!* or the WASO *Concert Catalogue*, both free from the WATC. Around the time of the Festival of Perth there are a number of free concerts under the stars in Supreme Court and Queens gardens and in Kings Park.

Comedy Perth has a good comedy scene although those that survive the smoke, late nights and audience abuse, generally gravitate to stand-up heaven in Melbourne. The rear bar of the *Brass Monkey*, corner of William and James Sts, Northbridge, seems to be the latest venue (Wednesday and Thursday from 8.30 pm, $8); they welcome 'try outs' on Thursday nights. Otherwise, it is an international act at the *Burswood Casino*.

Pubs & Live Music Some of the popular places for live music in Northbridge are the *Brass Monkey*, corner of William and James Sts; the *Metropolis City* (☎ 9228 0500) at 146 Roe St, an interior clone of Freo's old stalwart, which really goes off most nights and is great for bands; *Novak's Tavern*, on the corner of James and Lake Sts, which has cheap jugs for $4.50 during happy hour; *Rosie O'Grady's*, Lake St, which has Irish bands most nights of the week; the *Bog* –

don't you just love the name – Newcastle St, open until 6 am, where drinkers are serenaded through their hangovers with Irish tunes (ouch!); the revamped *Northbridge Hotel*, corner of Lake and Brisbane Sts with live music on Wednesday and Sunday; and the *Aberdeen Hotel*, 84 Aberdeen St, which has bands most nights.

In nearby Oxford St, the *Leederville Hotel* has a great Sunday afternoon session. Mondays and Tuesdays will find many backpackers at the *hip-e-club*, behind the Leederville Village, enjoying free entry and meal (eg macaroni, spaghetti bolognaise) and one complimentary drink – the club provides a free bus back to local hostels.

Thursday and Sundays at the *Continental* (*'Conti'*) in Bay View Terrace, Claremont, were once popular; the *Loft*, 237 Hay St, East Perth, is good for a mix of Goth, Indie and other; and the Sunday blast at the *Ocean Beach Hotel* (*'OBH'*), Cottesloe North, never waivers in its ability to surprise even the most timid of drinkers.

Perth has the usual pub-rock circuit with varying cover charges depending on the gig. Popular venues include the *Indi Bar & Bistro*, Hastings St, Scarborough, where 'slam' is king; the *Swanbourne Hotel*, 141 Claremont Crescent, Swanbourne; the *Shents*, 207 Nicholson Rd, Shenton Park; the *Junction*, Great Eastern Highway, Midland (Thursday to Sunday nights); *Gobbles*, 613

Perff 4 Kids

If you are travelling with kids in tow, see the main chapter listing for the following diversions: It's a Small World (Perth), Underwater World (Hillary's Boat Harbour), Energy Museum (Fremantle), Perth Zoo (South Perth), Omni Theatre (Perth), Caversham Wildlife Park (West Swan), Adventure World (Bibra Lakes), Pioneer World (Armadale), Whiteman Park (West Swan) and the Scitech Discovery Centre (West Perth).

Other 'family friendly' places are the grounds of Burswood Park where the children can run around and explore; Botanic Mini Golf, Burns Beach Rd, Wanneroo; Heritage Mini Golf, swan Bank Rd, Maylands; the Children's Playground, May Drive, Kings Park; Dizzy lamb park, corner of Karaborup and Wanneroo Rds, Carabooda (open 10 am to 5 pm Sunday and public holidays); The Maze, Neaves Rd, Bullsbrook (open Tuesday to Sunday); and the Cameleer Park Camel Farm (closed on Friday), 300 Neaves Rd, Wanneroo; and Gumnut World, 30 Prindiville Drive, also in Wanneroo and open daily from 9.30 am to 4 pm.

If you want a place for the kids to play while you enjoy a glass of white wine and a plate of fish, try the *Surf Club Fish Cafe* in North Fremantle or *Lamont's Winery* in the Swan Valley. ■

Wellington St, Perth; and *SLAM at the Sands*, White Sands Hotel, 240 West Coast Highway; the *Grosvenor Hotel*, corner of Hill and Hay Sts, East Perth, where live music is belted out Wednesday to Sunday; and the *Babylon Hotel*, 901 Albany Hotel, East Victoria Park. At the latter, you can choke on your pizza as you attempt to 'interpret' that Babel-onian next to you.

Discos & Nightclubs Learn the difference between funk, acid jazz, techno and house, and then prepare to sweet talk the steroided door 'bitches'. Perth has plenty of places where you can dance into the wee small hours. Mix with 'models' fresh from gym sessions in Claremont and St George's Terrace 'executives', not so fresh from Wanneroo and Armadale.

In the city centre are the *Buzz Bar*, Shafto Lane; *Brannigan's* in the Mercure International Hotel, Irwin St; the *Racquet Club*, Piccadilly Square, corner of Lord and Short Sts; *Club 418*, formerly Rumours, at 418 Murray St (Friday and Saturday nights); *Geremiah's* in The Orchard Hotel, Milligan St; *Club 418*, 418 Murray St; *Planet* at 329 Charles St, North Perth; and *Margeaux* in the Parmelia Hilton, Mill St.

Northbridge has a few late-night venues for hard-core ravers. *Kremlin*, 69 Lake St, has its legion of fans. *O2 (Oxygen)* in the James St nightclub, at No 139, buzzes most buzzy nights. For rave, go to *Krush*, next door and upstairs from O2 (above Novak's Tavern). The *Post Office*, corner of Parker and Aberdeen Sts, handles a slightly older crowd, with aplomb (especially on Thursday at the over-30s session). And the *Ozone* at 44 Lake St, upstairs in the Redheads Tavern complex, has one more oxygen 'free radical' than the O2; both upstairs and downstairs go off on weekends.

Gay & Lesbian Venues These include ; the *Court Hotel*, corner of Beaufort and James Sts (live music Friday and Sunday and 'gay friendly' accommodation); *Dual Control* *(DC's)*, 105 Francis St, for live shows on the weekend and 'men only' night on Wednesday); and *Connections* ('Connies'), James St, for dance music and floorshows.

Freo is probably heart (and soul?) of the lesbian scene – a sociable place is *Lola's Bar & Cafe*, 237 Queen Victoria St, North Fremantle; it is open Wednesday to Sunday from about 4 pm until late. Check in the *Westside Observer* ($1), available from the Arcane Bookshop, William St, New Editions in South Terrace, Fremantle, or any of the above-mentioned places, for more venues and activities.

Casino Perth's glitzy *Burswood Casino*, built on an artificial island off the Great Western Highway, is open all day, every day. Its setup seems pretty similar to other Australian casinos, with the usual gaming tables (roulette and blackjack), a two-up 'shed', Keno, poker machines and extensive off-course betting. The casino is also host to a cavalcade of prominent local and foreign entertainers.

Spectator Sport
The people of Perth, like most other Australians, are parochial in their support of local sporting teams. The West Coast Eagles and the Fremantle Dockers, Perth's two representatives in the Australian Football League (AFL), the Perth Wildcats in the National Basketball League and the Western Reds in the Super League, regularly play interstate teams in Perth. Check the *West Australian* for game details.

The venerated shrine in Perth for interstate AFL games, and games between local clubs, is Subiaco Oval. Details of matches can be found in the sporting section of the Friday and Saturday *West Australian*.

At least one of the test matches of an international cricket series (or a one day game of that competition) is usually played in Perth, keeping interested eastern TV viewers glued to their sets until late. Games are played at the Western Australian Cricket Association (WACA) which is close to the centre of the city.

Things to Buy

Perth has a number of excellent outlets for Aboriginal arts & crafts including the Creative Native Gallery, at 32 King St; Ganada at 71 Barrack St; and Artists in Residence Gallery at The Lookout, Fraser Ave, Kings Park. Other crafts can be found at the various markets – see the Market section earlier in this chapter.

For camping and climbing equipment, there's Paddy Pallin, 891 Hay St and, across the road, Mountain Designs, at No 862.

Getting There & Away

Air Qantas Domestic (☎ 13 1313) and Ansett Australia (☎ 13 1300) have direct flights to/from Sydney, Melbourne, Adelaide, Ayers Rock and Alice Springs. In most cases, flights to Queensland (Brisbane and Cairns) involve stops in Melbourne or Sydney and flights to Darwin have one stop (either Port Hedland or Alice Springs).

Discounted return airfares are in a state of flux, but you should be able to get return tickets between Perth and Adelaide for around $440, Melbourne $510, Sydney $540 and Brisbane $660. Discount fares are subject to conditions (see the Air section of the Getting There & Away chapter).

Ansett Australia and Qantas Domestic also have flights to Perth from North Queensland via Alice Springs. Apex return fares from Alice Springs are $503, and $621 from Cairns. Darwin to Perth flights go via Alice Springs or Port Hedland – Ansett Australia flies from Darwin to Perth along the coast daily (with possible stops at Broome, Karratha, Port Hedland or Kununurra); the Apex return fare from Perth to Darwin via Alice Springs is $699.

Skywest (☎ 9334 2288), out on the Great Eastern Highway, flies to WA centres such as Albany, Carnarvon, Esperance, Exmouth, Kalgoorlie, Geraldton, Monkey Mia, Meekatharra and Wiluna.

Bus Greyhound Pioneer (☎ 9328 6677) operates daily bus services from Adelaide to Perth from the Westrail Centre, West Parade, East Perth (Interstate Railway Station). The daily journey from Perth to Darwin along the coast takes around 56 hours by bus and costs $325. Greyhound Pioneer also operates a three times weekly service to Port Hedland (and with connections to Darwin) via the more direct, inland route through Newman. It saves three hours and is the same price.

Westrail (☎ 13 2232) operates bus services from the East Perth terminal to a number of WA centres. South West Coachlines (☎ 9324 2333) buses depart from the City Bus Port to Bunbury, Margaret River and capes Naturaliste and Leeuwin. See the Bus section in the Getting Around chapter for destinations and prices for both companies.

Train Perth is the starting and ending point of one of the world's great train journeys – the 65 hour trip between the Pacific and Indian oceans (see the Getting There & Away chapter).

The only rail services within WA are the limited *AvonLink* from Perth to York, the *Prospector* to Kalgoorlie and the *Australind* to Bunbury. Westrail Terminal in West Parade, East Perth, is for all WA rail services and Westrail buses, and trains arriving from the east coast. Reservations can be made by phoning ☎ 13 2232.

The *Australind* has two services every day, except Sunday when there is only one, in both directions. These leave Perth at 10 am and 7 pm and Bunbury at 6.30 am and 3.40 pm; the trip takes over two hours. Towns stopped at are Armadale, Mundijong, Serpentine, North Dandalup, Pinjarra, Waroona, Yarloop, Cookernup, Harvey and Brunswick Junction.

The *Prospector* has at least one service in each direction every day and there are some other limited services during the week; the trip takes about 7½ hours. Major stops are Midland, Toodyay, Northam, Meckering, Cunderdin, Kellerberrin, Merredin and Southern Cross. From Monday to Thursday it departs in the morning at around 9.30 am (it pays to check as this is only an indication) and on Friday and Sunday the train departs at 4.10 pm from both ends; on Saturday the train departs Perth at 6 pm and Kalgoorlie at 7.15 am.

Hitching We *don't* recommend hitching (see the Hitching warning in the Getting Around chapter). But if you must, hostel notice boards are worth checking for lifts to points around the country. If you're hitching out of Perth to the north or east, take a train to Midland. For travel south, take a train to Armadale. Trans-Nullarbor hitching is not easy, and the fierce competition between bus companies and discounted airfares have made such travel much more attractive.

Ferry The Rottnest Island Getting There & Away section has details on ferries from Perth, Hillary's Boat Harbour and Fremantle to Rottnest.

Getting Around

Perth's central public transport organisation, Transperth, operates buses, trains and ferries. There are Transperth information offices (☎ 13 2213) in the Plaza Arcade (off Hay St Mall); the City Bus Port on Mounts Bay Rd at the foot of William St; and at the Wellington St bus station. They all provide advice about getting around Perth and provide a system map and timetables. These offices are open from 7.30 am to 5.30 pm Monday to Friday; the Plaza Arcade office is open from 8 am to 5.30 pm Saturday, noon to 6 pm Sunday. The free pamphlet and map *Public Transport to Tourist Spots Around Perth* is very useful.

Free Transit Zone A free transit zone which includes all Transperth bus and trains is provided every day within the central city area – from Northbridge, in the north, to the river in the south, and from Kings Park in the west to the Causeway in the east. This allows free travel at all times within city boundaries, described above for buses. It also includes train travel between Claisebrook and City West stations. Also see the CAT system in the Bus section.

The Airport Perth's airport is busy – the city's isolation from the east coast means that planes arrive and depart at all hours.

The domestic and international terminals are 10km apart and taxi fares to the city are around $16 and $20 respectively. The privately run airport bus (☎ 9479 4131) meets all incoming domestic and international flights and provides transport to the city centre, hotels and hostels. It claims to meet all flights, but travellers have reported that sometimes it doesn't turn up – if this occurs late at night, a taxi is the best option.

The airport bus costs $6 from the domestic terminal and $8 from the international terminal; terminal to terminal is $6/4 for adults/children. To the airport terminals, there are scheduled runs every couple of hours from 4.45 am to 10.30 pm. Call them for hotel and hostel pick-ups and timetable information.

Alternatively, you can get into the city for $2.30 on Transperth bus Nos 200, 202, 208 and 209 to William St. It departs from the domestic terminal every hour or so (more frequently at peak times) from 5.30 am to 10 pm on weekdays and for nearly as long on Saturday; Sunday services are less frequent. It leaves from bus stand No 39, on St George's Terrace, to the domestic terminal. Some backpacker places pick up guests at the airport.

Bus There are two free Central Area Transit (CAT) services in the city centre. The buses are state of the art and there are computer readouts (and audio) at the stops telling you when the next bus is due. Using the two, you can get to most sights in the inner city.

The Red CAT operates east-west from Outram St, West Perth, to the WACA, in East Perth; the service is every five minutes, Monday to Friday, from 7 am to 6 pm. The Blue CAT operates north-south from the river to Northbridge, roughly in the centre of the Red CAT route; services are every 7.5 minutes, Monday to Friday, from 7 am to 6 pm. A modified version of the Blue CAT runs every 10 minutes on weekends – Friday from 6 pm to 1 am, Saturday 8.30 am to 1 am and Sunday from 10 am to 5 pm.

On regular buses, a short ride of one zone is $1.60, two zones $2.30 and three zones $3. Zone 1 includes the city centre and the inner suburbs (including Subiaco and Claremont), and Zone 2 extends all the way to Fremantle, 20km from the city centre. A MultiRider ticket gives 10 journeys for the price of nine. A MaxiRider ($5.50) ticket allows weekend travel for two adults and as many as five children, anywhere on Transperth.

The Perth Tram (☎ 9367 9404) doesn't run on rails – it's a bus that takes you around some of Perth's main attractions (such as the city, Kings Park, Barrack St jetty and the Burswood Casino) in 1½ hours. It is $12/6 for adults/kids, and it leaves from 565 Hay St (near Barrack St) at least six times daily.

There is also a tram in Subiaco, which operates weekdays from Linney's in Rokeby Rd; the cost is $6/3 for adults/children.

Train Transperth (☎ 13 2213) operates the Fastrak suburban train lines to Armadale, Fremantle, Midland and the northern suburb of Joondalup from around 5.20 am to midnight on weekdays with reduced services on weekends. During the day, some of the Joondalup trains continue to Armadale and some Fremantle trains run through to Midland. Free train travel is allowed between Claisebrook and City West stations.

All trains leave from the city station on Wellington St. Your rail ticket can also be used on Transperth buses and ferries within the ticket's area of validity.

Car & Motorcycle Driving in the city centre takes a little bit of getting used to as some streets are one way and many street signs are not prominent.

In the city you will have no trouble getting fuel from 7 am to 9 pm from Monday to Saturday but on Sunday it is a different story. You will have to find out which fuel outlets

are rostered to be open (usually from 7 am to 10 pm). For rostering details call ☎ 11573.

Rental Hertz (☎ 9321 7777), Budget (☎ 13 2727), Avis (☎ 9325 7677) and Thrifty (☎ 9481 1999) all have offices, along with many more local firms mentioned in the Getting Around chapter.

Taxi Perth has a good system of metered taxi cabs, and there are taxi ranks throughout the city and in nearby Fremantle. The two main companies are Swan Taxis (☎ 9322 0111, 9335 3944) and Black & White or Green & Gold (☎ 9333 3333). A taxi service for the disabled, officially available from 8.30 am to 4.30 pm Monday to Friday, can be booked on ☎ 9333 3377.

Bicycle Cycling is a great way to explore Perth. There are many bicycle routes along the river all the way to Fremantle and along the Indian Ocean coast. Get the free *Along the Coast Ride*, *Around the River Ride* and *Armadale to Perth* booklets from the WATC in Forrest Place.

At WA Bicycle Disposal Centre (☎ 9325 1176) at 47 Bennett St, East Perth, you can buy a bike knowing that you get a guaranteed buy-back price after a certain time. About Bike Hire (☎ 9221 2665) on Riverside Drive near the Causeway Bridge also rents cycles for about $15 per day. Many backpackers' places have free or rental bikes for guests.

Ferry Transperth ferries (☎ 13 2213) cross the river every day from the Barrack St jetty to the Mends St jetty in South Perth every half an hour (more frequently at peak times) from 6.45 am to 7.15 pm for 90c (one zone). Take this ferry to get to the zoo.

Around Perth

The area around Perth has a wealth of attractions and activities. There is the historic port city of Fremantle, the traffic-free holiday resort of Rottnest Island, the picturesque Avon Valley, a string of large towns – Rockingham and Mandurah – to the south, and the beaches and national parks to the north.

Most of these places, with the exception of Lancelin, the Pinnacles, Green Head and Leeman, are only an hour or so away.

South of Perth

The coast south of Perth has a softer appearance than the often harsh landscape to the north. This is another popular resort area for Perth residents and many have holiday houses along this stretch of coast.

FREMANTLE
* *pop 25,000*

Fremantle ('Freo' to the locals), Perth's port, has a population of 25,000 and lies at the mouth of the Swan River, 19km south-west of the city centre. Over the years, Perth has sprawled to engulf Fremantle, which is now more a suburb of the city than a town in its own right. Despite recent development, Freo has a wholly different feeling than gleaming, skyscrapered Perth. It's a place with a real sense of history and an extremely pleasant atmosphere.

The town has a number of interesting old buildings, some excellent museums and galleries, lively produce and craft markets, and a diverse range of pubs, cafes and restaurants. A visit to Fremantle will be one of the highlights of your trip to WA. The town is also considered the alternative lifestyle centre of WA.

History
This region was settled many thousands of years ago by the Nyoongar people. Several

HIGHLIGHTS

* Marvelling at the *Duyfken* reconstruction at the superb Maritime Museum in Fremantle
* Sipping coffee and people-watching on Freo's 'cappuccino strip', South Terrace
* Pedalling around Rottnest Island looking for birds, whales and cuddly quokkas
* Wandering among the quaint historic towns of the Avon Valley
* Gasping at the views of Perth from the Zig Zag Rd, near Kalamunda, en route to the picturesque Araluen Gardens
* Swimming with dolphins near Rockingham
* Day-tripping to the intriguing and hauntingly beautiful Pinnacles Desert
* A ride on the Hotham Valley tourist railway from Pinjarra to Dwellingup

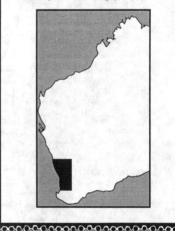

trails joined on the south side of the Swan River at the hub of intertribal trading routes; here was a natural bridge almost spanning the Swan. Known to the Aborigines as Munjaree, groups quickly occupied various parts of the area.

Fremantle's modern, European history began in 1829 when the HMS *Challenger* landed, captained by Charles Howe Fremantle.

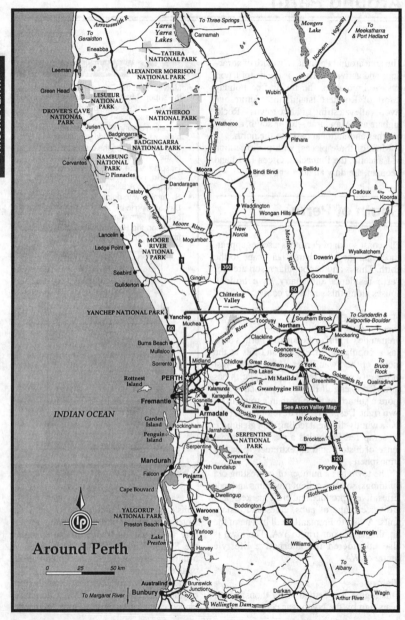

Around Perth

0   25   50 km

He took possession of 'the whole of the west coast in the name of King George IV'.

Like Perth, the settlement made little progress until taking on convict labour. These hard-worked labourers constructed most of the town's earliest buildings, some of them among the oldest and most treasured in WA. As a port, Fremantle was abysmal until the brilliant engineer CY O'Connor (see the boxed aside 'Where Water is like Gold!' in The Southern Outback chapter) built an artificial harbour in the 1890s.

In 1987, the city was the site of the unsuccessful defence of what was, for a brief period, one of Australia's most prized possessions – the America's Cup yachting trophy. Preparations for the influx of tourists transformed Fremantle into a more modern, colourful and expensive city. Many of the residents, however, protested that their lifestyle and the character of their community would be damaged by the development.

Information

The information office, once housed in the Fremantle Town Hall has, sadly, closed down. Some sort of tourist information place should open up in the future but at the moment the void is filled by the Queen of Tarts Cafe (☎ 9335 9977) in Margaret St. It is open 9 am to 5 pm Monday to Saturday, Sunday 10 am to 3 pm. Among the free brochures are a number of guides, and information on Heritage Trails and National Trust walking tours – *Manjaree Track*, *Convict Trail* and *Old Foreshore*.

You can get information on all WA's national parks at CALM's WA Naturally shop (☎ 9430 8600) at 47 Henry St (on the corner of Croke St); it is open daily (except Tuesday) from 10 am to 5.30 pm.

History Museum & Arts Centre

The museum, housed in an impressive building on the corner of Ord and Finnerty Sts, was originally constructed by convict labourers as a lunatic asylum in the 1860s. It houses a fine collection including exhibits on Fremantle's early history, including a small section on Aboriginal history, the colonisation of WA and the early whaling industry. There is a focus on the diverse nationalities which make up the Freao population. It is open from 11 am to 4 pm weekdays, 1 to 5 pm on weekends; entry is free.

The arts centre, which occupies one wing of the building, is open daily from 10 am to 5 pm and Wednesday evening from 7 to 9 pm; admission is also free.

Maritime Museum

The Maritime Museum, on Cliff St, near the waterfront, occupies a building constructed in 1852 as a commissariat store. The museum has a display on WA's maritime history with particular emphasis on the history, recovery and restoration of the famous wreck *Batavia*, other Dutch merchants and some more recent wrecks.

At one end of the *Batavia* gallery is a huge stone facade intended for an entrance to Batavia Castle. It was being carried by the *Batavia* as ballast when she sank. The dominant feature of the gallery, however, is the reconstruction of a part of the hull of the ship from recovered timbers, which you can view from ground level as well as from a mezzanine floor above.

Another interesting exhibit is the original de Vlamingh plate. When de Vlamingh retrieved Hartog's inscribed plate (see the History section in the Facts about Western Australia chapter) from Hartog Island, he replaced it with another. Hartog's plate is preserved in a museum in the Netherlands.

At the time of writing, the front of the museum was shielded by a huge shed. Here, an exact replica of the *Duyfken* ('Little Dove'), a Dutch *jacht* (scout ship) for the Moluccan fleet in the 1600s, is being built. Many of the craftspersons worked on the earlier reconstruction of James Cook's *Endeavour*, and to watch them at work is a fascinating experience. There is no entry fee and some great souvenirs are sold.

This rather intriguing, not-to-be-missed museum is open daily from 10.30 am to 5 pm; entry is free.

AROUND PERTH

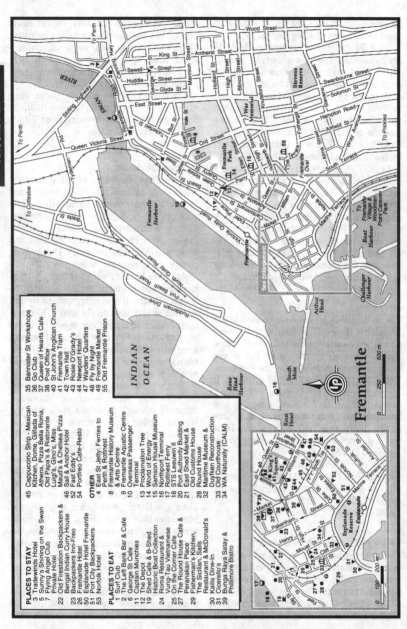

PLACES TO STAY
5 Tradewinds Hotel
7 Sunny's Shining on the Swan
8 Flying Angel Club
22 Old Firestation Backpackers &
    Bengal Indian Curry House
23 Backpackers Inn-Freo
26 Fremantle Hotel
50 Esplanade Hotel Fremantle
51 Port City Backpackers
53 Norfolk Hotel

PLACES TO EAT
1 Surf Club
6 The Left Bank Bar & Cafe
6 George St Cafe
11 Captain Munchies
12 The Depot
19 Shed Cafe & B-Shed
    Historic Boat Collection
24 Roma Restaurant &
    Vung-Tau Vietnamese
27 On The Corner Cafe
27 The Red House Cafe &
    Perpaka Place
29 Fisherman's Kitchen,
    The Sicilian, Sails
    Restaurant & McDonald's
30 Kailis Dine-In
31 Cicerello's
39 Bunga Raya Satay &
    Phillimore Bistro

45 Cappuccino Strip - Mexican
    Kitchen, Dome, Gilfada of
    Athens, Pizza Bella Roma,
    Lld Papa's & Ristorante
    Maud's & Chelsea Pizza
46 Sail & Anchor Hotel
52 Fast Eddy's
54 Portfreo Cafe-Resto

OTHER
4 East St Jetty: Ferries to
    Perth & Rottnest
8 Fremantle History Museum
    & Arts Centre
9 Fremantle Aquatic Centre
10 Overseas Passenger
    Terminal
13 Proclamation Tree
14 World of Energy
15 Samson House Museum
16 Northport Terminal
17 STS Leeuwin
18 Rottnest Ferry
20 E Shed Market &
    Old Customs House
21 East Shed Market &
28 Round House
32 Maritime Museum &
    Duyken Reconstruction
33 Old Courthouse
34 WA Naturally (CALM)
35 Bannister St Workshops
36 Go Club
37 Queen of Hearts Cafe
38 Post Office
40 St John's Anglican Church
41 Fremantle Tram
42 Town Hall
43 Rosie O'Grady's
44 Newport Hotel
47 Warders' Quarters
48 Fly by Night
49 Fremantle Market
55 Old Fremantle Prison

Fremantle

Fremantle Market

The colourful Fremantle Market at the corner of South Terrace and Henderson St, is a prime attraction. Originally opened in 1897, the market was reopened in 1975 and draws crowds looking for anything from craftwork to vegetables, jewellery and antiques; there is also a great tavern bar where buskers often perform. The market is open from 9 am to 9 pm on Friday, 9 am to 5 pm on Saturday, and 10 am to 5 pm Sunday. Late Sunday afternoon is the time for fruit and vegetables sold off cheap before closing time.

Round House

On Arthur Head, at the western end of High St, near the Maritime Museum, is the Round House. Built in 1831, it's the oldest public building in WA. It was originally a local prison (in the days before convicts were brought into WA). It was the site of the colony's first hanging.

Later, the building was used to hold Aborigines before they were taken to Rottnest Island. To the Nyoongar people, the Round House is a sacred site because of the number

The stone Round House actually has 12 sides.

of their people killed while incarcerated here. One local remarked ironically that, although WA was initially settled as a penal colony, the first thing the authorities did was to build a prison using convict labour to house local Aborigines.

Incidentally, the tunnel underneath the Round House was cut by a whaling company in 1837 for access to Bathers Bay. The Round House shop and information office is housed in one of the nearby pilots' cottages. The building is open from 10 am to 5 pm daily; admission is free. The site provides good views of Fremantle, especially historic High St.

Convict-Era Buildings

Many other buildings in Fremantle date from the period after 1850, when convict labour was introduced. The *Convict Trail* brochure, available from the Queen of Tarts Cafe, outlines the places of interest from this era. They include the **Old Fremantle Prison**, one of the unlucky convicts' first building tasks.

To a certain extent, the prison with its 5m-high walls, dominates modern Fremantle. It operated as a prison from 1855 until 1991. The prison is open from 10 am to 6 pm daily; admission is $10/4. The best time to visit is on Wednesday and Friday for the torchlight tours; these are also $10.

Beside the prison gates, at 16 The Terrace, is a **museum** on the convict era in WA. The entrance for both is on the Terrace.

Later Landmarks

Fremantle boomed during the WA gold rush and many buildings were constructed during, or shortly before, this period. They include **Samson House**, a well-preserved 1888 colonial home in Ellen St, which is open from 1 to 5 pm on Thursday and Sunday – tours of the house are run by volunteer guides. The fine **St John's Anglican Church** of 1882, on the corner of Adelaide and Queen Sts, contains a large stained-glass window.

Other buildings of the era include the **Fremantle Town Hall** (1887) in King's Square; the former **German consulate**

building built in 1902 at 5 Mouat St; the **Fremantle Train Station** of 1907; and the Georgian-style **old customs house** on the corner of Cliff and Phillimore Sts. The **Victoria Grandstand** of Fremantle Oval (1897) is a good example of the once popular timber and iron pavilion, complete with lace work and towers.

The **water trough**, in the park in front of the station, has a memorial to two men who died of thirst on an outback expedition. The **Proclamation Tree**, near the corner of Adelaide and Edwards Sts, is a Moreton Bay fig, planted in 1890.

Victoria Quay Docks

From the observation tower on top of the **Port Authority Building** in Cliff St, you can enjoy a panoramic view of Fremantle Harbour. You must take the escorted tours which are conducted from the foyer every weekday at 1.30 pm only. Nearby are the **East Shed Markets** which are open from 10 am to 9 pm Fridays, and 9 am to 5 pm on weekends.

For boat freaks, there is a **collection of boats** in B Shed, Victoria Quay, including a pilot boat, Aboriginal craft and working marine engine. It is open from 10 am to 3 pm weekdays, and 11 am to 4 pm on weekends; admission is free.

The training ship, **STS Leeuwin II**, a 55m three-masted barquentine, is based at B Berth, Victoria Dock (☎ 9430 4105). This ship undertakes day, weekend and five day sailing trips. There are occasionally 10 day trips – real 'eco-adventures' – to the Kimberley Coast; they cost from $1250/890 for adults/students.

Other Attractions

Fremantle is well endowed with parks, which include the popular **Esplanade Reserve**, beside the picturesque fishing-boat harbour off Marine Terrace.

The city is a popular centre for craft workers of all kinds and one of the best places to find them is at the imaginative **Bannister St Workshops**.

The **World of Energy**, at 12 Parry St, has some entertaining and educational displays tracing the development of gas and electricity. It is open from 10.30 am to 4.30 pm on weekdays, 1 to 4.30 pm on weekends; admission is free.

Organised Tours

The Fremantle Tram (☎ 9339 8719), despite the name, is actually a bus like the Perth Tram. It does a 45 minute historical tour of Fremantle with full commentary for $7; a harbour tour is also available for $7 and a Top of the Port tour for $10. You can combine the tour with a cruise to Perth, a tour of Perth on the Perth Tram and a return ticket to Fremantle for $34.

Places to Stay

At the corner of Cockburn and Rockingham Rds is the *Fremantle Village Caravan Park* (☎ 9430 4866) with noisy en-suite sites/chalets (courtesy of its proximity to a very busy highway) for $20/70 for two. The *Woodman Point Caravan Park* (☎ 9434 1433), 10km south of Freo on Cockburn Rd, is well set up with a pool and playground but also suffers from vehicle noise. A tent/caravan site is $13/17 for two, and the chalets are from $68 to $75 for a double.

Port City Backpackers (☎ 9335 6635), a YHA-affiliated place at 5 Essex St, is in a terrific location, equidistant between The Esplanade and South Terrace. Dorm beds are $13/14, and double rooms $30/32 for YHA members/nonmembers. It has a peaceful courtyard, and also offers exceptional $200 trips out to Nyoongar country to select, prepare and then paint your own didgeridoo.

Backpackers Inn-Freo (☎ 9431 7065), 11 Pakenham St, was undergoing extensive renovations when we visited. When completed, it will be a good place to stay with a secure recreation area, good cafe (with backpacker specials) and comfortable rooms. Dorms or twins are $14.50, singles/doubles $19.50/32.50 and a 'honeymoon suite' $38.

The *Old Firestation Backpackers* (☎ 9430 5454) at 18 Phillimore St has dorms for $12, doubles for $30 and there are discounts for extended stays. The place has all sorts of security setups (including lockable cabinets near each bed), a separate area for women, a restaurant which offers specials for guests, and there is also bike hire ($3 per day).

The *Flying Angel Club Private Hotel* (☎ 9335 5321), in the International Seafarers' Centre, 78 Queen Victoria St, has B&B singles/doubles from $35/60.

The *Norfolk Hotel* (☎ 9335 5405), 47 South Terrace, has good-value B&B from $45/70, and arguably the best beer garden in Perth. The fully restored *Fremantle Hotel* (☎ 9430 4300), 6 High St, has rooms from $45 to $70.

In East Fremantle, at 66 Canning Highway, is the *Tradewinds Hotel* (☎ 9339 8188); the river views elevate the price to $108 for a studio or a one bedroom apartment. *Sunny's Shining on the Swan* (☎ 9339 1888), at 6 Canning Highway, is similar to the Tradewinds and costs $90/95.

The ritziest hotel in town is the four star *Esplanade Hotel Fremantle* (☎ 9432 4000) on the corner of Marine Terrace and Essex St. Very comfortable rooms for two from $200.

B&B accommodation is a popular alternative in this town. *Kilkelly's* (☎ 9336 1744), 82 Marine Terrace, has B&B from $65/85; *Fremantle Colonial Accommodation* (☎ 9430 6568) at 215 High St, a nonsmoking establishment, is $40/60; and *Danum House* (☎ 9336 3735), 6 Fothergill St, is $75/85.

Places to Eat

A highlight of Fremantle is the diverse range of cafes, restaurants, food halls and taverns. Many a traveller's afternoon has been whittled away sipping beer or coffee and watching life go by from kerbside tables. There is a concentration of places along South Terrace and another enclave at the western end of town near the fishing boat harbour with outdoor seating.

South Terrace Cafes and restaurants in this area include the popular *Old Papa's & Ristorante Luigi's*, at No 17, which has coffee and gelati (and comes recommended

by cricket's great fast bowler Dennis Lillee); the trendy *Gino's* (the place to be seen) at No 1, *Dome*, across the road from Papa's, which has a multicultural arts centre upstairs; and the large *Miss Maud's* at No 33. All these places can be crowded on weekends if the weather is fine.

The historic *Sail & Anchor Hotel* (formerly the Freemason's Hotel, built in 1854), at 64 South Terrace, has been impressively restored to recall much of its former glory. It specialises in locally brewed Matilda Bay beers, and on the 1st floor is a brasserie serving snacks and meals.

Also on South Terrace is the *Mexican Kitchen*, with a range of Mexican dishes from $10 to $12 (half-price on Tuesday night). Across the road, *Chelsea Pizza* also has half-price specials Tuesday night. Nearby is *Pizza Bella Roma* and the *Glifada of Athens* with tasty souvlaki. A couple of backpackers recommended *Portfreo Cafe-Resto*, at the corner of Parry St and South Terrace, for its patisseries.

The *Up-Market Food Centre* on Henderson St, opposite the market, has stalls where you can get delicious and cheap Thai, Vietnamese, Japanese, Chinese and Italian food from $7.50 for a large fixed plate. It is open Thursday to Sunday from about noon to 9 pm, and can be very busy, especially on market days. *Foodtown*, at the South Terrace end of Essex St, is another good choice.

Fast Eddy's at 13 Essex St, not far from South Terrace, has the best value breakfast in town with bottomless cappuccinos and a 24-hour license. *Granita's*, in South Fremantle (the southern end of South Terrace), gets rave reviews from locals.

West End & Harbour The *Roma*, at 13 High St, is a reliable Freo institution, which serves home-made Italian fare including its famous chicken and spaghetti. Even the rich and famous have to queue to eat here. The nearby *Round House Cafe* is good for a cheap breakfast or a quick snack; next door is another good restaurant *Peranakan Place*, open Wednesday to Sunday from 6 pm. The *On the Corner Cafe*, the first place on High St,

AROUND PERTH

is another good breakfast place. For Vietnamese food, try the *Vung-Tau*, at 19 High St, with meals including a vegetarian menu from $7 to $10. A little out of the restaurant belt is the *Bunga Raya Satay* at 8 Cantonment St; it is popular with locals and noted for its good food (although the servings are small). Not far away, in the Old Firestation on Phillimore St, is the *Bengal Indian Curry House* with great $6 lunch specials. Across the road, the notorious 'skimpy bar' has metamorphosed into the trendy *Phillimore Bistro*.

There is also an enclave of restaurants at the eastern end of George St in East Fremantle. The *George St Cafe*, a fish and chip shop, has an excellent reputation.

For more fish and chips *Cicerello's* or *Kailis Dine-In* on the Esplanade by the fishing boat harbour, are Fremantle traditions. The *Fisherman's Kitchen* is at the back of the equally popular *Sails Restaurant*, upstairs at 47 The Mews. Fisherman's and Cicerello's have sit-down meals and takeaways.

If you want value for money, then the *Sicilian*, beneath Sails Restaurant, is where you will probably spend the evening – a huge plate of fish and chips and a mountain of salad costs $12. It is still as good as ever. If fast food takes your fancy there is a *McDonald's* nearby – just look for the flocks of well-fed seagulls.

Other The hipper-than-thou places are the *Left Bank Bar & Cafe*, on Riverside Rd down from the East St jetty, and the beachy, trendified *Surf Club* (which has both cheap and expensive sections) out at North Fremantle Beach. *Captain Munchies*, at 2 Beach St, will satisfy any urgent pangs of hunger. The *Depot*, across the road, is a more up-market place with good food and a dance garden.

Prickles, on the corner of Douro Rd and South Terrace, specialises in bush tucker – nouvelle cuisine Aussie meals (kangaroo, emu and crocodile), and a host of vegetarian dishes with a twist.

Entertainment

Freo fairly buzzes at night. There are many venues in town with music and/or dancing.

The home of the 'big gig' is the much-lauded *Metropolis* on South Terrace (which has recently been replicated in Perth's Northbridge). At the *Newport*, at No 2, there are live bands playing on most evenings. On weekends, down the road at the *Seaview Tavern*, at No 282, you can listen to 'indy' and 'tribal roots' music with Freo's feral community.

The *Railway* at 201 Queen Victoria St in North Fremantle, has R&B, rock and jazz, on alternate nights, Thursday to Sunday.

For Latin and folk music, try the *Fly by Night Club* in Queen St. It is frequented by talented musicians specialising in ethnic and 'World' music.

The *Go Club* in High St, entered with a free pass provided by the backpacker places, is a dance club with house and techno music. *Rosie O'Grady's*, on William St, is an Irish pub where you can hear live music (washed down with Guinness) three or four nights per week.

Recovery could well begin at the Fremantle Aquatic Centre in Ord St. It has a full-sized pool, gymnasium, spa and saunas; casual entry is $5.50. Or you could continue to party on the water with Fremantle Yacht Charters – sail to Rotto, spend an afternoon on the island, put in a full night, then sleep on board the yacht and sail back to Freo next morning ($75).

To communicate with the outside world, whilst sipping coffee, try the Net Trek Cafe, 8 Bannister St Mall, Fremantle.

Getting There & Around

The train between Perth and Fremantle runs every 15 minutes or so throughout the day for around $2.40. Bus Nos 106 (bus stand No 35) and 111 (bus stand No 48) go from St Georges Terrace to Fremantle via the Canning Highway; or you can take bus No 105 (bus stand No 40 on St Georges Terrace), which takes a longer route south of the river. Bus Nos 103 and 104 also depart from St

Georges Terrace (south side) but go to Fremantle via the north side of the river.

There are also daily ferries from Perth's Barrack St jetty to Freo for $14 one way.

The Fremantle airport shuttle (☎ (014) 083 446) departs Fremantle for the airport every two hours from 6 am to 10 pm; from the airport to Freo departures are every two hours from 7 am to 11 pm. The price of $10 includes drop-off/pick up at your accommodation.

Bicycles are available for hire from Bell Bike Hire (☎ 9430 5414); it is a mobile set up – ring and they deliver. The cost is $15 per day, or $30 per month!

ROCKINGHAM
• *pop 60,000*

Rockingham, 47km south of Perth, was founded in 1872 as a port, but that function, in time, was taken over by Fremantle. Today, Rockingham is a dormitory city, with most of the population commuting to Perth for work, and popular seaside resort with sheltered and ocean beaches and an attractive foreshore. The population has a fair smattering of British migrants.

The helpful, well-organised Rockingham tourist centre (☎ 9592 3464), at 43 Kent St, is open weekdays from 9 am to 5 pm, weekends from 10 am to 4 pm.

Things to See & Do

For kids there is **Marapana Wildlife World**, just south of Rockingham on Paganoni Rd, Karnup, with all the Aussie favourites. For the adults, there are a couple of **wineries** in the region. Baldivis Estate Winery, at 249a River Rd, Baldivis, is open from 11 am to 5 pm for cellar sales. Peel Estate, 10km south of Rockingham on the Mandurah Rd, is open from 10 am to 5 pm.

Worshippers of the industrial revolution can visit the **Kwinana power station**, the state's second largest after Muja (see the Collie section in the South-West chapter). Tours operate daily; check by calling ☎ 9410 8440.

Offshore Islands

Close to Rockingham is **Penguin Island**, home to a colony of fairy penguins from late March to early December, and **Seal Island**, with a colony of sea lions. (Penguin Island is closed during the breeding season from June to August.) Rockingham Sea Tours (☎ 9528 2004) has tours to the offshore islands Tuesday and Thursday (six hours), Wednesday and Sunday (eight hours); the cost for adults/children is $46/36 and includes morning tea and lunch as well as pick-up from Perth. Tours are cheaper if you start at the Shoalwater Visitor Centre at Mersey Point.

The naval base of **Garden Island** is nearby and open during daylight hours. Many pleasant beaches on the island can be reached by private boat. Shy tammar wallabies can occasionally be seen on the bush fringes.

Rockingham Dolphin Cruises (☎ (0418) 958 678) operate daily tours where you can swim with bottlenose dolphins; the cost is $120, all-inclusive from Perth.

Places to Stay

There are a number of caravan parks in Rockingham; enquire at the tourist office. They are the *Palm Beach* (☎ 9527 1515), at 37 Fisher St; the *Cee & See* (☎ 9527 1297), corner of Governor and Rockingham Rds; the *Rockingham Holiday Village* (☎ 9527 4240), on Dixon Rd; and *Point Peron Recreation Camp* (☎ 9527 1104) on Point Peron

Seal Island is home to a sea lion colony.

Rd. Pricewise, there isn't a great difference between them – tent/powered sites are about $8/12, on-site vans $35.

One budget place is the *CWA Rockingham* (☎ 9527 9560), 110 Parkin St. Units, each sleeping six, are about $50.

There are plenty of motels and hotels including the *Ocean Clipper Inn* (☎ 9527 8000), Patterson Rd, at $58/65 for singles/doubles; the *Leisure Inn* (☎ 9527 7777), on the corner of Read St and Simpson Ave, at $60 for a double; and the *Rockingham Motel Hotel* (☎ 9592 1828), 26 Kent St, at $40/50. For private self-contained units and B&Bs, contact the tourist centre.

Places to Eat
In a city this size you would expect a fair number of eateries, and Rockingham doesn't let you down. There are over 10 coffee shops and those happily hunting for a 'cuppa' will be rewarded at either the Rockingham Arcade or in the city centre. The full gamut of takeaways is available near the beaches.

There are at least 10 Asian restaurants including *Indian Delights*, at 26 Flinders Lane, for good-value curries.

Oscar's on the Bay, at 304 Safety Bay Rd, has great sea views; the *Gables*, a licensed place at 178 Safety Bay Rd, is open daily; and the *George 'n' Dragon* in the Shoalwater shopping centre specialises in family meals.

Two good places, side by side, are *Oliver's Cafe* at 45 Rockingham Rd and the *Promenade Cafe*, at No 43. The latter has a blackboard menu (from $10 to $15 for main meals) and is open for breakfast, lunch and dinner daily.

Getting There & Away
You can get to Rockingham on bus No 120 from Fremantle or a No 116 from bus stand No 48 in St Georges Terrace, Perth.

MANDURAH
• *pop 29,000*
Situated on the calm Mandurah Estuary, this is yet another popular beach resort and dormitory suburb, 75km south of Perth. The name comes from the Aboriginal *mandjar*

('meeting place'). Dolphins are often seen in the estuary, and the waterways in the area are noted for good fishing, prawning (March and April) and crabbing.

Things to See & Do
Things to see in town include the restored, limestone **Hall's Cottage** (open Sunday afternoon), built in the 1830s, and the **Parrots of Bellawood Park** (☎ 9535 6732), open daily (except Tuesday and Wednesday) from 10 am to 4 pm (admission is $5/2.50).

Full-day and short cruises are available on the MV *Peel Princess* (☎ 9535 3324) from the jetty in town (lunch cruise $28). Contact the Mandurah tourist office (☎ 9535 1155), 5 Pinjarra Rd, for ferry schedules, maps and other information.

Prolific bird life can be seen on **Peel Inlet** and the narrow coastal salt lakes, **Clifton** and **Preston**, 20km to the south.

There is no shortage of things to do, especially during the holidays and the options available for kids will render parents penniless. There are horse, boat, camel, sailboard, jet ski, yacht and cycle rides. There is a skating arena, golf (mini and 'real'), Sweethearts English Candy and the Castle Fun Park.

Places to Stay
Mandurah is one of those places close to a major city which gets congested with holiday-makers at certain times of the year. There is a string of caravan parks around town with tent and powered sites and on-site vans; enquire at the tourist office.

The *Blue Bay Motel* (☎ 9535 2743), on Oversby St about 200m from the beach, is good value with singles/doubles from $50/75. The *Mandurah Holiday Village* (☎ 9535 4963), 124 Mandurah Terrace, has cosy units with all the facilities from $70; *Albatross House* (☎ 9581 5597), 26 Hall St, has B&B for $45/90; and the *Linksview B&B* (☎ 9535 7808), 52 Portmarnock Circle, Halls Head, charges $30/60.

Places to Eat
There are numerous places to eat around

town including *Pronto's Cafe* on the corner of Pinjarra Rd and Mandurah Terrace. It has an all-you-can-eat pasta night on Friday for $10 – live music is often provided.

A big and tasty serve of fish and chips ($3.50) is available at *Jetty Fish & Chips* by the estuary near the end of Pinjarra Rd. Next door is *Yo-Yo's* for ice creams.

There are also a number of choices on Mandurah Terrace: *Peppercorns* at No 124 for family meals, *Silver Sands Tavern* at No 176 for pub meals, and *Doddi's* at No 115 for garden lunches.

The *Dancing Dolphin*, at 3 Rees Place, South Mandurah near the Dawesville Channel, is a good choice for seafood. Also on the Dawesville Channel is the *Port Bouvard Cafe* with great views of the estuary; it is open daily.

Getting There & Away

To get to Mandurah, catch bus No 116 from stand No 48 on St Georges Terrace, Perth, or bus No 117 from Fremantle. Westrail (☎ 9326 2477) also has a number of services which pass through Mandurah and stop at all the towns between Mandurah and Bunbury.

SOUTH-WESTERN HIGHWAY

From Armadale, 29km south of Perth, the South-Western Highway skirts the Darling Range then heads south to Bunbury via Pinjarra and Harvey.

Serpentine to Jarrahdale

This peaceful area of forest, 55km from Perth, includes the Serpentine National Park. On Falls Rd, at the base of the national park, are the **Serpentine Falls**; the entry fee is $4 per car. There are walking tracks and picnic areas near the Serpentine Dam.

Jarrahdale is an old mill town, established in 1871 and the old **post office** was built in 1880. The Serpentine-Jarrahdale tourist office (☎ 9525 5255) is in Paterson St, Mundijong. There is also a 7km **walking trail** from Jarrahdale to the South-Western Highway; it follows part of the old Rockingham-Jarrahdale timber railway.

There is bush camping at Gooralong

Brook, in an area soon to be included in the national park. There is also a caravan park (☎ 9525 2528) near Serpentine Falls with powered sites for $15 for two; converted railway carriages (☎ 9525 5256) – popular but cold accommodation – near Whitby Falls (from $60 to $80 for two); and converted railway carriages (☎ 9525 5780) in Jarrahdale ($40 for two). You can get good meals, Wednesday to Sunday, at the *Whitby Falls Coach House Restaurant*.

North Dandalup & Dwellingup

These towns, respectively 71km and 97km south of Perth, are jumping-off points for the nearby forests. **Old Whittaker's Mill**, off Scarp Rd near North Dandalup, is a great spot for bushwalking and camping.

Destroyed by fire in 1961, Dwellingup has been rebuilt and is now a busy timber town. It is the terminus for the popular Hotham Valley Tourist Railway. The Bibbulmun Track (see Bushwalking in the Activities section of the Facts for the Visitor chapter) passes Dwellingup, some 500m to the east. Here, at Nanga Mill and Pool, is a night stopover for walkers on the track.

The **Forest Heritage Centre** (☎ 9538 1352), Acacia St, in a rammed earth building in the shape of three leaves, interprets the forest. (If you read between the lines, it is really an apologia for the timber industry.) It's open daily from 10 am to 5 pm; entry is $5/2/10 for adults/children/families.

There are group camping facilities (☎ 9538 1001) in the Dwellingup region.

Pinjarra

Pinjarra (population 9100), 86km south of Perth, has a number of old buildings picturesquely sited on the banks of the Murray River.

The Murray tourist office (☎ 9531 1438), in Pinjarra, is in the historic building **Edenvale**, on the corner of George and Henry Sts. Behind the historic mud-brick post office is a pleasant picnic area and a **suspension bridge** – wobbly enough to test most people's coordination! **St John's Church**, built in 1861 from mud bricks, is beside the original 1862 **schoolhouse**. Picturesque **Cooper's Mill**, on Culeenup Island and only accessible by boat, was the first in the Murray region.

About 4km from the town is the **Old Blythewood Homestead**, an 1859 colonial farm and a National Trust property.

Places to Stay & Eat The caravan park (☎ 9531 1374) at 95 Pinjarra Rd has tent/powered sites for $12/13 for two and on-site vans from $28. The *Pinjarra Motel* (☎ 9531 1811), 131 South-Western Highway, has singles/doubles with breakfast for $40/50.

The *Heritage Tearooms* serves light meals such as sandwiches and quiches for around $6.50. Other restaurants are the *Copper Kettle*, George St; and the *River Resort Restaurant*, Murray Lakes.

Steam Trains: Pinjarra to Dwellingup

Hotham Valley Tourist Railway steam trains run from Pinjarra to Dwellingup through blooming wildflowers and jarrah forests from August to October. You can find out the timetable from the Forest Ranger service by calling ☎ 9221 4444. The cost for adults is $26.50/34.50 in tourist/1st class, for children it is $15/19.50.

A short trip from Dwellingup to Etmilyn on the Etmilyn Forest Tramway (in a steam train), which operates Tuesday, Thursday, Saturday and Sunday, is $9/4.50 for adults/children. There are also a number of other rail adventures offered – see the timetable.

Waroona, Yarloop & Harvey

Originally called Drakesbrook, Waroona is another popular holiday spot, 112km south of Perth. It is ideally situated with Preston and Clifton lakes to the west and the forests to the east. If you follow Preston Beach Rd from Waroona you reach **Yalgorup National Park**, which has bushwalking trails through the tuart trees. Some 13km south of Waroona is Yarloop where there are restored engineering workshops dating from the steam and horse-drawn eras.

Inland from the south-west coast is the town of Harvey, in a bushwalking area of

green hills to the north of Bunbury. This is the home of WA's Big Orange, standing 20m high at the Fruit Bowl on the South-Western Highway. There are dam systems (Harvey Weir and Stirling Dam) and some beautiful waterfalls nearby.

The tourist office (☎ 9729 1122) is on the South-Western Highway. Committed vegetarians can hurl vitriol in a tour of EG Green & Sons abattoirs (☎ 9729 1000).

Places to Stay There is a range of accommodation in this region. In Waroona, try the *Waroona Caravan Village* (☎ 9733 1518), the *Drakesbrook Guesthouse* (☎ 9733 1245) where B&B is $35 per person, or the *Nanga Dell Farm* (☎ 9538 1035), on Kyabram Rd, where a cabin is $50 for four.

In Yarloop, there is the 1890 timber *Old Mill Guest House* (☎ 9733 5264), at 113 Railway Parade, where B&B is $25/40.

Harvey has the *Rainbow Caravan Park* (☎ 9729 2239), 199 King St, where tent/powered sites are $10/12 and on-site vans are $25 for two. The *Wagon Wheels Motel* (☎ 9729 1408), Uduc Rd, has singles/doubles for $55/60.

Rottnest Island

'Rotto', as it's known by the locals, is a sandy island about 19km off the coast of Fremantle. It's 11km long, 5km wide and is very popular with Perth residents and visitors. What do you do on Rotto? Well, you cycle around, laze in the sun on the many superb beaches (the Basin is the most popular, while Parakeet Bay is the place for skinny-dipping), climb the low hills, go fishing or boating, ride a glass-bottomed boat (Rotto has some of the southernmost coral in the world and a number of shipwrecks), swim in the crystal-clear water or go quokka spotting.

History

The island was discovered by the Dutch explorer de Vlamingh in 1696. He named the island 'Rats' Nest' because of the numerous

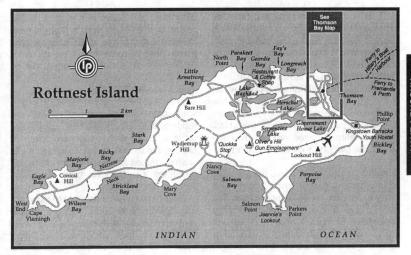

Rottnest Island

king-size 'rats' (quokkas) he saw there, but the Nyoongar knew it as Wadjemup.

There are signs of occupation dating from 7000 years ago when a hill on a coastal plain became the island after being cut off by rising seas, but it was uninhabited when the Europeans arrived. The Rottnest settlement was originally established in 1838 as a prison for Aborigines from the mainland – the early colonists had lots of trouble imposing their ideas of private ownership on the nomadic Aborigines. Although there were no new prisoners after 1903 the existing prisoners had to serve out their sentences until 1920.

After this the island soon became an escape for Perth society. Only in the last 30 years, however, has it really developed as a popular day trip. The island is considered a sacred site by the Nyoongar people because hundreds of their people died there; the buildings of the original prison settlement which held them are among the oldest in WA.

Information

There is an information office (☎ 9372 9752), open weekdays from 8.30 am to 5 pm, Saturday 9 am to 4 pm and Sunday 10 am to noon and 2.30 to 4 pm. It is just to the north of the jetty at Thomson Bay (the island's largest settlement) as you arrive. There, and at the museum, you can get useful publications, such as a walking tour of the old settlement buildings, Heritage Trail brochures, information on the various shipwrecks around the island and the *Rottnest Island Bicycle Guide* ($4). The latter has heaps of additional info on the island's flora & fauna.

Also, grab a copy of the brochure *Rottnest: WA's Holiday Isle*. Rottnest is very popular in summer when ferries and accommodation are heavily booked – plan ahead.

Things To See & Do

Rottnest Museum & Old Buildings There's an excellent museum with exhibits about the island, its history (including Aboriginal incarceration), wildlife and shipwrecks. You can pick up the *Vincent Way Heritage Trail* and the *Vlamingh Memorial Heritage Trail* walking-tour leaflets ($2/1, respectively) and wander around the interesting old convict-built buildings, including the octagonal 1864 'Quad' where the prison cells are now hotel rooms. The museum is open from 10 am to 4 pm in summer, 11 am to 4 pm in winter ($2).

There is also the excellent and free, one hour tour of the old buildings which takes in Vincent Way, the Aboriginal burial ground, the sea wall and boat sheds, the picturesque chapel and the Quad. The walk starts at the visitor centre at 11.15 am and 2 pm daily.

You can walk to **Vlamingh's Lookout** on View Hill, not far from Thomson Bay. You pass the old cemetery on the way and at the top you get panoramic views of the island. Also of interest is the recently restored **Oliver Hill Battery**, west of Thomson Bay.

Quokka-Watching The island has a number of low-lying salt lakes where you're most likely to spot the cuddly little quokkas. The quokka was one of the first marsupials spotted by Europeans and De Vlamingh unflatteringly described them as 'a kind of rat as big as a common cat, whose dung is found in abundance all over the island'.

The animal was known to the Aborigines as the *quak-a*, Europeanised into quokka. Quokkas were once found throughout the south-west but are now confined to patches of forest on the mainland and Rottnest. It is believed that there are 8000 to 12,000 on the island and you are bound to see one or two during your visit. Anniversary Park, on the right just after the last buildings of Thomson Bay (when heading to Kingstown), is a good spot to observe quokkas in the wild. Just walk off the road, sit down and watch.

Bus tours have regular quokka-feeding points (the 'quokka stop'), where the voracious marsupials seem to appear on demand. Quokka kicking, once a popular sport on the island, is now illegal!

Bird-Watching Rottnest is a great place for the avid twitcher as there are a number of habitats: coast, salt lakes, swamps, heath, woodlands and settlements. This means that you will see a great range of species.

Coastal birds include cormorants, reef heron, bar-tailed godwits, whimbrels, roseate, fairy, bridled and crested terns, oyster-catchers, and majestic ospreys.

There is a wedge-tailed shearwater colony at Radar Reef at the far western end of the

island and, at Phillip Point at the opposite end of the island, fairy terns nest on the sand. Parakeet Bay takes its name from the rock parrot, seen at many places on the coast feeding on sandfly larvae. Osprey can be seen along the southern coast from Strickland Bay to West End.

In the salt lakes you can see black swans, white-faced herons, red-necked avocets, ruddy turnstones, caspian terns, grey-tailed tattlers, stints and sandpipers. Even in Garden Lake, next to the village, you can see red-necked avocets, plovers and ruddy turnstones. Caspian terns breed near Government House Lake.

Ducks and teals are found in the swamps and turtledoves, welcome swallows and red-capped robins in the woodlands.

In the so-called disturbed areas are a great number of introduced birds such as the

The osprey patrols above water off Rottnest.

peafowl and natives such as the sacred king-fisher and rainbow bee-eater.

For more information, get *The Birdlife of Rottnest Island* by Denis Saunders & Perry de Rebeira (1985). For scientific names see the Bird Names glossary at the back of this book.

Rotto Underwater The glass-bottom boat *Underwater Explorer* allows viewing below the waterline for viewing shipwrecks and marine life. It departs hourly from 11.15 am from the jetty at Thomson Bay; an interesting 45 minute trip costs $15/8 for adults/children. Contact Boat Torque Cruises (☎ 9221 5844) to book in advance.

Some of Rotto's shipwrecks are accessible to snorkellers, but getting to them requires a boat. There are marker plaques around the island telling the sad tales of how and when the ships sank. Snorkelling equipment, fishing gear and boats can be hired from Dive, Ski & Surf (☎ 9292 5167) at Thomson Bay – one dive with all equipment provided is $50, two dives are $85.

Organised Tours

There's a two hour bus tour around the island for $9/4.50 for adults/children; there are daily departures at 11.15 am and 1.15 pm – again it is wise to book in the peak season. The tour visits the island's main **lighthouse** – built in 1895, it is visible 60km out to sea.

There is a light railway tour to Oliver's Hill gun emplacement; it leaves at 10.30 am from behind the Rottnest Hotel, then hourly (last trip at 1.30 pm), and costs $9/4.50. A tour and bike option is $15/7.50.

Sea Kayak Wilderness Adventure Tours (☎ (0411) 887 868) has a fascinating day trip (lunch provided) around the bays of the island for $120; it meets the Rottnest Express at Rottnest jetty at 8 am, fits you out with all your equipment and the paddle lasts until 3 pm.

Places to Stay

Most visitors to Rotto come only for the day but it's just as interesting staying on the island. You can camp for $12 (two people) in hired tents with rubber mattresses or get

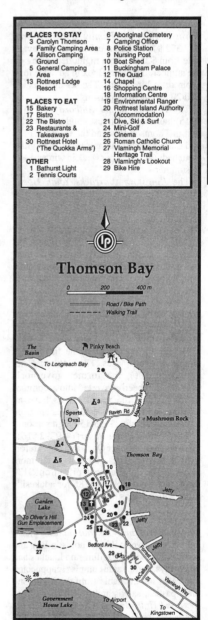

PLACES TO STAY
3 Carolyn Thomson Family Camping Area
4 Allison Camping Ground
5 General Camping Area
13 Rottnest Lodge Resort

PLACES TO EAT
15 Bakery
17 Bistro
22 The Bistro
23 Restaurants & Takeaways
30 Rottnest Hotel ('The Quokka Arms')

OTHER
1 Bathurst Light
2 Tennis Courts
6 Aboriginal Cemetery
7 Camping Office
8 Police Station
9 Nursing Post
10 Boat Shed
11 Buckingham Palace
12 The Quad
14 Chapel
16 Shopping Centre
18 Information Centre
19 Environmental Ranger
20 Rottnest Island Authority (Accommodation)
21 Dive, Ski & Surf
24 Mini-Golf
25 Cinema
26 Roman Catholic Church
27 Vlamingh Memorial Heritage Trail
28 Vlamingh's Lookout
29 Bike Hire

Thomson Bay

0   200   400 m

——— Road / Bike Path
– – – – Walking Trail

AROUND PERTH

tent sites at the *Allison Camping Ground* or *Carolyn Thomson Family Camping Area* (☎ 9372 9737). Safari cabins are also available from $25 to $66 a night, depending on the number of people. Book in advance for a cabin or to hire a tent. The set-up tents are $10/20 for one/four persons.

The *Rottnest Island Authority* (☎ 9372 9715) has over 250 houses and cottages for rent in Thomson Bay and the Geordie, Fays and Longreach Bay areas. Ocean-front villas (four beds) are $392 per week in winter, $492 in summer.

The *Kingstown Barracks Youth Hostel* (☎ 9372 9780), 1.2km from the ferry terminal, is housed in an old barracks built in 1936; the cost is from $14 for members and $17 for nonmembers (doubles are $34/40 for members/nonmembers). This place has more than the appearance of an army barracks – part of the complex is often shared with school groups on environmental awareness courses and hot water for a shower is only a reality if you get up before 6 am. The kitchen facilities are adequate and the salvation is the communal lounge with its pot-belly stove.

At the top end of the scale there are a couple of good places. The *Rottnest Hotel* (☎ 9292 5011), the former governor's mansion, has been converted into accommodation. All of the motel rooms have an en-suite and B&B singles/doubles are from $75/90 low season, $135/150 high season.

The *Rottnest Lodge Resort* (☎ 9292 5161) is based on the former Quad and boy's reformatory school. These days it is far more inviting. The units range in price from $130 for a standard double to $185 for a lakeside room which sleeps three.

Places to Eat

The *Rottnest Family Restaurant* has a pleasant balcony overlooking Thomson Bay and serves Chinese dishes, dim sum lunches and takeaways. In the same complex, cappuccino and cakes are available from the *Bistro* and pies, pasties, salads and health foods from the *Food Hall*. *Brolley's Restaurant*, in the Rottnest Hotel, also serves light and full

meals. There is the licensed *Garden Lake Restaurant* in the Lodge; sometimes there is entertainment.

The island has a general store and a bakery that is famous for its fresh bread and pies. There's also a fast-food centre in the Thomson Bay settlement. In the Lodge there is the *Governor's Bar* with a buffet on Tuesday, Wednesday and Thursday ($7). There's always the *Red Rooster*, also in the Thomson Bay shopping mall.

Geordie Bay has a licensed restaurant and coffee shop, open throughout the week during summer from 7 am to 7 pm. There is a liquor store attached.

Getting There & Away

Competition, bless it, has brought prices down for the ferry trip to Rotto. There are daily services, and many more services on weekends. The Rottnest Express (☎ 9335 6406) departs from C Shed Victoria Quay, Fremantle Port, daily at 7.30, 9.30 and 11.15 am, and 3.30 pm; adult/child fares are $28/8 for same-day return, $33/12 for an extended stay.

Oceanic Cruises (☎ 9430 5127) has done some monopoly busting and its *Supercat*, which leaves the East St jetty, Fremantle, costs only $25/8 for adults/children (same-day return); the extended stay cost is $30/12. From Pier 2, Barrack St jetty in Perth the fare is $35/12, or $40/15 for an extended stay.

Boat Torque (☎ 9430 7644, 9221 5844) leaves from Pier 4 Barrack St jetty, Northport (North Fremantle), East St jetty, and Hillary's Boat Harbour (north of Perth). Same-day return costs are slightly more expensive than those of Oceanic Cruises. Boat Torque's speedy, luxurious *Star Flyte* ferry from Barrack St jetty is $50/40 for a deluxe/economy return, and $33/28 from Northport. Boat Torque's *Sea Flyte*, from Hillary's Boat Harbour, is $37/27 for adults/backpackers.

Rottnest Airlines (☎ 9478 1322) has an $85 return special to Rotto, which includes lunch at the Lodge and a two hour guided tour of the island (admission to the island is $4.50/0.50 for adults/children). It provides transfers between Rottnest airport and Thomson Bay.

Getting Around

Bicycles are the time-honoured way of getting around the island. The number of motor vehicles is strictly limited, which makes cycling a real pleasure. Furthermore, the island is just big enough to make a day's ride good exercise.

You can bring your own bike over on the ferry (free at present from East St jetty) or rent one of the hundreds available on the island from Rottnest Bike Hire (☎ 9372 9722) in Thomson Bay. Adult/junior bikes cost $15/6 for the day – a refundable deposit of $10 is required and helmets and locks (bicycles are often stolen) are provided.

There are two bus services – the Settlement bus ($0.50) and the Bayseeker ($2). The latter does a loop around the whole island.

Darling Range

The hills that surround Perth are popular for picnics, barbecues and bushwalks. There are also excellent lookouts from where you can see Perth and further down the coast. Araluen with its constructed waterfalls, Mundaring Weir, Gooseberry Hill and Kalamunda national parks, and Lake Leschenaultia are all of interest.

One fascinating aspect of the Darling Ranges is their geological diversity – in the ranges you can explore evidence of the break up of Gondwanaland (formerly one of two ancient supercontinents). CALM provides a good free pamphlet *The Hills Forest*.

KALAMUNDA

The township of Kalamunda is about a 30 minute drive from Perth on the crest of the Darling Ranges. The area had its beginnings as a timber settlement in the 1860s but the clean air and magnificent bush later attracted Perth and Fremantle residents to this forest getaway. From Kalamunda, there are fine views over Perth to the coast.

The quaint mud-brick and shingle **Stirk's Cottage**, in Kalamunda, was built in 1881.

The **Gooseberry Hill National Park** with the amazing Zig Zag Rd is well worth the drive for spectacular views of the city. At **Kalamunda National Park** you can walk, rest and picnic in beautiful surroundings. There are also a number of wineries (Hainault Vineyard and Darlington Estate), plant nurseries and art & craft places nearby.

South of Kalamunda, just off the Brookton Highway, is **Araluen Botanic Park**, a real gem; you get to it from Gardiner Rd, Roleystone. It was originally constructed in the 1920s by the Australian Youth League as a bush retreat but it was neglected for many years and quickly became overgrown. In recent years, the almost 'archaeological' excavations have revealed elaborate garden terraces, waterfalls and an ornamental pool, all surrounded by many species of tall trees. Well worth a visit, it is open from 9 am to 6 pm daily and entry for cars/motorcycles is $5/2; there are barbecues and a popular restaurant.

Places to Stay & Eat

The *Kalamunda Hotel* (☎ 9257 1084), 43 Railway Rd, has singles/doubles for $35/50. Numerous B&B places are tucked away in the hills and valleys. At *Ville du Lac* (☎ 9293 3906), 58 Betti Rd, rooms are $30/60 and at the *Whistlepipe Cottage* (☎ 9291 9872), 195 Orange Valley Rd, B&B costs $35 per person.

Perth's tradition of good dining extends to the hills. If you are after coffee and a snack then try *Coffee Time*, *Village Coffee Shop*, *Barberry Cafe* and the *Kalamunda Cafe* in Kalamunda or *Le Croissant* on Gooseberry Hill Rd.

For a full meal you have the choice of the *Kalamunda Hotel* and *Williners Restaurant* on Railway Rd, the *Last Drop* and *Dons Family Restaurant* on Haynes St, and the *Copperwood* on Stirk St.

Getting There & Away

Get to Kalamunda from Perth on bus No 300 or 302 via Maida Vale from bus stand No 43 on St Georges Terrace; or bus No 292 or 305 via Wattle Grove and Lesmurdie also from bus stand No 43. Taking one route out and the other back makes for an interesting circular tour.

MUNDARING WEIR

Mundaring, in the ranges only 35km east from Perth, is the site of the Mundaring Weir – the dam built at the turn of the century to supply water to the goldfields over 500km to the east. The reservoir has an attractive setting and is a popular excursion for Perthites. There are a number of walking tracks.

The **CY O'Connor Museum** has models and exhibits about the water pipeline to the goldfields – in its time one of the world's most amazing engineering feats (see the boxed aside 'Where Water is like Gold!' in The Southern Outback chapter). The museum is open weekdays from 10.30 am to 3 pm, Saturday from 1 to 4 pm and Sunday 12.30 to 5 pm; it is closed on Tuesday.

North of the Great Eastern Highway, near the village of Chidlow, is the beautiful freshwater **Lake Leschenaultia**, ideal for picnics, bushwalking and swimming; there is an entry fee of $4 per car.

The 16 sq km **John Forrest National Park**, near Mundaring, has protected areas of jarrah and marri trees, native fauna, waterfalls and a pool. There is an admission fee of $5/3 for cars/motorcycles.

Places to Stay

The *Mundaring Caravan Park* (☎ 9295 1125), 2km west of town on the Great Eastern Highway, has powered sites for $7 for two. The *Djaril Mari YHA Hostel* (☎ 9295 1809), on Mundaring Weir Rd, is 8km south of town and costs $11 per person. The *Mundaring Weir Hotel* (☎ 9295 1106) is exceedingly popular with Perth escapees. Its quality units, constructed out of rammed earth, cost from $60 to $65 for two (add an extra $5 on Friday nights).

The historic *Mahogany Inn* (☎ 9295 1118), on the corner of the Great Eastern Highway and Homestead Rd, is well worth the $80/120 for single/double B&B.

WALYUNGA NATIONAL PARK

The river cuts a narrow gorge through the Darling Range at Walyunga National Park in Upper Swan. This 18 sq km park is off the Great Northern Highway, 40km north-east of Perth. There are walking tracks along the river and it's a popular picnic spot; there's an entry fee of $3 for each car. The **bushwalks** include a 5.2km return walk to Syd's Rapids, and a 1.7km Aboriginal Heritage Trail. Perhaps the best trail is the 10.6km Echidna Loop as it has tremendous views over the Swan and Avon valleys.

The park has one of the largest known campsites of the Nyoongar people and it was still in use last century. The area may well have been occupied by Aborigines for over 6000 years.

Avon Valley

The green and lush Avon Valley looks very English and proved a delight to homesick early settlers. In the spring, this area is particularly rich in wildflowers. In 1830, food shortages forced Governor Stirling to dispatch Ensign Dale to search the Darling Range for arable land – by August he had 'discovered' the Avon Valley. The valley was first settled in that year, only a year after Perth was founded, so there are many historic buildings in the area. The picturesque Avon River is very popular with canoeing enthusiasts.

Getting There & Away

Northam and Toodyay are connected to Perth with Avonlink; there are daily rail services from the East Perth terminal (one service only on Sunday). Fares from Perth to Toodyay are $9.70/19.40 one way/return, to Northam ($11.40/22.80).

Most people drive their own cars to York. You can also get there on the daily Westrail bus; the cost from Perth is $9.70. The best way to see the valley is by car as this allows you the flexibility to visit the many interesting places outside of the towns.

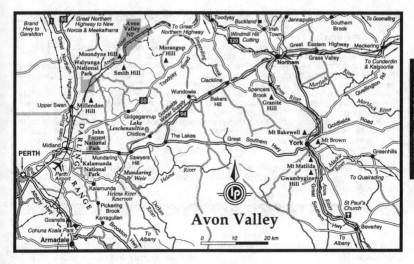

Avon Valley

TOODYAY
• *pop 800*

This charming, small town is only 85km north-east of Perth. There are numerous old classified and recorded buildings in this historic town, many of them built by convicts. Toodyay was declared an historic town by the National Trust in 1980.

Originally named Newcastle, the name Toodyay, from the Aboriginal *duidgee* ('place of plenty'), was applied in 1910. A big folk music festival is held here during the October long weekend.

Things to See & Do

The local tourist office (☎ 9574 2435) is in Connor's Mill, Stirling Terrace, which still houses a working flour mill. The kids have a lot of fun gristing their own wheat. It's open from 9 am to 5 pm (Sunday from 10 am); entry is $2.50/2 for adults/children.

The **Old Newcastle Gaol Museum**, on Clinton St, was built in the 1860s. The Moondyne Gallery tells the story of bushranger Joseph Bolitho Johns – see the boxed aside 'Moondyne Joe' in this section. The entrance fee is $3/2 for adults/children. Also

in town is the historic **St Stephen's Church**, built in 1862.

Some 5km from the town is the oldest inland **winery** in WA, Coorinja, which began operating in the 1870s; it specialises in fortified wines, particularly port. It is open daily, except Sunday.

Down the Perth road is the **White Gum Flower farm**, where native plants are cultivated for sale.

Places to Stay & Eat

Toodyay Caravan Park Avon Banks (☎ 9574 2612), Railway Rd, on the banks of the Avon River, has tent/powered sites for $8/12, on-site vans for $25 and chalets for $50; all prices are for two. It is noisy (as it's near the railway line and road) and the tent sites are as hard as rock. The *Broadgrounds Park* (☎ 9574 2534), off Racecourse Rd, has tent/powered sites for $5/15 (and camper's kitchen), on-site vans for $25 and chalets for $50.

The *Freemasons Hotel* (☎ 9574 2201) has basic B&B from $25 per person and inexpensive counter meals. On the same street is the *Victoria Hotel/Motel* (☎ 9574 2206) with singles/doubles for $20/40; add $10 if you

AROUND PERTH

Moondyne Joe

Every state should have a bushranger. The west's most famous bushranger was Joseph Bolitho Johns, known as Moondyne Joe, but he was more of a Harry Houdini than a Ned Kelly.

Transported to WA for larceny, he arrived in Fremantle in 1853 and was granted an immediate ticket of leave. In 1861 he was arrested on a charge of horse stealing, escaped from Toodyay gaol, was recaptured, and sentenced to three years' imprisonment.

He subsequently achieved infamy because of his ability to escape rather than the severity of his crimes. Between November 1865 and March 1867, he made four attempts to escape, three of them successful. He repeatedly returned to hide in the wild and inaccessible Darling Ranges while at large.

When eventually captured he was placed in a special reinforced cell with triple-barred windows in Fremantle. In 1867 when allowed out for exercise (you guessed it) he escaped and headed back to the hills east of Perth. He served more time in Fremantle prison when recaptured and was conditionally pardoned in 1873. After release he worked in the Vasse district and kept his nose clean until his death in 1900.

He is reputed to have discovered the caves near Margaret River, named after him. To find out more about Moondyne Joe, visit the Moondyne Gallery in Toodyay. The Moondyne Festival is held in Toodyay in May. ■

---

want a motel unit. Counter meals are available from $10.

On Duke St is *Lavender Cottage* (☎ 9574 4189), an elegant B&B where doubles are $75. *Pecan Hill Guesthouse* (☎ 9574 2636), to the west of Toodyay, has doubles for $75 midweek, and $85 on weekends.

There are a few eating places on Stirling Terrace including a bakery, *Wendouree Tearooms*, *Stirling House Cafe* (for light lunches and afternoon teas) and the *Lavender Cafe*. *Connor's Restaurant* is the best place in town, and is popular with day-trippers.

AVON VALLEY NATIONAL PARK

The park is 45km from Midland and access is along Toodyay, Morangup and Quarry roads. Features of the park are the granite outcrops, transitional forests and diverse fauna. The Avon River flows through the centre of the park in winter and spring but is usually dry at other times.

This is the northern limit of the jarrah forests, and the jarrah and marri are mixed with wandoo woodland. The two species of wandoo (*Eucalyptus accedens* and *E. wandoo*) grow in the heavy, clay soils; deep-rooted jarrah grows on the well-drained higher slopes; and the marri grows farther down the slope in moist, deep soil.

Many bird species make use of the diverse habitats in this forest – species seen are rainbow bee-eaters, a number of honey-eaters, kingfishers and rufous treecreepers. A number of animals and reptiles live in the understorey. Honey possums and western pygmy-possums hide among the dead leaves, and skinks and geckos are everywhere. Predators such as foxes and cats are a real problem and CALM is trying to eradicate them.

There are campsites with basic facilities such as pit toilets and barbecues; contact the ranger (☎ 9574 2540). A campsite is $5 for two, and entry to the park is free.

NORTHAM
• *pop 7500*

Northam, the major town of the Avon Valley, is a busy farming centre on the railway line to Kalgoorlie. The line from Perth once ended here and miners had to make the rest of the weary trek to the goldfields by road.

Northam is packed on the first weekend in August every year for the start of the gruelling 133km Avon Descent for power boats, kayaks and canoes. The friendly tourist office (☎ 9622 2100), in Minson Ave near the suspension bridge, is open daily from 9 am to 5 pm.

Things to See & Do

The 1836 **Morby Cottage** served as Northam's first church and school, and it now houses a museum open on Sunday; the entry fee is $2. The **old train station**, listed by the National Trust, has been restored and turned into a museum; it is open on Sunday from 10 am to 4 pm and admission is $2. Also of interest in town are the colony of **white swans** on the Avon River, descendants of birds introduced from England early this century.

If you have enough funds, try **ballooning** over the Avon Valley, on weekends from March to November; the cost is $160 per person.

Places to Stay

The *Northam Guesthouse* (☎ 9622 2301), 51 Wellington St, has cheap accommodation from $15 for the first night and $10 thereafter. On the same street, at No 426, is the *Grand Hotel* (☎ 9622 1024) with basic rooms and shared facilities for $20/40. The *Avon Bridge Hotel* (☎ 9622 1023), the oldest hotel in Northam, is also $20/40.

The only motel in town is aptly named the *Northam* (☎ 9622 1755), 13 John St; singles/doubles are $48/57. The *Shamrock Hotel* at 112 Fitzgerald St, is the best place in town with elegant en-suite bedrooms; a double will cost from $99.

Excellent out-of-town B&B choices are the farmstay *Egoline Reflections* (☎ 9622 5811), on the Toodyay Rd, which has single/double rooms for $85/110 (no children); *Brackson House* (☎ 9622 5262), 2 Old York Rd, for $80 a double; and *Stackallan Homestead)* (☎ 9622 7206), which is south of town, for $55/100.

Places to Eat

Near the tourist office are two tearooms, *Central Cafe* and *Lucy's*. *Tattersalls Hotel*, at 174 Fitzgerald St, also has lunch specials and is open for breakfast from 7 to 10 am. Next to Tattersalls Hotel, *Bruno's Pizza Bar* does tasty pizza to eat in or takeaway. The *Panda Chinese*, 59 Fitzgerald St, has main courses from $10 to $12. The *Whistling*

Kettle, 48 Broome Terrace, overlooks the river and is a great place to enjoy home-cooked food.

The Shamrock Hotel has a coffee shop, the best breakfast choice in town ($7.50), and the up-market *Gallery Restaurant* with Avon Valley yabbies for $14 and two courses for $35. If you want a steak, try the *Stonecourt Restaurant*, on the corner of Gordon and Chidlow Sts.

YORK
• *pop 2800*

The oldest inland town in WA, York is 97km from Perth. York was first settled in 1831, only two years after the Swan River Colony. Settlers saw similarities in the Avon Valley to their native Yorkshire, so Governor Stirling bestowed the name York on the region's first town.

Convicts were introduced to the York region in 1851 and helped in the development of the district; the ticket-of-leave hiring depot was not closed until 1872, four years after transportation to WA had ceased. During the gold rush, York prospered as a commercial centre, equipping miners who were travelling overland to Southern Cross and beyond. It is now a farming centre and a popular destination for locals looking to escape Perth for the weekend.

A stroll down the main street, with its restored old buildings, is a real step back in time. In fact, the many intact colonial and Victorian buildings have earned the National Trust classification of 'historic town'.

Orientation & Information

Most of the activity happens along Avon Terrace, very much the focal point of York. The tourist office (☎ 9641 1301) is in the old town hall; ask for a copy of the free booklet *York: The State's Festival Town*.

Things to See & Do

There are many fine, old buildings. The old **town hall**, the **Castle Hotel** (built in 1853), the old **police station**, **old gaol**, **courthouse** and **Settlers House** are all of interest. The old gaol and courthouse includes a main law court, old courtroom, prison cell block, prison exercise yard, trooper's cottage and stables with a carriage display. The **Residency**, Brook St, was built in the 1850s. It now houses a museum of York's history; it is open Tuesday to Thursday from 1 to 3 pm, weekends from 1 to 5 pm; entry is $2/1 for adults/children.

The **Holy Trinity Church**, on Pool St by the Avon River, was completed in 1854. It contains glass designed by the WA artist Robert Juniper (see under Arts & Culture in the Facts about Western Australia chapter)

and the high altar features his paintings. Also in the church is a rare pipe organ with eight bells. The suspension bridge near town was built in 1906 and it crosses the Avon River.

The classy **York Motor Museum** (a must for vintage-car enthusiasts) is on Avon Terrace. The cars in this museum range from an 1894 Peugeot to the Saudi Williams driven by Alan Jones, the 1980 world champion. It is open every day from 9 am to 5 pm – entry is $7/2 for adults/children.

Historic **Balladong Farm**, established in the 1830s, houses a museum which interprets

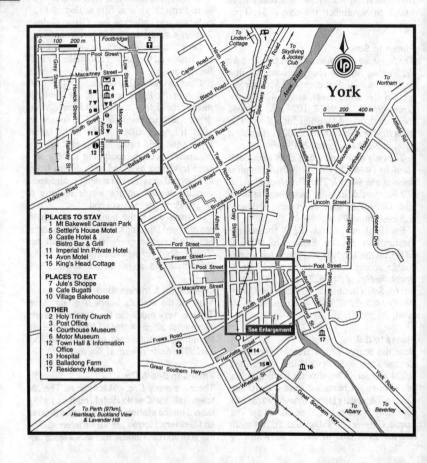

PLACES TO STAY
1 Mt Bakewell Caravan Park
5 Settler's House Motel
9 Castle Hotel &
    Bistro Bar & Grill
11 Imperial Inn Private Hotel
14 Avon Motel
15 King's Head Cottage

PLACES TO EAT
7 Jule's Shoppe
8 Cafe Bugatti
10 Village Bakehouse

OTHER
2 Holy Trinity Church
3 Post Office
4 Courthouse Museum
6 Motor Museum
12 Town Hall & Information
    Office
13 Hospital
16 Balladong Farm
17 Residency Museum

the lives of early pioneering families; there is a free 14 minute audiovisual presentation.

York has earned a reputation as the state's **skydiving** centre; the drop zone is at the racecourse, 3km from town. Many first-timers go there to do tandem jumps or accelerated free-fall courses. Skydive Express (☎ toll-free (1800) 355 833, 9444 4199), 353 Oxford St, Leederville, 6903, offers tandem jumps from 12,000/8000 feet for $300/220, accelerated free-fall jumps from 12,000/10,000 feet for $440/400; videos or photos are $80 extra.

Special Events

York is a festival town with no fewer than a dozen major events annually. The better patronised ones are the Jazz Festival in October and the Flying 50s Vintage & Veteran car race in August. Heritage Week is held in April (and some of the old houses are opened to the public), the agricultural show in September and car rallies in October.

Places to Stay

The only caravan park is the *Mt Bakewell Caravan Park* (☎ 9641 1421), which has tent/powered sites for $12/14, on-site vans for $30 for two. The old section of the historic, renovated *Castle Hotel* (☎ 9641 1007), on Avon Terrace, is good value with B&B singles/doubles from $30/60; the motel units are $70/100. The *Imperial Inn Private Hotel* (☎ 9641 1010), 83 Avon Terrace, is $36/60, room only.

There are a number of quality B&B and farmstays in the region; enquire at the tourist office. In town, *King's Head Cottage* (☎ 9641 1817), 39 Avon Terrace, is $50 for two; the *Settlers House Motel* (☎ 9641 1096), 125 Avon Terrace, is from $69/98, breakfast included; and *Linden Cottage* (☎ 9641 1421), at the foot of Mt Bakewell, is $50 for a double.

Places to Eat

All of the eateries are along Avon Terrace. *Cafe Bugatti* serves Italian food (spaghetti

bolognaise $8.50, lasagne $9), a great range of cakes and cappuccino.

The *York Village Bakehouse* sells freshly baked bread and cakes, and *Jule's Shoppe* has exquisite pasties and some vegetarian selections. The *Castle Hotel* serves good counter meals from $10 and has an à la carte restaurant or you can eat outside in the verandah cafe.

BEVERLEY

South-east of York, also on the Avon River, is Beverley, founded in 1838 and named after a town in Yorkshire. It is noted for its fine **aeronautical museum** open daily from 9 am to 4 pm. Exhibits include a locally constructed biplane *Silver Centenary*, built between 1928 and 1930.

The **grave** of a local Aborigine, Billy Noongale, who accompanied Sir John Forrest on his journey from Perth to Adelaide in 1870, is in Brooking St. The Beverley information office (☎ 9646 1555) is in Vincent St.

The **town hall** and **Beverley Hotel** are good examples of Art Deco architecture. The **Dead Finish Hotel** was built in 1872. With the advent of the railway, the town centre was moved closer to the train station, leaving the Dead Finish isolated; it is now a museum.

The 7 sq km **Avondale Discovery Farm**, 6km west of Beverley on Waterhatch Rd, has a collection of agricultural machinery, a homestead, a workshop and stables. Equidistant between York and Beverley is **Gwambygine Park** where there is a viewing tower over a permanent pool on the Avon River.

Places to Stay & Eat

The *Beverley Caravan Park* (☎ 9646 1200), on Vincent St, has tent sites for $12 for two. The ordinary *Beverley Hotel* (☎ 9646 1190), 137 Vincent St, has B&B for $24/47. The *Rosedale Farmstay* (☎ 9648 1031), on the York-Williams Rd charges $62.50 per person, and *Wonderlin Merino Stud* (☎ 9646 1239), 6km south of town, is $70.

Two delis, *Beverley* and *Marg's*, are both on Vincent St. The hotels serve counter meals.

North Coast

The coast north of Perth has great scenery with long sand dunes, but it quickly becomes the inhospitable terrain that deterred early visitors. The north coast really begins at Yanchep and its satellite town of Two Rocks and extends up through Nambung National Park, site of the Pinnacles, to the coastal town of Jurien.

To get to Lancelin, follow State Highway 60, which branches off to the north-west at Wanneroo. The Pinnacles (Nambung) and Jurien are reached from the Brand Highway (Highway 1) which runs inland.

Getting There & Away

Catch-a-Bus (☎ 9019) 378 987), which picks up from backpackers' in Perth on Wednesday, Friday and Sunday, runs to Seabird ($13), Ledge Point ($16) and Lancelin ($17); sailboards are $5 extra.

Coastal Coachlines (☎ 9652 1036) runs a service from Perth to Cervantes ($20.50), Jurien ($21.50), Green Head and Leeman on Friday, Monday and public holidays.

Daily there is a bus from opposite the Cervantes post office to the highway to meet the north and southbound Greyhound services; it is operated by Happyday Tours (☎ 9652 7244) who carry on to the Pinnacles (allowing you to use the Kilometre Pass).

YANCHEP

The first break in Perth's northward urban sprawl is Yanchep, 51km north of Perth, at the end of the Swan Coastal Plain. The name comes from the Aboriginal *yanget* after the bulrushes at the edge of the lakes.

Yanchep National Park has natural bushland with tuart forests, some fine caves (Crystal and Yondemp) and Loch McNess. You can go inside the limestone Crystal Cave; entry is $2/1 for adults/children.

The 28km **Yaberoo Budjara Aboriginal Heritage Trail** follows a chain of lakes used by the Yaberoo people; serious walkers can obtain a brochure from the national park

office. The park features such fauna as the honey possum, grey kangaroo, bandicoots, reptiles and a host of water birds. The koala, not indigenous to the west, can also be seen here in a special large enclosure (photos are $8). The national park information office (☎ 9561 1004) has plenty of ideas on activities in the area; the entry fee is $5 per car.

There is the Yanchep Stables (☎ 9561 1606) for those keen on horse-riding, and Blue Dolphin Dive Tours (☎ 9561 1106) for those wishing to explore the lagoon reefs.

Yanchep Sun City is a major marina with a modern shopping complex and Perth's only country beach resort.

On weekdays, one bus goes to Yanchep from the Wellington St bus station.

Places to Stay

There are a handful of places to stay. The *Yanchep Lagoon Lodge Guest House* (☎ 9561 1033), 11 Nautical Court, has doubles for $60. The *Yanchep Holiday Village* (☎ 9561 2244), 56 St Andrews Drive, specialises in family units, accommodating four to six, which cost from $330 to $590 weekly.

Also on Two Rocks Rd is the *Lodge Capricorn Motel* (☎ 9561 1106) with doubles from $95 to $125.

GUILDERTON & SEABIRD

Some 43km north of Yanchep is Guilderton, a popular holiday resort, at the mouth of the Moore River. The *Vergulde Draeck*, part of the Dutch East India Company fleet, ran aground near here in 1656. There is good fishing both in the Moore River and in the ocean. There is a caravan park (☎ 9577 1021) with tent/powered sites for $10/12 for two, and the three bedroom *CWA Guilderton Cottage* (☎ 9577 1040) from $35 for eight.

Seabird, 36km north of Guilderton, is a quaint fishing village. It also has a caravan park (☎ 9577 1038) close to a swimming area which is safe for children. On-site vans are $40 and cabins from $60 for two.

LEDGE POINT & LANCELIN

Ledge Point, 115km from Perth, is another

fishing town and a very popular holiday spot for Perth families. It is the starting point for the Ledge Point-Lancelin Sailboard Classic, held in January.

The coast road (State Highway 60) ends at Lancelin, a small fishing port 14km north of Ledge Point, but coastal tracks continue north and may be passable with a 4WD. Lancelin was possibly named after PF Lancelin, a French scientific writer, by the 1801 French expedition (which passed here in the *Naturaliste* and *Geographe*). Windswept Lancelin is the finishing point of the 24km annual sailboard race from Ledge Point. This race is now an important event on the world windsurfing calendar.

For those keen to learn **windsurfing** there is Werner's Hot Spot (☎ 9655 1553), 25 Ayres Crescent; beginners' boards are $20 per hour, weekly rentals of advanced boards $190. Lessons are also provided by the qualified instructors from Club Mistral (☎ 9655 1422); they are in the big yellow trailer seen on the beach from November to April. Another outfit is Lancelin Surfsports (☎ 9655 1422) – a one hour express/intense lesson is $15/30.

Fishing, boating, diving and swimming are options for those who have yet to stand up on a windsurfer; contact Lancelin Seaquest Charters (☎ 9655 1665) for diving.

You can get information (☎ 9655 1155), daily from 10 am to 4 pm.

Places to Stay & Eat

There is a plethora of accommodation in these towns but booking is strongly advised during holiday periods.

The *Ledge Point Caravan Park* (☎ 9655 1066) has powered sites/on-site vans for $13/45 for two. Other options are the *Fern Tree Court Holiday Units* (☎ 9655 1069), Jones St, with singles/doubles for $60/80; and the *Gilt Dragon Villas* (☎ 9655 1069), on the corner of Hill St and Harris Place, from $100 to $120 per day (the villas sleep four).

Lancelin has two caravan parks, the *North End* (☎ 9655 1115) and *Lancelin* (☎ 9655 1056), where tent/powered sites are $10/12 for two, and on-site vans from $32.

The tidy, purpose-built backpackers', the *Lancelin Lodge* (☎ 9655 2020) is in Hopkins St. It is run by two travellers, Trish and Trev, who have included many of the features they would have liked to have seen in accommodation while they were on the road (such as a fully equipped kitchen). A comfortable dorm bed is $15, and neat doubles are $40 ($50 in peak season).

There are also *Campbells Cottages* (☎ 9655 1181); the *Lancelin Holiday Village* (☎ 9655 1100); an inn/motel/hotel (☎ 9655 1005); *Ocean Front Flats* (☎ 9655 1029) and the *Windsurfer Beach Chalets* (☎ 9655 1454); the latter are $50 for two. Ask about the much cheaper weekly rates.

The preferred hang-out in Lancelin is the *Endeavour Tavern* near the jetty. Cafes include *Shipwrecks*, *El Tropo's* for Chinese and Italian and *Finny's Pizza* (a medium pizza is from $12 to $14); all three are in Gingin Rd. The *Offshore Cafe* at The Point has fish and chips, and vegetarian selections.

PINNACLES DESERT

The small seaport of **Cervantes**, 257km north of Perth, was named after an American whaling ship wrecked on nearby islands. This town is the entry point for the unusual and haunting (and not to be missed) Pinnacles Desert. The Cervantes Shell service station (☎ 9652 7041) acts as the tourist office, although the Pinnacles Beach Backpackers' has plenty of information.

In the coastal **Nambung National Park**, the flat, sandy desert is punctured with peculiar limestone pillars, some only a few cm high and others towering up to 5m.

These pillars are calcified spires, around 30,000 years old, which have been gradually uncovered by erosion. Some have eroded into extraordinary, weird shapes. To the south of the main group is an area known as the Tombstones, where dark spires protrude from the vegetated landscape. The different colour comes from lichen, which grows on the Pinnacles as they are protected from the sandblasting action of the wind. When Dutch sailors saw the Pinnacles from the sea they though they were the ruins of an ancient city.

If possible, try to visit the Pinnacles Desert early in the morning. Not only is the light better for photography but you will avoid the crowds which tend to clutter the view, especially in peak holiday times. Full moon over the Pinnacles is also not to be missed. The park is the scene of an impressive display of **wildflowers** from August to October – look out for daisies, leschenaultia, lilies, grevillea, banksia and kangaroo paw.

Nambung may have the appearance of a desert but it still contains a wealth of fauna and the observant will spy many animal and reptile tracks. Snakes, skinks, geckos, western blue tongue lizards, bearded dragons, kangaroos, brush wallabies and dunnarts are all present in the park. Bird species are plentiful with many raptors, honeyeaters, emus and wrens. The Australian or kori bustard was once prolific but has been affected greatly by predation.

Check in Cervantes before attempting to drive the road into the park – if conditions are bad, a 4WD may be necessary for the last 6km from the Hangover Bay turn-off but usually the road is OK, if somewhat bumpy, for normal vehicles. A coastal 4WD track runs north to Jurien, a crayfishing centre, and south to Lancelin (except when the Hill River is in flood). The sand dunes along the coast are spectacular.

Organised Tours

Cervantes Pinnacles Adventure Tours (☎ 9652 7236) operates daily tours from 33 Brown St. The Pinnacles tour includes a 4WD jaunt along the beach from Hangover Bay, refreshments, entrance fee to the Pinnacles and commentary ($27.50). There is another thrilling 4WD trip (also $27.50) up and over sand dunes, down narrow overgrown tracks to a 'rollercoaster hill' where the 4WD tackles the dunes. Once at the top you sandboard down a few times, before having a relaxing snack at a secluded beach. A combined trip – Pinnacles and sandboarding – is $44. There are also a number of combined 4WD/boat trips.

If you drive into the Pinnacles Desert yourself, there is a $5 car entry fee. There are

many tours to the Pinnacles from Perth. The occasional bus service operated to the park from the Cervantes Shell service station (☎ 9652 7041) is $12 per person (plus $2 entry).

Places to Stay & Eat

Accommodation in the area includes the *Pinnacles Caravan Park* (☎ 9652 7060) on the beachfront with tent/powered sites for $10/13 for two, and on-site vans from $25.

The new purpose-built *Pinnacles Beach Backpackers'* (☎ 9652 7377) at 91 Seville St was much needed. It has a well-equipped, airy kitchen, plenty of recreation space and tidy rooms; dorm beds are $15, en-suite doubles $50 and family rooms $40 for two (plus $8 for each child, which adds up).

Cervantes Pinnacles Motel (☎ 9652 7145), 227 Aragon St has singles/doubles for $60/75, while *Cervantes Holiday Homes* (☎ 9652 7115), on the corner of Valencia Rd and Malaga Court, has self-contained units from $40 for two.

The local pizza shop has small supremes for $10, medium vegetarians for $12.50 and large specials for $18. The Cervantes Shell service station has a takeaway; the *Ronsard Bay Tavern*, 219 Cadiz St, serves counter meals ($6.50 for chicken and chips); and the Cervantes Motel has the licensed *Europa Anchor Restaurant*.

JURIEN

This coastal town is 38km west of the Brand Highway and 266km north of Perth. (A coastal route runs due north from Cervantes but it is 4WD only.) Jurien, centre of a thriving crayfishing industry, is a great holiday destination for those who love boating, fishing and swimming. The **old jetty** was used in the late 1800s to load wool, from inland stations, onto boats bound for Fremantle and India. The Jurien tourist office (☎ 9652 1444) is in the BP service station on Bashford St.

Places to Stay

The caravan park (☎ 9652 1595) has tent/powered sites for $10/13, and on-site vans from $25 to $45. The *Jurien Bay Holiday*

PAUL STEEL

Around Perth
The Pinnacles, ancient limestone pillars surrounded by flat sandy desert, in Nambung
National Park

JEFF WILLIAMS

JEFF WILLIAMS

JEFF WILLIAMS

JEFF WILLIAMS

A	B
C	D

South-West Coast

A: The 60m climb up the Gloucester Tree, near Pemberton

B: The view from the Gloucester Tree

C: Bushtucker feast – bardi grubs and all

D: In search of bushtucker by canoe, Margaret River

Flats (☎ 9652 1172), Grigson St, are $40 for two. The *Jurien Bay Motel Hotel* (☎ 9652 1022), Padbury St, has singles/doubles for $50/65. There are a number of chalets in the town; enquire at the tourist office.

GREEN HEAD & LEEMAN
Green Head, on the coast 288km north of Perth, is blessed with the beautiful **Dynamite Bay**, great for snorkelling and swimming.

Leeman, 7km further north, was named after a navigator on the Dutch ship *Waeckende Boey* (sent to rescue survivors of the *Vergulde Draeck)*. It has a much more colourful past and now houses the workforce of a nearby mineral sands project.

There is a caravan park (☎ 9953 1131) in Green Head and a caravan park (☎ 9953 1080) in Leeman.

NATIONAL PARKS
In addition to Nambung, there are a number of other interesting national parks not too far north of Perth. **Stockyard Gully National Park**, named after one of the stopping places used by drovers on the North Road stock route, is reached from the Coorow-Green Head Rd; access is by 4WD only. Some 5.6km down Grover Rd is the ancient underground river system of Stockyard Gully tunnel, about 300m long (torches/flashlights are needed). Tours can be arranged through Jurien Bus & Charter Tours (☎ 9652 1036).

It is worth walking the 90 minute Badgingarra Trail in **Badgingarra National Park**. The park, on the west side of the Brand Highway and opposite the town of Badgingarra, was established to protect the wildflowers which grow there in numbers.

Between the Brand Highway and State Highway 116 (Midlands Way) there are a number of national parks noted for their wildflowers. **Watheroo** – 443 sq km of sandy plain north-east of Badgingarra – has some rare flora; the **Alexander Morrison National Park**, between Coorow and Green Head, is one of the best locations in the state to view wildflowers; and **Tathra**, east of Eneabba, preserves important flora & fauna.

Lesueur National Park This is one of the most diverse and rich flora areas in WA with over 900 species (perhaps 10% of the state's classified flora). It is a breeding area for Carnaby's black cockatoo.

The Lesueur Fault, Mt Lesueur and the Cockleshell Gully formation can all be explored. Cervantes Pinnacles Adventure Tours (☎ 9652 7236) operates an interesting trip to the Mt Leseur Trail ($50).

Hi-Vallee Farm (☎ 9652 3035), on Tootbardi Rd close to Mt Leseur National Park, is a great place to see the diverse wildflowers of the region. The Williams family explain whichever flora is flowering at the time; the cost is $6/16 without/with lunch. You can also camp here ($5 per person), stay in a self-contained caravan ($10) or have fullboard homestay (tremendous value at $26).

The South-West

The south-west of WA has a magnificent coastline, rugged ranges, national parks and the greenest and most fertile areas – a great contrast to the dry and barren country found in much of the state. You will find great patches of forest, famous surfing beaches, whale and dolphin-watching, prosperous farms, the Margaret River wineries and more of the state's beautiful wildflowers.

In this chapter, the south-west includes the southern coast from Bunbury to Augusta, taking in a number of wineries, and the 'tall trees' hinterland (Southern Forests)to the east. The main towns of the region are Bunbury, Busselton, Margaret River, Augusta, Manjimup, Pemberton and Northcliffe.

Getting There & Away
Westrail (☎ 13 22 32) buses go daily from Perth to Bunbury ($16.30), Busselton ($21.30), Yallingup ($24.50), Margaret River ($24.50) and Augusta ($29.10).

South-West Coachlines (☎ 9324 2333, 9754 1666 and 9791 1955) also services the region and has daily services from Perth to Bunbury ($16), Busselton ($20), Dunsborough ($22), Margaret River ($23) and Augusta ($28), and Monday to Friday services to Collie ($20), Donnybrook ($20), Bridgetown ($23), Manjimup ($27), Nannup ($24) and Balingup ($23).

The Easyrider Backpackers bus (☎ 9383 7848) also stops off at hostels in 13 of the south-west towns ($129 for a loop pass).

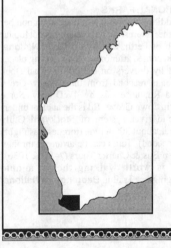

> ## HIGHLIGHTS
>
> - Watching the dolphins' spontaneous visits to Koombana Beach, Bunbury
> - The labyrinthine limestone caves between the Capes – especially stunning Lake Cave and the beautiful Jewel and Ngilgi caves
> - The lighthouse at the end of the world – Cape Leeuwin, where two oceans, the Southern and the Indian, meet
> - Margaret River – nirvana for a wine-drinking surfer – it has great surf breaks and some of Australia's premium wineries
> - The timber town of Pemberton and the surrounding forests – home of the Gloucester, Bicentennial and Diamond tree fire towers
> - The tourist drive and interpretive walks through the karri forest of Shannon National Park

Bunbury Region

BUNBURY
- *pop 26,000*

Western Australia's second largest town, some 180km south of Perth, is a port, an industrial town and a holiday resort. It is a pleasant place, worth at least a day in a trip to the south-west. Some scientific boffins actually identified Bunbury as being in a region with the 'most comfortable climatic environment for human existence'.

The town lies at the western end of Leschenault Inlet which Nicolas Baudin, commander of *Le Geographe*, sighted in 1803 and named after his botanist Jean

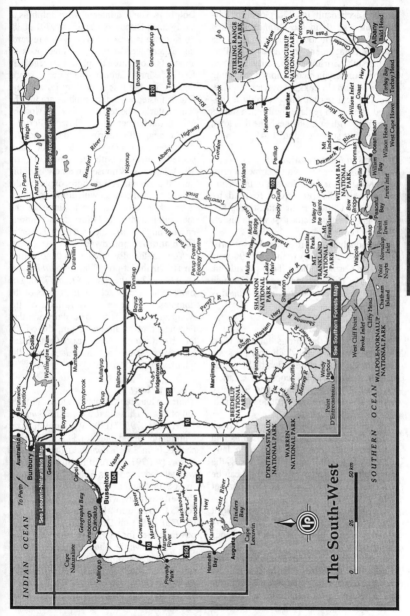

The South-West

Batiste Leschenault. In 1836, Governor Stirling sailed south in the *Sulphur* and met Henry William Bunbury, commander of the military detachment in Pinjarra, at Port Leschenault. Stirling supposedly renamed the port Bunbury in recognition of the young officer's efforts in trekking overland to meet him. The real reason was probably a concerted attempt to replace the French names on the map with English ones! The first town lots were not surveyed until 1841.

Orientation & Information

Bunbury is an easy town to come to grips with. Most of the facilities are in the centre of town in the rectangle formed by Wittenoom, Clifton, Blair and Stirling Sts. The main street is Victoria St which bisects the town centre.

The nonchalant Port of Bunbury tourist bureau (☎ 9721 7922) is in the 1904 train station on Carmody Place. They provide the free *Port of Bunbury Visitors Guide*, which includes an interesting stroll around this tidy town.

Things to See & Do

The town's old buildings include **King Cottage**, Forrest Ave, which now houses a museum; the **Rose Hotel**, Victoria St; and **St Mark's Church** (1842), corner of Charterhouse and Flynn Rds. Interesting **Bunbury Regional Art Galleries**, Wittenoom St, is in a restored 1897 convent.

The **Big Swamp Wildlife Park** on Prince Phillip Drive has kangaroos, possums and caged birds; it is open 10 am to 5 pm daily and entry is $3/1 for adults/kids. Across the road, some 70 species of water bird can be observed in a more natural environment from boardwalks (for free).

The daring can take a **microlight flight** from the airport with SW Microlights (☎ (015) 389 417); it is $60 for a half-hour introductory flight.

In February the Leschenault Inlet hosts the **International Dragon Boat Races**. At Easter you can witness the **Aqua Spectacular**, a water sports festival where the waterways are choked with all sorts of craft.

Dolphins You can interact with dolphins at the Dolphin Discovery Centre (☎ 9791 3088) on Koombana Beach. This can be a rewarding experience. Visits from three pods of about 100 bottlenose dolphins that regularly feed in the Inner Harbour usually occur several times a day but less frequently in winter; a flag is hoisted when the dolphins are in. The 'encounter' is better than that at Monkey Mia, and it happens much closer to Perth!

The area, staffed during the day by helpful volunteers, was set up in 1989, and dolphins started to interact with the public in early 1990. The trust is housed in a new building near the beach. A brochure explains the simple rules of contact with dolphins; otherwise ask a volunteer. The audiovisual and museum is a must ($5/4 for adults/children, casual entry). Across the road from the centre is a **mangrove boardwalk**.

You can literally dance with the dolphins on a trip in the jet-propelled *Dolphin Dancer* (☎ 9791 1827); the cost is $12.50/7.50. The more sedate can watch the high jinks of the dolphins in more leisurely fashion on the *Naturaliste Lady*. Trips go out daily, weather dependent, at 11 am and 2 pm; the cost is $15/10. In summer catch the boat outside the Discovery Centre, and in winter from the wharf.

Places to Stay

There are four caravan parks in town and two out of town. Those in town are the *Bunbury Village* (☎ 9795 7100), Washington Ave, with tent/powered sites for $12/13 for two, chalets from $55; *Koombana Bay Holiday Resort* (☎ 9791 3900), in Koombana Drive, with tent/powered sites from $13/15, chalets from $100; *Bunbury Glade* (☎ 9721 3800), Bussell Highway, with powered sites/cabins for $13/32; and the small *Punchbowl* (☎ 9721 4761) on Ocean Drive, with tent/powered sites for $11/13, on-site vans from $26. Out of town, the *Waterloo Village* (☎ 9725 4434), South-Western Highway, has powered sites/on-site vans for $12/35 for two; and the *Riverside Cabin Park* (☎ 9725 1234), Pratt Rd, Eaton, has on-site vans/chalets from $28/45.

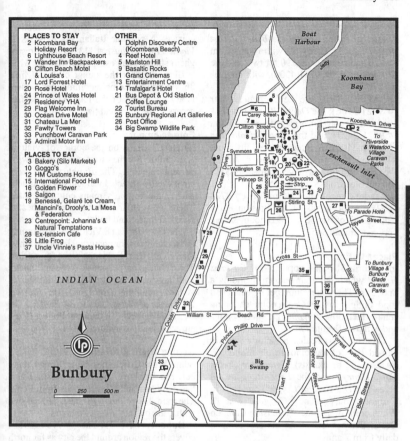

PLACES TO STAY
2 Koombana Bay
  Holiday Resort
6 Lighthouse Beach Resort
7 Wander Inn Backpackers
8 Clifton Beach Motel
  & Louisa's
17 Lord Forrest Hotel
20 Rose Hotel
24 Prince of Wales Hotel
27 Residency YHA
29 Flag Welcome Inn
30 Ocean Drive Motel
31 Chateau La Mer
32 Fawlty Towers
33 Punchbowl Caravan Park
35 Admiral Motor Inn

PLACES TO EAT
3 Bakery (Silo Markets)
10 Goggo's
12 HM Customs House
15 International Food Hall
16 Golden Flower
18 Saigon
19 Benessé, Gelaré Ice Cream,
  Mancini's, Drooly's, La Mesa
  & Federation
23 Centrepoint: Johanna's &
  Natural Temptations
28 Ex-tension Cafe
36 Little Frog
37 Uncle Vinnie's Pasta House

OTHER
1 Dolphin Discovery Centre
  (Koombana Beach)
4 Reef Hotel
5 Marlston Hill
9 Basaltic Rocks
11 Grand Cinemas
13 Entertainment Centre
14 Trafalgar's Hotel
21 Bus Depot & Old Station
  Coffee Lounge
22 Tourist Bureau
25 Bunbury Regional Art Galleries
26 Post Office
34 Big Swamp Wildlife Park

Bunbury

The efficiently run and friendly *Wander Inn – Bunbury Backpackers* (☎ 9721 3242) is close to the town centre and the ocean at 16 Clifton St. It costs $14 for a dorm bed, $32 for a double or twin. Their adventure tours and eco-safaris have been the subject of praise in many readers' letters. A trip to the forests, waterfalls and wildflowers around Wellington Dam, especially suited to backpackers, is $15/25 for a half-day/day. Phone ☎ toll-free (1800) 064 704) for a free pick-up from the train station.

The *Residency YHA* (☎ 9791 2621) is on the corner of Stirling and Moore Sts in an historic residence. Good dorm beds in this clean hostel are $15 ($13 for members), doubles are $28 and a family room is $35. They also rent bicycles for $10 per day.

The *Prince of Wales Hotel* (☎ 9721 2016) at 41 Stephen St has B&B doubles for $60. The *Rose Hotel* (☎ 9721 4533) is a clean, lavishly restored place; yet the rooms, $53/66 with breakfast, are rough and ready. The big hotel in town is the *Lord Forrest* (☎ 9721 9966), on Symmons St, with singles/doubles for about $110/145.

There are plenty of motels in town. The *Admiral Motor Inn* (☎ 9721 7322) is close to the town centre; singles/doubles are $70/80. Also close is the *Lighthouse Beach Resort* (☎ 9721 1311), Carey St, with rooms from $50/70 and suites from $90 for two; and the *Clifton Beach* (☎ 9721 4300), with doubles for $70.

On Ocean Drive are the *Chateau La Mer* (☎ 9721 3166); the *Ocean Beach* (☎ 9721 2033); the courageously named *Fawlty Towers* (☎ 9721 2427); and the *Flag Welcome Inn* (☎ 9721 3100). Singles/doubles are about $45/60 at the first three places. At the Welcome Inn singles range from $68 to $115 and doubles from $78 to $135.

Readers recommend *Taralea* (☎ 9728 1252), on the banks of the Preston River 12km south of Bunbury; B&B doubles are a very reasonable $45.

Places to Eat
In Victoria St is the popular *HM Customs House*, which has four outlets, including a brasserie. There are a number of cafes and food outlets in the Centrepoint shopping centre, including *Johanna's Coffee Lounge* and *Natural Temptations*.

There are lots of cafes in Victoria St, aptly named the 'cappuccino strip'. *Mancini's*, *Benessé* ($8 breakfasts), *Gelaré Ice Cream Café*, *Henry's* and the *Federation* are all here. The *Old Station Coffee Lounge* is in Carmody Place; trendy *Goggo's* is at 18 Wittenoom St; and the *Ex-Tension Cafe*, on Ocean Drive overlooking the sea, is open daily from 7 am.

Drooly's, at 70 Victoria St, does great pizzas for moderate prices, and is open from 5 pm until late. The *Rose Hotel*, on Victoria St, does good counter meals and has nine beers on tap. The *Golden Flower*, 57 Victoria St, is a reliable Chinese place. Those wanting to try tasty Vietnamese *pho* at $6.50 for a huge bowl, should go to the *Saigon* on Victoria St. And Tex-Mex is also represented at *La Mesa* at 52 Victoria St; a huge nachos is $7.50, and a mix of enchilada, taco and tostada is $10.50.

If you are after French cuisine then hop into the *Little Frog* on Rose St, which has a set menu at $25. *Louisa's*, 15 Clifton St, is

an award-winner with innovative modern cuisine. A popular Italian place is *Uncle Vinnie's Pasta House* at 113 Spencer St; spaghetti slurpers can escape satisfied for $15.

Bistro meals in the lounge of *Trafalgar's*, 36 Victoria St, come recommended – there is always a fish of the day ($12) and free access to the big salad bar.

Entertainment
Grand Cinemas, on the corner of Victoria and Clifton Sts, has four cinemas showing current releases. The *Bunbury Entertainment Centre* attracts local and overseas acts, and is the region's main cultural centre. There are regular performances of theatre, classical music and ballet.

The *Reef Hotel* at 8 Victoria St is currently the social focus for nocturnal Bunburyians – the verdant Reef Bar is the place for a drink. There is an active pub music scene in Bunbury with musicians performing at a number of venues including *Trafalgar's*, the *Parade*, the *Prince of Wales* and the *Burlington*. The *Westend Nightclub*, in the Lord Forrest Hotel, attracts the more mature clubbing type.

Getting There & Around
South-West Coachlines buses travel daily between Bunbury and Perth. Westrail also has daily bus and train services from Perth. The train *Australind* ($18) takes around two hours; the bus just over two hours.

Bunbury City Transit (☎ 9791 1955) covers the region around the city as far north as Australind and south to Gelorup. You can get a bus from the tourist bureau to the train station for free.

AROUND BUNBURY
Australind
Australind (population 800), yet another holiday resort, is a pleasant 11km drive north of Bunbury. The town takes its name from an 1840s plan to make it a port for trade with India. The plan never worked but the strange name (from 'Australia-India') remains.

The tiny **St Nicholas Church** (1860), on Paris Rd, is just 4m by 7m, and is said to be the smallest church in Australia. **Henton**

Cottage, built in 1842 from local materials, has arts and crafts for sale. There is a wonderful scenic drive between Australind and Binningup along **Leschenault Inlet**, a good place to net blue manna crabs.

Places to Stay Australind has two caravan parks: *Leschenault Inlet* (☎ 9797 1095), Scenic Drive; and the *Holiday Homes* (☎ 9725 1206), on the Old Coast Rd. *Castlehead B&B* (☎ 9797 0272), Elinor Bell Rd, is $30/55 a single/double; and *Leschenault B&B* (☎ 9797 1352), 14 Old Coast Rd, is $30/60.

Collie

Collie, WA's only coal town (with a regional population of 10,000), is 202km south of Perth. It has an interesting replica of a coal mine, an historical museum and a steam locomotive museum. There is some pleasant bushwalking country around the town and plenty of wildflowers in season.

The **Wellington Forest**, near Wellington Dam and Collie, offers a great deal of 'natural' recreational activities. Walking tracks include the lengthy Bibbulmun, the two day 24km Lennard Circuit, the four hour Wellington Mills and Sika circuits, and the 2½ hour Lookout Loop close to Honeymoon Pool. About 300 species of wildflowers grow in the Wellington Forest, some unique to the area.

The **Muja power station** is the state's non-nuclear answer to Three Mile Island; tours of the complex are available on Tuesday and Thursday at 11 am and 1.30 pm, Sunday at 1.30 pm. Far more interesting would be a **rafting** descent of the rapids of the Collie River. Book both trips at the Collie tourist office (☎ 9734 2051), Throssell St.

Places to Stay The *Mr Marron Holiday Village* (☎ 9734 2507), Porter St, has tent/powered sites for $10/12, on-site vans for $25 for two. As befits a mining town, there are a number of hotels offering accommodation. In Throssell St, the *Victoria* (☎ 9734 1138) has singles/twins for $30/40, as do the *Colliefields* (☎ 9734 2052) and *Federal* (☎ 9734 2010).

Donnybrook

South of Bunbury, 210km south of Perth and on the fringe of the forest region, is Donnybrook, centre of a vegetable and fruit-growing area. It was given its name by five Irish settlers in 1842 as it reminded them of home, a Dublin suburb. Apple-picking work is often available in season (apparently most of the year). The **Anchor & Hope Inn**, built in 1862 as a coach inn, is now a restaurant.

About 25km to the south of Donnybrook, in Mullalyup, is the historic 1864 **Blackwood Inn**, an old stage-coach post classified by the National Trust.

Donnybrook's tourist office (☎ 9731 1720) is in the old train station.

Places to Stay & Eat The *Brook Lodge* (☎ 9731 1520), on Bridge St, is a backpackers' hostel with kitchen and laundry facilities. It is slowly being renovated (and needs it) but the plus is that the owners help overseas travellers to find work; dorms are $12, twins and doubles $24 (or $80 per week). Just before the bridge leading to Brook Lodge, at 6 Bridge St, is the comfy, rambling *Donnybrook Backpackers'* (☎ 9731 1844); dorm beds are $13, or $78 per week. The owners also help you to seek work and provide transport to orchards and farms.

The *Donnybrook Motorlodge* (☎ 9731 1499), South-Western Highway, provides singles/doubles for $42/58.

The cosy *Blackwood Inn* (☎ 9764 1138), in Mullalyup, is the perfect winter retreat. It has spacious suites with open log fires, and B&B costs from $105 to $180 for doubles (no children under 18 years). The inn has a classy à la carte restaurant.

For a snack there is the *Copper Kettle Coffee Lounge* in the Central Arcade and a bakery on the South-Western Highway. The Anchor & Hope has a good restaurant.

Balingup

About 65km south of Bunbury is the arts and crafts village of Balingup. The Balingup tourist centre (☎ 9764 1018) is in the Old Cheese Factory craft centre on Nannup Rd. Other craft places include the Tinderbox for products created from herbs and the Village Pedlars for home crafts. There are a number of farmstays in the Balingup area; contact the tourist centre.

For light lunches, try the *Old Cheese Factory*.

Naturaliste to Leeuwin

The capes region (Naturaliste to Leeuwin) is easily defined – to the north-east are the holiday resorts of Busselton and Dunsborough; in the north-west corner is Cape Naturaliste and the surf of Yallingup; the south-west corner has Cape Leeuwin, several interesting caves, and remote Augusta at the confluence of two oceans, the Indian and Southern; and the regional epicentre is the laid-back town of Margaret River.

The cape region is known for its picturesque wineries, great surfing beaches and labyrinthine caves. Arts and crafts places are everywhere and there are accommodation options for all travellers. Mapanew's quarterly *Map and Guide to the South West Capes*, and the Cape Naturaliste Tourism Association's *Holiday Planner: South Western Australia*, are handy brochures.

BUSSELTON
• *pop 11,000*

Busselton, 230km south of Perth on the shores of Geographe Bay, is a popular holiday resort, especially with parents in the hunt for diversions for their frenetic kids. During the holidays the population quadruples, accommodation is fully booked, and the beaches and restaurants are crowded. At this time Busselton represents the worst habitat of the peripatetic species *Holidayus australii*.

In 1801, a French sailor named Vasse was lost at sea in Geographe Bay during a violent storm. The names Vasse for the river and district, Geographe for the bay and Naturaliste for the cape come from this time. The town itself is named after the Bussell family, early settlers in the area.

The reliable Busselton tourist office (☎ 9752 1288) is on the corner of Causeway Rd and Peel Terrace.

Things to See & Do

The town has a 2km **jetty** which was reputed to be the longest timber jetty in Australia, but a fair section of it was destroyed by Cyclone Alby in 1978. Likely the kids will gravitate to the fairground attractions of the **Nautical Lady**, which is based near the jetty.

The old **courthouse** has been restored

Established grass trees *(Xanthorrhoea preissii)* at Cape Naturaliste, their age indicated by the height of the trunk. A long straight flower spike grows from the crown of narrow leaves.

THE SOUTH-WEST

WINERIES
1 Wise Winery & Cafe Restaurant
4 Happ's Vineyard
5 Hunt's Foxhaven Estate
7 Wildwood Winery & Brasserie
8 Amberley Estate
9 Rivendell Gardens
10 Abbey-Vale Vineyard & Moonshine Brewery
11 Driftwood Estate
12 Cape Clairault Wines
13 Carbunup/Vasse River Wines
14 Brookland Valley Vineyard & Woodlands
15 Moss Brothers, Sandalford Wines, Cullen Wilyabrup, Evans & Tate, Fermoy Estate, Willespie, Hay Shed Hill, Pierro, Arlewood, Vasse Felix & Ribbon Vale Estate
16 Wright's Wines
17 Treeton Estate
19 Rosa Brook Estate
20 Chateau Xanadu
21 Cape Mentelle
23 Voyager Estate
24 Redgate Wines
27 Leeuwin Estate
28 Green Valley
29 Serventy Organic Wines
31 The Berry Farm

PLACES TO STAY
25 Surf Point Lodge
35 Hamelin Bay Caravan Park

PLACES TO EAT
2 Gunyulgup Restaurant
6 Crayfish Inn

OTHER
3 Yallingup Cave
18 Ellensbrook Homestead
22 Eagles Heritage
26 Georgette Shipwreck
30 Marron Farm
32 Clydesdale Museum
33 Mammoth Cave
34 Lake Cave (CaveWorks)

The Capes:
Leeuwin-Naturaliste

and now houses an impressive arts centre with a gallery, a coffee shop and artists' workshops; it is open from 9 am to 5 pm and there is no entry fee.

The **Old Butter Factory Museum** exhibits the history of Busselton and the Bussell family; it is open daily (except Tuesday) from 2 to 5 pm; entry is $3/1 for adults/kids.

About 7km east of Busselton is the 20 sq km **Ludlow Tuart Forest**, the only considerable natural stand of tuart in the world. Tuart has hard, coarse-grained timber, and can grow extremely large over a period of about 500 years. **Wonnerup House**, in the tuart forest, is a 1859 colonial-style house lovingly restored by the National Trust; it is open from 10 am to 4 pm daily and entry is $4/2 for an adult/child.

Places to Stay

There is a great deal of accommodation along this popular stretch of coast; enquire at the tourist office for more information.

The most central of the many caravan parks, *Kookaburra* (☎ 9752 1516), 66 Marine Terrace, has powered sites for $12, on-site vans for $20, cabins for $30 for two – accept this as a rough average for the other parks. The *Busselton Caravan Park* (☎ 9752 1175), at 163 Bussell Highway, has extremely friendly hosts; the *Acacia* (☎ 9755 4034) is on the Bussell Highway near Harvest Rd; the *Amblin* (☎ 9755 4079) is also on the Bussell Highway; *Lazy Days* (☎ 9752 1780) is at No 452; and *Vasse Beachfront* (☎ 9755 4044) is, yet again, on the Bussell Highway.

The small *Busselton Backpackers* (☎ 9754 2763), 14 Peel St, is a private house with limited kitchen facilities ($12 for dorms); ask at the tourist office for details.

The often booked-out *Motel Busselton* (☎ 9752 1908), 90 Bussell Highway, has comfortable units from $35 per B&B double. *Villa Carlotta Private Hotel* (☎ 9754 2026), at 110 Adelaide St, is good, friendly, organises tours and has singles/doubles for $40/60 with breakfast. Another guesthouse, the *Travellers Rest* (☎ 9752 2290), 223 Bussell Highway, has double B&B for $55.

There are many more B&Bs; check with the tourist office.

There are a number of holiday resorts in the region with a bewildering variety of accommodation. Some examples are the *Busselton Beach Resort* (☎ 9752 3444), corner of Geographe Bay Rd and Guerin St, which has singles/doubles from $80/100; the *Broadwater Resort* (☎ 9754 1633), on the corner of Bussell Highway and Holgate Rd, where one/two-bedroom units are from $150 to $205; the *Geographe Bay Resort* (☎ 9755 4166) on the Bussell Highway, where rooms are from $70/80; and the *Mandalay Holiday Resort* (☎ 9752 1328), 254 Geographe Bay Rd, with doubles/triples for $82/90.

Places to Eat

There are lots of takeaway places along this coastal strip, catering for travellers and the hordes which descend upon the place during holiday periods. *Geographe Pizza* is in Queen St, *Red Rooster* is on the Bussell Highway, and *Presto Pizza* is in the Boulevarde shopping centre.

There are a stack of more up-market places to eat in Busselton including *Michelango* at the Riviera Motel for Italian food, the *Golden Inn* on Albert St for Chinese food, and *Tiffins* in Queen St for Indian tandoori. Hotels such as the *Ship Resort*, Albert St, and the *Esplanade*, on Marine Terrace, are good for counter meals.

Enjoy the succulent seafood at the BYO *Cafe Enigma*, at the jetty end of Queen St, or at *A Lump of Rump*, also on Queen St, which has both seafood and vegetarian dishes. A local favourite is the *Equinox Café* on the beachfront; they have light meals and dinners (about $12 for a main).

Getting There & Away

You can get to Busselton by Westrail or South-West Coachlines (their depot is in Albert St). Geographe Bay Coachlines (☎ 9754 2026) has day tours to capes Naturaliste and Leeuwin, the caves, Augusta and Margaret River.

DUNSBOROUGH

Dunsborough, just west of Busselton, is a pleasant coastal town dependent on tourism. Like Busselton, its beaches suit families as they have shallow water for swimming. The helpful tourist office (☎ 9755 3299) is in the shopping centre on Naturaliste Terrace.

Both South-West Coachlines and Westrail have daily services to Dunsborough.

Things to See & Do

North-west of Dunsborough, the Naturaliste Rd, leads to excellent beaches such as **Meelup**, **Eagle Bay** and **Bunker Bay**, some fine coastal lookouts and the tip of **Cape Naturaliste**, which has a lighthouse and some walking trails. The lighthouse is open daily (except Monday) from 9.30 am to 4 pm; entry is $5/2 for adults/children.

In season you can see humpback whales, southern right whales and dolphins from the lookouts over Geographe Bay. At scenic **Sugarloaf Rock** there is the southernmost nesting colony of the rare red-tailed tropicbird; see the boxed aside 'The Bird Has Flown – Too Far South' in this chapter.

You can ride through the surrounding farms and countryside on horseback. Dunsborough Horse World (☎ 9755 3372) is on Mewett Rd, off Commonage Rd (near Simmo's Icecreamery), and Mirravale Riding School (☎ 9755 2180) is halfway between Dunsborough and Yallingup on Biddles Rd.

Places to Stay

The *Green Acres Beachfront Caravan Park* (☎ 9755 3087), in Dunsborough itself, has tent/powered sites from $11/12, on-site vans from $30 and park cabins from $30 for two (these prices rise in holiday periods).

In Quindalup is the *Three Pines Resort YHA* (☎ 9755 3107), on the beachfront at 285 Geographe Bay Rd; it is $16 ($14 for members) in dorms, and twins and family rooms are $18 per person. They hire bicycles ($6 per day) and canoes ($5 per hour).

There are a couple of up-market resorts in Dunsborough, including the *Dunsborough Bay Village Resort* (☎ 9755 3397), on Dunn Bay Rd, with chalets from $110 for two; and the Dunsborough *Resort Motel* (☎ 9755 3200), 536 Naturaliste Terrace, with double rooms from $75 to $95. The *Bayshore Resort* (☎ 9756 8353) at 374 Geographe Bay Rd, Quindalup, has all the facilities; the units are from $90 to $155 for two. The quality self-contained rammed-earth villas of *Whaler's Cove* (☎ 9755 3699), Lecaille Court, Dunsborough, have been recommended by readers.

The tourist office has an extensive list of private homes for homestays and to rent.

Places to Eat

The *Forum Food Centre* has a variety of eating places including a fine bakery, home of succulent lamingtons. *Dunsborough Health Foods*, in the shopping centre, sells

THE SOUTH-WEST

The Bird Has Flown – Too Far South

Keen bird-watchers will marvel at the sight of the red-tailed tropicbird (*Phaethon rubricauda*) soaring happily in the sea breezes above Sugarloaf Rock, south of Cape Naturaliste. The section of beaches between capes Naturaliste and Leeuwin is anything but the tropics – in fact, the last time this author saw a red-tailed tropicbird was on South Plaza Island in the equatorial Galapagos! Nevertheless, this stretch of coast is home to the most southerly breeding colony of red-tailed tropicbirds in Australia.

The tropicbird is distinguished by its two long red tail streamers – almost twice its body length. It has a tern-like bill and, from a distance, could easily be mistaken for a caspian tern. You'll have fun watching through binoculars as the inhabitants of this small breeding colony soar, glide, dive then swim with their disproportionately long tail feathers cocked up. They are ungainly on land and have to descend almost to the spot where they wish to nest. ■

wholemeal salad rolls and delicious smoothies and juices, and the bakery has tasty pies. and the *Golden Bay Chinese* restaurant is in the Dunsborough Bay Village Resort. For a Tex-Mex/cajun/creole blend, try *Little Havana*, open for dinner Thursday to Monday. An up-market choice is the reliable *Bay Cottage*, near the centre of town – main meals are from $25.

On Commonage Rd is *Simmo's Icecreamery*. It is a hit with the kids because not only are there 21 home-made flavours available but plenty of other diversions once they have devoured their ice cream.

YALLINGUP

Yallingup, a mecca for surfers, is surrounded by a spectacular coastline and some fine beaches. At Yallingup and Smith's Beach there are a number of **walking trails**.

Nearby is the mystical **Ngilgi Cave** which was discovered, or rather stumbled upon, in 1899. Formations include the white 'Mother of Pearl Shawl' and the equally beautiful 'Arab's Tent' and 'Oriental Shawl'. The cave is open daily from 9.30 am to 4.30 pm and you can look around by yourself or take a guided tour that also explores parts of the cave not open to most visitors; entry is $9/4 for adults/children. An adventure tour is $30 (minimum age 15); and an Aboriginal culture tour which covers mythology, bush food and medicine is $15/8.

The **Canal Rocks**, a series of rocky outcrops which form a natural canal, are off Caves Rd just outside of Leeuwin-Naturaliste National Park.

Surfing

Known colloquially to surfers as 'Yal's' and 'Margaret's' (when viewed from far-off Perth), the beaches between the capes offer powerful reef breaks, mainly left-handers (the direction you take after catching a wave). The wave at Margaret's has been described by surfing supremo Nat Young as 'epic', and by world-surfing champ Mark Richards as 'one of the world's finest'.

The better locations include Rocky Point (short left-hander), the Farm and Bone Yards

(right-hander), Three Bears (Papa, Mama and Baby, of course), Yallingup (breaks left and right), Injidup Car Park and Injidup Point (right-hand tube on a heavy swell; left-hander), Guillotine/Gallows (right-hander), South Point (popular break), Left-Handers (the name says it all) and Margaret River (with Southside or 'Suicides').

You can get a copy of the *Down South Surfing Guide*, free from the Dunsborough and Busselton tourist bureaus, which indicates wave size, wind direction and swell size. The **Margaret River Surf Classic** is held in November. Josh Palmateer (current WA champ) runs the Swell's Up Surf Academy (☎ 9757 3850); a two hour lesson at either Margaret's or Yal's is $25.

Places to Stay & Eat

The *Yallingup Beach Caravan Park* (☎ 9755 2164), on the beachfront at Valley Rd, has tent/powered sites for $10/12, on-site vans for $30 and park cabins for $35 for two; the *Caves Caravan Park* (☎ 9755 2196), corner of Caves and Yallingup Beach Rds, is slightly more expensive. *Caves House Hotel* (☎ 9755 2131), Caves Rd, established in 1903, is one of those 'old-world' lodges with ocean views and an English garden. The rooms are not cheap at $120 for two ($175 for suites); it's very much a honeymoon place.

There's a variety of holiday homes and cottages available; enquire at the Dunsborough or Margaret River-Augusta tourist offices. *Yallingup Farm Cottages* (☎ 9755 2261), corner of Caves Rd and Marrinup Drive, is a good example – the self-contained cottages (with potbelly stove for heating) are from $55 to $90. The popular *Yallingup Siding Carriages* (☎ 9755 1106) are on Glover Rd. these Quaint, recycled dwellings are value at $75 to $105 for two, depending on the season.

In Yallingup, the grub, not the surf, is 'up' at the *Yallingup Store* (especially known for its burgers) and at the *Surfside Restaurant*. Indulge yourself at the fully licensed *Caves House Restaurant*; *Flutes Cafe* at the Brookland Valley winery; the *Rocks Cafe* at Canal Rocks; the brasserie at *Wildwood Winery*,

8km south of Yallingup; or at the *Gunyulgup Restaurant*, a real gourmand's delight with meals from $25.

MARGARET RIVER

The attractive town of Margaret River (Margie's or Margaret's) is a popular holiday spot due to its proximity to fine surf (Margaret River Mouth, Gnarabup, Suicides and Redgate) and swimming beaches (Prevelly and Gracetown), some of Australia's best wineries and pleasant rural scenery.

It is somewhat of a festival centre with a food and wine bash in November, concerts at Leeuwin Estate in February, surf competitions in April and November, and the Wilyabrup craft and wine festival in October.

The Margaret River-Augusta tourist office (☎ 9757 2911) has a wad of information on the area including an extensive vineyard guide ($2.50); it is on the corner of the Bussell Highway and Tunbridge St.

Things to See & Do

There are a number of arts and crafts places in town including Margaret River Pottery and Kookaburra Crafts. The National Trust property, **Ellensbrook Homestead**, the first home of the Bussell family (built in 1855), is 8km north-west of town. It has been closed for some time but may reopen soon.

Eagles Heritage, 5km south of Margaret River on Boodjidup Rd, has an interesting collection of raptors in a natural setting; it is open daily from 10 am to 5 pm and costs $4.50/2.50 for adults/children.

One really interesting tour is the search for forest secrets with Helen of **Cave Canoe Bushtucker Tours** at Prevelly Park (☎ 9757 9084). This tour combines walking and canoeing up the Margaret River, teaches aspects of Aboriginal culture, uses of flora, tasting of bushtucker (smoked kangaroo and emu, quondongs, damper and bardi grub paté) and ends with a descent into an adventure cave. The three hour exploration costs a very reasonable $20/10 for adults/kids (my four-year-old loved every moment of it).

Margaret River Tour Co (☎ (041) 991 7166) goes to the wineries, the surf and the lighthouses; a half-day trip is $35, and a full day is $55. Milesaway Tours (☎ (1800) 818 102) has full-day canoe and adventure tours for $55/35 for adults/kids.

For the more adventurous there are abseiling, climbing and caving trips with Adventure in Margaret River (☎ 9757 2104); a half-day/full day outing is $60/80.

Caves Rd, the **old coast road** between Augusta, Margaret River and Busselton, is a good alternative to the direct road which runs slightly inland. The coast here has real variety – cliff faces, long beaches pounded by rolling surf, and calm, sheltered bays.

THE SOUTH-WEST

Historic Ellensbrook Homestead, near Margaret River

THE SOUTH-WEST

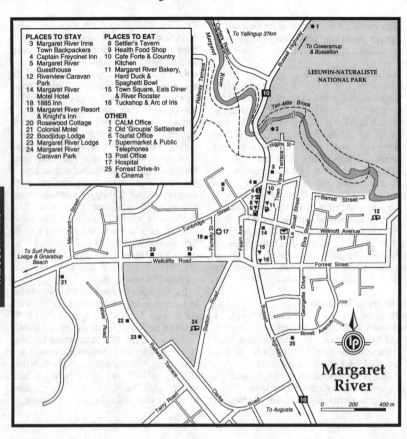

PLACES TO STAY
3 Margaret River Inne Town Backpackers
4 Captain Freycinet Inn
5 Margaret River Guesthouse
12 Riverview Caravan Park
14 Margaret River Motel Hotel
18 1885 Inn
19 Margaret River Resort & Knight's Inn
20 Rosewood Cottage
21 Colonial Motel
22 Boodjidup Lodge
23 Margaret River Lodge
24 Margaret River Caravan Park

PLACES TO EAT
8 Settler's Tavern
9 Health Food Shop
10 Cafe Forte & Country Kitchen
11 Margaret River Bakery, Hard Duck & Spaghetti Bowl
15 Town Square, Eats Diner & River Rooster
16 Tuckshop & Arc of Iris

OTHER
1 CALM Office
2 Old 'Groupie' Settlement
6 Tourist Office
7 Supermarket & Public Telephones
13 Post Office
17 Hospital
25 Forrest Drive-In & Cinema

Margaret River

0   200   400 m

Places to Stay

There are plenty of places to stay around Margaret River but unfortunately most are upwards of $50 per night. Cheap possibilities include the *Margaret River Caravan Park* (☎ 9757 2180), on Station Rd, which has tent/powered sites for $12/14, and on-site vans for $33 for two; and the *Riverview Caravan Park* (☎ 9757 2270) on Willmott Ave. Tenters beware of the latter unless you like sleeping on an angle. *Gracetown Caravan Park* (☎ 9755 5301) is 2.5km from the beach on Cowaramup Bay Rd; on-site vans are $30 and park cabins $40 for two.

Margaret River Lodge (☎ 9757 2532), a backpackers' hostel, is about 1.5km south-west of the town centre at 220 Railway Terrace. It's clean and modern with all the facilities (and they don't mind family groups); dorm beds are $12, four-bed bunk-rooms cost from $15 per person and doubles cost from $35 for two. Just down Railway Terrace, towards town, is *Boodjidup Lodge* (☎ 9757 3448) with singles/doubles from $20/36.

The name says it all – the *Margaret River Inne Town Backpackers* (☎ 9757 3698) is in town, at 93 Bussell Highway. It is in a converted house, slowly being extended, but has a great patio; dorms are $14, twins and doubles $32 and a triple room is $39.

One of the nicest backpackers' hostels you could hope to stay in is the *Surf Point Lodge* (☎ 9757 1777), on Riedle Drive, at Gnarabup Beach. In addition to its beachside location, the place has an air of class – it was built by travellers for travellers and has a large, fully equipped kitchen and many recreation areas – surfers will love the theme. There is also a courtesy bus to and from Margaret River. Dorm beds in four/eight-bed rooms are $15/16, twins and doubles are $40 and en-suite rooms $59.

The renovated *Margaret River Motel Hotel* (☎ 9757 2655) is very central; doubles are $75. The *Captain Freycinet Inn* (☎ 9757 2033), corner of Tunbridge St and the Bussell Highway, has singles/doubles for $80/98 and the *Colonial Motel* (☎ 9757 2633), on Wallcliffe Rd, is $85/90.

The *Margaret River Guesthouse* (☎ 9757 2349) at 22 Valley Rd has B&B from $60 to $80 for a double. *Croft Guesthouse* (☎ 9757 2845), at 54 Wallcliffe Rd, is a comfortable place run by a friendly couple; B&B is from $50/65. There are many other cottages, B&Bs and farmstays; enquire at the tourist

THE SOUTH-WEST

Margaret River Wineries

The region between capes Leeuwin and Naturaliste is famous for its wineries. The Mediterranean-type climate and well-drained soils are ideal conditions for the production of wine grapes. The first grapes were only planted in 1967 and those initially established were rhine riesling and cabernet sauvignon. Since then, many varieties including pinot noir, merlot, shiraz, cabernet franc, chardonnay, sauvignon blanc, verdelho and semillon have been planted. In general, the wines are expensive but worth it. Don't expect a heavy red – these wines are produced from grapes grown in sandy soil, resulting in light textures and flavours.

The region provides a mere 1% of Australia's wine but it is estimated that it provides 10% of premium bottled wine. The *Margaret River Regional Vineyard Guide*, available from tourist offices ($2.50), lists over 35 wineries found between the capes. A good place to start is the Margaret River Regional Wine Centre, at 9 Bussell Highway, Cowaramup, open Monday to Saturday from 10 am to 8 pm.

Every year in summer since 1985, Leeuwin Estate has hosted performances by famous local and international acts in the winery's natural amphitheatre – the London Philharmonic, Royal Danish and Berlin State orchestras, Dame Kiri Te Kanawa, Diana Ross, James Galway, Shirley Bassey, Joan Armatrading, George Benson, Ray Charles and Tom Jones – to name just a few.

Wineries in the region include:
North
  Happs, Rivendell Gardens, Abbey-Vale (merlot shiraz, verdelho), Wise Winery, Amberley Estate (shiraz), Hunt's Foxhaven Estate, Wildwood Winery, Driftwood Estate, Carbunup Estate/Vasse River Wines, Cape Clairault, Wright's Wines.
Wilyabrup & Cowaramup
  Pierro (chardonnay), Fermoy Estate (merlot, chardonnay), Evans & Tate, Brookland Valley, Willespie, Hay Shed Hill (pinot noir, semillon), Ribbon Vale (semillon, sauvignon blanc), Arlewood Estate, Moss Wood, Moss Brothers, Vasse Felix, Sandalford Wines, Cullens Wilyabrup, Treeton Estate, Woodlands.
Margaret River
  Rosa Brook Estate (cabernet merlot, autumn harvest riesling, botrytis riesling), Cape Mentelle, The Berry Farm (fruit and berry wines), Leeuwin Estate (chardonnay, pinot noir, cabernet sauvignon), Serventy Organic Wines (pinot noir, pinot rosé and shiraz – produced without herbicides and insecticides), Redgate (pinot noir), Voyager Estate (chardonnay).

A few favourite wines from the area, in no order of merit: Cullen's cabernet merlot, Voyager chardonnay, Leeuwin Estate chardonnay and pinot noir (the least expensive ones), Redgate cabernet, Amberley shiraz, Vasse Felix shiraz, Cape Mentelle cabernet sauvignon, Brookland Valley chardonnay and Pierro chardonnay. ■

office or check the free *Margaret River Regional Accommodation Guide*.

The *1885 Inn* (☎ 9757 3177), Farrelly St, is the place to stay if you have the money; doubles are $100. The country-style *Noble Grape* (☎ 9755 5538), on the Bussell Highway in Cowaramup, comes highly recommended with rooms furnished with antiques; B&B is from $55/75.

The *Margaret River Resort* (☎ 9757 0000) in Wallcliffe Rd is an expensive option but worth it if you have the dollars; an upstairs double at the front will cost from $120. In its Knight's Inn you can get a selection of English beers and the smorgasbord in the restaurant is good value at $10.

Places to Eat

Among the many places to eat in Margaret River is the *Settler's Tavern*, on Bussell Highway, which has good counter meals from $10 to $12 – they also have live music on weekends. The Margaret River Motel Hotel has counter meals in its *Rivers Bar & Bistro* and the *Margaret River Guesthouse* has a restaurant with a blackboard menu which reflects what is available in the district at the time (from $15).

There are a great number of eateries on Bussell Highway between the tourist office and Wallcliffe Rd. At the southern end is the *Margaret River Tuckshop*, a bit of an institution with friendly owners, and the *Arc of Iris*, a quick bypass to the Aquarian generation – a Thai meal will cost from $8 to $12. *Cafe Forte* serves great Aussie cuisine and a hearty meal will cost $15 or so.

Moving north, the *River Rooster* and *Eats Diner* are in the Town Square complex. North of Willmott Ave is the *Spaghetti Bowl*, the *Margaret River Bakery* and the oddly named *Hard Duck*. The *Country Kitchen*, nearby, is famed for its burgers, omelettes and pastas.

More expensive is the licensed *1885 Inn*, Farrelly St, with continental fare and a good selection of regional wines. About 10km north, in Cowaramup, the *Flame Tree* is reputed to be both expensive and good.

Getting There & Around

South-West Coachlines and Westrail both have daily bus services between Perth and Margaret River; the trip is around five hours.

The Wanderer Bus can get you around town, out to Surf Point Lodge, the Gnarabup and Surfers' Point beaches and perhaps the wineries (eg Cape Mentelle); the cost for a single trip is $3 (or $6 round trip). Catch it outside the tourist office.

Bikes can be rented by the hour or day from the Margaret River Lodge.

AUGUSTA

A popular holiday resort, Augusta is 5km north of Cape Leeuwin. The cape, the most south-westerly point in Australia, has a rugged coastline, a **lighthouse** (open daily, except Monday, from 9 am to 4 pm, $3) with views extending over the Indian and Southern oceans. Not far away is a salt-encrusted **waterwheel**, built in 1895.

Cape Leeuwin took its name from a Dutch ship which passed here in 1622. The **Matthew Flinders memorial**, between Groper Bay and Point Matthew on the Leeuwin Rd, commemorates Flinders' mapping of the Australian coastline, which commenced at the cape on 6 December 1801.

The tourist office (☎ 9758 1695), in a souvenir shop at 70 Blackwood Ave, is open from 9 am to 5 pm daily.

The interesting **Augusta Historical Museum**, also on Blackwood Ave, has exhibits relating to local history; it is open daily from 10 am to noon and 2 to 4 pm and entry is $1 for adults.

There are some good beaches between Augusta and Margaret River, including **Hamelin Bay** and **Cosy Corner**.

Organised Tours

Scenic flights over the cape are conducted by Leeuwin Aviation ($32 for 20 minutes, $98 for the two capes); book with the Margaret River tourist office.

Whale-watching is good from Cape Leeuwin between May and September. Naturaliste Charters (☎ 9755 2276) has three

THE SOUTH-WEST

The magnificent humpback whale can be seen breaching around Cape Leeuwin in winter.

THE SOUTH-WEST

hour trips to see southern right and humpback whales, bottlenose dolphins, a colony of NZ fur seals on Flinders Island (June to September) and, occasionally, pygmy blue whales; the cost is $40/20 for adults/children. A new operator, the *Leeuwin Lady* (☎ 9758 1770), based in the dive shop on Blackwood Ave, also has three hour tours for $40.

There are more sedate cruises up the Blackwood River from the Ellis St jetty on the *Miss Flinders* (☎ 9758 1944). It departs, September to June, at 2 pm on Tuesday, Thursday and Saturday and on Wednesday between Christmas and Easter; the cost is $14/7 for adults/children (discounts available to backpackers).

Places to Stay

The *Doonbanks Caravan Park* (☎ 9758 1517) is the most central with tent/powered sites for $12/13, on-site vans for $25 and park cabins from $40 for two. Three other caravan parks in the area are *Flinders Bay* (☎ 9758 1380), right on the beach in Albany Terrace; *Turner* (☎ 9758 1593), Blackwood Ave; and *West Bay* (☎ 9758 1572), on the Bussell Highway 2km north of town (on-site vans are $50).

The *Hamelin Bay Caravan Park* (☎ 9758 5540), 8km west of Karridale, has tent/powered sites from $12/14, on-site vans from $25 and park cabins from $37 for two. Fishing and swimming at the lovely beach are popular pastimes.

There are a number of basic *campsites* in the Leeuwin-Naturaliste National Park, including ones on Boranup Drive, Point Rd and Conto's Field, near Lake Cave; camping is $5 per person.

The purpose-built, federation-style YHA affiliate *Baywatch Manor Resort* (☎ 9758 1290), 88 Blackwood Ave, has all the facilities and comfortable rooms, but it is definitely not a party place. It is disabled-equipped and dorm beds are $15, doubles and twins $38 for two (linen included).

The *Augusta Motel Hotel* (☎ 9758 1944), Blackwood Ave, has singles from $40 to $80 and doubles from $45 to $85, depending on the season; and the *Georgiana Molloy Motel* (☎ 9758 1255), 84 Blackwood Ave, has singles from $55 to $70 and doubles from $65 to $85.

Some of the self-contained holiday flats have reasonable rates but they may have minimum-booking periods in the high season; enquire at the tourist office.

Places to Eat

The *Augusta Motel Hotel* does good meals and has an à la carte restaurant, or head for *Squirrels*, next to the hotel, where you can find delicious burgers (piled high with salad), Lebanese sandwiches and various health foods. The *August(a) Moon Chinese Restaurant* is in the Matthew Flinders shopping centre on Ellis St. The bakery, known for its pizzas (from $8 to $16), buns and home-baked pies, and *Cosy's Corner* for its $6 breakfasts and tasty foccacia, are both on Blackwood Ave.

Down on Albany Terrace, you can watch the Blackwood River meet the waters of Flinders Bay while drinking coffee and eating pasta at the 'last cafe before Antarctica', the *Colourpatch*.

LEEUWIN-NATURALISTE CAVES

There are a number of limestone caves (perhaps 350) dotted throughout the Leeuwin-Naturaliste Ridge between the capes, which are often collectively called the 'Hidden Wilderness Caves'. These include Jewel (the most picturesque), Lake, the Mammoth and the Moondyne Adventure Cave.

In **Mammoth Cave**, 21km south of Margaret River, a fossilised jawbone of *Zygomaturus trilobus*, a giant wombat-like creature, can be touched. Other fossil remains have revealed a great deal about prehistoric fauna of the south-west region.

The limestone formations are reflected in the still waters of an underground stream in the **Lake Cave**, 25km from Margaret River. The vegetated entrance to this cave is spectacular and includes a karri tree with a girth of 7m. The interpretive centre, CaveWorks (☎ 9757 7411), has computerised displays, a cave model, audiovisuals and a boardwalk.

Fossil remains of a Tasmanian tiger *(thylacine)* have been discovered in the **Jewel Cave**, which is 8km north of Augusta – the remains are believed to be 25,000 years old. It is the unusual formations which attract visitors underground, however, and the Jewel has a 5.9m straw stalactite, so far the longest seen in a 'commercial' cave.

Guided cave tours, the only way to see these caves, run daily for $9 (Jewel $10). Both Jewel and Lake are open on the half hour from 9.30 am until 4 pm, Mammoth is open on the hour from 9 am until 4 pm and Moondyne at 10 am and 2.30 pm (these times vary, so contact CaveWorks).

Moondyne Cave, also 8km north of Augusta, was presumably discovered by and named after the bushranger Moondyne Joe (see the boxed aside 'Moondyne Joe' in the Around Perth chapter). This cave is unlit and an experienced guide takes the visitor on a caving adventure; all equipment is provided on this two hour trip which costs $25.

Of all the caves discovered between the capes only these four, and Ngilgi Cave near Busselton, are open to the public.

Southern Forests

A visit to the forests of the south-west is a must for any traveller to WA. Interspersed between the forests are many interesting towns, a variety of attractions and a host of things to do. The forests are magnificent – towering jarrah, marri and karri trees protect the natural, vibrant undergrowth. Unfortunately, parts of these forests are threatened by logging.

The area of 'tall trees' (not 'tall timber', as that predetermines their fate) lies between the Vasse Highway (State Highway 10) and the South-Western Highway, and includes the timber towns of Bridgetown, Manjimup, Nannup, Pemberton and Northcliffe. A trip will be more rewarding if you have CALM's free brochure, *Karri Country*.

Getting There & Away

Westrail Perth-Pemberton buses run daily, via Bunbury, Donnybrook and Manjimup; the trip takes about five hours. From Albany it's three hours, and the service is twice weekly.

Westrail has a daily service from Perth via Bunbury, and South-West Coachlines has a weekday service from Perth.

The Perth-Albany Westrail bus goes

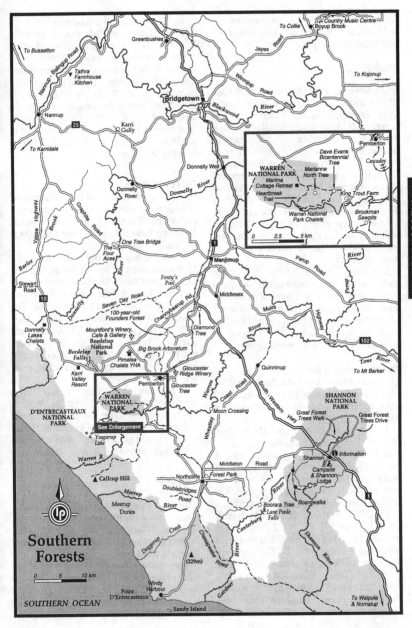

THE SOUTH-WEST

Southern Forests

SOUTHERN OCEAN

through Northcliffe daily (except Monday and Thursday), but you need your own transport to get to Windy Harbour.

BRIDGETOWN
• *pop 4000*

Bridgetown, a quiet country town on the Blackwood River and centre of the Blackwood Valley, is in an area of karri forests and farmland. It has some old buildings, including **Bridgedale House**, which was built of mud and clay by the area's first settler in 1862 and has been restored by the National Trust; it is open daily, except Tuesday and Wednesday, from 10 am to 4 pm (admission is by donation). There is a local history display and a captivating **jigsaw collection** in the tourist office (☎ 9761 1740) on Hampton St. The staff are enthusiastic volunteers, so you'll have no trouble fitting the pieces together.

Interesting features of the Blackwood Valley are the burrawangs (grass trees) and large granite boulders. There's a panoramic view over the town from **Sutton's Lookout** off Phillips St. About 10km north of Bridgetown on the South-Western Highway is **Greenbushes**, once a tin-mining centre.

Places to Stay & Eat

The *Bridgetown Caravan Park* (☎ 9761 1053), South-Western Highway, has tent/powered sites for $12/14, and on-site vans from $28 for two.

At the basic *Freemasons Motel Hotel* (☎ 9761 1725) singles/doubles are $25/41 with breakfast. The best place in town is the *Bridgetown Motel* (☎ 9761 1641), 38 Hampton St, in a beautifully renovated federation-style house; rooms range from $58 to $130 a double, depending on the facilities.

The *Old Well* (☎ 9761 2032) on Gifford St has B&B for $35/65 and *Lauren Brook* (☎ 9761 1676) is $70/120. Ask at the tourist office about many other B&Bs. There are also many self-catering cottages in the area: *Lucieville Farm Chalets* (☎ 9761 1733), 8km south of town, are from $252 for a week; and *Leyburn Farm Cottages* (☎ 9761 7506), 28km to the north, are $300 with breakfast.

In Greenbushes, the *Exchange* (☎ 9764 3509), Blackwood Rd, has single/twin rooms for $25/35, motel units for $35/45.

For snacks and takeaways in Bridgetown, there is the *Bridgetown Cafe*, the *Pottery* and *DJ's Coffee Lounge* on Hampton St. For up-market meals ($25), the *Geegelup Joy Restaurant* is open Wednesday to Sunday. In Greenbushes, the old *Post Office Cafe* is the best choice. Entertainment may well be in the form of a Saturday-night good old-fashioned country dance.

BOYUP BROOK

In this small town, 31km north-east of Bridgetown, there is a flora reserve, a country music centre (5km from town on the Dinninup-Arthur River Rd) and a large butterfly and beetle display.

Nearby is **Norlup Pool** with glacial rock formations, and to the north, **Wilga**, which is an old timber mill with vintage engines.

After witnessing the country & western collection you will probably need to rest. The *Flax Mill Recreation Camp & Caravan Park* (☎ 9765 1136), Flax Mill Rd, has camping and caravan sites; the *Barracks Accommodation* (☎ 9765 1437), Railway Parade, is $10 per person; and there are several farmstays and B&Bs near town.

For the latter, contact the tourist office on the corner of Abel and Bridge Sts (☎ 9765 1444); they have a fine leaflet on the town.

There are a couple of delis in Boyup Brook where you can get a decent sandwich – one is in Bridge St and the other in Abel St.

NANNUP
• *pop 1100*

Nannup (with a population of 550 rednecks, 550 alternatives), 50km west of Bridgetown, is a quiet, historical, picturesque town in the heart of forest and farmland, and our favourite in the south-west.

The tourist office (☎ 9756 1211), at the 1922 police station in Brockman St, is open daily from 9 am to 3 pm. They sell an excellent booklet (50c) that points out places of interest around town and details a range of scenic drives in the area, including a Blackwood River Rd drive and forest drives.

Things to See & Do

There is a sawmill (one of the largest in WA), an arboretum, some fine old buildings and several craft shops. Nannup is home of the mythical **'tiger'**, spotted by many 'clear-thinking people' before the ingestion of Nannup weed, and along one of the scenic drives is the notice: 'No shooting or feeding of thylacines'. There's a $25 reward offered for an authenticated photograph of a striped solipsist.

Canoeing the Blackwood River

The Blackwood River begins in the salt lake system to the east of Wagin and Katanning. It then flows for over 400km through forests and farmland and near many towns before emptying into the ocean east of Augusta.

It is most suited to Canadian-style canoes which can be hired in Nannup, Boyup Brook and Bridgetown. The best time to paddle the river is in late winter and early spring when the water levels are up. There is a series of guides entitled *South-West Canoeing Guide: Blackwood River*, available from local tourist offices; carefully read the safety instructions regarding equipment and what to do in the event of a capsize.

On Wednesday and Saturday, Milesaway Tours (☎ (1800) 818 102) takes full-day trips on the river through jarrah forest; the cost is $55/35 for adults/children, and a bush breakfast and lunch is included.

Places to Stay & Eat

The *caravan park* (☎ 9756 1211), on Brockman St near the banks of the river, has powered sites for $11 for two. The backpackers' lodge, the rustic *Black Cockatoo* (☎ 9756 1035), 27 Grange Rd, is the place to 'kick back and mellow out' (their words not mine); rooms with a difference are from $12 a night and entry into paradise is priceless. If you choose an eco-stay, and work your butt off gardening or tidying up, you may get a free bed.

There are a great number of B&Bs,

farmstays, bush cottages and even a yuppie lodge available; enquire at the tourist office.

The *Blackwood Cafe*, Warren Rd, has good light meals such as quiche, soup and sandwiches; and the *Nannup Hotel* dishes out counter meals. Many gourmands come here just to sample the famous meaty Nannup tiger pies ($2) or 'tiger' sandwiched in a croissant.

Old Templemore, opposite the Telecentre, incorporates an antique tool museum (items are for sale) with great cafe-style food, and the *Good Food Shop*, Warren Rd, lives up to its organic reputation (indulge in a trout roll for $4).

MANJIMUP
• *pop 4650*

Manjimup is the commercial centre of the south-west, a major agricultural centre noted for apple-growing and reviled for wood-chipping. If you detest the whine of dirt bikes, avoid Manjimup in June when the '$15,000 Race' is held.

The impressive **Timber Park Complex** on the corner of Rose and Edwards Sts includes various museums, old buildings and the Manjimup tourist bureau (☎ 9771 1831); it is open daily from 9 am to 5 pm. It's pro-logging, but that's this town's raison d'etre.

One Tree Bridge, or what's left of it after floods in 1966, is 22km down the Graphite Rd. It was constructed from a single karri log carefully felled to span the width of the river. The **Four Aces**, 1.6km from One Tree Bridge, are four superb karri trees believed to be over 300 years old. **Fonty's Pool**, a great spot to cool off on a hot summer day, is 10km south-west of town along Seven Day Rd.

Nine km south of town, along the South-Western Highway, is the **Diamond Tree Fire Tower**. You're allowed to climb this 51m karri; there's a nature trail nearby.

Places to Stay & Eat

The *caravan park* (☎ 9777 1575) has a hostel with dorm beds and cooking facilities for $12 per night – it can get busy in apple-picking season (March to June) when beds are $75 weekly. No alcohol is permitted and, as they say emphatically, 'If you can't live with that – stay somewhere else!' They also have powered sites/on-site vans from \$13/26. Two other caravan parks, *Warren Way* (☎ 9771 1060; 2km north of town) and *Fonty's Pool* (☎ 9771 2105; 10km southwest of town), also have tent and powered sites, on-site vans and cabins.

A backpackers' hostel, the *Barracks* (☎ 9771 1154), is opening up at 8 Muir St; the twin rooms should be OK for \$30 for two (write and tell us more, we saw it before it opened).

There is a big, basic hotel on Giblett St (☎ 9771 1322) with singles/doubles from \$35/48. There are three motels: the *Overlander* (☎ 9771 1477), *Manjimup Motor Inn* (☎ 9771 1900) and the *Kingsley* (☎ 9771 1177). The Motor Inn and the Kingsley have facilities for disabled travellers. For farmstays, cottages and B&Bs contact the tourist bureau.

In Mottram St, across the railway line, is the pulsating *Manji-Mart*, a takeaway and usually the last place to close sometime after midnight. Try the *Blue Marron Restaurant*, Channybearup Rd near Eagle Springs, which serves marron and trout, the *Creative Collectables* next to the Timber Park for lunches, the *Tuk Tuk* for Thai meals, the hotel (a timber millers' haunt) for counter meals, and the *Billabong Restaurant* in the Kingsley for à la carte.

PEMBERTON
• *pop 1200*

Deep in the karri forests is the delightful town of Pemberton. The child-friendly, well-organised Karri visitors' centre (☎ 9776 1133), Brockman St, incorporates the tourist office, pioneer museum and karri forest discovery centre (the kids will love the frog and the possum). Get the excellent *What to See & Do in Big Tree Country* map (\$1) or the *Pemberton and Northcliffe: Kingdom of the Karri* pamphlet from the visitors' centre.

Things to See & Do
Pemberton has some interesting **craft shops** specialising in handcrafted timber products; the **Big Brook Arboretum** which features

'big' trees from all over the world and the eastern states; the **Pemberton Sawmill** where you can go on guided tours and observe timber being sawn; the pretty **Pemberton Pool** surrounded by karri trees (ideal on a hot day); and a **trout hatchery** that supplies fish for the state's rivers.

There are **Forest Discovery Tours** (☎ 9771 2915) from Manjimup and Pemberton, apologist guided exercises for the extractive timber industry. Tours are held at Pemberton at 10.30 am and 12.30 pm from the Forest Industries Centre, Brockman St (\$10/2 for adults/children). Ask them how long it takes these trees to grow. CALM preserves the ancient forests and allows others to cut them down – oxymoronic, eh? For the other side of the equation, take a walk with Andy Russell's Pemberton Hiking Co (☎ 9776 1559).

If you are feeling fit, you can make the scary 60m climb to the top of the **Gloucester Tree** (this is not for the fainthearted and only one visitor in four ascends!) The view makes the climb well worthwhile. To get to the tree just follow the signs from town. The tree was named after the Duke of Gloucester, who visited in 1946. The **Dave Evans Bicentennial Tree**, at 68m the tallest of the 'climbing trees', is in Warren National Park, 11km south of Pemberton.

Also of interest in the area are the spectacular **Cascades** (when the water level is high), the over 100 years old **Founders Forest** (once a wheat field) and **Warren National Park** where camping is allowed in designated areas. The biggest karri, some 89m high, is in the park. There are also two great forest drives in the park: the **Heartbreak Trail** (16km) and the **Maidenbush Trail**. Both pass through 400-year-old karri stands.

Pemberton also has a burgeoning **wine industry**, with reds attracting favourable comparison to those from Burgundy in France. Ask at the visitors' centre for the free *Wineries & Vineyards of the Pemberton Wine Region*.

The Pemberton Tramway
The scenic Pemberton Tramway (☎ 9776 1322), one of the area's main attractions, was constructed between 1929 and 1933. It was part of the

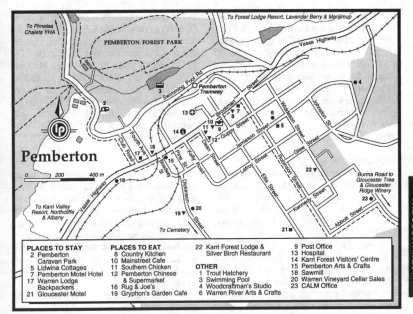

Pemberton

0   200   400 m

To Pimelea
Chalets YHA

To Forest Lodge Resort, Lavender Berry & Manjimup

PEMBERTON FOREST PARK

Vasse Highway

To Karri Valley
Resort, Northcliffe
& Albany

To Cemetery

Burma Road to
Gloucester Tree
& Gloucester
Ridge Winery

THE SOUTH-WEST

PLACES TO STAY	PLACES TO EAT		22 Karri Forest Lodge &	9 Post Office
2 Pemberton	8 Country Kitchen		Silver Birch Restaurant	13 Hospital
Caravan Park	10 Mainstreet Cafe			14 Karri Forest Visitors' Centre
5 Lidwina Cottages	11 Southern Chicken		**OTHER**	15 Pemberton Arts & Crafts
7 Pemberton Motel Hotel	12 Pemberton Chinese		1 Trout Hatchery	18 Sawmill
17 Warren Lodge	& Supermarket		3 Swimming Pool	20 Warren Vineyard Cellar Sales
Backpackers	16 Rug & Joe's		4 Woodcraftman's Studio	23 CALM Office
21 Gloucester Motel	19 Gryphon's Garden Cafe		6 Warren River Arts & Crafts	

planned line between Bunbury and Albany and was in use for passengers and goods until 1986.

Trams leave Pemberton train station daily at 10.45 am and 2 pm to Warren River ($12.50/6.50 for adults/children) and to Northcliffe ($19.50/9.50) at 10.15 am on Tuesday, Thursday and Saturday. The route travels through lush karri and marri forests with occasional photo stops; a commentary is also provided. The trip is incredibly noisy and only worthwhile if you don't have a car.

Beedelup National Park This enchanting forest park should not be missed. There is a short but scenic walk which crosses Beedelup Brook near **Beedelup Falls**; the bridge was built from a karri log. There is also a walk-through karri – vandals from an earlier age cut the 3m by 4m hole with a chainsaw. It's sobering to think that there are 150 tonnes of tree towering above.

For the keen bird-watcher there are

numerous species to be found flitting in and around the tall trees. One of the most striking, the red-winged fairy wren, is seen in the undergrowth of the forests.

National Park Tours Southern Forest Adventures (☎ 9776 1222) has 4WD tours of the forest and coastal areas around Pemberton. One half-day trip takes in karri forest as well as the spectacular Yeagarup dune system of d'Entrecasteaux National Park; it costs $40 and includes a barbecue lunch (a trip to the dunes alone is $25/18 for adults/children). A two day safari to d'Entrecasteaux and the cliffs of Windy Harbour is $120. Canoeing trips on the Warren River with the same operator are from $30/20.

Perup, 50km east of Manjimup, is the centre of a 400 sq km forest which has populations of rare mammals, including the numbat, tammar wallaby, ringtail possum and southern brown bandicoot. The tour is overnight because most of the animals are nocturnal. You leave Pemberton with Perup Tours (☎ 9776 7273) on Friday at 2 pm and return at noon on Saturday; the cost is $95/55 (a $25 entry fee is payable to CALM) and includes dinner and accommodation.

Pemberton Scenic Bus Tours does a forest industry tour weekdays at 10.30 am; a three hour scenic tour weekdays at 2 pm, weekends at 10.30 am and 2 pm; and tours to Perup (see earlier).

Places to Stay

Camping is permitted in Warren National Park (☎ 9776 1207) and in some areas of the Pemberton Forest (☎ 9776 1200). The picturesque caravan park (☎ 9776 1300) has tent/powered sites for $11/13, on-site vans for $26 and cabins for $34 for two.

Pimelea Chalets YHA (☎ 9776 1153), in a beautiful forest location at Pimelea, costs a hefty $14 a night (nonmembers $15). It's 10km north-west of Pemberton – readers have reported problems getting transport to this hostel. The place was not attended when we visited (for the second time).

In town, the centrally located *Warren Lodge* (☎ 9776 1105), on Brockman St, has backpackers' beds from $13, and twins/doubles for $30/38. It requires some tender loving care and improvement of facilities. And remember, you are the paying guest and should be treated as such.

The *Pemberton Motel Hotel* (☎ 9776 1017) is a grand old building on Brockman St with double units for $55, with breakfast. The *Gloucester Motel* (☎ 9776 1266), in Ellis St, has tidy, clean units for $40/60.

Perth-ites flush with funds head for the *Karri Valley Resort* (☎ 9776 2020), on the Vasse Highway. This is a very beautiful place sited at the edge of a lake and surrounded by magnificent karri forest. It has motel rooms from $131, and two to three-bedroom chalets from $181. Similar, but much more economical, is the *Forest Lodge Resort* (☎ 9776 1113), 2km north of Pemberton on the Vasse Highway, which has lodge rooms with en-suites for $95 (with a spa $140); all prices are for two. The *Broadaxe Restaurant* is on the premises.

For more information on the plethora of farmstays, cottages and B&Bs, enquire at the Karri visitors' centre. Readers recommend the fine *Marima Cottage Retreat* (☎ 9776 1211) on Old Vasse Rd in Warren National Park; single and double B&B is from $90. Another recommended place is *Warren National Park Chalets* (☎ 9776 1188), on the Hawke Rd near the Bibbulmun Track – self-contained two-bedroom chalets, with verandah and potbelly stove, are only $80.

Places to Eat

The town, for its size, has many places to eat; most have local trout and marron on their menus. The *Pemberton Patisserie* has tasty pies and cakes; the *Country Café* near the hotel has good old-fashioned home-cooking; while the *Mainstreet Cafe* on Brockman St has basic, cheap food such as hamburgers and Lebanese rolls. As befits the deep south, *Southern Chicken* is on the corner of Dean and Brockman Sts.

Gryphon's Garden Cafe, in Dickinson St, attached to a fantastic arts and crafts gallery, has a pleasant setting, is good for breakfast and has daily blackboard specials (it's closed on Thursday). The *Pemberton Chinese*, next to the supermarket on Dean St, is open Tuesday to Sunday from 5 pm.

NORTHCLIFFE
- *pop 800*

Northcliffe, 32km south of Pemberton, has a **pioneer museum** and a **forest park** close to town with good walks through stands of grand karri, marri and jarrah trees – a brochure and map of the trails is available from the tourist office (☎ 9776 7203), by the museum on Wheatley Coast Rd. Bikes can be hired from Trail 'n' Track (☎ 9776 7010) at 82 Zamia St; it is $16 for a day or $75 for a week.

The popular and picturesque **Lane Poole Falls** are 19km south-east of Northcliffe; the 2.5km track to the falls leaves from the 50m Boorara lookout tree.

Windy Harbour, on the coast 29km south of Northcliffe, has prefab shacks and a sheltered beach, although true to its name, it is very blustery. The cliffs of the magnificent

d'Entrecasteaux National Park can be accessed from here.

Places to Stay & Eat
Opposite the school, the *Northcliffe Caravan Park* (☎ 9776 7193) has tent sites for $5.50 (power is $3 extra). *Northcliffe Hotel* (☎ 9776 7089), the only pub in town, has basic backpackers' beds with shared facilities for $15, singles/doubles for $25/30 (meals are available).

Out of town, *Meerup Springs Cabins* (☎ 9776 7216), Double Bridges Rd, are $60 for two ($10 per extra person); and *Round-Tuit Holidays* (☎ 9776 7276), Muirillup Rd, has B&B for $40/60. At Windy Harbour, the only place to stay is the camping area (☎ 9776 8398) where tent sites are $6 for two.

The *Hollow Butt* coffee shop, on Zamia St and Wheatley Coast Rd, has light meals and cakes. The *Petrene Estate* (☎ 9776 7145), on Muirillup Rd 2km from town, has good lunches from $5 to $10.

SHANNON NATIONAL PARK
This 53,500 hectare national park, on the South-Western Highway, 50km south of Manjimup, is well worth a visit. There is a covered information shelter on the north of the highway (near the entrance to the drive). The free CALM publication *Shannon National Park and the Great Forest Trees Drive*, by Caris Bailey, is very informative.

CALM has markedly improved facilities, and the 48km **Great Forest Trees Drive** is well worth doing. On the drive you learn about the old-growth karri forest by tuning into 100 FM when you see the signs (there are eight). Those wishing to know more could consult *The Great Forest Trees Drive* ($12.95), a detailed map and guidebook.

The drive is split in two by the highway, but both sections are worthwhile. In the north you have the option to walk the 8km **Great Forest Trees**, crossing the Shannon River at one point; and in the south boardwalks give access to stands of giant karri at **Snake Gully** and **Big Tree Grove**. There is also a 3.5km walk to the Shannon Dam and a 5.5km circuit to Mokare's Rock, where there is a boardwalk (to protect the environment) and great views.

There is a fine camping area (☎ 9776 1207) in the spot where the original timber-milling village used to be (the mill was closed in 1968). Camping fees are $8 for two adults ($3 for an additional adult) and $1 for school-age children. If you use a hut, equipped with potbelly stoves, it is $5 – all fees are on a self-registration basis. The self-contained *Shannon Lodge* is available for groups (of up to 10); contact CALM (☎ 9776 1207).

THE SOUTH-WEST

The South Coast

To the east of the capes and the karri forests is the vast area of the south coast, sometimes called the 'Great Southern'. It includes the coastline from Walpole in the west to Cape Arid, east of Esperance. The scenery is magnificent and the main scenic road often hugs the coastline.

This large area has some of the state's best coastal parks: d'Entrecasteaux, Walpole-Nornalup, William Bay, West Cape Howe, Fitzgerald River and Cape Le Grand. The towns throughout this area each have their own distinctive characters and include Denmark, 'old' Albany and Esperance.

Inland, north of Albany, are two of the best mountain parks in Australia – the 'ecological islands' of the Stirling Ranges, which rise abruptly 1000m above the surrounding plains; and the karri forest and ancient granite spires of the Porongurups.

Getting There & Away

Skywest (☎ 9334 2288) flies daily from Perth to Albany (☎ 9841 6655) and Perth to Esperance (☎ 9071 2002) (see the Airfares Chart in the Getting Around chapter).

Westrail's daily Perth-Albany ($44.70, via the south coast) service, which passes through Denmark ($39.30), takes about seven hours. Denmark, via Albany, is $39.30. It is $36.70 to Walpole, by a combination of the *Australind* and coach. (Westrail concessions are half of the full fare.)

The daily, six hour Westrail, Perth-Albany (via Williams) bus service stops in Mt Barker ($30.60 – for the Stirling Ranges); the fare from Perth to Albany is $35.10 one way.

Westrail has a bus three times a week from Kalgoorlie to Esperance ($33.50), an Esperance-Albany service ($45.90) and a 10 hour Perth-Esperance ($52.60) service, that runs on Monday via Jerramungup, Wednesday and Friday via Lake Grace, and Tuesday and Thursday via Hyden. It is $18 to Norseman, where connections with Greyhound can be made, on the latter service.

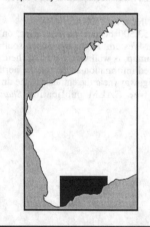

WALPOLE-NORNALUP

The South-Western Highway almost meets the coast at the twin inlets of Walpole and Nornalup. The heavily forested **Walpole-Nornalup National Park** covers 180 sq km

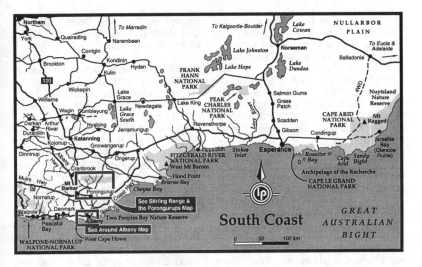

around Nornalup Inlet and the town of Walpole; it contains beaches, rugged coastline, inlets and the revamped **Valley of the Giants** (see later in this section).

There are a number of scenic drives, including the Knoll Drive 3km east of Walpole; the Valley of the Giants Rd; and **Mt Frankland**, 29km north of Walpole. At Mt Frankland you can climb to the summit for panoramic views or walk around the trail at its base. Opposite Knoll Drive is **Hilltop Rd** which leads to a giant tingle tree; this road continues to the **Circular Pool** on the Frankland River. The Frankland River is popular with canoeists.

About 13km west of Walpole via Crystal Springs is a 4WD road to Mandalay Beach, where the **Mandalay**, a Norwegian barque, was wrecked in 1911. It seems to appear every 10 years out of the sands as a result of the sea washing the sand away.

Details of things to see and do are available from the Walpole tourist office (☎ 9840 1111) at the Pioneer Cottage, in Pioneer Park, or from CALM (☎ 9840 8263), South Coast Highway, Walpole.

In particular, read CALM's *Finding the Magic* which costs $1.50; it includes a tree-spotter's guide and the Ocean Drive is outlined in it. This includes the hauntingly beautiful **Conspicuous Cliffs beach**, which is not far from the western end of the Valley of the Giants Rd.

Valley of the Giants

Four species of rare eucalypts grow in this region within 4km of each other, and nowhere else in the world: red, yellow and Rates tingle inland, and the red flowering gum closer to the coast. See Flora in the Facts for the Visitor chapter. Pleasant shady and ferny paths lead through the forests, which are frequented by bushwalkers.

The Valley of the Giants is the best place to see the giant tingles. Recently an impressive **Tree Top Walk**, a 600m-long ramp, was built allowing visitors to get high up into the canopy of the giant trees. At its highest point it is 40m above the ground and the views below and above are simply stunning. (It is even wheelchair accessible.) If it has one fault, it is that the sights are not well interpreted from the ramp – to many people it is just a bunch of big trees.

At the right end of the ramp is the entrance to the **Ancient Empire**, a boardwalk at ground level at the base of the giant trees, some of which are 16m in circumference, including one that soars to 46m. Kids particularly love to look for the faces of 'forest giants' in the gnarled tree roots.

The Valley of the Giants (☎ 9840 8263) is open March to November from 9 am to 5 pm, December to February from 8 am to 6 pm; entry to the Tree Top Walk is $5/2/12 for adults/kids/families. The Ancient Empire walk is free.

The statuesque international model Elle McPherson was one of the first visitors to walk the ramp, apparently a kindred spirit of the giants.

Bushwalking – Nuyts Wilderness

One of the state's finest coastal walks, in the Nuyts Wilderness, is close to Walpole. It combines ocean beaches, rocky headlands, idyllic estuaries and magnificent flora. There are karri and jarrah forests near Deep River, extensive heathlands on the walk to the sea and a bewildering variety of flowers, including jug orchids and kangaroo paw.

An easy, two day circuit walk which takes in Lost Beach and Thompson Cove is described in Lonely Planet's *Bushwalking in Australia* by John & Monica Chapman.

From the Nuyts car park to Thompson Cove is 7km and there are possible side trips to Crystal Lake and Mt Hopkins. The best time to do this walk is in spring because the wildflowers are prolific.

Organised Tours

Cape to Cape Ecotours (☎ 9752 2334) runs day trips around the area for $60, which includes lunch on Nornalup Inlet and the Valley of the Giants.

Wilderness Cruises (☎ 9840 1036) has daily trips through the Walpole and Nornalup inlets and the river systems at 10 am (also 2.30 pm from October to April); snacks are included, all for $15/8 for adults/children.

Places to Stay & Eat

There are a number of campsites in the Walpole-Nornalup National Park including tent sites ($5) at Peaceful Bay, Crystal

Springs and Coalmine Beach. There are CALM huts at Fernhook Falls and Mt Frankland ($10 per person).

The *Tingle All Over Backpackers'* (☎ 9840 1041), on the South Coast Highway in Walpole, was closed when we visited – and backpackers were left stranded in the rain outside the front door. If you are lucky to find it open, it is $12 for a budget bed.

We also get both good and bad press for the rustic *Dingo Flat YHA Hostel* (☎ 9840 8073) on Dingo Flat Rd off the Valley of the Giants Rd, 18km east of Walpole. You need a car or cycle to get to this hostel, or if you ring ahead they may pick you up at Bow Bridge (there is a phone in the local shop). Budget beds are from $11.

The *Rest Point Tourist Centre* (☎ 9840 1032) is 5km west of Walpole on the southern side of the inlet. They have tent and powered sites, A-frame cabins and units. Fully equipped three-bedroom cottages (sleeping six);are a bargain for $95.

The *Walpole Motel Hotel* (☎ 9840 1023) has single/double units for $46/55. The *Jesmond Dene Lodge* (☎ 9840 1107) is on the South Coast Highway in Nornalup, near the Frankland River; a unit is from $65 to $80 for two.

There are also many farmstays and cottages in the area; enquire at the tourist office. A more novel form of accommodation would be on a houseboat. *Houseboat Holidays* (☎ 9840 1310), Boronia Ave, Walpole, has 10-berth houseboats for hire; again, enquire at the tourist office.

You can get counter meals at the *Walpole Hotel* and there are at least three cafes on the South-Western Highway.

PEACEFUL BAY

The road to Peaceful Bay, one of those archetypal, get-away-from-it-all places, is 24km east of Walpole. This is a beach area for those keen on fishing and swimming. There is a caravan park (☎ 9840 8060) with powered sites/on-site vans from $12/20 for two, and *Peaceful Bay Chalets* (☎ 9840 8169) with units from $42 for two.

DENMARK
- *pop 3500*

Denmark), or Koorabup ('place of the black swan'), was once settled by Aborigines (3000-year-old fish traps have been found in Wilson Inlet). Named by an early explorer after his friend, the town was established to supply timber for the goldfields. About 54km west of Albany, it has some fine beaches in the area (especially Ocean Beach for surfing) and is a good base for trips into the karri forests.

Today it is an arts and crafts centre with quite a large 'hippie' population. It is also a popular holiday spot with a good selection of restaurants and accommodation.

Information

The friendly Denmark tourist office (☎ 9848 2055), housed in an old church on Strickland St, has Heritage Trail brochures including the **Mokare Trail** (a 3km trail along the Denmark River) and the **Wilson Inlet Trail** (a 6km trail that starts from the river mouth. They provide the free booklet and map, both called *Discover Denmark*. The Environment Centre (☎ 9848 1644) on Strickland St has an extensive library and bookshop.

Things to See & Do

There are fine views from **Mt Shadforth Lookout** while the **William Bay National Park**, 14km west of Denmark, has fine coastal scenery of rocks and reefs. There are also scenic spots such as Greens Pool, Elephant Rocks, Madfish Bay, Tower Hill and Waterfall Beach.

Places to Stay

There are several caravan parks in town, the closest being the idyllic *Rivermouth Caravan Park* (☎ 9848 1262), 1km south of the town centre on Inlet Drive; tent/powered sites are $10/13, and on-site vans are from $28 for two. Other caravan parks are *Ocean Beach* (☎ 9848 1105), 8km south of town; *Wilson Inlet* (☎ 9848 1267), 4km south; and *Rudgyard Beach* (☎ 9848 1169), 9km east.

The *Associate YHA Hostel* at Wilson Inlet Caravan Park, over 4km south of Denmark,

isn't much chop. The dingy dorm in the park's most dilapidated building is $10 per night – four or so people could get together and get something better in town. Denmark sure needs a real backpackers' hostel.

Edinburgh House (☎ 9848 1477, toll-free (1800) 671 477), on the South Coast Highway in the centre of town, is a friendly place with a large TV lounge and clean single/double en-suite rooms for $45/70. The *Denmark Unit Motel Hotel* (☎ 9848 2206), Holling Rd, has singles/doubles for $20/35 and motel units for $50/70; and the *Denmark Motel & Cottages* (☎ 9848 1147) on Inlet Drive has units from $50/65.

There are many types of farmstays, B&Bs, chalets and cottages in the Denmark area; the tourist office keeps a current list.

A small selection of those with good settings are: the *Kon Tiki Cottage* (☎ 9848 1265), 19 Adams Rd, with a two bedroom cottage for $65/100 in the low/high season (if you stay two nights); *Riverview Cottage* (☎ 9848 1873) on Scotsdale Rd with doubles from $75 to $100; the *The Grange B&B* (☎ 9848 2319), Mt Shadforth Rd, for $135 for two with a full 'farmhouse' cooked breakfast; and the A-frame *Tree Tops Cottage* (☎ 9848 1265), Payne Rd, for $100 (minimum two nights). *Waters Edge B&B* (☎ 9848 1043), 9 Inlet Drive, has tidy en-suite rooms; expect to pay $40/70.

Places to Eat

There are three bakeries: *Bill's* and *Day's Lunch Bar*, both on the highway, and the *Denmark* on the corner of Fig Tree Square. *Russell's Hunger Buster*, a fast food place, is near the corner of Walker and Strickland Sts, and *Kettles Deli* is on the corner of the highway and Holling Rd.

Bellini's, also in Holling Rd, has a great balcony with views of the river. The food is Greek even though the name is Italian, but you are in Denmark, Australia. It is open daily for lunch and dinner, except Tuesday; a meal will set you back about $20.

Just around the corner, on the highway, is the *Blue Wren Cafe*, open from 8 am to 8 pm most days (or when they feel like it). They

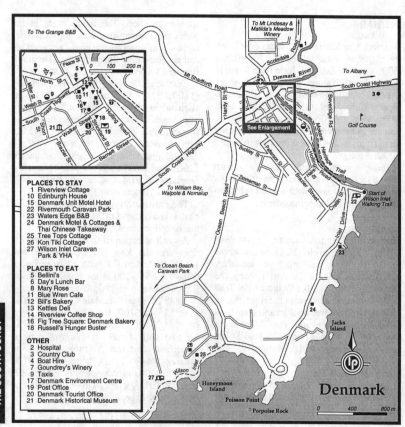

PLACES TO STAY
1   Riverview Cottage
10 Edinburgh House
15 Denmark Unit Motel Hotel
22 Rivermouth Caravan Park
23 Waters Edge B&B
24 Denmark Motel & Cottages &
    Thai Chinese Takeaway
25 Tree Tops Cottage
26 Kon Tiki Cottage
27 Wilson Inlet Caravan
    Park & YHA

PLACES TO EAT
5   Bellini's
6   Day's Lunch Bar
8   Mary Rose
11 Blue Wren Cafe
12 Bill's Bakery
13 Kettles Deli
14 Riverview Coffee Shop
16 Fig Tree Square: Denmark Bakery
18 Russell's Hunger Buster

OTHER
2   Hospital
3   Country Club
4   Boat Hire
7   Goundrey's Winery
9   Taxis
17 Denmark Environment Centre
19 Post Office
20 Denmark Tourist Office
21 Denmark Historical Museum

Denmark

have a pasta night on Thursday. The *Riverview Coffee Shop*, 18 Holling Rd, has good German food – no meal is over $12. The *Hillside Restaurant* (☎ 9848 1147), out on Inlet Drive, has large fish baskets for about $20; bookings are essential.

The *Mary Rose*, on North St next to Goundrey's Winery, is a quaint place with a pleasant balcony, and it serves tasty light meals – they also have vegetarian dishes.

Matilda's Meadow, Hamilton Rd, serves meals incorporating local produce and they stock a variety of regional wines. There are great views over the vineyards and you can choose to dine alfresco or inside; it is closed Monday and Tuesday for meals.

ALBANY
- *pop 26,000*

The town of Albany is the commercial centre of the southern region and the oldest European settlement in the state. It was established in 1826, three years before Perth. The area was previously occupied by Aborigines and there is much evidence, especially around Oyster Harbour, of their earlier presence.

Albany's excellent harbour, on King

George Sound, made it a thriving whaling port. Later Albany was a coaling station for British ships bound for the east coast. In WWI, it was the gathering point for troopships of the 1st Australian Imperial Force (AIF) before they sailed for Egypt and the Gallipoli campaign.

The coastline around Albany contains some of Australia's most rugged and spectacular scenery. There are a number of pristine beaches in the area where you don't have to compete for sand space – try the misnamed Misery, Ledge or Nanarup beaches.

Information

The informative Albany tourist bureau (☎ 9841 1088, toll-free (1800) 644 088) is in the old train station in Proudlove Terrace. It's open from 8.15 am to 5.30 pm weekdays, and from 9 am to 5 pm weekends. Get the free *Albany* guide (and a free map) which lists places to eat and stay, and things to do.

If you need some reading material, the Gemini book exchange is opposite St John's Church in York St. The post office is at 218 York St; most of the banks are on York St; and the CALM office is on the Albany Highway next to the RACWA.

Old Buildings

Albany has some fine old colonial buildings – **Stirling Terrace** is noted for its Victorian shopfronts. The informative **Albany Residency Museum**, opposite the Old Gaol, was originally built in the 1850s as the home of the resident magistrate; it is open daily from 10 am to 5 pm. Displays include seafaring subjects, flora and fauna and Aboriginal artefacts. Housed in another building is 'Sea & Touch', a great hands-on experience for children and adults focusing on the marine and animal world (eg sea urchins, possum fur, bones).

Next to the museum is a full-scale replica of the brig **Amity**, the ship that brought Albany's founding party to the area in 1826; it is open daily from 9 am to 5 pm and there is a $2/0.50 entry fee for adults/children.

The **old gaol**, built in 1851, was originally intended as a hiring depot for ticket-of-leave convicts. Most were in private employment

by 1855 so it was closed until 1872, when it was extended and reopened as a civil gaol. Now a folk museum, it is open daily from 10 am to 4.15 pm (this includes entry into Patrick Taylor Cottage).

The restored **old post office**, built in 1870, now houses the Inter-Colonial Museum. It has an interesting collection of communications equipment from WA's past; it is open daily and admission is free.

The 1832 wattle-and-daub **Patrick Taylor Cottage** is open daily. The farm at **Strawberry Hill**, 2km from town, is one of the oldest in the state, established in 1827 as the government farm for Albany. It is open daily from 10 am to 5 pm; entry is $3.50/2/ for adults/children.

Other historic buildings in town include the train station, St John's Anglican Church and the courthouse. A guided walking-tour brochure of colonial buildings is available from the tourist office, but the *First Settlement Heritage Trail* ($2) is far more detailed.

Views

There are fine views over the coast and inland from the twin peaks, **Mt Clarence** and **Mt Melville**, which overlook the town. On top of Mt Clarence is the Desert Mounted Corps Memorial, originally erected in Port Said as a memorial to the events of Gallipoli. It was brought here when the Suez crisis in 1956 made colonial reminders less than popular in Egypt.

To climb Mt Clarence follow the track accessible from the end of Grey St East; turn left, take the first turn on the right and follow the path by the water tanks. The walk is tough but the views from the top make it worthwhile. The easiest way is along Apex Drive.

There are also panoramic views from the lookout tower on Mt Melville; the turn-off to the tower is off Serpentine Rd.

Other Attractions

The **Princess Royal Fortress**, Mt Adelaide, was built in 1893 – as Albany was a strategic port, its vulnerability to attack loomed as a potential threat to Australia's security. The restored buildings, gun emplacements and fine

THE SOUTH COAST

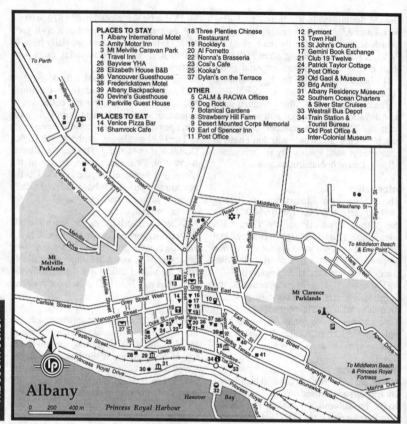

PLACES TO STAY
1 Albany International Motel
2 Amity Motor Inn
3 Mt Melville Caravan Park
4 Travel Inn
26 Bayview YHA
28 Elizabeth House B&B
36 Vancouver Guesthouse
38 Frederickstown Motel
39 Albany Backpackers
40 Devine's Guesthouse
41 Parkville Guest House

PLACES TO EAT
14 Venice Pizza Bar
16 Shamrock Cafe

18 Three Plenties Chinese
   Restaurant
19 Rockley's
20 Al Fornetto
22 Nonna's Brasseria
23 Cosi's Cafe
25 Kooka's
37 Dylan's on the Terrace

OTHER
5 CALM & RACWA Offices
6 Dog Rock
7 Botanical Gardens
8 Strawberry Hill Farm
9 Desert Mounted Corps Memorial
10 Earl of Spencer Inn
11 Post Office

12 Pyrmont
13 Town Hall
15 St John's Church
17 Gemini Book Exchange
21 Club 19 Twelve
24 Patrick Taylor Cottage
27 Post Office
29 Old Gaol & Museum
30 Brig Amity
31 Albany Residency Museum
32 Southern Ocean Charters
   & Silver Star Cruises
33 Westrail Bus Depot
34 Train Station &
   Tourist Bureau
35 Old Post Office &
   Inter-Colonial Museum

Albany

0 200 400 m

Princess Royal Harbour

THE SOUTH COAST

views make it well worth a visit. Particularly poignant are the photos of the troop transports on their way to Gallipoli. The fortress is open daily from 9 am to 5 pm; admission is $3/1/7 for adults/children/families.

On Middleton Rd is Albany's most bizarre sight **Dog Rock**, a deformed and painted boulder that looks like a dog's head.

Whale-Watching

The whale-watching season is from July to mid-October – southern right and humpback whales can be observed near the bays and coves of King George Sound. Southern

Dog Rock – complete with painted collar

JEFF WILLIAMS

JEFF WILLIAMS

JEFF WILLIAMS

JEFF WILLIAMS

A	B
C	D

South Coast

A: Ancient forest near Walpole
C: The view from Frenchman's Peak, Cape Le Grand National Park

B: Natural Bridge, Torndirrup National Park
D: Amongst the giant karri, Valley of the Giants, near Walpole

South Coast

A: The tail of a humpback whale
B: The grandeur of Cape Le Grand (from Frenchman's Peak), near Esperance

Ocean Charters (☎ 9841 7176) takes trips out to the whales and also operates diving, fishing, underwater photography and snorkelling tours on demand. Silver Star Cruises (☎ 9841 3333) and Spinners Charters (☎ 9841 7151) also take tours. A two to three hour cruise is about $20/12 for adults/children.

Organised Tours

The *Silver Star* leaves the town jetty four times weekly for a 2½ hour cruise around King George Sound; the cost is $22/12 for adults/children. Spinners Charters departs from Emu Point Marina, Southern Ocean Charters from the town jetty.

Escape Tours (☎ 9841 2865) operates from the tourist bureau and has many local half/full-day tours around Albany for $30/60. Albany Taxi Tours (☎ 9844 4444) charges $30 per hour for tours (a maximum of four passengers). There are 4WD tours with Do-a-Tour (☎ 9844 3509) and extended tours with Design a Tour (☎ 9842 2809). Ask the tourist bureau for information on these and others.

Places to Stay

Caravan Parks & Hostels There are caravan parks aplenty in Albany. The closest are *Mt Melville Caravan Park* (☎ 9841 4616), 1km north of town on the corner of Lion and Wellington Sts; and the spotless *Middleton Beach Caravan Park* (☎ 9841 3593) on Middleton Rd, 3km east of town. Both have tent/powered sites for $12/14, and tidy park cabins for about $45 for two.

Other parks include the *Tourist Village* (☎ 9841 3752), on the Albany Highway 4km north of town; *Panorama* (☎ 9844 4031), Frenchman Bay Rd; *Cheyne Beach* (☎ 9846 1247), Cheyne Beach Rd; *Happy Days* (☎ 9844 3267), at 21 Millbrook Rd, 10km north of town; *Emu Beach* (☎ 9844 1147), Medcalf Parade, Emu Point; *King River Palms Waterfront* (☎ 9844 3232), also 10km north on Chester Pass Rd; *Kalgan River Caravan Park* (☎ 9844 7937), north-east of Albany on Nanarup Rd near the Lower King Bridge; *Oyster Harbour* (☎ 9844 7164),

Elizabeth St, Lower King, 10km north-east of town; and *Rose Gardens* (☎ 9844 1041), Mermaid Ave, Emu Point.

Albany Backpackers (☎ 9841 8848), centrally located on the corner of Stirling Terrace and Spencer St, is the best travellers' option – its a backpackers' place as such places should be, with free cake and other pluses. With discount a dorm is $11, a single is $20, a twin/double is $32. This place has all the necessities; they hire mountain bikes for $12/24 for a day/week. The cafe below offers half-price pizzas to those living above.

The rambling *Bayview YHA* (☎ 9842 3388), 49 Duke St, is 400m from the centre; dorms cost $13, singles $20, twins and doubles $32 for two (kids are $8 extra). They rent out items such as surfboards ($10 per day), bicycles ($10) and kites ($2).

Guesthouses & B&Bs Albany also has a number of reasonably priced guesthouses and B&B places; enquire at the tourist office.

Some of the places on the tourist office's list are: *Parkville Guest House* (☎ 9841 3704), at 136 Brunswick Rd, from $25/38 including breakfast; and divine *Devines Guesthouse* (☎ 9841 8050), 20 Stirling Terrace, from $35/55. *Elizabeth House B&B* (☎ 9842 2734), Festing St, is good value for $28/50; and the *Vancouver Guesthouse* (☎ 9842 1071), on Stirling Terrace, is similar.

The *King River Homestead* (☎ 9844 7770), 64 Bushby Rd, is located in bushland overlooking the estuary; all rooms have a bath and a double is from $60 to $65.

The *Coraki Holiday Cottages & Villas* (☎ 9844 7068) are about a 10 minute drive from Albany, on Lower King River Rd on the banks of Oyster Harbour; self-contained cottages in this pretty setting are from $50 to $75 (minimum of two nights).

Hotels & Motels There are many hotels and motels in Albany, many of which are on the Albany Highway. The *Amity Motor Inn* (☎ 9841 2200), at No 234, has single/double units from $50/60; the *Quality Inn Motel* (☎ 9841 1177), at No 369, has rooms from

$55/60; the *Travel Inn* (☎ 9841 4144), at No 191, is from $75/83; and the *Albany International* (☎ 9841 7399), at No 270, is from $55/65. In town there is the *Frederickstown Motel* (☎ 9841 8630), near the corner of Frederick and Spencer Sts, with singles/doubles from $62/72. An out of town choice is the *Emu Point Motel* (☎ 9844 1001), corner of Mermaid Ave and Medcalf Parade; rooms are from $39/49.

The town's finest (and most expensive) accommodation is the *Mercure Grand Hotel* (☎ 9842 1711), formerly the Esplanade, at Middleton Beach; rooms, with everything that opens and shuts, are from $129 to $199 (but there are all sorts of weekend and other specials).

This is a small selection of the available accommodation; the tourist bureau has more details, especially on self-catering options.

Places to Eat

Albany You will not starve if you wander along Stirling Terrace. *Dylan's Cafe on the Terrace*, at No 82, has an excellent range of light meals including hamburgers and pancakes at reasonable prices; it is open late most nights, early for breakfast and has a takeaway section. Also on the terrace is *Kooka's*, at No 204, in a restored old house, where you pay about $35 for an excellent, three course meal. Other 'sterling' choices are the *Penny Post Restaurant* in the old post office, the *Harbourfront Steak & Grill* and three pubs *The London, Royal George* and *White Star* with the ubiquitous counter meal.

Breakfasts at *Eatcha Heart Out* at 154 York St and *Cosi's Cafe* on Peel Place are recommended. The *Shamrock Cafe* on York St is a favourite of the impecunious; breakfasts are $4 and a bottomless coffee or tea is $1.60.

There are also a couple of pizza places on York St including *Al Fornetto* and the *Venice Pizza Bar* (open daily); the latter wins our Silver Fork Award for value.

Rookley's, 36 Peel Place, has an alfresco courtyard and specialises in lunches, deli meals and fine takeaways. It is in the evenings. Expect to pay $5 to $7 for a tasty roll with unusual ingredients. *Nonna's Brasseria*, across from Al Fornetto, is Albany's yuppie alternative with a fairly expensive Italian menu; it is, however, open until late.

The *Lemon Grass Thai*, 370 Middleton Rd, has a good range of Thai food (including vegetarian meals); and *Three Plenties* Chinese, York St, and has $5 lunch specials, and doesn't cook with MSG.

Middleton Beach & Emu Point At Middleton Beach there is the trendy *Beachside Cafe* – with great fish and chips – and the *Middleton Beach Fish & Chips*, close to the Mercure Grand Hotel. The latter has crisp golden chips and a diverse catch of groper, schnapper, shark and flounder. The Mercure Grand Hotel has a couple of restaurants – the *Legends Bar & Cafe* and the licensed *Genevieve's Restaurant*.

It is the setting, more so than the food, which attracts diners to Emu Point. Restaurants in the vicinity of the view include *Emu Point Cafe*, Mermaid Ave, and *Cravings Waterfront Bistro*; both are BYO.

Entertainment

As rural as it is, Albany always seems to have a vibrant nightlife. On our last visit, *Maggie's*, at 338 Middleton Rd, and *Club 19 Twelve*, at 120 York St, were the latest of the late-night venues – Maggie's has bands Thursday to Sunday. There are usually bands at the *Earl of Spencer Inn*, corner of Earl and Spencer Sts, on weekends.

The *Town Hall Theatre* has regular shows. There are cinemas on the Albany Highway.

Getting Around

Love's runs bus services around town from Monday to Friday, and Saturday morning. Buses will take you along Albany Highway from Peel Place to the roundabout; others go to Spencer Park, Middleton Beach, Emu Point and Bayonet Head (once a week).

Albany Car Rentals (☎ 9841 7077) has cars from $40 per day with unlimited kilometres. Avis (☎ 9842 2833) and Budget (☎ 9841 2299) have offices in town. Rainbow Coast (☎ 9842 2456) has 4WDs from $50 daily.

You can rent bicycles from Albany Backpackers on Stirling Terrace; the cost is $10 per day. Emu Beach Caravan Park also rents out bikes (see Places to Stay).

AROUND ALBANY

South of Albany, off Frenchman Bay Rd, is a stunning stretch of coastline that includes **the Gap** and **Natural Bridge**, rugged natural rock formations surrounded by pounding seas; the **Blowholes**, especially interesting in heavy seas when spray is blown with great force through the surrounding rock; the **rock-climbing** areas of Peak Head and West Cape Howe National Park; steep, rocky coves such as **Jimmy Newhill's Harbour** and **Salmon Holes**, popular with surfers but considered quite dangerous; and **Frenchman Bay**, which has a caravan park, a fine swimming beach and a grassed, shady BBQ area. This is a dangerous coastline so be aware of freakish, large waves.

Whaleworld Museum

The Whaleworld Museum, at Frenchman Bay, 21km from Albany, is based at Cheynes Beach Whaling Station (which ceased operations in November 1978). There's a rusting 'Cheynes IV' whalechaser and station impedimenta (such as whale oil tanks) to inspect outside. The museum screens a gore-spattered film on whaling operations and it has examples of harpoons, whaleboat models and scrimshaw (etchings on whalebone).

It is open daily from 9 am to 5 pm, and admission is $5/2 for adults/children. The museum also has a superb collection of marine mammal paintings by noted US artist Richard Ellis. Listen carefully and you will hear the haunting, mournful songs of the humpbacks, not far away out at sea.

National Parks & Reserves

There are a number of excellent natural areas near Albany. From west to east along the coast you can explore many different habitats and see a wide variety of coastal scenery. The 17 sq km **William Bay National Park** has coastal dunes, granite boulders, heathlands and mature karri forest.

West Cape Howe National Park, 30km west of Albany, is a 35 sq km playground for naturalists, bushwalkers, rock-climbers and anglers. Inland, there is coastal heath, areas of lakes and swamp and karri forest. With the

THE SOUTH COAST

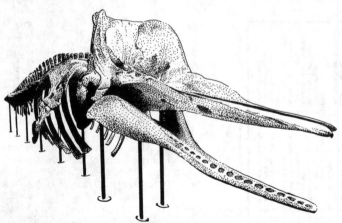

This 11m sperm whale was one of the last killed by the Cheynes Beach Whaling Company in 1978.

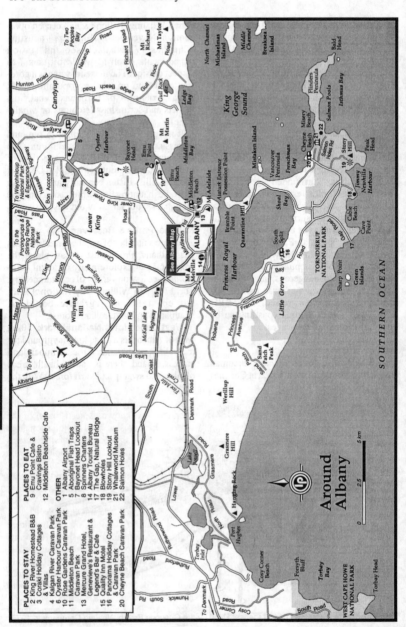

THE SOUTH COAST

PLACES TO STAY
1 King River Homestead B&B
& Villas
3 Coraki Holiday Cottages
4 Kalgan River Caravan Park
6 Oyster Harbour Caravan Park
10 Rose Gardens Caravan Park
11 Middleton Beach
Caravan Park
13 Mercure Grand Hotel;
Genevieve's Restaurant &
Legend's Bar & Cafe
15 Quality Inn Motel
16 Panorama Holiday Cottages
& Caravan Park
20 Cheyne Beach Caravan Park

PLACES TO EAT
9 Emu Point Cafe &
Cravings Bistro
12 Middleton Beachside Cafe

OTHER
1 Albany Airport
5 Aboriginal Fish Traps
7 Bayonet Head Lookout
8 Spinners Charters
14 Albany Tourist Bureau
17 The Gap, Natural Bridge
18 Blowholes
19 Stony Hill Lookout
21 Whaleworld Museum
22 Salmon Holes

Around
Albany

0   2.5   5 km

SOUTHERN OCEAN

exception of the road to Shelley Beach, access is restricted to 4WD and walkers.

Torndirrup National Park includes the region's two very popular attractions, the Natural Bridge and the Gap, as well as the Blowholes, Jimmy Newhill's Beach and Bald Head. The views are spectacular. Whales are frequently seen from the cliffs and the park's varied vegetation provides habitats for many native animals and reptiles. Keen walkers can tackle the hard 10km return **bushwalk** (six-plus hours) over Isthmus Hill to Bald Head, at the eastern extremity of the park.

Some 20km east of Albany is **Two People's Bay**, a nature reserve of 46 sq km with a good swimming beach, scenic coastline and a small colony of the noisy scrub bird (once thought to be extinct – see the boxed aside 'Noisy Scrub Bird' in this chapter). The title 'Baie des Deux Peuples' leaves you in no doubt as to who gave this place its name – there is a 2km heritage trail of that 'nom' in the reserve.

Probably the best of the national parks, but the least visited of them, is the 39 sq km **Waychinicup National Park**, which includes Mt Manypeaks and other granite formations. At the moment there is a problem with dieback, restricting walking in the area.

Noisy Scrub Bird

This little, near-flightless bird lives up to its name as it has a powerful, ear-piercing call. The noisy scrub bird (*Atrichornus clamosus*) almost joined the thylacine to extinction. It was sighted in jarrah forest at the foot of the Darling Scarp, near Perth, in 1842, and the last recorded specimen was collected near Torbay in 1889. It was then thought extinct until rediscovered in 1961 in Two People's Bay.

In 1983, breeding pairs were transferred to similar habitats in Mt Manypeaks Nature Reserve (now part of Waychinicup National Park) to reseed populations where the bird had died out. Later, in 1987, another colony was established at Walpole-Nornalup. It is now believed that there are well over 100 breeding pairs. ■

THE MOUNTAIN NATIONAL PARKS

To the north-east of Denmark and almost due north of Albany are two spectacular mountainous national parks: the Stirling Range and the Porongurups. The best time to visit both parks is in late spring and early summer when it is beginning to warm up and the wildflowers are at their best. From June to August it is cold and wet and hail is not uncommon. Occasionally, snow falls on the top of the ranges.

Further information on these parks can be obtained from the following CALM centres: Porongurup National Park, Bolganup Rd, RMB 1112, Mt Barker 6324; Stirling Range National Park, Chester Pass Rd, c/o Amelup via Borden 6338; and South Coast Regional Centre, Albany Highway, Albany 6330.

CALM produces two informative booklets on this region – *Mountains of Mystery: A Natural History of the Stirling Ranges* and *Rugged Mountains Jewelled Sea: The South Coast from Eucla to Albany*.

The Porongurups

The beautiful Porongurup National Park (24 sq km) has 1100 million-year-old granite outcrops, panoramic views, beautiful scenery, large karri trees, and some excellent bushwalks. The range is 12km long and 670m at its highest point.

In the Porongurups, karri trees grow in the deep red soil (known as karri loam) of the upper slopes. It is unusual to find such large trees growing this far east of the forests between Manjimup and Walpole, but the correct soil, combined with an annual rainfall of over 700mm, accounts for this outlier of forest. Beneath these trees is a beautiful display of wildflowers in season. A **wildflower festival** is held in October.

There are a number of **bushwalking** trails. These range from the short, 10 minute Tree in the Rock stroll, the intermediate Castle and Balancing Rocks (two hours) to the harder Hayward and Nancy Peaks (four hours) and excellent Devil's Slide and Marmabup Rock (three hours) walks. A scenic 6km drive along the northern edge of the park starts near the ranger's residence.

THE SOUTH COAST

Rock-Climbing

This is a highly technical and potentially dangerous sport. The moral is don't climb if you don't know how. The Great Southern is the hub of WA's climbing scene with West Cape Howe, Torndirrup, Porongurup and the Stirling Range national parks. Contact Bushed! for Adventure (☎ 9842 2127), 334 Middleton Rd, Albany, for more advice and information. (Bushed! also offers climbing guides, abseiling, walking and canoeing trips.)

West Cape Howe is remote 'out there' climbing territory where a group size of three should be the minimum. The area has multi-pitch climbs on granite sea cliffs, all usually reached by abseil. Climbs are scaled by the level of difficulty; 30 would be regarded as suitable for the experienced climber while 10 is somewhat easier. Classics include Tombstone (20), the Elite (18) and Vulture St (17).

Torndirrup includes the Gap, Natural Bridge and Amphitheatre granite climbing areas. Most of the climbs are single pitch and classics include Horrie Cometh (17) and Surfs Up (15).

The Porongurups have a number of long climbs on weathered white granite; it is requested that you register with the CALM ranger.

Bluff Knoll in the Stirlings is the closest WA gets to offering a real mountaineering experience and has been the scene of many 'epics'. Climbs can be up to 350m long involving a dozen or more pitches and as many hours to complete. Again, let the CALM ranger know of your intentions and log out when climbing has ended. ■

Places to Stay & Eat There is no camping within the national park but there's a tourist park (☎ 9853 1057) in Porongurup township with tent/powered sites for $12/14, and on-site vans for $35 for two; and a small backpackers' hostel (☎ 9853 1110) at the back of the tearooms with dorm beds for $13, doubles for $30 (and hearty meals for $6.50).

The *Porongurup Chalets*, on the corner of Bolganup and Porongurup Rds, cost from $50 to $70 for four; the *Bolganup Homestead Units* (☎ 9853 1049) are from $70 to $80; and *Karribank Lodge* (☎ 9853 1022), on Main St, has singles/doubles from $55 to $90. There are also a number of farmstays and B&Bs in the region which cost around $65 for two; enquire in Albany, Cranbrook or Mt Barker.

The Stirling Range

This national park (1156 sq km) consists of a single chain of peaks, 10km wide and 65km long. Running most of its length are isolated peaks which tower above broad valleys covered in prickly shrubs and heath. The range is also noted for its spectacular colour changes through blues, reds and purples. The range was first visited in 1832 by Ensign Dale in search of grains and, three years later,

Surveyor General Roe named the range. In his diary he recorded:

The remarkable and picturesque mountains being as yet unknown collectively by any distinguishing appellation...I called them 'Stirling Range' after the Governor of the Swan River Colony, by whom they were about to undergo a closer personal examination.

Because of the combination of height and climate there are a great number of localised plants in the range. It is estimated that over 1500 species of plants occur naturally, 60 of which are endemic. The most beautiful are the Darwinias or mountain bells. Ten species of these mountain bells, which only occur above 300m, have been identified, and only one of them occurs outside the range. One particularly beautiful example is the Mondurup bell.

The bells are not the only plants with such a restricted distribution. The Talyuberlup bell, with its finger-like buds, is known only from a few localities; you can see it on the Mt Talyuberlup walk.

This park is one of the best **bushwalking** locations in the state. Keen walkers can choose from a number of high points: Toolbrunup (for views and a good climb), Bluff Knoll (at 1073m the highest peak in the

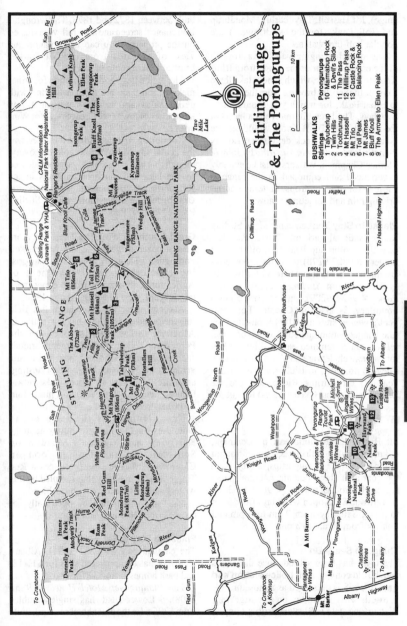

Stirling Range & The Porongurups

0   5   10 km

BUSHWALKS

Stirlings
1 Talyuberlup
2 Twin Hills
3 Toolbrunup
4 Mt Hassell
5 Mt Trio
6 Toll Peak
7 Mt James
8 Bluff Knoll
9 The Arrows to Ellen Peak

Porongurups
10 Marmabup Rock & Devil's Slide
11 The Pass
12 Millinup Pass
13 Castle Rock & Balancing Rock

range), Mt Hassell, Talyuberlup, Mondurup and Toll Peak (for the wildflowers) are popular half-day walks.

The most challenging walks are a crossing of the eastern sector of the range from Bluff Knoll to Ellen Peak, which should take three days, or the shorter traverse from the Arrows to Ellen Peak, for which you should allow two days. The latter alternative is a loop but the former, from Bluff Knoll, would require a car shuttle. For track details see Lonely Planet's *Bushwalking in Australia* by John & Monica Chapman. Walkers must be suitably experienced and equipped as the range is subject to sudden drops in temperature, driving rain and sometimes snow.

Places to Stay You can camp in the Stirling Range National Park on Chester Pass Rd, near the Toolbrunup Peak turn-off; call the ranger (☎ 9827 9278) for details. Facilities are limited, and tent sites are $5 for two.

The well-run *Stirling Range Caravan Park* (☎ 9827 9229), on the park's north boundary, is also on Chester Pass Rd. Tent/powered sites are $10/14, on-site vans (the budget option) are $30 for two or three, self-contained rammed-earth cabins are $49 for two and chalets are $59/67 for two/three. They do drop-offs to Bluff Knoll and Ellen Peak for the Stirling Ridge, and provide handy 'mud maps' (sketch maps) for guests.

MT BARKER
- *pop 4500*

Mt Barker, 55km north-east of Denmark, 64km south of the Stirling Ranges and about 20km west of the Porongurups, is very much the centre of the mountain national parks region. The tourist bureau (☎ 9851 1163), at 57 Lowood St, is open weekdays from 9 am to 5 pm, Saturday from 9 am to 2 pm and Sunday from 10 am to 3 pm.

Things to See & Do

The town has been settled since the 1830s and the old convict-built **police station and gaol** of 1868 is preserved as a museum.

South-west of town on the Egerton-Warburton estate is **St Werburgh's chapel**,

built between 1872 and 1873. The wrought-iron chancel screen and altar rail were shaped on the property. You can get a panoramic view of the area from the Mt Barker **Lookout**, 5km south of town.

The region has a good reputation for wine-making, and there are many **wineries** with cellar sales and tastings within a few kilometres of town (see Great Southern Wineries below).

Kendenup, 16km north of Mt Barker, was the actual site of WA's first gold discovery, though this was considerably overshadowed by the later and much larger finds in the Kalgoorlie area. Also north of Mt Barker is **Cranbrook**, an access point to the Stirling Range National Park.

Great Southern Wineries

There are more than a dozen wineries in the Mt Barker/Porongurups/Denmark area. This is surprising considering the Department of Agriculture only established an experimental vineyard, west of Mt Barker, in 1966.

Alkoomi, near Mt Frankland, has rich, full-flavoured reds (they have a cellar in Albany); the vineyards based on the Porongurup soil produce divergent varieties such as Castle Rock liqueur muscat, Jingalla verdelho and Karrivale late-harvest riesling; and the Mt Barker vineyards boast Plantagenet fleur (light red) and pinot noir, and Chatsfield traminer.

Near Denmark is the town-bound Goundrey in the historic butter factory, Karriview and Matilda's Meadow on Scotsdale Rd and Tingle-Wood on Glenrowan Rd. The latter produces a Red Tingle, à la the tree (as yet unsampled by this writer) which is a cabernet-shiraz blend.

Most of the wineries are open daily for tastings from 10 am to 4 or 5 pm.

Places to Stay & Eat

The caravan park (☎ 9851 1691), Albany Highway, has tent/powered sites for $10/12, and park homes from $32 for two.

The *Plantagenet Motel Hotel* (☎ 9851 1008), 9 Lowood Rd, has singles/doubles from $20/36 (in the older hotel section), units for $28/46 and counter meals for around $10. The *Mt Barker Hotel* (☎ 9851 1477), 39 Lowood Rd, has basic twin rooms at $25 per person. For those wanting to sample country air there is the quaint 1869 stone cottage, *Abbeyholme B&B* (☎ 9851 1101), to the south of town on the Albany Highway. It is $35/60; they prepare great vegetarian meals.

Two places on Lowood Rd, *Gene's Kitchen* and *Lockwood's Bread Shop*, have home-style meals; and the BYO *Sophie's Restaurant*, 34 Albany Highway, has lunches on weekends and dinner from Wednesday to Sunday.

ALBANY TO ESPERANCE

From Albany, the South Coast Highway runs north-east along the coast before turning inland to skirt the Fitzgerald River National Park and finishing in Esperance. The distance is 476km.

Ongerup & Jerramungup

Ongerup, a small wheatbelt town 153km north of Albany, has an annual wildflower show in September/October with hundreds of local species on show. The Ongerup-Needilup district (within a 40km radius of Ongerup) has over 1300 recorded species, ranging from the 30m salmon gum to small 25mm trigger plants. Two excellent nature reserves are Cawallelup, 19km to the south, and Vaux's Lake, 19km north.

In Jerramungup, there is an interesting **Military Museum** in Tobruk Rd; all the restored vehicles are in working order. The tourist centre (☎ 9835 1119) is also here.

There are a caravan park (☎ 9828 2090) and hotel (☎ 9828 2001) in Ongerup, and a caravan park (☎ 9835 1174) in Jerramungup. The *Jerramungup Farmstay B&B* (☎ 9835 1002) is on a 30 sq km sheep and wheat property 2km south of town; singles/doubles are $35/50.

Bremer Bay

This fishing and holiday town (population 200), which sits at the western end of the Great Australian Bight, is 61km from the South Coast Highway. The BP service station (☎ 9837 4093), Gnombup Terrace, acts as the information office.

From July until November, Bremer Bay is a good spot to observe **southern right whales**. These whales come in to many bays in the area to give birth to their calves. Sometimes they are as close as 6m from the shore, and can be seen from many vantage points on the coastline – Point Ann and Dillon Bay are good observation points.

The caravan park (☎ 9837 4018) has powered sites for $14, and park cabins for $30 for two; and the hotel (☎ 9837 4133) has singles/doubles for $62/72. Readers recommend the *Bremer Bay B&B* (☎ 9837 4136), in Old Myamba on Bremer Bay Rd, 7km from town; it is $40/50.

A nice place to stay within Fitzgerald River National Park is the historic 1858 *Quaalup Homestead* (☎ 9837 4124), Gairdner Rd; a bunk bed is $10, single/double units are $47.50/60 (with breakfast), a chalet is $55, and a cottage is from $85 to $100.

Ravensthorpe

The small town of Ravensthorpe (population 400) was once the centre of the Phillips River goldfield; later, copper was also mined here. Nowadays, the area is dependent on farming. Every September a wildflower show is held in town.

The tourist office (☎ 9838 1277), in the Going Bush Craft Shop in Morgans St, provides a detailed visitor map and information guide to the region.

The ruins of a disused government smelter and the Cattlin Creek Mine (copper) are near town. West of town is the **WA standard time meridian**, indicated by a boulder with a plaque on it.

Places to Stay & Eat The *caravan park* (☎ 9838 1050) has tent/powered sites for $10/12, and on-site vans at $25 for two. The *Palace Motor Hotel* (☎ 9838 1005), classified by the National Trust, has backpackers' beds for $20 per person, and single/double motel units for $38/48.

Tempt yourself with the sumptuous selection of cakes at the *Country Kitchen*.

At Munglinup, 90km east of Ravensthorpe, is the *Singing Winds* (☎ 9075 1018), which provides B&B at reasonable rates for long-distance cyclists.

Hopetoun

There are fine beaches and bays around Hopetoun (population 300), which is also the eastern gateway to the Fitzgerald River National Park.

For tourist information, go to Chatterbox Crafts (☎ 9838 3228) in Veal St; they provide a map and information guide.

About 5km north of town is **Dunn's Swamp**, an ideal location for a picnic, bushwalking and bird-watching. West of town is the landlocked **Culham Inlet**, a beaut spot for fishing (especially black bream) and east of town is the very scenic **Southern Ocean East Drive**, which features beaches and the Jerdacuttup Lakes.

The world's longest fence – the 1822km long **rabbit-proof fence** – enters the sea in the south at Starvation Bay, east of Hopetoun and 40km south of the South Coast Highway. It starts at Eighty Mile Beach on the Indian Ocean, north of Port Hedland.

Places to Stay & Eat The *caravan park* (☎ 9838 3096) has tent/powered sites for $11/13, and on-site vans for $27 for two; and the *Port Hotel* (☎ 9838 3053), Veal St, has singles/doubles for $15/30 (backpackers pay $10 per person). The *Hopetoun Motel & Chalet Village* (☎ 9838 3219) has units for $55 for two, chalets for $55 for four.

You can get meals from the hotel, lunches from *Marg's Cafe* or takeaways from the BYO *Starboard Cafe*; all are in Veal St.

Fitzgerald River National Park

This 3300 sq km park is one of two places in WA with a UNESCO Biosphere rating and is one of the most fascinating places to explore in the whole state. The park contains a very beautiful coastline, sand plains, the rugged Barren mountain range and deep, wide river valleys.

The **bushwalking** is excellent and the wilderness route from Fitzgerald Beach to West Beach is recommended – there is no trail and no water but camping is permitted (you will need to plan water drops yourself at the end of access roads). Clean your shoes at each end of the walk to discourage the spread of dieback; also register with the ranger on Quiss Rd or Hamersley Drive.

Shorter walks in the park are East Mt Barren (three hours), West Mt Barren (two hours) and Point Ann (one hour).

Wildflowers are most abundant in spring but there are flowers in bloom throughout the year. This park is botanically significant in Australia with 20% of the state's described species. In the park are half the orchids in WA (over 80 species) and 70 of these occur nowhere else; 22 mammal species including honey possums, dibblers – highly endangered with only a few hundred left – and tammar wallabies; 200 species of birds including the ground parrot and western bristlebird; 41 reptile and 12 frog species; and 1700 species of plants. Many of the plant species have not yet been named by botanists. To top off the list of superlatives, this is the home of the royal hakea and Quaalup bell, and southern right whales are seen offshore from August to September.

The fires of 1989, which swept through

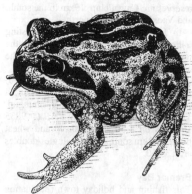

A pobbledonk – or Western Banjo Frog *(Limnodynastes dorsalis)* if you wish to be formal – endemic to WA.

48% of the park, have done little to diminish the magnificent wildflower display. Fitzgerald River is still an ecotourism highlight.

You can gain access to the park from Bremer Bay and Hopetoun or from the South Coast Highway along Devils Creek, Quiss and Hamersley Rds. There is accommodation in Bremer Bay, at Quaalup Homestead (in the park) and in Hopetoun.

ESPERANCE
• *pop 12,000*

Esperance, on the coast 200km south of Norseman, was named in 1792 when the *Recherche* and *L'Esperance* sailed into the bay to shelter from a storm. Although the first settlers came to the area in 1863, it was during the gold rush in the 1890s that the town really became established as a port. When the gold fever subsided, Esperance went into a state of suspended animation until after WWII.

In the 1950s, it was discovered that adding missing trace elements to the soil around Esperance restored fertility, and since then the town has rapidly become an agricultural centre. It has deservedly become a popular resort due to its temperate climate, stunning coastal scenery, blue waters, good fishing and dazzling, sandy beaches. The seas offshore are studded with the many islands of the Archipelago of the Recherche. Distinctive Norfolk Island pines line the foreshore.

Information
The helpful Esperance tourist bureau (☎ 9071 2330) on Dempster St, in the museum village, is open daily from 9 am to 5 pm. Here you can book tours along the coast and to the islands, or pour over their extensive pamphlet collection. The post office is on the corner of Andrew and Dempster Sts, and there are public toilets in the museum park.

Things to See & Do
The **Esperance Municipal Museum** consists of various old buildings, including a gallery, smithy's forge, cafe and craft shop.

The museum itself, on James St between the Esplanade and Dempster St, is open daily from 1.30 to 4.30 pm and contains a Skylab display – when the USA's Skylab crashed to earth in 1979, it made its fiery re-entry right over Esperance.

The interesting 36km **Great Ocean Drive** includes spectacular vistas from Observatory Point and the Rotary Lookout on Wireless Hill; Twilight Bay and Picnic Cove, popular swimming spots; and the Pink Lake, stained by a salt-tolerant algae called *Dunalella salina*.

There are about 100 small islands in the **Archipelago of the Recherche**. Colonies of seals, penguins and a wide variety of water birds live on the islands. Woody Island is a wildlife sanctuary.

Kids will enjoy **Telegraph Farm**, 21km out on the South Coast Highway. This commercial protea farm has a host of animals such as buffalo, camels, deer and birds. It is closed Monday and Friday; a tour is $6/3 for adults/children. You can look at various products made from shark and fish leather at Mermaid Leather, 76 Wood St; it's open daily, except Monday, from 2 to 5 pm.

Organised Tours
Vacation Country Tours (☎ 9071 2227) include a town-and-coast tour for $22 and a Cape Le Grand tour for $38. More adventurous alternatives are Aussie Bight Expeditions (☎ 9071 7778) which has 4WD safaris to secluded beaches and bays, and to national parks.

Tours on the Bay of Isles are a must. McKenzies *Seabreeze* (☎ 9071 5757) regularly tours the bay; the cost is $39/16 for adults/children. Expect to see NZ fur seals, Australian sea lions, sea eagles, Cape Barren geese, common dolphins and a host of other wildlife. McKenzies operates the daily ferry to Woody Island in January and February ($25/13).

The Esperance Diving Academy (☎ 9071 5111) conducts dive charters and diving courses. They have island cruises in their *Southern Image* over the Christmas school holidays ($28/14).

THE SOUTH COAST

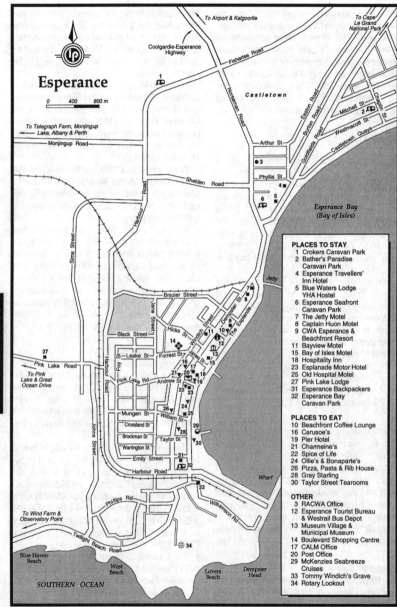

Esperance

0   400   800 m

To Telegraph Farm, Monjingup
Lake, Albany & Perth

To Airport & Kalgoorlie

To Cape
Le Grand
National Park

Coolgardie-Esperance Highway

Fisheries Road

Castletown

Monjingup Road

Arthur St

Shelden Road

Phyllis St

*Esperance Bay
(Bay of Isles)*

Sims Street

Harbour Road

Brazier Street

Jane Street

Jetty

Black Street

Hicks

Forrest St

Leake St

Foy St

Pink Lake Road

Andrew St

To Pink
Lake & Great
Ocean Drive

Mungan St

Crossland St

Brockman St

Warrington St

Emily Street

Harbour Road

Phillips Rd

To Wind Farm &
Observatory Point

Twilight Beach Road

Blue Haven
Beach

West
Beach

Lovers
Beach

Dempster
Head

SOUTHERN OCEAN

Williamson Rd

Wharf

William St

Taylor St

Dempster St

The Esplanade

Castletown Quays

Mitchell St

Chaplin St

Westmacott St

Goldfields Road

Burton Road

Easton Road

Norseman Road

THE SOUTH COAST

PLACES TO STAY
1   Crokers Caravan Park
2   Bather's Paradise
    Caravan Park
4   Esperance Travellers'
    Inn Hotel
5   Blue Waters Lodge
    YHA Hostel
6   Esperance Seafront
    Caravan Park
7   The Jetty Motel
8   Captain Huon Motel
9   CWA Esperance &
    Beachfront Resort
11 Bayview Motel
15 Bay of Isles Motel
18 Hospitality Inn
23 Esplanade Motor Hotel
25 Old Hospital Motel
27 Pink Lake Lodge
31 Esperance Backpackers
32 Esperance Bay
    Caravan Park

PLACES TO EAT
10 Beachfront Coffee Lounge
16 Carusoe's
19 Pier Hotel
21 Charmeine's
22 Spice of Life
24 Ollie's & Bonaparte's
26 Pizza, Pasta & Rib House
28 Gray Starling
30 Taylor Street Tearooms

OTHER
3   RACWA Office
12 Esperance Tourist Bureau
    & Westrail Bus Depot
13 Museum Village &
    Municipal Museum
14 Boulevard Shopping Centre
17 CALM Office
20 Post Office
29 McKenzies Seabreeze
    Cruises
33 Tommy Windich's Grave
34 Rotary Lookout

Places to Stay
There are half a dozen caravan parks around Esperance that provide campsites and on-site vans and cabins; the usual rates for tent/powered sites are $12/14, on-site vans are $25, and park cabins $40 for two. The most central of the parks are the *Esperance Bay Caravan Park* (☎ 9071 2237), on the corner of the Esplanade and Harbour Rd, near the wharf; and the *Esperance Seafront Caravan Park* (☎ 9071 1251) on the corner of Goldfields and Norseman Rds. Others not far away are *Bather's Paradise* (☎ 9071 1014), on the corner of Westmacott and Chaplin Sts; the well-kept and efficiently run *Crokers* (☎ 9071 4100), 629 Harbour Rd, which deservedly wins awards; and *Pink Lake* (☎ 9071 2424) on Pink Lake Rd.

The large, popular *Blue Waters Lodge-YHA* (☎ 9071 1040), on Goldfields Rd, is 2km north of the centre. It is $14 in dorms, and singles and twins are $32. It has a nice breakfast area with views over the water.

Also good value is the tidy, comfortable *Esperance Backpackers* (☎ 9071 4724, (018) 93 4541), 14 Emily St. It has all the facilities, has dorm beds for $14, and twins and doubles for $30. They run tours for their backpackers to the national parks with 'scurfing' (surfing the sandhills) included for $40; fishing is $25.

The well-run *Esperance Travellers' Inn Hotel* (☎ 9071 1677), on the corner of Goldfields Rd and Phyllis St, has clean singles/doubles for $40/50. The *Pink Lake Lodge Private Hotel* (☎ 9071 2075), 85 Pink Lake Rd, is $55/65; the *CWA Esperance* (☎ 9071 1364), 23 The Esplanade, has units from $25 to $40; and the *Esperance Chalet Village* (☎ 9071 1861), 6km east of town on Frank Freeman Drive, has A-frame self-contained chalets from $50 to $95 (depending on the season).

There are numerous motels with rates from about $55/70 for singles/doubles. The *Bay of Isles Motel* (☎ 9071 3999) is at 32 The Esplanade; the *Bayview* (☎ 9071 1533) is in Dempster St; the *Esperance Motel Hotel* (☎ 9071 1555) is in Andrew St; the *Captain Huon* (☎ 9071 2383) is at 5 The Esplanade; the *Jetty* (☎ 9071 5978) is at 1 The Esplanade; the *Hospitality Inn* (☎ 9071 1999) is also on the Esplanade, as is the *Beachfront Resort* (☎ 9071 2513), at No 19.

See the tourist bureau for a list of B&Bs.

Places to Eat
The town has a good number of cafes. Sip at the *Beachfront Coffee Lounge*, *Taylor Street Tearooms* or the *Village Cafe*; the latter is in the museum enclave. The best known of the takeaways is *Pizza, Pasta & Rib House*, on the corner of William and Dempster Sts, but there are also a number of fish and chip places. If you like cooking fish then buy fillets of gnanagi – coat them in flour and lightly cook in butter with a sprinkling of lemon pepper.

Coffee lounges which serve meals are the *Island Fare* in the Boulevard shopping centre, and *Charmeine's* in the Dutton Arcade, Dempster St. The *Spice of Life* on Andrew St has a varied health-food menu including zucchini slice, vegetarian pasties, and Lebanese rolls chock-full of salad.

Ollies on the Esplanade is open from 7 am until 11 pm, seven days – you can get a cappuccino, soup or a three course meal and they don't mind kids. The Pier Hotel bistro has good meals (about $15) and a well-stocked 'all-you-can-eat' salad bar. *Carusoe's* in the Centrepoint Arcade, Dempster St, has bistro meals for about $12.

Some up-market choices are the licensed *Peaches* in the Bay of Isles Motel, the very classy *Bonaparte's Seafood* above Ollie's, *Seasons* in the Hospitality Inn and the BYO *Gray Starling*, Dempster St.

Getting Around
There is a taxi rank by the post office. Hire bicycles from Esperance Mini Golf, on the Esplanade, for $6 per hour ($22 daily).

NATIONAL PARKS
There are four national parks in the Esperance region. The closest and most popular is **Cape Le Grand**, which extends 60km east of Esperance. The park has spectacular coastal scenery, some good white-sand

THE SOUTH COAST

The once numerous New Zealand fur seal
(*Arctocephalus forsteri*)

beaches and excellent walking tracks. There are fine views across the park from Frenchmans Peak, at the western end of the park, and good fishing, camping and swimming at Lucky Bay and Le Grand Beach. Make the effort to climb the peak (a 3km walk) as the views from the top and through the 'eye' (the huge open cave at the top) especially in the late afternoon, are superb.

Just over 6km east of Cape Le Grand is **Rossiter Bay**. This is where Eyre and Wylie, during their epic overland crossing in 1841, fortuitously met Captain Rossiter of the French whaler *Mississippi*.

Farther east is the coastal **Cape Arid National Park**, at the start of the Great Australian Bight and on the fringes of the Nullarbor Plain. It is a rugged and isolated park with abundant flora and fauna, good bushwalking, beaches and campsites. Whales and seals are regularly spotted off the coast and Cape Barren geese are often seen. Most of the park is only accessible by 4WD, although the Poison Creek and Thomas River sites are accessible in normal vehicles. Sites such as Mount Ragged require 4WD.

Mt Ragged and the Russell Range were islands during the late Eocene period (40 million years ago) and there are wave-cut platforms on their upper slopes. The world's most primitive species of ant was found thriving near Mt Ragged in 1930.

Other national parks in the area include the **Stokes Inlet National Park**, 90km west of Esperance, with an inlet, long beaches and rocky headlands backed by sand dunes and low hills; and the **Peak Charles National Park**, 130km to the north. Close to Esperance is the **Monjingup Lake Botanical Park**, on Telegraph Rd (off the South Coast Highway); it has a boardwalk across the lake, interpretive displays and excellent bird-watching. For information about these national parks, contact CALM (☎ 9071 3733) in Dempster St, Esperance.

If you are going into the national parks, take plenty of water as there is little or no fresh water in most of these areas. Also, be wary of spreading dieback and get information about its prevention from park rangers.

Places to Stay & Eat

There are limited-facility campsites at Le Grand Beach and Lucky Bay in Cape Le Grand (☎ 9075 9022; $8 for two); on the shores of the inlet at Stokes (☎ 9076 8541, $8 for two); in Peak Charles (☎ 9076 8541; free); and at Seal Creek, Jorndee Creek and Thomas River at Cape Arid (☎ 9075 0055;

Dieback

Many of the national parks along the south coast (and huge areas outside the parks) are infected with dieback, a plant disease caused by the fungus *Phytophthora cinnamomi*. This microscopic fungus lives in the soil and attacks the root systems of plants causing them to rot. As a result, plants cannot take up water or nutrients through their roots and die of 'starvation'.

The fungus is spread by vehicles and on the feet of bushwalkers. You can help prevent its spread by keeping to formed roads and by observing 'no go' road signs in the conservation reserves. There are also places where you are instructed to clean mud and soil from your boots before you enter reserves. The CALM rangers will provide information on the prevention and spread of the disease. ∎

THE SOUTH COAST

free). Apply for permits with the ranger at the park entrances. The *Orleans Bay Caravan Park* (☎ 9075 0033), near the eastern end of Cape Le Grand, is a good, friendly place to stay; tent/powered sites are $11/13 for two, cabins are $30 for two and chalets $50 for four.

If heading into the national parks make sure you stock up with supplies from the supermarkets in Esperance. Just off Merivale Rd, on the way to Le Grand, is *Merivale Farm*, known throughout the free world for cakes and tempting tortes.

The Southern Outback

East, beyond the expansive wheatbelt, lies a huge region of semi-desert and desert, the southern outback. Towns are few and far between, the distances are great and much of the attraction is found in the isolation of this frontier. The goldfields include the mining towns of Kalgoorlie-Boulder, Kambalda and Norseman and the many ghost towns in-between which appear and, just as quickly, fade into the spinifex. East of the goldfields is the famed Nullarbor Plain and the sealed Eyre Highway to the eastern states.

Eastern Goldfields

Fifty years after its establishment in 1829, the WA colony was still going nowhere, so the government in Perth was delighted when gold was discovered at Southern Cross in 1887. That first strike petered out pretty quickly, but following more discoveries, WA profited from the gold boom for the rest of the century. It was gold that put WA on the map and finally gave it the population to make it viable in its own right, rather than just a distant offshoot of the eastern colonies.

The major strikes were made in 1892 at Coolgardie and nearby Kalgoorlie, but in the whole goldfields area, Kalgoorlie is the only large town left. Coolgardie's period of prosperity lasted only until 1905 and many other gold towns went from nothing to populations of 10,000, then back to nothing, in just 10 years. Nevertheless, the towns capitalised on their prosperity while it lasted, as the many magnificent public buildings grandly attest.

Life on the early goldfields was terribly hard. This area of WA is extremely dry – rainfall is erratic and never great. Even the little rain that does fall, quickly disappears into the porous soil. Many early gold-seekers, driven more by enthusiasm than by common sense, died of thirst while seeking the elusive metal. Others succumbed to the

HIGHLIGHTS

- Exploring the old ghost towns of the gold-fields (and panning for gold) – Coolgardie, Kanowna, Kookynie, Broad Arrow, Ora Banda, Niagara and Gwalia
- The modern frontier town of Kalgoorlie-Boulder – 'Golden Age' architecture, 'two-up', raucous pubs and the enormity of mining operations
- 4WD drive adventures along the Canning Stock Route, Gunbarrel Highway, Warburton Road and the Trans-Australia Railway
- The Eyre Highway – Australia's greatest sealed road adventure from Perth to Adelaide
- Bird-watching at the Eyre Bird Observatory and walks along the lonely Great Australian Bight
- Remote Eucla with its sandhills and slowly disappearing telegraph station

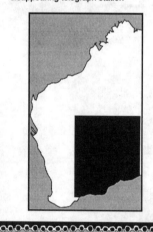

diseases that broke out periodically in the unhygienic shantytowns. The supply of water to the goldfields by pipeline in 1903 was a major breakthrough (see the boxed aside 'Where Water is like Gold!' in this chapter) and ensured the continuation of mining.

Today, Kalgoorlie-Boulder is the main goldfields centre and mines still operate

THE SOUTHERN OUTBACK

208

TONY WHEELER

JEFF WILLIAMS

RICHARD NEBESKY

| A |
| B |
| C |

Southern Outback
A: Nullarbor sunset, Eyre Highway
B: The real Aussie pub still exists – Exchange Hotel, Kalgoorlie
C: Eucla Telegraph Station, Eyre Highway, Southern Nullarbor

The red sand of the central deserts of Australia – the reason why a large portion of inner Australia is known as 'the red centre'

Central Desert

In the arid centre of Australia life is most conspicuous in shaded gorges and along dry river courses where river red gums, home to colourful and noisy parrots, are able to tap deep reserves of water. On this ancient, eroded landscape, sparse vegetation and red sandy soils are infrequently and temporarily transformed by rain into a carpet of wildflowers. Tell-tale tracks in the sand lead to clumps of spinifex grass and burrows. Small marsupials and mice are mostly nocturnal; the rare and endangered bilby was once common to much of Australia but is now only found in the deserts of central Australia. A few of the lizards, such as the thorny devil, will venture out into the heat of the day for a feed of ants. Among the scattered mulga and desert oak, mobs of kangaroos, the males brick-red and over two metres tall, seek shelter from the sun; but seemingly impervious to the heat, emus, with an insulating double layer of feathers, continue the search for seeds and fruit. In the evenings rock-wallabies emerge from rocky outcrops to browse on nearby vegetation. Most animals breed in the cooler winter – their eggs and young attracting the attention of dingoes, eagles and perenties.

BERNARD NAPTHINE RICHARD I'ANSON RON & VIV MOON

Flora and fauna of the central deserts – emus, Sturt's desert pea
and kangaroos

DENIS O'BYRNE RICHARD I'ANSON

Left: River red gums line a dry creek bed
Right: Major Mitchell cockatoos

BERNARD NAPTHINE DAVID CURL BERNARD NAPTHINE

Thousands of years ago, as the climate changed and lakes dried up,
animals like the thorny devil adapted to life in the arid desert

A	B
C	D

Southern Outback

A: Tossing pennies in the Two-Up School, near Kalgoorlie

C: Poppet head, Kalgoorlie goldfields

B: Eerie desolation, Eyre Bird Observatory

D: Mining operations near the Superpit, Kalgoorlie-Boulder

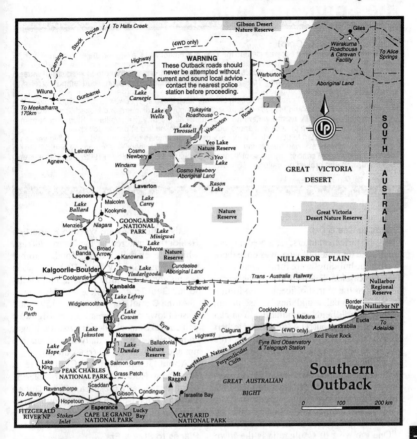

there. Elsewhere, a string of fascinating ghost and near-ghost towns, often surrounded by carpets of wildflowers, make a visit to WA's gold country a must.

COOLGARDIE
- *pop 1800*

A popular pause in the long journey across the Nullarbor, and also the turn-off for Kalgoorlie, Coolgardie really is a ghost of its former self. Its history far outweighs its reality. You only have to glance at the huge town hall, warden's court and post office building to appreciate the size that Coolgardie once was.

A reef of gold was discovered here in 1892 by the prospector Arthur Bayley and his mate Bill Ford, and called 'Bayley's Reward'. By the turn of the century the population of Coolgardie had boomed to 15,000, there were two stock exchanges, six newspapers, over 20 hotels and three breweries. The gold then petered out and the town withered away just as quickly.

The helpful tourist office (☎ 9026 6090), in the Warden's Court in Bayley St, is open daily from 9 am to 5 pm. The BP service station, corner of Hunt St, has an ATM. The post office is just across the road.

Where Water is like Gold!

At the turn of the century, it became clear to the WA government that the large-scale extraction of gold, the state's most important industry, was unlikely to continue in the Kalgoorlie goldfields without a reliable water supply. Stop-gap measures, like huge condensation plants that produced distilled water from salt lakes, or bores that pumped brackish water from beneath the earth, provided temporary relief.

In 1898, however, the engineer CY O'Connor proposed a stunning solution: he would build a reservoir near Perth and construct a 556km pipeline to Kalgoorlie. This was long before the current era of long oil pipelines, and his idea was opposed violently in Parliament and looked upon by some as impossible, especially as the water had to go uphill all the way (Kalgoorlie is 400m higher than Perth). Nevertheless, the project was approved and the pipeline laid at breakneck speed.

In 1903, water started to pour into Kalgoorlie's newly constructed reservoir; and a modified version of the same system still operates today. For O'Connor, however, there was no happy ending: long delays and continual criticism by those of lesser vision resulted in his suicide in 1902, less than a year before his scheme proved operational. ■

Things to See & Do

Many historical markers, scattered in and around the town, tell of what was once there or what the buildings were formerly used for. The **Goldfields Exhibition**, in the same building as the tourist office, is open from 9 am to 5 pm daily and has a fascinating display of goldfields memorabilia. You can even find out about US President Herbert Hoover's days on the WA goldfields. It's worth the $3/1 entry fee for adults/children, which includes a film.

The **train station** in Woodward St also operates as a museum; you can learn the incredible story of the Varischetti mine rescue. In 1907, a miner was trapped 300m underground by floodwater and rescued by divers 10 days later.

One km west of Coolgardie is the **town cemetery**, which includes many old graves, such as those of explorer Ernest Giles (1835-97) and several Afghan camel drivers. Due to the unsanitary conditions and violence on the goldfields, it's said that 'one half of the population buried the other half'. The old **pioneer cemetery**, used from 1892 to 1894, is near the old oval at the end of Forrest St.

Just before you reach the cemetery, on the north side of the road, is a private dwelling that prides itself on its garishness. The **junk garden** is positively awful. Another of Coolgardie's odd sights is **Ben Prior's Open Air Museum**, diagonally opposite the tourist office, an historic junk garden in a state of disrepair.

Other attractions are **Warden Finnerty's Residence**, restored by the National Trust, which is open daily except Monday from 1 to 4 pm and Sunday from 10 am to noon (admission $2); nearby is the lightning-dissected **Gaol Tree**, complete with leg irons.

At the **Camel Farm** (☎ 9026 6159), 3km west of town on the Great Eastern Highway, you can take camel rides or organise longer camel treks; it is open daily from 9 am to 5 pm and admission is $2 (rides are $3).

About 30km south of Coolgardie is **Gnarlbine Rocks**, an important watering point for the early prospectors. The **Queen Victoria Rock Nature Reserve**, with primitive camping, is a farther 18km south.

Places to Stay & Eat

The *Coolgardie Caravan Park* (☎ 9026 6009), 99 Bayley St, has excellent tent/powered sites for $9/12 and on-site vans for $32. Parents with kids will appreciate the playground. The other van-choked caravan park, *The Haven* (☎ 9026 6123), has poor but cheaper tent/powered sites; on-site vans are from $20 to $25. The YHA has closed.

There are a couple of historic hotels in Bayley St with long, shady verandahs: the *Goldrush Lodge* (☎ 9026 6446), which has singles/doubles for $25/35, and the *Denver City Hotel* (☎ 9026 6031) with rooms for $30/45. The tautological *Coolgardie Motor Inne Motel* (☎ 9026 6002), 10 Bayley St, has good rooms for $55/70; and the *Coolgardie Motel* (☎ 9026 6080), 49 Bayley St, is about $55/70.

The *Denver City* does counter lunches and teas. The pizza shop, next door, has the doughy things from $12 to $18 depending on the size and topping. There are a couple of roadhouses on Bayley St that do meals, and restaurants in the motels.

Getting There & Away

Greyhound passes through Coolgardie on its Perth to Adelaide runs; the one-way fare from Perth to Coolgardie is $85, to Adelaide it's $207. The local operator Perth Goldfields Express (☎ 9021 2655) runs on weekdays from Coolgardie to Kal; the bus departs at 8 am and returns at 3.20 pm; the fare is $2.75.

The *Prospector*, from Perth to Kalgoorlie, stops at Bonnie Vale train station, 14km away, daily except Saturday; the one-way fare from Perth is $56.50, with a meal. For bookings call the tourist office or Westrail (☎ 9326 2222).

For motorists' interest, the price of fuel in Coolgardie is the same as that in Kal.

KALGOORLIE-BOULDER
- *pop 25,000*

Kalgoorlie ('Kal' to the locals), some 600km from Perth, is a real surprise – it's a prosperous, humming metropolis, vying with Bunbury to be the state's second largest town. The longest-lasting and most successful of WA's gold towns, it rose to prominence much later than Coolgardie.

There is no doubt that this town invokes traveller ambivalence. Walk into the wrong bar and a group of dishevelled, hoary miners will turn slowly and observe you as if you were some sort of 'bad smell' that had wafted in. Don't be surprised if the lady at the bar appears somewhat *dishabille* in bra, panties, suspenders and high heels – it might be a 'skimpy' night. And if you're not in thongs, shorts and checked shirt you have failed to meet the 'dress-down' standards. Hey, this is Kal and if you don't like it, then the standard retort would be 'bugger off!'.

In spite of the overwhelming 'macho' feel and air of crassness, there is something appealing about Kal. This is Australia's raw edge – larrikin-like, threatening and at the same time loving, with warts and all – that influences the alter ego of many urban dwellers.

History

In 1893, Paddy Hannan, a prospector, set out from Coolgardie for another gold strike with a couple of Irish mates but stopped at the site of Kalgoorlie. He found enough gold lying on the surface to spark another rush.

As in so many places, the surface gold soon dried up, but at Kalgoorlie the miners went deeper and more and more gold was found. These weren't the storybook chunky nuggets of solid gold – Kalgoorlie's gold had to be extracted from the rocks by a costly and complex process of grinding, roasting and chemical action – but there was plenty of it.

Kalgoorlie quickly reached fabled heights of prosperity, and the enormous and magnificent public buildings erected at the turn of

---

Architectural Styles

Kalgoorlie-Boulder boasts an interesting collection of architectural styles, many unconventional. Nowhere is this better represented than along Hannan St. Expect to see curious blends of Victorian gold boom, Edwardian, Moorish and Art Nouveau styles. The turn-of-the-century styles have melded to produce a bizarre mix of ornate facades, colonnaded footpaths, recessed verandahs, stuccoed walls and general overstatement.

Buildings to look out for in Hannan St include the Kalgoorlie Miner and Old Western Argus building (Nos 117-119); Exchange Hotel (No 135); Palace Hotel (Nos 135-139); Exchange building (Nos 149-151); Lasletts (No 181); York Hotel (No 259) – don't miss its staircase; the town hall; and the City Markets (No 276). In Maritana St, look out for Hannan's Club and the Maritana buildings. ■

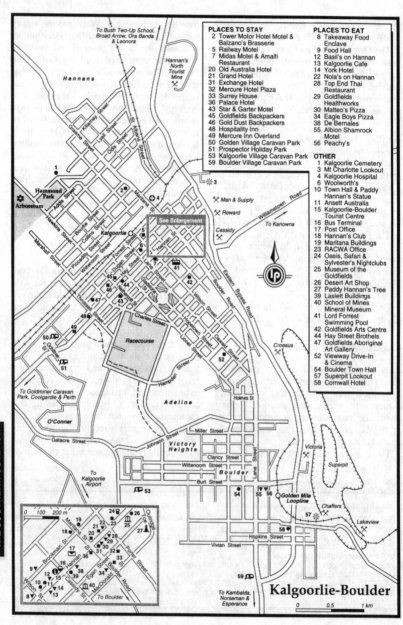

PLACES TO STAY
2 Tower Motor Hotel Motel & Balzano's Brasserie
5 Railway Motel
7 Midas Motel & Amalfi Restaurant
20 Old Australia Hotel
21 Grand Hotel
31 Exchange Hotel
32 Mercure Hotel Plaza
33 Surrey House
36 Palace Hotel
43 Star & Garter Motel
45 Goldfields Backpackers
46 Gold Dust Backpackers
48 Hospitality Inn
49 Mercure Inn Overland
50 Golden Village Caravan Park
51 Prospector Holiday Park
53 Kalgoorlie Village Caravan Park
59 Boulder Village Caravan Park

PLACES TO EAT
8 Takeaway Food Enclave
9 Food Hall
12 Basil's on Hannan
13 Kalgoorlie Cafe
14 York Hotel
22 Nola's on Hannan
28 Top End Thai Restaurant
29 Goldfields Healthworks
30 Matteo's Pizza
34 Eagle Boys Pizza
55 De Bernales
55 Albion Shamrock Motel
56 Peachy's

OTHER
1 Kalgoorlie Cemetery
3 Mt Charlotte Lookout
4 Kalgoorlie Hospital
6 Woolworth's
10 Town Hall & Paddy Hannan's Statue
11 Ansett Australia
15 Kalgoorlie-Boulder Tourist Centre
16 Bus Terminal
17 Post Office
19 Hannan's Club
19 Maritana Buildings
23 RACWA Office
24 Oasis, Safari & Sylvester's Nightclubs
25 Museum of the Goldfields
26 Desert Art Shop
27 Paddy Hannan's Tree
39 Laslett Buildings
40 School of Mines Mineral Museum
41 Lord Forrest Swimming Pool
42 Goldfields Arts Centre
44 Hay Street Brothels
47 Goldfields Aboriginal Art Gallery
52 Viewway Drive-In & Cinema
54 Boulder Town Hall
57 Superpit Lookout
58 Cornwall Hotel

Kalgoorlie-Boulder

THE SOUTHERN OUTBACK

the century are evidence of its fabulous wealth. After WWI, however, increasing production costs and static gold prices led to Kalgoorlie's slow but steady decline.

In 1934 there were bitter race riots in twin towns Kalgoorlie and Boulder. On 29 and 30 January, mobs of disgruntled Australians roamed the streets angrily setting fire to foreign-owned businesses and shooting at foreigners. They were supposedly upset at preference being given by shift bosses to southern European immigrants. The disturbance had died down by the time police reinforcements and volunteers arrived by train from Perth.

With the substantial increase in gold prices since the mid-1970s, mining of lower-grade deposits has become economical and Kalgoorlie is again the largest producer of gold in Australia. Large mining conglomerates have been at the forefront of new open-cut mining operations in the Golden Mile – gone are the old headframes and corrugated iron homes. Mining, pastoral development and a busy tourist trade ensure Kal's continuing importance as an outback centre.

Orientation

Although Kalgoorlie sprang up close to Paddy Hannan's original find, the mining emphasis soon shifted a few kilometres away to the Golden Mile, an area which was probably the wealthiest gold-mining locale for its size in the world. The satellite town of Boulder developed to service this area. The two towns amalgamated in August 1989 into the City of Kalgoorlie-Boulder.

Kalgoorlie itself is a grid of broad, tree-lined streets. The main street (Hannan St), flanked by imposing public buildings, is wide enough to turn a camel train – a necessity in turn-of-the-century goldfield towns. You'll find most of the hotels, restaurants and offices on or close to Hannan St.

Information

There's a helpful tourist centre (☎ 9021 1966, 9021 1413) on the corner of Hannan and Cassidy Sts where you can get a good free map of Kal and friendly advice; a number of other area maps are for sale. The office is open from 8.30 am to 5 pm Monday to Friday, from 9 am to 5 pm on weekends. The daily newspaper is the *Kalgoorlie Miner*. There are laundrettes in McDonald St and in Boulder Rd.

Kal can get very hot in December and January; overall the cool winter months are the best time to visit. From late August to the end of September, however, the town is packed because of wildflower tours and the local horse-racing round, and accommodation of any type can be difficult to find.

The RACWA office (☎ 9021 1511) is on the corner of Porter and Hannan Sts. The post office is at 204 Hannan St and the train station is on the corner of Wilson and Forrest Sts. There is an attended public toilet ($0.30) near the tourist centre.

Hannan's North Tourist Mine

One of Kalgoorlie's biggest attractions is the Hannan's North Tourist Mine just off Gold-fields Hwy. You can take the lift cage down into the bowels of the earth and make a tour around the drives and crosscuts of the mine, guided by an ex-miner.

The $15 (children $7.50, family $38) entry fee covers the underground tour, an audiovisual, a tour of the surface workings and a gold pour. Underground tours are on demand daily (more frequently during peak season) and the complex is open from 9.30 am to 4.30 pm. Fully enclosed shoes must be worn underground.

Golden Mile Loopline

You can make an interesting loop around the Golden Mile by catching the 'Rattler', a tourist train complete with commentary which makes an hour-long trip daily at 10 am. On Sunday it also goes at 11.45 am, on demand. It leaves from Boulder station, passing the old mining works. The cost is $9/5 for adults/children. For more information call ☎ 9021 7077.

In the early part of this century, the Loopline was the most important urban transport for Kal and Boulder and the Golden Gate station was once the busiest in WA.

Museum of the Goldfields

The impressive Ivanhoe mine headframe at the northern end of Hannan St marks the entrance to this excellent museum. It is open daily from 10 am to 4.30 pm (admission is by donation) and has a wide range of exhibits including an underground gold vault and historic photographs. A lift takes you up to a viewing point on the headframe where you can look out over the city and mines and down into delightfully untidy backyards. The tiny **British Arms Hotel** (the narrowest hotel in Australia) is part of the museum.

Kalgoorlie Attractions

The **Mt Charlotte Lookout** and the town's reservoir are a few hundred metres from the north-eastern end of Hannan St, off the Goldfields Hwy. The view over the town is good but there's little to see of the reservoir, which is covered to limit evaporation. This is the reservoir, however, which is the culmination of the genius of CY O'Connor – the water in it took 10 days to get there from Mundaring Weir.

The **School of Mines Mineral Museum**, on the corner of Egan and Cassidy Sts, has a geology display including replicas of big nuggets discovered in the area. It's usually open from 10 am to 12.30 pm, Monday to Friday (closed on school holidays).

Along Hannan St, you'll find the imposing **town hall** and the equally impressive **post office**. There's an art gallery upstairs in the decorative town hall, while outside is a replica of a statue of Paddy Hannan holding a water bag. The original is inside the town hall, safe from nocturnal painters.

A block back, north-west from Hannan St, is Hay St and one of Kal's most notorious 'attractions'. Although it's quietly ignored in the tourist brochures, Kal has a block-long strip of **brothels** where working ladies beckon passing men (sometimes driving past in huge bedecked rigs) to their true-blue, and pink, Aussie galvanised-iron doorways. A blind eye has been turned to this patronage for so long that it has become an accepted and historical part of the town.

Kalgoorlie also has a legal **two-up school** in a corrugated-iron amphitheatre 6km north

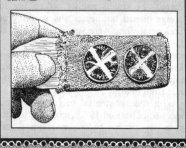

Two-up School
Two-up is a frenetic, uniquely Australian gambling game where two coins are tossed and bets are placed on the result. Among the gamblers' yelps, a lot of money seems to change hands. It is open from 4 pm until after dark. ■

of town, 1km off the Goldfields Hwy – follow the signs from Hannan St.

On Outridge Terrace is **Paddy Hannan's tree**, marking the spot where the first gold strike was made. **Hammond Park** is a small fauna reserve with a miniature Bavarian castle. It's open daily from 9 am to 5 pm. Not far away is a pleasant **arboretum**.

Boulder Attractions

The **Goldfields War Museum** in Burt St was undergoing renovation at the time of writing. The **Boulder train station** was built in 1897.

The **Super Pit** lookout, just off the Goldfields Hwy, near Boulder, is open from 6 am to 6 pm daily (it is closed when blasting is in progress). The view from the lookout is awesome and the big trucks at the bottom of the huge hole look like kid's toys.

On Hopkins St is the **Cornwall Hotel**, which was involved in the notorious Pittman and Walsh murders.

Organised Tours

Goldrush Tours (☎ 9021 2954) is the main tour operator in Kal. Book through the tourist office or from Goldrush Tours in Hay St. They have tours of Kal ($35), Coolgardie and nearby ghost towns.

THE SOUTHERN OUTBACK

There's also a gold-detector tour for avid fossickers, August and September wildflower tours and Aboriginal cultural tours. Two reputable operators are Geoff Smith's Bush Tours (☎ 9021 2669) and Geoff Stokes (☎ 9093 3745) Aboriginal bush tours.

Starting from $25, you can see Kal and the Golden Mile mining operations from the air with Goldfields Air Services (☎ 9093 2116) and AAA Charters (☎ 9021 6980). Pro Rotor (☎ (041) 986 0969) charges $30 per person for a 10 minute helicopter flight.

Places to Stay

Caravans & Camping There are a number of caravan parks in Kal; all prices below are for two people. The closest to the city centre are the *Golden Village* (☎ 9021 4162), 406 Hay St, 2km south-west of the train station, which has tent/powered sites for $14/17.50, and chalets and villas for $65 ($70 in peak season); and the *Prospector Holiday Park* (☎ 9021 2524) on the Great Eastern Highway with tent and powered sites for $15, standard and en-suite cabins for $42/48. The Prospector has a pool, a grassed area for campers and a campers' kitchen – one of the best in WA, so thumbs up.

The other caravan parks are the *Boulder Village* (☎ 9093 1266), Lane St, Boulder; *Kalgoorlie Village* (☎ 9093 2780), Burt St, Boulder; and the *Goldminer* (☎ 9021 3713), on the Great Eastern Highway.

Gold Stealing Detection Murders

During April 1926, Detective Sergeant Pittman of the Gold Stealing Detection staff and Inspector John Walsh went missing. They were found shot, dismembered, partially burnt and dumped in a mineshaft.

The police were determined to get the killers and did, eventually, when Teddy Clarke, licensee of the Cornwall Hotel and a gold-stealer, turned King's evidence. His barman Phillip Treffene and one William Coulter, a punter and backer of bookies, were found guilty of the murders and hanged at Fremantle gaol. ■

Hostels There are two good purpose-built places on Hay St; both pick up from transport on request. *Goldfields Backpackers* (☎ 9091 1482, mobile (017) 11 0001), at No 166, has a pool, fully equipped kitchen and comfy TV lounge; dorms (with comforts such as linen, mirrors and towel racks) are $15, doubles are from $36 to $38 and triples are $18 per person. The characterful homestay (☎ 9091 1482) next door at No 164 is a former brothel; B&B rooms are $30/50.

The *Gold Dust Backpackers* (☎ 9091 3737), at 192 Hay St, is very similar to Goldfields in facilities; dorms are $15, twins $30, doubles $35 and triples $45. *Surrey House* (☎ 9021 1340), 9 Boulder Rd, has shared rooms for $20 per person; it's an option if the purpose-built places are full.

Hotels & Motels There are several pleasantly old-fashioned hotels right in the centre of Kal, including the *Palace Hotel* (☎ 9021 2788), corner of Maritana and Hannan Sts, with en-suite singles/doubles for $40/60. The *Exchange Hotel* (☎ 9021 2833), Hannan St, has rooms from $35/50; it is well placed in the heart of town. Other pubs are the *Grand* (☎ 9021 2353), 90 Hannan St, for $30/50; and the *Piccadilly* (☎ 9021 2109), at 164 Piccadilly St, for $25/40.

There is no shortage of good-quality motels. On Hannan St at No 409 is the *Midas* (☎ 9021 3088) with singles/doubles from $85/100; at No 497 the *Star & Garter* (☎ 9091 3004) for $65/75; at lower Hannan the *Mercure Inn Overland* (☎ 9021 1433) with rooms for $99; at the corner of Maritana the superbly renovated *Old Australia* (☎ 9021 1320) with singles/twins for $60/75 (en-suite rooms are $80/95); and on lower Hannan at the corner of Throssell St, the *Hospitality Inn* (☎ 9021 2888), with standard rooms for $91 and executive rooms for $120.

The *Mercure Hotel Plaza* (☎ 9021 4544), in Egan St, has en-suite rooms from $137; and at the *Tower Motor Hotel Motel* (☎ 9021 3211), corner of Maritana and Bourke Sts, rooms are $75.

Perhaps the town's nicest accommodation is the *Railway Motel* (☎ 9088 0000), 51

Forrest St; standard rooms are $124, with kitchenettes $130, and deluxe spa units $145 (all rooms are $30 less on weekends).

Places to Eat

Kalgoorlie The tourist office produces a small restaurant guide – a good place to start. There is a food hall in Brookman St, open from 11.30 am to 2.30 pm and from 5 to 9 pm.

On Wilson St, between Brookman and Hannan Sts, is a small enclave of takeaway places including the *Fu Wah* Chinese restaurant, a bakery and a takeaway *Pizza Hut*. At 277 Hannan St is the *Kalgoorlie Cafe*, which has burger-type fast food.

For pizza, try *Pizza Cantina*, 211 Hannan St, *Matteo's* at No 123, or *Eagle Boys* in Boulder Rd. *Basil's on Hannan*, at No 268, once *the* place for breakfast, was very disappointing on our last visit.

There are plenty of counter-meal pubs, restaurants and cafes in Kal, particularly along Hannan St. The *York Hotel* has counter meals in its Steak House for $14, and meals in the saloon bar for around $7.50. The *Grand Hotel* does counter meals ($9) and usually has cheap lunch specials on offer ($2.50). The *Exchange* and the *Palace* both have restaurants with main courses from around $10 to $15.

The *Goldfields Healthworks*, at 75 Hannan St, has a lunch bar with an interesting menu – most of it vegetarian. Nearby, the *Top End Thai*, at 71 Hannan St, is good for a splurge – a wide range of prawn, curry and noodle dishes costs from $14 to $18. Across the road at No 84 is *Nola's on Hannan*, a BYO Italian place with hearty soups for $4.50 and daily pasta specials from $10.

The more up-market *de Bernales*, 193 Hannan St, does tasty food (and game specials) from $12 to $16 and has a pleasant verandah opening onto the street – a good place to sip a beer and watch life go by.

The *Amalfi*, at 409 Hannan St in the Midas Motel, is at the top end of the dining scale; it is à la carte, fully licensed and dishes cost from $22. A perennial favourite is *Balzano*

Brasserie, in the Tower at 11 Maritana St; à la carte meals are from $16.

Boulder You can get counter meals at the very reliable *Albion Shamrock Hotel* ($10). You can also try the *Wah On* Chinese restaurant, 110 Burt St, next to the Goldfields War Museum, and *Peachy's* takeaway at 16 Burt St.

Entertainment

Visiting artists perform regularly at the *Arts Centre* in Cassidy St. In the same complex is the Goldfields Art Gallery with local and travelling exhibitions.

Pubs feature heavily in the night scene. *Balzano Brasserie* in the Tower (see Places to Stay) and *de Bernales* on Hannan St are great places for a soothing ale.

Nightclubs include *Hendrix* in the Midas Motel, the *Oasis*, *Safari* and *Sylvesters* – all in the same building – at the top end of Hannan St. Careful, it can get rough in this area at times.

Things to Buy

The Goldfields Aboriginal Art Gallery in Dugan St, and the Desert Art shop, next to the Museum of the Goldfields, have crafts for sale. Kal is a good place to buy gold nuggets fashioned into relatively inexpensive jewellery – shop along Hannan St.

Getting There & Away

Air Ansett flies from Perth to Kal and returns several times daily. The Ansett office is at 314 Hannan St.

Skywest has a direct flight daily – it has discounts such as special weekend fares ($196 return, 21 day advance purchase). To contact Skywest and Ansett, ring ☎ 13 13 00.

Bus Greyhound (☎ 9021 7100, 13 20 30) buses pass through Kalgoorlie en route from Perth to Sydney, Melbourne and Adelaide. Goldfields Express (☎ 9021 2954, 9328 9199) has a twice-weekly Perth to Kal service which also heads north to Laverton ($50 from Kal), Leinster ($55) and Leonora ($35). Check timetables carefully as some of these buses pull into Kal at an ungodly hour when everything is closed and finding a place to stay can be difficult.

Westrail (☎ 9021 2023) runs a bus three times a week from Kal to Esperance – once via Kambalda and Norseman and twice via Coolgardie and Norseman; the trip takes 5½ hours and costs $18 to Norseman, $33.50 to Esperance. There are daily Westrail services between Perth and Kal (see the Getting Around chapter).

Train The daily *Prospector* from Perth takes around 7½ hours and costs $58.80, including a meal. In Perth, you can book seats at the WATC in Forrest Place or at the Westrail terminal (☎ 9326 2222). It's wise to book at the tourist centre as this service is fairly popular, particularly in the tourist season. The *Indian-Pacific* and *Trans-Australian* trains also go through Kalgoorlie twice a week.

Getting Around

Between Kal and Boulder, there's a regular bus service (get a timetable from the tourist office). Goldenlines (☎ 9021 2655) travels to Boulder, either directly or via Lionel St, between 8 am and 6 pm. There are also daily buses to Kambalda and Coolgardie (during school term only).

You can rent cars from Hertz (☎ 9091 2625), Budget (☎ 9093 2300), Avis (☎ 9021 1722) and Halfpenny Hire (☎ 9021 1804). If you want to explore farther afield, you'll have to drive, hitch or take a tour as public transport is limited. A taxi to the airport costs around $9. You can hire bicycles from Johnston Cycles (☎ 9021 1157), 76 Boulder Rd, and Hannan Cycles (☎ 9021 2467) in Maritana St; a deposit is required.

NORTH OF KALGOORLIE

The road north is surfaced from Kalgoorlie to the three 'Ls' – Laverton (361km northeast), Leinster (368km north) and Leonora-Gwalia (237km north). Off the main road, however, traffic is virtually nonexistent and rain can quickly close unsealed roads. There are a number of towns of interest along the way including Kanowna, Broad Arrow, Ora Banda, Menzies and Kookynie.

Getting There & Away

Skywest has several flights from Perth to Laverton (every day except Saturday), Leinster (Monday to Thursday) and Leonora (daily except Saturday). Skywest has flights to Wiluna on Tuesday, Thursday and Friday.

Goldfields Express (☎ 9021 2954) has a service from Perth to Leonora, Laverton and Leinster on Wednesday, Friday and Sunday. The bus heads to Perth from these towns on Monday, Wednesday and Friday. There is no regular bus service to Wiluna; most people get there in their own 4WD vehicles in order to do one of the great outback tracks from there.

Kanowna

This is the most fascinating of the goldfields ghost towns in terms of history. It is just 18km from Kal-Boulder along a dirt road. In 1905, Kanowna had a population of 12,000, 16 hotels, two breweries, many churches and an hourly train service to Kalgoorlie. Today, apart from the train station platform and the odd pile of rubble, absolutely nothing remains.

It is now the starting point, each September, for the Balzano barrow race – where teams push a miner's barrow to Kal.

Broad Arrow & Ora Banda

With a population of 20, compared with 2400 at the turn of the century, Broad Arrow is definitely a shadow of its former self. One of the town's original eight hotels still operates in a virtually unchanged condition. The town was featured in *The Nickel Queen*, the first full-length feature film made in WA. The stone train station featured in the film was demolished in 1973.

Ora Banda, 28km west of the Kal-Menzies Rd, has shrunk from a population of 2000 to less than 50. The *Ora Banda Historic Inn* (☎ 9024 2059), built in 1911, is a neat place to stay, representing the closest thing to civilisation for miles; double rooms are from $45 to $65.

THE SOUTHERN OUTBACK

Menzies & Kookynie

Another typical goldfields town, Menzies is 132km north of Kal. It has about 230 people today, compared with 5000 in 1900. Many early buildings remain, including the train station with its 120m platform (1898) and the imposing town hall (1896) with its clockless clock tower. The ship bringing the clock from England, the SS *Orizaba*, sank south of Rottnest Island.

There are no rivers in the area and the surrounding countryside is mostly flat with eucalypts, salmon gum and blackbutt trees. If there is adequate winter rainfall, marvellous displays of **wildflowers** can be seen from August to September.

Kookynie is a small ghost town, 69km south-east of Leonora, surrounded by old mine workings and tailings. The *Grand Hotel* (☎ 9031 3010), built in 1894, has big verandahs and spacious rooms. There is also an interesting little museum in town with a collection of photographs and antique bottles. About 10km from Kookynie is the **Niagara Dam**, built with cement carried from Coolgardie by a caravan of 400 camels.

Well worth a visit, especially in spring, is the 500 sq km **Goongarrie National Park**. It includes large areas of mulga, prolific bird life of the arid region and wildflowers in season. The park is reached on a reasonable road south-east of Menzies.

Places to Stay & Eat In Menzies, the caravan park (☎ 9024 2041), Shenton St, has tent/powered sites for $7/9; and the *Menzies Hotel* (☎ 9024 2043), 22 Shenton St has B&B singles/doubles for $40/70. Meals can be obtained from the *Caltex Roadhouse* and the hotel. Unwind with a beer (and barbecued food) in the beer garden of the *Grand Hotel* in Kookynie. Full board at the Grand (one of the 'grandest') is $59.50 per person.

Leonora-Gwalia

Named after the wife of a WA governor, Leonora is 237km north of Kalgoorlie. It has a population of 2000 and serves as the railhead for the nickel from Windarra and Leinster. Climb to the summit of **Mt Leonora** to get a great view of the town or wander down to the **cenotaph** to see the 1927 restored hearse.

The tourist office (☎ 9037 6044) is in the shire offices on Power St.

In adjoining Gwalia (a ghost town), the Sons of Gwalia Goldmine, the largest in WA outside Kalgoorlie, closed in 1963 and much of the town shutdown until an increase in gold prices led this and other mines in the area to reopen. In the late 1890s, the mine was managed by Herbert Hoover, later to become president of the USA.

The Gwalia Historical Society is housed in the 1898 **mine office** – this fascinating local museum is open daily. Also of interest are the restored State Hotel, Patronis Guesthouse and the mine manager's house. The pamphlet *Historic Gwalia Heritage Trail* describes the places of interest on a fascinating 1km walk around the town.

Places to Stay The caravan park (☎ 9037 6568) in Rochester St has tent/powered sites for $10/15 for two; the motel (☎ 9037 6181), in Tower St, has singles/doubles for $75/85; the *Whitehouse Hotel* (☎ 9037 6030) has single rooms only for $30; and the *Central Hotel* (☎ 9037 6042), Tower St, is $40/50.

The Gwalia Beer Strike

The Gwalia State Hotel was the first and last of the government-owned state hotels in operation in WA. Built in 1903 in an attempt to cut down the sly-grog trade, the hotel did well as salaries in Gwalia were relatively high.

In March 1919, about 50 residents voted to boycott the hotel until certain conditions were met. They wanted some control over the brands of beer offered, cleanliness and the price and size of glasses. They also wanted the manager dismissed.

It was to their credit that these thirsty workers maintained the boycott until September – the number of sly-grog prosecutions in that time increased, however. During the 'strike', the hotel was used as a hospital when a serious influenza epidemic sweeping the state hit town. ∎

Laverton

From Leonora-Gwalia, you can turn north-east to Laverton, 361km north of Kalgoorlie, where the surfaced road ends. The population here declined from 1000 in 1910 to 200 in 1970 when the Poseidon nickel discovery (beloved of stock-market speculators in the late 1960s and early 1970s) revived mining operations in nearby Windarra. The town now has 1500 people. There are many abandoned mines in the area.

From here, it is a mere 1710km north-east to Alice Springs (see Warburton Rd & Gunbarrel Highway later in this chapter).

Places to Stay The *Desert Pea Caravan Park* (☎ 9031 1072), Weld Ave, has tent/powered sites from $8/11. The *Desert Inn Motel Hotel* (☎ 9031 1188), 2 Laver St, has single/double hotel rooms for $50/70, and motel units for $55/75.

The *Laverton Downs Station* (☎ 9037 5998) is 25km north of Laverton; B&B is $32, and dinner, bed and breakfast $55 per person.

Leinster

North of Leonora-Gwalia, the road is now surfaced to Leinster (population 1000), another modern nickel-mining centre. **Agnew**, 23km west of Leinster, is an old gold town that has all but disappeared. The old brick gaol at **Lawlers**, 25km south-east of Leinster on the Agnew-Leonora Rd , is all that is left of that township.

From Leinster, it's 170km north to Wiluna and another 180km west to Meekatharra. From Meeka, the surfaced Great Northern Highway runs 765km south-west to Perth or 860km north to Port Hedland.

The *Leinster Lodge Motel* (☎ 9037 9241), on the corner of Mansbridge and Agnew Rds, has singles/doubles for $50/70.

Wiluna

Remote Wiluna marks the end of civilisation eastwards until Alice Springs. As the local shire puts it: 'Wiluna is a dusty outback town that hasn't got a lot of the creature comforts. What Wiluna has got is friendly people and a real bush atmosphere.'

When gold was mined in the district, Wiluna had a population of 9000 and was a prosperous town. Today, it's an administrative centre with a mainly Aboriginal population. You can obtain tourist information from the shire office (☎ 9981 7010) in Scotia St.

11km east of town is the Desert Gold **orange orchard**, proof that the desert can bloom.

Wiluna is the starting or finishing point of two of Australia's great driving adventures – the **Canning Stock Route** and the **Gunbarrel Highway** (see Warburton Rd & Gunbarrel Highway).

The Canning runs south-west from Halls Creek to Wiluna, crossing the Great Sandy and Gibson deserts. As the track has not been maintained for over 30 years it's a route to be taken seriously. If you intend taking this route get the *Australian Geographic Book of the Canning Stock Route* (1992) which has all the maps and info you'll require.

Places to Stay & Eat Most visitors come in their own 4WD transport and head to the local caravan park (☎ 9981 7021); tent/powered sites are $10/12.50 for two. The *Club Motel Hotel* (☎ 9981 7012), Wotton St, has singles/doubles (and, obviously, a captive market) for $45/65, and motel units for $80/95.

You can get counter meals from the *Club* which also has a licensed restaurant for dinner. Provisions for the inevitable long journeys (whichever way you leave town) are available from the Canning Trading Co or Ngangganawili Community store, both on Wotton St.

Warburton Rd & Gunbarrel Highway

For those interested in an outback experience, the unsealed road from Laverton to Yulara (the tourist development near Uluru) via Cosmo Newbery Aboriginal Land and Warburton, provides a rich scenery of red sand, spinifex, mulga and desert oaks.

The road, while sandy in places, is suitable for conventional vehicles, although a 4WD would give a much smoother ride. Although this road is often mistakenly called the Gunbarrel Highway, the genuine article actually runs some distance to the north, and is very rough and only partially maintained.

THE SOUTHERN OUTBACK

You should take precautions relevant to travel in such an isolated area – tell someone (shire office or local police) of your travel plans and take adequate supplies of water, petrol, food and spare parts.

The route passes through Aboriginal land and permission to enter must be obtained in advance if you want to leave the road. Petrol is available at Laverton, Warburton (where basic supplies are also available) and Yulara. In an emergency, you may be able to get fuel at the Docker River settlement.

The longest stretch without fuel is between Laverton and **Warburton** (570km). The *Warburton Roadhouse & Caravan Facility* (☎ (08) 8956 7656) has accommodation (camping and self-catering), fuel and food supplies; tent sites are $4 for one, cabins $10 for one and demountable rooms $60 for two. The Warburton township is an Aboriginal community on private land and not open to the public. Central Land Council permits must be obtained; contact ☎ (08) 8951 6211.

At **Giles**, 231km north-east of Warburton and about 105km west from the Northern Territory border, there is a meteorological station with a friendly 'Visitors Welcome' sign and a bar – it is well worth a visit. The *Warakurna Roadhouse & Caravan Facility* (☎ (08) 8956 7344) has accommodation, fuel and food supplies, and you can arrange tours to the meteorological station there.

Don't even consider doing this route from November to March due to the extreme heat. See the Getting Around chapter for more details. For nearly 300km west from Giles, the Warburton Rd and Gunbarrel Highway run on the same route. Taking the old Gunbarrel Highway (to the north of the Warburton Rd) all the way to Wiluna is a much rougher and far more serious trip requiring a 4WD.

SOUTH OF KALGOORLIE
Kambalda
Kambalda (population 5000) died as a gold-mining town in 1906, but nickel was discovered there in 1966, and today it is a major mining centre. Kambalda is split into two parts, East and West, about 4km apart.

East was the original centre but when nickel was found in an area due for housing expansion, the mining company simply built another town away from the nickel deposits.

The tourist office (☎ 9027 1446), on Emu Rocks Rd (the Norseman road), Kambalda West, provides a map of the area.

Kambalda is on the shores of Lake Lefroy, a large salt pan and a popular spot for **land-sailing**. The yachts can travel at 100km/h across the smooth salt lake. The first land sailors were prospectors who mounted wheels on a 5m sailboat. Watch the boats sail on Sundays from November to April.

The view from **Red Hill Lookout** in Kambalda East is well worth checking out. If you have binoculars you will be able to watch the land-sailing from here.

Places to Stay The miners seem to have the monopoly on accommodation here. If for some reason you get stuck, try the caravan park (☎ 9027 1582) in Gordon Adams Rd, Kambalda East; powered sites/on-site vans are $12/30 for two. In Bluebush Rd, Kambalda West, there is a motor hotel (☎ 9027 1582) with singles/doubles for $70/80.

Widgiemooltha
No trip to WA could be considered complete or fulfilled if Widgie was not on the itinerary. At the roadhouse (☎ 9091 3863) they pride themselves on the 'truckies brekkie', a stomach-bursting three-sausage, several slices of bacon, two or three eggs, three pieces of toast monster. Don't use the outside dunny – the resident redback will chew a major portion out of your posterior.

A place to stay – the demountables up the back, just beyond the smell of the toilet – may be opened soon to independent travellers. For entertainment, the expansive Widgie bar is something else – it hums vibrantly.

Norseman
To most people, Norseman (population 2500) is just a crossroads where you turn east for the trans-Nullarbor Eyre Highway journey, south to Esperance along the Leeuwin Way or north to Coolgardie and

Perth. The town, however, also has gold mines, some of which are in operation.

The tourist office (☎ 9039 1071), at 68 Roberts St, is open daily from 9 am to 5 pm. Next to the tourist office is a tourist rest park, open from 9 am to 5 pm. The **Historical & Geological Collection** in the old School of Mines has items from the gold-rush days; it's open from 10 am to 1 pm daily (except Thursday and Sunday); entry is $2/1 for adults/children.

You can get an excellent view of the town and the surrounding salt lakes from the **Beacon Hill Mararoa Lookout** down past the mountainous tailings. The tailings, one of which contains 4.2 million tonnes of rock, are the result of 40 years of gold-mining.

The graffiti-covered **Dundas Rocks** are huge boulders, 22km south of Norseman. Also worth a look are the views at sunrise and sunset of the dry, expansive and spectacular **Lake Cowans**, north of Norseman.

South of Norseman, halfway along the road to Esperance, is the small township of **Salmon Gums** (population 50), named after the gum trees, prevalent in the area, which acquire a seasonal rich-pink bark in late summer and autumn.

See the Kalgoorlie Getting There & Away section for bus information.

Places to Stay & Eat The tidy *Gateway Caravan Park* (☎ 9039 1500), Princep St, has tent/powered sites for $13/15, and on-site vans/cabins for $28/36 for two.

There is no real backpackers' hostel in town but *Lodge 101* (☎ 9039 1541), at 101 Princep St, has a limited number of dorm beds for $15, which will do at a pinch. They also have B&B from $25 per person.

The *Norseman Hotel* (☎ 9039 1023), on the corner of Robert St and Talbot Rd, has B&B singles/doubles for $30/50; at the *Railway Hotel Motel* (☎ 9039 1115) they are $25/35. The *Norseman Eyre Motel* (☎ 9039 1130), Robert St, is $62/69, which is similar to the *Great Western* (☎ 9039 1633), Princep St.

Vegetarian cyclists, just having finished the Nullarbor, will go wild at *Pure Health*, 91B Roberts St. Health foods are for sale,

and there are naturopathy and massage consultations. Ahhh!

Bits & Pizzas has a wide range of eat-in or takeaway meals, and also cooked breakfasts. The BP and Ampol roadhouses have a wide range of takeaways or dine-in meals.

The Eyre Highway

It's a little over 2700km between Perth and Adelaide – not much less than the distance from London to Moscow. The long and sometimes lonely Eyre Highway crosses the southern edge of the vast Nullarbor Plain. Nullarbor is bad Latin for 'no trees' but there is actually only a small stretch where you see none at all. Surprisingly, the road is flanked by trees most of the way as this coastal fringe receives regular rain, especially in winter.

The road across the Nullarbor takes its name from John Eyre, the explorer who made the first east-west crossing in 1841. It was a superhuman effort that took five months of hardship and resulted in the death of Eyre's companion, John Baxter. In 1877, a telegraph line was laid across the Nullarbor, roughly delineating the route the first road would take.

Later in the century, miners on their way to the goldfields followed the same telegraph line route across the empty plain. In 1896, the first bicycle crossing was made and in 1912 the first car was driven across, but in the next 12 years only three more cars managed to traverse the continent.

In 1941, the war inspired the building of a transcontinental highway, just as it had the Alice Springs to Darwin route. It was a rough-and-ready track when completed, and in the 1950s only a few vehicles a day made the crossing. In the 1960s, the traffic flow increased to more than 30 vehicles a day and in 1969 the WA government surfaced the road as far as the South Australian border. Finally, in 1976, the last stretch from the South Australian border was surfaced and now the Nullarbor crossing is a much easier drive, but still a long one.

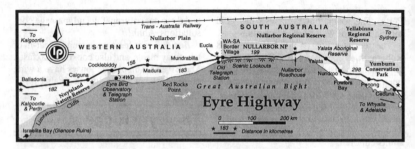

The surfaced road runs close to the coast on the South Australian side. The Nullarbor region ends dramatically on the coast of the Great Australian Bight, at cliffs that drop steeply into the ocean. It's easy to see why this was a seafarer's nightmare, for a ship driven onto the coast would quickly be pounded to pieces against the cliffs, and climbing them would be a near impossibility.

The Indian-Pacific railway runs north of the coast and actually through the Nullarbor Plain – unlike the main road, which only fringes the great plain. One stretch of the railway runs dead straight for 478km – the longest piece of straight railway line in the world.

Information

At the western end of the highway, there's a tourist office (☎ 9039 1071) in Norseman (see the Eastern Goldfields section in this chapter). At the eastern end in South Australia, the first tourist office is in Ceduna (☎ (08) 8625 2780), in Poynton St. There is a much larger facility in Port Augusta – the Wadlata Outback Centre (☎ (08) 8641 0793), 41 Flinders Terrace.

All of the roadhouses have stacks of pamphlets relating to tourist sights in the area and for the towns on either side.

Books & Maps A number of helpful publications cover the Nullarbor. One of the most comprehensive is the free *Across Australia*, available in Perth and Adelaide. The RACWA has a series of interlinking maps, available for a small fee from their offices.

Crossing the Nullarbor

See the Getting There & Away chapter for air, rail, hitching and bus information across the Nullarbor.

Car Although the Nullarbor is no longer a torture trail where cars get shaken to bits by potholes and corrugations or where you're going to die of thirst waiting for another vehicle if you break down, it's still wise to avoid difficulties whenever possible.

The longest distance between fuel stops is about 200km, so if you're foolish enough to run out of petrol midway, you'll have a nice long round trip to get more. Getting help for a mechanical breakdown can be equally time-consuming and very expensive, so make sure your vehicle is in good shape and that you've got plenty of petrol, good tyres and at least a basic kit of simple spare parts.

The cost of fuel varies greatly – diesel varies from 73c a litre in Adelaide to 97c in Balladonia, to 81c in Esperance. Unleaded petrol is 97c in Norseman, $1.02 in Cocklebiddy.

Carry some drinking water (4L per person) just in case you do have to sit it out by the roadside on a hot summer day. Remember, there are limited fresh-water facilities between Norseman and Ceduna.

There are no banking facilities between Norseman and Ceduna so take plenty of cash. All roadhouses, except Mundrabilla, have EFTPOS and take major credit cards.

Take it easy on the Nullarbor – plenty of people try to set speed records and plenty more have messed up their cars when they've run into kangaroos at night. There are many rest areas – make use of them!

Bus & Train As the Eyre is the most important transcontinental route, there are daily scheduled bus services all the way from Perth to Adelaide with Greyhound. There is also a rail option – one of the world's great railway journeys (see Indian-Pacific in the Getting There & Away chapter).

Bicycle The Nullarbor (Eyre Highway) is a real challenge to cyclists. They are attracted by the barrenness and distance, certainly not by the interesting scenery. As you drive across you see many cyclists, at all times of the year, lifting their water bottles to their parched mouths or sheltering under one of the lone trees that enliven the barren stretches.

Excellent equipment is needed and adequate water supplies have to be carried. The cyclist should also know where all the water tanks are located. Adequate protection (hats, lotions etc) from the sun should be used even in cloudy weather. The prevailing wind for most of the journey is west to east, the most preferable direction to be pedalling.

THE EYRE HIGHWAY – WA TO SA
From Norseman, where the Eyre Highway begins, it's 727km to the Western Australia/South Australia border, near Eucla, and a farther 482km to Ceduna (from an Aboriginal word meaning 'a place to sit down and rest') in South Australia. From Ceduna, it's still another 783km to Adelaide via Port Augusta. In the immortal words of a trans-Australian truckie: 'It's a bloody long way!'.

Places to Stay & Eat
The *Baladonia Hotel Motel* (☎ 9039 3453) has singles/doubles from $58/68 and its dusty caravan facility has tent/powered sites for $10/14. At Caiguna, the *John Eyre Motel* (☎ 9039 3459) has rooms for $50/65 and a caravan facility with tent/powered sites from $5/12 for two.

In Cocklebiddy, the *Wedgetail Inn Hotel*

Under the Nullarbor
Beneath the uninhabited and barren landscape of the Nullarbor lies a wealth of interest. And yes, I do mean *beneath*. The Nullarbor is an ancient limestone seabed, up to 300m thick in places. About 20 million years ago shells and other marine organisms began to settle and some three million years ago the bed was gently raised, forming a huge plateau 700km long and up to 300km wide.

Within this raised plateau is Australia's largest network of caves, formed over the millennia as rain seeped through cracks in the surface limestone. The caves vary from shallow depressions to elaborate, deep caves with immense chambers. About 50 of the caves are entered via passages which begin in large sinkholes or dolines; others can only be accessed through narrow, vertical blowholes.

The best known of the caves is Koonalda in South Australia, entered through a huge sinkhole. This cave contains a large main chamber, 70m below the surface, which has a 45m-high domed ceiling. Aborigines quarried flint from this cave over 20,000 years ago and they left unexplained incisions on the main entrance passage.

More caves exist on the WA side of the border. West of Eucla are the Weebubbie and the Abrakurrie caves. The Weebubbie Cave is currently closed due to a collapse at its entrance. The Abrakurrie Cave contains the largest chamber of the Nullarbor caves, 180m long and 45m wide and with a 40m-high ceiling; it is reached by a steeply sloping passage from the sinkhole entrance.

The Cocklebiddy Cave, 12km north of the Eyre Highway, has one of the longest underwater passages known in the world. The Mullamullang Cave east of Cocklebiddy is the most extensive cave network known in Australia and contains the Salt Cellars – superb mineral formations.

All this said, *never* enter any of these caves without an experienced guide and proper equipment. Many lives have been lost (especially in Cocklebiddy Cave) and the vertical access to a number of the caves requires highly specialised equipment. Those keen to venture underground should contact CALM in Perth or the South Australia National Parks & Wildlife Service in Ceduna for more information. ■

Motel (☎ 9039 3462) has expensive fuel, pricey rooms from $66/76 for two/three and its caravan facility has tent/powered sites for $6/12. The RAOU's *Eyre Bird Observatory* (☎ 9039 3450) housed in the Eyre Telegraph Station, south of Cocklebiddy has accommodation (see the 'Birds of the Bight' below).

The *Madura Pass Oasis Inn* (☎ 9039 3464) has rooms from $49 to $76 for two and its caravan facility has tent/powered sites from $8/15. Mundrabilla has a caravan facility with sites for $8/12 and cabins for $30, while the *Mundrabilla Hotel* (☎ 9039 3465) has rooms from $45/55.

Eucla is the border town and an important stop-off. The *Amber Motel Hotel* (☎ 9039 3468) has doubles from $68; its Eucla Pass economy section has tent/powered sites for $4/10 (showers are $1) and basic rooms for $15/30. The *WA-SA Border Village* (☎ 9039 3478) has sites from $6/10, cabins from $35 a double and motel units from $60/68.

All of the roadhouses serve food, but a wise traveller will have crossed with a well-stocked food-cooler.

Norseman to Cocklebiddy
• *441km*

From Norseman, the first settlement you reach is **Balladonia**, 191km to the east. After Balladonia, near the old station, you may see the remains of old stone fences built to enclose stock. Clay saltpans are also visible in the area. **Newmann's Rocks**, 50km west of Balladonia, are also worth seeing. The Crocker family has a fine art gallery (☎ (08) 9039 3456), with paintings of the Eyre Highway. Phone between 9 am and 4.30 pm to arrange a visit.

The road from Balladonia to Cocklebiddy is a lonely section. To Caiguna, it includes one of the world's longest stretches of straight road – 145km, the so-called 90 Mile Straight.

Caiguna, over 370km from Norseman, is a good place to stop. Some 10km south of Caiguna is the memorial to John Baxter, Eyre's companion, who was killed on 29 April 1841 by hostile Aborigines.

At Cocklebiddy are the stone ruins of an Aboriginal mission. **Cocklebiddy Cave** is

the largest of the Nullarbor caves. In 1984 a team of French explorers set a record here for the deepest cave-dive in the world.

With a 4WD, you can travel south of Cocklebiddy to **Twilight Cove**, where there are 75m-high limestone cliffs, or to the **Eyre Bird Observatory** (see the later Alternative Routes section).

Cocklebiddy to Eucla
• *276km*

Some 93km east of Cocklebiddy is **Madura**, close to the hills of the Hampton Tablelands. At one time, horses were bred here for the Indian Army. You get good views over the plains from the road.

The ruins of the **Old Madura Homestead**, several kilometres west of the new homestead by a dirt track, have some old machinery and other equipment. Caves in the area include the large **Mullamullang Caves**, north-west of Madura, with three lakes and many side passages.

The **Mundrabilla Roadhouse** is on the lower coastal plain, with the Hampton Tablelands as a backdrop. From Mundrabilla it is 66km to Eucla or 79km to the border.

Eucla & the WA/SA Border

Just before the South Australian border is Eucla, which has picturesque ruins (just the chimneys stick out now) of an old **telegraph repeater & weather station**, first opened in 1877. The telegraph line now runs along the railway line, far to the north. The station, 5km from the roadhouse, is gradually being engulfed by the sand dunes. You can also inspect the historic jetty, which is visible from the top of the dunes. The dunes around Eucla are a truly spectacular sight.

The 3340 hectare **Eucla National Park** is only a 10 minute drive from the town. It features the Delisser Sandhills and the high limestone Wilson Bluff. The mallee scrub and heath of the park is typical of the coastal vegetation in this region.

At Eucla, many people have their photo taken with the international sign pinpointing distances to many parts of the world; it's near a ferro-concrete sperm whale, a species

A	B
C	

Midlands
A: Dominican Chapel of St Hyacinth, Yalgoo
B: Our Lady of Mt Carmel Church, Mullewa
C: Wave Rock, near Hyden

A	B
	C
D	E

Central West Coast

A: Kalbarri coastline
B: Hawk's Head Lookout, Kalbarri
C: Yardie Creek Gorge,
   Cape Range National Park
D: St Francis Xavier Cathedral,
   Geraldton
E: Dolphins, Monkey Mia

Birds of the Bight

The Eyre Bird Observatory (☎ 9039 3450) provides accommodation by prior arrangement only. Established in 1977, it is housed in the Eyre Telegraph Station, an 1897 stone building in the Nuytsland Nature Reserve, surrounded by mallee scrubland and looking up to spectacular roving sand dunes which separate the buildings from the sea. A wide range of desert flora and fauna are studied. Twitchers can expect to see many pink cockatoos, brush bronzewings and the odd furtive malleefowl. There are many raptors along all sections of the highway dispensing with road kills. By far the most spectacular is the wedge-tailed eagle. A small museum at the rear of the station has exhibits from the days of the telegraph line and of the legendary stationmaster, William Graham.

Harold Anderson, eccentric US millionaire and one-time visitor, was convinced Armageddon was nigh. He subsequently donated all the books that he thought would form the perfect account of the earth and its history to the observatory. Eyre's isolation made it just the place to sit out the firestorms and nuclear winters that would wrack the rest of the world. He returned to the USA, collated the books and dispatched them to Australia via Qantas. Not long after his return he was murdered, never to see the books on the shelves at the observatory. They are still there, alongside all the written paraphernalia an avid birder needs.

Full board is the usual arrangement: $60 per person for the first night, $55 each subsequent day ($10 discount for YHA and RAOU members, $30 for children under 14). Return transport to the bird observatory from Cocklebiddy or the Microwave Tower can be arranged for about $30. If travelling independently, you will need a 4WD to get there, as it is about 50km south-east of Cocklebiddy. 4WDs have to descend the escarpment, then drive through about 12km of sand to reach the observatory. From the buildings there is a 1km walk, via the dunes, to the beach and the lonely Great Australian Bight. ∎

seldom seen in these parts. Another popular photo stop is at the **Travellers' Cross**. This is atop the escarpment which overlooks the ruins of old Eucla.

At **Border Village**, 13km from Eucla, connoisseurs of kitsch will appreciate a 5m-high fibreglass kangaroo. Remember to set your watch forward 1½ hours – or 2½ hours when daylight-saving time is operating in South Australia.

Border Village to Nullarbor Roadhouse
• *185km*

Between the WA/SA border and Nullarbor Hotel/Motel and Roadhouse, the Eyre Highway runs close to the coast, and there are six spectacular **lookouts** over the Great Australian Bight – be sure to stop at one or two.

After about 90km, you reach a turn-off (4WD only) to the well known **Koonalda Cave**. It has a 45m-high chamber, entered by ladder. Like other Nullarbor caves, it's really for experienced cave explorers only. All caves in this part of South Australia are strictly regulated; to enter them, you usually must be accompanied by a National Parks & Wildlife officer.

Around **Nullarbor Roadhouse** are many caves, which should be explored only with extreme care (again, they are recommended to experienced cave explorers only). Watch out for wombat holes and poisonous snakes in the area. A dirt road leads to a beach, 30km away – ask directions at the roadhouse.

Nullarbor National Park (593,000 hectares) and **Nullarbor Regional Reserve** (2.28 million hectares) contain part of the largest arid limestone landscape in the world. The treeless terrain is best appreciated travelling north of the Eyre Highway along Cook Road.

Nullarbor SA to Nundroo (South Australia)
• *145km*

The road passes through the Yalata Aboriginal Reserve (600,000 hectares), and Aborigines often sell boomerangs and other souvenirs by the roadside. You can also buy these in the **Yalata Community Roadhouse**.

Winter and early spring are a good time for whale-watching (southern right whales). The best viewing point is **Twin Rocks**, at the Head of the Bight, and for 7km west of the rocks. The turn-off to Twin Rocks is about

20km east of the Nullarbor Roadhouse. Get a $2 permit from the Nullarbor or Yalata roadhouses. The edge of the Nullarbor is at **Nundroo**, 52km from Yalata.

Nundroo to Ceduna (South Australia)
• *152km*

South-east of Nundroo is the ghost town of **Fowlers Bay**. There is good fishing here, and nearby is **Mexican Hat Beach**.

You can make a short detour south of Penong to see the Pink Lake, Point Sinclair and **Cactus Beach**, a surf beach with left and right breaks that is a 'must' for any serious surfer making the east-west journey.

Eastbound from Penong to Ceduna, there are several places with fuel and other facilities. **Ceduna**, effectively the end of the solitary stretch from Norseman, is equipped with supermarkets, a backpackers' hostel, banks and all the comforts of a big town.

ALTERNATIVE ROUTES
Esperance to Balladonia

For those travelling in the south-west of WA, there is one good alternative route from Esperance. You can cut north-east to the Eyre Highway from near Cape Arid National Park utilising the 4WD-only Balladonia Road. To get there, head out from Esperance on Fisheries Rd, and when Grewer Rd comes in on the right, turn left. This becomes Balladonia Road and allows you to traverse part of Cape Arid National Park.

On this route you will pass Mt Ragged, the highest point in the Russell Range, where there is a tough walk to the top (3km return, three hours). Good topographic coverage is found in the 1:250,000 AUSLIG series *Balladonia* and *Malcolm*. Good information on the national park is in the CALM pamphlet *Cape Arid & Eucla*.

You have to be self-sufficient with both fuel and water, and after the caravan park at

Duke of Orleans Bay (south of the route), there are no facilities until Balladonia.

North into the Nullarbor

Possibly the best detour into the Nullarbor is in South Australia: drive north through the Nullarbor National Park and the regional reserve, east along the transcontinental railway line to Ooldea, and then south through Yalata Aboriginal Reserve to the Eyre Highway. From Eucla or Border Village, it is a full day of driving, best broken into two days. Take plenty of water. Because of rough sections of road a 4WD vehicle would be preferable.

If you take two days, you will need two permits: a bush-camping permit for Nullarbor Regional Reserve (available from South Australian National Parks & Wildlfe Service in Ceduna ☎ (08) 8625 3144) and a permit to cross Yalata Aboriginal Reserve (available from Yalata Roadhouse ☎ (08) 8625 6990). There is a fuel outlet at Cook (☎ (08) 8641 8506), but it is not always open when you need it – phone ahead to find out its hours.

From Border Village, it is 146km to the Cook turn-off. If you go to a few (or all) of the Nullarbor lookouts, this stretch of sealed road will take some time. It is 107km north to Cook.

Turn right and follow the rough road which parallels the transcontinental railway on its south side to Watson, passing by Fisher and O'Malley stations. Cross to the north side of the line at Watson, follow the improved road to Ooldea and then cross to the south again (the Telecom repeater station should be to your left) – it is about 141km from Cook to Ooldea. Proceed south to the Eyre Highway, crossing Ifould Lake, a large saltpan, on the way. Leave the gates in this section as you found them, and make sure you close the dog-barrier gate.

The Midlands

This chapter covers three different areas – if you look at a map they are all connected, extending from the base of the Pilbara down to the wheatbelt towns some 300km or so south of the Great Eastern Highway.

That so vast an area is covered in a small chapter suggests that there is little to see. Generally this is true, but there are some exceptions: the gold towns in the Murchison Valley, the Wildflower Way and Midlands Scenic Way, the much-photographed Wave Rock and wheatbelt towns with 'real dinki-di' inhabitants are all worthwhile.

Wheatbelt

East of the Darling Range and stretching north from the Albany coastal region to the areas beyond the Great Eastern Highway (the Perth to Kalgoorlie road) are the WA wheatlands. The area is noted for its unusual rock formations, the best known being Wave Rock, near Hyden; and for its many Aboriginal rock carvings and namma (water holes).

Some towns considered part of the wheatbelt have been covered in other chapters where they are part of a distinct and well known route north or east. For ease of description, the wheatbelt has been divided into four areas: north-eastern wheatbelt, Great Eastern Highway and central & southern regions. CALM produces the informative *Voices of the Bush – A Wheatbelt Heritage*.

The towns with names ending in 'up' and 'in' denote the presence of water and are Aboriginal appellations for namma holes.

NORTH-EASTERN WHEATBELT

This vast area is north of the Great Eastern Highway (Golden Way) and east of the Great Northern Highway. It begins at the towns of Goomalling and Wongan Hills and stretches over 200km to Mukinbudin. There are few attractions here but the odd marooned motor-

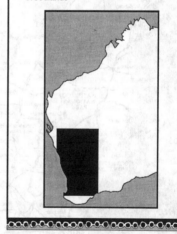

HIGHLIGHTS

- The amazing sculpted form of Wave Rock near Hyden
- The Wildflower Way's incredible transformation after the spring rains
- Walga Rock shelters – one of WA's most significant Aboriginal art sites
- The intriguing monastery town of New Norcia
- The goldfields towns of Yalgoo, Cue and Sandstone where you can sneak a look at life as it was 100 years ago
- The refreshing and fauna-rich Dryandra Woodlands

ist may glean some satisfaction from his or her isolated circumstances.

Goomalling & Dowerin

There is a **museum** in Goomalling, 132km north-east of Perth, which features a rare, though esoteric, windmill display. Rumour has it that Don Quixote's curiosity got the better of him and he visited here. Namma holes are found in Oak Park where his horse was probably watered.

Some 25km away, in Dowerin, there is

The Midlands

0 50 100 km

KALBARRI
NATIONAL
PARK

Kalbarri

Toolonga
Nature
Reserve

To Port Hedland

Wilga Mia
Ochre Mine

Meekatharra

Nannine

Tuckanarra

Cue

Walga
Rock

Lake
Austin

Mt Magnet

Sandstone

Northampton

Yalgoo

Mullewa

Pindar

Geraldton

Walkaway

Mingenew

Payne's Find

Dongara

Port Denison

Morawa

Perenjori

Three Springs

Yarra Yarra
Lakes

Carnamah

Latham

Mongers
Lake

Eneabba

Coorow

Lake
Moore

Leeman

Wubin

Green
Head

WATHEROO
NATIONAL
PARK

Dalwallinu

Kalannie

Beacon

Wialki

Bonnie Rock

Jurien

Coomberdale

Cervantes

NAMBUNG
NATIONAL
PARK

Pinnacles

Berkshire Valley
Folk Museum

Moora

Burakin

Koorda

Bencubbin

Cadoux

Wheatbelt

Way

Mukinbudin

Lake
Brown

Bullfinch

New
Norcia

Wongan
Hills

Dowerin

Wyalkatchem

MOORE RIVER
NATIONAL PARK

Goomalling

Trayning

Tammarin
Rock

Lake Campion

Westonia

Merredin

Southern Cross

Gingin

Bindoon

Toodyay

Meckering

Tammin

Great

Eastern

Highway

Muchea

Cunderdin

To Kalgoorlie
& Adelaide

INDIAN
OCEAN

Northam

York

Greenhills

Shackleton

Bruce Rock

Mt Walker

PERTH

Beverley

Quairading

Naraneen

Anderson
Rocks

Fremantle

Armadale

Dale

Corrigin

King Rocks

Wave Rock

Rockingham

Bannister

Brookton

Pingelly

Kondinin
Lake

Kondinin

Graham
Rock

Mandurah

Wickepin

Kulin

Hyden

SE Hyden

Waroona

Dryandra
Woodland

Albert Facey's
Homestead

Lake
Grace
North

Lake Grace

Harvey

Narrogin

Newdegate

Lake
King

Williams

Kukerin

Bunbury

Collie

Darkan

Arthur
River

Dumbleyung

Lake Grace
South

Holland
Rocks

Lake
Lockhart

Lake
Magenta

Capel

Donnybrook

Wagin

Dumbleyung
Lake

Nyabing

Pingrup

Busselton

Boyup
Brook

Woodanilling

Katanning

Lake Cairocup

Mindarabin

To Margaret River
& Augusta

Kojonup

Broomehill

To Mt Barker & Albany

another **museum** which shows the lifestyle of early settlers. **Hagbooms Lake** is home of the Dowerin Salt Lake Sailor's Club; there are races at Easter.

There is a caravan park (☎ 9629 1101) in Goomalling with tent/powered sites for $5/10; and the *Caratel Caravan Park/Motel* (☎ 9631 1135) in Dowerin, with powered sites for $12 and single/double rooms for $38/48.

Wyalkatchem

It is worth the drive to this town, 191km north-east of Perth, just to be photographed next to the sign on the way into town. The 'town with the odd, unexplained name' has two **museums**. One has a great collection of antique farm machinery and vehicles and the other houses a collection of old household items. There's a granite outcrop, **Uberin Rock**, 28km north of Dowerin on the Uberin Rd.

Like most towns out the back of beyond there is a nondescript caravan park (☎ 9681 1166) with sites for $12. Try *Robyn's Rest* for coffee, sandwiches and cakes.

Trayning & Nungarin

The most interesting fact about Trayning is the evolution of its name. In the Aboriginal language *duri-dring* means 'snake crawling in grass near campsite'. Over time this was transliterated into D'r'nin and was, eventually, pronounced 'Trayning'. Ponder this beneath the twin ancient **granite outcrops** at Yarragin, north-east of Kununoppin. Opposite, is **Billycatting Rock**, another massive granite outcrop and a 25 sq km flora & fauna reserve. Trayning also saw the formation of the first trotting club in Australia. Every October, trotting is held in conjunction with the Gala Wool Day.

In **Nungarin** you have to make the decision whether or not to turn north to Mukinbudin or south to the Great Eastern Highway. Either toss a coin or make a decision in the *Nungarin Hotel* (☎ 9046 5084) which has great meals, is lovingly furnished with antiques and run by friendly people.

There are, you guessed it, a caravan park (☎ 9683 1001) and hotel (☎ 9683 1005) in Trayning.

Wongan Hills

To the Aborigines this was a place of wongan ('whispering'). Wongan Hills is 184km north-east of Perth and is something of a gateway to the State Highway 99 access to the north agricultural region.

Near the town are a number of **rock formations** which rise abruptly from the landscape. These all make good vantage points to observe the annual wildflower display, especially the fields of *Verticordia* seen each November. Dingo Rock is 26km east of town, the Mt O'Brien Lookout is on the Piawaning Rd, the granite rocks of the Gathercole Reserve are on Moonijin Rd and the Xmas Rock walk is just north of the Wongan Hills caravan park.

A great place to see wildflowers is **Reynoldson's Flora Reserve**, 15km north of Wongan Hills on the old Ballidu Rd.

About 10km west of town on Calingiri Rd is **Lake Ninan**, a good place to observe water birds. For more information contact the Wongan Hills tourist centre (☎ 9671 1157) in the old train station.

Places to Stay & Eat There is a caravan park (☎ 9671 1009) on Wongan Rd where tent/powered sites are $7/11 for two people. The *Civic Hotel Motel* (☎ 9671 1022) on Fenton St has single/double rooms for $30/45 and motel units for $55/65; and the *Wongan Hills Guesthouse* (☎ 9671 1015), 1 Moore St, has B&B for $25/40. The bakery at 23 Fenton Place turns out good cakes, pies and country-style bread.

Koorda

The Aboriginal name 'Koorda' means either 'married person' or 'to separate or divide'. Koorda, 235km north-east of Perth, is best known for its **corn dolly** workshops, held in November. A corn dolly is a dolly made of corn – believe me! To get to **Redcliffe**, an unusual geological formation near the town, enquire at the Koorda tourist centre (☎ 9684 1219), Haig Rd.

The *Koorda Caravan Park* (☎ 9684 1219), Scott St, has tent sites for $7; and the *Koorda Hotel* (☎ 9684 1226), Railway St, has single/

double rooms for $27.50/40. You can get takeaway food or dine in *Helen's Kitchen* on Ninghan St.

Bencubbin & Mukinbudin

In Bencubbin, there is another one of those lovingly collected piles of trash and treasure that townsfolk have labelled the **Bates Museum** after Norman Bates' motel in Hitchcock's *Psycho*. The shire **museum**, in the old Road Boards building, has a piece from a meteorite found near the town.

About 12km south-east of town are the curious **Pergandes sheepyards**, which are constructed of granite slabs and looking like a mini version of Stonehenge.

There are also a number of interesting **rock formations** near Mukinbudin including Chiddarcooping, Yanneymooning, Elachbutting and Beringbooding. The town got its name from a rock formation called Muckenbooding, and it was later shortened to its present form.

If you get out this far you are probably going to have to stay somewhere. Bencubbin has a caravan park (☎ 9685 1202) and hotel (☎ 9085 1201). Mukinbudin also has a caravan park (☎ 9047 1103) and hotel (☎ 9047 1133). Let's face it, you didn't come all this way for *nouvelle cuisine* – local steak, peas and spud from the Mukin' cafe are a good compromise.

GREAT EASTERN HIGHWAY

This highway (State Highway 94), also known as the Golden Way, starts in Perth and passes through the towns of the Avon Valley before reaching the many agricultural towns on the way to Kalgoorlie. For much of its length it is paralleled by the pipes which carry water from Mundaring Reservoir to Kalgoorlie-Boulder (see the boxed aside 'Where Water is like Gold!' in The Southern Outback chapter).

Meckering & Cunderdin

The small town of **Meckering**, 24km west of Cunderdin, was badly damaged by an earthquake in 1968. The original faultline can be seen 11km from town on the Quellington (York) Rd.

The first town of reasonable size which you reach after Northam is **Cunderdin**, 156km from Perth. The museum and tourist centre (☎ 9635 1291), at 100 Forrest St, is housed in an old pumping station used on the goldfields water pipeline.

There is a caravan park (☎ 9635 1258) on Olympic Ave with on-site vans for $30 for two. The *Cunderdin Motor Hotel* (☎ 9635 1104), on Main St, has singles/double rooms for $40/60. This pub serves good meals including a hearty Sunday roast for $6.50.

Kellerberrin

Further to the east is Kellerberrin (203km from Perth), which has an **historical museum** in the old agricultural hall (built in 1897) and a lookout on **Kellerberrin Hill**. The tourist centre (☎ 9045 4006) is at 110 Massingham St.

The **Milligan Homestead** and outbuildings, 10km north of town, are a fine example of vernacular architecture as they are constructed of local fieldstone.

Kokerbin Rock, 30km south of Kellerberrin, is a prominent granite outcrop and is reputed to be the third-biggest monolith in Australia. There are great views of the endless fields of wheat from its summit.

Like many towns in the area, a great attraction is the profusion of **wildflowers** in spring. Two of the best places to see them are the Durakoppin Wildlife Sanctuary, 27km to the north, and Charles Gardner National Park, 35km south-west.

Kellerberrin has a caravan park (☎ 9045 4066) with tent/powered sites for $2/8 for two; the *Shell Roadhouse Motel* (☎ 9045 4007) with singles/doubles for $35/45; and a couple of delis.

Merredin

Merredin, the largest centre in the wheatbelt (population 3500), is 260km east of Perth on the Kalgoorlie railway line and the Great Eastern Highway. It has a tourist office (☎ 9041 1666) on Barrack St.

The 1920s train station has been turned into a charming **museum** with a vintage

1897 locomotive and an old signal box with 95 signal switching levers.

There are several short drives in the Merredin area which allow you to view **wild-flowers** in season.

Mangowine Homestead, 65km north of Merredin, has been restored by the National Trust.

There are also some interesting **rock formations** around Merredin, including Kangaroo Rock, 17km to the south-east; Burracoppin Rock to the north; and Sandford Rocks 11km east of Westonia.

Places to Stay & Eat On the Great Eastern Highway, *Merredin Caravan Park* (☎ 9041 1535), has tent/powered sites for $10/13 for two and on-site vans for $28. The *Merredin Motel* (☎ 9041 1886), 10 Gamenya Ave, has single/double units from $30/45 and the *Merredin Olympic Motel* (☎ 9041 1588), Great Eastern Highway, has singles/doubles for $40/50. *Potts Motor Inn* (☎ 9041 1755), also on the Great Eastern Highway, has singles/doubles for $54/64.

The *Commercial Hotel*, Barrack St, does counter meals (there's a $2.50 lunch-time

special) and the *Gum Tree* in the Merredin Motel is a good choice for dinner.

Southern Cross

Although the gold quickly gave out, Southern Cross (population 2200) was the first gold-rush town on the WA goldfields. The big rush soon moved east to Coolgardie and Kalgoorlie. Like the town itself, the streets of Southern Cross are named after the stars and constellations. The **Yilgarn History Museum** in the old courthouse has local displays; it deserves a visit. If you follow the continuation of Antares St south for 3km, you will see a couple of active open-cut mines.

Situated 368km east of Perth, this is really the end of the wheatbelt area and the start of the desert; when travelling by train the change of landscape is very noticeable. In the spring, the sandy plains around Southern Cross are carpeted with wildflowers.

Places to Stay & Eat There is a caravan park (☎ 9049 1212) on Coolgardie Rd which has powered sites for $12 for two, and on-site vans from $20 to $25 for two.

There are two hotels in Antares St and the pick of them is the *Palace Hotel* (☎ 9049 1555), a beautifully restored place with exquisite stained-glass windows, which has rooms for $30 per person; the restaurant serves great pizzas. The *Southern Cross Motel* (☎ 9049 1144) on Canopus St has singles/doubles for $53/65.

CENTRAL & SOUTHERN REGIONS

This is the area south of the Great Eastern Highway and east of the Albany Highway (State Highway 30). It stretches from Brookton/Pingelly out to Hyden/Wave Rock in the north and from Kojonup out to Grace and King lakes in the south. The considered highlight is Wave Rock but many motorists will think that this formation hardly merited the 700km return drive from Perth. This region also includes wildflowers in season, the magnificent Dryandra Woodland and the homestead of Albert Facey.

Get a free copy of *Central South Travellers Guide*.

Get familiar with one of Australia's major exports while travelling through the Wheatbelt.

Pingelly

The name Pingelly, 160km south-east of Perth, comes from the Aboriginal word for the area 'Pingeculling'. There are a number of historic buildings in the town such as the courthouse which is now the museum. **Boyagin Rock Reserve**, 26km north-west of the town, is an important remnant of natural bush on the edge of the wheatbelt.

There is a hotel (☎ 9887 1001) and a motel (☎ 9887 1015) in the town and numerous farmstays (☎ 9887 1375) outside town. The *Exchange Tavern* in Pasture St serves good counter meals.

Dryandra Woodland

This state forest (☎ 9881 1113) of 270 sq km is on the western edge of the central southern wheatbelt. It is a remnant of the open eucalypt woodlands which once covered much of the wheatbelt but which were cleared for agriculture. The woodlands are predominantly wandoo, powderbark and brown mallet and the plateaus have pockets of jarrah associated with *kwongan* (heath and shrublands).

At least 20 species of native mammal have been found in the park including the state's fauna emblem, the numbat. The small kangaroo-like woylie and tammar wallaby are other ground-dwelling mammals found here. It is a fine bird-watching area with over 100 species (including mallee fowl) and, in spring, there are many wildflowers.

There is a good 5km walk, the **Ochre Trail**, which has an ochre pit once quarried by the local Nyoongar people. The ochre was valued for body decoration and rock art. The 27km **Contine Bridal Trail** takes about five hours on horseback. There is also a 25km **radio drive trail** (tune to 100 FM).

Dryandra is accessible from the York-Williams Rd on the west side and the Narrogin-Wandering Rd on the east side. It is 160km south-east of Perth and 20km north-west of Narrogin. There is no camping in the forest but you can stay in the *Lions Dryandra Village* (☎ 9884 5231); accommodation in either the bunkhouse or cottages is $10 per person.

Narrogin

This town, 189km south-east of Perth, is an agricultural centre in the heart of WA's richest farming land. Narrogin has a **courthouse museum** in Egerton St, an axe-handle factory and a 'foxes lair' park. The fox problem has been eliminated and, today, the park has pygmy possums and red-tailed wambengers. There is also an old **butter factory** in Federal St; home to a collection of antiques and arts & crafts.

The Narrogin tourist centre (☎ 9881 2064), in Egerton St, has volunteer staff who really enjoy their work. It is open weekdays from 9.30 am to 4.30 pm, Saturday from 9 am to noon. You can get the excellent pamphlets *Narrogin Heritage Trail* and *Narrogin Centenary Pathway* to help you find the interesting sights in town.

To the east of Narrogin (and just to the south of Wickepin) is the **Albert Facey Homestead** (see the boxed aside 'The Fortunate House' below).

Places to Stay & Eat The caravan park (☎ 9881 1260) has tent sites for $11 for up to four. The *Hordern Hotel Motel* (☎ 9881 1015), Federal St, has single/double hotel rooms for $20/35 and motel units for $30/50. The *Narrogin Motel* (☎ 9881 1660), 56 Williams Rd, has singles/doubles for $45/55 and the *Wagon Way Motel* (☎ 9881 1899), 78 Williams Rd, has rooms for $55/63.

There are a few local farmstays. *Chuckem*

The Fortunate House

The Albert Facey Homestead, 39km to the east of Narrogin, is worth a visit, especially if you have read Albert Facey's popular book *A Fortunate Life* (see the boxed aside 'Albert Facey' in the Facts about WA chapter). The 86km self-drive Albert Facey Heritage Trail begins at the homestead and visits many of the places around Wickepin which are mentioned in the book. Entrance to the homestead, which has a rambling collection of Facey memorabilia, is $2 per person. ■

Farm (☎ 9885 9050), 27km away, has B&B for $50 per person; and *Stoke Farm* (☎ 9885 9018), 11km south of town, costs $75 for DB&B.

There is a great little cafe, on the main street, which pours a highly acceptable cappuccino.

Williams & West Arthur

Named after William IV, the town doesn't assume the regal proportions of its namesake and, at best, it merits the label 'pleasant'. It has an eponymous caravan park, hotel and motel.

The region of West Arthur has an interesting **slab cottage**. This was built in the 1900s from timber slab and stone and is situated on the Quindanning Rd. The best woollen quilts in the state are made at the **Woolshed** in Duranillin, near Darkan.

Quairading & Bruce Rock

If you wish to immerse yourself in agricultural delight, then the road to Quairading and Bruce Rock, 160km and 240km east of Perth respectively, are the places. Pigs, goats, sheep, cattle, lupins, peas, wheat and barley abound. Punctuating this sylvan scene are a number of prominent rock formations, including Kokerbin Rock (see under Kellerberrin earlier in this chapter).

Quairading ('home of the small bush kangaroo') has a tourist centre (☎ 9645 1001) on Jennaberring Rd. There is a caravan park (☎ 9645 1001) and a motel (☎ 9645 1054) in town. For those who came out here for the peace of the country, try *Quairading Farm Holidays* (☎ 9645 1086); B&B is $30/45 for one/two persons.

On the way to Bruce Rock you pass through Shackleton, home of the **smallest bank** in Australia, just 4m by 3m. Bruce Rock has a tourist centre (☎ 9061 1169) in Johnson St, two **museums**, a caravan park (☎ 9061 1169) with a backpackers' section ($5 per person) and a motel (☎ 9061 1174) with singles/doubles for $35/45. Again, country life can be experienced at *Breakell Farm* (☎ 9065 1042); B&B is about $35 per person.

Kulin & Kondinin

Only a short drive from town, along 86 Gate Rd, is the **Rabbit-Proof Fence**, built during the height of the rabbit plague between 1901 and 1907. The rabbits beat the constructors of the fence to the west side so the erection of the fence was a bit of a joke.

Jilakin Rock, 16km from Kulin, is a spectacular grey granite monolith which overlooks a lake of some 12 sq km. Near the lake's edge is a stand of jarrah trees, rare in the wheatbelt and usually associated with forests 140km to the west. **Buckley's Breakaway**, 58km east of Kulin, is a set of unusual kaolin formations with reddish-brown gravel caps.

Eco-hounds would probably drive further east to the 320 sq km **Dragon Rocks Nature Reserve**, some 17km east of Buckley's Breakaway. Over 70 species of birds including mallee fowl and the wedge-tailed eagle have been seen in the reserve. The park also boasts 10 different species of orchid. Sandy plain wildflowers abound throughout the region in spring.

Kulin has a caravan park (☎ 9880 1368) and a motel hotel (☎ 9880 1201). Nearby Kondinin has a caravan park (☎ 9889 1006), hotel (☎ 9889 1009) and motel (☎ 9889 1190).

Corrigin

This archetypal wheatbelt town, 68km south of Bruce Rock and 230km south-east of Perth, has a folk museum with a collection of farm machinery, a craft cottage and a miniature railway. The tourist office (☎ 9063 2203) is in Lynch St.

About 5km out of town is a 'buried bone' **dog cemetery**. This homage to 'persons' best friends' must be one of the more bizarre sights in all of WA. Corrigin also has an **emu farm**, a couple of **yabbie farms** and a **marron farm**; all are open from 10 am to 4 pm daily.

Places to Stay & Eat There is a caravan park (☎ 9063 2103) in Kirkwood St with powered sites for $10. Dogs (reincarnated perhaps?) are allowed on a leash.

The *Windmill Motel* (☎ 9063 2390) on the

Brookton Highway has singles/doubles for $48/58 and its guesthouse is $30/40.

There are a couple of farmstays: *Minda-long* (☎ 9065 8055), on Barber Rd about 28km west of Corrigin, is $25 per person and *Kelly Cottage* (☎ 9063 7011), Bullaring/Gorge Rock Rd, is about $50 for two.

If you dine in town, insist on yabbies with your salad. The morning and afternoon teas at *Kym's Coffee Shop & Takeaway*, Goyder St, are quite reasonable.

Hyden & Wave Rock

Wave Rock, 350km south-east of Perth and 4km east of the town of Hyden, south of Merredin and Southern Cross, is worth a visit if you are nearby , otherwise it's an awfully long day trip from Perth. The perfect surfer's wave is 15m high and 100m long and frozen in solid rock marked with different colour bands. The bands are caused by the runoff of waters containing carbonates and iron hydroxide. Unfortunately, a small concrete wall along its top detracts from its natural majesty.

Other interesting rock formations in the area bear names like the **Breakers, Hippo's Yawn** and the **Humps**. Hippo's Yawn is a 20 minute walk from Wave Rock, and well worth the visit. The walls of **Mulka's Cave**, 21km from Hyden, feature Aboriginal hand paintings. The tourist centre (☎ 9880 5182) at the Wave Rock Wildflower Shop provides information on how to get to these formations. Wave Rock also has the second-biggest **lace collection** in the world (the Margaret Blackburn collection), which begs more than one question.

The area is dotted with wheat and sheep farms. At night during seeding time, huge tractors operate in all directions on the darkened landscape. Ask the farmers if you can accompany them on a few circuits of a field.

Many people stop in the area to work during the seeding and harvesting season and it is likely that you will meet an international gathering of workers at the local pub.

A Westrail bus to Hyden leaves Perth on Tuesday and returns on Thursday; it costs $30.60 one way and the trip takes five hours.

Places to Stay & Eat At Wave Rock, the caravan park (☎ 9880 5022) has tent/powered sites for $9/12 for two, and cabins at $52 for one or two. The only backpackers', *Wave-a-Way* (☎ 9880 5103), is at the corner of Kalgarin Lake and Worland Rds in Kalgarin, 30 minutes' drive south-west of Wave Rock; it is on a wheat and sheep property. Dorm beds are $15. Two other farmstay choices are: *Glenorie* (☎ 9880 5151), 9km north of Hyden, with B&B for $25 per person; and *Turromo Farm* (☎ 9866 8066), Hyden and Newdegate Rds, with B&B for $20.

The comfortable *Hyden Wave Rock Hotel* (☎ 9880 5052), 2 Lynch St, has singles/doubles from $50/70.

Meals are available at the *Hyden Roadhouse* or the hotel. At Wave Rock, there is a coffee shop. It is strongly suggested that you bring your own picnic lunch.

Wagin

Pronounced 'way-jin' (and don't you forget it), this rural centre (population 2300) is 220km south-east of Perth. The Wagin tourist centre (☎ 9861 1177) is in Arthur Rd.

Wagin has a 15m-high fibreglass ram (a tribute to the surrounding merino industry and a sense of bad taste). There is also an **historical village** at the local showgrounds with some restored buildings and a vintage tractor display. There is also bushwalking around **Mt Latham** ('Badjarning'), a granite rock 6km to the west.

Places to Stay The caravan park (☎ 9861 1177), on the corner of Arthur Rd and Scadden St, has tent/powered sites for $9/10. The *Palace Hotel* (☎ 9861 1003) on Tudhoe St has simple singles/doubles for $20/40; and the *Wagin Motel* (☎ 9861 1784), 57 Tudhoe St, has rooms for $50/60. The *Rockleigh Farmstay* (☎ & fax 9862 2029), housed in a nice restored building, is recommended by readers; B&B costs $27 per person.

Katanning

This town, south of Wagin and 277km south of Perth, has a large Muslim community from Christmas Island, who worship at their own **mosque** in Andrews Rd. Other attractions include the old **flour mill** on Clive St, which houses the tourist centre (☎ 9821 2634) and the ruins of an old winery. The tourist centre is open weekdays from 10 am to 4 pm, Saturday from 10 am to noon.

The **saleyards** here are the second-biggest inland saleyards in Australia (Wagga Wagga, New South Wales, is the biggest).

The caravan park (☎ 9821 1066) in Aberdeen St has tent/powered sites for $4/10. The *Katanning Motel* (☎ 9821 1657), Albion St, with singles/doubles from $35/60, also has a restaurant.

Two cafes, *PM's* in Clive St, and *BKW* on Austral St, are good for coffee and lunches; and *Hung Win's*, a Chinese place in Carew St, is open daily.

Kojonup

This town (population 1100), 39km southwest of Katanning and on the southernmost extremity of the wheatbelt, was established in 1837 as a military outpost to protect the mail run from Perth to Albany. The name is derived from the Aboriginal *kodja* meaning 'stone axe'. The tourist office (☎ 9831 1686) is in the old train station in Benn Parade.

The **military barracks museum** still survives from the colonial era (circa 1845) and is worth a look.

Places to Stay & Eat There is a caravan park (☎ 9831 1127), the *Hillview Motel* (☎ 9831 1160) and *Commercial Motel Hotel* (☎ 9831 1044) in town.

The wise would choose to stay at one of the many farmstays in the district. You could try *Kalpara Cottage*, Tenner Rd (☎ 9832 3016), at $35 per person B&B; *Karana Farm* (☎ 9832 3072), 20 minutes' drive west on Blackwood Rd, at $40 for two; *Kengerrup Cottage* (☎ 9834 1057), off the Albany Highway, at $40 for two; and *Proandra Flowers Farmstay* (☎ 9832 8065), off Boscabel Rd, at $45 for a house which accommodates five people.

You can get takeaways, a meal and coffee at *Clarky's Cafe*, at 124 Albany Highway, or from the roadhouse.

Dumbleyung, Kukerin & Lake Grace

All of these towns are on State Highway 107. Dumbleyung is to the north-east of Lake Dumbleyung (where Donald Campbell broke the world speed record on water, setting 442.08 km/h in *Bluebird* in 1964). Today the lake hosts a variety of bird life. There is a good view of the lake from Pussy Cat Hill. Surprise, there is a caravan park and hotel in Dumbleyung.

Kukerin is 39km east of Dumbleyung. During the wildflower season there is a worthwhile drive through the **Tarin Rock Nature Reserve**.

Lake Grace, 345km from Perth, takes its name from the shallow salt lake which is 9km west of town. The **Inland Mission Hospital**, built in 1925 by the famous Flynn of the Inland, has recently been restored as a hospital museum. There is a caravan park (☎ 9865 1263) with powered sites for $9 for two, a motel hotel (☎ 9865 1219) and a motel (☎ 9865 1180). You will have no trouble locating any of them – if you hit the desert, you have gone too far.

Lake King, at the end of State Highway 107, is where an old sand track heads off to Frank Hann and Peak Charles national parks. Lake King is a great place to see wildflowers in season. It has a caravan park (☎ 9874 4060) and tavern/motel (☎ 9874 4048); singles/doubles at the latter are $50/60.

Central Midlands

There are two road options inland of Dongara and Geraldton and both branch off from the Great Northern Highway.

The first option, State Highway 116, is known locally as the Midlands Scenic Way. The road heads north from Bindoon and passes towns such as Moora, Coorow, Carnamah and Mingenew. The Midlands Rd emerges from its inland route at the coastal town of Dongara.

Towns such as Dalwallinu, Perenjori, Morawa and Mullewa are part of the second option, the Wildflower Way – famous for its brilliant spring display of wildflowers, including wreath leschenaultia, native foxgloves, everlastings and wattles (see under Wildflower Way in this chapter and the Wildflower section in the Facts about WA chapter). This area is also a gateway to the Murchison goldfields; there are old goldmining centres and ghost towns around Perenjori. One little-known feature of these routes are the wealth of buildings built by the enigmatic Monsignor John Hawes (see the boxed aside 'Monsignor John Hawes' in the Central West Coast chapter). The road heads north from the town of Wubin, which is around 210km north of where the Great Northern and North-West Coastal highways split near Muchea.

THE SCENIC WAY
New Norcia

This village, 132km north of Perth, is decidedly incongruous. It was established as a Spanish Benedictine mission in 1846, by Dom Rosendo Salvado and Dom Jose Serra, and named after Nursia in Italy where St Benedict was born. It is still occupied by about 20 Benedictine monks who own and operate the town. It has changed little since its inception and boasts a fine collection of buildings with classic Spanish architecture – 27 of the buildings are classified by the National Trust.

The buildings which house the **museum** and **art gallery** are worth seeing for their old paintings (including works by Spanish and Italian masters), manuscripts and religious artefacts. They also house the tourist centre (☎ 9654 8056) which is open from 10 am to 4.30 pm daily.

There are daily tours of the monastery for $10 (children $5) which include the 150 year old bakery, chapels and other cloistered, secret places. Search in vain for the secret recipe for the liqueur Dom Benedictine along the 2km self-guided **New Norcia Heritage Trail**. You can get the excellent *New Norcia Heritage Trail* brochure, which traces the development of the settlement, from the museum.

One of the interesting features of the trail is the **abbey church**, opened in 1861, and built from bush stones, mud plaster and rough-hewn tree trunks. Inside is the tomb of Dom Rosendo Salvado.

Westrail ($13 one way from Perth) and Greyhound buses pass through New Norcia twice weekly.

Places to Stay & Eat Just past the museum is the historic *New Norcia Hotel* (☎ 9654 8034) which has interesting decor, including a grand staircase; singles/doubles are from $33/50. You can experience monastic life by staying in the *Monastery Guesthouse* (☎ 9654 8002); full board is $40 per person for bed, prayer and all meals. Otherwise, try the farmstay *Napier Downs* (☎ 9655 9015) in Wannamal, 15km south of New Norcia; half-board/full board is $80/130 for two.

The sourdough bread, baked at the monastery, is simply delicious and known to many as the 'the staff of life'; it is available from the museum. Also baked in the woodfired oven is a panforte-style nut cake, best enjoyed with port or coffee. You can get a good home-cooked meal from *Salvado's Restaurant* in the New Norcia Roadhouse, open from 7 am to 8 pm, or from the New Norcia Hotel (if you are staying there).

Moora

The first town of any size in the area is Moora, 172km north of Perth, on the banks of the Moore River. The Moora tourist office (☎ 9651 1401) is at 34 Padbury St. There is a display of crafts and artefacts (all for sale) by local Aborigines at Yuat Artifacts (☎ 9651 1290), Padbury St; it is open weekdays from 8.30 am to 4.30 pm.

Some 19km east of town is the **Berkshire Valley Folk Museum**, in an old flour mill established in 1842. It is open from noon to 4 pm every Sunday, August to October (wildflower season), and every second Sunday, April to July. About 12km north of Moora is **Coomberdale** where there is one of the largest displays of dried flowers; flowers can also be seen growing (sorry, no time lapse) and being processed for export.

The **Moora Heritage Trail** takes in a number of historic homesteads

Places to Stay & Eat The *Moora Caravan Park* (☎ 9651 1401), Dandaragan St, has tent/powered sites for $9/15. The *Moora Drovers Inn* (☎ 9651 1108), also on Dandaragan St, is a restored 1909 historic building where singles/doubles are $35/45; the motel units are $40/50. About 40km north of Moora, near Watheroo National Park, is the *Watheroo Station Tavern* (☎ 9651 7007), a nice place with cheap singles/doubles from $13/30.

If you crave adventurous food, forget it! The cafes tried out in this town were distinctly ordinary.

Coorow

This town is in the heart of wildflower country and there are two good drives in the region; brochures are available from the shire office (☎ 9952 1103) in Main St. The **Darling Fault** is 12km west of the town along Green Head Rd. To the west of this line is the Perth Basin – one of the deepest sedimentary basins in the world. About 50km south of the town is **Watheroo National Park**, a good example of sandy plain country with a number of rare species of flora.

Places to Stay *Coorow Caravan Park* (☎ 9952 1103), in Station St, has tent/powered sites for $5.50/9 and there is one hotel (☎ 9952 1023) in Main St with pub-style singles/doubles for $30/40.

Carnamah & Three Springs

The town of Carnamah is 46km north of Coorow. To the west of town is the **Yarra Yarra Lake**, a salt-lake system in which the water ranges in colour from blood-red to azure. Just east of town is the **McPherson Homestead**, completed in 1880, and currently being restored.

Three Springs, close to Carnamah, is in the heart of wildflower country and the shire office (☎ 9954 1001), on Railway Rd, provides details of wildflower drives.

Places to Stay The *Carnamah Caravan Park* (☎ 9951 1055), next to Niven Park, has tent/powered sites for $6.50/8.40; and the *Carnamah Motel Hotel* (☎ 9951 1023), McPherson St, has singles/doubles for $15/30, or motel units for $45/60.

In Three Springs, the *Commercial Motel Hotel* (☎ 9954 1041), a 1928 Federation-style hotel, has singles/doubles for $25/37 (breakfast is an extra $9 per person).

Mingenew

This town has a small historical **museum** in the old Roads Board building. The tourist office (☎ 9928 1081) is on Midlands Rd.

Some 32km north-east of town on the gorge of the Irwin River is the coal seam discovered by the Gregory brothers in 1846.

The real attraction of this area is the carpet of **wildflowers** seen in August and September. Depot Hill National Park (14.5km west of town on the Dongara road), Yandanooka and Manarra are places where you will see a great range.

Places to Stay & Eat *Mingenew Caravan & Camping Park* (☎ 9928 1081), in Lee Steere St, has tent/powered sites for $8/10. To the south of town in Yandanooka is *Langton Holiday Farm* (☎ 9972 6062), a farmstay where B&B is from $30 per person (dinner is $15 per person extra).

You can get passable food at the *Old Post Office Tearooms* and the usual 'road' fare from the roadhouses on Midland Rd.

THE WILDFLOWER WAY

For those wanting to see the famous carpet of wildflowers, mainly everlastings, from July to November, this is the area to drive through. There are many organised tours which take in the wildflowers but the best mode of transport is a car.

Dalwallinu

The name of this town, 248km north-east of Perth on the Great Northern Highway, means 'to rest awhile'. It is the start of the Wildflower Way and August and September are the best months to visit. There is a caravan park (☎ 9661 1253) and a motel hotel (☎ 9661 1102) in town. *Ye Olde Convent Lodge* (☎ 9661 1216), on the corner of the Great Northern Highway and Kalanie Rd, is a restored guesthouse; Half-board singles/doubles are $39/58.

Wubin

This is the actual junction of the Wildflower Way and the Great Northern Highway. The wildflowers seen in August and September are again the attraction. There are a number of scenic **rock formations** near the town such as Buntine, to the east, and Wubin Rocks, 7km along the Great Northern Highway.

Perenjori

There are a number of reasons to drive the 350km from Perth to Perenjori. Apart from wildflower displays from August to October, this town is on the fringe of mining and station country and there are some interesting drives in the region. The tourist office (☎ 9973 1125) is in Fowler St.

The town itself has the unusual Catholic **Church of St Joseph** designed by Monsignor John Hawes (see the boxed aside

---

Not-So-Wild Flowers

A number of enterprising farmers in the Mingenew area have combined the growing and processing of wildflowers with wheat and sheep farming. The farmers can choose from the 3600 different species of wildflower which grow freely in the region. Popular varieties are the yellow *Verticordia serrata*, white wax *(Chamelaucium alba)* and the red kangaroo paw *(Anigozanthos manglesii)* – the latter is the state's floral symbol.

The flowers are picked before they bloom and exported to Europe and Japan at a time when these parts of the world are in the depths of winter. Designer plants which suit cut-flower and pot-plant markets are even being grown in controlled environments, but nothing quite lives up to the splendour of native wildflowers in their bush setting. ∎

'Monsignor John Hawes' in the Central West Coast chapter). The skeletal white church with its clerestory (upper stage of main walls) of round windows seems an incongruity in this wheatbelt town.

At the rear of the tourist office is a **museum** which houses memorabilia from the early pioneering days of the district. There is a namma (water hole), **Camel Soak**, 47km east of Perenjori. These namma were familiar to the Aborigines and were essential stops as they journeyed between regions.

Places to Stay & Eat The *Perenjori Caravan Park* (☎ 9973 1002), on Crossing Rd, has tent/powered sites for $6/11.

In town, there is the country-style *Graham's Bakery* for the usual pies, pastries and sausage rolls. The bread is baked in a 70 year old oven.

Morawa

This town has more wildflowers in its vicinity for those in search of the stamen, pistil and petal. Those undertaking the Monsignor Hawes Heritage Trail would be here to see the **Church of the Holy Cross** with its curious one room stone hermitage (maybe the smallest presbytery in the world), used by the retiring Monsignor Hawes. The church itself is a fine piece of Spanish mission architecture, made of local stone and Cordoba tiles.

The tourist office (☎ 9971 1204) is at 5 Jose St and the small **museum** with its displays of farming machinery is on Prater St. During the wildflower season a trip out to **Koolanooka Springs**, 24km east of town, is recommended.

The caravan park (☎ 9971 1380) is on White Ave and the *Morawa Motel Hotel* (☎ 9971 1060), at the corner of Solomon and Manning Sts, has single/double rooms for $15/30 and motel units for $40/55.

Mullewa

Again, the two main reasons for visits to this town are wildflowers and the architecture of Monsignor John Hawes. Flower lovers head for the unique wreath flower, while those following the Monsignor Hawes Heritage Trail go to **Our Lady of Mt Carmel Church** in Doney St and the **Priest House** in Bowes St. The tourist office (☎ 9961 1110) is at 5 Jose St. The Wildflower Show is held in the last week of August.

At ease with his pastoral duties, Hawes put his heart and a portion of unused soul into building the church. The Romanesque design is also seen in hillside churches in southern Europe. In a letter, Hawes wrote:

I am building into these stones at Mullewa, poor little feeble church that it is, my convictions, aspirations and ideals as to what a church should be ... my heart is in these stones!

Next to the church, Hawes built a house for himself and furnished the interior with jarrah pieces of his own design. It is more or less a museum honouring Hawes, although his actual buildings tell you much more about him. The house, well worth a look, is open from Monday to Friday from 10 to 11.45 am and 1.30 to 3 pm.

Just east of Mullewa, on the Mt Magnet Rd, is **Mass Rock**. Hawes used to ring a bell to let the shy Aborigines know that he was about to perform mass. Part of the rock has been flattened to serve as an altar, and although Hawes drew up plans for a Spanish mission-style archway and belltower for 'Mission Dolores', they were never built.

In the pioneer cemetery, 1km north of town, there is a **headstone** to Selby John Arnold, carved by Hawes. Arnold, who died in tragic circumstances, was an altar boy to Hawes and the headstone is the result of a promise made to the boy's parents. The prolific monsignor also drew the preliminary sketches for St Mary's Agricultural School in Tardun, south-east of Mullewa.

The trail in search of the enigmatic Monsignor Hawes is one of the highlights of a visit to WA (it is around 210km long). The juxtaposition of his curious yet functional architectural styles with the surrounding monotony of scrub and farms has to be seen to be believed.

Places to Stay *Mullewa Caravan Park* (☎ 9961 1161), 1 Lovers Lane, has facilities for the disabled; tent/powered sites are $7/12 for two. The *Club Hotel* (☎ 9961 1131) at 30 Maitland Rd has singles/doubles for $25/40, and motel units at the *Railway Motel Hotel* (☎ 9961 1050) on Grey St are $55/75.

There are a few station stays north of Mullewa in the Murchison: *Meeberrie* (☎ 9963 7971), *Tallering* (☎ 9962 3045) and *Wooleen* (☎ 9963 7973), for example. Check prices with each station; usually a full days' board is about $85.

GREAT NORTHERN HIGHWAY: WUBIN TO MEEKATHARRA

Although most people heading for the Pilbara and the Kimberley travel up the coast, the Great Northern Highway from Perth to Port Hedland is much more direct. The road is sealed the total distance of 1636km. The first part of this road, from Wubin to Meekatharra, skirts the Central Midlands on its eastern side.

The highway is one of Australia's least interesting, passing through country that is flat and featureless. The Murchison River goldfields, and the towns of Mt Magnet, Cue and Meekatharra help break the monotony.

The Great Northern Highway (State Highway 95), begins near Muchea, passes through Bindoon, New Norcia and Dalwallinu before heading north-east from Wubin. It is 272km from Perth to Wubin, 297km from Wubin to Mt Magnet, and 196km from Mt Magnet to Meekatharra.

Getting There & Away

Skywest flies from Perth to Mt Magnet, Cue and Meekatharra Monday, Wednesday and Friday. There are also flights to Meekatharra Tuesday, Friday and Sunday.

The Great Northern Highway is served by two bus services: Greyhound goes from Perth to Port Hedland on Friday, Wednesday and Sunday; and Westrail has less frequent services as far as Meekatharra. Fares from Perth with Westrail are Mt Magnet ($56), Cue ($60.50) and Meekatharra ($67.30).

Mt Magnet

Gold was found at Mt Magnet in the late 19th century and mining is still the town's sole justification, with gold being mined at the Hill 50 Mine. Mt Magnet was named after a prominent nearby hill which contained magnetic rocks. The town, however, was not developed until the gold rush. The Mt Magnet tourist office (☎ 9963 4172) is in Hepburn St.

You can get a panoramic view of the town and the huge open-cut pits from Warramboo ('Camping Place') Hill. About 7km north of town in an area of breakaways (cliffs) are **The Granites**, a popular picnic spot where Aboriginal rock art can still be seen. Eleven km north of town are the ruins of **Lennonville**, once a busy town. The modern magnet is often the wildflowers which carpet the landscape in spring.

Places to Stay & Eat The accommodation situation in town is bad. The seemingly unattended *Mt Magnet Caravan Park* (☎ 9963 4198) has tent/powered sites for $7/13. On no account rent their leaky, broken down on-site vans ($25, rain water free). The *Commercial Club Motel Hotel* (☎ 9963 4021) and *Grand Motel Hotel* (☎ 9963 4110) have very ordinary singles/doubles for $50/70 and $55/75 respectively.

Some 40km south-west of Magnet is *Wogarno Sheep Station* (☎ 9963 5846) which charges $80 each per night for full board. A bed in the shearers' quarters is $14. About 61km west of Mt Magnet, on the road to Yalgoo, *Murrum Station* (☎ 9963 5843) has tent and caravan sites for $5 and comfortable, clean beds in the shearers' quarters for $15 per person.

The town does not exert much of a culinary pull. There is a fish and chip shop on Main St, meals are available from the *Magnet Chinese & Takeaway*, the *Grand* has fish and chips for $7, and you can get light meals and takeaways from the *Crib Tin Cafe*. The hamburger van operates after the pubs have closed; all the locals will know where it is parked.

Yalgoo

This town is well worth the 127km drive west of Mt Magnet. In the 1890s, the town was the centre of a thriving goldfield; gold and gemstones are still found in the area. Wildflowers are also an attraction between July and September.

And guess what? The ubiquitous 'building monsignor' made it out to Yalgoo, designing and then helping to build the **Dominican Chapel of St Hyacinth**. The manual labour calloused his hands to such an extent he feared they might damage his silk vestments.

The Shire of Yalgoo office in Shamrock St is also the tourist office (☎ 9962 8042); it will provide a key to open the chapel. The courthouse **museum** is in Gibbons St behind the Telstra building. The **old train station** is one of the few remaining buildings from the old Mullewa-Meekatharra line.

Places to Stay There is a *caravan park* (☎ 9962 8042) in Stanley St with tent/powered sites $8/12 for two. The motel hotel (☎ 9962 8031), Gibbons St, has singles/doubles for $30/45, and motel units for $45/55.

There are station stays in the vicinity: *Barnong* (☎ 9963 7991), *Thundelarra* (☎ 9963 6575) and *Yuin* (☎ 9963 7982). Full board for one at Thundelarra is from $65; and at Yuin, an establishment which prefers sheep to children, it is $85. These stations usually have beds in the shearers' quarters for $15 per person.

Sandstone

This town is not on the Great Northern Highway but lies 160km east of Mt Magnet, on a road that is usually impassable after heavy rain. The historic town is surrounded by a bronzed, rusty sandstone landscape, hence its name. There were four principal mines in the area during the peak mining period, 1908-1912: Oroya, WA Development, Wanderrie and Black Range. If you venture out this far make sure you obtain a copy of the *Sandstone Heritage Trail* pamphlet.

South-east of town is the basalt **London Bridge**, over 350 million years old. On the road to the bridge, among the breakaways, is an old brewery and storage site.

Abandoned mining settlements around Sandstone include Youanmi, Montague, Paynesville, Berrigrin and Barrambie.

The *Alice Atkinson Caravan Park* (☎ 9963 5859) has tent/powered sites for $7.50/10 for two, and on-site vans for $35. The food situation in town is a mystery.

Cue

Cue, the 'Queen of the Murchison', 80km north of Mt Magnet, has some interesting old buildings of solid stone. The National Trust has classified **Austin St** because of its many buildings featuring goldfields architecture; these include the Cue Public Buildings, Bank of New South Wales, band rotunda and Gentlemen's Club. Away from the main street are an old gaol, historic primary school

The interesting but dilapidated corrugated-iron Masonic Hall in Cue

and the Masonic Lodge. Sneak a look inside **Bell's Emporium** to see what a shopping trip was like 100 years ago.

There are a number of **ghost towns** in the vicinity of Cue. The sister town of **Day Dawn** is 5km to the south. It once had a population of 3000 in the heyday of the Great Fingall Mine; about all that is left standing is the Great Fingall office and the gaunt chimneys of the Cue-Day Dawn Hospital. Mining has resumed around the ruins.

Other nearby ghost towns are Austin Island, Austin Mainland (20km south on Lake Austin), the 'Dead Finish' (10km west), Pinnacles (24km east) and Tuckanarra (40km north).

Some 30km west is the **Big Bell Mine**. The original town has a few remaining old buildings but access to the mine is restricted as mining has resumed.

Places to Stay & Eat The *Cue Caravan Park* (☎ 9963 1107) has tent/powered sites at $7/12 for two and the *Murchison Club Motel Hotel* (☎ 9963 1020), in Austin St, has overpriced single/double units for $80/95 – they can charge what they like as there is a desperate accommodation shortage. The *Dorsett Guest House* (☎ 9963 1286), 6 Austin St, is in a converted hotel (built in 1892) and singles/doubles are $40/55.

Like a number of towns in the Murchison, there are station stays available. *Nallan Station* (☎ 9963 1054), 11km north of Cue, has shearer's quarters/cottage/homestead rooms for $12/20/65 per person; 'homesteaders' have all meals included.

The Murchison Club Hotel has a restaurant. You can get a coffee from the *Breakaway Cafe* in Austin St.

Wilgie Mia & Walga Rock

The Murchison region has a number of significant Aboriginal sites. Two of the most celebrated are the Wilgie Mia Red Ochre Mine and Walga Rock.

Wilgie Mia is 64km north-west of Cue via Glen Station. Red ochre has possibly been mined here by the Aborigines for more than 30,000 years. They used stone hammers and wooden wedges to remove thousands of tonnes of rock in order to get to the ochre, believed to have been traded as far away as Queensland. There is no doubt that Wilgie Mia features a great deal in stories from the Dreaming.

Walga Rock (also known as Walganna), about 50km south-west of Cue via Austin Downs Station, is a rock monolith which juts 50m out of the surrounding scrub. It is one of the most significant Aboriginal art sites in WA. The 60m rock-shelter at its base houses a gallery of desert-style paintings of lizards, birds and animals and hand stencils in red, white and yellow ochre. Not surprisingly, *walga* means 'ochre painting' in the Warragi language. The red ochre comes from Wilgie Mia, 65km to the north-east.

At the northern end of the gallery, a ship, with twin masts, funnel and four wavy lines beneath, is depicted. Several theories have been advanced as to its origins, including one that it was painted by shipwrecked sailors.

Meekatharra

Meekatharra (population 1200), 765km north of Perth and 540km north-east of Geraldton, is a mining and administrative centre. The name means 'place of little water'. At one time it was a railhead for cattle brought down from the Northern Territory and the East Kimberley along the Canning stock route. There are shells of various old gold towns and workings in the area.

Five km north of town, off the Gascoyne Junction Rd, are **Peace Gorge** and **The Granites**, an area of rock formations.

From Meekatharra, you can travel south via Wiluna and Leonora (see The Southern Outback chapter) to the Kalgoorlie goldfields. It's over 700km to Kalgoorlie, more than half of it on unsealed road.

Places to Stay & Eat The *Meekatharra Caravan Park* (☎ 9981 1253) has expensive tent/powered sites for $11/12.50 for two, and the *Meekatharra Motel Hotel* (☎ 9981 1021), on Main St, has single/double units for $35/50. More expensive are the rooms at the *Royal Mail Hotel* (☎ 9981 1148), Main St, at $55/75. The *Auski Inland Motel Hotel* (☎ 9981 1433), also on Main St, tops the range at a whopping $95/102.

Readers have made recommendations on places to eat. In this 'place of little water' there are a few gems. In Main St, there is the *Balcony Coffee Shop* with a functioning cappuccino machine. One reader reports one of the 'great chefs of the Outback' at the Auski Inland Motel restaurant.

Another reader dobbed in the *Royal Mail* where you get two courses for $15, and reports that it is rollicking on Friday nights. The pizzas in the *Commercial* ('The Commie') are good value and cost from $10 to $18 – try their cocktail 'Sex in the Bush' (a mere $7), or risk ordering one of the 'yuppie beers' from their blacklist. The brave may venture into the *Meekatharra* for a beer – be careful, as fights are rife.

Central West Coast

This chapter covers a huge area of the WA coast and interior. It extends from Dongara-Port Denison to the Gascoyne River and Carnarvon (about 600km as the crow flies) and out to the eastern apex of Mt Augustus, 350km from the Indian Ocean.

The Batavia Coast lies in this area and has much of historical and scenic interest: the gorges of Kalbarri National Park; the World Heritage area of Shark Bay with ancient stromatolites; the shell beaches and the dolphins of Monkey Mia; the world's largest rock at Mt Augustus; and the rugged Kennedy Ranges in the Gascoyne.

Batavia Coast

Since 1985, the strip of coast from Green Head and Leeman to Kalbarri has been referred to as the Batavia Coast, evoking the memory of the many shipwrecks which have occurred along the coast, especially that of the *Batavia* (see the boxed aside 'Dutch Shipwrecks' in this chapter).

The Batavia Coast combines rich history with many features of natural beauty. Sneak a look at the past in Greenough Hamlet, Northampton, Walkaway, the convict ruins near Port Gregory and the museums of Geraldton. There are many areas of abundant wildflowers, particularly beside the magnificent gorges of Kalbarri National Park as well as left and right of the Brand Highway. The abundant fauna of the Houtman Abrolhos, once known only as the site of shipwrecks or a place to gather crayfish (rock lobster), is finally being appreciated.

The distance from Perth to Geraldton is 421km. From Perth, follow the Brand Highway (National Highway 1) through the towns of Gingin and Badgingarra, and past the turn-off to Jurien and the Pinnacles Desert (see under North Coast in the Around

HIGHLIGHTS

- The spectacular sea cliffs, remote river gorges and wildflowers of the Kalbarri area
- The cathedral and museums in Geraldton, and the nearby historic hamlets of Greenough and Walkaway
- The ancient stromatolites of Hamelin Pool, Shark Bay
- The 'world-famous' dolphins of Monkey Mia, Shark Bay
- A sunset dip in the hot tubs of François Péron National Park
- Diving among the stunning coral beds around the Houtman Abrolhos Islands
- Climbing to the top of Mt Augustus, the world's largest single rock

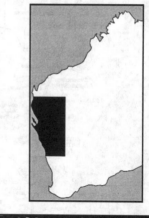

Perth chapter). The towns of Green Head and Leeman can be reached from the turn-offs at Halfway Mill or Eneabba. The Brand Highway joins the Midland Rd (State Highway 116) 8km east of Dongara-Port Denison and more or less hugs the coast from there to Geraldton.

Many national parks, famed for wildflower displays, are found to the west and east of the highway (see the Around Perth chapter for

243

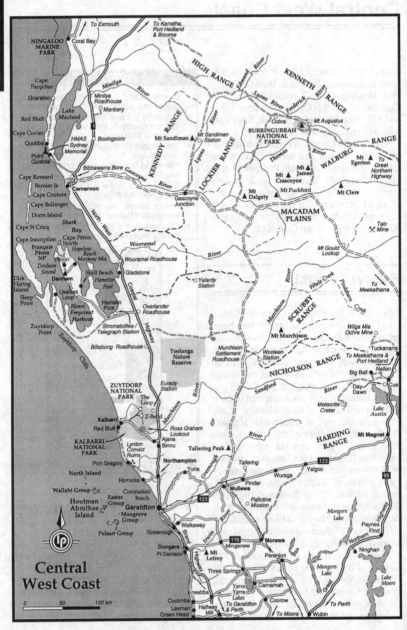

Central
West Coast

Dutch Shipwrecks

During the 17th century, ships of the Dutch East India Company, sailing from Europe to Batavia (now Jakarta), would head due east from the Cape of Good Hope then beat up the WA coast to Indonesia. It only took a small miscalculation for a ship to run aground on the coast and a few did just that, usually with disastrous results. The west coast of Australia is often decidedly inhospitable and the chances of rescue at that time were remote.

Four wrecks, once belonging to the Dutch East India Company, have been located, including the *Batavia* – the earliest and, in many ways, the most interesting.

In 1629, the *Batavia* went aground on the Houtman Abrolhos Islands, off the coast of Geraldton. The survivors set up camp, sent off a rescue party to Batavia in the ship's boat and waited. It took three months for a rescue party to arrive and in that time a mutiny had taken place and more than 120 of the survivors had been murdered. The ringleaders were hanged, and two mutineers were unceremoniously dumped on the coast just south of modern-day Kalbarri.

In 1656, the *Vergulde Draeck* struck a reef about 100km north of Perth and although a party of seven survivors made its way to Batavia, no trace, other than a few scattered coins, was found of the other survivors who had straggled ashore.

The *Zuytdorp* ran aground beneath the towering cliffs north of Kalbarri in 1712. Wine bottles, other relics and the remains of fires have been found on the cliff top. The discovery of the extremely rare Ellis van Creveld syndrome (rife in Holland at the time the ship ran aground) in children of Aboriginal descent poses the question: did the *Zuytdorp* survivors pass the gene on to Aborigines they assimilated with 300 years ago?

In 1727, the *Zeewijk* followed the ill-fated *Batavia* to destruction on the Houtman Abrolhos. Again a small party of survivors made its way to Batavia but many of the remaining sailors died before they could be rescued. Many relics from these shipwrecks, particularly the *Batavia*, can be seen today in the museums in Fremantle and Geraldton. A good account is the *Islands of Angry Ghosts* by Hugh Edwards (1966) who led the expedition which discovered the wreck of the *Batavia*. ∎

---

information on the national parks near Cervantes and Jurien).

DONGARA-PORT DENISON

The main road comes back to the coast 360km north of Perth at Dongara. This is a pleasant little town with fine beaches, plenty of places serving crayfish and a main street lined with Moreton Bay figs. Dongara, which means 'Meeting Place of Seals' in Aboriginal, was first settled in 1850 and was surveyed for use as a town site in 1852. A jetty was built at nearby Port Irwin (later known as Denison) in 1860.

The Dongara-Port Denison tourist office (☎ 9927 1404) is in the old police station at 5 Waldeck St; it is open weekdays from 9 am to 5 pm, weekends from 10 am to 2 pm. It provides a comprehensive free pamphlet.

Russ Cottage, on Point Leander Drive, was built in 1870; it is open on Sunday from 10 am to noon. The **Royal Steam Flour Mill**, easily seen from the Brand Highway, was built about 1894. Dongara's **Old East End**

is a collection of four restored stone colonial buildings and stables dating from 1860; there is a resident blacksmith and entry to the complex is free.

Just over the Irwin River is Port Denison. The Irwin river mouth is a great place to watch birds such as pelicans and cormorants.

Places to Stay & Eat

There are four caravan parks in these twin coastal towns. Two recommended ones are the *Dongara Denison Beach* (☎ 9927 1131), on Denison Beach, with powered sites/on-site vans for $14/28; and the very friendly *Seaspray* (☎ 9927 1165), 81 Church St, with powered sites/on-site vans for $12/26. The latter is sheltered from the sea breezes by a large grassed wall. The other parks are the *Dongara Strata* (☎ 9927 1840), Point Leander Drive; and the *Dongara Denison Tourist Park* (☎ 9927 1210), George St.

The *Dongara Backpackers* (☎ 9927 1581) is at 32 Waldeck St. It is a comfortable, friendly place with rooms in an old house or

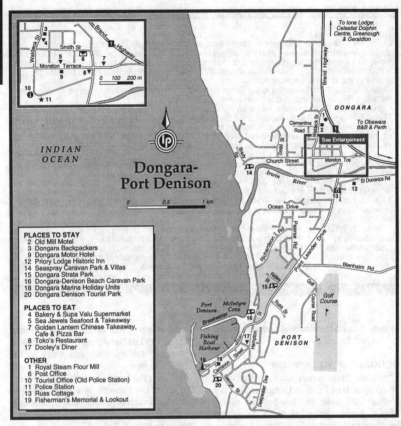

INDIAN
OCEAN

Dongara-
Port Denison

PLACES TO STAY
2 Old Mill Motel
3 Dongara Backpackers
9 Dongara Motor Hotel
12 Priory Lodge Historic Inn
14 Seaspray Caravan Park & Villas
15 Dongara Strata Park
16 Dongara-Denison Beach Caravan Park
18 Dongara Marina Holiday Units
20 Dongara Denison Tourist Park

PLACES TO EAT
4 Bakery & Supa Valu Supermarket
5 Sea Jewels Seafood & Takeaway
7 Golden Lantern Chinese Takeaway,
   Cafe & Pizza Bar
8 Toko's Restaurant
17 Dooley's Diner

OTHER
1 Royal Steam Flour Mill
6 Post Office
10 Tourist Office (Old Police Station)
11 Police Station
13 Russ Cottage
19 Fisherman's Memorial & Lookout

in a nearby train carriage. There is a pleasant
verandah overlooking the volleyball court;
the cost is \$12/26 for dorm/twin rooms.

The *Old Mill Motel* (☎ 9927 1200), on the
Brand Highway by the Royal Steam Flour
Mill, has single/double units for \$45/55; the
Dongara Motor Hotel (☎ 9927 1023),
Moreton Terrace, has rooms for \$50/60; and
the *Dongara Marina Holiday Units* (☎ 9927
1486), 4 George St in Port Denison, are from
\$65 to \$93 for two.

The *Priory Lodge Historic Inn* (☎ 9927
1090), 9 St Dominics Rd, is a good accommodation alternative (it was built in 1881)

with rooms for \$20/30; and *Obawara B&B*
(☎ 9927 1043), 5km east of Dongara, is a
farm property with doubles for \$60 (DB&B
is \$90 for two).

New Age devotees will find inspiration in
the ley lines and chakra points of the *Iona
Lodge: Celestial Dolphin Centre* (☎ 9927
1206), to the north-west of Dongara.

Some 58km south of Dongara is the
Western Flora Caravan Park (☎ 9955 2030),
special because it is in the heart of one of the
most diverse and dense floral regions in the
world. Several tracks branch out from the
park into the wonderland of native plant

species; a must for foreign visitors. Powered sites/on-site vans are $13/25 for two, and two-room chalets with TV are $45. There are backpackers' cabins for $12 per person.

In Dongara, try *Toko's Restaurant* at 38 Moreton Terrace. Also on Moreton Terrace is the *Sea Jewels Seafood & Takeaway* for delicious fish and chips, chilli mussels and garlic prawn rolls (and if you can afford it, crayfish). The *Golden Lantern*, a Chinese place at the end of Moreton Terrace, is close to a cafe and a pizza bar. The bakery on Waldeck St sells a range of sticky buns. There is a barbecue area and a restaurant in the motor hotel.

On a fine day the verandah at *Dooley's*, on Ocean Drive in Denison, is popular.

GREENOUGH

Further north, about 20km south of Geraldton (and 400km north of Perth), is Greenough, once a busy little mining town but now a quiet farming centre. The fascinat-ing **Greenough Historical Hamlet** contains 11 19th century buildings restored by the National Trust; guided tours are run daily and it is well worth a visit ($4/2/10 for adults/children/families). The Pioneer Museum, open daily from 8 am to 4 pm, has some fine historical displays. You should allow a day to explore this area if you are staying in Geraldton for a few days. Get a copy of the *Greenough-Walkaway Heritage Trail* pamphlet from the Geraldton-Greenough tourist office.

The large stone **flour mill** was built by the Clinch family in 1858. Opposite is **Cliff Grange**, a beautifully restored nine room National Trust property which is open to the public from 9 am to 4.30 pm, Wednesday to Sunday. Out on Company Rd is the restored **Hampton Arms**, formerly a wayside inn (see Places to Stay).

Look for the flood gums in the local paddocks – the **'leaning trees'** (*Eucalyptus*

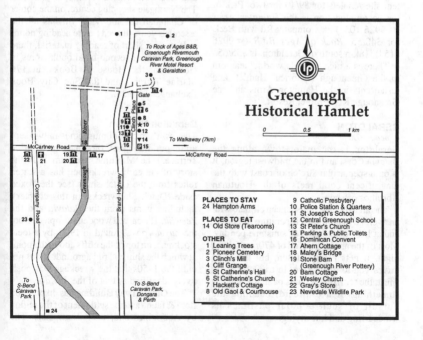

Greenough Historical Hamlet

0   0.5   1 km

To Rock of Ages B&B, Greenough Rivermouth Caravan Park, Greenough River Motel Resort & Geraldton

To Walkaway (7km)

McCartney Road

PLACES TO STAY		9 Catholic Presbytery
24 Hampton Arms		10 Police Station & Quarters
		11 St Joseph's School
PLACES TO EAT		12 Central Greenough School
14 Old Store (Tearooms)		13 St Peter's Church
		15 Parking & Public Toilets
OTHER		16 Dominican Convent
1 Leaning Trees		17 Ahern Cottage
2 Pioneer Cemetery		18 Maley's Bridge
3 Clinch's Mill		19 Stone Barn
4 Cliff Grange		(Greenough River Pottery)
5 St Catherine's Hall		20 Barn Cottage
6 St Catherine's Church		21 Wesley Church
7 Hackett's Cottage		22 Gray's Store
8 Old Gaol & Courthouse		23 Nevedale Wildlife Park

To S-Bend Caravan Park

To S-Bend Caravan Park, Dongara & Perth

camaldulensis) – deferring to the strong salt winds off the ocean.

It is about 7km east from Greenough Hamlet to Walkaway, another interesting old township, with the atmospheric old *Walkaway Tavern* and an old train station **museum**. Some 20km from Walkaway is **Ellendale Pool**, a great picnic spot at the foot of cliffs which provides welcome respite from the long grind on Highway 1.

Places to Stay & Eat

The *Greenough Rivermouth Caravan Park* (☎ 9963 5845), 14km north of Greenough Hamlet at Cape Burney, has tent/powered sites for $12/15 for two, on-site vans for $25 and cabins for $45; there is a camper's kitchen. Not far away is the classy *Greenough River Motel Resort* (☎ 9921 5888) which has singles/doubles for $60/75.

The poorly located *S-Bend Caravan Park* (☎ 9926 1072), on the prominent S-bend on the Brand Highway south of Greenough, has tent sites/chalets for $9/40 for two. Pick of the accommodation is the *Hampton Arms* (☎ 9926 1057) on Company Rd with B&B for $40/55. *Rock of Ages B&B* (☎ 9926 1154), 18km south of Geraldton, is $55/65.

There is a nice 'ye olde worlde' tearoom in the Greenough Historical Hamlet, and restaurants in the Hampton Arms and the Greenough River Motel Resort.

GERALDTON
• *pop 35,000*

Geraldton is the major town along the Batavia Coast and in the midwest region. It is on a spectacular stretch of coast with the magnificent coral reefs of the Houtman Abrolhos offshore.

The area has a Mediterranean climate with an average maximum temperature of 28.8°C and at least eight hours of sunshine per day. Most of the annual rainfall of 470mm falls at night. It gets plenty of sun, but the wind drives you to distraction. In true optimistic spirit, the tourist brochures paint the wind as something of a drawcard, enabling the pursuit of such popular pastimes as windsurfing and kite-flying.

If you are tempted by crayfish fresh from the boat then this is the place to come as the town is the centre of the multimillion-dollar crayfish industry.

Orientation & Information

Geraldton stretches for nearly 16km along the Indian Ocean coast, from Drummonds Cove in the north to Greenough River in the south. The main part of the city and its harbour is in the centre. On Marine Terrace and Chapman Rd you will find most of the businesses and services.

The Geraldton-Greenough tourist office (☎ 9921 3999; fax 9964 2445) is in the Bill Sewell complex on Chapman Rd, diagonally across from the train station and beside the Northgate shopping centre. It is open from 8.30 am to 5 pm weekdays, from 9 am to 4.30 pm Saturday and public holidays and 9.30 am to 4.30 pm on Sunday.

The main post office is on Durlacher St and most of the banks are in The Mall area. The Northgate shopping centre, on the corner of Chapman Rd and View St, has all the essentials you will need before heading north.

If you are short of reading material, there are a couple of second-hand book stores in Geraldton: the House of Books, at 176 Marine Terrace, and the Sun City Book Exchange at No 36.

Geraldton Museum

The town's excellent museum is in two separate buildings not far apart on Marine Terrace. The Maritime Museum tells the story of the early wrecks and has assorted relics from the Dutch ships (see the boxed aside 'Dutch Shipwrecks' in this chapter), including items from the *Batavia* and the *Zeewijk*. The carved wooden sternpiece from the *Zuytdorp* was found in 1927, by a local stockman, on top of the cliffs above the point at which the ship had run aground. It was not until the 1950s that the wreckage was positively identified as that of the *Zuytdorp*.

The Old Railway Building has displays on flora & fauna and the settlement of the region by Aborigines and, later, Europeans. The

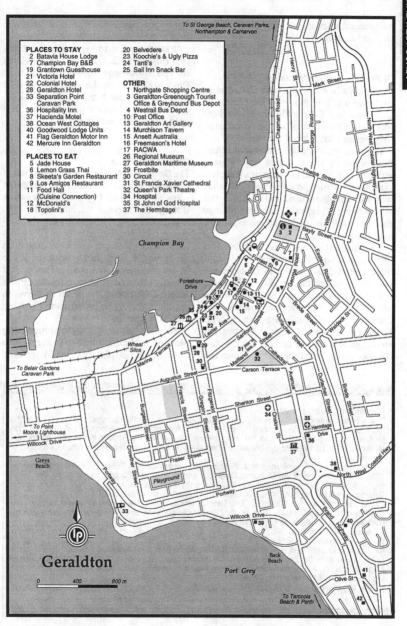

PLACES TO STAY
2 Batavia House Lodge
7 Champion Bay B&B
19 Grantown Guesthouse
21 Victoria Hotel
22 Colonial Hotel
28 Geraldton Hotel
33 Separation Point
Caravan Park
36 Hospitality Inn
37 Hacienda Motel
38 Ocean West Cottages
40 Goodwood Lodge Units
41 Flag Geraldton Motor Inn
42 Mercure Inn Geraldton

PLACES TO EAT
5 Jade House
6 Lemon Grass Thai
8 Skeeta's Garden Restaurant
9 Los Amigos Restaurant
11 Food Hall
(Cuisine Connection)
12 McDonald's
18 Topolini's

20 Belvedere
23 Koochie's & Ugly Pizza
24 Tanti's
25 Sail Inn Snack Bar

OTHER
1 Northgate Shopping Centre
3 Geraldton-Greenough Tourist
Office & Greyhound Bus Depot
4 Westrail Bus Depot
10 Post Office
13 Geraldton Art Gallery
14 Murchison Tavern
15 Ansett Australia
16 Freemason's Hotel
17 RACWA
26 Regional Museum
27 Geraldton Maritime Museum
29 Frostbite
30 Circuit
31 St Francis Xavier Cathedral
32 Queen's Park Theatre
34 Hospital
35 St John of God Hospital
37 The Hermitage

To St George Beach, Caravan Parks,
Northampton & Carnarvon

Champion Bay

Foreshore
Drive

*Wheat
Silos*

— To Belair Gardens
Caravan Park

— To Point
Moore Lighthouse

Greys
Beach

Playground

Geraldton

0   400   800 m

Port Grey

Back
Beach

To Tarcoola
Beach & Perth

museum complex is open daily from 10 am to 4 pm; admission is free.

St Francis Xavier Cathedral

Geraldton's St Francis Xavier Cathedral is just one of a number of buildings in Geraldton and WA's midwest designed by Monsignor John Hawes (see the boxed aside 'Monsignor John Hawes' below.

Construction of the Byzantine-style cathedral began in 1916, a year after Hawes arrived in Geraldton, but his plans were too grandiose and the partially built cathedral was not completed until 1938. This is the most striking of Hawes' Australian buildings and the interior is unlike any cathedral you may have seen!

The architecture is a blend of styles. The twin towers, with their arched openings, a large central dome similar to Brunellesci's famous cupola of the Duomo in Florence, Italy, and a tower with a coned roof, would not be out of place in the Loire Valley, France. The interior is just as striking with Romanesque columns, huge arches beneath an octagonal dome and zebra striping within the stone walls. When completed, Hawes felt

that he had 'caught the rhythm of a poem in stone'.

While he was working on the St John of God Hospital in Cathedral Ave, Hawes lived in **The Hermitage** across the road, in Onslow St. He had designed this unusual dwelling, built for him in 1937 by a local contractor, as a possible place to retire; it is open by appointment only.

Other Attractions

The **Geraldton Art Gallery**, on the corner of Chapman Rd and Durlacher St, is open daily; entry is free. The **Lighthouse Keeper's Cottage** on Chapman Rd, built in 1870 and now the Geraldton Historical Society's headquarters, is open Thursday from 10 am to 4 pm. You can look out over Geraldton from the **Waverley Heights Lookout**, on Brede St, or watch the crayfish boats at Fisherman's Wharf, at the end of Marine Terrace. **Point Moore Lighthouse**, on Willcock Drive, in operation since 1878, is also worth a visit but you can't go inside.

There also tours to the **crayfish processing plant** on weekdays from November to June (9.30 am and 1.30 pm); entry is a $1 donation.

Monsignor John Hawes

The architect-cum-priest Monsignor John Hawes has left a magnificent legacy of buildings in the midwest. He was born in Richmond, England, in 1876. After receiving architectural training in London he converted to Anglicanism and, following his ordination in 1903, worked in the London slums as a missionary. He then went to the Bahamas where he used his architectural skill to rebuild a number of churches.

Two years later, he converted to Catholicism and went to study in Rome. He came to Australia in 1915 at the invitation of the Bishop of Geraldton and worked as a country pastor in the Murchison region. In the 24 years from 1915 until 1939 he worked tirelessly as a parish priest at Mullewa and Greenough and, as well, designed 24 buildings, 16 of which were later built.

His best works are the **Church of Our Lady of Mt Carmel** and the **Priest House** in Mullewa, the **Church of the Holy Cross** in Morawa, the **Church of St Joseph in Perenjori** and the unforgettable **Cathedral of St Francis Xavier** in Geraldton.

Hawes left Australia in 1939 after witnessing the opening of his controversial Geraldton cathedral the previous year. Plans for a cathedral in Perth had been rejected and the cathedral he had struggled for 22 years to build was now complete. His only regret at leaving Australia was that his fox terrier Dominie was to be left behind. He went to Cat Island in the Bahamas and lived as a hermit in a small stone building on a hilltop. He died in a Miami hospital in 1956 and his body was brought back to a tomb he had built for himself on Cat Island.

The *Monsignor Hawes Heritage Trail* pamphlet is available from the tourist office in Geraldton. ∎

Organised Tours

Touch the Wild Safaris (☎ 9921 8435) organises trips into the hinterland around Geraldton, and you get the chance to see a wide range of flora & fauna. The cost for adults is $65 for a half-day, $80 for a full day; children are $15 less.

Red Earth Safaris (☎ 9964 1543) has wildflower tours, Kalbarri day trips ($55) and outback safaris ($165). Mid-West Tours (☎ 9921 5089) ranges far wider to Mt Augustus, the wildflowers and the Murchison goldfields.

There are also boat and plane trips to the outlying islands of the Houtman Abrolhos (see that section later). Top Cat Boat Charter (☎ (015) 990 047) have diving, fishing and windsurfing tours (the cost is $100 per day per person, with a minimum of six).

Special Events

Geraldton celebrates the Seafood Festival on the long weekend in June celebrating the Queen's birthday. The Festival of Geraldton happens in the October school holidays for four days; there are dragon boat races, parades and partying.

Places to Stay

Camping The closest caravan parks to the city centre are *Separation Point* (☎ 9921 2763), at the corner of Portway and Separation Way; and *Belair Gardens* (☎ 9921 1997), on Willcock Drive at Point Moore; both have powered sites/on-site vans for about $13/30 for two. The excellent *Sun City Tourist Park* (☎ 9938 1655), Bosley St, Sunset Beach, is a little way north of town but well worth it for its beach location; tent/powered sites are $12/15, and the tidy park cabins are from $45 for two. There are other parks; ask at the tourist office.

Hostels The *Batavia House Lodge* (☎ 9964 3001), on the corner of Chapman Rd and Bayly St in the Bill Sewell complex, has good facilities and beds for $12 per night; a double is $25. The *Chapman Valley Farm Backpackers* (☎ 9920 5160), 25km out of town, is in an historic homestead. They pick up from Geraldton at 11 am; beds are $12.

Guesthouses & Hotels Geraldton has plenty of old-fashioned seaside guesthouses, particularly along Marine Terrace. The *Grantown Guesthouse* (☎ 9921 3275), at No 172, has singles/doubles for $22/44, including breakfast.

Cheap rooms are also available at some of the older-style hotels such as the *Colonial*, Fitzgerald St; the *Victoria*, Marine Terrace; and the *Geraldton* ('Gero'), Gregory St; count on about $20 per person.

B&Bs For information on B&Bs contact the tourist office. Good examples are *Champion Bay* (☎ 9921 7624), 31 Snowdon St, at $80 for a double; and *Bluntisham* (☎ 9938 1448), Sexton Drive (12km from town), at $50 a double, with cooked breakfast.

Motels & Units The *Hacienda Motel* (☎ 9921 2155), on Durlacher St, has singles/doubles at $50/60; family units are available. The *Mercure Inn Geraldton* (☎ 9921 2455), on the Brand Highway, is one of those old dependables at $96 for one or two people; the car is allowed in free. Another 'chain' place is the *Hospitality Inn* (☎ 9921 1422), 169 Cathedral Ave, from $80 to $97 for two. The *Flag Geraldton Motor Inn* (☎ 9964 4777), at 107 Brand Highway, is an old favourite of travelling salespersons. The rooms, with all the comforts, are from $70 to $80, and a light breakfast is included.

Ocean West Cottages (☎ 9921 1047), on the corner of Hadda Way and Willcock Drive at Mahomets Beach, has self-contained cottages for around $65 a double. *Goodwood Lodge Units* (☎ 9921 5666), on the corner of the Brand Highway and Durlacher St, also has self-contained units for $55.

The *African Reef Resort Motel Hotel* (☎ 9964 5566), at 5 Broadhead Ave, Tarcoola Beach, is the best of the city's places to stay, with every facility imaginable; holiday units are from $55 to $80, and comfortable rooms from $90 to $95 for two.

Places to Eat

The *Cuisine Connection*, in Durlacher St, is a food hall with Indian, Chinese and Italian food, roasts and fish and chips. The food is excellent and you should be able to get a good feed for $7. Fast-food junkies who have made the long haul from Darwin will think they have entered nirvana: *Chicken Treat*, *Hungry Jacks*, *Pizza Hut*, *McDonald's*, *KFC* and *Red Rooster* all occupy real estate in this town.

There are a number of small snack bars and cafes along Marine Terrace including: *Thuy's Cake Shop*, at No 202, which is open from 6 am for breakfast; and *Belvedere*, at No 149, with standard cafe food at down-to-earth prices. *Hardy's*, on Chapman Rd in the Bill Sewell complex, is also open for breakfast and lunches, including monster burgers. The *Sail Inn Snack Bar*, by the museum on Marine Terrace, sells burgers and fish and chips.

Chinese restaurants include the *Golden Coins*, on Marine Terrace; *Rose Chinese & Thai* in Forrest St; and the *Jade House* at 57 Marine Terrace. *Lemon Grass* at 18 Snowdon St, and *Tanti's*, at 174 Marine Terrace, are both popular Thai restaurants; expect to pay from $14 for a main meal.

At 105 Durlacher St, *Los Amigos* is a deservedly popular Mexican place (licensed). Fancier restaurants include *Reflections* on Foreshore Drive, *Skeetas Garden Restaurant* on George St and the *Boatshed* on Marine Terrace for great seafood. *Topolini's Cafe*, at 158 Marine Terrace, is a popular Italian place.

The African Reef has two good restaurants, the *Stanford* and *Reef Cafe*; at the latter a full meal is about $18.

Entertainment

Occasionally a live band plays at the Geraldton Hotel ('Gero') in Gregory St and, if you recently turned 20, chances are you would be meeting your mates here or at the Freemason's ('Freo') in The Mall, or at the *Frostbites* and *Circuit* nightclubs.

Getting There & Around

Skywest has flights from Perth to Geraldton daily. There are also flights from Geraldton to Broome, Carnarvon, Karratha and Exmouth on Tuesday and Thursday.

Westrail and Greyhound have regular services from Perth to Geraldton for around $40 one way. Westrail services continue northeast to Meekatharra (two days weekly) or north to Kalbarri (three weekly). Greyhound continues on Highway 1 through Port Hedland and Broome to Darwin. Westrail stops at the train station, while Greyhound stops at the Bill Sewell complex.

There is a local bus service (☎ 9921 1034) which provides access to all nearby suburbs.

HOUTMAN ABROLHOS ISLANDS

There are 108 islands in this archipelago, about 60km off the Geraldton coast. The island groups are Wallabi, Easter and Pelsaert; North Island stands alone at the top of the archipelago.

The beautiful but treacherous reefs surrounding the islands have claimed many ships over the years. The first to nearly run aground was Frederick de Houtman of the Dutch East India Company and it is believed that the name Abrolhos comes from the Portuguese expression *Abri vossos olhos* ('Keep your eyes open'). The most famous wreck was that of the *Batavia* on 5 June 1629 with 300 people aboard (see the boxed aside 'Dutch Shipwrecks' earlier in this chapter). The survivors' shelters were probably the first European structures on Australian soil.

Guano (bird poo) was taken from the islands in the late 1800s and again during WWII when there were phosphate shortages. The islands are now the centre of the area's crayfishing industry and about 200 boats are licensed to fish there.

The most attractive feature of the islands is the wide range of fauna. Nearly 100 species of birds, some endangered, use the islands as their home. Reptiles thrive in the harsh environment and over 20 species have been recorded. Also found on some islands are the rare tammar wallaby and the Abrolhos bush rat (a subspecies of *Rattus fuscipes*).

It is below the water, however, that the Abrolhos really come into their own. The

Abrolhos are the most southerly coral islands of the Indian Ocean and the Acropora family of corals, of which the well known staghorn is a member, are found in abundance. Interwoven into this rough sea carpet are sea anemones, plate corals, the hard Tubastrea corals and seaweeds such as sargassum. One species of coral, *Gonipora pendulus*, is found only on Australia's west coast.

Getting There & Away

You are not allowed to spend the night on any of the Abrolhos Islands so all excursions are day trips. Air and diving tours to these protected and spectacular islands are available from Geraldton – check with the tourist office for details. Bird-watching tours are also conducted to the southern Abrolhos.

Force 5 Charter (☎ 9921 6416) runs trips to the Houtman Abrolhos; a day trip is $100, and a weekend away is $300. Shine Aviation Services (☎ 9923 3600) flies over the islands; the cost is $110 in a fixed-wing plane, and $160 in a seaplane (snorkelling equipment is provided on the latter trip).

NORTHAMPTON

• *pop 1500*

Northampton, 50km north of Geraldton, was settled soon after the establishment of the Swan River colony. Copper was discovered nearby at Wanerenooka in 1842 and lead was discovered six years later. Convicts were brought into the region to relieve labour shortages and there was a convict-hiring facility established at Lynton near Port Gregory from 1853 to 1856.

The Northampton tourist office (☎ 9934 1488) is in the old library on Hampton Rd.

The agricultural centre of Northampton has a number of **historic buildings** and is now making an initial foray into tourism.

St Mary's Convent, on Hampton Rd, was designed by the peripatetic Monsignor Hawes and built entirely of local stone. An early mine-manager's home, **Chiverton House**, is now a fine municipal museum ($2 entry). The stone building was constructed between 1868 and 1875. The Gwalla Church **cemetery** also tells its tales of old times.

Places to Stay & Eat

There is a caravan park (☎ 9934 1202) on the North-West Coastal Highway, with powered sites at $10 for two. Budget accommodation, with all facilities, can be found in the *Nagle Centre* (☎ 9934 1488), which was formerly the Sacred Heart Convent. It's $12 per person in two and four-bed rooms.

The *Miners Arms* (☎ 9934 1281) has singles/doubles at $30/50 and the *Northampton Motor Hotel* (☎ 9934 1240) costs $40/50 ($60 for triples).

Eurady Station (☎ 9936 1038), well to the north of Northampton, is a great place for foreign travellers who have never experienced the Outback; it's not flash, but B&B is a miniscule $20 and dinner is only $8 extra.

You can get a coffee and a snack at the *Northampton Tourist Cafe*, takeaways from the two roadhouses or counter meals from any of the hotels. The *Palette Cafe* is the fanciest place in town; lunches are $10.

HORROCKS BEACH & PORT GREGORY

From Northampton you can head west to the coast along a scenic road and, if conditions are right, north up the coast to Kalbarri.

Horrocks Beach, 22km west, is a popular holiday resort with a safe, sheltered bay. This area is an angler's paradise with catches of tailor, whiting and skipjack off the beach. Boaties can head further out in pursuit of dhufish, schnapper and blue bone groper.

It is 43km from Northampton to Port Gregory, the oldest port on the midwest coast. It is named after the explorer AC Gregory, who discovered lead in the Murchison River in 1848. Today, Port Gregory supports a commercial fishing fleet and is popular as a holiday centre.

On the way to the coast you pass the numerous ruins of the **Lynton Convict Settlement**. It was established as a convict hiring facility (for ticket-of-leave men) in 1853 and abandoned four years later.

The **Hutt Lagoon**, just before Port Gregory, is a dry salt lake that sometimes looks like a small pink inland sea. The pink colour is due to naturally occurring beta-carotene, a dye used for food colouring.

From Port Gregory you can head north on the east side of the lagoon along the very scenic Grey Rd to Kalbarri (check to see if it is suitable for 2WD); this route takes you past all the sights of the southern part of Kalbarri National Park. It should all be sealed by the year 2000. Somewhere inland from here was the secessionist Hutt River Province, once a tourist destination, but now just a colourful piece of WA's history.

Places to Stay

The *Port Gregory Caravan Park* (☎ 9935 1052), Sandford St, and the *Horrocks Beach Caravan Park* (☎ 9934 3039) have tent/powered sites for $9/12, and on-site vans for $25 for two. *Killara Cottages* (☎ 9934 3031) at Horrocks has three and four-bed cottages from $200 per week.

The *Lynton B&B* (☎ 9935 1040), next to the Lynton convict settlement, costs a reasonable $25, and has backpackers' beds in a bunkhouse for $15 per person. *Glenore Lookout Lodge* (☎ 9935 1017), off the road to Port Gregory, has doubles for $75.

KALBARRI
• *pop 2900*

Kalbarri, a popular spot with backpackers and holiday-makers, is on the coast at the mouth of the Murchison River, 66km west of the main highway. The area is appreciated for its coastline, scenic gorges and the poignant history of the west coast's Dutch shipwrecks.

In 1629, two *Batavia* mutineers (Wouter Loos and Jan Pelgrom) were marooned as punishment at Wittecarra Gully, an inlet just south of the town; it is marked today by an historical cairn. The *Zuytdorp* was wrecked about 65km north of Kalbarri in 1712. Although diving on the *Zuytdorp* is very difficult as a heavy swell and unpredictable currents batter the shoreline, divers from the Geraldton Museum did manage to raise artefacts in 1986.

The Kalbarri tourist office (☎ 9937 1104, freecall (1800) 63 9468) on Grey St is open daily from 9 am to 5 pm. The post office is on Porter St.

Things to See & Do

The **Rainbow Jungle**, an interesting rainforest bird park 4km south of town towards Red Bluff, has a number of endangered species of parrot; entry is $5/2 for adults/children and it's open daily from 9 am to 5 pm. **Recollections** on Grey St ($2 for adults) is a collection of dolls, shells, gemstones, and other memorabilia; there is a cafe attached.

Boats can be hired on the river (☎ 9937 1245) and tours can be made on the river's lower reaches on the *Kalbarri River Queen*; the cost is $14/7 for adults/kids.

There are some excellent **surfing** breaks along the coast – Jakes Corner, 3.5km to the south, is reputed to be amongst the best breaks in the state.

You can go **horse-riding** through rugged bush at the Big River Ranch (☎ 9937 1214); a three hour beach ride is $35.

Water-based activities are the domain of Kalbarri Boat Hire (☎ 9937 1245), on the foreshore opposite Murchison Caravan Park; a canoe safari up the river with a barbecue breakfast is $25 for adults.

The less energetic can feed the **pelicans** by the water in Grey St; feeding time is 8.45 am daily (when the birds are there).

Organised Tours

For tours over the Murchison River gorges, take a flight with Kalbarri Air Charter (☎ 9937 1130) from $29.

Kalbarri Coach Tours organises visits to the Loop, Z-Bend and ocean gorges ($30). It also runs a canoeing adventure tour into the gorges ($40) taking in the Fourways gullies.

Kalbarri Safari Tours (☎ 9937 1011) is a new and untested outfit – it has full day tours to the Murchison River gorges for $35 or Lucky Bay & Coastal Gorges for $75. The more adventurous can abseil into the gorges with Gordon ($40). The tourist office will provide details.

Icon Ocean Adventures (☎ 9937 1062) runs several cruises – whale watching, sunset cruises and deep-sea fishing. These operate from July to October; see the tourist office for details.

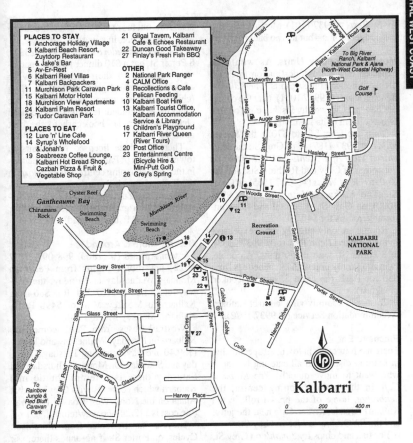

PLACES TO STAY
1 Anchorage Holiday Village
3 Kalbarri Beach Resort, Zuytdorp Restaurant & Jake's Bar
5 Av-Er-Rest
6 Kalbarri Reef Villas
7 Kalbarri Backpackers
11 Murchison Park Caravan Park
15 Kalbarri Motor Hotel
18 Murchison View Apartments
24 Kalbarri Palm Resort
25 Tudor Caravan Park

PLACES TO EAT
12 Lure 'n' Line Cafe
14 Syrup's Wholefood & Jonah's
19 Seabreeze Coffee Lounge, Kalbarri Hot Bread Shop, Cazbah Pizza & Fruit & Vegetable Shop

21 Gilgai Tavern, Kalbarri Cafe & Echoes Restaurant
22 Duncan Good Takeaway
27 Finlay's Fresh Fish BBQ

OTHER
2 National Park Ranger
4 CALM Office
8 Recollections & Cafe
9 Pelican Feeding
10 Kalbarri Boat Hire
13 Kalbarri Tourist Office, Kalbarri Accommodation Service & Library
16 Children's Playground
17 Kalbarri River Queen (River Tours)
20 Post Office
23 Entertainment Centre (Bicycle Hire & Mini-Putt Golf)
26 Grey's Spring

Kalbarri

Places to Stay

Kalbarri is a popular resort and accommodation can be tight at holiday times.

Camping & Caravans There are several caravan parks: the *Murchison Park* (☎ 9937 1005), Grey St, with powered sites for $13; the *Anchorage* (☎ 9937 1181), Anchorage Lane, with tent sites/on-site vans for $10/32 for two; and the *Tudor* (☎ 9937 1077), Porter St, with on-site vans and cabins from $28 to $38 (the kids will love the mini-zoo, others will be dismayed by the circumstances of the fauna). *Red Bluff* (☎ 9937 1080), on Red

Bluff Rd, 4km south of town, has on-site vans/chalets from $28/35 for two. There are barbecues on Wednesday and Saturday nights with hearty serves of meat and salad.

Hostels The clean, modern and 'kid-friendly' *Kalbarri Backpackers* (☎ 9937 1430), 2 Mortimer St, has dorms from $11, and family and disabled units from $40; it has been recommended by a number of travellers and would have to be one of the best of its type in WA. The owners organise snorkelling gear free of charge and point you in the right direction for other activities.

Av-Er-Rest (☎ 9937 1101), Mortimer St, also has budget rooms – but it is no backpackers'.

Motels & Holiday Units As would be expected in a holiday destination there are plenty of holiday units/resorts. The *Kalbarri Beach Resort* (☎ 9937 1061), near the corner of Grey and Clotworthy Sts, has comfortable two-bedroom units from $65.

Units are from $65 to $70 in the *Sunsea Villas* (☎ 9937 1187) at 18 Grey St; the *Murchison View Apartments* (☎ 9937 1096) on the corner of Grey and Rushton Sts; and the *Kalbarri Reef Villas* (☎ 9937 1165) on Coles St. The *Kalbarri Motor Hotel* (☎ 9937 1000), on Grey St, is central and has comfortable rooms for $40/50.

Rooms are only slightly more expensive in the *Kalbarri Palm Resort* (☎ 9937 2333), at 8 Porter St, with its 50 units. A double, twin and family unit with kitchenette is from $50 for B&B (an extra $5 with a cooked breakfast).

To stay in a family villa, contact Kalbarri Accommodation Service (☎ 9937 1072).

Places to Eat
There are four cafes in town, all specialising in seafood dishes and all catering for those who want to move quickly. The *Kalbarri Cafe* in the main shopping centre; the *Seabreeze*, home of the prawn roll, in the Kalbarri Arcade; *Rivers Cafe* near the jetty; and the BYO *Lure 'n Line* in Grey St.

For fish and chips try *Jonah's* on Grey St, and for pizza go to *Cazbah Pizza* in the shopping centre. There is a bakery (hot-bread shop) in the Kalbarri Arcade which serves up a range of pies, rolls and cakes, and *Duncan Good Takeaway* with cheap Mexican, Chinese and European dishes. In the same arcade is a fruit and vegetable shop for self-caterers. Nearby, at the *Gilgai Tavern*, you can get a decent counter meal for $7.

Vegetarians can get all their wholefood supplies at *Syrup's*, between the tourist office and Kalbarri Motor Hotel.

Finlay's Fresh Fish BBQ, Magee Crescent, in an old ice works, is a special place for a meal (most are less than $10). The decor is no frills but the meals and salads are filling – the atmosphere, in a word, is great.

The *Kalbarri Palm Resort* (☎ 9937 2333), 8 Porter St, has a $10 dinner (which guarantees entrance to their cinema showing current reel films). A giant potato with filling (chicken or meat curry) and access to the salad bar is included. It is the only licensed cinema in Australia – book early for the front couches.

There are three licensed restaurants in town: the *Palm* of Palm Resort fame, *Echoes* in the main shopping centre and *Zuytdorp* in the Kalbarri Beach Resort.

Behind the Zuytdorp is *Jake's*, a 1970s-style bar, with great counter meals ($9 for steak or grilled fish with salad).

Getting There & Around
Western Airlines (☎ (1800) 998 097, 9277 4022) has return flights from Perth on Monday, Wednesday and Friday; the one-way/return fare is $167/334. It is $86 from Kalbarri to Monkey Mia (or $498 Perth, Kalbarri, Monkey Mia to Perth).

Westrail buses from Perth come into Kalbarri on Monday, Wednesday and Friday ($59.40 one way) returning Tuesday, Thursday and Saturday. On Monday, Thursday and Saturday there is a return shuttle into Kalbarri which connects with Greyhound at Ajana on the North-West Coastal Highway (the cost is $13/24 one way/return).

Bicycles can be rented from Murchison Cycles, on Porter St; if no-one is there, ask at the Mini-Putt complex next door.

KALBARRI NATIONAL PARK
This national park has over 1860 sq km of bushland including some scenic gorges on the **Murchison River**. The Murchison starts near Peak Hill, 80 km north of Meekatharra. It once flowed over a smooth red plain of Tumblagooda sandstone but shifting of the earth's surface in the region, about two million years ago, caused the river to erode deep into the rock. This created the meandering 80km gorge.

From Kalbarri, it's about 40km to the **Loop** and **Z-Bend Gorge**, two impressive

The western grey kangaroo can be spotted in Kalbarri National Park.

gorges with steep banded cliffs. Further east along the Ajana-Kalbarri Rd are two lookouts: **Hawk's Head** (a must-see) and **Ross Graham** (he was a noted conservationist).

Short **walking trails** lead into the gorges from the road access points but there are also longer walks. The walk around the Loop, which begins and ends at Nature's Window, takes six hours. It takes about two days to walk between Z-Bend, a narrow ravine, and the Loop. The 38km walk from Ross Graham Lookout to the Loop requires a strenuous four days.

South of Kalbarri town there is a string of cliff faces where you can take in rugged, beautiful seascapes. These include **Red Bluff** (a red sandstone outcrop) and the banded **Rainbow Valley**. **Pot Alley**, **Eagle Gorge** and **Natural Bridge** have been sculpted by the surrounding seas. All these sights can be reached by car; the road has recently been sealed. There is an 8km **coastal walking trail** which takes from three to five hours; the drop-off is Eagle Gorge, and the pick-up at Natural Bridge.

The park puts on a particularly fine display of wildflowers in the spring including everlastings, banksia, grevillea, kangaroo paw, acacia and the ubiquitous grass tree. More than 850 varieties of wildflower have been recorded in the park, many of which can be seen from the roads. There is also a great range of fauna. In addition to euros, rock wallabies, red and western grey kangaroos, another nine species of mammal are found. Emus are frequently spotted and over 170 bird species have been recorded.

Shark Bay

Shark Bay World Heritage and Marine Park has some spectacular beaches, important seagrass beds, the stromatolites at Hamelin Pool and the famous dolphins of Monkey Mia. The peninsulas and nearby islands are important sanctuaries for many endangered species such as the Shark Bay mouse and the greater stick-nest rat (see the boxed aside 'A Story of Survival' in this section). Shark Bay is undoubtedly one of Australia's best, but as yet undeveloped, eco-tourism destinations.

History

Prior to colonisation, the Shark Bay region was part of the traditional lands of the Nganda and Malgana people. There was an abundant supply of seafood such as shellfish and turtles, and fossilised mudwhelks have been found in midden sites near Little Lagoon. More evidence of earlier Aboriginal occupation has been found near Eagle Bluff and in caves near Monkey Mia. Evidence has been dated back 22,000 years.

The first recorded landing on Australian soil by a European took place at Shark Bay in 1616 when the Dutch explorer Dirk Hartog landed on the island that now bears

---

Shark Bay's World Heritage Listing

Shark Bay is one of only 12 places on earth to have satisfied all four natural criteria for World Heritage listing. World Heritage sites must:

- be outstanding examples representing a major stage of the earth's evolutionary history
- be outstanding examples representing significant ongoing geological processes, biological evolution and human interaction with the natural environment
- contain superlative natural phenomena, formations or features
- contain important and significant natural habitats where threatened species of outstanding universal value still survive ∎

his name. He nailed an inscribed plate to a post on the beach but a later Dutch visitor, de Vlamingh, collected it. It's now in a museum in the Netherlands, although there's a reproduction in the Geraldton Museum.

The many French names are the legacy of the French explorers in the *Géographe* and *Naturaliste* (June 1801) but the name Bay of Sharks (now Shark Bay) was given much earlier by William Dampier in August 1699 (see under History in the Facts about Western Australia chapter). Mr Goodwin, Dampier's cook, is the first known European to be buried on Australian soil.

Shark Bay is the name loosely applied to the two fingers of land which jut into the Indian Ocean and the lagoons which surround them. Denham, the main population centre of Shark Bay, is 132km off the main highway from the Overlander Roadhouse. Monkey Mia, on the eastern finger, is 26km north-east of Denham on a sealed road.

KALBARRI TO DENHAM

Between the Kalbarri turn-off and Shark Bay there is, well, not much! Aficionados of roadhouses will be delighted by the *Billabong* (☎ 9942 5980), a perfect architectural example of this roadside attraction, perched halfway between Geraldton and Carnarvon. Equally enthralling is the *Overlander* (☎ 9942 5916), on the way to Shark Bay.

On the way into Denham, the first turn-off (27km from the highway) is a 6km road to **Hamelin Pool**, a marine reserve which has the world's best known colony of **stromatolites** (see the boxed aside in this chapter). An interpretive boardwalk has been constructed, lessening damage to the delicate structures.

Go into the old **Telegraph Station** (☎ 9942 5905), established in 1884, to get information on these unique life forms before tackling the boardwalk. This is the only intact repeater station left in WA and served as a telephone exchange until 1977. There is a dusty caravan park, barbecues and small tearooms at Hamelin.

Just over 50km from Hamelin is the 2000 sq km **Nanga Station**, with its old homestead building constructed of cut shell blocks. The complex has a liquor licence and is the only station licensed in Australia. There is also a small pioneer museum, BYO restaurant and a sheltered bay for swimming and fishing. Integrated into the station is the *Nanga Bay Resort* (☎ 9948 3992) which has basic bunkhouse accommodation for $12 per person, cabins for $45, chalets from $80 and holiday units for $90 for two. Catamarans, sailboards and dinghies can be hired at the beach.

The 110km stretch of **Shell Beach** is solid shells nearly 10m deep! In places in Shark Bay, the shells *(Fragum erugatum)* are so tightly packed that they can be cut into

---

Bird-Watching

The Shark Bay region contains a variety of habitats, making it a great location for birdwatching. In addition to being at the northern limit of the range of many birds of the south-west, it is a preferred location for birds of the arid and semi-arid zones, and for marine birds, waterbirds and shorebirds.

At the southern end of Shark Bay look for, among others, these south-western species: the blue-breasted fairy wren *(Malurus pulcherrimus)*, brown-headed honeyeater *(Melithreptus brevirostris)* and golden whistler *(Pachycephala pectoralis)*.

On the Péron Peninsula, the crimson chats *(Ephthianura tricolor)*, southern whiteface *(Aphelocephala leucopis)*, white-winged fairy wren *(Malurus leucopterus)*, chiming wedgebill *(Psophodes occidentalis)* and rare thick-billed grass wren *(Amytornis textilis)* may be observed. Incidentally, you will probably hear the wedgebill ask 'Did you get drunk?' before you spot it.

Marine birds are numerous and include the wedge-tailed shearwater, terns and the white-bellied sea eagle. The mangroves at the north of the peninsula attract, to the southern limit of their range, the mangrove grey-fantail *(Rhipidura phasiana)* and yellow-white-eye *(Zosterops lutea)*. ■

Stromatolites

The dolphins at Monkey Mia didn't solely contribute to the listing of Shark Bay as a World Heritage region. Perhaps the biggest single contributor was the existence of stromatolites (rocky formations) at Hamelin Pool. These structures are thousands of years old having evolved over 3½ billion years.

Hamelin Pool is suited to the growth of stromatolites because of the clarity and hypersalinity of the water. In essence, each stromatolite is covered in a form of cyanobacterial microbe shaped like algae which – during daily photosynthesis – wave around. At night the microbe folds over, often trapping calcium and carbonate ions dissolved in the water. The sticky chemicals they exude adds to the concretion of another layer on the surface of the stromatolite.

These are the most accessible stromatolites in the world, spectacularly set amidst the turquoise waters of Hamelin Pool. A boardwalk has been constructed so that damage to these unique structures will be minimised; there are interpretive signs explaining the various types of stromatolite and their development. Stay on the boardwalk and be careful not to disturb the structures; they have been growing for thousands of years. ■

blocks and have been used for buildings in many parts of Shark Bay. The **barrier fence** on the Taillefer Isthmus has been designed to keep out feral animals, once contributors to the decline in native mammal populations (such as the Shark Bay mouse).

At **Eagle Bluff**, halfway between Nanga and Denham, there are superb views from the cliff. If you look hard enough you will see marine creatures such as manta rays frolicking in the water and white-bellied sea-eagles overhead (hence the bluff's name).

DENHAM

The name Denham comes from Captain Henry Denham who charted the waters of Shark Bay in 1858 in HMS *Herald*. He was an early graffitist, having inscribed his name into rock on the cliff face at Eagle Bluff. A section of this rock collapsed into the sea and has been relocated to Pioneer Park in the town. Denham, once a pearling port, boasts a street paved with pearl shell. It is also the most westerly town in Australia. There is also a shell craft museum, a church and a restaurant made of shell blocks.

These days, if it weren't for a group of friendly dolphins, Denham would probably still be a sleepy fishing village. This town has the Shark Bay tourist office (☎ 9948 1253) at Knight Terrace, which is open daily from 8.30 am to 6 pm. The CALM office (☎ 9948 1208), Knight Terrace, has a great deal of information on the World Heritage area

including the free *Shark Bay* booklet and *Shark Bay: Discover Monkey Mia & Other Natural Wonders* ($5.95).

Things to See & Do

There is an interesting **walk** along the shore from Denham to the Town Bluff – the two rows of curved rocks are believed to be an Aboriginal fish trap. A couple of kilometres

Millions of tiny shells line the 110km shore at Shell Beach.

down the road to Monkey Mia is the shallow and picturesque **Little Lagoon**. About 4km from Denham on the Monkey Mia Rd is the turn-off to the fascinating, wild **François Péron National Park** (see later in this section).

Organised Tours

There is a wildlife cruise (weather permitting) to Steep Point on the MV *Explorer* for $85 – book at the tourist office in Denham (minimum of 10 people). Shark Bay Safari Tours (☎ 9948 1247) has various tours around Shark Bay and the World Heritage area; again, enquire at the tourist office. On Wednesday it runs a full-day tour to Cape Péron in François Péron National Park ($70). Every day, except Monday and Friday, the yacht *Shotover* does a morning and sunset dolphin cruise for $29.

Topday 4WD tours (☎ 9948 1880) goes to Shell Beach ($39), Shell Beach and the stromatolites ($69) and to Cape Péron ($70). Enquire at the tourist centre; there are discounts for Greyhound pass holders.

For flightseeing, see Monkey Mia.

Places to Stay

The *Denham Seaside Caravan Park* (☎ 9948 1242), Knight Terrace, is a friendly place on the foreshore with tent/powered sites for $10/12, on-site vans for $35 for two. *Shark Bay Caravan Park* (☎ 9948 1387) on Spaven Way and the *Blue Dolphin* (☎ 9948 1385) on Hamelin Rd, in Denham, are similarly priced.

Accommodation in Shark Bay can be very tight and expensive during school holidays. The recently renovated *Bay Lodge* (☎ 9948 1278), a budget place at 95 Knight Terrace on the Denham foreshore, has beds in shared units which cost $12, and two-bedroom self-contained units for $46.

There are a number of holiday cottages and villas in Shark Bay. The friendly, well-run *Shark Bay Holiday Cottages* (☎ 9948 1206), Knight Terrace, has backpackers' beds for $12 in four-bed, self-contained rooms, as well as cottages at $40 for two. The *Denham Holiday Village* (☎ 9335 5550), on the corner of Capewell Drive and Sunter

Place, has three-bedroom brick cottages and the *Denham Villas* (☎ 9948 1264), 4 Durlacher St, has self-contained villas; both cost from $65. Units in the *Tradewinds Holiday Village* (☎ 9948 1222) on Knight Terrace are from $60 to $70 per night.

The up-market choice is the *Heritage Resort Hotel* (☎ 9948 1133), also centrally located on Knight Terrace; the units are not cheap at $120 for doubles but you get all the facilities you would expect at this price.

Shark Bay Accommodation Service (☎ 9948 1323) has a number of private cottages and units available, usually by the week.

Places to Eat

There are a number of takeaways and the *Loaves & Fishes Bakery* along Knight Terrace. The other dining choices are also along Knight Terrace: the *Shark Bay Hotel* has counter meals, or there's the more expensive shell-block *Old Pearler* restaurant (lunch specials are $10, main dinner meals are from $18 to $22 and crayfish is the speciality, in season). The *Heritage Resort Hotel* serves bar meals and has a good à la carte *restaurant* specialising in seafood dishes.

Getting There & Away

Air Western Airlines (☎ (1800) 998 097) has return flights from Perth on Monday, Wednesday and Friday; the one-way fare is $167 to Kalbarri and a further $86 from Kalbarri to Monkey Mia.

Bus North from Kalbarri, it's a fairly dull, boring and often very hot run to Carnarvon. The Overlander Roadhouse, 290km north of Geraldton, is the turn-off to Shark Bay. Greyhound has a connecting bus service from Denham to Overlander to connect with interstate buses on Saturday, Monday and Thursday (both north and southbound). The fare from Perth to Denham is $120. It's $23/42 one way/return from Denham and Monkey Mia to the Overlander Roadhouse.

A daily local bus departs Denham (near the tourist office on Knight Terrace) at 8.45 am and 5 pm for Monkey Mia and returns at 9.15 am

---

A Story of Survival – the Stick-Nest Rat

In a minuscule portion of geological time, some 200 years, over a dozen non-flying mammal species of Australia's arid zone have become extinct. Introduced species such as donkeys, camels, cats, foxes and rabbits have destroyed habitats and preyed upon many native species.

The innocuous greater stick-nest rat *(Leporillus conditor)* builds its humble nest of intertwined sticks above ground (most of its cousins burrow) which leaves it vulnerable to trampling by roving stock.

Prior to colonisation the rat was found throughout southern Australia from the central west coast of WA to western New South Wales. It was last recorded on the mainland in the 1920s and from then on a small population of about 1000 were confined to Franklin Island in the Nuyts Archipelago, off the coast of South Australia.

A successful captive breeding programme began in South Australia in 1985 and, in 1990, 40 of the rats were fitted with radio-collars and released on Salutation Island in Shark Bay. The conditions and vegetation of the island resembled those of Franklin Island; importantly, there were no introduced predators. At last check the rat was doing OK and even finding time to breed.

Not so lucky are: the desert and pig-footed bandicoots; desert-rat kangaroo; eastern and central hare-wallabies; crescent nail-tailed wallaby; white-footed rabbit; lesser stick-nest and central rock rats; and big-eared, long-tailed and short-tailed hopping mice. ■

---

and 5.30 pm; the fare is $14 return. There is also another daily service at 8 am (7.15 am Friday) for $14; ask at the tourist office.

FRANÇOIS PÉRON NATIONAL PARK

This truly magnificent national park is appropriately named after the French naturalist who visited Shark Bay with Nicolas Baudin's *Géographe* expedition in 1801 and 1803. Baudin died of tuberculosis on the return voyage so it was left to Péron to write up the narrative and scientific accounts of the expedition in his *A Voyage of Discovery to the Southern Hemisphere* (1809).

The 400 sq km park is known for its arid scenery, tracts of wilderness and the landlocked salt lakes or *birridas*; which range from 100m to 1km wide. At the tip of the peninsula is Cape Péron with its dramatic colour contrasts, the place to spot turtles, dolphins, dugongs and manta rays.

The observant may see the rare thick-billed grass wren in the low acacia shrubland. There are many other species to observe – see the boxed aside on bird-watching earlier. Several species of snake, such as the mulga and gwardar, are found in the park but perhaps the most famous of the reptiles is the thorny or mountain devil.

There are two artesian bore tanks, one which has water at 35°C and the other at a hot 43°C in the grounds of the *Péron Home-stead* – you may soak in one of these (sunset is a great time). The station itself is a reminder of the peninsula's former use for grazing. There are campsites with limited facilities at Big Lagoon, Gregories, Bottle Bay, South Gregories and Herald Bight.

Always carry your own supplies of drinking water, carry out all rubbish, light fires only in the rings provided, do not collect firewood (as it provides protection for fauna), watch out for stonefish in shallow waters and keep well back from the cliffs at Cape Péron. Entry to the park is $3 for a day visit and $20 for a vehicle with four passengers for seven nights.

The road to the homestead is suitable for 2WD vehicles but a 4WD will be necessary to go any further into the park. Stick to the roads and *don't* try to cross any of the birridas – you will get bogged. For those without 4WD there is a tour option with Shark Bay Safari Tours (☎ 9948 1247) – see Organised Tours under Denham earlier.

MONKEY MIA

This pleasant spot with the unusual name is 26km from Denham. Several theories exist as to how the name came about. In 1834, a schooner *Monkey* supposedly anchored in Shark Bay and *mia* is Aboriginal for 'house or home', hence 'Home of the Monkey'. This is disputed as records indicate the

Monkey was never near the east side of the Péron Peninsula. Then there was the pearling boat which had a monkey as a mascot ('monkey' was slang at the time for Mongolian pearlers and was the colloquial expression for shepherd etc). We will probably never know for sure.

You pass the Dolphin Information Centre (☎ 9948 1366) just as you enter the beach viewing area ($5 per vehicle); there is lots of information on the region and on the dolphins and you can see a captivating 45 minute video on many aspects of Shark Bay.

The Dolphins of Monkey Mia
It's believed that bottle-nose dolphins have been visiting Monkey Mia since the early 1960s, although it's only in the last decade or so that it's become a world-famous event.

Monkey Mia's dolphins simply drop by to visit humans; they swim into knee-deep water and nudge up against you, even take a fish from you if it's offered. The dolphins generally come in every day during the winter months, less frequently during the summer. They may arrive singly or in groups of five or more, but as many as 13 were recorded on one occasion. They seem to come in more often in the mornings.

The entry fee to the reserve is $5/2 per adult/child (a family pass is $10).

Organised Tours
There are numerous flightseeing tours: Monkey Mia Air Charter (☎ 9948 1307) has a Zuytdorp Cliffs tour from $47 per person, and an 'Around the Bay' tour for $67 (minimum numbers are required).

Seagrasses
You will see seagrasses, appearing as a dark shadow, in the crystal-clear waters of Shark Bay and washed up on the beaches of Denham and Monkey Mia. Shark Bay is known to have 12 species of seagrass growing in 4000 of its 13,000 sq km, including the 1030 sq km Wooramel Bank seagrass meadow, the largest in the world.

Seagrasses are not seaweeds. Seaweeds are plants without flowers or roots. In contrast, seagrasses have complex root systems, are green flowering plants and can survive in the highly saline waters of the bay. In fact, seaweeds and animals grow on the seagrasses as epiphytes. The meadows are important nurseries for small fish and act to slow water movement. They also provide the most essential part of the diet of the dugong. ■

The dugong grazes in seagrass meadows.

You can see the dolphins from a boat. Both the *Aristocat* and *Shotover* cruise to the dolphins ($29), or do a four hour trip around the bay ($34). The *Shotover* sails out to the dugongs and in the 2½ hour trip you'll probably see these shy mammals ($34/17).

There are also cruises on the *Blue Lagoon Pearl* to see a pearl farm at Red Bluff ($18/7); Monday trips to Dirk Hartog Island on the *Sea Eagle* (☎ 9948 1113, $100); and cruises to Steep Point for fishing with Explorer Charters & Cruises (☎ 9948 1246, $110).

There are a number of Shark Bay Discovery 4WD tours from the resort (☎ 9948 1320). The full-day Péron/Project Eden tour is the best as it covers the cape's native mammal reintroduction program and ends with a dip in the hot tubs ($70/30 for an adult/child). The Steep Point and Zuytdorp Cliffs trip involves a scenic flight and 4WD trip to the 60m cliffs ($149/89).

Places to Stay & Eat
The *Monkey Mia Dolphin Resort* (☎ 9948 1320) has a wide range of accommodation including expensive tent/powered sites from $15/17.50 for two (a beach-front site is $21.50), backpackers' beds in two-tent condos for $12, tented condos for $65 for four, on-site vans from $25 for two, and chalets at $130 for three; discounts apply off season.

The *Péron Cafe* serves light meals and takeaways. At the *Bough Shed Restaurant* you can join the elite and watch the dolphins feed – a private box at Marineworld?

There is a campers' store, open daily until 6 pm.

The Gascoyne

The Gascoyne region takes its name from the 764km Gascoyne River, which together with its major tributary, the Lyons River, has a catchment area of nearly 70,000 sq km. Seldom does the Gascoyne flow above ground west of the Kennedy Range.

There are a number of attractions within this vast region but a good deal of driving is necessary to get to them. North of Carnarvon is an interesting stretch of coastline with blowholes and rocky capes. To the east is the impressive north-south running Kennedy Range and the massive bulk of Mt Augustus.

Station stays are popular with foreign travellers (see the boxed aside 'Station Stays' in the Coral Coast & Pilbara chapter).

CARNARVON
* *pop 9000*

Carnarvon is at the mouth of the Gascoyne River. It's noted for its tropical fruit, particularly bananas, and fine climate. It can get very hot in the middle of summer and is periodically subjected to floods and cyclones. Subsurface water, which flows even when the above-ground river is dry, is tapped to irrigate riverside plantations. Salt is produced at Lake Macleod near Carnarvon, and prawns and scallops are harvested in the area. The main street of Carnarvon is 40m wide, a reminder of the days when camel trains used to pass by.

The Carnarvon tourist office (☎ 9941 1146), on Robinson St, is open daily from 8.30 am to 5.30 pm; in the off season from 9 am to 5 pm. If you are not driving the next leg of your journey you may wish to read a book – the Wise Owl Book Exchange, just past the Caltex service station (on the corner of Robinson St and Babbage Island Rd), has books for sale or trade.

Things to See & Do

Carnarvon once had a NASA **tracking station**. It opened in 1966 and was closed in 1975 (it is now called the OTC station); you can drive to the pedestal of the parabolic dish but the building is not open; there are great views of Carnarvon.

The **Fascine**, lined with palm trees, is a pleasant place for a stroll. Carnarvon's **'one mile' jetty** was a popular fishing spot (it is not open at the moment) as is the little jetty at the prawning station. The small, furnished **Lighthouse Keeper's Cottage Museum** is beside the jetty ($1 entry); it is open from 10 am to noon and 2 to 4 pm daily.

Pelican Point, 5km to the south-west, is a popular swimming and picnic spot. Other good beaches, also south and off the Geraldton Rd, are **Bush Bay** (turn-off 20km) and **New Beach** (37km).

Munro's Banana Plantation, on South River Rd, has a very informative plantation tour ($4) at 11 am daily. After the tour, you can indulge yourself in fantastic fresh-fruit ice cream or smoothies. They sell a banana cookbook which includes banana cures for such ills as diarrhoea, ulcers and depression. **Westoby Plantation**, on Robinson St, is open from 10 am to 4 pm daily, except Tuesday ($4).

The **Tropical Bird Park** at 55 Angelo St has 55 aviaries; it is open Tuesday to Sunday from 9.30 am to 4.30 pm and entry is $4/2 for adults/children.

Carnarvon is a great place for fishing – all the secrets are revealed in *The Best Fishing Around Carnarvon*, free from the tourist office.

Organised Tours

Tropical Tripper Tours departs from the tourist office and offers half-day tours around town for $15 and an all-day tour that includes Lake Macleod, Cape Cuvier, the *Korean Star* wreck and blowholes for $40.

A couple of local surfers know where the 'full-bore barrels with plenty of length' are; enquire at the tourist office.

There are helicopter scenic flights from Carnarvon airport with Gascoyne Helicopter Services (☎ 9941 2494); these cost from $50 per person (minimum of two).

Paggi's (☎ 9941 1587) has scenic air tours down to Shark Bay and out over Mt Augustus; call and ask for prices.

Places to Stay

Camping & Caravans You shouldn't have any trouble finding a caravan park in Carnarvon; the closest to the centre of town is the *Carnarvon Tourist Centre Caravan Park* (☎ 9941 1438), 90 Robinson St, which has powered sites/on-site vans at $13.50/29 for two. The *Marloo Caravan Park* (☎ 9941 1439), on Wise St, is well set up for senior campers with a kitchen, laundry and great bathroom facilities; campsites are $10 for two (you must be 55 or over to stay here – revel in your age).

Other caravan parks have similar rates: on Robinson St are *Carnarvon Caravan Park* (☎ 9941 8101), *Plantation* (☎ 9941 8100), and the *Wintersun* (☎ 9941 8150). The *Norwesta* (☎ 9941 1277) is at 12-20 Angelo St; and *Startrek* (☎ 9941 8153) is on the North-West Coastal Highway.

Hostels *Carnarvon Backpackers* (☎ 9941 1095), at 46 Olivia Terrace, has dorm beds from $10 (it is a good place to find picking work). The *Backpackers' Paradise* (☎ 9941 2966), an associate YHA hostel on Robinson St, has shared accommodation from $12; it also has doubles (which can be family rooms) from $30. There is a cafe attached which has good-value meals.

Hotels, B&B & Motels Carnarvon has some old-fashioned hotels with old-fashioned prices. The *Port Hotel* has rooms from $25/50 in its older section. The *Carnarvon Hotel Motel* (☎ 9941 1181), Olivia Terrace, has comfortable rooms for $35/55.

The *Gateway Motel* (☎ 9941 1532), on Robinson St, has rooms at $75. There are self-contained holiday units at the *Carnarvon Close Holiday Resort* (☎ 9941 1317), 96 Robinson St, at $55 for two. The *Fascine*

Lodge Motel (☎ 9941 2411), 1002 David Brand Drive, costs $80/85; and the *Hospitality Inn Motel* (☎ 9941 1600), West St, is from $74 a double.

The top accommodation in Carnarvon is the Maslen family's the *Outcamp* (☎ 9941 2421) at 16 Olivia Terrace, on the Fascine. This is a luxurious B&B in the town's best location. The cost is a mere $45/75 for singles/doubles for the great facilities, so treat yourself. For information about station stays see the boxed aside 'Station Stays' in the Coral Coast & Pilbara chapter.

Places to Eat

On Robinson St are *Fascine* and *Kaycee's*, both standard coffee lounges. *River Rooster*, also on Robinson St next to the Tourist Centre Caravan Park, has takeaways and pasta at reasonable prices; you can eat in or take away. Next to it are *PizzaLand* and *BurgerLand*. Readers recommend the *Old Post Office Café*, at Backpackers' Paradise – it's open from 6 pm until late and for Sunday breakfast.

The *Carnarvon Bakery*, 21 Robinson St, has home-made pies and sandwiches, as does

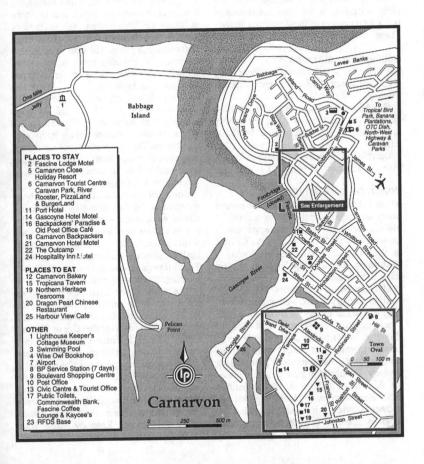

PLACES TO STAY
2 Fascine Lodge Motel
5 Carnarvon Close
  Holiday Resort
6 Carnarvon Tourist Centre
  Caravan Park, River
  Rooster, PizzaLand
  & BurgerLand
11 Port Hotel
14 Gascoyne Hotel Motel
16 Backpackers' Paradise &
  Old Post Office Café
18 Carnarvon Backpackers
21 Carnarvon Hotel Motel
22 The Outcamp
24 Hospitality Inn Motel

PLACES TO EAT
12 Carnarvon Bakery
15 Tropicana Tavern
19 Northern Heritage
  Tearooms
20 Dragon Pearl Chinese
  Restaurant
25 Harbour View Cafe

OTHER
1 Lighthouse Keeper's
  Cottage Museum
3 Swimming Pool
4 Wise Owl Bookshop
7 Airport
8 BP Service Station (7 days)
9 Boulevard Shopping Centre
10 Post Office
13 Civic Centre & Tourist Office
17 Public Toilets,
  Commonwealth Bank,
  Fascine Coffee
  Lounge & Kaycee's
23 RFDS Base

Carnarvon

0   250   500 m

Jenny's Hot Bread Kitchen, on the corner of Robinson and Angelo Sts in the Supa Valu supermarket. The *Northern Heritage Tea-rooms*, 44 Olivia Terrace, comes and goes; when it is resurrected it has great home-made meals. The *Carnarvon* and *Gascoyne* hotels both have good counter meals. The *Harbour View Cafe*, at the boat harbour, is renowned for its excellent seafood and salads – read the visitors' book (pan fried prawns are $8, a fish basket is $13).

The *Dragon Pearl*, Francis St, has Chinese food. If you're looking for a more up-market place, *Sails Restaurant* in the Hospitality Inn, or the excellent restaurant (with a takeaway) in the *Tropicana Tavern*, Camel Lane, are both good choices.

Getting There & Around

Skywest flies to Carnarvon from Perth daily – enquire about the large range of special fares.

Greyhound buses pass through Carnarvon on their way north or south. The one-way fare, Perth to Carnarvon, is $114 ($202 return).

Bicycles and helmets are available for hire from Backpackers' Paradise.

NORTH OF CARNARVON

About 14km north of town, the **Bibbawarra Bore**, an artesian well sunk to a depth of 914m, is being developed into a spa bath. It has a continuous flow of water at 65°C. West of the bore, 22km from Carnarvon, is **Miaboolya Beach**, popular with anglers using light or heavy line.

The spectacular blowholes, 70km to the north of Carnarvon, are well worth the trip. They can be reached by the Bibbawarra Bore Track or from the North-West Coastal Highway. Water is forced through holes in the rock to a height of 20m. One km south of the Quobba Station homestead is the **HMAS Sydney Memorial** which commemorates the ship sunk off the coast by the German raider *Kormoran* on 19 November 1941.

Cape Cuvier, where salt is loaded for Japan, is 30km north of the blowholes, and nearby is the *Korean Star*, grounded by

Cyclone Herbie on 21 May 1988 (do not climb over the wreck as it is dangerous).

Places to Stay

There's a fine beach about a km south of the blowholes with a primitive campsite (no fresh water available) and shanty town. You can camp at *Quobba Station* for about $5 per person; power is limited but water is available.

KENNEDY RANGE

This spectacular eroded plateau is some 160km east of Carnarvon; it runs north from Gascoyne Junction for 195km and in places is 30km wide. The southern and eastern sides have eroded, forming dramatic 100m-high cliffs which are dissected with steep-walled canyons. The resulting mesa, which slopes quickly on the west side, is covered with red sand dunes and spinifex.

The park was explored by the Gregory brothers in 1858 and they named the range after the then governor of WA. The many artefacts attest to much earlier use by Aboriginal groups. The semiprecious coloured chert was used to make stone tools. The ranges were explored for minerals and the mining potential was deemed low.

Some 295 species of plant have been recorded in the park and 40% of these are annual wildflowers – much of the park has not yet been explored. Euros and rock wallabies are the most visible mammals and birds are seen around permanent waterholes. The cliff eyries are perfect vantage points for the magnificent wedge-tailed eagle.

The many marine fossils in the sandstone strata relate to the Permian period, some 250 million years ago, when the Gascoyne was a shallow ocean basin off the edge of the Australian continent. These can be seen in a number of places on the eastern escarpment.

The eastern escarpment can be reached in a 2WD vehicle but driving in the rest of the park is not recommended. If you don't fancy driving you can fly over it or get someone else to take you there. West Coast Safaris (☎ 9941 1146) and Kennedy Range Tours (☎ 9943 0550) take trips to the Kennedy

Range. A three day trip including the range and Mt Augustus would cost around $475. Neither fuel nor water is available in the park so you have to come with adequate supplies.

Places to Stay

Bush camping is permitted at designated sites by the eastern escarpment of the Kennedy Range, near the entry to The Temple. There is accommodation at the *Mt Sandiman Homestead* (☎ 9943 0546), 240km north-east of Carnarvon via Gascoyne Junction; backpackers can stay in the old jackeroo (or jilleroo) quarters.

MT AUGUSTUS (BURRINGURRAH)

Mt Augustus, in Burringurrah National Park, 450km from Carnarvon, is the biggest rock (monadnock) in the world but certainly not the most spectacular; it is twice the size of Uluru but the partial vegetation cover makes it far less dramatic. The granite underneath the layered rocks of the mount is estimated to be 1650 million years old.

There are three main sites where Aboriginal engravings can be seen. **Ooramboo** has engravings on a rock face and there is a spring nearby; at **Mundee** the engravings are in an overhang; and **Beedoboondu**, the starting point for the climb to the summit, the engraved flintstone rocks and a mostly dry waterfall.

The rock can be climbed from the car park near Beedoboondu. The excursion can take at least six hours and is 12km return. There is a shorter walk of 6km (2½ hours return) from Ooramboo which also offers elevated views.

Most visitors get to Mt Augustus via remote **Gascoyne Junction**, which is 164km inland (east) from Carnarvon. The old pub (the Junction Hotel) is the general store and the only source of cold beer before you get to Mt Augustus or Meekatharra.

A copy of CALM's excellent *National Parks of the Gascoyne Hinterland*, covering the Kennedy Ranges and Augustus ($2), is well worthwhile.

Places to Stay

Camping is not allowed in the area of Mt Augustus. The *Junction Hotel* (☎ 9943 0504), where the Lyons River meets the Gascoyne River, has single/double rooms for $40/50. Close to Mt Augustus is *Cobra Station Motel* (☎ 9943 0565), with tent sites for $9, guesthouse rooms for $35/45 for two, and motel rooms for $50/60 (it was formerly the Bangemall Inn which was established for miners at the nearby El Dorado Goldmine).

The *Mt Augustus Outback Tourist Resort* (☎ 9943 0527), only 5km from the monadnock, has tent/powered sites at $12/16 for two, and single/double units for $40/60.

Coral Coast & The Pilbara

The Coral Coast extends from Coral Bay to Onslow and is, without doubt, one of the richest eco-tourism destinations in the world. The Pilbara, composed of the oldest rocks in the world, is an ancient, arid region with a glut of natural wonders. It stretches from Onslow to north of Port Hedland and inland beyond the Karijini (Hamersley Range) National Park and several modern mining towns.

Coral Coast

The Coral Coast is replete with wildlife, amazing vegetation, a coral reef and a perfect climate. Anyone with time should endeavour to visit, if only for a chance to observe wildlife you cannot hope to see elsewhere (see Interaction with Marine Life under Ningaloo Marine Park later). Apart from the eco-tourism possibilities, this is a place to take it easy – lie on the beach and enjoy the magnificent climate, snorkel across the very accessible reef and have a meal of prawns or freshly caught fish.

CARNARVON TO NORTH-WEST CAPE

From Carnarvon to Exmouth, via the North-West Coastal Highway, is about 370km. It is about 145km from Carnarvon to the first major roadhouse, at Minilya. From this 'backpacker unfriendly' roadhouse it is another 8km to the turn-off to the North-West Cape via the Cape Rd. Minilya has powered sites for $12, and small single/double cabins for $25/35.

The road to *Warroora Station* (☎ 9942 5920) is 25km from Highway 1, and from there it is 23km on a dirt road; campsites are $5, singles in the shearers' quarters and stockmens' rooms are $15 and small self-contained overseers' shacks are $35 per person. Some 80km up the Cape Rd is the turn-off to Coral Bay. The next major turn-

HIGHLIGHTS

- Swimming with the mighty whale sharks at Ningaloo Reef near Exmouth
- Walking and driving through Cape Range National Park near Exmouth – Shothole Canyon, the Charles Knife Rd, Yardie Creek and Mandu gorges
- The oases of Millstream-Chichester National Park in the heart of the red rocks of the Pilbara
- The gorges of the Hamersley Range and the view from Oxer's Lookout, where four spectacular gorges meet
- Relaxing at Cossack, a well-preserved historic town close to many natural attractions
- Aboriginal culture on the Dampier Peninsula and Archipelago
- A station stay to experience the 'real' Australia (complete with stockmen, shearing sheds and sheep caked in Pilbara dust)
- A cruise to the Montebello Islands, a pristine marine wilderness and great bird-watching destination

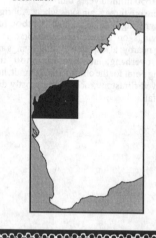

off is the road which heads off east to Giralia Station; this is being progressively sealed and is a good short cut to the North-West Coastal Highway (Hwy 1).

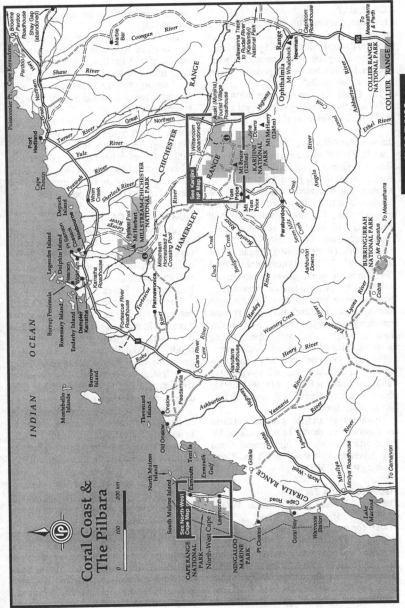

Coral Coast &
The Pilbara

CORAL COAST

CORAL BAY

This town, 150km south of Exmouth and a whopping 1200km north of Perth, is an important access point for Ningaloo Marine Park and a popular diving centre. Between April and November the temperature hovers around a pleasant 28°C.

The Coral Bay tourist bureau (☎ 9942 5988) is in the Coral Bay Arcade; get a copy of *Coral Bay: Ningaloo Reef*.

Underwater Activities

Coral Bay is at the southern base of Ningaloo Marine Park and a great place for snorkelling. The idyllic lagoon is sandwiched between the Ningaloo coral reef and the coastline and is a great spot for swimming and sunbathing. For those who love to get all their gear off, there is a secluded beach known as 'skinny dip corner'.

Coral Dive (☎ 9942 5940), Ningaloo Reef Dive (☎ 9954 5836) and Dominator (☎ 9942 5995) arrange scuba adventures, operate PADI dive courses, fill tanks and rent equipment. A good time to dive is during the coral-spawning in March and April. You can rent snorkelling equipment for $10 per day from the beach or go 'snuba' diving (using an air hose) for $40/20 for adults/children.

For those who don't wish to go underwater there are the Glass Bottom Boats (☎ 9942 5885) and Sub-Sea Explorer (☎ 9942 5955) trips which leave from Coral Bay; they cost $25 for three hours.

This area is also a fishing mecca and there are a number of charter boats available for game and deep-sea fishing: contact Coral Bay Adventures (☎ 9942 5955) and Coral Cruiser (☎ 9942 5955).

Places to Stay & Eat

The clean *Peoples Park Caravan Village* (☎ 9942 5933) has tent/powered sites for $14/16 for two (more expensive for ocean frontage). The *Bayview Holiday Village* (☎ 9942 5932) has tent/powered sites from $13/15. There is a backpackers' area with kitchen facilities; the cost is $14 per night. *Coral Bay Backpackers'* (☎ 9942 5934) is in a building behind the Ningaloo Reef Resort;

you also get access to the resort's pool and bar for $15.

The *Coral Bay Lodge* (☎ 9942 5932), on the corner of Robinson and French Sts, is associated with the Bayview and has double units from $86 to $110; and the *Ningaloo Reef Resort* (☎ 9942 5934) has tidy, well-appointed rooms from $95 for two ($10/5 for an extra adult/child).

The *Coral Bay Supermarket* has fresh bread, milk, fish and meat for self-caterers. *Fin's Cafe* opens early for those needing a caffeine fix before heading off to fish or dive; it has a nice alfresco dining area. The *Coral Cove Restaurant* in the Ningaloo Reef Resort has backpackers' specials for $10.

NORTH-WEST CAPE

North-West Cape, a finger of land jutting north into the Indian Ocean, offers a bewildering array of activities for travellers – mainly because of the excellent eco-tourism opportunities at Coral Bay, Ningaloo Marine Park and Cape Range National Park.

The cape was once occupied by Aborigines but about 150 years ago disease wiped them out. In this weathered country much of the evidence of their presence has faded rapidly. The Mandu Mandu Creek Rockshelter in the Cape Range is currently being investigated; so far, evidence of the use of shellfish and fish by Aborigines has been dated back 34,000 years.

During WWII, the area near Wapet Creek on the eastern side of the cape was used as an advance and refuelling base for US submarines; codenamed Operation Potshot, the facility was destroyed by a cyclone in 1945.

Recently the cape was again in the news because of the hush-hush US Navy communications base north of Exmouth which, fortunately, was rendered obsolete at the end of the Cold War.

The cape is a fabulous eco-tourism destination with whale sharks, humpback whales, manta rays and colourful schools of fish in and around Ningaloo Reef. In addition, there are many mammals, marine and land reptiles, and abundant bird life. If you only see one part of WA, this should be it!

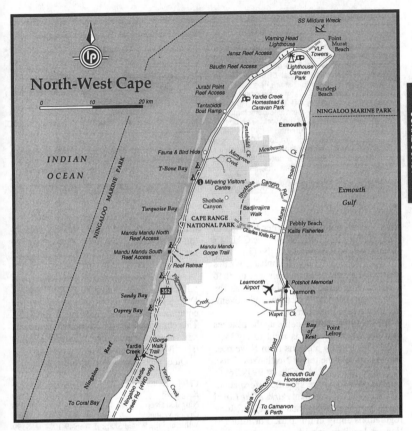

NINGALOO MARINE PARK

Running alongside the North-West Cape for 260km, from Bundegi Reef in the north-east to Amherst Point in the south-west, is the stunning Ningaloo ('Point of Land') Reef. This miniature version of the Great Barrier Reef is actually more accessible – in places it is less than 100m offshore. The lagoons enclosed by the reef vary in width from 200m to 6km.

Within the marine park are eight sanctuary zones – no fishing, only observing. Dugongs are observed, greenback turtles lay their eggs along the cape beaches and placid whale sharks can also be seen just beyond the reef's waters.

Over 220 species of coral have been recorded in the waters of the park, ranging from the slow-growing bommies to delicate branching varieties. For eight to nine nights after the full moon in March, there is a synchronised mass spawning of coral with eggs and sperm being released into the water simultaneously. Once fertilised, the larvae drifts until it settles and begins to build a skeleton, eventually forming into juvenile coral.

Up on the arid coast of Cape Range National Park, fossil corals and fossilised

Whale Sharks

Sharks have always been the subject of morbid fascination for visitors to Australia, especially the deadly great white which frequents the Southern Ocean. However the largest of the sharks (and indeed all fish), the whale shark, is a gentle giant. One of the few places in the world where you can see this leviathan is off Ningaloo Reef, near Exmouth. To swim with them is to participate in one of the natural wonders of the world. The best time to visit is at the end of summer.

The whale shark weighs up to 40,000kg, is up to 18m long and drifts slowly across ocean currents filtering water for the plankton and small fish it feeds on. They also eat an awful lot of rubbish. In the stomach of one, a wallet, a boot, a bucket and part of an oar were discovered. The whale shark's scientific name 'rhini-odon' means 'file tooth', referring to its 300 or more bands of minute teeth. ■

shark's teeth point to an earlier location of the reef. For more information, see CALM's *Coral Reefs of Western Australia* ($3).

Every June and July, humpback whales pass close by the coast on their way north to their calving grounds, probably near the Montebello Islands. In October and November they return to Antarctica.

In November, turtles come up the beaches at night when the tide is right to lay their eggs. This usually happens from November to January near the top of North-West Cape.

Contact the CALM office (☎ 9949 1676) in Exmouth for more specific information. Get a copy of the excellent *Parks of the Coral Coast* pamphlet from there; special fishing regulations apply in this park. For information on local marine life, get the excellent *The Marine Fishes of North-West Australia* (G Allen & R Swainston, 1988).

It would be environmentally suicidal to allow marine-drilling anywhere in the North-West Cape region. The WA government legislated in 1994 to prevent drilling in the marine park – we can only hope this decision remains the status quo.

Interaction with Marine Life

Whale shark observing goes on from late March to mid-June. The largest number of whale sharks is seen off the Tantabiddi and Mangrove Bay areas. The season begins at the time of coral-spawning and there is a plankton bloom at the same time. The best way to see them is by licensed charter vessel (after they have been initially spotted by aircraft).

About 12 boats were allowed to take trips out to the whale sharks in 1997. Exmouth Diving Centre (☎ 9949 1201) provides full equipment and daily refreshment for $250. This company has a good encounter success rate. Their advanced diving course is $320 (six dives) and their rescue course $450.

Other reputable operators are:

Company	Telephone	Fare
King Dive	☎ 9949 1094	$199
Ningaloo Deep	☎ 9949 1663	$250
Diving Ventures	☎ 9421 1052	$214
Willie and the Whale Shark	☎ 9949 1004	$199
Ningaloo Blue	☎ 9949 1119	$199
Sea-Trek Diving Ventures	☎ 9949 2635	$214

It is not guaranteed that you will see manta rays every day. Enquire at the dive centres as they will know where they are. Manta rays are seen from July to November. You can fly underwater with them as part of a normal dive charter; this costs $30 per dive and with daily rental of equipment it is $60.

The Exmouth Diving Centre organises trips to the Muiron Islands, 10km north-east of the cape, on demand. These islands are a breeding sanctuary for three species of turtle: green, loggerhead and hawksbill. During dives it is possible to hand-feed the 1.5m potato cod at the 'cod house'. You can see all the marine attractions as you gain an accredited diving qualification.

Two German readers recommend Western Australia Getaway Scuba (☎ 9949 2661) for small, personalised diving trips. Diving on the west side with all gear supplied is $110, on the east side $90.

EXMOUTH
- *pop 3200*

Exmouth was established in 1967 largely as a service centre for the huge US navy communications base. The Yanks have gone and it now provides a good focus for the many great eco-activities in the area. On no account should it be allowed to become a supply and administrative centre for multinational companies drilling in and around Ningaloo Marine Park!

The helpful Exmouth tourist office (☎ 9949 1176), recently relocated to the Exmouth Cape Tourist Village (see Places to Stay), has a video on all aspects of the reef. It's open daily from 8.30 am to 5 pm. The CALM office (☎ 9949 1676) is on Maidstone Crescent.

Things to See & Do
The Ocean Exhibits **shell museum** on Pellew St is open daily (except Sunday). The **town beach** at the end of Warne St is a popular swimming spot.

About 13km south of town is **Pebbly Beach**, a safe swimming beach covered in colourful pebbles. The wreck of the **SS Mildura**, beached in 1907, and the **Vlaming Head Lighthouse** are north of town and have sensational views.

Part of North-West Cape is dominated by the 13 low-frequency transmitter stations of Harold Holt Communications Station. Twelve are higher than the Eiffel Tower and serve to support the 13th, which is 396m high – the tallest structure in the southern hemisphere.

Organised Tours
There is a host of tours in the area ranging from gulf and gorge safaris to reef and fishing tours. Perhaps the most informative is Neil McLeod's Ningaloo Safari Tours (☎ 9949 1550). The full-day safari, called 'Over the Top' (10 hours, $95) has been recommended by many travellers (including me); it takes in the Cape Range, Ningaloo Reef, Yardie Creek and Vlaming Head lighthouse. Neil's mum makes a great boiled fruitcake.

Other tour operators, with similar itineraries, are Exmouth Eco Tours (☎ 9949 2809, $95), West Coast Safaris (☎ 9949 1625, $95) and WestTrek Safaris (☎ 9949 2659, $85). Exmouth Backpackers' (☎ 9949 1101) arranges budget trips for backpackers, regardless of numbers.

The Ningaloo Coral Explorer (☎ 9949 2424), a glass-bottom boat, operates coral-viewing trips over Bundegi Reef on the east coast. Ningaloo Ecology Cruises (☎ 9949 2255) operates from Tantabiddi on the west coast. The cost is $20/45 for adults/family.

Sea Kayak Wilderness Adventures (☎ 9949 1990) runs a fantastic sea kayak full-day paddle from Tantabiddi to Turquoise Bay; it costs $130, all equipment included.

Exmouth Air Charters (☎ 9949 2182) conducts scenic flights over the reef ($55/60 for 30/45 minutes, minimum of two).

Places to Stay
The well-kept, tidy *Exmouth Cape Tourist Village* (☎ 9949 1101), on the corner of Truscott Crescent and Murat Rd, has powered/en-suite sites for $17/21, cabins with cooking facilities from $32 to $46 and comfortable self-contained chalets for $60. Some chalets have been converted into a backpackers' place and beds are $14 per night; this includes access to a very cold pool.

The *Exmouth Caravan Park* (☎ 9949 1331), on Lefroy St, was once a poor choice but the council has improved it greatly. Tent/powered sites are $12/15, on-site vans $35 and $45; all prices are for two.

At Vlaming Head, the *Lighthouse Caravan Park* (☎ 9949 1478) has powered sites for $16, on-site vans for $35, cabins for $50 and delightful chalets (with great views) for $60; all prices are for two. There is good surfing nearby.

CORAL COAST

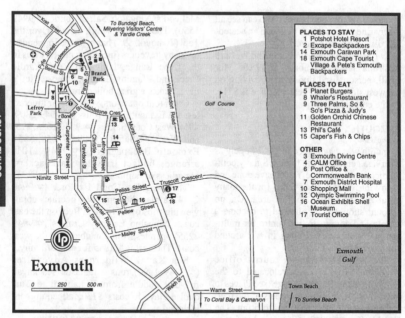

PLACES TO STAY
1 Potshot Hotel Resort
2 Excape Backpackers
14 Exmouth Caravan Park
18 Exmouth Cape Tourist
Village & Pete's Exmouth
Backpackers

PLACES TO EAT
5 Planet Burgers
8 Whaler's Restaurant
9 Three Palms, So &
So's Pizza & Judy's
11 Golden Orchid Chinese
Restaurant
13 Phil's Café
15 Caper's Fish & Chips

OTHER
3 Exmouth Diving Centre
4 CALM Office
6 Post Office &
Commonwealth Bank
7 Exmouth District Hospital
10 Shopping Mall
12 Olympic Swimming Pool
16 Ocean Exhibits Shell
Museum
17 Tourist Office

Exmouth

The huge *Potshot Hotel Resort* (☎ 9949 1200), Murat Rd, has all types of accommodation. The *Excape Backpackers* (☎ 9949 1201) looks as though it is the old staff quarters for the Potshot; the plus is that $15 gets the budget traveller access to all of the resort's fancy facilities. The Potshot itself has self-contained holiday units from $125 for four, two-bedroom villas from $85 to $110, and resort units for $95/105 for singles/doubles. All in all, it is a nice place with spa pools scattered around the grounds.

Private houses can be rented by Ray White (☎ 9949 1144) from $400 a week.

Places to Eat

There are a number of takeaways in the main shopping area of town, including *So and So's Pizza*, *Three Palms*, *Judy's* and *Whaler's Restaurant*, which has a nice verandah. *Phil's Café*, on the corner of Lefroy St and Maidstone Crescent, is open at night for takeaways.

Fish and chips are a regional speciality. In town go to *Caper's* – clever name, but bring your own tomato sauce as they actually charge for it! Out of town try *MG Kailis'* prawn palace, 25km south, open May to November. Here the annual prawn catch is as much as one million kg – perhaps this fact explains the many Porsches nearby.

The BYO *Golden Orchid* Chinese, behind the shopping centre, is open seven nights. The *Potshot Hotel* has buffet and à la carte meals, a great pool bar and a cocktail lounge. *Planet Burgers*, opposite the Exmouth Diving Centre, has all your fatty favourites.

Getting There & Away

There are periodic Skywest services between Learmonth (37km from Exmouth) and Carnarvon, Geraldton and Karratha (Tuesday and Thursday), and daily services to Perth.

Three times a week there is a Greyhound service to Exmouth from Perth (Sunday, Wednesday and Friday). From Exmouth to

Perth, services are Saturday, Monday and Thursday; the cost is $167.

There is a shuttle bus (the postie), Monday to Saturday, which goes from Exmouth to Minilya roadhouse to meet Greyhound. The cost one way is $15; a good option if you don't have your own vehicle.

Car After giving rides to numerous backpackers, I can only suggest that the North-West Cape is the place to have your own car. If you land in Exmouth without transport you probably won't see much.

CAPE RANGE NATIONAL PARK
The 510 sq km park, which runs down the west coast of the cape, includes the modern Milyering visitors' centre, a wide variety of rare flora & fauna, 50km of good swimming beaches, gorges (including scenic Yardie Creek) and rugged scenery.

Things to See & Do
The impressive Shothole and Charles Knife gorges are, respectively, 16km and 23km south of Exmouth. The **Shothole Gorge** is not like those in the Pilbara. Weathering has not occurred from permanent water but through periodic downpours and wind. The wind is a feature of the climate – it blows continually, usually from west to east.

The view from above **Charles Knife Gorge** is memorable. In front are the eroded limestone walls of the gorge and far beyond, the azure waters of Exmouth Gulf. The two gorges are connected by the 8km return **Badjirrajirra Walk**; CALM provides an interesting and free pamphlet.

There is a 4WD-only track which crosses the range near Learmonth. It is not recommended you take the drive yourself as it is easy to get lost. About halfway along this 45km track is **Owl's Roost Cave**, which you descend into by climbing down a wild fig root. Along the sandy track are flowering shrubs and trees including species of wattle, grevillea and banksia. The view as you come down from the range to Ningaloo Reef near Osprey Bay is nothing short of stunning.

The Milyering visitors' centre (☎ 9949 2808) is 52km from Exmouth on the west coast. Built in rammed-earth style, it is solar-powered and has waste disposal. A comprehensive display of the area's natural and cultural history can be seen here. It is usually open from 10 am to 4 pm during tourist season ($5 per car).

The saltwater **Yardie Creek Gorge** is 38km to the south of Milyering on a newly sealed road. Here, the deep blue waters of the gorge are held back by a sand bar. You can easily see the black-footed wallaby on the multicoloured canyon walls and a number of species of birds in and around the water. The 1.5km walk from the car park to the top of the gorge is recommended. CALM provides a *Visitor and Walk Trail Guide*.

One hour boat tours are conducted up the gorge on Monday, Wednesday and Saturday; the cost is $15/8 for adults/children. A trip up the gorge is usually included as part of the many day trips out of Exmouth.

4WD vehicles can continue south to Coral Bay from Yardie Creek following the coast. The road is signposted and there is a turn-off to the picturesque Point Cloates lighthouse.

Places to Stay
Basic tent and caravan sites are available in larger camps in the park (☎ 9949 1676) at $5 per double. Make sure you bring plenty of water; there are no supplies in the park.

Just outside the park and 34km from Exmouth is *Yardie Creek Homestead* (☎ 9949 1389), basking in its isolation, but with a small shop; powered sites are $14, an on-site van $38, and chalets $60 (prices for two).

Safari-style and 'backpacker-friendly' accommodation is provided at the *Reef Retreat* (☎ 9949 1776), on the beach opposite the entrance to Mandu Mandu Gorge Rd. The big marquee (a big circus tent) houses the kitchen, bedrooms and common room – it's a neat place to stay. The cost is $15 per night, with breakfast and camping fee included. Transport can be arranged from Exmouth in a 4WD for $17.50 each way. First reports from travellers (and LP readers) are good.

CORAL COAST

Station Stays

If you really want to sample a slice of genuine station life in the red sandy country, then head out to one of the station stays.

As an example, on the Bullara-Giralia Rd, 43km from the North-West Coastal Highway, is the 265,000 hectare *Giralia Station* (☎ 942 5937). There is a variety of accommodation here including dinner, bed & breakfast from $60 (bookings essential and BYO), shearers' quarters from $10 to $15, and camping and caravan sites for $6; all prices are per person. The homestead is near many features in the Pilbara and Gascoyne regions. If you want to sample activities on the station, which runs 25,000 merino sheep, just ask.

There are plenty of other places in the region (a number are covered in the text). In the Kennedy Ranges there is Mt Sandiman Station (☎ 9943 0550) – see the Central West Coast chapter; Manberry Station Stays (☎ 9942 5926) and Gnaraloo (☎ 9942 5927) north of Carnarvon; Nallan Station (☎ 9963 1054) near Cue; Erong Springs (☎ 9981 2910), east of Gascoyne Junction; Eurady Station (☎ 9936 1038), just off the North-West Coastal Highway; Yalardy (☎ 9942 5904), north-east of the Overlander Roadhouse; Wooleen Station (☎ 9963 7973) on the Murchison River; and Cobra Station (☎ 9943 0534) and Mt Augustus Station (☎ 9943 0527) in the Outback at the head of the Gascoyne River. Get a copy of the free *Gascoyne Station Stays* and go Outback! ∎

MINILYA TO KARRATHA

From Minilya it is about 110km north to the dirt road that heads west to Giralia Station – now sealed and used as a short-cut to the North-West Cape. (You may have missed it but about 50km north of Minilya you crossed the Tropic of Capricorn.) The Yannarie River crossing is 41km north of the Giralia Station turn-off and Barradale Roadhouse, shown on maps, is closed.

Don't despair as it is only another 70km to *Nanutarra Roadhouse* (☎ 9943 0521), on the Ashburton River, which is open 24 hours. There is a caravan facility with tent sites/powered sites/air-conditioned cabins at $10/12/35 for two; there is also a restaurant, but the showers and toilets here are a disgrace. The informal *Ashburton River Travellers' Park* has tent/powered sites for $3/6, station accommodation for $15. It's by the river and run by one 'Tex' whose motto is 'Pick a possie and I'll be down later'.

There is a turn east to the mining towns of the Pilbara (Tom Price and Paraburdoo) and Karijini (Hamersley Range) National Park after Nanutarra. North of this, perhaps 35km, is the road to Onslow.

Some 78km from the Onslow junction is another easterly road to Pannawonica, a mining town 46km off the highway. From this road junction it is another 41km up the

highway to the *Fortescue River Roadhouse* (☎ 9184 5126), the last of the roadhouses before Karratha and some 544km north of Carnarvon; tent/powered sites are $6.60/15 and hotel rooms $35 for two.

All in all, it's a long way between drinks.

ONSLOW
• *pop 650*

The original Onslow, near the mouth of the Ashburton River, came into being in 1883. It was the centre for pearling, mining and pastoral industries. Old Onslow was abandoned in 1925 and relocated to Beadon Bay. The 'new' town, 81km from the North-West Coastal Highway, has the distinction of being the southernmost WA town to be bombed in WWII (in 1943). It was used by the British, in the 1950s, for nuclear testing in the Montebello Islands.

Onslow is often hit by cyclones and, in 1963, one flattened the town. Today, Onslow is the mainland base for offshore oil exploration and production, and a supply base for Barrow Island (80km to the north) and the Saladin Islands. Many people visit Onslow in winter for the superb fishing.

The Onslow tourist office (☎ 9184 6001) is in the historic shire building on Second Ave.

Things to See & Do

Located on Second Ave is the Onslow Goods Shed **museum**, which displays items of historical interest. There is good swimming and **fishing** in the area; anglers head for the Beadon Creek Groyne and Four Mile Creek or out to sea for deep-sea fishing.

Old Onslow ruins, 48km south of town, include a gaol and a post office; worth a look if you accidentally end up in the region.

Places to Stay & Eat

The *Oceanview Caravan Park* (☎ 9184 6053), Second Ave, has tent/powered sites for $12/14 and park cabins from $30 to $50 for two; the new *Beadon Bay Village* (☎ 9184 6007), on Beadon Creek Rd, also has tent and powered sites. The units at *Onslow Sun Chalets* (☎ 9184 6058), Second Ave, are $65/75 for singles/doubles.

Haute cuisine is not one of Onslow's strong points – there is a bakery, a fish and chip shop called the *Beadon Creek Food Bar*, and the *Main Street Cafe* – the opportunity to do-it-yourself is immense. In the waters off Onslow are at least a dozen varieties of table fish, so bait your hook and then cook your catch.

Getting There & Away

You really need your own transport to get in and out of Onslow. Greyhound buses will drop you at the junction of Onslow Rd and the North-West Coastal Highway but you have to hitch the 81km to town.

DIRECTION & MACKEREL ISLANDS

Offshore, 11km and 22km respectively from Onslow, are Direction Island and the 10 Mackerel Islands (☎ 9184 6058, Onslow Sun Chalets). The tariff of $610 to $710 for full board for a week includes boat transfers to the 6km by 1.5km coral atoll, Thevenard, in the Mackerels.

Crayfish and oysters are rife for those who know where to look, as are Spanish mackerel, schnapper, groper and red emperor for the keen fisher. Direction Island has its own reef on one side and a beach on the other. One major plus is that the islands support many species of bird life, including the majestic osprey.

Montebello Islands

The Montebellos are a group of more than 100 flat limestone islands off the north-west coast of WA between Onslow and Karratha. They range in size from Hermite, the largest at 1000 hectares, to small islets and rocks of about one hectare. In 1992 they were gazetted as a conservation park administered by CALM.

In 1622, the survivors of the shipwreck of the *Tryal* camped here before setting off north to the East Indies. The islands were named by the French explorer Baudin in 1801 after the battle of Monte Bello. The pearlers who came next introduced the black rat and the cat, which ensured the extinction of the golden bandicoot and the spectacled hare-wallaby on the island.

In 1952 the British, in an operation codenamed Hurricane, detonated an atomic weapon mounted on HMS *Plym* anchored in Main Bay off Trimouille Island. Two further atomic tests were carried out in 1956, on Alpha and Trimouille islands.

Some 40 years later we can finally step ashore and get close to a real 'ground zero', the point of detonation of an atomic weapon. (I wonder how long the radiation warning signs last before being souvenired). 'Ladies and gentlemen, your guide today is Dr Strangelove and he would like to show you a number of mutating species of fish and a coral reef that *always* glows in the dark'...

Fortunately, nature is resilient. The islands have thriving populations of both land and marine fauna and more than 100 plant species, including a stand of mangroves. The legless lizard *Aprasia rostrata* is found only on Hermite Island. (Was it legless before 1952?) Two species of marine turtle are known to nest on the islands, as are a number of sea birds. Vignerons will love the names applied to many of the bays: hock, champagne, burgundy, claret and moselle, for example.

Beautiful mountains the islands are not. They are, rather, silent witnesses to the awesome destructive power of '$E=mc^2$' and the miraculous, recuperative powers of nature. ∎

The Pilbara

The Pilbara (meaning 'freshwater fish'), which contains some of the hottest country on earth, is the iron-ore and natural-gas producing area accounting for much of WA's prosperity. Gigantic machines are used to tear the dusty red ranges apart. It's isolated, harsh and fabulously wealthy. The Pilbara towns are almost all company towns: either mining centres where the ore is wrenched from the earth or ports from which it's shipped abroad. Exceptions are the mystical islands of the Dampier Archipelago, the gorges of Karijini National Park and historic towns like Marble Bar and Cossack.

If you are travelling away from the main coastal highway in this area in your own vehicle, always carry a lot of extra water – 20L per person is a sensible amount – and check that you have enough fuel to get to the next refuelling station. If travelling into remote areas, tell someone your travel plans. Don't leave your vehicle if you are stranded.

KARRATHA
• *pop 10,800*

Karratha ('good country'), the commercial centre for the area, is on Nickol Bay and some 1535km from Perth. It's the fastest-growing town in the Pilbara, due to the rapid expansion of Hamersley Iron and Woodside LNG projects.

This rich town is now the hub of the coastal Pilbara. Ask the average householder how much they pay for air-conditioning and you will realise that Karratha gets hot in summer; winter is the best time to visit.

The Fe-NaCl-NG Festival (pronounced 'fernarkling') is held in August each year. The title combines the chemical abbreviations of the region's main natural resources – iron, salt and natural gas.

Information
The Karratha & District tourist office (☎ 9144 4600), on Karratha Rd just before you reach the T-intersection of Dampier and Millstream Rds, has heaps of information on what to see and do in the Pilbara. CALM's north-west regional office is in the SGIO building, Welcome Rd.

Travellers coming from the north will revel in the offerings at Karratha's shopping complex in Welcome Rd. There is a Coles, K-Mart, Woolworth's, Chain Reaction and over 50 other speciality shops. There is a laundrette in the Millars Well shopping centre. Sounds funny to cover these in a guidebook? Wait and see!

Things to See & Do
There are good views from the lookout at **TV Hill**, and **Miaree Pool**, 35km to the south-west, is scenic and a good place to cool off. The Karratha **salt flats** are a great place to go bird-watching; dawn and dusk are the best viewing times.

The **Jaburara Heritage Trail** near town is replete with evidence of Aboriginal occupation: carvings, grindstones, etchings and middens are all located on the 3.5km trail which starts near the tourist office. Jaburara (pronounced 'Yabura') is the name of the former Aboriginal inhabitants of the Karratha region. At first glance the trail looks like a huge pile of rocks sticking out of the spinifex; don't be fooled as it is an enlightening journey into the past.

Aboriginal carvings along the ridge depict various life forms and totemic themes. They were carved with chert and dolerite tools and are estimated to be 5000 to 6000 years old. Flat rocks adjacent to one of the creeks on

---

Pebble-Mound Mouse

This mouse (*Pseudomys chapmani*), which is unique to the Pilbara, is a recent discovery. It is found living between clumps of spinifex in shallow burrows upon which it heaps a relatively flat mound of pebbles.

The carefully selected pebbles are small but the actual mound can be up to 50cm high. The pebbles are meticulously placed around the entrance of the burrow to provide insulation and moisture. ■

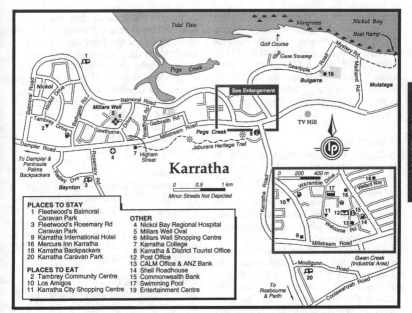

the trail were used for grinding spinifex and other seeds. The **talu sites**, or spiritual repositories, are represented predominantly by physical features. The major talu here is the large dolerite outcrop Warramurrangka, the 'giant flying fox'.

It is likely that you will see the euro (wallaroo) on the trail. The short-beaked echidna (spiny anteater or 'biggada' to the Aborigines) is another common animal found in the region.

You may also see evidence of the pebble-mound mouse but it is unlikely that you will see this diminutive creature (see under Pebble-Mound Mouse in this chapter). Reptiles include Australia's largest lizard, the perentie or racing goanna. The *Terminalia canescens*, a tree that grows in creek beds here, is a reminder of a former, much different tropical climate.

Tackle this walk in the early morning; it will be more rewarding if you take *Jaburara Heritage Trail* ($1.50) with you.

Places to Stay

There are three caravan parks in Karratha: *Fleetwood's Balmoral Rd* (☎ 9185 3628) is a permanents' haunt and *Fleetwood's Rosemary Rd* (☎ 9185 1855) is a temporaries' haunt – very temporary after my experience in one of the shoddiest caravans ever rented. At the latter, powered/ensuite sites are $16.50/24 and on-site vans are $47.50. *Karratha Caravan Park* (☎ 9185 1012), a little out of town on Mooligunn Rd, has powered sites for $15 and on-site vans for $35 for two.

Sadly, we have had lots of letters saying that *Karratha Backpackers* (☎ 9144 4904), Wellard Way, is tainted by beer-swilling semipermanents, who are rude to foreign female travellers. It seemed OK on our visit with a friendly host, and the rooms and facilities (laundry, TV room, etc) were good value for the money ($15 for a dorm, $30 for a single, $50 for a family). Let us know more.

The up-market choices are expensive. The

Karratha International Hotel (☎ 9185 3111), on the corner of Millstream and Balmoral Rds, is $132 for singles or doubles; and the *Mercure Inn Karratha* (☎ 9185 1155), Searipple Rd, is also $132. Both of these places have pools, although the kid-friendly Tambrey Community Centre (no accommodation; see Places to Eat) is the best place for a dip.

Places to Eat

On Balmoral Rd, *Los Amigos*, opposite the BP station, has Mexican food (Wednesday is 'el cheapo' night with four courses for just $12.50).

For a snack, there are a number of cafes and takeaways in the Karratha City shopping centre, including *Adriennes*, *Paradiso Pizza* and *Wendy's Super Sundae*.

A little out of town, the *Tambrey Community Centre* has a tavern and serves good counter meals ($13.95 for a huge Sunday grill), and the Karratha International has the licensed *Finches Restaurant* and the bistro *Gecko's*. There is a bottle shop opposite with a good selection of wines.

Getting There & Away

By far the most convenient way is by air and Qantas/Airlink and Ansett Australia have direct daily jet services from Perth. Skywest operates periodic services to Broome, Exmouth and Port Hedland.

Greyhound (☎ 13 2030) has daily services (about $126) from Perth; they use the Shell roadhouse on Searipple Rd as their depot. Most people coming to Karratha, however, arrive by car.

The Karratha Backpackers (☎ 9144 4904) has a courtesy bus from the Shell roadhouse. A local taxi is $33 from Karratha to Dampier.

DAMPIER
• *pop 1600*

Dampier, 20km from Karratha, is on King Bay and faces the other 41 islands of the Dampier Archipelago (named after the explorer William Dampier who passed by in 1699).

Dampier is a Hamersley Iron town and the port for Tom Price and Paraburdoo iron-ore operations. Now, gas from the huge natural-gas fields of the North-West Shelf is piped ashore nearby on the Burrup Peninsula. From there, it is piped to Perth and the Pilbara, or liquefied as part of the huge Woodside Petroleum project and exported to Japan and South Korea.

Dampier has mild, sunny winters with temperatures in the high twenties, but in summer it is very hot.

Information

The Dampier Community Association (☎ 9183 1072) is located just outside the shopping centre. Permits to drive along Hamersley Iron's service road to Karijini National Park are obtainable from the security office (☎ 9143 6224) at their Seven Mile depot on Dampier Rd.

Things to See & Do

An inspection of the **port facilities** can be arranged (☎ 9144 4600); the cost is $5/3 for adults/children. The William Dampier Lookout provides a fine view over the harbour and the **Woodside LNG Visitors' Centre** (☎ 9183 8100) is open weekdays, 10 am to 4 pm during the tourist season.

Train enthusiasts are well catered for in this region. There is the Pilbara Railways Historical Society **museum**, 10km before Dampier on the Dampier Rd, which features the *Pendennis Castle*, one of the fastest steam engines in the world. The museum is open weekdays from 10 am until 2 pm and on Sunday from 9 am to noon; trips along the Hamersley Iron railway are periodically organised by the society (☎ 9183 1157).

Nearby **Hearson's Cove** is a popular beach and picnic area, as is **Dampier Beach**. The explorer FT Gregory landed at Hearson's Cove in 1861 – it was his positive reports that led to settlement of the region.

The **Burrup Peninsula** has some 10,000 Aboriginal rock engravings depicting fish, turtles, euros, wallabies and a Tasmanian tiger. It is one of the most prolific sites for prehistoric rock art in the world. Particularly fascinating are the 'climbing figures', a short walk off the road near the North-West Shelf Project's onshore treatment plant. As you look back from the cluster of ancient rocks, the retorts, storage tanks and other ugly impedimenta of the modern age block the view of the sea which the ancient carvers would once have seen.

Dampier Archipelago National Park This
archipelago of over 40 islands was formed some 6000 to 8000 years ago when rising sea levels flooded coastal valleys. The islands are in a 45km radius of Dampier and it is 20 minutes by boat to the nearest island and about two hours to the farthest.

The islands have seen the coming and going of pearling, attempts at pastoralism and whaling. For about three years in the late 1800s there was a whaling station on Malus Island which processed humpback whales harpooned from longboats.

The relative isolation of the islands from predators has meant there are a number of nesting colonies of birds such as fairy and bridled terns, and four species of turtle use the beaches for egg-laying. A number of mammal species, including the Rothschild's rock wallaby, inhabit the islands.

Access to all the islands is by boat from the ramps at Dampier, Point Samson, Wickham, Cossack and Nickol Bay (Karratha). In winter, a North West Sports Fishing charter boat (☎ 9185 2242) cruises the archipelago. Do-it-yourselfers can hire 14 foot aluminium 'superducks' from Getaway Boat Hire (☎ 9185 1214) for $80 for six hours; the boats are permitted up to five nautical miles from the mainland. The free *The Dampier Archipelago: Islands in the Sun* is useful.

The Dampier Archipelago is renowned as a game-fishing mecca and each year it hosts the Dampier Classic.

Depuch Island, accessible by boat from a road that heads north from Whim Creek, is a mystical, spiritual place with many petroglyphs. Check with CALM in Karratha about access conditions to the island.

Places to Stay & Eat
Apart from the transit caravan park (☎ 9183 1109) on the Esplanade, which has tent/powered sites for $7/14 for two, there is a backpackers' hostel in the *Peninsula Palms* (☎ 9183 1888) on the Esplanade; the cost is $15 in a building we only saw before it was fully renovated (write and tell us about it); enquire at the main hotel desk. The Palms also has single/double budget units at $50/60, and deluxe units for $75/90. (In one publication it is described as 'uncharismatic' and I would have to agree.) Also in Dampier is the *Mercure Inn* (☎ 9183 1222), the Esplanade, which has comfortable singles from $75 to $95, doubles from $110.

Barnacle Bob's, also on the Esplanade and overlooking Hampton Harbour, is good for fish and chips ($8.50). There is a Chinese restaurant in the shopping centre and the *Harbour Lights* restaurant is part of the Peninsula Palms complex; a buffet at the latter is $16.50.

ROEBOURNE AREA
The Roebourne area is a busy little enclave of historic towns and modern port facilities. Cape Lambert, near Wickham, is the port for the iron ore mined at Pannawonica, Point Samson is a great fishing spot and Cossack is a very picturesque and historic town. This area holds the beginnings of European settlement of the north-west.

Aboriginal History
Aborigines have occupied the area around Roebourne for at least 20,000 years, according to radiocarbon dating of recovered artefacts. The Ngaluma people inhabited the flood country from the Maitland River to Peawah River, which covers about 6400 sq km. There were three divisions of this grouping: two were west and east of the Harding River and the other occupied the Burrup Peninsula and were known as the Jaburara.

Numerous shell middens remain, including a number just on the outskirts of Karratha. The Ngaluma constructed spinifex fishing nets and etched symbolic motifs into thousands of rocks. When the first settlers came, they employed the Aborigines as labourers and shepherds and paid them with goods. Introduced diseases, such as smallpox and measles, soon took their toll.

For a while there was an uneasy peace between the two groups. There were a number of massacres and in one clash in 1868, known as the 'Flying Foam massacre', between 40 and 60 Aborigines were killed in retaliation for the spearing of four settlers. The Aborigines who remained were forced into working on pastoral leases, and others were forced to dive for pearl shells.

In the 1930s, several neighbouring Aboriginal tribes – the Gurruma, Injibandi, Banjima and Marduthunia – were moved into reserves in Roebourne and Onslow, in an effort to reduce administrative costs. The main groups today in the Roebourne area are Injibandi and Ngaluma. The Jaburara are gone but their curious etchings survive.

Information
The Roebourne District tourist office (☎ 9182 1060) is in the Old Gaol, Queen St, Roebourne. For information about activities in Point Samson go to the fisheries building (☎ 9187 1414) in Point Samson Rd.

There is a laundrette in the Victoria Hotel-Mt Welcome Motel complex in Roebourne and a good supermarket in Wickham. Get a copy of the *Emma Withnell Heritage Trail* brochure ($1.50); it outlines a 52km walk/drive through Cossack, Roebourne, Wickham and Point Samson.

Roebourne
Roebourne (population 1700), 39km from Karratha, is the oldest existing town in the Pilbara. It has a history of grazing, gold and copper-mining, and was once the capital of the north-west.

It is the oldest town between Port Gregory, near Geraldton, and Palmerston, Northern Territory, and there are still fine historic buildings to be seen. These include an **old gaol**, the 1888 **Union Bank**, a **church** built in 1894 and the **Victoria Hotel**, which is the last of the five original pubs. The town was once connected to Cossack, 13km away on the coast, by a horse-drawn tram.

Places to Stay & Eat There is the *Harding River Caravan Park* (☎ 9182 1063) with tent/powered sites at $10/12 for two. The *Mt Welcome Motel Hotel* (☎ 9182 1001), in Roe St, has single/double units for $45/65.

The *Roebourne Diner*, good for eat-in and takeaway, and the more up-market *Poinciana Room*, are in the hotel complex. Also on Roe St is a snack bar, open daily, and a BP roadhouse for takeaways and supplies.

Cossack
This is a fascinating town with many intact early buildings. It was originally known as Tien Tsin Harbour after the barque which carried the first settlers there in 1863. It was given its present name when the HMS *Cossack*, with Governor Weld aboard, visited the town in 1871.

Cossack was a bustling town and the main port for the district in the mid to late 19th century. Cossack's boom was short lived and Point Samson soon supplanted it as the chief port for the area. The sturdy old buildings date from 1870 to 1898, and much of the town is being restored as a continuing 1988 bicentennial project.

The town now includes an **art gallery** in the post office (built in 1884), a **museum** in the 1895 stone-brick courthouse and budget accommodation in the police barracks (built in 1897). Other buildings in the town are Galbraith's store (1891), the bakehouse, a custom house/bond store (1896), the post and telegraph building (1884), schoolhouse (1897) and mining Registrar's quarters and mercantile store (1895).

Beyond town, there's a **pioneer cemetery** with a small Japanese section dating from the pearl-diving days. In fact, this is where pearling actually began; it later moved to Broome in the 1890s. There are a couple of lookouts and excellent beaches in the area; the cooler, drier months are best for a visit.

Obtain copies of *Cossack Historic Walk* and *Cossack: The First Port in the North-*

West (50c each). All proceeds go towards restoration of the town.

The Staircase to the Moon (moonlight reflected on the tidal flats), viewed from Reader's Point Lookout, is legendary. It comes across an average of 50km of marsh and lasts for ages. For trivia buffs, all seven of the species of mangrove found in the Pilbara occur near the Cossack boat ramp.

Places to Stay *Cossack Backpackers* (☎ 9182 1190) is one of those gems of the road. In the old police barracks you can truly get away from it all. The dorm/family rooms are $12/35, there is a kitchen, refrigerators and hot and cold showers. There is also a small shop nearby. As there are no places to eat (except a basic cafe in the Customs House), bring your own food. The managers will pick you up from the bus depot in Wickham; they do two runs each day.

Wickham & Point Samson

Wickham is a Robe River Iron town, handling their ore-exporting facilities 10km away at Cape Lambert, where the jetty is 3km long (one of the highest and longest open ocean wharves in Australia).

Point Samson, beyond Wickham, took the place of Cossack when the old port silted up. In turn, it has been replaced by the modern port facilities of Dampier and Cape Lambert. The name comes from Michael Samson, who accompanied Walter Padbury, the first settler, on his 1863 journey.

There are good beaches at Point Samson and at nearby **Honeymoon Cove**. You can explore **Samson Reef** at low tide for coral and oysters. If you have any queries about the area, the friendly people at Point Samson Fisheries (☎ 9187 1414) will answer them.

Places to Stay & Eat In Wickham, *Wickham Lodge* (☎ 9187 1439), in Wickham Drive, has singles/doubles for $70/78. The price includes air-con, TV, laundry service and a continental breakfast. *Samson Accommodation* (☎ 9187 1052), at 56 Samson Rd, Point Samson, has units from $80/90 for doubles/triples. The *Solveig Caravan Park* (☎ 9187

1414), Samson Rd, has tent/powered caravan sites for $13/15 for two. *Delilah's B&B* (☎ 9187 1471) in Point Samson is $45/85.

At Point Samson, *Trawlers Tavern* is a bar/restaurant overlooking the pier. Underneath, in the same building, is *Moby's Kitchen*, where you can get excellent fish, chips and salad ($8). It's popular with locals on weekends.

WHIM CREEK

The site of the first significant Pilbara mineral find was at Whim Creek, 80km east of Roebourne. It once had a copper mine and all that is left is the great, old *Whim Creek Hotel* (☎ 9176 4953) with tent and caravan sites (formerly free, but now $10 for two people), backpackers' beds for $12 and singles/doubles for $30/35. The restaurant has barraburgers for $7.50, 10 inch hot dogs for $3.50 and cappuccinos for $2.80.

'COMPANY' TOWNS

The Pilbara is the home of the company town. (For a start there needs to be a salary earner in the family to at least pay the air-con bill.) It was big companies that built most of the towns as dormitories for their workers and administrative bases for their mining projects.

Dampier, Karratha, Newman, Parabur-doo, Pannawonica and Tom Price all owe their existence to big mining companies. They invariably have a variety of sports facilities which always fall second in popularity behind the tavern or workers' club. Sky TV, dirt-bike racing, stock cars, takeaway food and 'eclectic' videos are the stock in trade of these communities.

Tom Price

This iron-ore town, south-west of Wittenoom, is the 'big daddy' of the Pilbara's company towns and belongs to Hamersley Iron. Built in 1962, it is even named after a mining expert, Thomas Moore Price of the giant US Kaiser Steel Corporation. The umbilical cord of the town is the railway line to Dampier, on the coast.

Check with Hamersley Iron (☎ 9189 2375) in Tom Price about inspecting the open-cut mine works – if nothing else, the scale of it will impress you. Conducted weekdays only, the tours cost a hefty $12/6 for adults/children.

Mt Nameless (1128m), 4km west of Tom Price, is the highest accessible mountain in the state. It offers good views of the area, especially at sunset.

Places to Stay & Eat The *Tom Price Caravan Park* (☎ 9189 1515) has tent/ powered sites for $12/14, on-site vans for $40 and chalets for $65; all prices are for two. *Hillview Lodge* (☎ 9189 1110), Stadium Rd, has budget rooms for $50 for two and deluxe rooms from $119. The *Mercure Inn Tom Price* (☎ 9189 1101) is also expensive with singles, twins and double units all $94; there is a babysitting service.

The *Red Emperor, Karijini Cafe* and the *Milk Bar Tom Price & Chinese Takeaway* (their title) in the shopping mall, provide reasonable food. The *Mercure Inn Tom Price* and *Hillview Lodge* both have standard counter meals. Self-caterers can buy ingredients from Charlie Carters in Central Rd.

Paraburdoo
This Hamersley Iron town, some 79km south of Tom Price, was built in 1970 to service local iron-ore operations. In the local Aboriginal language, 'Piru-Pardu' loosely translated means 'meat feathers' after the abundance of sulphur-crested cockatoos in the area. Paraburdoo's airport is the closest commercial airport to Karijini National Park. The tourist office (☎ 9189 5374) is part of the Paraburdoo Caravan Park at 1 Camp Rd.

Each Thursday at 12.40 pm there are mine tours; book these on ☎ 9189 5200. About 6km south of town is the **Radio Hill Lookout** (Mt Paraburdoo). There are a number of swimming holes and springs near town such as Kelly's Pool, Ratty Springs, Howie's Hole, Nanjilgardy Pool and Palm Springs.

Places to Stay & Eat The cheap option is the *Paraburdoo Caravan Park* (☎ 9189 5374) on Camp Rd; powered sites are $15 and cabins are $30/47 for singles/doubles. At

the corner of Rocklea and Tom Price Rds is the *Mercure Inn Paraburdoo*; there is a choice of 'old' rooms at $65/85 and 'new' rooms at $94/105. There is a restaurant in the Paraburdoo Hotel and Charlie Carters supermarket in Ashburton Ave.

Pannawonica
This is definitely a 'company town', built to house workers from the Robe River Iron Associates open-cut mining operations. It is 46km off the North-West Coastal Highway on the way to Millstream-Chichester National Park. There is a tavern and hotel (☎ 9184 1073) in Pannawonica Drive; B&B is $65/75 for singles/doubles. If you wish to see iron ore loaded into trucks and transferred to another form of transport (still awake?) then ring Pannawonica Mine Tours (☎ 9184 1142) 24 hours in advance.

MILLSTREAM-CHICHESTER NATIONAL PARK
The impressive 2000 sq km Millstream-Chichester National Park lies 150km south of Roebourne. It is reached by gravel road from the North-West Coastal Highway; the signposted turn-off is 27km past Roebourne. The main feature is **Pyramid Hill**, a volcanic remnant comprised of reddish breccia and tuff, some 1800 million years old.

Millstream-Chichester includes a number of freshwater pools formed by a spring from the underflow of the Fortescue River. **Python Pool**, different from the rest of Millstream, is a deep water hole at the base of a cliff. It was once an oasis for Afghani cameldrivers and still makes a good place for a swim.

The road which heads over the Chichester Range is sealed for a good deal of the climb and descent. At the top of the range is **Mt Herbert** (366m), a good lookout and starting point for the **Chichester Range Camel Trail**, an 8km, two hour walk through a rugged part of the range and via McKenzie Spring down to Python Pool. From the lookout you can see what constitutes most of the park – clay tablelands, basalt ranges and a cloak of pincushion spinifex.

The main part of the park is centred around

Millstream Homestead and access is via a 30km loop road which is 11.5km off the Hamersley Iron Rd. The **Chinderwarriner Pool**, near the visitors' centre in Millstream, is another pleasant oasis with pools, palms (including the unique Millstream palm) and lilies; it is well worth a visit.

The lush environment is a haven for birds and other fauna such as flying foxes and kangaroos. Over 20 species of dragonfly and damselfly have been recorded around the pool. The old homestead has been converted into an information centre with a wealth of detail on the Millstream ecosystems and lifestyle of the Yinjibarndi people.

The park also has a number of walking and driving trails including the Homestead Walk, the 6.8km Murlunmunyjurna Trail and Cliff Lookout Drive (6km).

Places to Stay & Eat

There are basic campsites (☎ 9184 5144) at Snake Creek (near Python Pool), Crossing Pool and Deep Reach; tent sites are $5 for two and $3 for each adult. You cannot buy food out here; stock up in Karratha before tackling the interior Pilbara.

KARIJINI (HAMERSLEY RANGE) NATIONAL PARK

This national park, second-largest in the state after Rudall River, contains rugged scenery which has few equals in Australia. It is about five hours from Roebourne and 3½ hours from Port Hedland. If you are in the Pilbara do not, on any account, miss the gorge country.

The traditional owners of the region are the Panyjima, Innawonga and Kurrama Aboriginal people. The name of the park was changed to Karijini to recognise the significance of these people, who have lived here for at least 20,000 years.

There is an Aboriginal interpretive centre (☎ (014) 511 1285) at the junction of Juna Downs, Joffre Falls and Yampire Gorge Rds, in the south-east corner of the park. It is run by Aborigines and they are enthusiastic and informative. Get a copy of the free *Karijini: Visitor Information/Walk Trail Guide*.

Flora & Fauna

The park is rich in wildlife and you may encounter euros, red kangaroos and the rare Rothschild's rock wallaby when driving. You may even see the Pilbara ningaui – pronounced 'nin-gowie' – an almost mythological creature which comes out at night to hunt for food. Reptiles love this environment and many species are seen, especially in the gorges. Birds are also attracted to the semi-permanent pools in the gorges or the nesting eyries along the cliffs.

One of the great features of the park is the profusion of wildflowers which vary with the seasons. There always seems to be something in flower. In the cooler months, look for yellow flowering sennas (cassias) and acacias, mulla-mulla and bluebells.

The Gorges

The gorges of Karijini are spectacular both in their sheer rocky faces and their varied colours.

There is now a sealed road from the Great Northern Highway to the interpretive centre. This access road is about 35km south of the Auski (Munjina) Roadhouse and 160km north of Newman. Eventually the road will be sealed all the way to Tom Price, on the western edge of the park, thus opening up

Giant termite mounds can be seen around Dales Gorge.

THE PILBARA

THE PILBARA

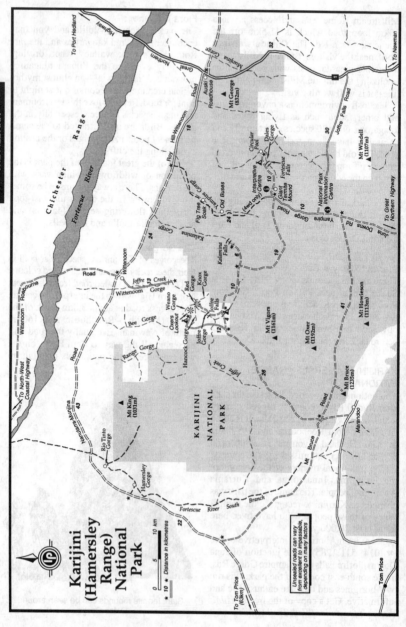

Karijini (Hamersley Range) National Park

0   5   10 km

★ 10   Distance in kilometres

Unsealed roads can vary from excellent to impassable, depending on many factors

---

'Miracle Mile' & Knox Slide

If you want a totally different impression of the awesome scenery in Karijini, try the 'Miracle Mile' (MM) & Knox Slide with local identity Dave Doust.

The MM starts early in the morning. You first go to Oxer's Lookout, then to Hancock Gorge where the adventure starts. You descend a steep track into the gorge and follow it down to where it narrows, allowing bridging on either wall of the gorge. At Kermit's Pool there is time for a swim before you climb around a waterfall using Oxer's Handle (find out for yourself what this is). Negotiate the next narrow ledge without using your hands. It gets worse. Down the harrowing and frighteningly steep Hade's Stairs and around the corner to the end of Hancock Gorge.

Prepare to get wet – the next stage is a swim across Junction Pool. Here you can partake of some Cadjeput courage and fling yourself from a tree. Climbing starts again as you head up the 100-Foot Waterfall into Weano Gorge. This is not for the faint-hearted. Next (it goes on!), the side of Deep Pool is negotiated by a goat track. Into the water again through two pools into Handrail Pool and the MM is over. It is, unsurprisingly, one of the best experiences of most participant's lives.

In the afternoon you can continue into Knox Pool. This includes the Knox Slide. Sit on your bum, slide down a rock, then drop 7m into a deep, cold pool. You paid for it! Usually there are no complaints. How do you get out? – only Dave knows the secret. ∎

---

that area. After 26km, turn north on the Juna Downs Rd and follow the newly sealed road to the interpretive centre. You pass a self-registration station where you pay entry fees ($5 per car).

Dales Gorge is a good place to start your exploration of the many gorges. The 10km road into Dales Gorge starts just south of the interpretive centre; there is a freshwater tank close to the turn-off for those needing to replenish supplies. About 200m along the Dales Gorge track is a turn-off to the right; it takes you to a **giant termite mound**, popular with 'I've been there' snapshooters.

At the end of this road you can get to **Circular Pool** and a nearby lookout, and by a footpath to the bottom of **Fortescue Falls**. The walk from Circular Pool along Dales Gorge to the falls is recommended; you will be surprised by how much permanent water is in the gorge.

Next, head west on the Joffre Falls road. A turn-off after 19km leads to **Kalamina Gorge** (6km) and then another turn-off (after 30km) leads to **Knox Gorge** (6km). It is only 1km down this road to the often dry but nonetheless spectacular **Joffre Falls**. Near Knox Gorge is a 1.5km return walk to Red Gorge lookout.

From the Knox Gorge turn-off it is 3km west to a T-junction. Head north from this junction for another 14km to the remarkable **Oxers Lookout**, at the point where **Red**, **Weano**, **Joffre** and **Hancock** gorges all meet. This is one of the Outback's greatest sights. If you wish to get down into the gorge proper, take the steps down to Handrail Pool (turn right at the bottom) in Weano Gorge.

At the T-junction on Joffre Falls road you can head south to Tom Price. Follow Joffre Falls Rd for 26km until it meets Mt Bruce Rd. Turn right for 2km and then head south for another 5km until you meet the Marandoo Rd. Turn right on Marandoo Rd and after 35km it joins the Paraburdoo-Tom Price Rd; it is another 10km north-west to Tom Price. You'll pass **Mt Bruce** (1235m), Western Australia's second-highest peak, on this route. Incidentally, the state's highest mountain is **Mt MeHarry** (1245m), near the south-east border of Karijini National Park.

About 29km north of Tom Price you can take a side trip on the Nanutarra-Munjina road. After 41km on this road you reach the turn-off to the **Hamersley Gorge**, only 4km from the main road. The evidence of the force of nature, reflected in the folded ribbons of rock, adds to the awe-inspiring landscape. Not far north is the small **Rio Tinto Gorge**, appearing like a dry gulch in all those cowboy movies of old.

Wittenoom, at the northern end of the

Karijini, is now virtually a ghost town, although a few inhabitants still cling tenaciously to their beleaguered homes. Likely, there will be nothing there when you visit, as Perth's bureaucrats are doing everything they can to close it down – probably to avoid the possibility of future litigation. It has been removed from all official maps.

Wittenoom had an earlier history as a blue asbestos mining town, but mining finally halted in 1966. A number of miners and baggers who once worked at the Wittenoom Gorge mine have subsequently 'died of the dust' (or mesothelioma, a debilitating lung condition). There are still many potential compensation cases outstanding.

To the seasoned traveller there is, however, an irresistible appeal about this place. Perhaps it unlocks all those hidden images of western moviedom: rolling tumbleweeds, lone gunslingers, scowling Jack Palance-types and cowering townsfolk.

The now infamous **Wittenoom Gorge** is immediately south of the former town. A surfaced road runs the 13km through this gorge, passing old asbestos mines and a number of smaller gorges and pretty pools.

Travel down the road, 24km east from Wittenoom, and there's a turn-off to the **Yampire Gorge** where blue veins of asbestos can be seen in the rock. **Fig Tree Soak**, in the gorge, was used by Afghani cameldrivers as a watering point. The road may be closed in future because of the asbestos risk.

Organised Tours

There are a number of tour operators in the area, including Dave's Gorge Tours (☎ 9189 7026) which has received rave reviews from travellers to the tune of 'it's the best experience that I've had'. Contact Dave for details.

Design-a-Tour (☎ 9144 1460), based at Auski Roadhouse, has one day tours of Karijini and the gorges for $70, including lunch. They have two day tours from Tom Price and Port Hedland for $190. Lestok Tours (☎ 9189 2032), based in Tom Price, has a day trip to Karijini for $35/15 for adults/children.

Snappy Gum Safaris (☎ 9185 1278) runs

Asbestos Warning
Even after 25 years, there is a health risk in Wittenoom township, and in Wittenoom and Yampire gorges, from airborne asbestos fibres. Avoid disturbing asbestos tailings in the area and keep your car windows closed on windy days. If you are concerned, seek medical advice before going to these areas. ■

two day camping safaris to Karijini ($190) but mainly concentrates on Millstream-Chichester National Park (day tour $70). A four day Pilbara safari is $695, all-inclusive.

A great way to see the gorges is by helicopter. One trip departs from the Auski Roadhouse (☎ 9176 6979, 30 minutes, $135) and another from the Bee Gorge turnoff west of Wittenoom (☎ 9189 7075, 40 minutes, $140).

Places to Stay & Eat

There are several basic campsites within the Karijini including Dales Gorge, Weano Gorge and the Joffre Intersection ($5 for a tent site for two, extra adult $3); contact the rangers (☎ 9189 8157) for information.

All of Wittenoom's accommodation is basic (and under imminent threat of closure). The *Gorges Caravan Park* (☎ 9189 7075), Second Ave, has tent sites from $12, and cabins from $35 for two. *Wittenoom Bungarra Bivouac Hostel* (☎ 9189 7026), 71 Fifth Ave, has beds at $7 per night; this is the base for Dave's Gorge Tours. *Nomad Heights* (☎ 9189 7068), on First Ave, is a small arid/tropical permaculture farm; it is $7. *Wittenoom Holiday Homes* (☎ 9189 7096) on Fifth Ave has cottages from $55 for two.

Some 42km east of Wittenoom, on the Great Northern Highway, is the asbestos-free *Auski Tourist Village* (☎ 9176 6988). Its 'negative' mineral status and the fine hamburgers in the restaurant are its only saving graces. The ablution block is a bitterly cold winter's morning walk from the vastly overpriced cabins – $45 for the barest of necessities. Tent sites in the caravan facility

KEREN FLAVELL

JEFF WILLIAMS

JEFF WILLIAMS

JEFF WILLIAMS

A	
B	C
D	

Central West Coast, Coral Coast & The Pilbara

A: The Korean Star shipwreck,
   north of Carnarvon

B: Aboriginal petroglyphs, Jaburara
   Heritage Trail, near Karratha

C: Stromatolites, Shark Bay World
   Heritage Area

D: The 'climbing figures', Burrup
   Peninsula, near Dampier

RICHARD I'ANSON

JEFF WILLIAMS

KEREN FLAVELL

Coral Coast & The Pilbara

A: Outback north of Newman, in the Pilbara
B: Swimming with a whale shark, Ningaloo Reef
C: Coastline of North Carnarvon

are $10 for two and the motel rooms, basking in their lack of competition, are $110 for two.

Other places outside the park are Tom Price and Newman (see those sections). The *Mt Florance Station* (☎ 9189 8151), halfway between Millstream and Karijini, has camping for $5 per person, and beds in the shearers' quarters for $12.

NEWMAN
• *pop 5500*

Newman, a town which only came into existence in the 1970s, is on the Great Northern Highway. It is 414km north of Meekatharra and 450km south of Port Hedland.

Newman is a modern company town built solely to service the mine. The friendly, helpful Newman tourist office (☎ 9175 2888) is at the corner of Fortescue Ave and Newman Drive. The **museum** and art gallery, built of rammed earth and financed by BHP Iron Ore, is adjacent to the tourist office.

Near the town, the iron-ore mountain, **Whaleback**, is being systematically taken apart and railed to the coast some 426km away. Guided tours (☎ 9175 2888) of these operations (and the largest open-cut, iron-ore mine in the world) leave across from the tourist office at 8.30 am and 1 pm daily; safety helmets are provided, the tour is 1½ hours long and it costs $3.

The highlight of Newman is undoubtedly the northern road out of it. This is one of the most **scenic drives** in the state as the highway weaves its way through the Hamersley and Ophthalmia ranges. Wildflowers are seen along the road from June to October.

There are Aboriginal **rock carvings** at Wanna Munna, 70km from town, and at Punda, off the Marble Bar road. Two nearby pools of note on the Waterhole Circuit (map available from the tourist office) are **Stuarts Pool**, a difficult but adventurous trip by 4WD, and **Kalgan's Pool**, a day outing (also 4WD-only) from town.

Places to Stay & Eat

There are several caravan parks in the area, the closest to town being the *Newman Caravan Park* (☎ 9175 1428), on Kalgan

Drive; tent/powered sites are $12/15 for two, backpackers' cabins are $25 for two (with TV and a nearby caravan with cooking facilities) and park cabins are $60. Other parks are the *Capricorn Caravan Park Roadhouse* (☎ 9175 1535), on the Great Northern Highway 18km south of town, with powered sites/rooms for $10/30 for two; and *Dearlove's Caravan Park* (☎ 9175 2802), Cowra Drive, with tent/powered sites for $10/15 for two, and on-site vans from $30.

If you are over 50 you get a discount (and will probably need it) from the *Mercure Inn Newman* (☎ 9175 1101), Newman Drive, which has double rooms from $132. The *All Seasons Newman Hotel* (☎ 9177 8666), Newman Drive, also has backpackers' beds for $30, and tidy doubles for $130.

In addition to the roadhouses, there are a number of takeaways including the *Boulevarde Coffee Shop*, *Chicken Treat* and the *Chinese Kitchen* in the Boulevarde shopping centre. On Hilditch Ave, there's the *Thai Restaurant* and in the All Seasons Newman Hotel they have fine counter meals with an endless salad bar.

Getting There & Away

Ansett Australia (☎ 13 1300) has at least one jet each day to Perth.

Greyhound Pioneer (☎ 9175 1398) has a service from Perth to Port Hedland (with connections to Darwin) via Newman on Sunday, Wednesday and Friday and in the other direction on Sunday, Tuesday and Friday.

MARBLE BAR
• *pop 350*

Reputed to be the hottest place in Australia, Marble Bar had a period in the 1920s when temperatures topped 37°C for 160 consecutive days. On one occasion, in 1905, the mercury soared to 49.1°C. From October to March, days over 40°C are common – though it is dry heat and not too unbearable.

The town is 203km south-east of Port Hedland. It takes its name from a bar of red jasper across the Coongan River, 6km west of town. The tourist office (☎ 9176 1041) is opposite the Ironclad Hotel.

In town, the 1895 **government buildings** on the corner of Francis and Contest Sts, made of local stone, are still in use. In late winter, as the spring wildflowers begin to bloom, Marble Bar is a pretty place and one of the most popular Pilbara towns to visit.

The **Comet Gold Mine**, 10km south of Marble Bar, is still in operation and has a mining museum and display centre; it is open daily. **Coppins Gap/Doolena Gorge**, about 70km north-east of Marble Bar, is a deep cutting with impressive views, twisted bands of rock and an ideal swimming hole.

Places to Stay

The *Marble Bar Caravan Park* (☎ 9176 1067), on Contest St, has tent sites/on-site vans for $15/35 for two. Single/double rooms at the *Iron Clad Hotel* (☎ 9176 1066), a distinctive drinking spot, are from $60/80; they also have backpackers' accommodation from $20. The *Marble Bar Travellers Stop Motel* (☎ 9176 1166) has rooms for $35, motel units for $70/80.

COLLIER RANGE & RUDALL RIVER (KARLAMILYI) NATIONAL PARKS

Two of the most isolated and interesting of the state's national parks are found in the Pilbara. Both parks are true wilderness areas, accessible only by 4WD. Travellers have to be self-sufficient with fuel, water, food and first-aid equipment; seek permission from property owners before using their roads.

The **Collier Range** is the more easily accessible as the Great Northern Highway bisects it near the quaint Kumarina Roadhouse, 256km north of Meekatharra. Here, at the upper reaches of the Ashburton and Gascoyne rivers, the ranges vary from low hills to high ridges bounded by cliffs.

In the far west of the park near Coobarra there are sand dunes, then spinifex plains and, in the north-east, mulga, which is seasonally interspersed with mulla-mulla.

Even more remote is the **Rudall River (Karlamilyi) National Park**, a breathtakingly beautiful desert region of 15,000 sq

km, which is accessible only to experienced drivers with 4WD vehicles. The best time to visit is July and August when daytime temperatures are tolerable – in the desert the nights can be exceptionally cold.

The park is reached via two routes. The first is from Marble Bar along the Telfer Rd to the northern park boundary, about 420km. (Permission to use this route must be obtained from the Newmont Holdings' Perth office.) The second route is from Newman via Balfour Downs on the Talawana Track to the southern boundary, about 260km. To give you an indication of the area you are entering, the Canning Stock Route skirts the park to the east and No 24 Well is to the south-east.

The Martu people still live in this area and, as recently as the 1980s, established the Punmu and Parnngurr communities in the park.

Plateaus of sandstone and quartzite carved by glaciers 280 million years ago, sand

Emus are seen at the northern and southern ends of the Canning Stock Route.

plains covered with spinifex and desert oak, dunes and salt lakes, are all features of the landscape. Wattles and hakeas line some watercourses and eucalypts are found by the Rudall River. Over 70 species of birds have been recorded and the rabbit-eared bandicoot (also dalgyte or bilby – see the boxed aside 'The Bilby' in the Broome Region chapter) may still exist in the area.

At least two vehicles, equipped with Royal Flying Doctor Service radios, are needed for this trip and visitors must be *totally* self-sufficient. There are absolutely no facilities in this park.

PORT HEDLAND
• *pop 18,000*
This port, billed as the 'port of big ships', handles a massive tonnage and is the place from which Pilbara's iron ore is shipped overseas. The town itself is built on an island connected to the mainland by causeways, and the main highway into Port Hedland enters along a 3km causeway. The satellite community of South Hedland was established with a planned population of 40,000 and is where many of Port Hedland's inhabitants live.

Even before the Marble Bar gold rush of the 1880s, the town had been important. It became a grazing centre in 1864 and during the 1870s, a fleet of 150 pearling luggers had been based there. By 1946, however, the population had dwindled to a mere 150. Iron-ore mining operations in the Pilbara ensured a rebirth of the port's importance. The port now has the greatest export tonnage of any in Australia and is the only facility capable of handling two ships in excess of 250,000 tonnes at one time.

The port is on a mangrove-fringed inlet – there are plenty of fish, crabs, oysters and birds around. The port and iron-ore eyesores are feted at the expense of the prolific natural wonders in the area.

Information
The helpful tourist bureau (☎ 9173 1711), which has showers ($1.50), is at 13 Wedge St, across from the post office. It's open from 8.30 am to 5 pm during the week, from 8.30 am to 4.30 pm on weekends. It provides an excellent keyed map of the town. You have to give the staff a guernsey for their enthusiasm – few other tourism employees have to promote a town caked in red dust with a port area that at night looks like the opening scenes from *Bladerunner*!

Things to See & Do
You can visit the wharf area or view it from the 26m **observation tower** behind the tourist office (you have to sign a waiver to climb it and you'll need closed-in shoes, $2/1 for adults/children). Below are huge ore carriers, stockpiles of ore and a town encrusted in red Pilbara dust. The iron-ore trains are up to 2.6km in length. From Monday to Friday, at 10 am, there's a 1½ hour BHP Iron Ore & Port Tour which leaves from the tourist office (adults/kids $10/2).

Pretty Pool, 7km east of the town centre on the waterfront, is a safe tidal pool where shell collectors will have fun – beware of stonefish. Visits can also be made to the **Royal Flying Doctor Service base**, Richardson St, between 10 am and 2 pm on weekdays. There are **Aboriginal petroglyphs** (rock engravings), including turtles and a whale, near the BHP main gate at Two Mile Ridge; you have to approach the Aboriginal office in the Boulevard shopping centre for permission to see them.

Whale & Turtle-Watching
These eco-paupers receive little publicity in a town where red dust and iron ore are sovereign.

The flatback turtle nests between October and March on some of the nearby beaches, including Munda, Cooke Point, Cemetery Beach and Pretty Pool. Nesting density is low on city beaches with only a few turtles nesting each night. At Munda, up to 20 turtles may nest in a night. Enquire at the tourist office about their location during the nesting season.

Whale-watching trips are operated by Big Blue Dive (☎ 9173 3202). These take four hours, leave on weekdays only and cost about $60 per person; trips are dependent on

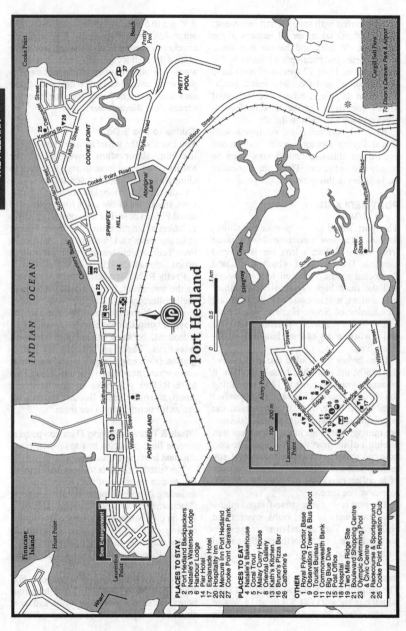

PLACES TO STAY
2 Port Hedland Backpackers
3 Natalie's Waterside Lodge
6 Harbour Lodge
14 Pier Hotel
17 Esplanade Hotel
20 Hospitality Inn
22 Mercure Inn Port Hedland
27 Cooke Point Caravan Park

PLACES TO EAT
4 Natalie's Bakehouse
5 Coral Trout
7 Malay Curry House
8 Oriental Gallery
13 Kath's Kitchen
16 Bruno's Pizza Bar
26 Catherine's

OTHER
1 Royal Flying Doctor Base
9 Observation Tower & Bus Depot
10 Tourist Bureau
11 Commonwealth Bank
12 Big Blue Dive
15 Post Office
18 Hospital
19 Two Mile Ridge Site
21 Boulevard Shopping Centre
23 Olympic Swimming Pool
   & Civic Centre
24 Racecourse & Sportsground
25 Cooke Point Recreation Club

tides and numbers. The majestic humpback is often seen in pods of five to six.

Places to Stay

Camping & Caravanning You can camp by the airport at *Dixon's Caravan Park* (☎ 9172 2525) when space permits; powered sites are $16 for two. More convenient, however, is the revamped *Cooke Point Caravan Park* (☎ 9173 1271), on Athol St, which is also adjacent to Pretty Pool; powered sites in this very presentable park are $17 for two, and excellent park cabins are $65. *South Hedland Caravan Park* (☎ 9172 1197), on Hamilton Rd, South Hedland, is the third park in the area, but recent development projects have filled its accommodation with workers.

Budget Accommodation The dusty *Port Hedland Backpackers* (☎ 9173 3282) is at 20 Richardson St between Edgar and McKay Sts. The homely atmosphere and friendly hosts make up for the lack of luxuries. Dorm beds/twin rooms cost $14/32 and the place has a kitchen and (in these parts) much-needed laundry facilities. They run economical three day camping trips to Karijini for $220.

The *Harbour Lodge* (☎ 9173 2996), at 11 Edgar St, has a fully equipped kitchen; double/ family rooms are $40/45.

Hotels & Motels On the corner of Anderson St and the Esplanade, there's the decaying *Esplanade Hotel* (☎ 9173 1798) which has rooms from $45 per person. The usual cost for motel rooms at the *Pier Hotel* is $75/85.

Natalie's Waterside Lodge (☎ 9173 2635) at 7 Richardson St is a good choice as you at least get what you pay for; comfortable doubles are $80, or $420 per week (and the views of the port and ore piles are free).

The *South Hedland Motel* (☎ 9172 2222), in Court Place, is currently full of project workers; a single here is from $100 (when you can get it and if you want it).

The most expensive motels are the *Hospitality Inn* (☎ 9173 1044), Webster St, with singles and doubles from $138; the *Mercure*

Inn Port Hedland (☎ 9173 1511), Lukis St, with rooms for $139; and the *Mercure Inn Airport* (☎ 9172 1222), on the North-West Coastal Highway, opposite the airport, with rooms also from $139.

Places to Eat

The *Pier* and the *Esplanade* hotels do counter meals at lunch time; about $10 per person. The air-con *Salty's Bistro* in the Mercure Inn Port Hedland has a good buffet.

There are plenty of supermarkets if you want to fix your own food and also a number of coffee bars and other places where you can get a pie or pastie. *Natalie's Bakehouse*, on Richardson St, has been heartily recommended for its home-made salad rolls. Nearby is the *Coral Trout* with a BYO restaurant and takeaway section where you can get fish and chips; the mackerel is superb. *Kath's Kitchen*, Wedge St, is open from 5 am to 8.30 pm and has basic good meals such as gigantic breakfasts for about $8.

The *Oriental Gallery*, on the corner of Edgar and Anderson Sts, does a good-value weekday lunch. There are other Asian restaurants: the *Dynasty Gardens* and *Malay Curry House*.

Up in Cooke Point, on Keesing St, is *Catherine's*, one of the more expensive options in town. The *Cooke Point Recreation Club* has a pizza bar.

Getting There & Away

Air Qantas has at least one jet service daily to Perth. Ansett Australia has daily flights to Perth and also frequent flights, many operated by Skywest, to and from Broome, Derby, Geraldton, Karratha and Kununurra.

Ansett Australia (☎ 9173 3122) is in the Boulevard shopping centre on Wilson St.

Bus It's 230km from Karratha to Port Hedland and a farther 604km to Broome. Greyhound (☎ 13 2030) runs from Perth to Port Hedland and north to Broome and Darwin. Their office is in the Homestead, Throssell St, South Hedland.

Apart from the coastal route, Greyhound has another service that takes the inland route from Perth to Port Hedland via Newman three times weekly (with connections to Darwin). Northbound the bus departs Port Hedland on Sunday, Wednesday and Friday; southbound to Perth it departs on Sunday, Tuesday and Friday.

Getting Around

The airport is 13km from town; the only way to get there is by taxi, which costs $15. There's a Hedland Bus Lines service (☎ 9172 1394) between Port Hedland and South Hedland; it takes 40 minutes to an hour and operates Monday to Friday ($2.20). You can hire cars at the airport from the usual operators. Osborne Rentals (☎ 9140 2411) in the light industrial area has cheaper rates.

The Kimberley

The rugged Kimberley, at the northern end of WA, is one of Australia's last frontiers. Despite enormous advances in the past decade, this is still a little-travelled and very remote area of great rivers and magnificent scenery. The Kimberley suffers from climatic extremes – heavy rains in the Wet followed by searing heat in the Dry – but the irrigation projects in the north-east have greatlychanged the economic life of the region.

Nevertheless, rivers and creeks can rise rapidly following heavy rainfall and become impassable torrents within 15 minutes. Unless it's a very brief storm, it's quite likely that the watercourses will remain impassable for some days. The Fitzroy River can become so swollen at times that after two or three days rain it grows from its normal 100m width to a spectacular torrent more than 10km wide. Highway 1 through the Kimberley is sealed most of the way, but there are several notorious crossings which are still only fords rather than all-weather bridges.

The best time to visit is between April and September. By October it's already getting hot (35°C), and later in the year daily temperatures of more than 40°C are common until it starts to rain. On the other hand, the Wet is a spectacular time to visit – ethereal thunderstorms, lightning, flowing waterfalls and a swathe of rejuvenated landscape.

Kimberley attractions include the spectacular gorges on the Fitzroy River, the huge Wolfe Creek meteorite crater, the remote Gibb River, Mitchell Plateau and Kalumburu roads, the tidal waterfalls of Talbot Bay, Purnululu (Bungle Bungle) National Park and the Indian Ocean oasis of Broome and Cable Beach.

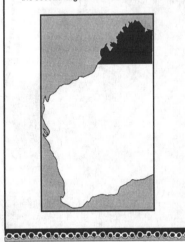

HIGHLIGHTS

- The exotic Indian Ocean getaways of multicultural Broome, or Cable Beach and Eco Beach
- Exploring the Dampier Peninsula with its rich Aboriginal culture (and watching sunset by the red pindan cliffs at Cape Leveque)
- Whitewater rafting down one of the horizontal tidal waterfalls at Walcott Inlet
- A 4WD adventure along the Gibb River or Kalumburu roads, with a sidetrip to Mitchells Falls or Drysdale River National Park
- A cruise along the remote Kimberley coast, passing waterfalls and dodging huge crocodiles
- Driving into and exploring the Devonian Reef national parks and taking a boat trip through Geikie Gorge
- Camping out near the mystical Purnululu (Bungle Bungle) Range (or even better, a helicopter flight above and alongside it)
- Peering into Wolfe Creek meteorite crater, the second largest known crater in the world

Books & Maps

The most descriptive book of the Kimberley is the excellent *The Kimberley: Horizons of Stone* (1992) by Alisdair McGregor & Quentin Chester. Modern and thorough coverage is given in Australian Geographic's *The Kimberley* (1990) by David McGonigal; this book includes an excellent touring map.

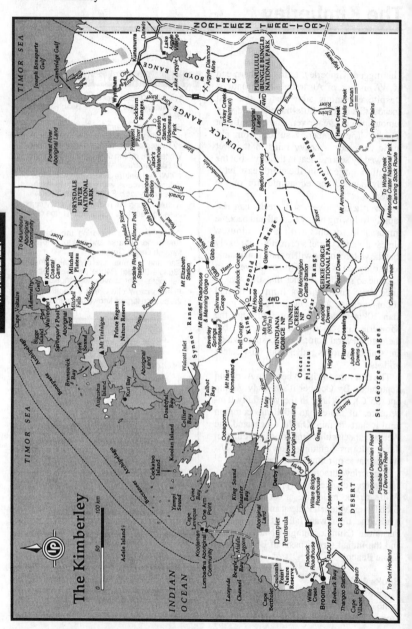

Broome Region

The Pilbara and the Kimberley are separated by the westerly edge of the Great Sandy Desert which extends all the way from the Northern Territory to the Indian Ocean. From the time you cross the De Grey River, there is almost nothing until you reach Broome, an isolated town which has become something of a travellers' haunt. Broome is nestled on the north side of Roebuck Bay and to the north is the Dampier Peninsula, home to a number of Aboriginal communities.

PORT HEDLAND TO BROOME

It is 610km from Port Hedland to Broome on what is probably Australia's most boring stretch of highway. Consequently, it proves to be a difficult day's drive. Get a copy of the handy leaflet, *Port Hedland to Broome*, from the Broome tourist office.

About 84km from Port Hedland is the **De Grey River** and just over 20km beyond that is the turn off to **Goldsworthy** and **Shay Gap**, former mining towns. It is now hard to believe these were once sizable towns.

Some 20km or so before the Pardoo Roadhouse is a turn-off to *Pardoo Station* (☎ 9176 4930), some 13km in towards the coast. The station comes recommended by a number of backpackers; camp/powered sites are $7/9, and budget beds are $15/7 for adults/children. A day visit is $5 per adult.

Just before the roadhouse (153km) is the turn-off to **Cape Keraudren**, which is 14km to the west on a dirt road. There is great fishing, picturesque tidal creeks and expansive beaches here ; campsites, from April to October, are $5. There are no facilities and water is not available (bring your own). The roadhouse (☎ 9176 4916) has tent/powered sites for $8/12, and there are budget cabins for $20/35.

Many shells are washed ashore on the magnificent stretch of **Eighty Mile Beach**, 245km from Port Hedland and 10km in towards the coast. The caravan park (☎ 9176 5941) is a great place to stay and tent/

powered sites are $12/16 for two, and cabins $55 for two ($5 for an extra adult).

Sandfire Roadhouse (☎ 9176 5944), 291km north of Port Hedland, is very much an enforced fuel stop for most. The *Droughtmaster Bar* is worth a look and the place to buy a great neoprene stubby holder. In the adequate caravan facility, tent/powered sites are $10/12 for two, single/twin motel units with shared facilities are $20/30, and units with en-suites are $50 for two.

Port Smith (☎ 9192 4969) is on a tidal lagoon, 23km from the highway turn-off (140km south of Broome). It is a beautiful place with unpowered sites only for $6 per person. Fishing is popular, with threadfin salmon, mangrove jack, trevally and whiting being the usual catches.

Eco Beach Wilderness Retreat

The area now called Eco Beach, near Cape Villaret and the southern end of Roebuck Bay, has long been settled by the Yawuru people. In 1699, Dampier landed here, but the cape's name was bestowed by the 1801 French expedition, to commemorate a French maritime captain. The region was later settled by pastoralists and named Thangoo Station. Sadly, the Aborigines were moved off their traditional land by these pastoralists just before WWII and sent to mission stations near Broome.

Eco Beach is only 27km by sea and 130km by road from Broome (and yet light years removed from the ethos of that town). There is a 15km stretch of white sandy beach, timber huts on stilts with superb views of the Indian Ocean, and abundant marine and bird life. Activities include nature walks, horse-riding, fishing, swimming and snorkelling, and generally relaxing. There are no five-star luxuries, no TVs, telephones or room service, but the fend-for-yourself theme, the silence, remoteness, clear starry skies and minimal impact on the environment, all compensate. A kilometre or so along the beach, near red pindan cliffs, are **rock formations** which look something like a miniaturised Bungle Bungle range. 'Paradise' comes at a price – hordes of mosquitoes descend after rain, so be prepared.

A two day package to Eco Beach is $199 per person with all meals and transfers included, far less than you would pay at a more conventional resort. Singles/twins are $100 ($10 for an extra person) and 4WD transfers are $40 return. You can fly with Broome Aviation for $60. Contact numbers are ☎ 9192 4844, fax 9192 4845, e-mail ecobeach@tpgi.com.au.

Wholesome meals, made from local ingredients, are served daily at *Jack's Bar* (adding up to $45 if you have three). There is no self-catering, a downside for the place.

The road entrance is between the 500 and 450km Port Hedland road markers (heading south from Broome). The entrance is marked with a white drum and is directly across from a communications tower; you'll need to have obtained a gate key beforehand.

BROOME

For many travellers, Broome is Australia's archetypal getaway: palm-fringed beaches, clear, blue waters and a relaxed atmosphere. But it is also noted for its Chinatown and the influences of early Japanese pearlers.

Although still relatively isolated, Broome has been discovered. Today, it is something of a travellers' centre with the attendant good and bad characteristics. By all means, slip into 'Broome time' but watch out for thieves.

History

The Roebuck Bay region was known to the local Djuleun Aborigines as 'Nileribanjen'. The surrounding mudflats and shallows were rich in shellfish, fish and mudcrabs and the Djuleun traded spears and pearl shell; the latter eventually contributed to the end of their traditional way of life.

In 1864, a syndicate was formed to investigate the story of a convict who had found gold at Camden Harbour, near Kuri Bay, in 1856. Many eager pastoralists backed this expedition and, when gold was not found, a number of them put together another expedition to introduce sheep to the 'land in the vicinity of Roebuck Bay which would bear favourable comparison with some of the best runs in Victoria'.

The Aboriginal inhabitants of Roebuck Bay resented the intrusion of the pastoralists, especially their fencing of traditional water holes. In November 1864, three members of the pastoralists' expedition were murdered by Aborigines, which resulted in open conflict. The pastoralists withdrew in 1867 only to be replaced by pearlers, working north from Cossack, in the 1870s.

The town was gazetted in 1883 and named after the then governor, Sir Frederick Napier Broome. Pearling in the sea off Broome started in earnest in the 1880s. Broome still remained very much a shantytown until the submarine telegraph cable was laid from Cable Bay, west of Broome, to Java in 1889. This kept the pearling industry in close touch with price fluctuations and the industry began to expand rapidly. It peaked in the early 1900s when the town's 400 pearling luggers, worked by 3000 men, supplied 80% of the world's mother-of-pearl shell. However, it slowly declined in importance and it was not until the 1950s that it was revived, but on a much smaller scale. Today only a handful of boats operate.

Pearl-diving was a very unsafe occupation, as Broome's Japanese cemetery attests. The divers were from various Asian countries and the rivalries between the different nationalities were always intense and sometimes took an ugly turn.

When Japan entered WWII in 1941, the 500 Japanese in Broome were interned for the duration of the war. On 3 March 1942, following the bombing of Darwin in February, the Japanese bombed Broome. A number of flying boats were destroyed and about 70 Dutch refugees were killed. Many pearl luggers anchored in the harbour were destroyed by the Australian army as part of its 'scorched earth' policy, which left nothing of use for the Japanese if they invaded.

Today, the main industry is beef and Broome's modern meatworks can process 40,000 head during the season. Tourism is the other major industry and Broome's attractions and festivals bring hordes of visitors. Fortunately, local Aborigines are playing a major part in this cultural renaissance. Thanks to a progressive shire council any town development involves consultation with the Aboriginal community.

Orientation

The Great Northern Highway (Broome Rd) becomes Hamersley St in town. The two centres of Broome's development and growth are the southern part of town (near the corner of Hamersley and Saville Sts) and Chinatown. The museum is here, as is the Seaview shopping centre opposite. Paspaley shopping centre is in Chinatown and the large Boulevard shopping centre is out near the airport. Cable Beach is 4km north-west of Broome post office.

Information

The efficient Broome tourist bureau (☎ 9192 2222), corner of the Great Northern Highway (Broome Rd) and Bagot St, is just across the sports field from Chinatown. It's open daily from 8 am to 5 pm, April to November, and in the interim from 9 am to 5 pm Monday to Friday and 9 am to 1 pm weekends. It distributes a useful monthly guide to what's happening in and around Broome, the *Discover Broome* town map and the annual *Kimberley Holiday Planner*. Another handy freebie is *Broome Time*.

The post office is in Paspaley shopping centre and there are banks in Carnarvon St.

Chinatown

The term 'Chinatown' is used to refer to the old part of town, although only one block or so is multicultural and historic. Some of the plain and simple wooden buildings that line Carnarvon St still house Chinese merchants, but most are now restaurants, pearl dealers and tourist shops. The bars on the windows are to minimise cyclone damage.

The Carnarvon St phone booth sign is in English, Chinese, Arabic, Japanese and Malay. There is a **statue** of three men in Carnarvon St: Hiroshi Iwaki, Tokuichi Kuribayashi and Keith Dureau, who were all involved in the cultured pearl industry.

Pearling

A pearling lugger, the *Cornelius*, can occasionally be seen at the old Streeters jetty off Dampier Terrace, and there are cruises ($65) from the port jetty, subject to weather.

Broome Historical Society Museum (☎ 9192 2075), on Saville St, has exhibits on Broome's history, and on the pearling industry and its dangers. It's in the old customs house and from April to November is open weekdays from 10 am to 4 pm, weekends from 10 am to 1 pm; it's open fewer hours from November to May.

Mother-of-pearl has long been a Broome speciality. Between Carnarvon St and Dampier Terrace in Chinatown are a number of **pearl shops**. The main places are Paspaley Pearling Co in Short St; Broome Pearls, the Pearl Emporium and Linney's Pearls in Dampier Terrace; and Anastasia's Pearl Gallery in Carnarvon St. There is also the Shell House in Guy St.

The **Japanese Cemetery**, near Cable Beach Rd, testifies to the dangers that accompanied pearl-diving when equipment was primitive and knowledge of diving techniques limited. In 1914, 33 divers died of the bends, while in 1908 a cyclone killed 150 sailors caught at sea. The Japanese section of the cemetery is one of the largest and most interesting and was renovated in 1983.

Behind the neat Japanese section is the interesting but run-down allotment containing European and Aboriginal graves.

Other Attractions

Across Napier Terrace from Chinatown is Wing's Restaurant with a magnificent **boab tree** beside it. There's another boab tree behind, outside what used to be the old police lock-up, with a rather sad little tale on a plaque at its base. The tree was planted by a police officer when his son (later killed in France in WWI) was born in 1898. The boab tree is still doing fine.

The 1888 **courthouse** was once used to house the transmitting equipment for the old cable station. The cable ran to Banyuwangi in Java, the ferry port across from Bali. The 1900 **Matso's Store**, corner of Hamersley

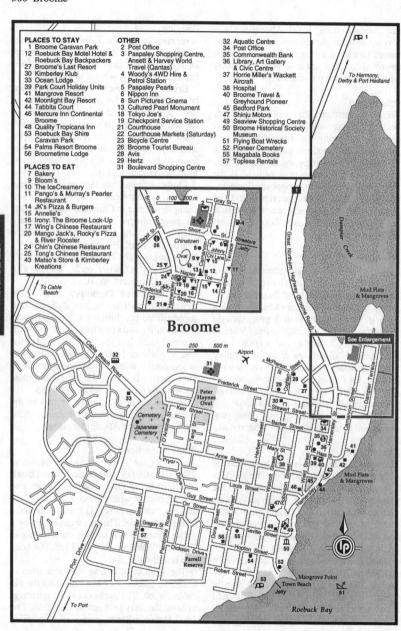

PLACES TO STAY
1 Broome Caravan Park
12 Roebuck Bay Motel Hotel & Roebuck Bay Backpackers
27 Broome's Last Resort
30 Kimberley Klub
33 Ocean Lodge
39 Park Court Holiday Units
41 Mangrove Resort
42 Moonlight Bay Resort
44 Tabbita Court
46 Mercure Inn Continental Broome
48 Quality Tropicana Inn
53 Roebuck Bay Shire Caravan Park
54 Palms Resort Broome
56 Broometime Lodge

PLACES TO EAT
7 Bakery
9 Bloom's
10 The IceCreamery
11 Pango's & Murray's Pearler Restaurant
14 JK's Pizza & Burgers
16 Irony: The Broome Lock-Up
17 Wing's Chinese Restaurant
20 Mango Jack's, Rocky's Pizza & River Rooster
24 Chin's Chinese Restaurant
25 Tong's Chinese Restaurant
43 Matso's Store & Kimberley Kreations

OTHER
2 Post Office
3 Paspaley Shopping Centre, Ansett & Harvey World Travel (Qantas)
4 Woody's 4WD Hire & Petrol Station
5 Paspaley Pearls
6 Nippon Inn
8 Sun Pictures Cinema
13 Cultured Pearl Monument
18 Tokyo Joe's
19 Checkpoint Service Station
21 Courthouse
22 Courthouse Markets (Saturday)
23 Bicycle Centre
26 Broome Tourist Bureau
28 Avis
29 Hertz
31 Boulevard Shopping Centre

32 Aquatic Centre
34 Post Office
35 Commonwealth Bank
36 Library, Art Gallery & Civic Centre
37 Horrie Miller's Wackett Aircraft
38 Hospital
40 Broome Travel & Greyhound Pioneer
45 Bedford Park
47 Shinju Motors
49 Seaview Shopping Centre
50 Broome Historical Society Museum
51 Flying Boat Wrecks
52 Pioneer Cemetery
55 Magabala Books
57 Topless Rentals

Broome

and Anne Sts, has been beautifully restored and now houses an art gallery and restaurant.

Farther along Weld St, by the library and civic centre in Bedford Park, is a **Wackett aircraft** that used to belong to Horrie Miller, founder of MacRobertson Miller Airlines, once Ansett WA, now Ansett Australia. The plane is hidden away in a modern but absurdly designed building that most people pass without a second glance.

There's a **pioneer cemetery** near Town Beach at the southern end of Robinson St. In the bay, at the entrance to Dampier Creek, there's a landmark, **Buccaneer Rock**, dedicated to William Dampier and HMS *Roebuck*.

If you're lucky enough to be in Broome on a cloudless night when there is a full moon, you can witness the **Staircase to the Moon**. The reflections of the moon from the rippling mudflats creates a wonderful golden-stairway effect, best seen from Town Beach. The effect is most dramatic about two days after full moon, as the moon rises after the sky has had a chance to darken. A lively market is held on this evening, and the town takes on a carnival air. Check with the tourist office for exact dates and times.

The new **Aquatic Centre** on Cable Beach Rd is open weekdays from 6 am to 6 pm, weekends from 9 am to 6 pm; entry is $2.50.

Organised Tours

There are a number of tours to make in and around Broome. The *Spirit of Broome* (☎ 9193 5025) is a small hovercraft which makes daily one hour trips ($45) around Roebuck Bay, stopping at points of interest. You can twilight cruise in the original pearl lugger *Cornelius* ($65) or in the replica lugger *The Willie* ($45).

There are also some good guided bushwalks. Paul Foulkes (☎ 9192 1371) concentrates on environmental features close to Broome, such as the palaeontologically important dinosaur footprints ($15/7.50 for adults/kids), the mangroves ($25/12.50), remnant rainforest ($25/12.50) and a hidden valley ($25/12.50).

Other unusual options include Harley Davidson motorcycle tours ($25) with the incomparable Roger; jet boat tours up Dampier Creek ($30/20); and Astro Tours' examinations of the star-studded Kimberley night sky ($30). For these tours, enquire at the tourist office.

Special Events

Broome is something of a festival centre. Some of the many excuses to party include:

March
Chinatown Street Party A party for which the whole multicultural population of Broome turns out. There are many local wares for sale, foodstalls and heaps of entertainment.

April
Dragon Boat Classic Paddlers from all over Australia meet annually for this carnival. For two days the town entertains the racers.

Late May/early June
Broome Fringe Arts Festival Local artists highlight 'fringe arts'. There are markets, art displays, poetry workshops and contemplative celebrations of the 'different'.

August
Shinju Matsuri (Festival of the Pearl) This excellent festival commemorates the early pearling years and the town's multicultural heritage. When the festival is on, the town population swells and beds are hard to find, so book ahead. Many traditional Japanese ceremonies are featured, including the Obon Festival. It concludes with a beach concert and a huge fireworks display. Don't miss the dragon boat races.

November
Mango Festival The town celebrates that stickysweet fruit deplored by mothers with small children. Events include mango-tasting, mardi gras and Great Chefs of Broome Cook Off.

Places to Stay

Camping Camping in Broome isn't cheap. The *Roebuck Bay Shire Caravan Park* (☎ 9192 1366) is conveniently central; tent/powered sites are $14/16.50 for two, and onsite vans are $40. *Broome Vacation Village* (☎ 9192 1057), Port Drive, has powered/ensuite sites from $15/18 for two; fortunately it has new owners attempting their best to overcome the place's once bad reputation. *Broome Caravan Park* (☎ 9192 1776), on the Great Northern Highway, 4km north of town, has tent/powered sites from $10/13 for two, on-site vans from $25, and cabins from $54.

Hostels Budget beds in Broome were hard to come by until recently. The new *Kimberley Klub* (☎ 9192 3233, fax 9192 3530), Frederick St, sets the Australian standard for purpose-built backpacker places (and it is family friendly). It's impressive, with a fully equipped kitchen, a bar and barbecue area overlooking the swimming pool, a sand volleyball court, a big TV/games room, a travel advisory service, shuttle bus, and so on. In eight/four/two bed rooms it is $14/16/19 per person, and there are singles and doubles for $45 per room (all high-season prices). Through Double-UA Extreme (☎ 9447 7971), it arranges 4WD, camping and mountain-bike tours to Cape Leveque (two days, $229), and to the remote Kimberley (five day Kununurra-Broome is $595). It's also sponsoring rafting on the spectacular Talbot Falls (watch this space).

On Bagot St, close to the centre and just a short stagger from the airport, is *Broome's Last Resort* (☎ 9193 5000), the overflow for the Kimberley Klub's noisier (perhaps more travelled) patrons. It has a pool, poky kitchen and oodles of character. Dorm beds are from $12, doubles (some with air-con) are $38; all rooms have shared facilities.

Roebuck Bay Backpackers (☎ 9192 1183), part of Roebuck Bay Motel Hotel on Napier Terrace, is, if nothing else, central. It's the roughest of the town's backpacker places in appearance and standards, but if you stay here you get to use the adjoining motel pool and you're close to the backpacker haunt Rattle & Hum. A dorm bed is $10 and budget doubles, still suffering from leaky showers and musty carpets, are $38 for two.

Hotels, Motels & Resorts During school holidays and other peak times, getting beds can be difficult; book ahead if possible.

The *Ocean Lodge* (☎ 9193 7700), on Cable Beach Rd near the junction of Port Drive, occasionally has backpackers' beds for $12; its well-equipped with self-contained units are $55 to $100, depending on size. The swimming pool is this place's biggest plus.

The once legendary *Roebuck Bay Motel Hotel* (☎ 9192 1221), corner of Carnarvon St and Napier Terrace, Chinatown, has single/double motel units for $65/85. The *Broometime Lodge* (☎ 9193 5067), 59 Forrest St, has tiny singles/twins/doubles with fan and air-con for $50/70/80 – it's a neat, quiet place, but way overpriced for its obscurity and poor location. The travellers we spoke to there seemed happy enough.

The *Mercure Inn Continental Broome* (☎ 9192 1002), a 'nice-enough' place on Weld St, has doubles from $88 to $110. *Mangrove Resort* (☎ 9192 1303), between the 'Conti' and Chinatown is the best place to see the staircase to the moon (the reflection of the moon on the tidal flats), but it's not cheap: $95 to $120 for doubles.

The *Palms Resort Broome* (☎ 9192 1898), corner of Hopton and Herbert Sts, has a range of units from $96 to $204. *Park Court Holiday Units* (☎ 9193 5887), Haas St, has units with all facilities from $50 to $130 (and cheaper weekly rates). *Quality Tropicana Inn* (☎ 9192 1204), corner of Saville and Robinson Sts, has great gardens and reasonable air-con rooms from $92.

B&B options are *Harmony* (☎ 9193 7439), Broome Rd (4km north of town), for $70/100 for doubles/triples; and *Tabbita Court* (☎ 9193 6026), Anne St, with doubles from $100 ($120 in the high season).

Places to Eat

Light Meals & Fast Food Getting a place to stay in Broome may be a hassle but eating out is no sweat. *Bloom's*, Carnarvon St, serves a very generous cappuccino and has excellent croissants. *Mango Jack's*, on Hamersley St, has hamburgers and kebabs and also dispenses fish and chips. In the same precinct as Mango Jack's, there's a *River Rooster* and *Rocky's Pizza*, which turns out distinctly average pizzas. Another pizza place is *JK's Pizzas & Burgers*, Napier Terrace, which is open from 8 pm until late.

There's an average, pricey bakery in Chinatown, corner of Carnarvon and Short Sts. Seaview shopping centre also has a bakery, as well as a *Charlie Carter's Food-mart*. The Paspaley shopping centre also has a handy Charlie Carter's. The *IceCreamery*, in Carnarvon St is, not surprisingly, busy most times of the year. *Tanami Moon* in Johnny Chi Lane has economical lunches. For fresh food go to the Saturday Courthouse Markets.

Pubs & Restaurants The Roebuck Bay Motel Hotel, the 'Roey', has *Pearlers Restaurant*, an alfresco dining area; Palms Resort Broome has the buzzing *Beer & Satay Hut*; and the Quality Tropicana Inn has the popular *Pure Steel*.

Chin's Chinese restaurant, on Hamersley St, has a variety of dishes from all over Asia. Prices range from $7 for a nasi goreng to $12 for other dishes. The takeaway is popular. Other Chinese specialists are *Wing's*, on Napier Terrace; *Tong's*, around the corner; *Son Ming* on Carnarvon St; and *Murray's Pearler*, on Dampier Terrace.

Annelie's is a continental restaurant on Napier Terrace opposite the Roey; reports from locals are all good and the lunches are cheap – eg turkey, camembert and avocado in a huge roll costs $4.50. The *Tea House*, in a mud-brick building with an outdoor dining area, is at the end of Saville St. It has a great variety of Thai and seafood dishes and BYO is permitted. The crowd at *Matso's*, on Hamersley St, seemed to be the most content – *feng shui* mixed with the best local food.

More expensive places include some of the restaurants in the resorts and motels. The Mangrove Resort reputedly has the best seafood restaurant in town, *Charters*, and a cafe, the *Palms*, which is a great spot for lunch. *Pango's*, a new place on Dampier Terrace, is a little slice of Bali with an Asian menu and Pindan decor; a starter is about $9, a main meal $14 to $15. *Irony: The Broome Lock-Up*, in Carnarvon St, serves vegetarian meals such as quiches and lasagnes, and also has cakes and a wide variety of coffees.

Cheffy's on the 19th (☎ 9192 2092), at the golf course overlooking Roebuck Bay, has meals from $5, a buffet roast for $10 and the greatest of garlic prawns.

Sun Pictures

Opened in 1916, Sun Pictures is believed to be the world's oldest operating picture garden. The silent movies were accompanied by music played by 'Fairy', the pianist, and the Cummin-Wilson RCA projector was adapted for sound in 1933 – the first 'talkie' screened was the musical comedy *Monte Carlo*, starring Nelson Eddy and Jeanette MacDonald. There is nothing quite like watching a movie while lying back in a deck chair under the stars on a balmy tropical evening. The snack bar still serves that old favourite of Aussie kids and adults – the 'chocolate bomb'.

There is a display of old projectors used in the early years of operation, in the foyer. The history of the theatre, *Reflections of the Sun*, by Maria Mann, is available from Sun Pictures for $5. ■

Entertainment

Sun Pictures, 27 Carnarvon St in Chinatown, is an open-air cinema dating from 1916. It has a programme of recent releases and is probably the oldest running picture garden in the world. Watching the 'flicks' here, at least once, is a must for visitors to Broome.

Despite an attempt to improve its appearance, the *Roey* still rocks along – just stand clear of the occasional fight. Backpackers (both guests and visitors) are well protected in the Roey's *Rattle & Hum* bar; they're allowed free entry and a meal voucher which gets them a $4 dinner. Locals like the *Beer & Satay Hut* at Palms Resort for a casual drink.

Nightclubs in town, of the disco variety, include the *Nippon Inn* on Dampier Terrace and *Tokyo Joe's* on Napier Terrace (entry to each is $5).

Getting There & Away

Ansett flies to Broome regularly on its Perth to Darwin route. Ansett's office (☎ 9193 5444) is in the Paspaley shopping centre, Short St.

Greyhound Pioneer operates through Broome on its daily Perth-Darwin route. The Greyhound Pioneer terminal (☎ 9192 1561) is near the corner of Haas and Hamersley Sts.

THE KIMBERLEY

Getting Around

The Airport There are plenty of taxis at the airport. The Kimberley Klub and Last Resort are within walking distance. A taxi into Chinatown is $5, and to the beach $11.

Bus The Pearl Town Bus (☎ 9193 6000) plies hourly between the town, Cable Beach, the port and Gantheaume Point (Red Line service only). A sector fare is $2 ($1.50 for each additional sector, $1 per sector for children and $25 for a week of unlimited travel). The bus stops close to most places to stay.

Bicycle Cycling is the best way to see the area. There are a number of places that hire bicycles for $6 to $12 a day, including the backpackers' places. The Broome Cycle Centre, corner of Hamersley and Frederick Sts, hires bikes, does repairs and gives good advice. Broome is an easy area to ride around; it's flat and you'll usually have no problem riding to Cable Beach (about 4km) as long as it's not too windy.

Car Rental Hertz, Budget, ATC and Avis have rent-a-car desks at the airport. There are better deals if you just want something for bopping around town; Suzuki jeeps are popular. Topless Rentals (☎ 9193 5017) in Hunter St, Woody's (☎ 9192 1791) on Napier Terrace and Broome Broome (☎ 9192 2210) on Carnarvon St are all local operations.

AROUND BROOME

Cable Beach

Six km from town is Cable Beach, the most popular swimming beach in the Broome region. It's a classic beach – white sand and turquoise water as far as the eye can see. It takes its name from the cable which once linked Broome and Indonesia.

You can hire surfboards and other equipment from Broome Surf Cat Hire (☎ 9193 5551). Parasailing ($50) is popular; the operators are on the northern side of the rocks on Cable Beach. On this north side, beyond the rocks and out of the public gaze, topless-bathing is popular. You can also take vehicles

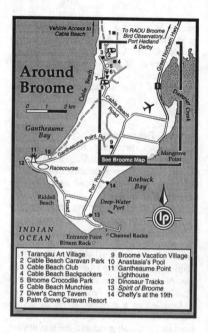

Around Broome

0   1   2 km

See Broome Map

INDIAN OCEAN

1 Tarangau Art Village
2 Cable Beach Caravan Park
3 Cable Beach Club
4 Cable Beach Backpackers
5 Broome Crocodile Park
6 Cable Beach Munchies
7 Diver's Camp Tavern
8 Palm Grove Caravan Resort
9 Broome Vacation Village
10 Anastasia's Pool
11 Gantheaume Point Lighthouse
12 Dinosaur Tracks
13 Spirit of Broome
14 Cheffy's at the 19th

(other than motorcycles) onto this part of the beach, although at high tide access is limited because of the rocks, so take care not to get stranded. Take caution if you're swimming between November and March as stingers are present.

Broome Camel Safaris, Red Sun and Ships of the Desert run **camel rides** along the beach. The best time is at sunset. The cost for adults/children is $25/20 per hour; book at the tourist office.

Also on Cable Beach Rd is **Broome Crocodile Park** with 1500 or so crocodiles. It's open, April to October, on weekdays from 10 am to 5 pm, weekends 2 to 5 pm; it has reduced hours the rest of the year. Wednesday to Sunday there are guided feeding tours at 3 pm; admission is $10/5/25 for adults/children/families.

Places to Stay & Eat *Cable Beach Caravan Park* (☎ 9192 2066), Millington Rd, has tent/powered sites for 15/18 for two. *Tar-*

angau Art Village (☎ 9193 5084), also Millington Rd, has tent/powered sites for $12/18, and on-site vans. In the adjoining art village you can sign up for Pilbara and Kimberley art safaris. *Palm Grove Caravan Resort* (☎ 9192 3336), Murray Drive, also has tent and van sites, as well as fully self-contained bungalows for $120/130 for two/three persons.

Cable Beach Backpackers (☎ 9193 5511), 33-37 Lullfitz Rd, is an ideal backpackers' hostel with an open-plan, fully equipped large kitchen, plenty of amusements, a swimming pool and a volleyball court. It is connected to town by local bus and it does pickups from Broome's Greyhound Pioneer terminal. It is only 200m from the beach and the best budget alternative at Cable Beach. It is $15 per person in four bed dorm rooms (or $40 for a twin).

The fully self-contained *Cable Beach-side Apartments* (☎ 9193 5545), on Murray Drive are $90/120 for one/two bedrooms in the low season (add another $30 in the high season).

The very up-market, beautifully designed *Cable Beach Club* (☎ 9192 0400) covers a large area, although it's not right on the beach. This place was set up by the British millionaire, Lord McAlpine, and is priced to attract more of his ilk; a studio room is from $255, and one/two bedroom bungalows from $335/495 (low season).

The resort has the expensive but superb *Club Restaurant* (☎ 9192 0400), the *Asian Affair* and the much more economical *Lord Mac's. Cable Beach Munchies*, across from the beach, is open daily for breakfast, lunch and dinner, and *Norma Jean's*, in the Divers' Camp Tavern, has cheap pub meals and burgers.

Gantheaume Point

The long sweep of Cable Beach eventually ends at Gantheaume Point, 7km south of Broome. The red, craggy cliffs have been eroded into curious shapes. At extremely low tides, **dinosaur tracks**, made 120 million years ago by a carnivorous species, are exposed. At other times you can inspect cement casts of the footprints on the cliff top.

Anastasia's Pool, an artificial rock pool believed to have been built by a former lighthouse keeper for his crippled wife, is on the north side of the point; it fills at high tide.

Willie Creek Pearl Farm

This pearl farm is 38km north of Broome, off Cape Leveque Rd. It offers a rare chance to see a working pearl farm and is worth the trip (entry is $17.50). The farm produces cultured pearls from the silver-lipped oyster *(Pinotada maxima)*. The road is open only to 4WD vehicles in the Wet, but to all vehicles in the Dry. There are daily tours from Broome ($40) with Broome Coachlines (☎ 9192 1068).

Broome Bird Observatory

The RAOU Broome Bird Observatory (☎ 9193 5600), 18km south of Broome on Roebuck Bay, is a twitcher's delight, and is rated as one of the top four non-breeding grounds for migrant Arctic waders. Officially opened in 1990, it is one of four such observatories in Australia – the others are Rotamah Island, Victoria; Barren Grounds, NSW; and Eyre, also in WA. Each year, Roebuck Bay receives 150,000 migrants from the northern hemisphere.

The observatory is a good base from which to seek out birds in a variety of habitats – mangroves, salt marshes, plains, pindan woodland, tidal flats and beaches. Please ring beforehand to find out the best viewing times. Over 250 species of birds have been spotted in the region, with migratory waders (shorebirds) seen there in abundance as well as over 20 species of raptors, including the white-breasted sea eagle, osprey and the rare grey falcon.

The RAOU organises two hour tours to see birds of the bush, shore and mangroves; the cost of each tour is $25/42 from the observatory/Broome (binoculars are provided).

The observatory is not signposted along Crab Creek Rd, but there is a dry weather track off the Great Northern Highway 3.7km north of town. Tent/powered campsites near the observatory are $12/16 for two. There are bunk rooms for $28 for two, and a five bed, self-contained chalet for $60 a double ($10 for each extra person).

George Swann of Kimberley Birdwatching (☎ 9192 1246) takes trips around town, out to Roebuck Bay, Crab Creek and even to the local sewage plant. State-of-the-art watching equipment is provided, including tripod-mounted telescopes. Based on a minimum of four people, the cost of a three hour shorebird trip is $50, a five hour Broome environs trip is $80.

DAMPIER PENINSULA

It's about 220km from the turn-off, 9km out of Broome, to the Cape Leveque lighthouse at the tip of the Dampier Peninsula. This peninsula features spectacular red pindan cliffs, expansive blue water and is a flora & fauna paradise. It is also a great spot for watching humpback whales.

Originally the peninsula was inhabited by the Bardi people and during the early pearling days, a number of Aborigines dived for pearl shell. The communities now welcome visitors and offer bush-tucker walks and mudcrabbing tours.

Also north of Broome, on the western coast of Dampier Peninsula, is **Coulomb Point Nature Reserve**. This conservation area was set up to protect the unique pindan vegetation of the peninsula and may still harbour the endangered rabbit-eared bandicoot or bilby. You can see bilby's in the CALM nocturnal house in Herbert St, Broome; ask at the tourist office.

An excellent account of the plants and peoples of the Dampier Peninsula is found in CALM's *Broome and Beyond* by K Kenneally, DC Edinger & T Willing.

Beagle Bay Aboriginal Community (☎ 9192 4913), 120km from Broome, is a welcome diversion and has a beautiful church in the middle of a green, built by Pallotine monks and completed in 1918. Inside is an altar stunningly decorated with pearl shell. A fee of $5 is charged for entry into the community and you must contact the office on arrival; petrol and diesel are available from 8 am daily, except Sunday.

From Beagle Bay it is 12km to the turn-off to picturesque **Middle Lagoon** (☎ 9192 4002), which is 18km west on a manageable dirt road. The lagoon is a great place for snorkelling, swimming, boating and fishing.

The Bilby

The rare rabbit-eared bandicoot *(Macrotus lagotis)* dalgyte, or bilby, is found in the northern desert regions of WA. Endangered by predation and habitat destruction, this rabbit-sized marsupial ranges from the Northern Territory to the Indian Ocean.

The bilby has adapted remarkably to its desert environment. It has a narrow head with large rabbit ears and pointed snout and thus acute senses of smell and hearing. It has very poor eyesight, but this is not a problem as it is strictly nocturnal, spending the hot desert days deep inside its burrow (which is up to 3m below ground) and it only comes out in search of food late at night when the earth has cooled sufficiently. Its food consists of ants, termites, larvae and seeds and it seems to survive without drinking water.

Litters of up to three newborn attach themselves firmly to the mother's teats for over two months before they leave the pouch. ■

Unpowered sites are $8 and beach shelters with a pine floor are $30 for two ($10 for an extra person); water is available.

Just before Cape Leveque is **Lombadina Aboriginal Community** (☎ 9192 4936), which has a church built from corrugated iron on the outside, lined with paper bark and supported by mangrove timber. There are a number of carved artefacts for sale including trochus shell, ebony carvings and pearl-shell jewellery. One day and overnight mudcrabbing and traditional fishing tours are available; contact the Broome tourist office for details. Fuel (leaded, unleaded and diesel) is available on weekdays. There are four bed, backpacker-style units with refrigerators (linen and towels provided); the cost is $35 per person. Fully self-contained dongas – rough and ready beach dwellings – which sleep four are $120 (linen and towels provided).

Cape Leveque has a lighthouse and two wonderful beaches. Beyond it (5km) is **One Arm Point**, another Aboriginal community (☎ 9192 4930). There is accommodation at *Kooljaman* (☎ 9192 4970), ranging from tent/powered sites for $10/15, beach shelters ($30 for two), family units ($50) and cabins ($80 to $90); prices are slightly cheaper in the low season. Bush-tucker and mudcrabbing tours are available. All types of vehicle fuel, except LPG, can be purchased here. The restaurant is open April to November, and the store year-round.

Take note that while you can look around or purchase goods, Aboriginal communities won't want you to stay on their land. Permission to visit other areas must be obtained in advance. Also, check road conditions with the Broome tourist office before setting out.

Organised Tours

Halls Creek and Bungle Bungle Tours (☎ 9193 6802), Over the Top Adventure Tours (☎ 9193 7257) and Flak Track in Broome (☎ 9192 1487) all operate tours to the peninsula. Expect to pay about $170/290 for a one/two day 4WD trip; there are also fly/drive options.

West Kimberley

The west Kimberley is a vast area that includes Broome out to Fitzroy Crossing, the Devonian Reef national parks, the Gibb River and Kalumburu roads and the remote and rugged north-west coast. The main town of the region is Derby.

DERBY
* *pop 5000*

Derby, only 220km from Broome, is a major administrative centre for the west Kimberley and a good point from which to travel to the spectacular gorges in the region.

The area has been occupied by Aborigines for many thousands of years and there is much evidence of their art and signs of their earlier habitation around Derby.

In 1883, Derby was officially proclaimed a town site and the first wooden jetty was built two years later. The Australian Aerial Medical Service (later to become the Royal Flying Doctor Service) started operation at Derby airport in 1934, largely funded by donations from Victoria. In 1942, Derby was one of the Australian towns bombed by the Japanese during WWII.

It is part of the largest shire in Australia – 102,706 sq km – with over 45% of the shire population comprising Aborigines. Mowajum ('settled at last'), on the outskirts of Derby, was one of the first independent Aboriginal communities established in the Kimberley.

Derby has the second-highest tidal range in the world; the highest astronomical tide is 10.8m and the lowest astronomical tide is 0.3m, exceeded only by the Bay of Fundy in Nova Scotia, Canada (14.5m).

The road beyond Derby continues to Fitzroy Crossing (256km) and Halls Creek (288km farther on). Alternatively, there's the much wilder Gibb River Rd (GRR). Derby is on King Sound, north of the mouth of the Fitzroy, the mighty river that drains the west Kimberley region.

THE KIMBERLEY

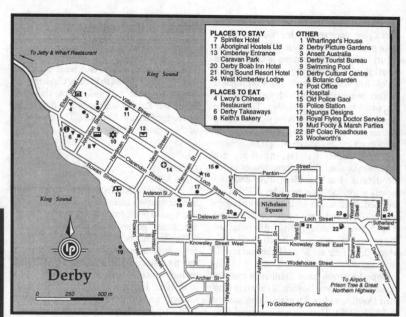

THE KIMBERLEY

PLACES TO STAY
7 Spinifex Hotel
11 Aboriginal Hostels Ltd
13 Kimberley Entrance
    Caravan Park
20 Derby Boab Inn Hotel
21 King Sound Resort Hotel
24 West Kimberley Lodge

PLACES TO EAT
4 Lwoy's Chinese
    Restaurant
6 Derby Takeaways
8 Keith's Bakery

OTHER
1 Wharfinger's House
2 Derby Picture Gardens
3 Ansett Australia
5 Derby Tourist Bureau
9 Swimming Pool
10 Derby Cultural Centre
    & Botanic Garden
12 Post Office
14 Hospital
15 Old Police Gaol
16 Police Station
17 Ngunga Designs
18 Royal Flying Doctor Service
19 Mud Footy & Marsh Parties
22 BP Colac Roadhouse
23 Woolworth's

Derby

0   250   500 m

Information

Derby tourist bureau (☎ 9191 1426), 1 Clarendon St, opens April to October, from 8.30 am to 4.30 pm on weekdays, 9 am to 1 pm on weekends. November to March, it is open on weekdays for the same hours, on Saturday from 9 am to noon.

Two supermarkets (Foodland in Clarendon St and Woolworths in Loch St) stay open after 5 pm. The BP Colac Roadhouse service station (☎ 9191 1278) is open daily from 6 am to 8 pm (Sunday 7 am to 7 pm).

Things to See & Do

Derby has a cultural centre and a botanic garden. There's a small museum and art gallery in **Wharfinger's House**, at the end of Loch St. Built in the 1920s, this has been restored as an example of early housing.

In the gardens, outside the shire buildings in Stanley Square, are the anchor and propeller of the SS *Colac*, which ran aground south of Derby in 1910. The original **old Derby**

police gaol, constructed in the late 1880s, is next to the present Derby police station. The **Royal Flying Doctor Service** building, in Clarendon St, is open for inspection weekdays from 8 am to noon, and 2 to 4 pm.

Derby's lofty **wharf** has not been used since 1983 for shipping, but it provides a handy fishing spot for the locals. The whole town is surrounded by huge expanses of mud flats, baked hard in the Dry. The mudflats are occasionally flooded by king tides.

The **Prison Tree**, near the airport, 7km south of town, is a huge boab tree with a hollow trunk 14m around. It is said to have been used as a temporary lock-up years ago. Nearby is **Myall's Bore**, a 120m-long cattle trough filled from a 322m-deep artesian bore.

Organised Tours

From Derby there are flights over King Sound to **Koolan** and **Cockatoo Islands**, both owned by BHP. You can't go there unless invited by a resident, but scenic flights are available to the adjoining islands of the **Buccaneer Archipelago**. Aerial Enterprises (☎ 9191 1132) and Derby Air Services (☎ 9193 1375) provide two hour flights for about $120 to the Buccaneer Archipelago; there's a minimum of four passengers.

Buccaneer Sea Safaris (☎ 9191 1991) does extended tours up the Kimberley coast (including the horizontal falls of Talbot Bay – see Tidal Waterfalls later in this chapter) in a large aluminium mono-hull.

Bush Track Safaris (☎ 9191 4644) operates four to 10 day tours into the remote Walcott Inlet area; these cost from $175 per day. West Kimberley Tours (☎ 9193 1442) operates tours to the Devonian Reef gorges ($80 per person) and Gibb River Rd gorges ($290 for two days).

Places to Stay

The *Kimberley Entrance Caravan Park* (☎ 9193 1055), Rowan St, has tent/powered sites for $12/15 for two, on-site vans for $40 a double. It is a nice, friendly place with free barbecues. *Aboriginal Hostels Ltd* (☎ 9191 1867), 233-235 Villiers St, charges $12 per person; a two course dinner here typically costs $8.50.

West Kimberley Lodge (☎ 9191 1031), at the edge of town, corner of Sutherland and Stanwell Sts, has singles/doubles for $30/45. A little out of town at Lot 4 Guildford St is *Goldsworthy Connection* (☎ 9193 1246); it has self-contained homes/cottages for $25/20 per person (there are minimum numbers).

The *Spinifex Hotel* (☎ 9191 1233), known as the 'Spinny' to all, on Clarendon St, has

THE KIMBERLEY

Boabs

Boab trees are a common sight in the Kimberley and also in the Victoria and Fitzmaurice river basins of the Northern Territory. The boab or *Adansonia gregorii* is closely related to the baobab of Africa and the eight varieties of *Adansonia* found on the island of Madagascar – it's probable that baobab seeds floated to Australia from Africa.

The boab is a curious-looking tree with branches rising like witches' fingers from a wide trunk that is sometimes elegantly bottle-shaped, and sometimes squat and powerful-looking. Boabs shed all their leaves during dry periods, further accentuating their unusual appearance. Evidently it's a successful policy, for boabs are noted for their rapid growth, hardiness and extreme longevity. Derby has some fine boabs, including a number transplanted along Loch St. ■

budget rooms at $40/50, motel units at $50/65, and there are backpackers' beds in the bunkhouse from $11 per person (fourth night free). This pub gets pretty noisy – a situation budget travellers either loath, love or even leave.

The *Derby Boab Inn Hotel* (☎ 9191 1044), on Loch St, is rather more motel-like; it costs $55/65. *King Sound Resort Hotel* (☎ 9193 1044), in Loch St, is the up-market place in this 'down-market town', with singles/doubles for $90/100; it has a squash court, pool and restaurant.

Places to Eat

Keith's Bakery, near the tourist bureau, is good for lunch and has a fine selection of sandwiches. The air-con *Jabiru Cafe* has a nice garden setting; *Derby Takeaways* is open daily until 11 pm; and *Albert's Kitchen* has cheap, tasty curries. All of these places are in Clarendon St.

The *Spinny, Derby Boab Inn* and *King Sound Resort* all do counter meals. At the Derby Boab Inn, there's a wide choice of good meals from $10 to $15; it is open six days a week. The specials at the Spinny cost from $6 and there is a spit roast at the King Sound Resort on Thursday from 6 to 9 pm.

At the end of Loch St there's *Lwoy's Chinese Restaurant*; at the jetty is the BYO *Wharf Restaurant & Takeaway* with local seafood specialities; and, 5km out of town, there is the *Boab Tea Gardens* for lunches and Devonshire teas.

Entertainment

Bands (or a disco) can usually be heard at the *Spinny* on weekends. If the locals get bored they will probably start a cockroach race (and bet on it) – no kidding. If you can tolerate it, there's a disco at *Chasers* in the King Sound Resort.

If you are lucky you may be able to make it to one of the legendary impromptu 'marsh parties' when barbecues are set up out in the mud, beer is consumed, 'mud footy' is played and a band plays into the night.

Less wild are the 'flicks' at the *Derby*

Picture Gardens, an open-air cinema on the corner of Johnston and Loch Sts.

Getting There & Away

Skywest flies to Broome, Carnarvon, Exmouth, Karratha. Port Hedland, Perth and Darwin. Skywest's (☎ 13 1300) agent in Derby is Traveland.

Greyhound Pioneer's daily Perth-Darwin service stops in Derby at the tourist office.

GIBB RIVER RD

This road was made to transport cattle from surrounding stations to the ports of Wyndham and Derby. At 670km, from Derby to the junction of the Great Northern Highway between Wyndham and Kununurra, it's more direct by several hundred kilometres than the Great Northern Highway (the Fitzroy Crossing and Halls Creek) route. All in all the Gibb River Rd is 647km from the junction of the Derby Highway to its end, described earlier.

It's almost all dirt, although it doesn't require a 4WD when it has been recently graded (not always the case). The road is impassable in the Wet and you should not attempt it from December to April. The best time is from May to November; ring the Main Roads Department (☎ (1800) 013 314) for up-to-date information on road conditions. There are a number of rules to observe in this area (and, indeed, in all off-road areas); see the boxed asides 'Responsible Camping' and 'Safe Driving' in this section.

Fuel is available at Mt House Station, Iminitji Store (diesel only), Mt Barnett

---

Responsible Camping
- Only camp in designated areas.
- Don't camp in river beds as they are subject to flash floods.
- When entering private property, get permission from the station owner first.
- Take extreme care to prevent bushfires and use only gas stoves for cooking.
- Don't use soap in creeks or rivers.
- Carry out all rubbish (don't bury it). ■

Roadhouse at Manning Gorge and El Questro Station. The distances mentioned are from Derby.

The Kimberley gorges are the major reason for taking this route. You could also make a side trip to the Windjana and Tunnel Creek gorges (see Devonian Reef National Parks in this chapter). Get a copy of The *Gibb River and Kalumburu Roads Travellers Guide* from the tourist offices.

There's no public transport along the Gibb River Rd – in fact there's very little traffic of any sort, so don't bother trying to hitch!

Derby to Mt Barnett

From Derby the bitumen extends 62km. It's 119km to the Windjana Gorge (21km) and Tunnel Creek (51km) turn-off and you can continue down that turn-off to the Great Northern Highway near Fitzroy Crossing (see under Devonian Reef National Parks).

The Lennard River bridge is crossed at 120km and at 145km you pass through the Yamarra Gap in the King Leopold Ranges. The country is rugged, punctuated by huge granite outcrops. At 181km is the Inglis Gap, where the road descends into the Broome Valley. The road passes Mt Bell (also known as Elephant Hill), one of the highest points in the range.

At 184km you can turn off to the beautiful **Mt Hart Homestead** (☎ 9191 4645) which is reached by a farther 50km of rough 4WD-only dirt road. You will need to have booked to stay here; B&B with dinner costs $95/50 for adults/children. Six km farther from the Mt Hart turn-off (at 190km) is the turn-off to

the **Bell Gorge**, 8km off the road along a 4WD-only track. This gorge is 5km long and has a waterfall just north of its entrance; the nearby pool is great for a quick, refreshing dip. You can camp here for $5/1 for adults/children. There is no access mid-December to mid-April. Some 237km from Derby is the Iminitji Store (☎ 9191 7471) and community; you can buy diesel here.

The signposted turn-off to **Mt House Station** (☎ 9191 4649) is at 246km. The station, nestled below the odd-shaped Mt House, about 10km down a side road, has fuel, stores and accommodation (by prior arrangement). B&B and dinner in the station homestead, with shared facilities (and the shadiest of verandahs), is $67 to $77 per person. The adventurous can push on from Mt House to the **Old Mornington Cattle Station** (☎ 9191 7035) on the Fitzroy River – it is a 180km round trip back to Mt House; you can camp for $8 per person or enjoy comfortable tent accommodation (with hot showers) for $85, fully inclusive.

At 251km, is the road into **Beverley Springs Homestead** (☎ 9191 4646). This is a working farm and station, 43km off the Gibb River Rd, with a variety of accommodation. Camping is $8 per person; chalets with B&B and dinner are $80; homestay with B&B and dinner is also $80; and self-contained two bedroom homes are $85 per house. You can also gain access to Walcott Inlet by arrangement.

The turn-off to **Adcock Gorge** is at 267km. This gorge is 5km off the road and is good for swimming. It has great rocks for jumping or diving off, although you should check for rocks beneath the water before doing so. If the waterfall is not flowing too fiercely, climb up above it for a good view of the surrounding country. You can camp at Adcock Gorge although the site is rocky and there's little shade.

Horseshoe-shaped **Galvans Gorge** is less than 1km off the road, at the 286km mark. The small campsite here has some good shade trees, and the gorge itself has a swimming hole. The rock paintings here include one of a Wandjina head.

THE KIMBERLEY

Mt Barnett & Manning Gorge

The *Mt Barnett Roadhouse* (☎ 9191 7007), 306km from Derby, is owned and run by the Aboriginal Kupingarri community. Ice is available and there's a small general store, open daily from 7 am to 6 pm, May to October. It's also the access point for Manning Gorge, which lies 7km off the road along an easy dirt track. There's an entry fee of $5/10 per person/family and this covers camping.

The campsite is by the waterhole, but the best part of the gorge is about a 1¼ hour walk along the far bank – walk around the right of the waterhole to pick up the track, which is marked with empty drink cans strung up in trees. It's a strenuous walk and, because the track runs inland from the gorge, you should carry some drinking water.

After the hot and sweaty walk, you are rewarded with this most beautiful gorge. It has a waterfall and some high rocks for daredevils.

Mt Barnett to Wyndham/Kununurra Rd

There is a turn-off to the **Barnett River Gorge**, after Mt Barnett, at 328km. This is another good swimming spot, 3km down a side road. If you scan the lower level of the cliff face on the far side you should be able to spot some Aboriginal paintings.

The **Mt Elizabeth Station** (☎ 9191 4644) lies 30km off the road at the 338km mark. Homestead accommodation is available but this must be arranged in advance ($90/45 per adult/child for B&B and dinner). The cost for camping is $7 per person; bookings are essential.

At 406km you come to the turn-off to the spectacular **Mitchell Plateau** (172km) and the **Kalumburu Aboriginal Community** (267km). This is remote, 4WD-only territory and should not be undertaken without adequate preparation; an entry permit is required (see under Kalumburu Rd later in this chapter).

There's magnificent scenery between the Kalumburu turn-off and Jack's (Joe's) Waterhole on **Durack River Station** (☎ 9161 4324) at 524km. There is no camp-

ing at Campbell Creek (451km) and at the Durack River (496km). At 476km there is a turn-off to **Ellenbrae Station** (☎ 9161 4325), 6km farther down a side road; camping is $7 and B&B with dinner is $80 per person.

Jack's Waterhole is 8km down a side road at 524km and apart from fuel, there's also homestead accommodation or camping here. The owners, the Sinnamon family, run a number of tours from Durack River Station to Oomaloo and Durack Falls. Camping is $6/1 per adult/child, and DB&B is $75 per person.

At 579km you get some excellent views of the Cockburn Ranges to the south, the Cambridge Gulf and the twin rivers (the Pentecost and the Durack). Shortly after (2km or so) is the turn-off to **Home Valley Station** (☎ 9161 4322) at 581km, which has camping ($6/1 for adults/children) and DB&B in the homestead for $50 per person. They conduct 4WD tours from the station.

The large **Pentecost River** is forded at 590km, and this crossing can be dodgy if there's water in the river. During the Dry it is no problem. There's no camping and if you're fishing, beware of saltwater crocodiles.

El Questro Station & Wilderness Park (☎ 9169 1777) is another place offering a variety of accommodation – from single/double bungalows for $97/130 to expensive homestead beds for a whopping $840/1280, all trips inclusive. For the poorer, riverside camping is $10 per person. El Questro lies 16km off the road at the 614km mark. This is also the access point for the **Chamberlain**, **Moonshine** and **El Questro gorges**. The latter has 60m towering escarpments with 9m between faces.

The last attraction on the road is **Emma Gorge** at 623km. The pleasant campsite lies 2km off the road and from here it's about a 40 minute walk to the spectacular gorge. Near the gorge is great wilderness cabin accommodation, run by El Questro; singles/doubles/family are $62/98/146. There's a licensed restaurant, bar and swimming pool. This gorge is close enough to

Kununurra to make it a popular weekend escape for residents of that town.

At 630km you cross King River (no camping) and at 647km you finally hit the bitumen road; Wyndham lies 48km to the north, while it's 52km east to Kununurra. The distance from Mt Barnett Roadhouse to the Wyndham/Kununurra Rd is 341km.

KALUMBURU RD

This is a natural earth road which traverses extremely rocky terrain in a very isolated area. Distances in the description are given from the junction of the Gibb River and Kalumburu roads, where the road commences. The junction is 419km from Derby Highway or 248km from the Great Northern Highway (Wyndham to Kununurra).

It is recommended that you obtain a permit before entering Kalumburu Reserve. Phone ☎ 9161 4300 (or fax 9161 4331) from 7 am to 12 noon on weekdays.

Gibb River Rd to Mitchell Plateau

The Gibb River is crossed at 3km and Plain Creek at 16km. The first fuel is at the **Drysdale River Station** (☎ 9161 4326) at 59km; the homestead is 1km down a side road. You can also buy supplies, and trailers and caravans can be left at the homestead ($2 per day or $10 per week).

At 62km you can turn off to the **Miner's Pool** picnic area. It is 3.5km to the river and the last 200m is slow going; there is an entrance fee of $2/1 for adults/children. Nearby are the Drysdale Cattle Yards (watch out for wild cattle) and the Drysdale River Crossing; you cannot camp here.

The road passes a couple of entrances to stations in the next 100km until it reaches the Mitchell Plateau turn-off at 172km. From this junction it is 70km along the Mitchell Plateau Road to the turn-off to the spectacular multi-tiered **Mitchell Falls**. The falls are a farther 16km downhill from this turn-off; from the last car park (13km) you need to walk for a farther 3km (allow a full day for the excursion). You usually cannot get into the falls until late May (when the Wet ends).

The Mitchell Plateau is also known for its ancient, tall fan palms, remnant rainforests, Wandjina paintings, the King Edward River and the Surveyor's Pool.

As this is a remote area, be sure to bring a large swag of basic necessities. In the Dry the falls are like any other with water falling from the centre of the terraces. In the Wet they are vastly different – the muddied water stretches from escarpment to escarpment and thunders down the completely submerged terraces.

You can camp at King Edward River (don't use soap in the watercourse), at Camp Creek (away from the Kandiwal Aboriginal Community) and at the Mitchell Falls car park. The well-heeled can arrange to stay at the *Kimberley Coastal Camp* (☎ 9161 4410, May to October), which is 7km by boat from Walsh Point, Point Warrender, Admiralty Gulf; it is $250 per person for each 24 hours and includes meals, fishing guides, transfers and gazebo-style rooms.

Mitchell Plateau to Kalumburu

From the Mitchell Plateau turn-off, the road heads north-east towards Kalumburu, crossing the Carson River at 247km. About 1km farther is a road to the east to Carson River Homestead on the fringe of the Drysdale River National Park. There is no access without prior approval from the Kalumburu Aboriginal Community.

The **Kalumburu Aboriginal Community** (☎ 9161 4300) is at 267km, about 5km from the mouth of the King Edward River and King Edward Gorge. The picturesque mission is set among giant mango trees and coconut palms, and there is accommodation (entry is $25 per vehicle and an additional fee is levied to camp at McGowan's Island and Honeymoon Beach) and a store. Food and all types of fuel are available, Monday to Friday from 7 to 11 am and 1.30 to 4 pm, and Saturday from 7 to 11 am.

There is lots to do and fishing and trekking trips are offered at reasonable rates; scenic flights over the area are also available.

The distance between the Mitchell Plateau turn-off and Kalumburu is 95km.

THE KIMBERLEY

Drysdale River National Park

Very few people get into Drysdale River, WA's most northern national park, which is 150km west of Wyndham. Apart from being one of the most remote parks in Australia – it has no road access – it is also the largest park in the Kimberley with an area of 4000 sq km. Furthermore, it is also the home of the mysterious, ancient Bradshaw art figures and the more recent Wandjina art figures (see the boxed aside 'Kimberley Art').

Included in the park are open woodlands, rugged gorges, waterfalls (Morgan and Solea) and the wide, meandering Drysdale River. Rainforest, thought not to exist in WA until 1965, is found in pockets along the Carson escarpment and in some gorges.

The flora & fauna is diverse. Over 600

Kimberley Art

The Kimberley is one of the greatest ancient art galleries in the world. Many antiquated paintings remain as a testimony to one of the richest periods of cultural achievement in Aboriginal history. The indigenous art found in the overhanging rock shelters has wrongly been attributed to space travellers, early European explorers and latter day visitors. The truth is, the ancient Bradshaw figures and the more recent Wandjina paintings are integral parts of Aboriginal culture, regardless of who put them there. But no one is sure, and controversy rages – many recent articles and TV programmes have presented a bewildering variety of explanations as to the origins of the art.

In 1838, the explorer George Grey, travelling in the Glenelg River region, was probably the first European to see the Wandjina paintings. These large mouthless figures in headdresses are among the most famous of Aboriginal paintings.

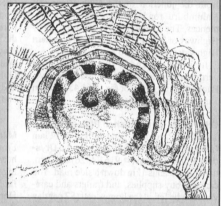

The Wandjina paintings have a lot in common with the Lightning Brothers paintings of Victoria River in the Northern Territory (and the lightning figures in the Kimberley) in both style and tradition. Wandjina paintings are believed to be the shadows of ancestors, imprinted on the rock as they pass by. Each Wandjina site has a living custodian and, to ensure good relations between Wandjina and people, the images should be retouched annually.

The major Wandjina site is Panda-Goornnya in the Drysdale River region. Other important areas in the Kimberley are the Sale, King Edward and Glenelg rivers, the Napier, Carr Boyd and Oscar ranges and Kalumburu.

The Bradshaw figures take their name from the first European to describe them – Joseph Bradshaw – who explored the area in 1891. He said: 'The bodies and limbs were attenuated and represented as having numerous tassel-shaped adornments appended to the hair, neck, waist, arms and legs, but the most remarkable fact in connection with these drawings is that wherever a profile face is shown, the features are of a most pronounced aquiline type, quite different from those of any native we encountered.'

The Bradshaws were there long before the Wandjinas, possibly 10,000 to 20,000 years ago, and their significance to the Aborigines has been long forgotten. These exquisite paintings are consistent from shelter to shelter as if painted by artists of the same 'school'. The Bradshaw figures are now all that we have left of one particular culture that flourished many thousands of years ago. They are found in shelters in the Drysdale River, often in the same place as Wandjina figures. Who knows how many have been painted over or weathered away? The source of the Bradshaws is the stuff of popular speculation. Various experts continue to debate the validity of their own theories as to the origins of the images. ■

plant species have been found in the park, a number of them unique. And of the 25 fern species, half are found only in the one gorge – Worriga. Mammals include the sugar glider, water rat, a species of planigale, the short-eared rock wallaby and plenty of bats. Some of the frogs and reptiles are known only from this park.

The King George River drains the northern part of the reserve. At the mouth of this river are the spectacular, split **King George Falls**, best seen from the air.

A permit is necessary to enter this national park and is obtainable from the CALM offices in Derby or Kununurra.

Organised Tours

Kununurra's Desert Inn (☎ (1800) 805 010) runs budget five day camping trips along the Gibb River Rd for $425. Kimberley Wilderness Adventures (☎ 9168 1711) has a five day Gibb River Rd Wanderer 4WD safari ($745) which leaves from Kununurra and finishes in Broome. Its six day Mitchell Plateau Explorer, which includes a fair slice of the Gibb River Rd, is $895.

There are guided full-day trips to the Mitchell Plateau from Kununurra. Kimberley Air Safaris (☎ 9169 1326) departs Kununurra at 6 am and returns at 5 pm; transport from the plateau airstrip to the falls is by 4WD. The total cost is $350 per person.

PRINCE REGENT NATURE RESERVE

This 600,000 hectare wilderness is one of Australia's most isolated reserves, and there are no roads into it; it is best seen from the air or its edges explored by boat.

Notable features include the mesa-like Mts Trafalgar and Waterloo, the near-vertical cliffs of the straight Prince Regent River and the extremely photogenic King Cascade. What is more, the region's isolation has ensured that the original fauna population has remained intact since European settlement.

Several companies operate flights over the region, including Kingfisher Aviation (☎ 9168 6160) and King Leopold Air (☎ 9193 7997); a half-day flight is about $350.

DEVONIAN REEF NATIONAL PARKS

The west Kimberley boasts three national parks, based on gorges which were once part of a western coral 'great barrier reef' in the Devonian era, 350 million years ago (see under Geology in the Facts about Western Australia chapter). The geological mysteries of this region are unravelled in the CALM pamphlet *Geology of Windjana Gorge, Geikie Gorge and Tunnel Creek National Parks* (1985) by Phillip Playford.

Geikie Gorge National Park

The magnificent Geikie Gorge, named after the British geologist Sir Archibald Geikie, is just 18km north of Fitzroy Crossing. Part of the gorge, on the Fitzroy River, is in a small national park only 8km by 3km. During the Wet, the river rises nearly 17m and in the Dry it stops flowing, leaving a series of water holes.

The vegetation around this gorge is dense and there is also much wildlife, including the freshwater crocodile. Sawfish and stingrays, usually only found in or close to the sea, can also be seen in the river. Euros and the rare black-footed wallaby live in the gorge. Visitors are not permitted to go anywhere except along the prescribed part of the west bank, where there is an excellent 1.5km walking track.

During the April to November Dry there's a 1½ hour boat trip up the river at 8 and 11 am and 3 pm. It costs $18 (children $2) and covers 16km of the gorge; tickets are sold at the CALM information centre at the gorge.

You can also visit the gorge, April to October, with Darngku Aboriginal guides (☎ 9191 5355) who show you a lot more than rocks and the water. These Bunuba people reveal interesting secrets of bush tucker, stories of the region and Aboriginal culture. The trip, which includes transport to the gorge, a river excursion and lunch beside the Fitzroy River, costs $75. It leaves Fitzroy Crossing tourist bureau at 8.15 am, returning at 1.30 pm.

Alternatively, you can fly over the Fitzroy gorges with Old Mornington (☎ 9191 7035); a one hour flight, which includes 'smoko' at Mornington Camp, is $90.

Windjana Gorge & Tunnel Creek

You can visit the spectacular ancient rock formations of Windjana Gorge and Tunnel Creek from the Gibb River Rd, or make a detour on the Leopold Station Rd off the main highway between Fitzroy Crossing and Derby, which adds about 40km to the distance.

The near-vertical walls at the Windjana Gorge soar 90m above the Lennard River which rushes through in the Wet, but becomes just a series of pools in the Dry. The deafening screech of corellas and the persistent horseflies will probably keep you out of the gorge during the middle of the day when they're at their worst.

Geologists are excited by the 3.5km long Windjana Gorge as the various deposits of an ancient reef complex are well exposed here. Fossil bones of a giant crocodile, 7m in length, have been found in the gorge, as have bones of the extinct giant marsupial *Dipro-*

todon. Nightly camping fees are $5 per person (children $1) and this includes firewood.

Three km from the river are the ruins of **Lillimilura**, an early homestead and then, from 1893, a police station.

Tunnel Creek is a 750m-long tunnel cut by the creek right through a spur of the Napier Range. The tunnel is 3m to 15m wide and you can walk all the way along it. You'll need a good light and sturdy shoes; be prepared to wade through very cold, chest-deep water in places. Don't attempt it during the Wet, as the creek may flood suddenly. Halfway through, a collapse has created a shaft to the top of the range.

Near the north entrance to the tunnel, cave paintings are evident and at the other entrance is the black dolerite and basalt which was fashioned by the Aborigines into stone axes. A cave near the tunnel was used as a hideout by Pigeon between 1894 and 1897.

Tidal Waterfalls

The Kimberley coastline is made up of sheer sandstone cliffs and basalt promontories with deep indentations made by inlets and bays. It is one of the remotest coasts in the world, mainly inaccessible from the land, and it is certainly one of the most treacherous. The tidal variation is enormous, fluctuating up to 10m, and the region is often hit by fierce cyclonic storms. It is as if nature constructed its own fortified Maginot Line to keep its beauty and wonders secret.

A remarkable feature of this coastline is the spectacular tidal 'waterfalls', which are not actual waterfalls but immense tidal currents which hurtle through the narrow coastal gorges. The speed that they attain, from 20 to 30 knots in places, gives the impression of a waterfall flowing horizontally.

The waterfalls are spectacular at **Talbot Bay**, north of King Sound. At the south end of the bay, two constricted gorges, both about 30m high and constructed of very hard sandstone, protect the Inner and Outer bays (flooded valleys). The high tide fills both bays with water and, when the tide is outgoing, the water in the bays is released. The narrow gorges restrict the outflow, resulting in a vertical difference of 1m between the first bay and the open sea of Talbot Bay, and of 2m between the first and second bays. Water then thunders through both the outer 70m-long gorge and the impressive 100m-long inner gorge.

The Aborigines of the now-extinct Meda tribe and the Worora people knew the waterfalls as 'Wolbunum' and once had a system of bidi (tracks) running to these valleys where food was abundant. Nowadays, many people see the waterfalls from the air and, occasionally, some brave them in a powerful motorboat or in a rubber raft. The landward journey to the falls is considered extremely difficult, harsh terrain, lack of water and the tangle of vegetation all combine to impede progress.

At the time of writing what you are about to read was hearsay – if it happens (say 1998) it will be one of the 'great' outdoor adventures. Kimberley Wilderness Promotions (☎ 9191 1426, mobile (041) 992 9115, or Broome's Kimberley Klub ☎ 9192 3233), based in Talbot Bay from April to November, plans to offer rafting trips through the horizontal falls in specially designed rafts (the 'Crocs I and II') steered by the enigmatic Goanna, a local character. Accommodation is aboard the houseboat *Goanna 1* (if you stay overnight). The cost of a one day rafting experience (from Broome or Derby), with flying boat transfers, will be $400. ■

Pigeon Heritage Trail

Windjana Gorge, Tunnel Creek and Lillimilura were the scene of the adventures of an Aboriginal tracker called Jundumarra or 'Pigeon'. In November 1894, Pigeon shot two police colleagues and then led a band of dissident Aborigines, skilfully evading search parties for over two years. In the meantime he killed another four men, but in early 1897, Pigeon was trapped and killed in Tunnel Creek. He and his small band had hidden in many of the seemingly inaccessible gullies of the adjoining Napier Range. Get hold of a copy of the *Pigeon Heritage Trail* from the Derby or Broome tourist office ($1.50). ■

Organised Tours

Over the Top Adventure Tours (☎ 9193 7700, 9193 7257) in Broome operates popular budget two day trips combining Windjana Gorge, Tunnel Creek and Geikie Gorge, a good way of seeing three sites in one trip; the cost is $190. It also has access to the Mimbi Caves of the Gooniyandi people, the Dreamtime place of the blue-tongued lizard, on extended trips. The Kimberley Klub and the Last Resort in Broome can also advise on popular tours to the gorges. Darlngunaya Backpackers (☎ 9191 5140), Fitzroy Crossing, offers specials – $80 for tours to the Devonian Reef gorges, $70 to the Mimbi Caves.

FITZROY CROSSING

Aboriginal people have lived in this area for many thousands of years and the Bunuba people still live near the Fitzroy River banks. A tiny settlement where the road crosses the Fitzroy River, this is another place from which to get to the gorges and water holes of the area. The old town site is on Russ St, north-east of the present town. The **Crossing Inn**, near Brooking Creek, established as a shanty inn by Joseph Blythe in the 1890s, is the oldest pub in the Kimberley and still has lively nights. In the cemetery on Sandford Rd are the graves of many early European pioneers.

The Fitzroy River flows for 750km through the hills and plains of the King Leopold and Mueller ranges. It's a veritable Amazon when in flood – extending to well over 10km in width.

A lot of money went into the construction of the Fitzroy Crossing tourist bureau (☎ 9191 5355) on Flynn Drive; your repeated questions and visit will ensure future funding. If you are extremely lucky you may be able to visit a wholly owned and run Aboriginal cattle station such as Louisa Downs. The Yiyili and Ganinyi communities there will introduce you to an Australia you never knew existed (and, if you are allowed, be prepared to help in the daily chores); enquire at the tourist bureau.

Places to Stay & Eat

The multi-personality *Fitzroy River Lodge Motel Hotel & Caravan Park* (☎ 9191 5141), by the famous river crossing, has tent/powered sites at $8.50/17 for two, safari tents for $75/90 for singles/doubles and motel rooms for $100/115. It's damn expensive by anyone's reckoning, but it probably has the best equipped and one of the nicest campsites along the Kununurra-Perth stretch.

The *Crossing Motor Inn Motel Hotel* (☎ 9191 5080), Skulthorpe Rd, is another Kimberley schizophrenic. Its motel units look like something out of an abandoned mining camp and are definitely not good value for the $70/85, especially if you're forced to stop when the Fitzroy is in flood! The pub seems to be split into black and white sections, both of which can get pretty noisy.

In the Old Post Office on Geikie Gorge Rd, about 4km from town, you'll find the rather dirty, tatty *Darlngunaya Backpackers* (☎ 9191 5140), well in need of a spring clean; dorms are $12, and single and double rooms are $20. All backpackers get picked up and returned to the Greyhound Pioneer bus stop at the roadhouse (at some ungodly hour of the night). The tours they run from here are informative and good value, and compensate for the rough accommodation.

It is cheaper to prepare food for yourself in this town. If your margarine is runny and the cheese you bought the day before is off,

THE KIMBERLEY

then *Maxine's* in the Fitzroy River Lodge serves reasonable meals.

East Kimberley

The east Kimberley is roughly the area east of Fitzroy Crossing out to the Northern Territory border. It includes Halls Creek; Mirima (Hidden Valley), Wolfe Creek Crater and the Purnululu national parks; massive Lake Argyle; and the towns of Wyndham and Kununurra. The hub of the region is Kununurra, a relatively new town in the heart of the Ord River valley.

HALLS CREEK
• *pop 1200*

The area around the new town of Halls Creek, in the centre of the Kimberley and on the edge of the Great Sandy Desert, was traditionally the land of the Jaru and Kija people. Graziers took over in the 1870s and virtually used these people as slave labour on stations. When the stations were sold off, about a hundred years later, the Aborigines drifted to the nearest town.

Nights are often noisy and interrupted by shouting, fighting and the din from smashing bottles. Dawn brings with it the scene of an uncontrolled, nocturnal rampage with scattered debris and human bodies lying where they fell. Halls Creek is about as close as you get to Australia's real shame.

The region was the site of the 1885 gold rush, the first in WA. The gold soon petered out and today the town is a cattle centre, 15km from the original town site where some crumbling remains can still be seen.

Although Halls Creek is a comfortable enough little place, just remember it sits on the edge of a distinctly inhospitable stretch of country. The Halls Creek tourist centre (☎ 9168 6262), Great Northern Highway, is open April to September daily from 8 am to 4 pm; it is closed October to March in the Wet.

Things to See & Do
There's an Aboriginal art shop on the Duncan Highway where you can buy high-quality artefacts and paintings, produced by artisans from outlying communities. Outside the shire offices, on Thomas St, there is a statue of **Russian Jack**, a character of the 1885 gold rush.

Five km east of Halls Creek and about 1.5km off the road, there's a natural **China Wall** – so called because it resembles the Great Wall of China. This sub-vertical quartz vein with a block-type formation is short but picturesquely situated; it is off Duncan Highway.

Halls Creek **Old Town** is a great place for fossicking. All that remain of the once-bustling mining town of 3000 people are the ant-bed and spinifex walls of the old post office, the cemetery and a huge broken bottle pile where a pub once stood. 'Old Town' is the general term for the hilly area behind Halls Creek, and gold might be found anywhere there.

You can swim in **Caroline Pool, Sawpit Gorge** and **Palm Springs**. Palm Springs, a popular picnic and camping spot, is a natural spring located where the Black Elvire River crosses Duncan Rd; it once supported a market garden which supplied vegetables to the area. Caroline Pool is a natural waterhole off Duncan Rd near Old Halls Creek and Sawpit Gorge is a popular fishing and swimming spot on the Black Elvire River.

Places to Stay
Halls Creek Caravan Park (☎ 9168 6169), on Roberta Ave towards the airport, has tent/powered sites for $12/14 for two, on-site vans at $38 per double (usually filled by workers) and basic cabins at $15 a single.

Opposite is the *Kimberley Hotel* (☎ 9168 6101), which has a variety of overpriced standard rooms from $80/95, and deluxe motel units (they had better be!) for $110/130. This hotel best exhibits the rough and smooth sides of this frontier town as best seen in the bar (see the Places to Eat section following).

Shell Roadhouse Cabins (☎ 9168 6060), has five basic backpackers' cabins for $50 (or $15 per person, with up to four occupants); and the *Halls Creek Motel* (☎ 9168

Russian Jack

The goldfields and the rushes threw up many heroes: successful speculators, the lucky who found nuggets or struck it rich, Peter Lalor and the diggers of Eureka Stockade, the knucklemen, the Mountain Maid and the extremely odd and unusual.

Russian Jack was the Kimberley's hero, renowned for his feats of strength and endurance. He is believed to have carried a sick friend over 300km in his rough-and-ready wheelbarrow. He had originally pushed his barrow, with its 2m Derbyshafts and wide wheel specially made for the sandy tracks, all the way from Derby loaded with food, tools, blankets and water.

His loyalty to his mates and the job became legendary. One day he fell to the bottom of an open pit at Mt Morgan, about 23m down. After laying there injured for three days his only comment when they pulled him out was 'I've missed a shift'. ■

6001) has units for $65/80; both are on the Great Northern Highway.

At Old Halls Creek, the *lodge* (☎ 9168 8999) has tent/powered sites for $8/10 for two, and a small restaurant.

Places to Eat

The *Kimberley Hotel* has a distinctive Outback bar: Aborigines mainly drink in the area with grills and no furniture, while the whites usually retreat to a leafy oasis behind the hotel. Standard counter meals cost about $10 which you can eat outside at the tables on the grass; inside there's a surprisingly swish restaurant with smorgasbord meals at $15. The roadhouses on the Great Northern Highway have takeaway/restaurant facilities.

Getting There & Away

It's 371km north-east to Kununurra, 555km west to Derby. Greyhound Pioneer passes through Halls Creek early in the morning (northbound) and late at night (southbound).

WOLFE CREEK METEORITE CRATER

The 835m-wide and 50m-deep Wolfe Creek Meteorite Crater (14 sq km) is the second-largest known in the world with fragments of

the impacting meteorite being retrieved. It is estimated to be about two million years old. To the Aborigines, the crater is 'Kandimalal', a place where one of the snakes emerged from the ground.

Why the 'e' in 'Wolfe' when most maps don't have it? It was discovered in 1986 that the Halls Creek storekeeper and digger whom they named the crater after was one Robert Tennant Stow Wolfe.

The turn-off to the crater (the Tanami Desert Rd) is 18km out of Halls Creek towards Fitzroy Crossing and from there it's 112km by unsealed road to the south. It's easily accessible without 4WD in the Dry season from May to November; check with the Halls Creek shire office. You can camp (free) and get some limited supplies at the nearby *Carranya Station Homestead* (☎ 9168 0200), 7km south of the crater.

You can walk, Neil Armstrong-like, for about 200m along a track on the steep crater lip. Loose rocks make it unsafe, so take care. There is an information shelter and tables at the crater. The trees in the centre have only been growing since 1983, the year for the longest Wet on record.

If you can't handle one more outback road

you can fly over the crater from Halls Creek for about $100 per person with these local flight operators: Oasis Airlines (☎ 9168 6462), Kingfisher Aviation (☎ 9168 6162) and Crocodile Air (☎ 9168 6250).

HALLS CREEK TO KUNUNURRA

It is 359km from Halls Creek to Kununurra on what is a pretty nondescript piece of highway. The lone vestige of civilisation passed through is **Turkey Creek** (aka 'Warmun'), which wouldn't even be mentioned if it wasn't close to one of the natural wonders of the world, Purnululu (Bungle Bungle) National Park.

Turkey Creek, 163km north-east of Halls Creek, has a grubby caravan facility (☎ 9168 7882) and a roadhouse motel (☎ 9168 7882). A tent/powered site is $10/15 for two, motel units are $45/55 and caravan storage is $4 per day. If you're desperate, grab some grub from the roadhouse; your best bet is to bring fresh tucker from Derby or Kununurra.

PURNULULU (BUNGLE BUNGLE) NATIONAL PARK

I'm sure 'bungle' means superlative and 'bungle bungle' means multiple superlatives. The 350-million-year-old Purnululu (formerly the Bungle Bungles) are an amazing spectacle which shouldn't be missed: impressive rounded rock towers, striped like tigers in alternate bands of orange (silica) and blackish-green (lichen) – truly one of Australia's natural wonders. The whole massif is a plateau which is more than 200m above the surrounding plain and at its edges are the curious beehive domes.

Traditionally the land of the Kija and Jaru people, who still live in settlements in the eat Kimberley, there is much Aboriginal art and a number of burial sites in the area. The area was not 'discovered' by tourists until filmed by a TV crew in 1982; in 1995 it was estimated that over 9000 people drove in to see the beehive domes.

The national park of 3000 sq km is 165km (four hours) from Halls Creek and 305km (five hours) from Kununurra. The range is hard to get to and access is limited to 4WDs

with good clearance; no caravans or trailers are permitted. Visitors are asked to stay on authorised tracks as new tracks quickly erode in the Wet (Green) season. The park is officially closed from 1 January to March 31 and this is extended if the weather is bad.

Visitors to the park are charged an entry fee of $11/1 for adults/children; this covers use of facilities for seven nights in the park.

Things to See & Do

There is much to see once you have made the long trip to the park. It will all be a little bewildering unless you have information to interpret what you are looking at. Australian Geographic's *The Kimberley* contains a good deal of information.

Walking is the only means of access into the gorges so this is the main activity in the park. **Echidna Chasm** in the north or **Cathedral Gorge** in the south are each only about a two hour walk from car parks at the road's end. However, the soaring **Piccaninny Gorge** is a 30km round trip that comfortably takes two days to walk.

The restricted gorges in the northern part of the park can only be seen from the air. They too are a spectacular sight, choked in fan palms. In fact, some of the plants in the park are so newly discovered that they have not yet been named. Most of the park is undulating plain which supports spinifex and other grasses, acacia and grevillea shrubland and eucalypt woodlands.

The Kimberley's southerly patches of rainforest are found around Osmond Creek (see Rainforest boxed aside in the Facts about Western Australia chapter). About 130 bird species have been recorded in the park, the most visible being the spinifex pigeons and large flocks of budgerigars.

The rock formations are fragile – you're not allowed to climb them.

Scenic Flights

As the range is so vast, flights and helicopter rides prove to be money well spent. The chopper rides cost $120 for a 30 minute flight from Wilardi campsite, or $130 in a faster helicopter from Turkey Creek, on the

The Kimberley
The fantastic colours of Purnululu (Bungle Bungle) National Park

JEFF WILLIAMS

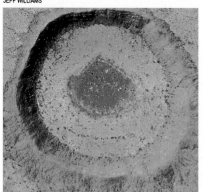

WESTERN AUSTRALIAN TOURIST COMMISSION

JEFF WILLIAMS

JEFF WILLIAMS

A	
B	C
D	

The Kimberley

A: Cable Beach, the most popular swimming beach near Broome

B: Wolfe Creek Meteorite Crater, the world's second largest at 14 sq km

C: Children parade in the Shinju Matsuri (Festival of the Pearl), Broome

D: Geikie Gorge during the Wet, when the river rises 17m

main highway. This latter flight is a popular option for people without a 4WD. Flights from Kununurra by land/float plane are $150/160 and they overfly Lake Argyle and the Argyle diamond mine. Out of Halls Creek, the flights to Purnululu are only $110.

The chopper rides, operated by Heliwork WA (part of Slingair; see below), are by far the more impressive of the two options, as you fly right in, among and over the deep, narrow gorges, while the light planes have to remain above 700m.

Operators of aerial tours of Purnululu and other Kimberley highlights, are:

Alan Clarke's Heliventures
    Fights from Kununurra over whole Kimberley, Prince Regent and Mitchell Falls, El Questro; helifishing (☎ 9168 7440)
Alligator Airways
    Fights from Kununurra over Lake Argyle, Argyle diamond mine and Purnululu (☎ 9168 1333)
Crocodile Air
    Flights from Halls Creek over Purnululu and Wolfe Creek Crater (☎ 9168 6250, 9168 6085)
East Kimberley Tours
    Flights from Kununurra over Purnululu (☎ 9168 2213)
Kingfisher Aviation
    Flights from Halls Creek and Kununurra over Purnululu, Wolfe Creek Crater and Prince Regent (☎ 9168 6160)
Oasis Airlines
    Flights from Halls Creek over Purnululu and Wolfe Creek (☎ 9168 6462)
Slingair
    Flights from Kununurra over Purnululu, Lake Argyle, Prince Regent and a full Kimberley panorama (☎ 9169 1300)

Places to Stay

From the main highway it's 55km to Three Ways. It's another 20 minutes north to *Kurrajong Camping Area* and 45 minutes south to *Bellburn Camping Area*. Bellburn Creek Campsite is mainly for the Fly/Drive visitors and licensed tour operators. *Kurrajong Camping Area*, for casual visitors, has long-drop toilets, supplied drinking water and fireplaces with firewood supplied. There is a small fee for overnight camping.

There is no rubbish disposal so take all of your rubbish out of the park.

Getting There & Away

The turn-off to the single access track to the park, known as Spring Creek Track, is 110km north of Halls Creek and 50km south of Turkey Creek (Warnum). This 4WD-only track traverses rugged country with numerous creek crossings. From the Three Ways intersection (ranger station) it is 15km to the Bellburn Camping Area (30 to 45 minutes); 21km to the Echidna Chasm car park (45 minutes); 7km to Kurrajong Camping Area (20 minutes); and 25km to the Piccaninny Creek car park (one hour). Although it's only 53km to Three Ways, in the park, from the Halls Creek to Kununurra road turn-off, the stretch takes two hours to drive.

The best option if you don't have a 4WD is to take one of the tours from Kununurra. Desert Inn 4WD Adventure (☎ (1800) 805 010) has popular two and three day trips ($220/365), while East Kimberley Tours (☎ 9168 2213) charges $295/425 for a day/overnight combined flight and 4WD trip; the park fee is an extra $30. There are several other operators and options.

WYNDHAM
• *pop 850*

It's possible only bird-watchers think the side trip to Wyndham, the most northerly town and harbour in WA, is actually worth the effort. It is a sprawling frontier town, suffering from Kununurra's boom in popularity, but its **Five Rivers Lookout** on top of Mt Bastion (380m) is still a must. From there you see the King, Pentecost, Durack, Forest and Ord rivers enter the Cambridge Gulf. It's memorable at sunrise or sunset.

There are paintings of great antiquity in the Wyndham region, evidence of the Aboriginal culture which thrived here for thousands of years. In 1819, Lieutenant Phillip Parker King in the *Mermaid*, sailed into the inlet where the town now stands; he named the gulf after the Duke of Cambridge.

Wyndham was the starting point for two record-breaking flights to England in 1931 and the finish of an England to Australia flight in 1933. It was also bombed by the Japanese in WWII and the wreck of the SS

Koolama, sunk during a raid, lies at the bottom of the gulf, not far from the wharf.

The tourist information centre in Wyndham has closed. Get information on the area from the Kununurra tourist bureau (see the following section for details).

Things to See & Do

A number of **historic buildings** survive in the old town – the port post office, Durack's store, the old Court House (now a museum, $2) and Anthon's Landing. These form part of a **port heritage trail**; the tourist office has copies of a map.

When the tide is right you can go down to the water's edge and observe (from a distance) large saltwater **crocodiles**. Failing this, you can see an 18m ferro-concrete saltwater crocodile at the entrance to town.

Near the town there's a rather desolate and decrepit **cemetery** where Afghan camel-drivers were buried last century. Near Moochalabra Dam, south of Wyndham, there are Aboriginal paintings of spiritual figures and animals and a prison boab tree. The **Grotto** is a good swimming hole just off the Wyndham to Kununurra road. **Crocodile Hole** is farther off the road and has a small population of freshwater crocodiles.

Not far from Wyndham is a protected bird sanctuary – **Marlgu Billabong** on Parry's Creek – where you will see many bird species including the black-necked stork or jabiru, brolga, magpie geese, sarus cranes, pygmy-geese and many varieties of duck. The **Moochalabra Dam** is a popular fishing and picnic spot about 25km away.

Kimberley Pursuits (☎ 9161 1029) offers mustering experiences ($85), two day horse-riding treks to Emma Gorge ($220) and four day treks near El Questro ($440).

Places to Stay & Eat

Three Mile Caravan Park (☎ 9161 1064), boasting the 'largest boab tree in captivity', has tent/powered sites for $10/12 for two. The better rooms in the *Wyndham Town Hotel* (☎ 9161 1003), on O'Donnell St, cost $65/80 for singles/doubles. Try the *Wyndham Community Club Hotel* (☎ 9161

1130), Great Northern Highway, for cheaper, but more basic beds (from $45/55).

There is a bakery on the Great Northern Highway, a coffee lounge in the Tuckerbox Store, a liquor store and a sole restaurant in Wyndham. Face it, you didn't drive all this way for cordon-bleu cookery.

KUNUNURRA
• *pop 4800*

In the Miriwoong language the region is known as 'Gananoorrang' – Kununurra is the European translation of this. As in most parts of the rugged Kimberley, the Aborigines have occupied the area for thousands of years. Nearby Hidden Valley is of great significance to the Aboriginal people and has ancient rock art and axe grooves.

Founded in the 1960s, the town of Kununurra is in the centre of the Ord River irrigation scheme and is quite a modern, bustling little town. In the past it was just a stopover on the main highway and there was little incentive to linger. Much of the history features in Mary Durack's *Kings in Grass Castles* and *Sons in the Saddle*. That has all changed in recent years with the increase in tourism and there are now enough recreational activities, most of them water-based, to keep you busy for a while.

The town is also a popular place to look for work. The main picking season starts in May and ends about September. Ask at the Desert Inn, Kununurra Backpackers or the tourist bureau.

Information

The excellent Kununurra tourist bureau (☎ 9168 1177), on Coolibah Drive, has information on the town and the Kimberley; from April to October it's open from 8 am to 5 pm daily (otherwise it has reduced hours). There is a laundrette (much needed in these parts) in Banksia St.

There's a 1½ hour time change between Kununurra and Katherine in the Northern Territory. Strict quarantine regulations apply when entering WA from the NT.

Mirima (Hidden Valley) National Park

This national park with a steep gorge, some

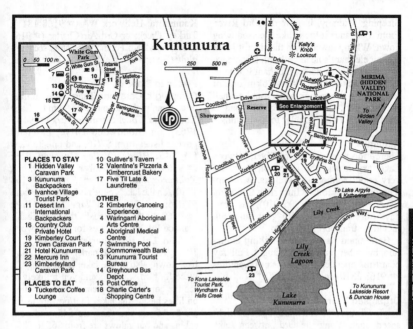

Kununurra

0   50   100 m

0   250   500 m

PLACES TO STAY
1 Hidden Valley
  Caravan Park
3 Kununurra
  Backpackers
6 Ivanhoe Village
  Tourist Park
11 Desert Inn
  International
  Backpackers
16 Country Club
  Private Hotel
19 Kimberley Court
20 Town Caravan Park
21 Hotel Kununurra
22 Mercure Inn
23 Kimberleyland
  Caravan Park

PLACES TO EAT
9 Tuckerbox Coffee
  Lounge

10 Gulliver's Tavern
12 Valentine's Pizzeria &
  Kimbercrust Bakery
17 Five Til Late &
  Laundrette

OTHER
2 Kimberley Canoeing
  Experience
4 Waringarri Aboriginal
  Arts Centre
5 Aboriginal Medical
  Centre
7 Swimming Pool
8 Commonwealth Bank
13 Kununurra Tourist
  Bureau
14 Greyhound Bus
  Depot
15 Post Office
18 Charlie Carter's
  Shopping Centre

THE KIMBERLEY

great views and a few short walking tracks, covers an area of 18 sq km. It is a rugged area of 300-million-year-old sandstone hills and valleys, often described as a 'mini Purnululu'. Mirima is the name given to the park by the Miriwoong people and the shelter and permanent water meant that it was a meeting place and corroboree ground.

Within the park you will see small boabs growing out of the valley walls. Given the size of boab fruit and seeds, it is believed that rock wallabies have carried them high up in their droppings. Other vegetation which thrives in the Hidden Valley are woollybutt and long-fruited bloodwood.

Three short walking trails within the park are the Lily Pool (100m return) where there are stone axe grooves; Wuttuwutubin ('short and narrow', 500m return) which enters a steep-sided gorge; and Didbagirring (1km return) which affords great views over Kununurra and the banded rock formations of the park.

Other Attractions
The **Waringarri Aboriginal Arts Centre** is on Speargrass Rd, at the turn-off to Kelly's Knob. You can admire the Aboriginal art of the east Kimberley and this is as good a place as any in WA to buy art and carvings.

There are good views of the irrigated fields from **Kelly's Knob Lookout**, close to the centre of town. During the Wet, distant thunderstorms can be spectacular when viewed from there, although caution is needed as the Knob itself is frequently struck by lightning.

Lake Kununurra (also called the Diversion Dam), an artificial lake beside the town, has plentiful bird life and several swimming spots. There's good fishing below the Lower Dam (watch for crocodiles) and also on the Ord River at **Ivanhoe Crossing**. If you're swimming there, be careful.

There are a number of unusual **rock formations** close to town. The Sleeping Buddha, also known as Carlton Ridge or the

Sleeping Mummy, is near the Ord River. From a distance it looks like a person lying down. When viewed from the river it looks like an elephant's head with trunk and ears, hence yet another name, Elephant Rock.

The **Packsaddle Plains**, 6km out of town, has a zebra rock gallery and a small wildlife park. Farther along this road is **Packsaddle Falls**, popular for swimming.

Activities

The **canoe** trips on the Ord River, between Lake Argyle and the Diversion Dam, are very popular amongst travellers. A recommended operation, Kimberley Canoeing Experience (☎ (1800) 805 010), has three day tours for $120, with gear supplied, including transport to the dam.

Barramundi is the major **fishing** attraction, but other fish are also caught. Full-day boat trips operated by Ultimate Adventures (☎ 9168 2310) cost about $180.

Organised Tours & Flights

Triple J Tours (☎ 9168 2682) operates high-speed boats along the Ord between Lake Argyle and Kununurra (55km). These are a real thrill and pass through beautiful scenery. The cost is $90/55 for an adult/child (with lunch), including return by bus.

Duncan's Ord River Tours (☎ 9168 1823) cruise on Lake Kununurra, visiting banana plantations on Packsaddle Plains, the zebra rock gallery and areas where bird life is prolific; the cost of the four hour tour is $50/30 for adults/children.

R&B Kimberley Ecotours (☎ 9168 2116) has two really interesting and informative wildlife tours, both thoroughly recommended. The morning tour, 6 to 8 am, focuses on wetland bird species ($30); and the evening tour, 5 to 7 pm, on freshwater crocodile biology and nocturnal wildlife.

Flights over Purnululu are popular and cost about $150 a person (discounts apply). They take about two hours and also fly over Lake Argyle, the Argyle and Bow River diamond projects and the irrigation area north of the town. Contact Alligator Airways (☎ 9168 1333) or Slingair (☎ 9169 1300) in

Kununurra; Heliwork WA (☎ 9168 1811), Turkey Creek; or Ord Air Charter (☎ 9161 1335), Wyndham. For more operators, see Purnululu (Bungle Bungle) National Park earlier.

Places to Stay

Camping & Caravans There are a number of caravan parks, a couple of them by Lake Kununurra. *Town Caravan Park* (☎ 9168 1763), on Bloodwood Drive, has tent/powered sites from $7/16, and on-site vans for $45. *Hidden Valley Caravan Park* (☎ 9168 1790), on Weaber Plains Rd, and *Kimberleyland Caravan Park* (☎ 9168 1280), on the lake's edge near town, are both $14/16; and *Ivanhoe Village Tourist Park* (☎ 9169 1995), previously the 'Coolibah', Ivanhoe Rd, has tent sites for $15 for two.

Kona Lakeside Tourist Park (☎ 9168 1031), the pick of the parks, is about 1km from town, also on the lake. Kona is a great place for bird-watchers and you're likely to see the comb-crested jacana darting around on lilies beside the lake. Tent/powered sites are $7/15, on-site vans are $45, and park cabins and bungalows are from $65 to $85.

Hostels There are two hostels. *Desert Inn International Backpackers* (☎ 9168 2702) is on Tristania St, opposite Gulliver's Tavern in the centre of town; dorm beds are $14, and twins are $30. This purpose-built complex, with full facilities including a spa pool, is a friendly and popular place.

At 112 Nutwood Crescent is *Kununurra Backpackers* (☎ 9169 1998). It's in a couple of adjacent houses about five minutes walk from the town centre; dorms are $13 and rooms $30 for two. The shaded pool is a big drawcard.

Hotels, Guesthouses & Motels Hotel accommodation is expensive with a big variation between low and high season tariffs. The *Country Club Private Hotel* (☎ 9168 1024), 76 Coolibah Drive, is the cheapest, but at $50/60 a single/double for small air-con rooms with no facilities, even it is grossly overpriced. Another place is *Kimberley Court* (☎ 9168 1411), corner of River Fig

Ave and Erythrina St; B&B is $85/95. The *Hotel Kununurra* (☎ 9168 1344), Messmate Way, is the town's main hotel. It has a motel section with standard rooms from $85 and deluxe rooms at $104. It has some grotty backpackers' rooms for $25 per person.

Mercure Inn (☎ 9168 1455), on the corner of Duncan Highway and Messmate Way, has high-season rates of $144 for all rooms ($10 less in the low season). Luxurious surroundings are found at the *Kununurra Lakeside Resort*, Casuarina Way, where deluxe singles/doubles are $103/117 ($20 less in the low season). There's a necessary pool.

Duncan House (☎ 9168 2436), 1921 Melaleuca Drive, is close to the lake; a comfortable single/double B&B is $60/75.

Places to Eat

The *Five Til Late Cafe*, on Banksia St, offers takeaway tucker and light meals; and *Valentines Pizzeria* and the *Kimbercrust Bakery*, both on Cottontree Ave, are open daily. Just off Coolibah Drive, the *Tuckerbox Coffee Lounge* serves good salads and excellent salad rolls ($2.50), and its small lunch-of-the-day servings at $3.50 are unbeatable value.

Gulliver's Tavern on Konkerberry Drive is a popular drinking place, and has good meals (fish and chips $6.50). The Country Club has the Chinese *Chopsticks* (mains $17.50) and at its *Kelly's Bar & Grill*, in a tropical setting, you get excellent steaks with potato and salad for $16.50. The Mercure Inn's *Ivanhoe's Gallery* is the best restaurant in town; a three course buffet is about $25.

Things to Buy

The Waringarri Aboriginal Arts Centre is on Speargrass Rd, at the turn-off to Kelly's Knob, and the Ochre Gallery is in the town centre. Both are good places to buy authentic Kimberley Aboriginal art.

Also of interest is Nina's Jewellery, in Konkerberry Drive. Here you can see the famous champagne diamonds from the Argyle mine. The friendly staff explain carat weight, cut, clarity and colour – the four Cs.

Getting There & Away

The Ansett office (☎ 9168 1622) is in the Charlie Carter's shopping centre; they fly to Darwin and Perth daily. Either Ansett or Skywest go to Broome Wednesday to Monday and Skywest flies to Derby Friday to Monday, and Wednesday. There is a cheap one-way fare from Kununurra to Darwin on Wednesday ($92).

Greyhound Pioneer (☎ 13 2030) passes through Kununurra on the Darwin to Perth route; it picks up and drops off in the shire office car park.

LAKE ARGYLE

Created by the Ord River Dam, Lake Argyle is the second-biggest storage reservoir in Australia, holding nine times as much water as Sydney Harbour. There are 96 islands in this huge, inland sea. Prior to its construction, there was too much water in the Wet season and not enough in the Dry. By providing a regular water supply the dam has encouraged agriculture on a massive scale.

At the lake there's a **pioneer museum** in the old Argyle Homestead. The reconstructed homestead of the Durack family was moved here when its original site was flooded. May to October it is open from 8.30 am to 4.30 pm daily; entry is $2.

Boats depart from there for the huge lake each morning and afternoon. Downstream of the lake is now green farmland. Encircling these flat lands are the small reddish mountains typical of the region.

There are two memorable trips on the inland sea. Lake Argyle Cruises (☎ 9168 7360) uses the *Bowerbird* for a two hour cruise ($25/12.50 for adults/children) and the *Silver Cobbler* for a half-day cruise ($80/50). There is ample opportunity to observe the bird life of the lake on the longer cruise, and keen anglers get the chance to go fishing. The enormity of Argyle is not appreciated until you are out in the middle of it.

Places to Stay

Lake Argyle Tourist Village (☎ 9168 7360), near the Ord Dam, has tent/powered sites for $9/12 for two, and expensive rooms ($65 for

326 East Kimberley – Argyle Diamond Mine

a single or double, $15 for each extra person). It is nothing flash, merely a resurrected workers' camp, but it has character and the bar is a great place to enjoy a meal or to pass an evening. It screens a video at 4.30 pm, showing the building of the huge neighbouring dam.

ARGYLE DIAMOND MINE

About 250km south of Kununurra is the huge Argyle diamond mine, the world's largest, which produces around 35% of the world's diamonds, although most are only of industrial

quality. The stones that get diamond merchant De Beer's excited, are the extremely rare and valuable pink diamonds, fine whites, champagne and cognac specimens.

Belray's six hour On-Site Tour (☎ 9168 1014) includes a flight over Purnululu (Bungle Bungle) National Park, a 4WD bus trip up the East Ridge Rd to overlook the mine pit, a tour round the $430 million process plant and a chance to look in the Diamond Viewing Room; the cost is equivalent to the purchase of a very small diamond, about $285 per person.

Australian Language Glossary

amber fluid – beer

ankle-biter – small child, *tacker*, *rug rat*

arvo – afternoon

avagoyermug – traditional rallying call, especially at cricket matches

award wage – minimum pay rate

back o' Bourke – back of beyond, middle of nowhere

backblocks – *bush* or other remote area far from the city

bail up – hold up, rob, *earbash*

bail out – leave

Balmain bug – see *Moreton Bay bug*

banana bender – resident of Queensland

banker – a river almost overflowing its banks (as in 'the Cooper is running a banker')

barbie – barbecue (BBQ)

barra – barramundi (prized fish of the north)

barrack – cheer on a team at sporting event, support (as in 'who do you barrack for?')

bastard – general term of address which can mean many things. While mostly used as a good-natured form of greeting ('*G'day*, you old bastard!'), it can also denote the highest level of praise or respect ('He's the bravest bastard I know!') or it can be the most dire of insults ('You lousy, lying bastard!')

bathers – swimming costume (Victoria, Western Australia)

battler – hard trier, struggler (the outback is full of 'great Aussie battlers')

beaut, beauty, bewdie – great, fantastic

big bikkies – a lot of money, expensive

big mobs – a large amount, heaps

bikies – motorcyclists

billabong – water hole in dried-up riverbed, more correctly an ox-bow bend cut off in the dry season by receding waters

billy – tin container used to boil tea in the bush

bitumen – asphalt, surfaced road

black stump – where the *back o' Bourke* begins

blaze – (a blaze in a tree) a mark in a tree trunk made by cutting away bark, indicating a path or reference point; also 'to blaze'

bloke – man

blowies – blowflies, bluebottles

bludger – lazy person, one who won't work and lives off other people's money (originally, a prostitute's pimp)

blue (ie **have a blue**) – to have an argument or fight

bluey – *swag*; also nickname for a red-haired person

bonzer – great, *ripper*

boomer – very big; a particularly large male kangaroo

boomerang – a curved flat wooden instrument used by Aborigines for hunting

booze bus – police van used for random breath testing for alcohol

boozer – pub

bottle – 750ml bottle of beer

bottle shop – liquor shop

bottlo – *bottle shop*

bowser – fuel pump at a service station (named after the US inventor SF Bowser)

brumby – wild horse

bruss – brother, *mate* (used by central Australian Aborigines)

Buckley's, Buckley's chance – no chance at all ('Across the Tanami? They've got Buckley's in that *shitbox*'). The origin of this term is unclear. Maybe it derives from the Melbourne department store of Buckley's & Nunn; or from the escaped convict William Buckley, whose chances of survival were considered negligible but who ended up living with Aborigines for 20 years; or from the Sydney escapologist Buckley, who had himself chained up in a coffin and thrown into Sydney Harbour, with dire results

bug – see *Moreton Bay bug*

Bulamakanka – place even beyond the *back o' Bourke*, way beyond the black stump (see *never-never*)

bull bar – outsize front bumper on car or truck used as the ultimate barrier against animals on the road

bull dust – fine, powdery and sometimes deep dust on outback roads, often hiding deep holes and ruts that you normally wouldn't drive into; also bullshit

bunfight – a quarrel over a frivolous issue or one that gets blown out of proportion

bungarra – any large (1.5m-plus) goanna, but specifically an Aboriginal name for Gould's goanna, prized as food

bunyip – mythical bush spirit said to inhabit Australia's swamps

burl – have a try (as in 'give it a burl')

bush – country, anywhere away from the city; *scrub*

bush (ie **go bush**) – go back to the land

bushbash – to force your way through pathless bush

bushranger – Australia's equivalent of the outlaws of the American Wild West (some goodies, some baddies) – the helmeted Ned Kelly was the most famous

bush tucker – food available naturally

BYO – Bring Your Own (booze to a restaurant, meat to a barbecue etc)

caaarn! – 'come on!'; traditional rallying call, especially at football games (as in 'Caaarn the Crows!')

cackle-berries – eggs; also 'hen-fruit', 'chook-nuts' and 'bum-nuts'

camp draft – Australian rodeo, testing horse rider's skills in separating cattle or sheep from a herd or flock

camp oven – large, cast-iron pot with lid, used for cooking in an open fire

cask – wine box (a great Australian invention)

Chiko roll – vile Australian junk food

chocka – completely full (from 'chock-a-block')

chook – chicken

chuck a U-ey – do a U-turn

chunder – vomit, technicolour yawn, pavement pizza, curbside quiche, liquid laugh, drive the porcelain bus, call Bluey

clobber – clothes

cobber – *mate*

cocky – small-scale farmer; cockatoo

come good – turn out all right

compo – compensation such as workers' compensation

cooee – shouting distance, close (to be within cooee of …)

cop, copper – police officer (not uniquely *strine* but common nevertheless); see *walloper*

counter meal, countery – pub meal

cow cocky – small-scale cattle farmer

cozzie – swimming costume (New South Wales)

crook – ill, badly made, substandard

crow eater – resident of South Australia

culvert – channel or pipe under road for rainwater drainage

cut lunch – sandwiches

cut snake – see *mad as a…*

dag, daggy – dirty lump of wool at back end of a sheep; also an affectionate or mildly abusive term for a socially inept person

daks – trousers

damper – bush loaf made from flour and water and cooked in a *camp oven*

Darwin stubby – 2L bottle of beer sold to tourists in Darwin

dead horse – tomato sauce

deli – delicatessen; milk bar in South Australia

digger – Australian or New Zealand soldier or veteran (originally, a miner); also a generic form of address assuming respect, mainly used for soldiers/veterans but sometimes also between friends

dijeridu – cylindrical wooden musical instrument played by Aboriginal men

dill – idiot

dingo – indigenous wild dog

dink – carry a second person on a bicycle or horse

dinkum, fair dinkum – honest, genuine ('fair dinkum?' – really?)

dinky-di – the real thing

distillate – diesel fuel

divvy van – police divisional van

dob in – to tell on someone

Dog Fence – the world's longest fence, erected to keep *dingoes* out of south-eastern Australia

donga – small transportable hut; also the *bush*, from the name for a shallow, eroded gully, found in areas where it doesn't rain often, so people don't go there

donk – car or boat engine

don't come the raw prawn – don't try and fool me

down south – the rest of Australia, viewed from the Northern Territory or anywhere north of Brisbane

drongo – foolish or worthless person

droving – moving livestock a considerable distance

Dry, the – the dry season in the north

duco – car paint

duffing – stealing cattle (literally: altering the brand on the 'duff', or rump)

dunny – outdoor lavatory

dunny budgies – *blowies*

earbash – talk non-stop

eastern states – the rest of Australia viewed from west of Queensland.

Esky – trademark name for a portable ice box used for keeping beer etc cold

fair go! – give us a break!

fair crack of the whip! – *fair go!*

feeding the ants – being in a very deceased condition out in the *donga*

FJ – most revered classic Holden car

flagon – 2L bottle (of wine, port etc)

flake – shark meat, often used in fish & chips down south

floater – meat pie floating in thick pea soup

flog – steal; sell; whip

fluke – undeserved good luck ('they had three flat tyres, no spare, no puncture kit, no water, but they fluked a lift into town on the monthly mail truck. Otherwise they'd still be there *feeding the ants*')

fossick – hunt for gems or semi-precious stones

from arsehole to breakfast – all over the place

furphy – a misleading statement, rumour or fictitious story, named after Joseph Furphy, who wrote a famous Australian novel, *Such is Life*, then reviewed the book for a literary journal of the time and criticised it; the public bought it by the ton. Or maybe this is a furphy and the term instead derives from the water or sewerage carrier made by his brother's company in Shepparton, Victoria; in WWI these carriers were places where the troops met, swapped yarns and information and no doubt construed a few furphies

galah – noisy parrot, thus noisy idiot

game – brave (as in 'game as Ned Kelly')

gander – look (as in 'have a gander')

garbo – person who collects your garbage

gibber – Aboriginal word for stone or boulder; gibber plain – stony desert

gidgee – a type of small acacia

give it away – give up

g'day – good day, traditional Australian greeting

good on ya – well done

grade – (to grade a road) to level a road, usually by means of a bulldozer fitted with a 'blade' that scrapes off the top layer and pushes it to the side

grazier – large-scale sheep or cattle farmer

Green, the – term used in the Kimberley for the wet season

grog – general term for alcoholic drinks

grouse – very good, unreal

homestead – the residence of a *station* owner or manager

hoon – idiot, hooligan, *yahoo*; also 'to hoon' or 'hooning around', often in a vehicle – to show off in a noisy fashion with little regard for others

how are ya? – standard greeting – expected answer: 'Good, thanks, how are you?'

how ya goin'? – *how are ya?*

HQ – second-most revered Holden car

Hughie – the god of rain and surf ('Send her down, Hughie!', 'Send 'em up, Hughie!'); also God when things go wrong ('It's up to Hughie now')

humpy – Aboriginal bark hut ('it was so cold, it would freeze the walls off a bark humpy')

icy-pole – frozen *lolly water* or ice cream on a stick

jackaroo – young male trainee manager on a *station*

jaffle – sealed toasted sandwich

jerky – dried meat

jillaroo – young female trainee on a *station*

jocks – men's underpants

joey – young kangaroo or wallaby

journo – journalist

jumped-up – arrogant, full of self-importance (a 'jumped-up petty Hitler')

jump-up – escarpment

Kal – Kalgoorlie-Boulder
kiwi – New Zealander
knackered – exhausted, very tired
knock – criticise, deride
knocker – one who *knocks*
Koori – Aborigine (mostly south of the Murray River)

lair – layabout, ruffian
lairising – acting like a *lair*
lamington – square of sponge cake covered in chocolate icing and coconut
larrikin – a bit like a *lair*; rascal
lay-by – put a deposit on an article so the shop will hold it for you
lemonade – Australian Seven-Up
lock-up – *watch house*
lollies – sweets, candy
lolly water – soft drink made of syrup and water
lurk – a scheme

mad as a cut snake – insane, crazy; also insane with anger
mallee – low, shrubby, multi-stemmed eucalypt. Also 'the mallee' – the *bush*
manchester – household linen
March fly – horsefly, gadfly
Margaret's – Margaret River (popular surfing spot)
mate – general term of familiarity, whether you know the person or not (but don't use it too often with total strangers)
Matilda – *swag*
middy – 285ml beer glass (New South Wales, Western Australia)
milk bar – general store
milko – milkman
mob – a herd of cattle or flock of sheep while *droving*; any bunch of people
Moreton Bay bug – (also known as *bug* or *Balmain bug*) an estuarine horseshoe crab closely related to the shovel-nosed lobster (good *tucker* with an unfortunate name)
mozzies – mosquitoes
mud map – map drawn on the ground with a stick, thus any rough map drawn by hand
mulga – arid-zone acacia; the *bush*, away from civilisation (as in 'he's gone up the mulga')

Murri – Aborigine (mostly in Queensland)
muster – round up livestock
mystery-bags – sausages, also *snags*
never-never – a place even more remote than *back o' Bourke*

namma – water hole
no-hoper – hopeless case
northern summer – summer in the northern hemisphere
north island – mainland Australia, viewed from Tasmania
no worries – *she'll be right*, that's OK
nulla-nulla – wooden club used by Aborigines

ocker – an uncultivated or boorish Australian
ocky strap – octopus strap: elastic strap with hooks for tying down gear and generally keeping things in place
off-sider – assistant or partner
on the piss – drinking alcohol ('they're on the piss tonight')
O-S – overseas (as in 'he's gone O-S')
outstation – an outlying *station* separate from the main one on a large property
OYO – own your own (flat or apartment)
Oz – Australia

pad – animal track ('cattle pad')
paddock – a fenced area of land, usually intended for livestock
pal – *mate*
pastoralist – large-scale *grazier*
pavlova – traditional Australian meringue and cream dessert, named after the Russian ballerina Anna Pavlova
perve – to gaze with lust
pineapple, rough end of – *stick, sharp end of*
piss – beer
pissed – drunk
pissed off – annoyed
piss turn – boozy party
plonk – cheap wine
pocamelo – camel polo
pokies – poker machines, found in clubs
pom – English person
pommy's towel – a notoriously dry object ('the Simpson Desert is as dry as a pommy's towel' – poms were considered not to bath as often as Australians)

possie – advantageous position (pronounced 'pozzy')

postie – mailman or -woman

pot – 285ml beer glass (Victoria, Queensland)

push – group or gang of people, such as shearers

quid – literally: a pound, $2. Still a common term in the *bush* for a non-specified amount of money, as in 'can you lend me a quid?' (enough money to last me until I'm not *skint*)

rapt – delighted, enraptured

ratbag – friendly term of abuse (friendly trouble-maker)

rat's coffin – meat pie of dubious quality

ratshit (R-S) – lousy

razoo – a coin of very little value, a subdivision of a rupee ('he spent every last razoo'). Counterfeit razoos made of brass circulated in the gold fields during *two-up* sessions, hence 'it's not worth a brass razoo'

reckon! – you bet!, absolutely!

rego – registration (as in 'car rego')

ridgy-didge – original, genuine, *dinky-di*

ripper – good, great (also 'little ripper')

road train – *semi-trailer*

roo bar – *bull bar*

root – have sexual intercourse

ropable – very bad-tempered or angry

Rotto –Rottnest Island

rubbish (ie **to rubbish**) – deride, tease

rug rat – small child, *ankle-biter*, *tacker*

salvo – member of the Salvation Army

sandgroper – resident of Western Australia

sanger – sandwich

scallops – fried potato cakes (Queensland), the edible muscle of certain molluscs (north Queensland), shellfish (elsewhere)

schooner – a 425ml beer glass in New South Wales, or a 285ml glass in South Australia (where a 425ml glass is called a 'pint')

scrub – stunted trees and bushes in a dry area; a remote, uninhabited area

sealed road – tarred road

sea wasp – box jellyfish

sedan – a closed car seating four to six people

see you in the soup – see you around

seismic line – *shotline*

semi-trailer – articulated truck

septic tanks – (also 'septics') rhyming slang for Yanks

session – lengthy period of heavy drinking

shanty – pub, usually unlicensed (proliferated in gold-rush areas)

sheila – woman, sometimes derogatory

shellacking – comprehensive defeat

she'll be right – *no worries*, it'll be OK

shitbox – neglected, worn-out, useless vehicle

shonky – unreliable

shoot through – leave in a hurry

shotline – straight trail through the bush, often kilometres long and leading nowhere, built by a mining company for seismic research

shout – buy round of drinks (as in 'it's your shout')

sickie – day off work through illness or lack of motivation

singlet – sleeveless shirt

skint – the state of being *quidless*

slab – package containing four six-packs of *tinnies* or *stubbies*, usually encased in plastic on a cardboard base; also called a 'carton' when packaged in a box (Victoria, Western Australia)

sleep-out – a covered verandah or shed, usually fairly open

sling off – criticise

smoke-oh – tea break

snag – sausage

sport – *mate*

spunky – good looking, attractive (as in 'what a spunk')

squatter – pioneer grazier who occupied land as a tenant of the government

squattocracy – Australian 'old money' folk, who made it by being first on the scene and grabbing the land

squiz – a look (as in 'take a squiz')

station – large sheep or cattle farm

stick, sharp end of – the worst deal

stickybeak – nosy person

stinger – box jellyfish

stoush – fist fight, brawl (also verbal)

stretcher – camp bed

strides – *daks*

strine – Australian slang (from how an *ocker* would pronounce the word 'Australian')

Stubbies – trademark name for rugged short shorts

stubby – 375ml bottle of beer

sunbake – sunbathe (well, the sun's hot in Australia)

super – superannuation (contributory pension)

surfaced road – tarred road

surfies – surfing fanatics

swag – canvas-covered bed roll used in the outback; also a large amount

swaggie, swagman – itinerant worker carrying his possessions in a *swag* (see *waltzing Matilda*)

ta – thanks

table drain – rainwater run-off area, often deep and wide, along the side of a dirt road

tacker – small child, *ankle-biter*, *rug rat*

takeaway – fast food, or a shop that sells it

tall poppies – achievers (*knockers* like to cut them down)

Taswegian – resident of Tasmania

tea – evening meal

terrorist – tourist

thingo – thing, whatchamacallit, hooza meebob, dooverlacky, thingamajig

thirst you could paint a picture of – the desire to drink a large quantity of foaming, ice-cold, nut-brown ale

thongs – flip-flops

tinny – 375ml can of beer; also a small aluminium fishing dinghy

Tip, the – the top of Cape York

togs – swimming costume (Queensland, Victoria)

too right! – absolutely!

Top, the – the tip of Cape York

Top End – northern part of the Northern Territory, sometimes also Cape York

Troopie – Toyota Landcruiser Troopcarrier (seats up to 11 people)

trucky – truck driver

true blue – *dinkum*

tucker – food

two-pot screamer – person unable to hold their drink

two-up – traditional heads/tails gambling game

uni – university

up north – New South Wales and Queensland when viewed from Victoria

ute – utility, pickup truck

vegies – vegetables

waddy – wooden club used by Aborigines

wag – to play truant ('to wag school')

wagon – station wagon, estate car

Wakka – Western Australian Cricket Association (the WACA)

walkabout – lengthy walk away from it all

wallaby track, on the – to wander from place to place seeking work (archaic)

walloper – police officer (from 'wallop', to hit something with a stick)

waltzing Matilda – to wander with one's *swag* seeking work or a place to settle (archaic)

washaway – washout: heavy erosion caused by running water across road or track

watch house – temporary prison at a police station

weatherboard house – wooden house clad with long, narrow planks

Wet, the – rainy season in the north

wharfie – dock worker

whinge – complain, moan

willy-willy – whirlwind, dust storm

woof wood – petrol used to start a fire (also 'bushman's lighter fluid')

woolly rocks – sheep

wowser – spoilsport, puritan

wobbly – disturbing, unpredictable behaviour (as in 'throw a wobbly')

wobbly boot – (as in 'to put on the wobbly boot') to have consumed too much alcohol

woomera – stick used by Aborigines for throwing spears

yabby, yabbie – small freshwater crayfish

yabby, to – to catch yabbies, a relaxed activity often involving *mates* and a *slab* or two ('they're going yabbying this *arvo*')

yahoo – noisy and unruly person, *hoon*

yakka – work (from an Aboriginal language)

Yal's – Yallingup (popular surfing spot)

youse – plural of you (pronounced 'yooz')

yobbo – uncouth, aggressive person

yonks – ages, a long time

yowie – Australia's yeti or bigfoot

Index

TEXT

LONELY PLANET

Phrasebooks

Lonely Planet phrasebooks are packed with essential words and phrases to help travellers communicate with the locals. With colour tabs for quick reference, an extensive vocabulary and use of script, these handy pocket-sized language guides cover day-to-day travel situations.

- handy pocket-sized books
- easy to understand Pronunciation chapter
- clear & comprehensive Grammar chapter
- romanisation alongside script to allow ease of pronunciation
- script throughout so users can point to phrases for every situation
- full of cultural information and tips for the traveller

'... vital for a real DIY spirit and attitude in language learning'
— *Backpacker*

'the phrasebooks have good cultural backgrounders and offer solid advice for challenging situations in remote locations'
— *San Francisco Examiner*

Arabic (Egyptian) • Arabic (Moroccan) • Australian *(Australian English, Aboriginal and Torres Strait languages)* • Baltic States *(Estonian, Latvian, Lithuanian)* • Bengali • Brazilian • British • Burmese • Cantonese • Central Asia (Uyghur, Uzbek, Kyrghiz, Kazak, Pashto, Tadjik • Central Europe *(Czech, French, German, Hungarian, Italian, Slovak)* • Eastern Europe *(Bulgarian, Czech, Hungarian, Polish, Romanian, Slovak)* • Ethiopian (Amharic) • Fijian • French • German • Greek • Hebrew • Hill Tribes • Hindi & Urdu • Indonesian • Italian • Japanese • Korean • Lao • Latin American Spanish • Malay • Mandarin • Mediterranean Europe *(Albanian, Croatian, Greek, Italian, Macedonian, Maltese, Serbian, Slovene)* • Mongolian • Nepali • Pidgin • Pilipino (Tagalog) • Portugese • Quechua • Russian • Scandinavian Europe *(Danish, Finnish, Icelandic, Norwegian, Swedish)* • South-East Asia *(Burmese, Indonesian, Khmer, Lao, Malay, Tagalog Pilipino, Thai, Vietnamese)* • South Pacific Languages • Spanish (Castilian) *(also includes Catalan, Galician and Basque)* • Sri Lanka • Swahili • Thai • Tibetan • Turkish • Ukrainian • USA *(US English, Vernacular, Native American languages, Hawaiian)* • Vietnamese • Western Europe *(Basque, Catalan, Dutch, French, German, Greek, Irish, Italian, Portuguese, Scottish Gaelic, Spanish (Castilian), Welsh)*

Lonely Planet Journeys

JOURNEYS is a unique collection of travel writing – published by the company that understands travel better than anyone else. It is a series for anyone who has ever experienced – or dreamed of – the magical moment when they encountered a strange culture or saw a place for the first time. They are tales to read while you're planning a trip, while you're on the road or while you're in an armchair in front of a fire.

These outstanding titles explore our planet through the eyes of a diverse group of international writers. JOURNEYS books catch the spirit of a place, illuminate a culture, recount a crazy adventure or introduce a fascinating way of life. They always entertain, and always enrich the experience of travel.

IN RAJASTHAN
Royina Grewal

As she writes of her travels through Rajasthan, Indian writer Royina Grewal takes us behind the exotic facade of this fabled destination: here is an insider's perceptive account of India's most colourful state, conveying the excitement and challenges of a region in transition.

SHOPPING FOR BUDDHAS
Jeff Greenwald

In his obsessive search for the perfect Buddha statue in the backstreets of Kathmandu, Jeff Greenwald discovers more than he bargained for ... and his souvenir-hunting turns into an ironic metaphor for the clash between spiritual riches and material greed. Politics, religion and serious shopping collide in this witty account of an enlightening visit to Nepal.

BRIEF ENCOUNTERS
Stories of Love, Sex & Travel
edited by Michelle de Kretser

Love affairs on the road, passionate holiday flings, disastrous pick-ups, erotic encounters ... In this seductive collection of stories, 22 authors from around the world write about travel romances. A tourist in Peru falls for her handsome guide; a writer explores the ambiguities of his relationship with a Japanese woman; a beautiful young man on a train proposes marriage ... Combining fiction and reportage, *Brief Encounters* is must-have reading – for everyone who has dreamt of escape with that perfect stranger.

Includes stories by Pico Iyer, Mary Morris, Emily Perkins, Mona Simpson, Lisa St Aubin de Terán, Paul Theroux and Sara Wheeler.

LONELY PLANET

Lonely Planet Travel Atlases

Lonely Planet has long been famous for the number and quality of its guidebook maps. Now we've gone one step further and produced a handy companion series: Lonely Planet trave atlases – maps of a country produced in book form.

Unlike other maps, which look good but lead travellers astray, our travel atlases have been researched on the road by Lonely Planet's experienced team of writers. All details are carefully checked to ensure the atlas corresponds with the equivalent Lonely Planet guidebook.

- full-colour throughout
- maps researched and checked by Lonely Planet authors
- place names correspond with Lonely Planet guidebooks
- no confusing spelling differences
- legend and travelling information in English, French, German, Japanese and Spanish
- size: 230 x 160 mm

Available now: Chile & Easter Island ● Egypt ● India & Bangladesh ● Israel & the Palestinian Territorie ● Jordan, Syria & Lebanon ● Kenya ● Laos ● Portugal ● South Africa, Lesotho & Swaziland ● Thailand ● Turkey ● Vietnam ● Zimbabwe, Botswana & Namibia

---

Lonely Planet TV Series & Videos

Lonely Planet travel guides have been brought to life on television screens around the world. Like our guides, the programs are based on the joy of independent travel, and look honestly at some of the most exciting, picturesque and frustrating places in the world. Each show is presented by one of three travellers from Australia, England or the USA and combines an innovative mixture of video, Super-8 film, atmospheric soundscapes and original music.

Videos of each episode – containing additional footage not shown on television – are available from good book and video shops, but the availability of individual videos varies with regional screening schedules.

Video destinations include: Alaska ● American Rockies ● Australia – The South-East ● Baja California & the Copper Canyon ● Brazil ● Central Asia ● Chile & Easter Island ● Corsica, Sicily & Sardinia – The Mediterranean Islands ● East Africa (Tanzania & Zanzibar) ● Ecuador & the Galapagos Islands ● Greenland & Iceland ● Indonesia ● Israel & the Sinai Desert ● Jamaica ● Japan ● La Ruta Maya ● Morocco ● New York ● North India ● Pacific Islands (Fiji, Solomon Islands & Vanuatu) ● South India ● South West China ● Turkey ● Vietnam ● West Africa ● Zimbabwe, Botswana & Namibia

The Lonely Planet TV series is produced by: Pilot Productions
The Old Studio
18 Middle Row
London W10 5AT, UK

FREE Lonely Planet Newsletters

We love hearing from you and think you'd like to hear from us.

Planet Talk

Our FREE quarterly printed newsletter is full of tips from travellers and anecdotes from Lonely Planet guidebook authors. Every issue is packed with up-to-date travel news and advice, and includes:

- a postcard from Lonely Planet co-founder Tony Wheeler
- a swag of mail from travellers
- a look at life on the road through the eyes of a Lonely Planet author
- topical health advice
- prizes for the best travel yarn
- news about forthcoming Lonely Planet events
- a complete list of Lonely Planet books and other titles

To join our mailing list, residents of the UK, Europe and Africa can email us at go@lonelyplanet.co.uk; residents of North and South America can email us at info@lonelyplanet.com; the rest of the world can email us at talk2us@lonelyplanet.com.au, or contact any Lonely Planet office.

Comet

Our FREE monthly email newsletter brings you all the latest travel news, features, interviews, competitions, destination ideas, travellers' tips & tales, Q&As, raging debates and related links. Find out what's new on the Lonely Planet Web site and which books are about to hit the shelves.

Subscribe from your desktop: www.lonelyplanet.com/comet

LONELY PLANET

Guides by Region

Lonely Planet is known worldwide for publishing practical, reliable and no-nonsense travel information in our guides and on our web site. The Lonely Planet list covers just about every accessible part of the world. Currently there are fifteen series: travel guides, Shoestrings, Condensed, Phrasebooks, Read This First, Healthy Travel, Walking guides, Cycling guides, Pisces Diving & Snorkeling guides, City Maps, Travel Atlases, Out to Eat, World Food, Journeys travel literature and Pictorials.

AFRICA Africa on a shoestring • Africa – the South • Arabic (Egyptian) phrasebook • Arabic (Moroccan) phrasebook • Cairo • Cape Town • Cape Town city map • Central Africa • East Africa • Egypt • Egypt travel atlas • Ethiopian (Amharic) phrasebook • The Gambia & Senegal • Healthy Travel Africa • Kenya • Kenya travel atlas • Malawi, Mozambique & Zambia • Morocco • North Africa • Read This First Africa • South Africa, Lesotho & Swaziland • South Africa, Lesotho & Swaziland travel atlas • Swahili phrasebook • Tanzania, Zanzibar & Pemba • Trekking in East Africa • Tunisia • West Africa • Zimbabwe, Botswana & Namibia • Zimbabwe, Botswana & Nambia Travel Atlas • World Food Morocco
Travel Literature: The Rainbird: A Central African Journey • Songs to an African Sunset: A Zimbabwean Story • Mali Blues: Traveling to an African Beat

AUSTRALIA & THE PACIFIC Auckland • Australia • Australian phrasebook • Bushwalking in Australia • Bushwalking in Papua New Guinea • Fiji • Fijian phrasebook • Healthy Travel Australia, NZ and the Pacific • Islands of Australia's Great Barrier Reef • Melbourne • Melbourne city map • Micronesia • New Caledonia • New South Wales & the ACT • New Zealand • Northern Territory • Outback Australia • Out To Eat – Melbourne • Out to Eat – Sydney • Papua New Guinea • Pidgin phrasebook • Queensland • Rarotonga & the Cook Islands • Samoa • Solomon Islands • South Australia • South Pacific • South Pacific Languages phrasebook • Sydney • Sydney city map • Sydney Condensed • Tahiti & French Polynesia • Tasmania • Tonga • Tramping in New Zealand • Vanuatu • Victoria • Western Australia
Travel Literature: Islands in the Clouds • Kiwi Tracks: A New Zealand Journey • Sean & David's Long Drive

CENTRAL AMERICA & THE CARIBBEAN Bahamas, Turks & Caicos • Bermuda • Central America on a shoestring • Costa Rica • Cuba • Dominican Republic & Haiti • Eastern Caribbean • Guatemala, Belize & Yucatán: La Ruta Maya • Jamaica • Mexico • Mexico City • Panama • Puerto Rico • Read This First Central & South America • World Food Mexico
Travel Literature: Green Dreams: Travels in Central America

EUROPE Amsterdam • Amsterdam city map • Andalucía • Austria • Baltic States phrasebook • Barcelona • Berlin • Berlin city map • Britain • British phrasebook • Brussels, Bruges & Antwerp • Budapest city map • Canary Islands • Central Europe • Central Europe phrasebook • Corfu & Ionians • Corsica • Crete • Crete Condensed • Croatia • Cyprus • Czech & Slovak Republics • Denmark • Dublin • Eastern Europe • Eastern Europe phrasebook • Edinburgh • Estonia, Latvia & Lithuania • Europe on a shoestring • Finland • Florence • France • French phrasebook • Germany • German phrasebook • Greece • Greek Islands • Greek phrasebook • Hungary • Iceland, Greenland & the Faroe Islands • Istanbul City Map • Ireland • Italian phrasebook • Italy • Krakow •Lisbon • London • London city map • London Condensed • Mediterranean Europe • Mediterranean Europe phrasebook • Munich • Norway • Paris • Paris city map • Paris Condensed • Poland • Portugal • Portugese phrasebook • Portugal travel atlas • Prague • Prague city map • Provence & the Côte d'Azur • Read This First Europe • Romania & Moldova • Rome • Russia, Ukraine & Belarus • Russian phrasebook • Scandinavian & Baltic Europe • Scandinavian Europe phrasebook • Scotland • Slovenia • Spain • Spanish phrasebook • St Petersburg • Switzerland • Trekking in Spain • Ukrainian phrasebook • Venice • Vienna • Walking in Britain • Walking in Ireland • Walking in Italy • Walking in Spain • Walking in Switzerland • Western Europe • Western Europe phrasebook • World Food Italy • World Food Spain
Travel Literature: The Olive Grove: Travels in Greece

INDIAN SUBCONTINENT Bangladesh • Bengali phrasebook • Bhutan • Delhi • Goa • Hindi & Urdu phrasebook • India • India & Bangladesh travel atlas • Indian Himalaya • Karakoram Highway • Kerala • Mumbai (Bombay) • Nepal • Nepali phrasebook • Pakistan • Rajasthan • Read This First: Asia & India • South India • Sri Lanka • Sri Lanka phrasebook • Trekking in the Indian Himalaya • Trekking in the Karakoram & Hindukush • Trekking in the Nepal Himalaya
Travel Literature: In Rajasthan • Shopping for Buddhas • The Age Of Kali

LONELY PLANET

Mail Order

Lonely Planet products are distributed worldwide. They are also available by mail order from Lonely Planet, so if you have difficulty finding a title please write to us. North and South American residents should write to 150 Linden St, Oakland CA 94607, USA; European and African residents should write to 10a Spring Place, London, NW5 3BH; and residents of other countries to PO Box 617, Hawthorn, Victoria 3122, Australia.

ISLANDS OF THE INDIAN OCEAN Madagascar & Comoros • Maldives • Mauritius, Réunion & Seychelles

MIDDLE EAST & CENTRAL ASIA Bahrain, Kuwait & Qatar • Central Asia • Central Asia phrasebook • Dubai • Hebrew phrasebook • Iran • Israel & the Palestinian Territories • Israel & the Palestinian Territories travel atlas • Istanbul • Istanbul to Cairo on a shoestring • Jerusalem • Jerusalem City Map • Jordan • Jordan, Syria & Lebanon travel atlas • Lebanon • Middle East • Oman & the United Arab Emirates • Syria • Turkey • Turkey travel atlas • Turkish phrasebook • Yemen
Travel Literature: The Gates of Damascus • Kingdom of the Film Stars: Journey into Jordan • Black on Black: Iran Revisited

NORTH AMERICA Alaska • Backpacking in Alaska • Baja California • California & Nevada • California Condensed • Canada • Chicago • Chicago city map • Deep South • Florida • Hawaii • Honolulu • Las Vegas • Los Angeles • Miami • New England • New Orleans • New York City • New York city map • New York Condensed • New York, New Jersey & Pennsylvania • Oahu • Pacific Northwest USA • Puerto Rico • Rocky Mountain • San Francisco • San Francisco city map • Seattle • Southwest USA • Texas • USA • USA phrasebook • Vancouver • Washington, DC & the Capital Region • Washington DC city map
Travel Literature: Drive Thru America

NORTH-EAST ASIA Beijing • Cantonese phrasebook • China • Hong Kong • Hong Kong city map • Hong Kong, Macau & Guangzhou • Japan • Japanese phrasebook • Japanese audio pack • Korea • Korean phrasebook • Kyoto • Mandarin phrasebook • Mongolia • Mongolian phrasebook • North-East Asia on a shoestring • Seoul • South-West China • Taiwan • Tibet • Tibetan phrasebook • Tokyo
Travel Literature: Lost Japan • In Xanadu

SOUTH AMERICA Argentina, Uruguay & Paraguay • Bolivia • Brazil • Brazilian phrasebook • Buenos Aires • Chile & Easter Island • Chile & Easter Island travel atlas • Colombia • Ecuador & the Galapagos Islands • Healthy Travel Central & South America • Latin American Spanish phrasebook • Peru • Quechua phrasebook • Rio de Janeiro • Rio de Janeiro city map • South America on a shoestring • Trekking in the Patagonian Andes • Venezuela
Travel Literature: Full Circle: A South American Journey

SOUTH-EAST ASIA Bali & Lombok • Bangkok • Bangkok city map • Burmese phrasebook • Cambodia • Hanoi • Healthy Travel Asia & India • Hill Tribes phrasebook • Ho Chi Minh City • Indonesia • Indonesia's Eastern Islands • Indonesian phrasebook • Indonesian audio pack • Jakarta • Java • Laos • Lao phrasebook • Laos travel atlas • Malay phrasebook • Malaysia, Singapore & Brunei • Myanmar (Burma) • Philippines • Pilipino (Tagalog) phrasebook • Read This First Asia & India • Singapore • South-East Asia on a shoestring • South-East Asia phrasebook • Thailand • Thailand's Islands & Beaches • Thailand travel atlas • Thai phrasebook • Thai audio pack • Vietnam • Vietnamese phrasebook • Vietnam travel atlas • World Food Thailand • World Food Vietnam

ALSO AVAILABLE: Antarctica • The Arctic • Brief Encounters: Stories of Love, Sex & Travel • Chasing Rickshaws • Lonely Planet Unpacked • Not the Only Planet: Travel Stories from Science Fiction • Sacred India • Travel with Children • Traveller's Tales

The Lonely Planet Story

Lonely Planet published its first book in 1973 in response to the numerous 'How did you do it?' questions Maureen and Tony Wheeler were asked after driving, bussing, hitching, sailing and railing their way from England to Australia.

Written at a kitchen table and hand collated, trimmed and stapled, *Across Asia on the Cheap* became an instant local bestseller, inspiring thoughts of another book.

Eighteen months in South-East Asia resulted in their second guide, *South-East Asia on a shoestring*, which they put together in a backstreet Chinese hotel in Singapore in 1975. The 'yellow bible', as it quickly became known to backpackers around the world, soon became *the* guide to the region. It has sold well over half a million copies and is now in its 9th edition, still retaining its familiar yellow cover.

Today there are over 350 titles, including travel guides, walking guides, language kits & phrasebooks, travel atlases, diving guides and travel literature. The company is the largest independent travel publisher in the world. Although Lonely Planet initially specialised in guides to Asia, today there are few corners of the globe that have not been covered.

The emphasis continues to be on travel for independent travellers. Tony and Maureen still travel for several months of each year and play an active part in the writing, updating and quality control of Lonely Planet's guides.

They have been joined by over 120 authors and 280 staff at our offices in Melbourne (Australia), Oakland (USA), London (UK) and Paris (France). Travellers themselves also make a valuable contribution to the guides through the feedback we receive in thousands of letters each year and on our web site.

The people at Lonely Planet strongly believe that travellers can make a positive contribution to the countries they visit, both through their appreciation of the countries' culture, wildlife and natural features, and through the money they spend. In addition, the company makes a direct contribution to the countries and regions it covers. Since 1986 a percentage of the income from each book has been donated to ventures such as famine relief in Africa; aid projects in India; agricultural projects in Central America; Greenpeace's efforts to halt French nuclear testing in the Pacific; and Amnesty International.

LONELY PLANET OFFICES

Australia
PO Box 617, Hawthorn, Victoria 3122
☎ 03 9819 1877 fax 03 9819 6459
email: talk2us@lonelyplanet.com.au

USA
150 Linden St, Oakland, CA 94607
☎ 510 893 8555 TOLL FREE: 800 275 8555
fax 510 893 8572
email: info@lonelyplanet.com

UK
10a Spring Place, London NW5 3BH
☎ 020 7428 4800 fax 020 7428 4828
email: go@lonelyplanet.co.uk

France
1 rue du Dahomey, 75011 Paris
☎ 01 55 25 33 00 fax 01 55 25 33 01
email: bip@lonelyplanet.fr
www.lonelyplanet.fr

World Wide Web: www.lonelyplanet.com *or* AOL keyword: lp
Lonely Planet Images: lpi@lonelyplanet.com.au